Reassembling Scholarly Communications

Reassembling Scholarly Communications

Histories, Infrastructures, and Global Politics of Open Access

Edited by Martin Paul Eve and Jonathan Gray

The MIT Press
Cambridge, Massachusetts
London, England

© 2020 Massachusetts Institute of Technology

This work is subject to a Creative Commons CC BY license.

Subject to such license, all rights are reserved.

The open access edition of this book was made possible by generous funding and support from Arcadia (a charitable fund of Lisbet Rausing and Peter Baldwin), the Open Society Foundations, the Open Knowledge Foundation, Birkbeck, University of London, and the Leverhulme Trust.

LEVERHULME
TRUST _____

This book was set in Stone Serif and Stone Sans by Westchester Publishing Services.

Library of Congress Cataloging-in-Publication Data

Names: Eve, Martin Paul, 1986- editor. | Gray, Jonathan, 1983- editor.
Title: Reassembling scholarly communications : histories, infrastructures, and
 global politics of open access / edited by Martin Paul Eve and Jonathan Gray.
Description: Cambridge, Massachusetts : The MIT Press, [2020] | Includes
 bibliographical references and index.
Identifiers: LCCN 2020000429 | ISBN 9780262536240 (paperback)
Subjects: LCSH: Open access publishing. | Communication in learning and
 scholarship. | Open access publishing--Social aspects. | Communication in learning
 and scholarship--Social aspects.
Classification: LCC Z286.O63 R43 2020 | DDC 001.2--dc23
LC record available at https://lccn.loc.gov/2020000429

149823138

In memory of Professor William Gray (1952–2019)

Contents

Grammatical and Terminological Notes   xi
Acknowledgments   xiii
Abbreviations and Glossary   xv

    Introduction   1
    Martin Paul Eve and Jonathan Gray

I   Colonial Influences

    1   Epistemic Alienation in African Scholarly Communications: Open Access as a *Pharmakon*   25
    Thomas Hervé Mboa Nkoudou

    2   Scholarly Communications and Social Justice   41
    Charlotte Roh, Harrison W. Inefuku, and Emily Drabinski

    3   Social Justice and Inclusivity: Drivers for the Dissemination of African Scholarship   53
    Reggie Raju, Jill Claassen, Namhla Madini, and Tamzyn Suliaman

    4   Can Open Scholarly Practices Redress Epistemic Injustice?   65
    Denisse Albornoz, Angela Okune, and Leslie Chan

II   Epistemologies

    5   When the Law Advances Access to Learning: Locke and the Origins of Modern Copyright   83
    John Willinsky

    6   How Does a Format Make a Public?   103
    Robin de Mourat, Donato Ricci, and Bruno Latour

7 Peer Review: Readers in the Making of Scholarly Knowledge   113
David Pontille and Didier Torny

8 The Making of Empirical Knowledge: Recipes, Craft, and Scholarly Communication   125
Pamela H. Smith, Tianna Helena Uchacz, Naomi Rosenkranz, and Claire Conklin Sabel

III Publics and Politics

9 The Royal Society and the Noncommercial Circulation of Knowledge   147
Aileen Fyfe

10 The Political Histories of UK Public Libraries and Access to Knowledge   161
Stuart Lawson

11 Libraries and Their Publics in the United States   173
Maura A. Smale

12 Open Access, "Publicity," and Democratic Knowledge   181
John Holmwood

IV Archives and Preservation

13 Libraries, Museums, and Archives as Speculative Knowledge Infrastructure   195
Bethany Nowviskie

14 Preserving the Past for the Future: Whose Past? Everyone's Future   205
April M. Hathcock

15 Is There a Text in These Data? The Digital Humanities and Preserving the Evidence   215
Dorothea Salo

16 Accessing the Past, or Should Archives Provide Open Access?   229
István Rév

Contents

V Infrastructures and Platforms

   17 Infrastructural Experiments and the Politics of Open Access   251
      Jonathan Gray

   18 The Platformization of Open   265
      Penny C. S. Andrews

   19 Reading Scholarship Digitally   277
      Martin Paul Eve

   20 Toward Linked Open Data for Latin America   285
      Arianna Becerril-García and Eduardo Aguado-López

   21 The Pasts, Presents, and Futures of SciELO   297
      Abel L. Packer

VI Global Communities

   22 Not Self-Indulgence, but Self-Preservation: Open Access and the Ethics of Care   317
      Eileen A. Joy

   23 Toward a Global Open-Access Scholarly Communications System: A Developing Region Perspective   331
      Dominique Babini

   24 Learned Societies, Humanities Publishing, and Scholarly Communication in the UK   343
      Jane Winters

   25 Not All Networks: Toward Open, Sustainable Research Communities   351
      Kathleen Fitzpatrick

   Conclusion   361
   Martin Paul Eve and Jonathan Gray

Bibliography   365
Contributors   423
Index   433

Grammatical and Terminological Notes

In this book, we spell the phrasal noun and postpositive compound adjective "open access," the prepositive compound adjective "open-access," and the heterogeneous group of individuals devoted to the advancement of open access, the "Open Access Movement" (although the extent to which there is a "movement" as such is a question that deserves ongoing scrutiny and empirical elaboration).

Contributors have used a variety of terms throughout this book to refer to the commonalities between Latin America, the Caribbean, the African continent, and elsewhere in a seemingly homogeneous bloc. Some of our contributors have preferred the term "Global South," while others find this concept to be patronizing and simplistic and have used "developing nations" or "developing countries" instead.[1] These latter variants, though, also have a potentially patronizing quality in suggesting a unified path to "development" that follows Anglo-American-European cultures, and so are disliked by others. Other possibilities that were not used include "less economically developed countries," "low- and lower-middle-income countries," and "the majority world." Every single one of these terms has its own advantages and drawbacks. In this book, we chose to leave contributors free to select their own terms, particularly when authors culturally identified themselves with the regions they were describing. In our own editorial sections of the book, we have used the terms "Global South" and "Global North" to refer to a worldwide division in equity of wealth as a result of colonial legacies and ongoing prestige practices. We recognize that this editorial decision will appeal to some readers and meet with scorn from others. We apologize, in advance, to the latter group and hope that our sincere desire and advocacy for a more equal and just knowledge world can excuse our infelicities of language.

Contributor biographical statements, including titles, are presented as specified by authors rather than being subject to any stylistic unification.

Acknowledgments

This book has had a long gestation and the editors would both like to extend their thanks to the many individuals in the world of open access, its attendant conversations, and its often tricky implementations.

Martin Paul Eve would like to thank his colleagues at Birkbeck, University of London and, in particular, all those who have worked with him on the Open Library of Humanities: Caroline Edwards, Andy Byers, Rose Harris-Birtill, Mauro Sanchez, Helen Saunders, Paula Clemente Vega, and Marija Katic. Martin has also had tremendous support from academic colleagues in the School of Arts at Birkbeck, especially from Anthony Bale as Dean, Heike Bauer as Head of Department of English, Theatre, and Creative Writing, and Isabel Davis as Head of Research. Other individuals continue to inspire him with their intellects and generosity in the open-access and other research spaces, including Janneka Adema, Juan Pablo Alperin, Josh Bolick, Joe Brooker (for discussions about "just blogging"), Susan Bruce, Michael Collins, Geoff Crossick, Kathleen Fitzpatrick, Hilary Fraser, Rupert Gatti, Alex Gil, Gary Hall, Richard Hall, Patricia Hswe, Ben Johnson, Eileen A. F. Joy, Matthew Kirschenbaum, Stuart Lawson, Mark Leach, Alan Liu, Sam Moore, Ross Mounce, Cameron Neylon, Daniel O'Donnell, Ernesto Priego, Rick Rylance, Johan Rooryck, Helen Snaith, Peter Suber, Demmy Verbeke, Don Waters, Peter Webster, and Jane Winters. The perils of such a list are, of course, that I have inevitably omitted people to whom I owe thanks and so I extend my apologies to those included in this sociology of absence. Thanks also from Martin to Gill Hinks, Ethel Gray, Rich Hinks, Alyce Magritte, Sue Eve-Jones, Juliet Eve, Lisa Holloway, Carin Eve, Anthony Eve, Julia Eve, and Sam Jones. Martin's greatest and final thanks go, though, to his wife, Helen.

Jonathan Gray would like to thank friends and colleagues at the Digital Methods Initiative (University of Amsterdam), the médialab at Sciences Po

(Paris), the Department of Digital Humanities at King's College London, the Public Data Lab and beyond for discussions, collaborations and experiments around "making research public," which have inspired and encouraged different aspects of this book—in particular Liliana Bounegru, Carolin Gerlitz, Anne Helmond, Lucy Kimbell, Bruno Latour, Noortje Marres, Michele Mauri, Sabine Niederer, Natalia Sanchez Querubin, Richard Rogers and Tommaso Venturini. He is also grateful to Bill Gray, to whom this work is dedicated, for showing the passage of sparks as an ongoing collective endeavor and for staying with us a little longer.

Both editors would like to express their thanks to the Open Society Foundations, the Open Knowledge Foundation, and to Birkbeck, University of London, who provided funding and support to make this volume itself open access. Martin Paul Eve would like to thank the Leverhulme Trust for his award of the 2019 Philip Leverhulme Prize that facilitated work on this volume. Thanks are due to Gita Manaktala at the MIT Press for taking the project on and Rebecca Kennison and other reviewers for providing insightful and penetrating peer review over multiple iterations of the manuscript—including recommendations to add several chapters to bring in other regional perspectives and infrastructural concerns. Finally, we are most grateful for the time, labor, input, and patience of all of the contributors herein, who have made this book what it is.

Note

Dimiter Toshkov, "The 'Global South' Is a Terrible Term. Don't Use It!," *RE-DESIGN* (blog), November 6, 2018, http://re-design.dimiter.eu/?p=969.

Abbreviations and Glossary

Unattributed quotations in this section refer to official self-identificatory text of the item in question.
- **aaaaarg.fail**: an online portal that provides pirate access to many journal articles and research books in violation of copyright law.
- **ABEC**: the Brazilian Society of Editors (Associação Brasileira de Editores Científicos). An organization representing scientific editors in Brazil.
- **Academia.edu**: a proprietary article-sharing repository and social networking site.
- **Afrofuturism**: aesthetic and philosophical explorations of links between African Diasporic cultures and new technologies.
- **AHA**: the American Historical Association. The largest learned society in the United States of America that represents historians.
- *AIME*: the *An Inquiry into Modes of Existence* project. A project initiated from the theoretical work of Bruno Latour.
- **Airbnb**: an online platform for arranging private lodgings.
- **AJOL**: African Journals Online. An online library of peer-reviewed, African-published scholarly journals.
- **Altmetric**: a company promoting and building services around Altmetrics, owned by Digital Science.
- **Altmetrics**: nontraditional bibliometrics and attention scores.
- **AmeliCA**: Open Knowledge for Latin America and the Global South (Conocimiento Abierto para América Latina y el Sur Global). A cooperative infrastructure for scientific communication controlled by an inter-institutional academy on a broad scale, led by Redalyc and CLACSO, with support from UNESCO.
- **APC**: Article Processing Charge. A business model for open access in which a publisher charges authors, institutions, or funders, rather than readers, to publish an article.

- **API**: an Application Programming Interface. A means of accessing data or services programmatically.
- **AR**: augmented reality. A virtual enhancement through the superposition of digital artefacts atop the "real" world.
- **ARL**: the Association of Research Libraries. A "membership organization of libraries and archives in major public and private universities, federal government agencies, and large public institutions in Canada and the US."
- **Article-Level Metrics**: citation metrics pertaining to individual articles rather than to journals.
- **arXiv**: a preprint server mostly for the natural sciences, supported by institutional memberships and hosted at Cornell University.
- **ASEES**: the Association for Slavic, East European, and Eurasian Studies. A learned society.
- **Authors Alliance**: an organization that seeks "to advance the interests of authors who want to serve the public good by sharing their creations broadly."
- **bepress**: an institutional repository platform owned by Elsevier.
- **BIREME**: the Latin American and Caribbean Center on Health Sciences Information (Biblioteca Regional de Medicina). A specialized center of the Pan American Health Organization/World Health Organization (PAHO/WHO) facilitating interoperability in health research.
- **BOAI**: the Budapest Open Access Initiative. One of three initial declarations on open access from ~2002, alongside the Bethesda Statement on Open Access Publishing and the Berlin Declaration on Open Access to Knowledge in the Sciences and Humanities.
- **BPC**: Book Processing Charge. A business model for open access in which a publisher charges authors, institutions, or funders, rather than readers, to publish a book.
- **CAPES**: the Coordination for the Improvement of Higher Education Personnel (Coordenação de Aperfeiçoamento de Pessoal de Nível Superior). A Brazilian federal government agency responsible for quality assurance in higher education institutions.
- **CERN**: the European Organization for Nuclear Research (Conseil Européen pour la Recherche Nucléaire). Operates the Zenodo repository and the Large Hadron Collider.
- **CiteULike**: a now-defunct social bookmarking site for academic papers.

Abbreviations and Glossary

- **CLACSO**: the Latin American Council of Social Sciences (Consejo Latinoamericano de Ciencias Sociales). An international nongovernmental association formed in 1967 by UNESCO, uniting almost 700 research centers in the Humanities and Social Sciences (HSS).
- **Clarivate Analytics**: a private analytics company.
- **COAR**: the Confederation of Open-Access Repositories. An organization that seeks to provide "greater visibility and application of research outputs through global networks of Open Access digital repositories."
- **CONICYT**: the Information Department of the Chilean National Council for Scientific and Technological Research (Comisión Nacional de Investigación Científica y Tecnológica). A Chilean government agency.
- **ContentDM**: a content management system for the presentation and preservation of digital collections.
- **ContentMine**: a text and data mining project focused on extracting noncopyrightable facts from the research literature.
- **COUNTER**: Project COUNTER. An organization that defines a standard for collecting metrics on scholarly articles.
- **CNPq**: the Brazilian National Council for Scientific and Technological Development (Conselho Nacional de Desenvolvimento Científico e Tecnológico). An organization of the Brazilian federal government dedicated to scientific research.
- **Creative Commons**: "a global nonprofit organization that enables sharing and reuse of creativity and knowledge through the provision of free legal tools."
- **DBPedia**: a project that extracts structured information from Wikipedia.
- **Depsy**: a software project to track the impact of research software itself.
- **DH**: Digital Humanities. A broad field encompassing the use or critique of computational aspects in the study of humanities disciplines.
- **Diamond open access**: any gold open-access system in which there is neither cost to the reader nor to the author.
- **Digital Science**: a London-based research technology company owned by Holtzbrinck Publishing Group.
- **DMCA**: the Digital Millennium Copyright Act. A 1998 law in the US that places legal restrictions on circumventing DRM technologies.
- **DOAJ**: the Directory of Open Access Journals. A list of open-access journals that fulfil a set of quality criteria for both academic

integrity and technical standards (pertaining, for example, to digital preservation).
- **DOAR**: *see under* OpenDOAR.
- **DOI**: Document Object Identifier. A unique and persistent identifier commonly used in scholarly publishing.
- **DORA**: the San Francisco Declaration on Research Assessment. A declaration that stresses the importance of article-level evaluation over journal-level proxies and particularly the impact factor (IF or JIF).
- **DRM**: Digital Rights Management. Measures to restrict unauthorized copying in the digital space. See also TPM.
- **Dublin Core**: a metadata standard.
- **Eigenfactor**: a rating of journals based on the weighted importance of incoming citation sources.
- **Elsevier**: the publishing division of RELX Group and the world's largest scholarly publisher by some measures.
- **EPUB**: a file format for e-books.
- **F1000**: Faculty of 1000, an open-access academic publisher in the life sciences. Now owned by Taylor & Francis.
- **Facebook**: a social networking site.
- **FAPESP**: the São Paulo Research Foundation (Fundação de Amparo à Pesquisa do Estado de São Paulo). A public foundation in Brazil that provides grants for research, education, and innovation in the state of São Paulo.
- **Fedora**: Flexible Extensible Digital Object Repository Architecture. An institutional repository architecture.
- **Figshare**: an open-access repository operated by Digital Science.
- **Finch Report**: an influential and controversial 2012 government-commissioned report (the Report of the Working Group on Expanding Access to Published Research Findings) in the UK that began its move toward open access to publicly funded research.
- **FOAF**: Friend of a Friend. An experimental linked information system.
- **4IR**: the Fourth Industrial Revolution. A term referring to recent technological developments, such as advances in communication and connectivity.
- **GDPR**: the General Data Protection Regulation. A 2018 European Union law protecting the rights of data subjects.

Abbreviations and Glossary   xix

- **Git:** a version-control system originally built by the originator of Linux, Linus Torvalds.
- **GOAP:** the Global Open Access Portal. A UNESCO initiative funded by Colombia, Denmark, Norway, and the United States Department of State, that gives an overview of open access to scientific information in 158 countries.
- **Gold open access:** open access at the site of publication.
- **Google:** originally a search engine that became a large suite of data and information services under a parent company called Alphabet.
- **Google Scholar:** Google's academic tracking service.
- **Green open access:** open access made possible by the use of a repository, rather than purely at the site of original publication.
- **Half-life index:** a measure of literature obsolescence that measures the time to the halfway point of all citations to an article, journal, or even discipline.
- **HathiTrust:** a large collaborative digital library.
- **HEFCE:** the Higher Education Funding Council for England. A now-defunct funding body for higher education in England that implemented a strong national open-access policy.
- **H-index:** the Hirsch index. A bibliographic measure that evaluates the number of publications (h) with h number of citations for an author.
- **HIPAA:** the Health Insurance Portability and Accountability Act. A piece of legislation in the United States of America that includes privacy protection for the dead.
- **HSS:** the Humanities and Social Sciences. Academic disciplines devoted to the study of human cultures, histories, and artifacts.
- **HTML:** the Hypertext Markup Language. An encoding format that underpins the World Wide Web.
- **Humanities Commons:** a social network and repository system built by the MLA.
- **Hybrid open access:** conditions under which a subscription journal yields options for making selected articles within that title openly accessible.
- **Hypothes.is:** a project that allows users to openly annotate web pages and documents.
- ***i*-10 index:** a bibliographic measure introduced by Google that evaluates the number of publications with at least ten citations.

- **ICSU**: the International Council for Science, formerly the International Council of Scientific Unions. An organization devoted to international cooperation in science.
- **IDEP**: the African Institute for Economic Development and Planning (L'Institut Africain de Développement Economique et de Planification). A subprogram of the United Nations Economic Commission for Africa.
- **IFAN**: the Fundamental Institute of Black Africa (Institut Fondamental d'Afrique Noire). A cultural and scientific institute in the nations of the former French West Africa.
- **IFLA**: the International Federation of Library Associations and Institutions. "The leading international body representing the interests of library and information services and their users."
- **Impact factor or journal impact factor**: a bibliometric indicator of the yearly average number of citations received by recent articles in a journal weighted against the total number of citable articles. Initially promulgated by the Institute for Scientific Information (ISI) and now by Clarivate Analytics.
- **ImpactStory**: an open-source tool that provides altmetrics, owned by the not-for-profit organization Our Research.
- **Internet of Things**: a system of networked devices and machines on the internet that is broader than conventional computers (e.g., smart heating systems).
- **IR**: Institutional Repository. A space where users can openly deposit research materials, affiliated with some form of institution.
- **ISI**: the Institute for Scientific Information. A citation indexing company now part of Clarivate Analytics.
- **Janeway**: an open-source platform for journal publishing developed by the Centre for Technology and Publishing at Birkbeck, University of London, for OLH.
- **JATS**: the Journal Article Tag Suite. An eXtensible Markup Language standard for the semantic encoding of scholarly articles.
- **JROST**: the Joint Roadmap for Open Science Tools. A community working on forward planning for software to help with open science.
- **JSTOR**: Journal STORage. A large online digital library.
- **Jussieu Call for Open Science and Bibliodiversity**: a manifesto that aims "to promote a scientific publishing open-access model fostering

bibliodiversity and innovation without involving the exclusive transfer of journal subscription monies to APC payments."
- **Kickstarter**: an online crowdfunding platform.
- **Kopernio**: Clarivate Analytics' discovery service for open-access content.
- **La Referencia**: the Latin American Federated Network of Institutional Repositories of Scientific Publications (Red de Repositorios de Acceso Abierto a la Ciencia). A network of open-access repositories in Latin America.
- **Latindex**: the Online Regional Information System for Scientific Journals from Latin America, the Caribbean, Spain, and Portugal (Sistema Regional de Información en Línea para Revistas Científicas de América Latina, el Caribe, España y Portugal). A bibliographical database of Ibero-American journals.
- **The Leiden Manifesto**: a set of principles for the responsible use of research metrics.
- **LGBTQIA+**: lesbian, gay, bisexual, transgender, queer/questioning, intersex, asexual/aromantic, plus community. An acronym developed to refer inclusively to a diverse set of sexual and gender identity cultures.
- **Library Genesis**: an online portal that provides pirate access to many journal articles and research books in violation of copyright law.
- **LinkedIn**: a professional social networking site.
- **LILACS**: Latin American and Caribbean Health Sciences Literature. A database founded in 1982 covering literature related to the health sciences in the countries of Latin America and the Caribbean.
- **LOCKSS**: Lots of Copies Keeps Stuff Safe. A peer-to-peer, distributed, redundant, open-source, and self-healing digital preservation system.
- **LOD**: Linked Open Data. An approach and set of conventions for publishing structured data on the web, informed by the work of web inventor Tim Berners-Lee.
- **Lyft**: a platform for arranging private transportation.
- **The *Making and Knowing Project***: a collaborative research and pedagogical initiative based at Columbia University that explores historical and methodological intersections between artistic making and scientific knowing.

- **MEDLARS**: the Medical Literature Analysis and Retrieval System. A database provided by the US National Library of Medicine (NLM).
- **MEDLINE**: a bibliographic database in the medical disciplines.
- **Megajournal**: a high-volume, multidisciplinary academic journal, sometimes based on a "technical soundness" standard of peer review, as in the case of *PLOS ONE*.
- **Mendeley**: a proprietary bibliographic reference manager owned by Elsevier.
- **Microsoft**: a software-development company.
- **MLA**: the Modern Language Association of America. A learned society in the United States of America representing scholars of language and literature.
- **Mukurtu**: a "free, mobile, and open source platform built with indigenous communities to manage and share digital cultural heritage."
- **NLM**: the United States National Library of Medicine. The world's largest medical library.
- **OA**: Open Access. Commonly used to designate conditions of academic publication in which there are no price barriers for readers and under which additional permissions beyond fair use/fair dealing are granted for re-users.
- **OA2020**: "a global initiative endorsed by a growing number of researchers, libraries, institutions and organizations committed to accelerating the transition to universal open access by transforming today's scholarly journals, currently locked behind paywalls, to open access."
- **OA Button**: a software project to document instances where users hit paywalls and thereby could not access research.
- **OAI-PMH**: the Open Archives Initiative Protocol for Metadata Harvesting. A standard for repository interoperability.
- **OBP**: Open Book Publishers. An open-access book publisher based at Trinity College, Cambridge.
- **OCLC**: the Ohio College Library Center, then the Online Computer Library Center. A global library cooperative.
- **OCSDNet**: the Open and Collaborative Science in Development Network. A set of "twelve researcher-practitioner teams from the Global South interested in understanding the role of openness and

collaboration in science as a transformative tool for development thinking and practice."
- **OfS**: the Office for Students. A regulatory body for higher education in the UK spun out of HEFCE.
- **OHP**: Open Humanities Press. An open-access book publisher.
- **OJS**: Open Journal Systems. A widely used open-source platform for journal publishing developed by PKP.
- **OLH**: the Open Library of Humanities. A consortially funded not-for-profit open-access publisher with no APCs.
- **Omeka**: a content management system designed primarily for the exhibition of digital cultural heritage objects.
- **OntoOAI**: a semantic web project that mapped RDF on top of OAI.
- **OpenAIRE**: Open Access Infrastructure for Research in Europe. Originally a network of Open Access repositories funded by the European Commission's Seventh Framework Programme (FP7) that grew from the DRIVER I & II projects. The latest iteration, OpenAIRE-Advance, seeks "to shift the momentum among its communities to Open Science as a trusted e-Infrastructure within the realms of the European Open Science Cloud."
- **OpenDOAR**: the Directory of Open Access Repositories. A website based in the UK that lists open-access repositories.
- **Open Science**: a broader paradigm than just open access to research publications encompassing the entire lifecycle of research.
- **Open Society Archives**: one of the largest archival repositories documenting grave violations of human rights.
- **ORCID**: Open Researcher and Contributor ID. A nonproprietary alphanumeric code, maintained by the nonprofit ORCID Inc., to uniquely identify academic contributors.
- **PAHO**: the Pan American Health Organization. The specialized international health agency for the Americas and the Regional Office for the Americas of the World Health Organization (WHO).
- **Palantir**: a private software company that specializes in data analytics.
- **PDF**: Portable Document Format. A standards-based format for preserving layout of documents between computing and display systems.
- **Pearson**: a UK-based publisher.
- **PECE**: the Platform for Experimental Collaborative Ethnography. A digital platform for "multi-sited, cross-scale ethnographic and historical

research" that makes explanatory pluralism and interpretive differences core to its inquiries.
- **PeerJ**: an open-access scientific mega-journal in the biological and medical sciences.
- **PKP**: the Public Knowledge Project. A software organization that develops OJS.
- **Plan S**: a set of principles to which many academic funders, worldwide, have subscribed, pledging an acceleration of the timescale to achieve full open access.
- **PLOS**: the Public Library of Science. An open-access scholarly publisher.
- **Principle of Respect for Context**: a philosophy for the reuse of personal data advanced by Helen Nissenbaum, which advocates for contextual reuse.
- **Projet SOHA**: Open Science in Francophone Africa and Haiti (Science Ouverte Haïti Afrique). A project exploring "the obstacles preventing the adoption of open science in universities in Haiti and Francophone Africa" and providing "tools to overcome them."
- **Publons**: a third-party peer-review website operated by Clarivate Analytics.
- **PubMed**: a search engine for the MEDLINE database of references and abstracts.
- **PubPeer**: an independent third-party peer-review website.
- **punctum books**: an open-access book publisher.
- **Pure**: institutional repository software developed by Elsevier.
- **Radical Open Access Collective**: "a community of scholar-led, not-for-profit presses, journals and other open access projects."
- **RCUK**: Research Councils UK. The forerunner to UKRI.
- **RDF**: a Resource Description Framework. A machine-comprehensible data paradigm.
- **RE**: Research England. A funder of higher-education research in England, spun out of HEFCE.
- **Redalyc**: Red de Revistas Científicas de América Latina y el Caribe, España y Portugal. A publishing system for peer-reviewed, open-access journals from Latin America, the Caribbean, Spain, and Portugal.
- **REF**: the Research Excellence Framework. A periodic research assessment exercise in the United Kingdom that informs the allocation of state research funding.

Abbreviations and Glossary

- **RELX**: the parent company of Elsevier.
- **ResearchGate**: a proprietary article sharing repository and social networking site.
- **RIO**: the *Research Ideas and Outcomes* journal. An open-science platform designed to encapsulate any type of research output and to make it publicly accessible.
- **ROAR**: the Registry of Open Access Repositories. A database of open-access institutional repositories and their contents.
- **The Royal Society**: a learned society founded in 1660 and the United Kingdom's national Academy of Sciences.
- **ScholarLed**: "a consortium of five scholar-led, not-for-profit, open access book publishers that was formed in 2018."
- **ScholarlyHub**: a germinative effort to create a nonprofit digital commons.
- **SciELO**: the Scientific Electronic Library Online. A bibliographic database and cooperative publishing model for open-access journals, predominantly in South America.
- **Sci-Hub**: an online portal that provides pirate access to many journal articles and research books in violation of copyright law.
- **Scopus**: an abstract and citation database owned by Elsevier.
- **SIDALC**: the Alliance of Agricultural Information Services (Servicio de Información y Documentación Agropecuario de las Américas). An online agricultural library from twenty-two countries of Latin America and the Caribbean.
- **SJR**: the Scimago Journal Ranking. A bibliometric system that combines the number of citations received by a journal and the prestige of the journals where such citations occur.
- **Snapchat**: a multimedia messaging app.
- **SocArxiv**: a preprint server for the social sciences owned by the not-for-profit Center for Open Science.
- **Solr**: a search platform/architecture.
- **SPARC**: the Scholarly Publishing and Academic Resource Coalition. A "global coalition committed to making Open the default for research and education."
- **Springer Nature**: an academic publishing company born of the 2015 merger of Springer Science+Business Media, Nature Publishing Group, Palgrave Macmillan, and Macmillan Education.

- **SSRN**: formerly the Social Science Research Network, now just known by its acronym. A preprint server for the social sciences owned by Elsevier.
- **STEM**: the disciplines of Science, Technology, Engineering, and Mathematics. Often used in contrast to HSS or combined in the acronym STEAM (Science, Technology, Engineering, Arts, and Mathematics).
- **TEI**: the Text Encoding Initiative. "A consortium which collectively develops and maintains a standard for the representation of texts in digital form."
- **Thomson Reuters**: a global conglomerate with a heavy investment record in data analytics.
- **TPM**: Technical Protection Measures. See also DRM.
- **Twitter**: a micro-blogging platform.
- **Uber**: a platform for arranging private transportation.
- **Uber Eats**: a food delivery service built on top of Uber.
- **UberRUSH**: a now-defunct parcel delivery service built on top of Uber.
- **Ubiquity Press**: a for-profit provider of open-access publishing services.
- **Ubuntu**: a Zulu concept advancing communal justice *en route* to promoting an egalitarian society.
- **UKRI**: United Kingdom Research and Innovation. The UK's national funding bodies.
- **UNESCO**: the United Nations Educational, Scientific and Cultural Organization. A branch of the United Nations that "seeks to build peace through international cooperation in Education, the Sciences and Culture."
- **Unpaywall**: a database of harvested open-access content and associated suite of software tools to enable the discovery of this content, developed by the not-for-profit ImpactStory/Our Research.
- **UrbanBellhop**: a platform that provides hospitality services for those running short-term property lets.
- **VHL**: the Virtual Health Library. A "decentralized and dynamic information-source collection, designed to provide equitable access to scientific knowledge on health," maintained by BIREME.
- **WHO**: the World Health Organization. The specialized health agency of the United Nations.
- **Wikipedia**: an extremely large-scale, crowd-sourced encyclopedia run by the not-for-profit Wikimedia Foundation.

Abbreviations and Glossary

- **Wordpress**: a content-management and blogging system.
- **WoS**: Web of Science. A citation database established by the Institute for Scientific Information (ISI) and now owned by Clarivate Analytics.
- **WWW**: the World Wide Web. An interconnected series of hypertext documents on the internet.
- **XML**: eXtensible Markup Language. A flexible semantic format for the representation of digital information.
- **Zenodo**: an open-access repository developed by OpenAIRE and operated by CERN.
- **Zotero**: an open-source bibliographic reference manager.

Introduction

Martin Paul Eve and Jonathan Gray

It can be tempting to view digital publishing in terms of a fundamental paradigm shift; a "disruptive innovation" that breaks as radically with its past as did Gutenberg's printing press.[1] As commonly noted by economists and policy makers, the ability instantly to copy material between visual display units across vast geographical distances, after all, is of a fundamentally different character to the dissemination of the rivalrous materiality of print. Yet path dependencies and social histories from print forebears condition the ways in which publishing acts in the digital space. One need only consider that the metaphor of "scrolling," for instance, persists in the digital era, centuries after that form of writing was most frequently replaced by the pages of the codex. For publishing, the digital environment is at once a rupture and a continuation, reformed by "new" accelerating technologies, recapitulated by "old" traditions of the academy.

Questions of intersecting traditions and technologies also have relevance, though, for the ongoing rapid transformations of research and learning that are taking place in the early twenty-first century. It is to this issue that this book devotes itself: how has the translation of publishing into the digital space, and the subsequent imaginaries, practices, and infrastructures of "openness" that have logically followed, been conditioned by histories, present discussions, and future projections of the scholarly communications environment?

The contributors to this volume have provided a range of pithy responses to these questions, designed as stimuli for the interested reader. None of the chapters herein yields a conclusive historical or future direction but each frames, either through a theoretical lens or empirical engagement, an apparatus with which we can begin to understand the present moment for scholarly communications beyond a merely instrumental orientation. In this introduction we outline the reasons for this volume's composition, the rationales for the formats of the chapters herein, and the logic behind the project descriptions that comprise parts of this book's contents.

* * *

The traditional story of open access goes like this: the most commonly cited moment of change for contemporary scholarly communications came in 2002 with the publication of the three declarations on open access: the "triple-Bs" of Bethesda, Budapest, and Berlin.[2] Open access, by these definitions, refers to conditions under which price and permission barriers for accessing peer-reviewed research work are removed.[3] That is, using the power of the internet and the World Wide Web to duplicate material at an infinitesimal cost-per-copy—using, that is, the move of publishing to the digital space—the Open Access Movement proposed to make research work freely available to anyone who wishes to read it.

Such a stance is premised on the idea that education is fundamentally different to other forms of commodity in two ways. First, in that education should be freely available to anyone, since a widespread well-educated population, worldwide, confers benefits upon us all. Second, in that higher education, where much research is produced, operates on an economic model that is conducive to the dissemination of such work. This is because academics are not paid based on the volume of their research that is *sold* but are rather given a salary to conduct the research work because it has social, scientific, or humanistic import. Academics and researchers are among the few classes of worker who are not primarily measured and assessed by sales (although this is less true in the brave new world of tuition fees and student recruitment, where insufficient enrollments can imperil a department's survival).[4] This dissociation of sales as a metric lends a type of academic freedom, a freedom from the market in order to investigate niche ideas and hunches that may not come off. Research is a risky business and the freedom to follow an instinct, not knowing the result in advance and not being beholden to its commercial potential, is important. Hence, it has been argued, academics with stable jobs and/or tenure are ideally placed to be able to give their work away to readers, for free. This is where open access enters.

There are several forms of open access, usually assigned on a color spectrum of "gold" and "green" but even going so far as "platinum" and "diamond" (although these last two are category errors: gold and green do not denote business models, while platinum and diamond do). Gold open access refers to conditions where a publisher makes the material openly available to read and reuse (but again, it does not specify any particular business model to make this possible). By contrast, green open access refers to instances where an author deposits a version of the work into a subject or institutional repository. Arguments for the change to open access have been spread across a range of axes, from taxpayer funding via easing library budgets through to the public good.[5] As above, open access is possible, in this area of cultural production (academic research), it is claimed, because researchers are free to give their work away; they are paid a salary by their institution, rather than making a living by selling their research work. The benefits would be a world in which nobody was unable to access research material that could further their understanding of the universe.

When couched in such terms, open access sounds easy, logical, and almost inevitable. However, the social, technical, and economic conditions of academic research publication practice make the entire endeavor far thornier than might be imagined.[6] On the economic side, scholarly publishing is big business. Particularly in the natural sciences, where a handful of large commercial publishers dominate the landscape, profit levels are regularly in the region of 30 percent (even while smaller mission-driven publishers can often be just one lawsuit away from bankruptcy).[7] This is the case even as the costs of subscribing to all academic serials have risen by nearly 400 percent above inflation since 1986.[8] Yet, for those entities whose existence depends on profiting from selling research publications, open access poses a potentially serious threat.

Indeed, for publishing entities that have staff and bills to pay, open access implies a change in business practice. For although green open access has not been shown definitively to cause any revenue loss in terms of subscriptions, if the publisher is giving material away then it must, by default, find another source of revenue to sustain its operations and/or surplus/profit. The most well-known, although by some measures not the most widespread, adaptation of publishers' business models is to levy an article processing charge.[9] The logic runs that, if one cannot sell material to readers, then one might instead sell professional publishing services to authors.

On the surface, this makes sense. It appears to be merely a direct inversion of the current economic model. However, this is not so. For such a system both radically changes the distribution of payments from the subscription environment that has existed for many years while also creating new exclusions. By reducing the ways in which payments are currently distributed–from hundreds or thousands of subscribers around the world all paying less than the cost of an article and moving instead to a single payer who must cover the entire cost—the processing charge model effects a substantial concentration of costs within high-output, research-producing universities.

This economic cost-concentration can be demonstrated through a simple thought experiment. Imagine that there are 100 people in a room. Each of these people has $10. The academic speaker will give them a talk, but the venue wants $50 to cover its costs (and any profit/surplus). There are 40 such talks per year. There is a final indefinitely large group of people (let us call them "the general public") who might want to hear the talk but who can afford to pay nothing. The total cost all year of running all the events is $2,000. The total pool of funds is $1,000. By default, then, some events are not viable to run under this economic model.

Under subscription logic, each person pays $0.50 and gets access to the talk. If a person does not pay, s/he/they may not hear the talk. This logic is implemented to introduce a classical economic system. With the funding available, each person can choose to attend this talk or another. However, each of the 40 talks is different and doesn't cover the same material. The attendees do not really know whether a talk will be useful to them in advance. They can attend 50 percent of the talks. This model spreads costs but limits access; 50 percent of the talks could be attended by 100 percent of the attendees but nobody from the "general public" group gets to hear the talks. Further, it is unlikely that all 100 participants will attend the same 40 talks, so knowledge of the talks' contents is diffuse. It is also the case that, in reality, not every speaker has $10. Some would have $20 and others only $0.50. Some believe this is, nonetheless, the best way of ensuring the venue is compensated and remains open for talks because it incentivizes people to pay. The speaker doesn't necessarily get the largest possible audience from this model. This is also the most unrealistic part of the thought experiment. In reality, some participants have $90 and some only have $1, often as a result of colonial legacies of global wealth distribution.

Under an article processing charge (APC) or book processing charge (BPC) logic for gold open access, the speaker will pay the venue's cost of $50 and let anybody hear the talk for no charge. This makes sense to the academic as her only motivation is to be heard (she is one of the lucky ones who has an academic post). The problem is, she, the speaker, only has $10 herself. This model concentrates costs (sometimes impossibly so) but allows the theoretically widest access. In this particular case, though, an idealized logic led to no access since no single individual can afford the total cost. APCs and BPCs have a problem within the current distribution of resources.

Another alternative model has been proposed to help with the economics. Under consortial open-access funding logic, five people attend each talk. They each spend their full allowance of $10 on that single talk. However, they let everybody else attend any talk for which they have paid, in expectation of reciprocity and for the public good. They record the talk and let others view this for no charge. This model spreads costs and allows broader access than the subscription model; 50 percent of the talks could be heard by not only 100 percent of the attendees but also by the group who can't afford to pay. This appears to be the logical choice for those present, but some are worried that they may pay while others might not return the favor.

There are also arguments that the $50 venue fee is extortionate, since it appears that 35 percent of it ($17.50) is pure profit for the venue organization, which is in fine financial health and is motivated by return for its shareholders, rather than the dissemination of education. Some point out that were this closer to 6 percent ($3.00), as it is in other sectors, the organization would still be fine and could pay all its staff but each talk would only cost around $35. At that rate, it would be possible to host approximately 29 of the planned talks and, with the distribution in the different models, allow other groups to have access. A new startup venue is willing to offer the space at much cheaper rates. The problem is, though, that speakers are rewarded by their institution with promotions and jobs if they speak at venues that are already known. The new venue does not carry such reputational clout, even as it performs the same functions as the older venues (including organizing the screening of the talks for quality). Of course, in reality, not all "venues" are for-profit publishers; many are university presses who are under much tighter financial constraints, even as they are viewed as revenue rather than cost centers.

Yet, as reductive as it is in some ways, the above scaled-down thought experiment shows a few of the challenges for implementing open access on the ground. The situation is even worse when it comes to open-access books, for which the production costs are much, much higher.[10] The economics of distribution—at the global, national, institutional, and disciplinary levels—are critical to our understanding of what it means to transition to a world in which academic content is free on the reader side, even while it is not free to produce or, importantly, to publish.[11] Economics, though, is not the only contested political area for open access. Among accusations that open access will encourage plagiarism, or degrade the quality of academic work, has come the more recent assertion that open access is entangled with the neoliberalization of academia and the academy, as well as the commodification and platformization of online spaces and digital infrastructures.[12]

* * *

Neoliberalism, an often poorly defined and overused term, can nonetheless be specified as the extension of economizing, quantifying thought to all areas of life and, in particular, the replacement of politics with economics.[13] Born out of the ordoliberalism movement in early twentieth-century Austria, the most forceful and notable proponents were those known as the Chicago School of Economics.

It is easy to chart a narrative of neoliberal incursion into higher education. In the UK, for instance, the proliferation of target-driven assessment mechanisms and financialization appear to confirm the notion that the bastions of liberal humanist thought have been colonized by quantifying urges that seek to metricize and operationalize education in utilitarian fashions.[14] This neoliberalization certainly also extends to scholarly publishing. The recent demands that Stanford University Press be self-sustaining—that is, as a revenue, rather than cost, center for the university—can be and have been read in this light of neoliberal politics.[15]

The actual history of higher education is more complex than this, though. Racial and class-based iniquities in access to university before the late-twentieth century (and still persisting in many spaces, particularly through the hierarchy of prestige between different schools) make a mockery of the idealized prehistory to which such narratives sometimes resort. Furthermore, critics of the Research Excellence Framework (REF) in the UK are slow to point out that this exercise is firstly one that disburses public money, gleaned through general taxation, to universities for research, and secondly one that reshaped the landscape of UK higher education to be more inclusive. It is not likely that new, younger universities would have been given a share of the funding pie without mechanisms such as the REF. This is to say neither that there are not terrible consequences of metricization—for individuals and for the higher education system as a whole—nor that we should not continue to fight for a system of universities that bring a true social good, but it is to note that overly linear and simplistic narratives of the purpose and context of such structures do not capture the whole story.[16] Higher education had a perfectly unequal and checkered history long before it became neoliberal.

That said, open access has become associated, for better or worse, with such assessment mechanisms. Over the previous two decades, research funders realized that who pays the piper calls the tunes and they began mandating for open access to publicly funded research work. This has led to the unfortunate situation in which many scholars encounter open access for the first time as a product of a need to comply with systems of bureaucracy and finance, rather than any genuinely critical engagement with scholarly communication practices in the digital age.[17] Of course, this varies from region to region and sometimes discipline to discipline. It is notoriously difficult to mandate in the United States, for instance, apart from in the instances of federal and/or private funding. Likewise, funders have less clout in the humanities disciplines, where project research funding has dried up to nearly desert status. Nonetheless, from this entanglement comes the critique that open access is a means by which neoliberal government agendas of "knowledge transfer" and "impact" can be forced upon researchers.[18] In this respect, many from the humanities disciplines have argued that open access should not apply to their work and is being driven by the agenda of the natural sciences. However, such a world would be a worrying space, for it would be one in which the general availability of natural-scientific research would be coupled with the near-total digital invisibility of the humanities disciplines.

In particular, though, criticism has fallen in this respect on the more liberal of the Creative Commons licenses and especially those without an NC (noncommercial) or ND (nonderivative) clause.[19] Prominent commentators, such as John Holmwood, have voiced fears that without a noncommercial clause, private higher education providers (who can issue degrees without doing any teaching in the UK, for instance) will swoop in to bundle open-access research content into textbooks, thereby undercutting the research university in its present form.[20] Given the current standard of discourse around higher education in government policy circles, this is a far from irrational fear.

Unfortunately, though, the law is often unhelpful when it comes to the interpretation of the "noncommercial" clause. Often, charitable organizations—with missions that we might wish to support for ethical reasons—conduct "commercial" activities in order to fund their operations. Indeed, universities are commercial in this sense. To this end, a court in Germany ruled that noncommercial meant *strictly* for personal use.[21] Likewise, in terms of allowing derivatives, or otherwise, it is unclear whether a course pack that used a mere excerpt might be ruled as a derivative rather than a compilation. In the quest to fight neoliberalization, the arguments against open licensing find themselves spinning too broad a web and, in the process, catching legitimate scholarly uses that could be worthwhile. The response has, on occasion, been to call for new licenses. Perhaps, it is reasoned, it is just that the Creative Commons licenses are not suited for scholarship. Yet, these licenses have been developed and legally tested over decades by some of the finest legal minds in the world. To rewrite them for scholarly purposes with watertight-enough language to facilitate "good" uses against those that are deemed undesirable would be extremely difficult. Further, it is not clear, even within the academy, what is agreed upon as acceptable. Are we seriously to have different licenses that must be legally tested for history than for biomedicine and computer science? It certainly might also be argued, under the "taxpayer argument," that since commercial entities pay taxes, and that tax money supports university research in some cases, that the mandate for open licenses should stand (though this resort to taxpayer arguments could, itself, be construed as a neoliberal exercise).[22]

Yet the fundamental contradiction remains that those who most loudly protest, say, precarious working conditions within universities, but who also contest open access on the grounds that it is neoliberal, find themselves in a double bind. For in perpetuating the unequal situation of access to research, which remains the precondition for producing further research and thereby securing a faculty position, those who disdain open access become those who uphold a system which remains extremely difficult for those outside of the university to benefit from and participate in. Further, it is hard also to ignore the fact that worldwide access (in both read and write modes) to scholarship from the Global North is almost exclusively the preserve of scholars from this region.[23] In attacking the claimed neoliberalism of open access in general—as opposed, say, to just the APC model—such scholars (inadvertently) uphold a system of neocolonial access to knowledge, as several commentators in this volume point out.

It is also curious that often those most opposed to the supposed neoliberalization of the academy are also those who will speak, in throwaway comments, of "top journals" and the importance of their perpetuation. Yet, it is this reliance on a proxy measure for quality—Impact Factors or even just prestige—that allows the neoliberal systems of assessment to continue to function. For how long do we really think that systems such as the UK's REF or European funding structures would last if panels could not find recourse to a frame of value within which a work is situated? Put otherwise: if panels had to read 200 book manuscripts as part of a search, rather than judging 200 books placed at well-regarded university presses, would the system not crumble away?

This evaluative reliance on "containers" is absolutely entangled with the current system of open access. Although, for a long time, the standing of a journal has determined the price that a publisher could charge for a subscription, in the present moment this is being made entirely transparent. For instance, in its recent IPO, SpringerNature explicitly noted that "[s]ome of our journals are among the open access journals with the highest Impact Factor, providing us with the ability to charge higher APCs for these journals than for journals with average Impact Factors."[24] Elsevier, the largest scientific publisher in the world, notes that its pricing of open-access fees is also based upon measures of the journal's standing, rather than purely upon the labor the publisher has provided through its services.[25] Research material has become a positional good, in which the status of the venues in which it appears bear more upon its market worth than the actual content of the work. (Although, one might also consider the same effect under a subscription model and conclude that it would be worse. Imagine, for instance, if the most important articles in biomedicine, with huge implications for public health, cost the most to access. Yet this is, to some extent, what a pricing system based on prestige implies.)

Such a stance only makes clear what has been fairly obvious to anybody in an academic library purchasing department for some time: that the symbolic economy of prestige in academia translates, as Pierre Bourdieu would appreciate, into a real-world financial economy.[26] Indeed, what appears as a matter of academic judgement and of practices protected by laws of academic freedom has dire market consequences for access to knowledge around the world. The ways in which we appraise "excellence" determine what, and who, is able to read and now to publish material.[27] Choices by academics of where to publish—on one set of criteria of appraisal—determine the ability of people around the world to afford access to that work.

* * *

All of this is to say that open access is intensely messy. Open access is perceived through a set of contested institutional histories, argued over various theoretical terrains in the present, and imagined via diverse potentialities for the future. And it is at this point, amid such an untidy set of circumstances, that this book makes its intervention. At the present moment, we are overdetermined by an inflexible historical understanding of open research practices that risks leading us into either overly instrumental conceptions or critiques that foreclose the possibility of other arrangements. How, we wanted here to ask, might our thinking differ if we had an alternative historical frame of reference? What experiments have people conducted, in the present, that might lead to other possible trajectories? And what different futures can we foresee, even as we are historically determined in our imagination, from our current vantage point?

When we envisaged this collection, we specifically aimed to do something different to a conventional edited volume. Certainly, the contributions in this volume are rigorous and backed by often decades' worth of intellectual or practical experience of work in the area of this book. What we also wanted, though, were pithy, shorter chapters that would serve as introductions to different perspectives, as gateways to alternative approaches. We have achieved this in many cases, although some of the chapters simply required more space than others, hence some variance in length is to be expected. Finally, we wanted to construct an archive of practical initiatives and to preserve it as history. For it is only in the documentation of practical enterprises that one can see the forks in history's otherwise apparent determinism. That is, in hindsight everything can appear as though it could never have been different. By describing efforts to change the future, in our present, from around the world, the notion of "history as timeline" may be complemented by another conception of contingent branching events. We perceive this as a model akin to one of the baseball player Yogi Berra's famous malapropisms: "when you come to a fork in the road, take it."

Introduction

Chapters and Structure

This book is divided into six parts: colonial influences; epistemologies; publics and politics; archives and preservation; infrastructures and platforms; and global communities. Of course, these various parts should not be taken as an indication that we regard them as distinct entities or processes. They are rather a reflection of our editorial efforts to cluster together the various chapters around shared themes and into a reasonably well-balanced set of sections, and there are certainly overlaps and conversations between them. For how can one write of preservation and selection, for instance, without an appreciation of the value structures that we use to select? And these value structures of selection have been historically conditioned by worldwide colonial and then postcolonial positions, as well as epistemological concerns and biases, and infrastructural changes.

This volume opens with a section on colonial legacies. We as editors acknowledge that, as two (half) white men based in Europe, our positions on open access, open science, and other open digital transformations of research have been shaped not only by our geographical stance but also our own historical proximity to former empires and their associated social, cultural, political, and economic circuitry, which often continue to operate. The four chapters in this section reflect upon issues of global inequality and paint a very different picture to the tableau with which those from the Global North may be familiar.

Indeed, we open with a somewhat less optimistic chapter about the spread of open access. In his chapter, Thomas Hervé Mboa Nkoudou shows how the spread of particular business models for open access, in particular, can be intensely problematic. Thus, on the one hand, it is argued, while the widespread accessibility of work may be advantageous for those working on the African continent, the perpetuation of the article processing charge system is, on the other, incredibly dangerous. For Nkoudou, the frame of the *pharmakon*–the simultaneous poison and cure–is helpful for understanding this dual-edged phenomenon. Nkoudou ends with a series of proposals for how we can decolonize knowledge for a more epistemically just world.

In their chapter Charlotte Roh, Harrison W. Inefuku, and Emily Drabinski continue this theme and examine the important ways in which our present systems of scholarly communications worldwide, here and now, are rooted in colonial histories of empire that have fostered deep inequalities.

Roh et al. identify a set of perpetuations of race, ethnicity, gender norms, and inequalities in research production and promulgation that all have their roots within colonial systems of privilege.

All, though, is not lost. In chapter 3, Reggie Raju, Jill Claassen, Namhla Madini, and Tamzyn Suliaman detail the ways in which the concept of Ubuntu—a Zulu term advancing communal justice *en route* to promoting an egalitarian society—can be seen in new library publishing initiatives in South Africa. At present, for Raju et al., there is a serious problem in the current open publishing landscape: equitable participation is not fixed by the equitable ability to read. Without the more systemic and bottom-up approaches that they detail, it seems likely that open practices will merely continue to perpetuate damaging legacies.

Finally for this first section, Denisse Albornoz, Angela Okune, and Leslie Chan consider what it might take to transform our notions of pragmatic open access, in the present, into future realities that address inequality. Examining several worldwide systems of scholarly communications from decolonial and feminist perspectives aligned with thinkers such as Boaventura de Sousa Santos, Jean and John Comaroff, Walter Mignolo, Anne Mahler, Maria Lugones, Arturo Escobar, and Raewyn Connell, they propose a model that will address the social justice and educational issues that sit at the heart of open access. For "the infrastructures we build and the practices we enable," they write, "need intentionally to aim to highlight voices, worldviews and epistemologies that have been historically excluded from the system."

The second section of this book focuses on epistemologies; the ways in which we think about knowledge itself and how this shapes our understandings of digital and open transformations of research publishing. Opening this section, John Willinsky draws on his extensive research into the history of copyright and intellectual property to paint a picture that differs substantially from the mainstream narrative. Turning back to the Statute of Anne from 1710, Willinsky details the ways in which the original purpose of copyright—in the encouragement of learning—has been lost. Indeed, for Willinsky, if we want to take seriously proposals to modify contemporary copyright law, we could do no better than to retrace our historical steps. For the intentions that many now seek, Willinsky argues, were there from the start.

In a slightly different vein, while still thinking about the ways in which conditions of practice loop back into the theoretical considerations that inform them, Robin de Mourat, Donato Ricci, and Bruno Latour document their *An Inquiry into Modes of Existence* (*AIME*) project and the theoretical consequences that arise from it. Taking a social approach to infrastructure—and recognizing that there are competing demands upon any single system because any public is composed of multiple "modes of existence" (a fact reflected in the chapters in this volume, such as Babini's, that recognize different "publics" for research work)—this open project forces us to question the difference between books and blogs, and the challenges of understanding how different intersecting groups can be captured in infrastructure design. Indeed, in their analysis of how a "format" might itself constitute the public to which it speaks, their work touches on vital issues of remediation that have become central to much work in archival studies.[28]

Perhaps one of the most crucial "formats" though, for scholarly communications, is that of the "peer-reviewed work." To address this matter, we turn to the questions raised by David Pontille and Didier Torny in their chapter. Namely: how does the material that is published become so in the present day? What are the evaluative mechanisms that sort the wheat from the chaff? And, in conjunction with Aileen Fyfe's chapter, how can we understand the historical development of these systems of peer review into the present day? Tracing peer review back to the seventeenth century, Pontille and Torny yield a historically informed investigation into the roots of contemporary review practices, functioning, in their terms, as a technology. At the close of their piece, they turn to the ways in which future imagined structures of review sit within such paradigms of thought, but also counter them as continuous instances of judgment.

Finally for our section on knowledge cultures, Pamela H. Smith, Tianna Helena Uchacz, Naomi Rosenkranz, and Claire Conklin Sabel revisit our historical assumptions about epistemology and science in the light of their openly accessible web project. Indeed, Smith et al. draw our attention to the way in which early scientific experiments were conducted by Renaissance artists, historians, and humanists, blurring the distinctions between humanistic and scientific practices, but also focusing on the transmission of this knowledge and the genealogies of craft dissemination. Smith et al. achieve this by documenting their project—the *Making of Empirical Knowledge*—and the finds that they there unearth.

The third section of this book turns to different audiences and publics, and the politics of the open dissemination of research work. For Aileen Fyfe, in this space, we have overlooked a history of publication in which the desire to make scholarship widely available and free to read is far longer than we might otherwise presume. Turning to what is broadly acknowledged as the first scientific journal publication—*The Philosophical Transactions*—Fyfe traces the financial context of its production through gift economies and reprints to one with an *aspiration* for open access, in an era without the technological promise so hailed by the Budapest Declaration in later years.

That said, we are also notoriously bad at revising our pasts in a romantic light when it suits us, as Stuart Lawson shows. In their chapter, Lawson seeks to retell the story that we tell ourselves that public libraries have always been institutions of progressive social change. Instead, as Lawson details, these institutions were embroiled in conflicts of class, race, and empire. This is not to say that public libraries have not yielded public benefits, but it does give us cause for concern if we seek a historical narrative of actual library practices. Perhaps in contrast to Willinsky, Lawson posits, sometimes it is what we have become, rather than whence we came, that matters most.

Continuing this exploration of the present and the current status of open access is taken up in Maura A. Smale's chapter on the contemporary public library in the United States of America. Furthering other work in this volume on the different models of library infrastructure, Smale argues that libraries—whether they be public, academic, or even high school-level—should embrace open access for its transformative potential. Rooting her analysis in Sirkazhi Ramamrita Ranganathan's 1931 volume, *The Five Laws of Library Science*, Smale's chapter is perhaps among the more concrete and hopeful in this volume. At the same time, though, Smale's chapter also brings to the fore the very real dilemmas faced by libraries in our present. While this chapter may present familiar ground for many readers, the direness of the contemporary situation for libraries cannot be underscored enough.

Finally, for our section on publics and politics, John Holmwood turns in his chapter to the ways in which the openness of social media systems and scholarly research are part of a broader turn to neoliberal practices in government policy around higher education. Even as it may be well-intentioned, Holmwood warns, open access ends up providing data to organizations that wish harm to our universities–and this must be stopped. More broadly, though, Holmwood also questions the ways in which notions of truth, democracy, and public knowledge circulate in the digital era, bringing a political-economic slant to his chapter. Specifically, how are we to understand the spread of "fake news," even as more and more original research work becomes openly available?

The fourth part of this book turns its focus to archives and preservation. Bethany Nowviskie turns to the ways in which we might encode Afrofuturist thinking and assumptions into our current and future practices. For Nowviskie, as for Lawson, the colonial assumptions about knowledge production and reception condition the possibilities for our understanding. In Noviskie's thinking, we must understand openness as an openness to broader community ownership and involvement, openness to richer scholarly endeavors, and openness for creative or speculative ends.

In her chapter, April M. Hathcock documents the difficulties here in the silences of the archive that we are creating. Chiming with Roh et al.'s chapter on the inequalities of the scholarly communications system, Hathcock's analysis here makes clear the ways in which our choices of selection in the present—shaped by problematic histories and discriminatory contemporary politics—condition the futures of scholarship that are possible. Presenting a complex set of temporal conditions for thinking about digital preservation, Hathcock's chapter warns us of difficulties of archival silence. For one of the biggest concerns of scholarship in the present is that it be rigorously preserved for the future. Since the footnote constitutes, for the most part, our only way of verifying the epistemic claims of scholarship, such matters of preservation—but also matters of *what material is selected for preservation*—are paramount.[29]

Turning inward toward the academy, next, and Dorothea Salo identifies the ways in which problematic politics manifest themselves in university career pathways that continue to turn scholars toward print. Riffing on the well-known Stanley Fish essay, "Is There a Text in This Class?," Salo's "Is There a Text in These Data?" shows us how difficult it is to jettison print for reasons of scarcity and prestige, even as we might be tempted to think that a switch to digital open publishing is merely a matter of time.[30]

In contrast to this, though, is István Rév's chapter. Rév has spent a substantial amount of time working on sensitive archives; documentations of conflict, persecution, and other terrible events of great personal consequence. It would be of great benefit to the collective memory of our world for access to these archives to be open. Yet the dangers at the individual level are substantial and, Rév provocatively argues, the archive should destroy or keep inaccessible portions of its collection in order to serve the whole of society, rather than just historians.

Opening the fifth section of the book, on infrastructures and platforms, Jonathan Gray explores how scholarly communication infrastructures can be understood not just as neutral vehicles for the dissemination of outputs, but as embodying and enabling different forms of value, meaning, sociality, and participation around research activities. Drawing on a range of recent examples, he looks at how such "infrastructural experiments" can enable and materialize different kinds of collective action, participation, and imagination around who has access, what counts, what matters and how relations are organized.

Indeed, it is easy to argue that open access depends upon new technologies and that, as a consequence, a type of technological thinking has made its way into most thinking about open access—at the neglect of community and the social. In their chapter, Penny C. S. Andrews conducts an examination of the ways in which new technological constructions function as platforms, at once enclosing and elevating the scholarship that is platformed. This, though, comes with the dark side of enclosure and totalizing ideas of "platforms" that exhibit negative ideas of "open."

Further to this, as Martin Paul Eve illustrates in his chapter, the digital realm also offers us a solution to a particular problem of proliferation—so long as we can get access. Namely, in an era when there is more published than can possibly ever be read, text and data mining procedures might afford us methods for navigating the vast ocean of scholarship. Exploring initiatives such as The Content Mine led by Peter Murray Rust at Cambridge, this chapter asks, in counterpoint to Salo's, what it means to think of scholarship as data.

The infrastructures that would enable such technological advances are not always in place, though. Indeed, on the ground this type of computational initiative requires extensive work in order to implement machine-readable structures. In their chapter, Arianna Becerril García and Eduardo Aguado-López detail the ways in which such infrastructural improvements could result in greater discoverability and integration of South American research cultures within broader global databases.

Finally for this section, in his chapter, Abel Packer details the history, present, and future of the important SciELO platform in South America. For in many ways, the economic systems by which we are ensnared in the Global North are traps of our own devising. South American countries have pioneered the way in open access and achieved much more than their northern counterparts, as this chapter shows. As the Director of the SciELO project, Packer is uniquely placed to give an informed perspective on one of the longest-standing and most widespread open-access platforms on the planet. He here details the ongoing roadmap that will allow for technical standardization of the SciELO infrastructure and its potential futures.

The last section of this book is dedicated to ideas of community and global community in scholarly communication paradigms. We here open with Eileen A. Joy's chapter on the ethics of care in open-access publishing. For Joy, open access is about far more than the pragmatics of compliance with mandates. Instead, she highlights here the importance of scholar-led infrastructural provision but also the interdependence of open access with other structural problems within the academy, notably the precarity of academic staff. For, if the claim of academic freedom through employment stability is undermined, what is left for the arguments for the freedoms of open access?

Yet care, integration, and thought must be considered not just in local realms but also at the level of the international. Dominique Babini, then, continues this theme in her chapter, noting the preconditions for success in South America to work on a global scale. While acknowledging the challenges, Babini details the work of CLACSO and other organizations in crafting a system of scholarly communications that caters for multiple audiences and addresses, systemically, access challenges both inside and outside of the academy.

On such matters of communality, Jane Winters asks, in her chapter, about the future of learned societies in a world of open access, particularly in the United Kingdom. Winters notes that, for a substantial period of time now, "there has been no need to question or perhaps really even to think about the role of the learned society as publisher" but that this is changing below our very feet. In her chapter, Winters addresses the future of Societies in both economic and social terms but also points toward helpful early experiments in open practice from organizations that have, traditionally, been less enthusiastic about open access, such as the Royal Historical Society.

Likewise, and finally, Kathleen Fitzpatrick brings her expertise of working at the head of a large scholarly society—the Modern Language Association—to discuss the ways in which such entities can resist the constant commercialization of platforms in recent years. Partly leading on from Andrews's previous chapter and partly documenting the creation of MLA Core and Commons, Fitzpatrick fuses a theoretical and practical approach to building an open future for scholarly communications in the humanities disciplines.

Conclusions and Perspectives

In all, then, we intend for this book to perform a range of functions. First, we aim to provide a different set of perspectives on the histories of scholarly communications and to question the dominant narrative of the emergence of open access in the twenty-first century. We excavate a history of the present. Second, we examine how contemporary practices might suggest other alternative arrangements and trajectories, embedding different values and conceptions of the role of scholarship in the contemporary world. Third, we turn to the futures, imagined or in constitution, that might emerge from such differential thought. Throughout the volume we also intersperse case studies, to document for whichever future emerges the possibilities of difference that gave way to historical inevitability. There is of course the danger that this volume will quickly appear dated. Luckily our aim is not to provide a set of policy recommendations, economic models, or technical proposals, but rather to gather a range of perspectives drawing on research in different fields that we hope may continue to inform and inspire experiments and interventions around scholarly communications long after the conditions in which they currently operate have changed.

We also note that many, or even most, of the contributors in this volume are humanists or social scientists. This has been a deliberate decision: we originally set out to explore precisely what kinds of perspectives social and cultural inquiry might bring to the recomposition of scholarly communications. We acknowledge that this might perhaps not be a conventional approach for a book about open access. After all, the humanities can scarcely have said to have been at the forefront of these developments, and it has often been the natural sciences and "STEM" disciplines that have most significantly influenced the environments of research funding, evaluation, and policy. However, it is precisely because of the prominence of more narrowly economic, administrative, and instrumentally "policy-relevant" knowledge cultures that we have sought to surface other lines of inquiry and ways of making sense of the histories, contexts, conditions, and futures of scholarly production.[31]

Introduction

Finally, the texts herein are not intended to cohere into a single outlook, line of inquiry or program—and, as readers will notice, there are numerous differences and tensions between them. For example, Rév's view on openness from his archival perspective is very different to others working on scholarship that would not be published otherwise. We have attempted, also, to think of access in various ways, although future work might wish to engage further with critical disability studies and *accessibility* in that sense, as do a few of the chapters herein. The audiences for this book will also be varied. This book is not, in many ways, an "introduction to open access"; there are certainly other works that are better positioned to fulfill that role.[32] It may, for some, though, be an introduction to the ongoing task of bringing diverse, critical engagements with scholarly communications grounded in social and humanities research to bear on practical interventions to shape its future, as well as an introduction to the approaches of the various fields that have been working with this orientation for many years.[33] It is our hope that both newcomers and seasoned scholarly communication aficionados alike will find provocation in the coming pages, as well as prompts for the progressive recomposition of the systems, infrastructures, and environments across and through which research is shared, used, valued, commodified, challenged, pirated, promoted, and made meaningful.

Notes

1. Even if this view of Gutenberg is Eurocentric. See Clayton M. Christensen, *The Innovator's Dilemma: When New Technologies Cause Great Firms to Fail*, The Management of Innovation and Change Series (Boston: Harvard Business School Press, 1997) for the canonical discussion on disruption.

2. Leslie Chan et al., "Budapest Open Access Initiative," February 14, 2002, http://www.soros.org/openaccess/read.shtml; Peter Suber et al., "Bethesda Statement on Open Access Publishing," 2003, http://dash.harvard.edu/handle/1/4725199; "Berlin Declaration on Open Access to Knowledge in the Sciences and Humanities," October 22, 2003, https://openaccess.mpg.de/Berlin-Declaration.

3. For an introductory primer on open access, see Peter Suber, *Open Access*, Essential Knowledge Series (Cambridge, MA: MIT Press, 2012), http://bit.ly/oa-book.

4. See, for two perspectives on the challenges in the contemporary academy of maintaining that such conditions even exist: Peter Suber, "Open Access When Authors Are Paid," *SPARC Open Access Newsletter*, no. 68 (December 2, 2003), http://dash.harvard.edu/handle/1/4552040; punctum books, "THREAD on What We Feel

Is One of the Most Under-Attended Issues in the Academic Publishing Landscape: Author Compensation. How Can the World's Knowledge Increase When More Than 70% of All Teaching Lines in the US Are Adjunctified & Many Post-PhD Scholars Have No Uni Employment?," Tweet, @punctum_books (blog), March 8, 2019, https://twitter.com/punctum_books/status/1104105017827643392.

5. Peter Suber, "The Taxpayer Argument for Open Access," *SPARC Open Access Newsletter*, no. 65 (September 4, 2003), http://dash.harvard.edu/handle/1/4725013.

6. See Martin Paul Eve, *Open Access and the Humanities: Contexts, Controversies and the Future* (Cambridge: Cambridge University Press, 2014), chap. 2, https://doi.org/10.1017/CBO9781316161012.

7. Heather Morrison, "Elsevier 2009 $2 Billion Profits Could Fund Worldwide OA at $1,383 per Article," *The Imaginary Journal of Poetic Economics* (blog), accessed January 21, 2013, http://poeticeconomics.blogspot.co.uk/2010/04/elsevier-2009-2-billion-profits-could.html.

8. Association of Research Libraries, "ARL Statistics 2009–2011," 2014, https://www.arl.org/arl-statistics-survey-statistical-trends/.

9. See Directory of Open Access Journals, "Journals by Publication Charges," accessed January 20, 2014, https://www.doaj.org/ for the extent to which APCs are charged.

10. See Martin Paul Eve et al., "Cost Estimates of an Open Access Mandate for Monographs in the UK's Third Research Excellence Framework," *Insights: The UKSG Journal* 30, no. 3 (2017), https://doi.org/10.1629/uksg.392.

11. For more see Martin Paul Eve, "Open Publication, Digital Abundance, and Scarce Labour," *Journal of Scholarly Publishing* 49, no. 1 (2017): 26–40, https://doi.org/10.3138/jsp.49.1.26.

12. Jeffrey Beall, "Predatory Publishers Are Corrupting Open Access," *Nature News* 489, no. 7415 (2012): 179, https://doi.org/10.1038/489179a; Jeffrey Beall, "The Open-Access Movement Is Not Really about Open Access," *TripleC: Communication, Capitalism & Critique. Open Access Journal for a Global Sustainable Information Society* 11, no. 2 (2013): 589–597; Peter Mandler, "Open Access for the Humanities: Not for Funders, Scientists or Publishers," *Journal of Victorian Culture* 18, no. 4 (2013): 551–557, https://doi.org/10.1080/13555502.2013.865981; Peter Mandler, "Open Access: A Perspective from the Humanities," *Insights: The UKSG Journal* 27, no. 2 (2014): 166–170, https://doi.org/10.1629/2048-7754.89. See also, for instance Gary Hall, "Should This Be the Last Thing You Read on Academia.Edu?," *Academia.Edu*, 2017, https://www.academia.edu/16959788/Should_This_Be_the_Last_Thing_You_Read_on_Academia.edu.

13. William Davies, *The Limits of Neoliberalism: Authority, Sovereignty and the Logic of Competition* (Thousand Oaks, CA: SAGE, 2014); Wendy Brown, *Undoing the Demos: Neoliberalism's Stealth Revolution* (New York: Zone Books, 2015).

14. See, for just a selection, Bill Readings, *The University in Ruins* (Cambridge, MA: Harvard University Press, 1996); Stefan Collini, *What Are Universities For?* (London: Penguin, 2012); Dubravka Žarkov, "On Intellectual Labour and Neoliberalism in Academia—Or, in Praise of Reviewers," *European Journal of Women's Studies* 22, no. 3 (2015): 269–273, https://doi.org/10.1177/1350506815591920; Richard Hall, *The Alienated Academic: The Struggle for Autonomy Inside the University* (London: Palgrave, 2018), https://doi.org/10.1007/978-3-319-94304-6; Tressie McMillan Cottom, *Lower Ed: The Troubling Rise of for-Profit Colleges in the New Economy* (New York: The New Press, 2018); Stuart Lawson, "Open Access Policy in the UK: From Neoliberalism to the Commons" (Doctoral thesis, Birkbeck, University of London, 2019), https://ethos.bl.uk/OrderDetails.do?uin=uk.bl.ethos.774255/; Liz Morrish and Helen Sauntson, *Academic Irregularities: Language and Neoloberalism in Higher Education*. (New York: Routledge, 2020), https://doi.org/10.4324/9781315561592.

15. Elise Miller, "The People, the Money, the Books: Inside Stanford University Press," *The Stanford Daily* (blog), June 5, 2019, https://www.stanforddaily.com/2019/06/05/the-people-the-money-the-books-inside-stanford-university-press/.

16. For more on this, see James Wilsdon, "Independent Review of the Role of Metrics in Research Assessment," 2015, http://dx.doi.org/10.4135/9781473978782.

17. For more on mandates, see Samuel Moore, "Common Struggles: Policy-Based vs. Scholar-Led Approaches to Open Access in the Humanities" (Doctoral thesis, King's College London, 2019), https://hcommons.org/deposits/item/hc:24135/.

18. Sarah Kember, "Opening Out from Open Access: Writing and Publishing in Response to Neoliberalism," *Ada New Media* (blog), April 21, 2014, https://adanewmedia.org/2014/04/issue4-kember/; Žarkov, "On Intellectual Labour and Neoliberalism in Academia"; David Golumbia, "Marxism and Open Access in the Humanities: Turning Academic Labor against Itself," *Workplace: A Journal for Academic Labor*, no. 28 (2016), https://doi.org/10.14288/workplace.v0i28.186213.

19. John Holmwood, "Markets versus Dialogue: The Debate over Open Access Ignores Competing Philosophies of Openness.," *Impact of Social Sciences* (blog), October 21, 2013, http://blogs.lse.ac.uk/impactofsocialsciences/2013/10/21/markets-versus-dialogue/.

20. For more on this in the US context, see Cottom, *Lower Ed*.

21. Creative Commons, "Case Law," 2013, http://wiki.creativecommons.org/Case_Law; Glyn Moody, "German Court Says Creative Commons 'Non-Commercial' Licenses Must Be Purely For Personal Use," Techdirt, 2014, https://www.techdirt.com/articles/20140326/11405526695/german-court-says-creative-commons-non-commercial-licenses-must-be-purely-personal-use.shtml.

22. See, again, Suber, "The Taxpayer Argument for Open Access."

23. For more on this, see Leslie Chan, Barbara Kirsop, and Subbiah Arunachalam, "Towards Open and Equitable Access to Research and Knowledge for Development," *PLOS Medicine* 8, no. 3 (2011): e1001016, https://doi.org/10.1371/journal.pmed.1001016.

24. SpringerNature, "Prospectus Dated April 25, 2018," 2018, 59.

25. Elsevier, "Pricing," 2018, https://www.elsevier.com/about/our-business/policies/pricing#Dipping.

26. See Eve, *Open Access and the Humanities*, chap. 2.

27. Samuel Moore et al., "Excellence R Us: University Research and the Fetishisation of Excellence," *Palgrave Communications* 3 (2017), https://doi.org/10.1057/palcomms.2016.105.

28. See, for instance, Hannah McGregor, "Remediation as Reading: Digitising The Western Home Monthly," *Archives and Manuscripts* 42, no. 3 (2014): 248–257, https://doi.org/10.1080/01576895.2014.958864; Faye Hammill and Hannah McGregor, "Bundling, Reprinting, and Reframing: Serial Practices Across Borders," *The Journal of Modern Periodical Studies* 9, no. 1 (2019): 76–100.

29. Anthony Grafton, *The Footnote: A Curious History* (Cambridge, MA: Harvard University Press, 1999).

30. Stanley Fish, *Is There a Text in This Class? The Authority of Interpretive Communities* (Cambridge, MA: Harvard University Press, 1990).

31. Anna Severin et al., "Discipline-Specific Open Access Publishing Practices and Barriers to Change: An Evidence-Based Review," *F1000Research* 7 (2018): 1925, https://doi.org/10.12688/f1000research.17328.1.

32. John Willinsky, *The Access Principle: The Case for Open Access to Research and Scholarship, Digital Libraries and Electronic Publishing* (Cambridge, MA: MIT Press, 2006); Suber, *Open Access*; Eve, *Open Access and the Humanities*.

33. For just two recent volumes in such a vein, see Nancy Maron et al., "Open and Equitable Scholarly Communications: Creating a More Inclusive Future" (Chicago: Association of College and Research Libraries, 2019), https://doi.org/10.5860/acrl.1; Kevin L. Smith and Katherine A. Dickson, eds., *Open Access and the Future of Scholarly Communication: Implementation*, Creating the 21st-Century Academic Library 10 (Lanham, MD: Rowman & Littlefield, 2017).

I Colonial Influences

1 Epistemic Alienation in African Scholarly Communications: Open Access as a *Pharmakon*

Thomas Hervé Mboa Nkoudou

Twenty years into the twenty-first century, it must regrettably be admitted that open access (OA) has not fulfilled the lofty ambitions set out in the Budapest Open Access Initiative (BOAI) in 2002. Instead of reducing publication costs, accelerating the dissemination of scientific information, ensuring the visibility of scientific publications, and promoting barrier-free access to scientific information, OA now often seems to reinforce and to create new inequalities. As Ulrich Herb has noted:

> Open access has changed. At the beginning of the millennium, it was portrayed in a romanticising way and was embedded in a conceptual ensemble of participation, democratisation, digital commons and equality. Nowadays, open access seems to be exclusive: to the extent that commercial players have discovered it as a business model and article fees have become a defining feature of gold open access, open access has increasingly transformed into a distinguishing feature and an exclusive element. ... Open access is increasingly becoming an instrument that creates exclusivity, exclusion, distinction and prestige. These functions, however, are obscured by symbolic gift giving strategies and presented as altruistically staged, so that in the discourse of the open access community and in media reporting on open access, the both euphemistic and largely obsolete prosocial story-telling of open access dominates.[1]

Regarding these unmet OA promises, it is important to think about their consequences in the context of the African continent. It is such thinking that is the aim of this chapter—in which, drawing on postcolonial theory, I will examine OA through the lens of the *pharmakon*. The term *pharmakon* comes from the Greek word *pharmakos* (φάρμακον), which refers to a purification ritual that took place in ancient Greece. During this rite, criminals were expelled from the city to purge the polis of the evil that affected it.[2] It may seem ambiguous, but from this ritual, the (criminal) evil is still used to heal the city. In his essay on Plato's *Pharmacy*, and in a more recent context,

Derrida provides a modern and philosophical interpretation of this ritual; he highlights the ambiguity of the term *pharmakon* which can mean both medicine and poison.[3] It is from this perspective that OA can be compared to a *pharmakon*. As I will show in the remainder of this chapter, it is simplistic to consider OA as a unified phenomenon: in some situations, it acts as a poison; in others, as a cure.

The first part of this chapter describes the context in which OA has been adopted in Africa. The second part is an attempt to demonstrate that OA, as here implemented, acts as a poison that causes epistemicides and linguicides in Africa and whose most insidious manifestation is epistemic alienation. Finally, in the third section, I recognize that OA still holds great hope for the African continent—depending on how it is adopted. For these reasons, I here suggest a strategy that will recover the healing potential of open access. By carrying out cognitive decolonization and redesigning OA as a tool of cognitive justice and liberation, this strategy, following Tlostanova and Mignolo, is about learning to unlearn in order to relearn.[4]

There are also a few important up-front clarifications. First, while writing this text, my identity is important: I fully assume my African standpoint. Second, the African academic communities I am talking about here are from universities located in sub-Saharan Africa; there is a specificity to my remarks that can be elided if we treat "Africa" as a homogeneous whole. Third, the intention of this text is not to retreat into a false and unnecessary dichotomy between the West and Africa. That said, historical and comparative approaches remain useful to understand better the current realities of scholarly communication. Finally, this text is inspired by the fieldwork initiated by the Open Science research project in Haiti and French-speaking African countries, also covered in this book by Denisse Albornoz, Leslie Chan, and Angela Okune.[5] One of the outcomes of this research project was the identification of cognitive injustices, including epistemic alienation, as obstacles to the adoption of open access.

The Biased Beginnings of Open Access in Africa

History shows that, in the contemporary sense, early OA practices began in North America and Europe, with the first online peer-reviewed journal, *New Horizons in Adult Education*, launched in early 1987 by the Syracuse University Kellogg Project.[6] Following this, many new OA services sprang to life on the

World Wide Web. One of the best known and longest running of these is *arXiv*, the first online preprint server, used by physicists to share their papers since 1991. The term "open access" was itself formalized and clearly defined only in 2002, after the Budapest Open Access Initiative (BOAI).[7] This first meeting opened the gate to a cascade of similar summits ending every time with declarations, plans, or programs for open access. From 2002 to the present day, most of these major meetings have taken place in Western countries and under the impetus of the actors from these countries.

Looking to Africa, the promises of OA after the BOAI in 2002 seemed irresistible if we were to address the lack of access to scientific information in African universities. This was probably the beginning of OA in Africa. Taking the well-known theory of Everett Rogers, the spread of OA is here understood as a result of a diffusion process.[8] This is aligned, though, with the notion that the visibility of African scientific production is always dependent on Western initiatives, even when it comes to using open technologies that African practitioners (including librarians and computer scientists) could appropriate in complete autonomy and at a lower cost. The Western origin of OA is, then, clear. This comes with significant challenges for its wholesale import into new African contexts.

Early Mismatching in the African Context

Considering the lack of a strong cultural attachment to OA in African academic communities, it is worth examining the history of its adoption. Even at a first glance, we can see that OA faces different challenges in Africa than in Western countries. Many factors suggest that OA is a matter for the rich countries of the Global North, where basic infrastructural matters, such as regular and reasonable salaries for academics, public research grants, access to the internet, electricity, well-supported libraries, and comfortable and safe workplaces have long been settled.[9] On this basis, it makes little sense to say that we are dealing with the "same" OA in both contexts and the motivations to fight for OA cannot necessarily be assumed to be the same. This disjunction stems from the failure to account for African realities since the beginning of the diffusion of OA.

Indeed, since the beginning of OA, there have been local barriers to uptake that, unfortunately, persist to this day. These include lack of infrastructure, lack of internet access in African universities, and the low digital literacy of most scholars. These barriers inhibit OA, and particularly green OA, whose promises seemed most to meet Africa's needs. In this latter case, the barriers consist of a scarcity of institutional repositories, librarians untrained in matters of open access, and the passivity of library staff with respect to introducing OA into academic practice.[10] In addition, the absence of local funder interest in OA and the lack of financial resources in African universities, compound libraries' expenditure on so-called "prestigious" journals. These barriers are the root of the failure of OA to meet its promises of rapid dissemination and access to scientific information on the African continent.

Another hope for OA was to make visible and accessible to Western scholars unknown and neglected research from the Global South.[11] However, in addition to the barriers mentioned above, this vision for OA faces resistance (involuntary or not) from African researchers. Among the reasons that can explain this resistance, the first is that the desire to make African knowledge visible was not truly an African initiative. The idea originated from the difficulty faced by some Western scholars in discovering knowledge produced in the Global South. The second was that many African researchers perceive OA as a threat to the supposed income they believe they will receive from their scientific publications. It must be said that, in Africa, the publication of an academic book and the rights that a person could derive from it are erroneously seen as possible income sources. This false perception is reinforced by a lack of knowledge about copyright and open licenses. Third, the scarcity of funding and grants for research leads to a lack of incentives for Africans to engage in OA. For while in some Western countries there are incentives (carrots) and mandates (sticks) that facilitate the adoption of OA, this is often because research is publicly funded. This is not always the case in Africa, where researchers are self-funded or supported by Western programs (although this can be different in a few countries, such as South Africa).

Thus, although the 2002 BOAI declaration was paved with good intentions, it did not address the realities of its adoption on the African continent.

Is Open Access a Poison for Africa?

From 2002 to the present day, OA has evolved positively but also been deeply perverted. In this section, I will focus on the dramatic development of OA and its consequences in the African academic milieu.

At its birth, OA was a broadly unified and idealistic movement with the green and gold routes; supported by a small but strong community of scientists, librarians, and research sponsors, advocating for free access to information and protesting against the high costs of publications. Over time, this romantic vision of OA has undergone fundamental changes that have distorted it toward market orientation, control, and governance of information and research.

The capitalist/market orientation of contemporary OA is evidenced by the economic language of the major laws, declarations, and policies.[12] For example, the 2012 Finch Report in the UK called for accountability, efficiency, and economic growth.[13] In the OA2020 initiative, libraries are considered as the organizers of the cash flows in the subscription system and the initiative is seen as an improvement of research evaluation.[14] In the same vein, the European Commission's 2016 publication considers that "open science is as important and disruptive a shift as e-commerce has been for retail. Just like e-commerce, it affects the whole 'business cycle' of doing science and research—from the selection of research subjects, to the carrying out of research and to its use and re-use—as well as all the actors and actions involved up front (e.g., universities) or down the line (e.g., publishers)."[15]

These changes and a shift toward economic thinking began with the growing interest in OA by commercial publishers. These entities have now infiltrated the decision-making spheres—often lobbying at the highest levels of politics—and created an imbalance in their favor within the discourse of open access.[16] That said, it is clear that green OA is a harder route to commercially exploit than is gold. Regarding the domination of commercial publishers in OA communities, it is hardly surprising, then, that article processing charges (APCs) have gained importance as the dominant and most prominent, even if not the most widespread, business model for open-access journals.[17] For this reason, I here focus on APCs, without wishing to ignore other, potentially better, models for gold OA. The sad truth, though, is that many African researchers cannot afford the costs required for authors to publish in APC-based journals. Hence, this model can be considered as a vehicle of continued exclusion.

In addition, there is a tight relationship between APC pricing and a journal's Impact Factor (IF). The higher a journal's IF, the higher the costs of APCs are set.[18] Thus, APCs consolidate the market strategy of publishers, whose approaches have always been based on the mirrored spaces of economics and prestige. This is encouraged at the local level by the promotion and tenure system which, despite declarations such as the San Francisco Declaration on Research Assessment (DORA), is still embedded in traditional practices of scientific publications and often gives more importance to high IF journals. This importance is given at the expense of local scientific production and open journals, which local promotion and tenure systems often consider to be of poor quality. This disregard of published work in journals outside these criteria is also visible at the global level. Indeed, academic institutions of the Global North will not usually recognize journals from Africa as being of high quality and sometimes these titles are not listed in scientific databases commonly used in Western universities (e.g., Scopus, Web of Science). Of this, Chan notes that

> historically institutions, and in particular publishers, from the [G]lobal North have largely established the quality standards for journals. Things like peer review, citation formats, writing or rhetoric styles, and external markers such as journal Impact Factor. Confronted with academic journals from countries of the [G]lobal South that they are not familiar with, librarians but also scientists, often assume that if these quality markers are absent or not recognisable, then the journals are of lesser or even questionable quality. This assumption is wrong but it continues today.[19]

In the end, the APC model represents the most visible capitalist trajectory of OA. It sets up a financial barrier to publish in "prestigious" journals; a form of exclusion that in almost all cases rules out researchers from African universities. It also consolidates the myth of the Impact Factor, leading to the exclusion of some journals according to their geographical origin. This second form of exclusion further allows us to make a parallel with Wallerstein's theory of capitalism, in which academia can be considered like a world system with scientific publication as the commercial unit.[20] Europe and North America sit at the center of the system, and countries of the Global South, including Africa, are placed at the periphery.

Coloniality of Knowledge in Open Access

In the thinking of Suárez Krabbe, coloniality refers to the fact that the relationship between colonialism and coloniality is structural and persisting, in opposition to the idea that colonialism is over.[21] Based on the insight that colonial societies have systematically banished indigenous forms of knowledge, coloniality of knowledge is a theoretical concept first developed by

Aníbal Quijano, and later by Walter Mignolo.[22] The concept describes the ongoing colonial access to, as well as the distribution, production, and reproduction of, knowledge, and the often subtle processes that ultimately exclude and occlude alternative *epistemes* (or ways of knowing). My interest in this section is to show how coloniality of knowledge manifests in OA in the context of the African continent.

If one examines platforms that harvest information available on the web, it quickly becomes apparent that most information resources come from the North. Web of Science, for example, reveals that Africa produces less than 1 percent of scientific articles in the world. This African contribution is shared between North Africa (44 percent) and sub-Saharan Africa (56 percent), but this nuance should be noted: production in sub-Saharan Africa is largely dominated by English-speaking countries. Indeed, in the sub-Saharan level, Francophone Africa produces only 2.75 percent of articles; this means that, at the global level, its contribution is almost zero (0.01 percent).[23] Do these proportions reflect the reality of scientific production? Clearly not—there are many high-quality articles written in Africa, but they are not included in web platforms such as the Web of Science. This is either because a large number of them exist in a physical format (hard copies) that prevents their circulation, diffusion, and sharing on the web; or because many African journals do not meet the infrastructural requirements of these web platforms. It is true that these platforms existed before the beginning of OA. But they also joined the OA movement, and now harvest almost all the OA resources that circulate on the web. As a result, the scientific information disseminated by these platforms reaches the majority of internet users in Africa, to a greater extent than local scientific productions. This situation strongly contributes to an ongoing coloniality of knowledge.

Fifty years ago, we would have found a reason for this exclusion, in that the costs associated with the production and distribution of physical (printed) documents were very high. In the contemporary era, this argument is not relevant, since the internet, the web, and OA have reduced production costs substantially and made the subsequent dissemination of information instantaneous. The paradox is that, despite this coloniality, Africans do not seize the opportunity of green OA to disseminate the grey literature that is abundant in African universities. Indeed, OpenDOAR and ROAR show that there are currently just three institutional repositories (IR) in sub-Saharan French-speaking Africa, compared to 130 in the rest of sub-Saharan Africa, including 33 in South Africa and 26 in Kenya.[24] The repository located in

Cameroon contains 31 documents and is not associated with any university, but rather with an association for the promotion of science. The Senegalese deposit of the African Institute for Economic Development and Planning (IDEP) also is not associated with any university, while the deposit of Institut Fondamental d'Afrique Noire (IFAN) is inaccessible. This exposes clearly a difficulty for the adoption of OA in African universities and particularly in sub-Saharan French-speaking Africa. Hence, these IRs do not reflect the actual scientific production of African universities. Under these conditions, how can we avoid a coloniality of African scientific production, if researchers do not have the possibility to self-archive and contribute themselves to the circulation of their work even through green OA?

Epistemic Alienation

We can define epistemic alienation as the distortion of one's native way of thinking, and of seeing and speaking of one's own reality. In Africa, this cognitive distortion is led by the adoption (unconscious or not) of Eurocentric philosophical, sociological, and historical thought—used to speak of, to describe, and to study African realities. Epistemic alienation is symptomatized by epistemicide: destruction of local epistemologies that are replaced, in this case, by a Western paradigm.[25] The African university system is one of the main causes of epistemic alienation because these institutions simply replicate Western universities, without any effort to contextualize missions, curricula, and structure. And indeed, these postcolonial universities are still dependent on the West; this dependence can be economic, scientific, or related to the language of instruction.[26]

On economic dependence, Piron et al. consider that postcolonial scientific research remains fundamentally outward facing and organized to meet a theoretical, scientific, and economic demand of the center of the system.[27] In other words, the fact that African policy makers do not always prioritize research funding in their countries makes them dependent on the scientific agendas of donors, most of whom are from the North. Extended to equipment, documentation, and scientific paradigms from the North, this dependence profoundly affects the African researcher's way of thinking. And current OA policies are not helping to change this situation, because many of them are international and shaped for Western contexts. There are a few true and effective African OA policies, which are not just replications or extensions of Western OA policies. But this situation would be a little different if government economic policies were to financially support common thinking on how to find solutions to local problems.

A scientific dependence is visible in the way in which Western authors and materials are frequently cited in scientific papers, theses, and dissertations produced in African universities. In French-speaking African countries, for example, one can note the prevalence of French authors in humanities and social sciences. By way of anecdote, this calls to mind a question I asked of a Cameroonian sociologist: "Do you think that Pierre Bourdieu can better describe our realities than what your colleagues here, at the University of Yaoundé I, wrote?" Because of the universal fame of authors such as Pierre Bourdieu, using them as a reference instead of a local author is prevalent in the practice of many African researchers, despite the difference in the specificity of the context. This choice is sometimes justified by claims of unawareness of the work of local colleagues and that all to which they have access, online/offline, or even OA, are the papers of authors like Pierre Bourdieu. This situation is not ideal for the humanities and social sciences, but the same issues are present in hard sciences. By way of another example, attending a friend's thesis defense in geology, I was outraged when the jury asked the candidate why he didn't cite an overseas journal with a high Impact Factor; despite the fact that he had already cited all the relevant locally contextualized literature. Afterwards, I asked my friend why he used, and why the jury encouraged him to use, Western journals. In his view, local journals are not serious; most of them disappear one to two years after their launch. Even if they continue to function, their periodicity is not always respected. The bias toward the citation of Western material that emerges from this, though, means that issues that are specific to Africa are pursued with less vigor, and OA accentuates this problem. This is because most OA scientific publications available and diffused on the web, with high visibility, are from the North. In this logic, OA aggravates epistemic alienation by reinforcing the use of the scientific work from the center of the world-system, while consolidating Eurocentric thought as the global theoretical reference or normative model, to the detriment of local epistemologies.

However, we should not place the entire blame for this situation on Western people, systems, and countries. This situation may be the responsibility of the local researchers themselves, due to their lack of OA literacy and practices. We can point the finger at librarians, who are not advising their institutions of current OA practices and the necessity to establish OA policies or infrastructures, such as institutional repositories and open journals. We can also put the blame on leaders of academic institutions who do not prioritize OA in their policies. We could also blame the editors of local journals for allowing their titles to die out. In addition, promoters of local journals need to be trained and supported by decision makers and OA policies. One can point to the fact that in countries such as South Africa, efforts are being made to change this reality.[28] But we must accept the obvious—that South Africa is not at the same level of development as many African countries. To do otherwise is to hide the realities of the majority of Africa.

On the matter of language, it must also be recognized that African researchers face a real dilemma. All have a first African language, with English, French, Spanish, or Portuguese being only secondary languages. Therefore, Africans feel obliged to undertake the difficult exercise of translating their thoughts into the colonial languages imposed in academic curricula. Added to the above, the inherent looseness of translation lends imprecision to the dissemination of African knowledge within a context dominated by Eurocentrism and English as the *lingua franca*. This linguistic distortion contributes to the marginalization and denial of African languages and fatally to their linguicide. This is another epistemic alienation that the current practices of scholarly communication and OA promote. Julia Schöneberg puts it very well in these terms:

> Translations make knowledge available to Eurocentric-dominated realms that they wouldn't otherwise appear in. Also, publications receive less recognition if not published in (mostly) English "high-ranked" journals and publishers. Vernacular language is rarely acknowledged as "academically relevant."[29]

While there are celebrated cases, such as Ngũgĩ wa Thiong'o, who chooses to write in his native language, who reads and how many people can read these languages? Indeed, African researchers face the difficult choice between sacrificing the relevance of their ideas in the local community, for the visibility that writing in English provides; or the opposite.[30]

The debasement of OA has had disastrous consequences in the African academic milieu. Amongst them is epistemic alienation, symptomatized by epistemicides (killing of indigenous people's knowledge), and linguicides (killing of indigenous people's languages). It is true that epistemicides and linguicides preexisted OA; but the way OA is going at the global level, and the lack of awareness at the local level, reinforces and accentuates these preexisting problems. On this basis, open access currently contains within it the germs of epistemic poison for Africa.

Rethinking OA: A Decolonized Approach to Scholarly Communication

The fact that OA can be an epistemic poison for Africa does not mean that it should be abandoned. Indeed, OA offers African scholarship unprecedented *opportunities* to reach previously inaccessible audiences—nationally, regionally, and internationally. Thus, failing to embrace OA would mean missing a great opportunity to improve the dissemination, visibility, and impact of research findings from the African continent. Depending on how we approach it, OA can be a cure for these ills; that is why in this section I am borrowing from Tlostanova and Mignolo, to call for a process of "learning to unlearn in order to relearn."[31] This process follows a twofold approach: decolonize the way of thinking and redesign OA to make it more relevant to the African context.

Cognitive Decolonization as a Starting Point

Many strategies can be established to seize OA as an opportunity. The starting point is to decolonize the way of thinking of scholars from both South and North. It can be surprising to mention Western scholars here, but it is important for them to make an epistemological rupture to better understand all the potential, nuances, and limits that they cannot see, blinded by their context. I am lucky to have graduated in both systems, Western and African universities; I can guarantee that those experiencing only the Western reality, where academic conditions are optimal, will not be aware of the realities and barriers faced by African universities and researchers. That is why it is so important to decolonize the way of thinking of scholars from the North. To achieve cognitive decolonization, I suggest a dual approach.

First, we should privilege and prioritize recognition and representation of the perspectives, epistemologies, contexts, and methodologies that inform knowledge production globally and locally.[32] This will help to develop the confidence of academics in knowledge, history, and language from the periphery. To do this, we will use epistemological decolonization that deals with problems such as epistemicides, linguicides, cultural imperialism, and alienation, through a double task of "provincializing the center of the system" and "deprovincializing Africa."[33] "Provincializing the center of the system," then, is a process of "moving the center" by confronting the problem of overrepresentation of Western thought in knowledge, social theory, and education. According to Ndlovu-Gatsheni, "deprovincializing Africa" is "an intellectual and academic process of centering Africa as a legitimate historical unit of analysis and epistemic site from which to interpret the world while at the same time globalizing knowledge from Africa."[34]

Second, we should facilitate and promote the creation of socially relevant knowledge, independently of Western norms and standards.[35] This is the quest of epistemic freedom (which is the right to think, to theorize, and to interpret the world; to develop one's own methodologies, and to write from where one is located, unencumbered by Eurocentrism): to democratize "knowledge" from its current rendition in the singular into its plural form, "knowledges."[36] This search for epistemic freedom is aligned with the concept of cognitive justice, initially defined "as a recognition of diverse ways of knowing by which human beings across the globe make sense of their existence."[37] Indeed, Piron et al. define cognitive justice as an epistemological, ethical, and political ideal aimed at the emergence of socially relevant knowledge everywhere on the planet, not only in the countries of the North, but within an inclusive science open to all knowledge.[38]

Through this process, scholarship could be decolonized, empowered, and enabled to define and design the best ways to adopt OA according to local needs.

The Redesign of Open Access as a Tool of Cognitive Justice

Open access can be made a tool of cognitive justice if we take into account the enhancement of knowledge produced in the periphery, particularly in sub-Saharan Africa. To achieve this, I recommend a five-point approach:

First, we must *embrace open science as the next stage of OA*. While enabling access to knowledge and research results through a multiplicity of dissemination possibilities, open participatory science will also help us to seize the prevalent power relations that structure knowledge production into interconnecting hierarchies at local and global levels. As Chan notes:

> Open Science aims for the entire research process to become more open: including the production of the research question, methodologies, through to data collection, peer review, publication and dissemination. In that way, it is easier to look at who is participating in these processes of knowledge production and what kind of power they have in a given context. It allows us to be more cognisant of how power is prevalent in systems of knowledge production, and allows us to think of ways to democratise these processes—to make them more collaborative and equitable.[39]

Second, we should *explore alternative ways for communicating research, aside from a traditional, published journal article*. This is especially relevant because African scientific knowledge is mostly found in the grey literature (theses, dissertations, and research reports) and they are rarely online or freely accessible. As a result, they are invisible in Northern databases and do not demonstrate their full potential in many contexts. That is why it is crucial to promote and to reinforce green OA. Additionally, we should consider the fact that younger scientists are using blogs and wikis for collaborative research development rather than the more competitive mode of research production to which older researchers are accustomed. Attention to this "grey literature" is important.

Third, we require local criteria for research assessment and evaluation, adapted to African realities, without any constraint to satisfy the requirement to publish in prestigious journals. For, as Eve Gray has written: "a truly African-focused scholarly publishing programme, for example, should not necessarily follow the international dominance of scholarly journals, but should publish according to the needs of target audiences, whether that be articles, research reports, data sets, and monographs, as well as publications targeted at non-scholarly audiences, such as manuals and handbooks."[40]

Fourth, we *need to train and to attune local stakeholders in and to decolonized OA*. I totally agree with Piron et al. that African university libraries, if better funded and their staff better trained in decolonized OA, could play a major role in locating, archiving, and preserving local scientific documents as well as in the management of these archives.[41] This will help them gain confidence in their ability to create knowledge relevant to their community.

Fifth, for all these initiatives to be fully realized, it is imperative to *develop open-access policies that are sensitive to cognitive justice*. As Gray says in this regard: "policy formulation would thus need to grapple with issues of access and development impact, rather than just the question of academic prestige. Publication policy cannot privilege international publication over local but needs to focus primarily on the production of high-quality and relevant research to meet African development needs and only in second place deal with the need for international prestige."[42]

At the conclusion of this chapter, I have presented the case that OA, as it is deployed today, contains a poisonous element for Africa and that this will remain the case if nothing is done. But we can still remedy this situation if we adopt a decolonized approach to scholarly communication. In this regard, the five recommendations I am making here should sound an alarm bell for all actors in the OA community around the world so that, together, we can get OA back on track in the quest for the common good.

Notes

1. Ulrich Herb, "Open Access and Symbolic Gift Giving," in *Open Divide: Critical Studies on Open Access*, ed. Joachim Schöpfel and Ulrich Herb (Sacramento, CA: Library Juice Press, 2018), 69, https://doi.org/10.5281/zenodo.1206377.

2. Jan Bremmer, "Scapegoat Rituals in Ancient Greece," *Harvard Studies in Classical Philology* 87 (1983): 299, https://doi.org/10.2307/311262.

3. Jacques Derrida, "Plato's Pharmacy," in *Dissemination*, trans. Barbara Johnson (London: Continuum, 2004), 67–186.

4. Madina V. Tlostanova and Walter D. Mignolo, *Learning to Unlearn: Decolonial Reflections from Eurasia and the Americas* (Columbus: Ohio State University Press, 2012).

5. "Projet SOHA," Science Ouverte Haïti Afrique, accessed June 1, 2019, https://www.projetsoha.org/.

6. Although, as Abel Packer notes in his chapter, South American initiatives were also ahead of the curve in this respect.

7. See Leslie Chan et al., "Budapest Open Access Initiative," February 14, 2002. http://www.soros.org/openaccess/read.shtml.

8. Everett M. Rogers, *Diffusion of Innovations* (New York: Simon and Schuster, 2003).

9. For more on this basic infrastructural provision, see Maura A. Smale's chapter in this volume.

10. As Reggie Raju et al. have alluded to in their chapter in this book.

11. Leslie Chan, "Asymmetry and Inequality as a Challenge for Open Access—An Interview with Leslie Chan (Interview by Joachim Schöpfel)," in *Open Divide: Critical Studies on Open Access*, ed. Ulrich Herb and Joachim Schöpfel (Sacramento, CA: Library Juice Press, 2018), 169–182.

12. Jutta Haider, "Openness as Tool for Acceleration and Measurement: Reflections on Problem Representations Underpinning Open Access and Open Science," in *Open Divide: Critical Studies on Open Access*, ed. Ulrich Herb and Joachim Schöpfel (Sacramento, CA: Library Juice Press, 2018), 17–30.

13. Working Group on Expanding Access to Published Research Findings ("Finch Group"), "Accessibility, Sustainability, Excellence: How to Expand Access to Research Publications," August 20, 2012, 5, https://doi.org/10.2436/20.1501.01.187.

14. Max Planck Digital Library, "Roadmap," *Open Access 2020* (blog), 2017, https://oa2020.org/.

15. European Commission, "Open Innovation, Open Science, Open to the World—a Vision for Europe," Text, Digital Single Market—European Commission, May 30,

2016, 33, https://ec.europa.eu/digital-single-market/en/news/open-innovation-open-science-open-world-vision-europe.

16. See, for example, Martin Paul Eve, "Transcript of Meeting between Elsevier and the Minister for Higher Education in the UK, Jo Johnson," Martin Paul Eve, May 4, 2016, https://eve.gd/2016/05/04/what-elsevier-and-the-minister-for-higher-education-in-the-uk-jo-johnson-met-about/.

17. Nina Schönfelder, "APCs—Mirroring the Impact Factor or Legacy of the Subscription-Based Model? Regression Analysis," *National Contact Point Open Access* (blog), January 21, 2019, https://oa2020-de.org/en/blog/2019/01/21/APCregressionanalysis/.

18. Schönfelder, "APCs."

19. Chan, "Asymmetry and Inequality as a Challenge for Open Access."

20. For more on this, see Immanuel Maurice Wallerstein, *World-Systems Analysis: An Introduction* (Durham, NC: Duke University Press, 2004).

21. Julia Suárez Krabbe, "Introduction: Coloniality of Knowledge and Epistemologies of Transformation," *KULT. Postkolonial Temaserie* 6 (2009): 1–10.

22. For an overview, see Gesa Mackenthun, "Coloniality of Knowledge," Institut für Anglistik/Amerikanistik—Universität Rostock, April 19, 2016, https://www.iaa.uni-rostock.de/forschung/laufende-forschungsprojekte/american-antiquities-prof-mackenthun/project/theories/coloniality-of-knowledge/.

23. Thomas Hervé Mboa Nkoudou, "Le Web et la production scientifique africaine: visibilité réelle ou inhibée?," *Projet SOHA* (blog), June 18, 2016, https://www.projetsoha.org/?p=1357.

24. Florence Piron et al., "Le Libre Accès vu d'Afrique Francophone Subsaharienne," *Revue Française Des Sciences de l'information et de La Communication*, no. 11 (2017), https://doi.org/10.4000/rfsic.3292.

25. Thomas Hervé Mboa Nkoudou, "The (Unconscious?) Neocolonial Face of Open Access" (OpenCon 2017, Berlin, 2017), https://www.youtube.com/watch?v=-HSOzoSLHL0; Florence Piron et al., *Justice Cognitive, Libre Accès et Savoirs Locaux: Pour une Science Ouverte Juste, au Service du Développement Local Durable* (Éditions science et bien commun, 2016), https://scienceetbiencommun.pressbooks.pub/justicecognitive1/; Sabelo J. Ndlovu-Gatsheni, "The Dynamics of Epistemological Decolonisation in the 21st Century: Towards Epistemic Freedom," *Strategic Review for Southern Africa* 40, no. 1 (2018): 16–45.

26. Bonaventure Mve Ondo, "La Fracture Scientifique," *Présence Africaine* 175-176-177, no. 1 (2007): 585, https://doi.org/10.3917/presa.175.0585; Eric Fredua-Kwarteng, "The Case for Developmental Universities," University World News, October 30, 2015, https://www.universityworldnews.com/post.php?story=20151028020047530; Raewyn Connell, "Using Southern Theory: Decolonizing Social Thought in Theory,

Research and Application," *Planning Theory* 13, no. 2 (2014): 210–223, https://doi.org/10.1177/1473095213499216.

27. Piron et al., "Le Libre Accès vu d'Afrique Francophone Subsaharienne."

28. Again, see Raju et al.'s chapter.

29. Julia Schöneberg, "Decolonising Teaching Pedagogies—Convivial Reflections," *Convivial Thinking* (blog), August 14, 2018, https://www.convivialthinking.org/index.php/2018/08/14/decolonising-teaching-pedagogies-convivial-reflections/.

30. Francis Nyamnjoh, "Institutional Review: Open Access and Open Knowledge Production Processes: Lessons from CODESRIA," *South African Journal of Information and Communication*, no. 10 (2010): 67–72, https://doi.org/10.23962/10539/19772.

31. Tlostanova and Mignolo, *Learning to Unlearn*.

32. Nyamnjoh, "Institutional Review"; Piron et al., "Le Libre Accès vu d'Afrique Francophone Subsaharienne."

33. Ndlovu-Gatsheni, "The Dynamics of Epistemological Decolonisation."

34. Ndlovu-Gatsheni, "The Dynamics of Epistemological Decolonisation."

35. Piron et al., "Le Libre Accès vu d'Afrique Francophone Subsaharienne."

36. Ndlovu-Gatsheni, "The Dynamics of Epistemological Decolonisation."

37. Boaventura de Sousa Santos, ed., *Cognitive Justice in a Global World: Prudent Knowledges for a Decent Life* (Lanham, MD: Lexington Books, 2007); Shiv Visvanathan, "The Search for Cognitive Justice," India Seminar, 2009, http://www.india-seminar.com/2009/597/597_shiv_visvanathan.htm.

38. Piron et al., "Le Libre Accès vu d'Afrique Francophone Subsaharienne."

39. Chan, "Asymmetry and Inequality as a Challenge for Open Access."

40. Eve Gray, "Bridging the North-South Divide in Scholarly Communication: Threats and Opportunities in the Digital Era At the South-Eastern Frontier: The Impact of Higher Education Policy on African Research Publication," 2006, http://www.policy.hu/gray/docs/ASC_Codesria_conference_paper.doc.

41. Piron et al., "Le Libre Accès vu d'Afrique Francophone Subsaharienne."

42. Gray, "Bridging the North-South Divide in Scholarly Communication."

2 Scholarly Communications and Social Justice

Charlotte Roh, Harrison W. Inefuku, and Emily Drabinski

The Open Access Movement has disrupted academic publishing, convincing academics and policy makers that research should be published in venues without paywall barriers. Academic institutions across the globe, including Harvard University and the University of Nairobi, have passed open-access policies that require faculty to make their work openly accessible, whether or not they are directed to do so by funding agencies. National governments in the United States, Japan, Argentina, and elsewhere have used legislation and regulatory policies to mandate that taxpayer-funded research be made publicly accessible through open-access publication. Influential nongovernment and private agencies—such as the United Nations Educational, Scientific, and Cultural Organization, the Gates Foundation, and the Andrew W. Mellon Foundation—have followed. For many, the moral argument for this is straightforward: important and useful research, like education itself, is a public good to which everyone should have access, particularly when it is paid for with public money.[1]

This fundamental social justice message of the Open Access Movement—that knowledge is a public good—connects the field of scholarly publishing to other social justice concerns. Yet, the universal impact of open access cannot simply be assumed or asserted. Access does not necessarily mean equality, and sometimes does not even mean equality of access. In the words of Safiya Noble, "the gatekeeping function of publishing is fundamental to issues of social justice ... the classification and dissemination of knowledge has never been a neutral project, and is often working in a broader context of nation-building, and to a larger degree, cultural domination. Knowledge and its dissemination are social constructs, with a variety of attendant values that are privileged."[2]

Academic publishing, or scholarly communication as it is now called, finds its home and values in academic institutions that reflect and reinforce colonialist structures of power. These systems must themselves be transformed if open access is to make good on its promise as a project of justice and equity.

Rooted in Colonial Privilege

In the United States, works authored by federal government employees are in the public domain, but the idea that government-funded research should be open to the public is relatively new. Western scholarly publishing began as the correspondence of gentlemen who had the leisure and wealth to indulge their intellectual curiosities, whose letters evolved into the journals and monographs that are now seen as traditional and inevitable. In order to access academic newsletters and journals, scholars paid membership fees to scholarly societies or subscribed to lending libraries, as Aileen Fyfe and Stuart Lawson explore further in this volume.

As Western colonialism expanded, so did universities and their presses. Oxford University Press is a clear example of how knowledge production and dissemination emerged as an aspect of the colonial project. According to its website, "Oxford University Press is the world's largest university press with the widest global presence," an acclamation that is consonant with British plans to govern the globe. Further, the Press describes its growth in alignment with conquest: "from the late 1800s OUP began to expand significantly, opening the first overseas OUP office in New York in 1896. Other international branches followed, including Canada (1904), Australia (1908), India (1912), Southern Africa (1914)."[3] These branches were all built in places where the British Empire had established a strong colonial foothold. The claim that the Oxford University Press is the largest university press in the world may well be because the sun never set on the British Empire.

Similarly, Elsevier's success as the largest academic publisher in the world can be correlated with the success of the Dutch Empire. In addition, Elsevier's parent company, Reed Elsevier, was involved in the arms trade through conference services until outrage from its medical publishing clients forced divestiture in 2007.[4] It is no coincidence that the largest, most lucrative, and most influential academic publishers are headquartered in the Global North (Springer in Germany, Wiley in the United States). The power to shape scholarly communications on a global scale—facilitated by the legacy of colonial extraction and the imposition of systems and knowledge from those in power—continues to this day. Regardless of the subject matter, the academic publishing system, structured and controlled by commercial and university presses headquartered in Europe and North America, has produced a scholarly record dominated by scholarship from the Global North.

For example, a 2013 study of economics papers found that only 1.5 percent of economics articles in top-tier journal articles were about countries other than the United States, while only about three papers about the poorest 20 countries were published every two years.[5] While many point to the impact of the digital divide, contributions to the scholarly record from scholars in the Global South are hampered by more than unequal access to digital technologies.[6] Systemic obstacles include the perceived importance of global and local knowledge, language, and negative perceptions of research from the Global South, as covered by Packer, Babini, and others in this volume.

When selecting research topics, scholars from South America, Africa, and Asia often have to choose between focusing their research on a topic of local interest or choosing topics that are more likely to be published in the top journals in their field.[7] Journals with high impact factors have editorial boards composed primarily of researchers in North America and Western Europe, which means the scope of these journals is evaluated by the criteria of the Global North. When scholars from other parts of the world choose to research topics of local importance, whether poverty, tropical diseases, or local folklore, they risk relegation to the periphery of the scholarly record. Richard Horton, an editor of medical journal *The Lancet*, noted that "we editors seek a global status for our journals, but we shut out the experiences and practices of those living in poverty by our (unconscious) neglect. One group is advantaged while the other is marginalized."[8] The marginalization of non-Western topics spans disciplines. Francis Nyamnjoh, former head of the Council for the Development of Social Science Research in Africa, pointed out that "in the social sciences, where objectivity is often distorted by obvious or subtle ideology, African scholars face a critical choice between sacrificing relevance for recognition, or recognition for relevance."[9] These choices for publication relevance have real impact on lives. Jean-Claude Guédon and Alain Loute have pointed out that Zika was first discovered in 1947 but largely ignored by those outside the equatorial belt—including scholarly publications—until it threatened the United States in 2015–2016.[10]

Researchers also have to make a choice between writing in a language that will be accepted by journals published in the Global North or using their local language. Because English is the *lingua franca* of research, scholars must produce scholarship in English if they wish to be published in the "top" international journals. Portuguese scholars Vieira Santos and Nunes da Silva describe the power held by English-fluent scholars, writing that "researchers and reviewers from core Anglophone countries are in a position to dictate parameters to their less-privileged 'peers,' thus imposing not only standard research criteria, but also standard genre models, writing parameters, and publishing guidelines."[11] Ghanaian folklore scholar Kwesi Yankah shared a similar perspective, noting that "African scholars have lamented the marginalization of their manuscripts by Western publishers, who complain of 'intrusive' African vocabularies in titles and texts, intrusive because they are not mainstream languages [and therefore] could pose problems for marketing and smooth reading."[12] Lack of English fluency can also shape a reviewer's perception of submissions, and may be used as a shortcut to judge the overall quality of the paper. As Yankah continues, "Other times, manuscripts and contributions have been rejected for being rather 'descriptive,' 'too data-oriented,' 'lacking theoretical grounding,' or 'not in tune with global jargon and metadiscourse.'"[13] The reliance on Western academic English language and its norms excludes valuable content that does not fit its container, and shapes what counts as legitimate research, from the questions that can be asked to how they can be answered.

Scholarship from the Global South is too readily dismissed by researchers in the Global North, due to a publishing system whose standards of quality have been developed for academics in the Global North. Jeffrey Beall, who until recently maintained a list of publishers and journals he considers predatory, has been criticized for unfairly labeling publishers from developing countries predatory.[14] In 2015, Beall called the Latin American publisher SciELO a "publication favela."[15] Many commentators called out the cultural bias implicit in his use of the term "favela," stressing the importance of local and regional publishers and the indexing of SciELO in Web of Science and Scopus.[16] In using the term "predatory publishers" to describe publishers in the Global South, Beall tainted the publishers with a conceit of ill-intent, foreclosing the possibility of developmental or capacity issues, rather than examining the problematic capitalist infrastructure of traditional commercial publishing that asks scholars to give away their intellectual property and to pay for the privilege.[17] His inconsistent, and at times factually incorrect, criteria revealed the fallacy of having a checklist that failed to consider context, causing "irreversible reputational damage to authors, editors and publishers. ... [Blacklists] can stigmatize researchers by being associated with them and can be used in a discriminatory manner."[18] The fallout from Beall's blacklist goes on as the academic community continues to refer to its principles and conclusions to educate and make decisions on the legitimacy of publications.

The importance of a more nuanced and contextual approach to publication, as well as an understanding of access to the means of production rather than simply the output, cannot be overstated. For example, the publication of sustainable journals that meet the standards established by Northern scholars requires an understanding of Northern scholarly publishing, and a pool of scholars who have the time and resources to volunteer to serve on editorial boards and as peer reviewers, luxuries that are in short supply in many parts of the Americas, Asia, and Africa. An understanding of Northern scholarly publishing is also difficult for those left out of the process entirely—a study by Publons reported that the majority of peer reviewers are overwhelmingly from the United States.[19] As Moore et al. describe, these exclusions are amplified in the context of contemporary neoliberal commitments to "excellence" that reify peer review rather than making room for other possible norms of quality.[20] Western frameworks for academic publishing, however, do not preclude the value of scholarship. The old adage "don't judge a book by its cover" takes on new meaning on the internet, where physical containers and formats have even less relevance and content is—or rather should be—king.

Replicating Representation: Race, Ethnicity, and Gender

In addition to geographical and linguistic biases, several studies have shown troubling gender gaps in publishing output. Studies have examined the JSTOR corpus,[21] Web of Science,[22] and Scopus and Science Direct[23] to find that, although gender representation has improved in the last 20 years to include more women across all areas of study, authorship is still shockingly imbalanced, particularly for single and lead-authored publications.

Women are even underrepresented in the peer review process: a recent study by Lerback and Hanson examined the journals from the American Geophysical Union (AGU), the largest publisher of Earth and space science, and showed that authors and editors suggest women as reviewers less often.[24] While this may be unsurprising in contemporary scholarly publishing, historians have demonstrated that this has not always been the case, and therefore does not have to be.[25] The AGU has since made an effort to include more women in its reviewer pool, which has resulted in an increase in female-authored papers.

While editors may be aware of the gender gap in authorship and peer review, it is important to point out that this imbalance exists within the scholarly publishing industry as well.[26] It has been pointed out that publishing professionals are 60 percent female, but at the highest levels women represent less than a third of CEOs and fewer than one in five board chairs.[27] There is also a gender pay gap across the industry, as reported in the UK in 2018.[28] This is attributed to the differing roles men and women play in publishing institutions, but it also reinforces the reality that systemic injustices exist in publishing, too.

It is clear that gender biases exist at every level of publishing, alongside other biases in representation, including race, ethnicity, class, language, national origin, and ability. The academic publishing industry is, to put it bluntly, painfully white,[29] much like the rest of the publishing industry.[30] Unfortunately, ethnicity in authorship is difficult to disambiguate, but the Cooperative Children's Book Center at the University of Wisconsin–Madison has been keeping track of authorship since 1985, when they found that only 18 books were authored by African Americans.[31] That number has since risen to 122 books authored by African Americans, which comes nowhere near to representing the percentage of African American children in the United States. It is not difficult to see a correlation between the lack of representation in editorial voices and the lack of representation in authorship, for both mainstream and scholarly publishing, particularly when there are concrete examples of race-based missteps in peer review and publication.[32]

As Inefuku and Roh have argued, "If the editorial board, representing the master narrative, selects reviewers who from their perspective are qualified, the results are likely to reflect the same perspectives. This result is even more likely when one considers that the pool from which editorial board members and peer reviewers are drawn consists of tenured and tenure-track professors, who are, as mentioned previously, 84 percent white."[33] These demographics and the resulting biases should be more directly confronted in the composition of editorial boards and the selection of reviewers in order to disrupt the inequities of race, ethnicity, and gender inclusion in traditional scholarly publishing.

This lack of representation affects not only the diversity of books and other publications that are produced and made available, but individuals, whose careers are at stake because *publication is central to tenure and promotion*. Voices that are not represented in the scholarly canon are not just a loss for readers of that one book or article. Lack of publication causes an erasure of voices from our academic institutions, our scholarly record, and our culture and knowledge at large, as April M. Hathcock shows in her chapter.

Inequalities in Production

We have explored the impact of race, gender, national origin, and language on the scope of scholarly communication, arguing that the transformation to open-access publishing—often framed as a justice-based intervention— will fall short unless these fundamental issues of power are addressed. Understanding scholarly communication as a material practice can help identify points of potential leverage and resistance. Scholarly communication requires the input of many forms of labor, from the inception of a research project to the dissemination of findings and analysis. This work includes defining the scope of a journal, soliciting and selecting articles, conducting the sometimes many rounds of peer review necessary to make an article ready to publish, and the production tasks of copyediting, layout, proofreading, and the task of ensuring that all metadata are correct. In addition, scholars must read, research and write in the first place, generating the text upon which all this work is applied. Some of this work—assigning DOIs, formatting text, and so forth—is invisible to scholars who are rarely asked to perform it. In turn, the work of research and writing is often understood not as labor, but as a calling higher than the maintenance work that sustains the work of scholarship.

Regardless of the affective relationship scholars have to this work, the work exists and must be remunerated. Unlike the research, writing, reviewing, and editing that are largely dominated by white men from the Global North, production work is a race-to-the-bottom sector as companies outsource the dotting of i's and the crossing of t's to the cheapest, most disposable workers. Paid work in scholarly communications continues to be available, but at increasingly lower rates, disadvantaging workers globally.[34]

For scholars in the academy, the economic structure on the individual level remains much the same as it has. Scholars gain access to academic society journals through memberships, and university libraries subscribe to journal databases in order to make publications available to their patrons. The scholars themselves (except in the case of a small percentage of monographs or textbooks that sell quite well) do not profit monetarily, as it is assumed that their labor is paid by external sources—either their university salaries or through grants. This is true not only for authors, but for editors and reviewers as well. Some editors and reviewers are paid a small stipend, but generally it is a gift economy, and scholars see these duties as necessary to being engaged and responsible members of the academic community. While the gift economy works for scholars located at centers of power, it disadvantages those who work outside of them, including scholars who live and work in the Global South, write from nondominant race, gender, or class perspectives, or who are part of the growing academic "precariat," some of the 50 percent of college and university professors who teach without stable employment and for whom the work of scholarship cannot be expected to lead to the tenure and promotion that can make volunteer work on journals make sense as a use of professional time.[35]

The challenge of developing open-access models that compensate knowledge workers drives much of the conversation around this transformation of scholarly communications.[36] Inequities in that labor are unevenly distributed: the work of reading and writing is reserved for a narrowing band of elite US- and European-based scholars publishing in English on topics of interest to that elite in prestigious journals headquartered in the Global North. The piecework of production is increasingly outsourced to workers in other parts of the world, who watch their pay plummet as profits are transferred to corporate publishers. Meaningful resistance to dominant forms of scholarly publishing relies on making connections between workers who are disenfranchised at every level of this process. Seeing links between the scholar whose line of inquiry is insufficiently white or Western to be published in top journals and the Indian production worker impoverished by those same systems can lead to productive points of solidarity and shared concern.

Conclusion

Ria DasGupta has argued that "when we see that university diversity programs grow out of corporate and capitalist notions of progress, we can begin to understand why universities are perhaps only putting a band aid on injustice rather than challenging the deeply-rooted structural inequities which make the university welcoming for some and not others."[37] Scholarly research is complicit in the production of social inequalities that academic universities have perpetuated across the globe. Recently, many publishing institutions have begun to pay more attention to the "problem" of diversity, though this attention has not resulted in the kind of fundamental change that would result in the redistribution of opportunity and access. The kind of change called for by the current system requires deep-rooted, radical shifts in how knowledge is produced, how it is valued, and whose voices are authorized to speak in the academy. This calls for revolution rather than progression.

What does it mean to create a new environment, a new ecosystem of scholarly communication? While open-access publishing advances equitable access to reading scholarly work, it does not automatically reverse the biases and norms of scholarship itself. Without self-reflection and organized efforts to shift power in publishing, open-access efforts risk simply replicating biases and injustices endemic to the traditional scholarly communication system. Social justice in scholarly communications requires more than the provision of access to materials through the open web. It requires true global participation—from authorship, to the tools and means of production, and to the indexing of and access to the end product. Social justice in scholarly communication requires more than representation. It requires reckoning with the labor conditions of workers whose work facilitates the scholarly conversation. Beyond the tasks described here, an ethical scholarly communications practice would also engage in fights for the wages and working conditions of all laborers along the production chain, from the ivory tower intellectual typing on their computer in Cambridge to the factory worker in China whose labor produced that computer in the first place. An ethical scholarly communications practice would consider both the Nigerian scholar who is recognized throughout Africa, as well as the environmental and labor practices around the metals that create our publishing tools. Scholarly communications is a series of material practices that could be constructed otherwise—rooted in equity and justice rather that colonization and dominance. Sustaining that radical vision and advancing toward it are critical to an Open Access Movement that can transform the world.

Notes

1. For more on this, see Suber, "The Taxpayer Argument for Open Access."

2. Safiya Umoja Noble, "Social Justice and Library Publishing" (keynote presentation, Library Publishing Forum, Baltimore, MD, March 20–22, 2017), https://www.periscope.tv/w/1yNGaPXEjXbKj?t=1.

3. Oxford University Press, "About Us," accessed May 14, 2019, https://global.oup.com/about/.

4. Reuters, "Reed Elsevier Says to Exit Defence Industry Shows," *Reuters*, June 1, 2007, https://uk.reuters.com/article/uk-reedelsevier-defence-idUKL0135316020070601.

5. Jishnu Das et al., "U.S. and Them: The Geography of Academic Research," *Journal of Development Economics* 105 (2013): 112, https://doi.org/10.1016/j.jdeveco.2013.07.010.

6. Harrison W. Inefuku, "Globalization, Open Access, and the Democratization of Knowledge," *Educause Review* 52 (August 2017): 62–63.

7. Chiara Franzoni, Giuseppe Scellato, and Paula Stephan, "Changing Incentives to Publish," *Science* 333, no. 6043 (August 5, 2011): 702–703, https://doi.org/10.1126/science.1197286; Sarah Huggett, "Cash Puts Publishing Ethics at Risk in China: Impact Factors," *Nature* 490, no. 7420 (2012): 342, https://doi.org/10.1038/490342c; Evaristo Jiménez-Contreras et al., "Impact-Factor Rewards Affect Spanish Research," *Nature* 417, no. 6892 (2002): 898, https://doi.org/10.1038/417898b.

8. Richard Horton, "Medical Journals: Evidence of Bias against the Diseases of Poverty," *The Lancet* 361, no. 9359 (2003): 712, https://doi.org/10.1016/S0140-6736(03)12665-7.

9. Francis Nyamnjoh, "Institutional Review: Open Access and Open Knowledge Production Processes: Lessons from CODESRIA," *South African Journal of Information and Communication*, no. 10 (2010): 67–72, https://doi.org/10.23962/10539/19772.

10. Jean-Claude Guédon and Alain Loute, "L'Histoire de la Forme Revue au Prisme de L'Histoire de la 'Grande Conversation Scientifique,'" *Cahiers du GRM. publiés par le Groupe de Recherches Matérialistes—Association*, no. 12 (2017): para. 20, https://doi.org/10.4000/grm.912.

11. Joana Vieira Santos and Paulo Nunes da Silva, "Issues with Publishing Abstracts in English: Challenges for Portuguese Linguists' Authorial Voices," *Publications* 4, no. 2 (2016), https://doi.org/10.3390/publications4020012.

12. Kwesi Yankah, "African Folk and the Challenges of a Global Lore," *Africa Today* 46, no. 2 (1999): 13, https://doi.org/10.1353/at.1999.0017.

13. Yankah, "African Folk," 13.

14. Declan Butler, "Investigating Journals: The Dark Side of Publishing," *Nature* 495, no. 7442 (2013): 433–435, https://doi.org/10.1038/495433a.

15. Jeffrey Beall, "Is SciELO a Publication Favela?," *Emerald City Journal*, July 30, 2015, https://www.emeraldcityjournal.com/2015/07/is-scielo-a-publication-favela/; see also SciELO, "Rebuttal to the Blog Post 'Is SciELO a Publication Favela?' Authored by Jeffrey Beall," *SciELO in Perspective* (blog), August 25, 2015, http://blog.scielo.org/en/2015/08/25/rebuttal-to-the-blog-post-is-scielo-a-publication-favela-authored-by-jeffrey-beall/.

16. Harrison W. Inefuku and Charlotte Roh, "Agents of Diversity and Social Justice: Librarians and Scholarly Communication," in *Open Access and the Future of Scholarly Communication: Policy and Infrastructure*, ed. Kevin L. Smith and Katherine A. Dickson (Lanham, MD: Rowman & Littlefield, 2016), 107–128, https://repository.usfca.edu/librarian/8.

17. For more on this, see Martin Paul Eve and Ernesto Priego, "Who Is Actually Harmed by Predatory Publishers?," *TripleC: Communication, Capitalism & Critique: Open Access Journal for a Global Sustainable Information Society* 15, no. 2 (2017): 755–770, https://doi.org/10.31269/triplec.v15i2.867.

18. Jaime A. Teixeira da Silva and Panagiotis Tsigaris, "What Value Do Journal Whitelists and Blacklists Have in Academia?," *The Journal of Academic Librarianship* 44, no. 6 (2018): 781–792, https://doi.org/10.1016/j.acalib.2018.09.017.

19. Publons, "Global State of Peer Review," 2018, https://publons.com/static/Publons-Global-State-Of-Peer-Review-2018.pdf.

20. Samuel Moore et al., "Excellence R Us: University Research and the Fetishisation of Excellence," *Palgrave Communications* 3 (2017), https://doi.org/10.1057/palcomms.2016.105.

21. Jevin D. West et al., "The Role of Gender in Scholarly Authorship," *PLOS ONE* 8, no. 7 (2013): e66212, https://doi.org/10.1371/journal.pone.0066212.

22. Vincent Larivière et al., "Bibliometrics: Global Gender Disparities in Science," *Nature* 504, no. 7479 (2013): 211–213, https://doi.org/10.1038/504211a.

23. Alice Atkinson-Bonasio, "Gender Balance in Research: New Analytical Report Reveals Uneven Progress," Elsevier Connect, 2017, https://www.elsevier.com/connect/gender-balance-in-research-new-analytical-report-reveals-uneven-progress.

24. Jory Lerback and Brooks Hanson, "Journals Invite Too Few Women to Referee," *Nature* 541, no. 7638 (2017): 455–457, https://doi.org/10.1038/541455a.

25. Camilla Mørk Røstvik and Aileen Fyfe, "Ladies, Gentlemen, and Scientific Publication at the Royal Society, 1945–1990," *Open Library of Humanities* 4, no. 1 (2018): 1–40, https://doi.org/10.16995/olh.265.

26. Angela Cochran et al., "Mind the Gap: Addressing the Need for More Women Leaders in Scholarly Publishing" (Society for Scholarly Publishing Annual Meeting, Arlington, VA, 2015), https://youtu.be/sDS0lWz7lNU.

27. Cochran et al., "Mind the Gap."

28. "Gender Pay Gaps across the Book Trade Reported by Majority of Larger Businesses: Book Businesses Mostly Unflattered by Compulsory Disclosure of Gender Pay Gap Data," *The Bookseller*, no. 5795 (April 6, 2018): 6–9.

29. Albert N. Greco, Robert M. Wharton, and Amy Brand, "Demographics of Scholarly Publishing and Communication Professionals: Demographics of Publishing Professionals," *Learned Publishing* 29, no. 2 (2016): 97–101, https://doi.org/10.1002/leap.1017.

30. Jim Milliot, "The PW Publishing Industry Salary Survey 2015: A Younger Workforce, Still Predominantly White," Publishers Weekly, October 16, 2015, https://www.publishersweekly.com/pw/by-topic/industry-news/publisher-news/article/68405-publishing-industry-salary-survey-2015-a-younger-workforce-still-predominantly-white.html; Jason Low, Sarah Park Dahlen, and Nicole Catlin, "Where Is the Diversity in Publishing? The 2015 Diversity Baseline Survey Results," *The Open Book Blog* (blog), January 26, 2016, https://blog.leeandlow.com/2016/01/26/where-is-the-diversity-in-publishing-the-2015-diversity-baseline-survey-results/.

31. Cooperative Children's Book Center, School of Education, University of Wisconsin–Madison, "Publishing Statistics on Children's Books about People of Color and First/Native Nations and by People of Color and First/Native Nations Authors and Illustrators," 2019, https://ccbc.education.wisc.edu/books/pcstats.asp.

32. Tom Hesse, "A Journal's Apology Prompts Soul-Searching over Racial Gatekeeping in Academe," *The Chronicle of Higher Education*, April 21, 2017, https://www.chronicle.com/article/A-Journal-s-Apology-Prompts/239852; Kyle Powys Whyte, "Systematic Discrimination in Peer Review: Some Reflections," Daily Nous, May 7, 2017, http://dailynous.com/2017/05/07/systematic-discrimination-peer-review-reflections/.

33. Inefuku and Roh, "Agents of Diversity and Social Justice."

34. Simone Dahlmann and Ursula Huws, "Sunset in the West: Outsourcing Editorial Work from the UK to India—A Case Study of the Impact on Workers," *Work Organisation, Labour & Globalisation* 1, no. 1 (2007): 59–75.

35. American Association of University Professors, "Background Facts on Contingent Faculty Positions," AAUP, accessed May 14, 2019, https://www.aaup.org/issues/contingency/background-facts.

36. For more on this, see Peter Suber, "Open Access When Authors Are Paid," *SPARC Open Access Newsletter*, no. 68 (December 2, 2003), http://dash.harvard.edu/handle/1/4552040; punctum books, "THREAD on What We Feel Is One of the Most Under-Attended Issues in the Academic Publishing Landscape: Author Compensation. How Can the World's Knowledge Increase When More than 70% of All Teaching Lines in the US Are Adjunctified & Many Post-PhD Scholars Have No Uni Employment?"

37. Ria DasGupta, "Connecting Diversity Programs in Higher Education to the Legacy of HRE" (USF Symposium on Engaged Scholarship, San Francisco, CA, 2017).

3 Social Justice and Inclusivity: Drivers for the Dissemination of African Scholarship

Reggie Raju, Jill Claassen, Namhla Madini, and Tamzyn Suliaman

The Open Access Movement, which gained traction in the early 2000s, was driven in part by the philanthropic principle of sharing scholarly literature for the acceleration of research and the enrichment of education. The Budapest Open Access Initiative (BOAI), a founding document for the openness movement, encourages the philanthropic sharing of scholarly literature for the advancement of society.[1] Arunachalam and Aulisio, amongst others, stress this philanthropic ethos when they assert that open access frees up the spread of ideas and knowledge for the growth and development of humanity.[2] The fundamental premise, acknowledging the cost of subscriptions and licensing barriers, was that all other influences were equal and that this free and unrestricted online access to scholarly literature would advance scholarship and societal development. However, in Africa[3] and the better part of the Global South, the cost and licensing barriers are exacerbated by a myriad of other challenges such as poor access to the internet, frequent blackouts, poor information technology infrastructure, and dire lack of skills. Hence, for those in Africa and the Global South, the philanthropic principle thread must be reinforced with the social justice and inclusivity fiber. It must also consider, as does Bethany Nowviskie in this volume, the principles of Afrofuturism and especially the ways in which we can control and build our own infrastructures.

Africa is desperate to find solutions to the myriad of challenges that have a stranglehold on its development. To fast track a positive development trajectory, Africa needs to generate solutions to local challenges at an exponential rate. Hence, there is growing dependency on freely accessible channels of dissemination of scholarly information to ensure the sharing of research. As much as there is strong advocacy for free access, there has to be equal support for inclusive participation for local solutions by Global South researchers.

We here argue that African academic libraries need to provide, as a medium for the dissemination of research and educational content, a proactive "library as publisher" service. These services should be delivered for nonprofit purposes and be underpinned by "philanthropic-social justice" principles if they are to work in this environment. Such a diamond open-access publishing model is gaining momentum in Africa, albeit very slowly.[4] It is proposed that this "library as a publisher" service must become mainstream for academic libraries in Africa because it is a significant conduit for inclusive and free access to scholarship for the marginalized and can strongly promote unhindered participation. Further, it facilitates relatively unhindered participation in knowledge production. As pointed out by Roh, these library publishing services could allow for "new voices to find their way into disciplinary conversations, reach new audiences, both academic and public, and impact existing and emerging fields of scholarship and practice in a transformative way."[5]

We further turn here to the extent to which the principles of social justice can be seen as a driver for the openness movement. The chapter will also present an exemplar library publishing service with a social justice agenda to openly publish content on a coequality basis. This publishing service provides free access to scholarly content and unhindered participation by African researchers in the production and dissemination of African research.

Ubuntu and Social Justice

Africa, including South Africa, has been subjected to years of colonialization and, as a consequence, has been ravished in the postcolonial period by inequality and deprivation. This deprivation extends to access to scholarly literature, which has relegated Africa to the periphery of the world's knowledge production. We contend that the Open Access Movement and its social justice principles will usher in some level of equity and equal opportunity; further, it will facilitate the participation of new African voices in the research landscape. We base these initial arguments on the theses of John Rawls, who posits that social justice promotes the protection of equal access to liberties, rights, and opportunities, as well as taking care of the least advantaged members of society.[6] Further, Buck and Valentino, and Miller argue that at least part of the notion of social justice is concerned

Social Justice and Inclusivity

with ways in which information resources are accessible to the citizenry through social institutions.[7]

Koutras maintains that John Rawls's theory of social justice is centered on the notion that a society cannot be just until there is equality and that will include equal access to information.[8] Open access is viewed as a means for social justice because it gives opportunities to everybody to acquire knowledge through growing opportunities for equal access to information. However, what is often missing in these applications of Rawls's theory is the equity in the participation process of knowledge *creation*.

We believe that social justice and the African principle of Ubuntu could advance sharing for the eradication of information poverty and information unfairness. As pointed out by various authors, and despite claims to the contrary,[9] the Open Access Movement is guided by the principle that access to information, an absolute necessity for any level of growth and development, must be made freely available to all end users.[10] Social justice approaches to eradicating information poverty and injustice can use open access as the conduit for this eradication. Ubuntu, on the other hand, is a Zulu word advancing communal justice *en route* to promoting an egalitarian society.[11] The principles of fairness and justice underpin both Ubuntu and social justice. Academic libraries, be it from the perspective of the Global North (social justice) or from an African perspective (Ubuntu), have been rolling out open-access services to ensure information is made freely accessible to the widest reading audience possible. In response to an Ubuntu "agended" call for the open sharing of African scholarship, some academic libraries are now offering a "library as a publisher" service to take scholarly information to all parts of the "global village." This service brings to the fore and consolidates the social justice imperative of open access. Researchers, in this growing service model, are supported in their desire to share their research output for the growth of research and to find solutions to the myriad of challenges that beset African societies. Improved access to information will ensure that all sections of the "village" can contribute to the growth and development of the "global village."

Social Justice and Inclusivity through Library Publishing

In rolling out an Ubuntu "agended" library publishing service, some academic institutions have taken open-access publishing to an unprecedented level in South Africa by offering diamond open access. Raju lists six South African universities that offer a library publishing program.[12] The South African institutions that offer this "library as a publisher" provision are:

- University of Stellenbosch—26 titles;
- Free State University—9 titles;
- University of Kwa-Zulu Natal—8 titles;
- University of Cape Town—5 titles;
- University of South Africa—5 titles;
- University of the Western Cape—2 titles; and,
- Rhodes University—titles.

The underpinning philosophy in offering such services is that public universities in South Africa receive substantial funding from national government.[13] This funding is earmarked for, *inter alia*, the provision of innovative and relevant library services. Some of the academic libraries have taken the bold step of providing this innovative library publishing service, without any training in publishing. The authors hold the view that this service responds to the social responsiveness and transformation agendas of their institutions. This diamond open-access service delivers, amongst others, decolonized African scholarship through the creation of an alternative publishing model that facilitates the cocreation of knowledge, rather than merely its reception. The University of Cape Town (UCT) has extended its "library as publisher" service by publishing monographs and textbooks. Currently, UCT has seven monographs and two textbooks that have been published, with three more monographs that are currently being worked on for imminent publication. In the quest for social justice and an egalitarian society, access to knowledge and scholarship should not be dependent on economic affordability. The authors acknowledge that online access is a challenge in Africa (and Maura A. Smale notes, in her chapter, that this is true also in the United States). However, this service is, at the least, one barrier removed. Further, it promotes the principles of inclusivity, ensuring that African research output is included in the dissemination process.

Decolonization of the Colonized Publishing Landscape

The BOAI states that removing access barriers to scholarly content will accelerate research, enrich education and share the learning of the rich with the poor and the poor with the rich. This statement supports the need for academic libraries to make innovative contributions to the dissemination of scholarship and contribute to the disruption of the colonized publishing landscape. The envisaged continental diamond open-access library publishing platform will assist in removing barriers to participation and ensure freedom of African representation. The envisaged platform, using open-source software, makes provision for the publication of African scholarship via their academic libraries. The opening of opportunities for the publication of African books and journals will address the dearth of African scholarship and remove barriers to participation in knowledge production and dissemination.

We assert, from our perspective, that over a period of time, there has been an unintended but systematic colonization of the publishing landscape which the library publishing service needs to challenge. This allegation is supported by comments from authors such as Crissinger, who make the point that there have been assumptions about the Global South remaining ignorant and underdeveloped until it has access to the Global North's knowledge.[14] In an attempt to "eradicate" this ignorance and promote development, there has been a push for the Global North to focus on improving the flow of information to the Global South. This imperialist proposition supports the unidirectional flow of information instead of a facilitated process allowing for knowledge exchange. However, as pointed out by Burkett, the people of the Global South may be "poor" in terms of the information they can retrieve from the internet but what is not factored in is the richness in many other ways which could never be calculated in the Western scientific paradigm, and that would include, amongst others, social relationships, community, and cultural traditions.[15]

Bonaccorso et al. bring to the debate the contributing circumstances that fueled this colonizing process; namely, the exclusion of Global South researchers from the supply side of the academic publishing and communication process.[16] Building on this, we argue that there are two fundamental processes that propagate this exclusion: first, Global South researchers, in the main, do not have access to research already published (and that would include research produced in the Global South) for them to contribute adequately to the world's knowledge production. The second is the delegitimization of research emanating from the Global South. Roh presents a scenario that demonstrates how this delegitimization contributes to the colonization of the publishing landscape.[17] She highlights that economics papers written about the United States were more likely to be published in the top five economics journals and only 1.5 percent were about countries other than the United States. Hence, there has been a shift in contributions from researchers from Global South countries who have refocused their research and were reporting on the United States in order to get published. Thus, the publishing markets and impact factors are driving the global research agenda.

These unintended, but profit-driven processes have triggered, in the view of the authors, the colonization of the publishing landscape resulting in the marginalization of research voices from the Global South. The abovementioned inequalities in publishing for and by marginalized voices are compounded by economic circumstances—specifically, the inability of authors from the Global South to pay exorbitant article processing charges (APCs) in an environment where there is a push via the openness movement for the free sharing of research output.

Library publishing is meant to create fertile ground for new voices that can find their way into disciplinary conversations, reach new audiences, both academic and public, and positively alter the existing publishing landscape. There is a desperate need for the democratization and decolonization of the publishing landscape—and library publishing is one such service that can deliver on this need. This publishing service promotes social justice and the inclusion of African researchers and research output into mainstream research processes.

Unhindered Access versus Unhindered Participation

One of the primary purposes for the production of research is to find solutions to challenges that beset society. Therefore, it is important for research output to have the widest accessibility for the greatest consumption. However, consumption is a double-sided coin; on the one side there is consumption for action to resolve problems and on the other, there is consumption necessary for the construction of new knowledge—researcher consumption. In terms of researcher consumption, the uneven research landscape brings to the debate the whole issue of equitable access and discoverability. In terms of equitable access, what must be brought to the fore is equitable participation in the creation and sharing of new knowledge.

The fundamental principles of open access point to equitable access culminating in equitable participation. These social justice principles have been hijacked by the publishers who feed aspirations for improved citation (which is understandable given its association with tenure), promotion, greater possibilities of funding and such. However, it detracts from the fundamental principles of the openness movement, which are sharing and inclusivity.

In a highly uneven global research landscape, there is no equality—there are those researchers that are marginalized, those that are on the periphery, and then those that are at the epicenter. The "participation access" is extremely divergent, with researchers from the Global North being "more equal" than those from the Global South. As stated by Bonaccorso et al., "everyone may be free to read papers, but it may still be prohibitively expensive to publish them."[18] Prohibitive APCs are one of a myriad of challenges that contribute to this inequality. Authors from the Global South have to compete for space in a limited number of journals carrying a range of challenges, from lack of content to support the creation of new knowledge, to the inability to pay exorbitant APCs courtesy of legacy publishing processes. This absurd and unrealistic competition significantly contributes to the exclusion of the marginalized research voices of the Global South. Library publishing is envisaged to be that social justice service that can give voice to the marginalized: to give space for active and equitable participation of researchers from the Global South in knowledge production and dissemination.

Library Publishing in South Africa

South Africa is a fledgling democracy that has endured decades of colonized and apartheid governance. The system of apartheid compartmentalized higher education with the historically disadvantaged black institutions being dramatically under resourced. We would argue that, in order to counteract the negative effects of this history, advantaged institutions in the present have a moral obligation to share scholarly content for the advancement of research in the country as a whole and for the greater good of the public. McKiernan shares this view when she writes that "open scholarship can help universities fulfil their missions by sharing research outputs, so they have the quickest and broadest societal impact."[19] Raju, Raju, and Claassen hold the view that the sharing of scholarly output will have a domino effect of growing the culture of research, ultimately culminating in Africa moving away from the periphery of the world's knowledge production to the epicenter—moving away from being a net consumer to becoming a contributor to knowledge production.[20]

A significant contributor to this transformation from consumer to participant is the offer of a "library as a publisher" service. The rationale underpinning this service is one of the core principles of open access, namely philanthropy. The offer of a diamond open-access publishing service to promote social justice and Ubuntu, must be embraced by historically advantaged African institutions. There must be concerted collective efforts to mainstream the "library as a publisher" service to support equity first and then equality in the creation and dissemination of African research. This nonprofit publishing model is a seismic shift in thinking around benefits for the production and dissemination of research:

- for the author, who wants their research reviewed and circulated,[21] the shift is from "what is in it for me" to "I must share my research";
- for the reader, the shift is from, "I cannot access all research, therefore I cannot create knowledge" to "all research is discoverable and can be reused for knowledge production"; and
- for the publisher (the library), a contribution to shifting profit-driven motivation to making a meaningful social impact to grow the knowledge economy.

In this model, all three stakeholders move toward the same goal of driving the dissemination of African scholarship and thereby participating in creating new African knowledge, which must form part of the global knowledge economy.

The "library as a publisher" service is offered at some South African academic libraries that collectively produce more than 55 journal titles. The UCT Libraries have extended their service and are now publishing open monographs/textbooks.[22] It is acknowledged that there is no systematic publishing agenda, with each institution engaging in self-learning and independently experimenting with the software, given that all of the institutions are using the Public Knowledge Project's software products (Open Journal Systems or Open Monograph Press)—all institutions are proverbially reinventing the wheel. Indeed, there is very little sharing of skills and resources. Such a lack of skills and poor infrastructure are deterrents to those institutions that are not offering such a service.

African Continental Platform

In acknowledging the skills shortage and poor information technology infrastructure, there is a process afoot to develop a continental platform for the publication of open journals and books. There is proof of concept for the functioning of an aggregated institutional platform, which in due course will be extended into a national platform, a South African platform. This South African platform will be made available to any of the academic institutions in the country to use for the publication of their local journals and/or monographs. The intention is to expand this national platform with the collaboration of a number of African partners, toward the creation of the continental platform. In the current UCT publishing platform, there are monographs that have audio and visual clips to simulate laboratory situations to overcome the lack of such facilities. The capacity to magnify images in a dermatology textbook allows for doctors to probe skin conditions; the capacity for books to be read to users improves accessibility for the visually impaired and supports different learning styles, especially those readers coming from backgrounds where English is not their first language. These capacities address the issues of social justice and inclusion.

Conclusion

The current commercial research publishing landscape is dictated to by the profit motive; the dictate for the researchers is the need for improved citation count and the prestige of being published in high-impact journals. These criteria, among other issues, have skewed the publishing landscape, benefiting primarily the Global North at the expense of the Global South. There is a need for a disruptor to this publishing landscape and the library publishing service, driven by its social justice and inclusivity imperatives, will facilitate the dissemination of African scholarship and the equitable and equal participation by African researchers in knowledge production. This disruptor will advance the principles of Ubuntu as it will contribute to the eradication of information poverty and information unfairness.

The library publishing service will aid in redrawing the map of global knowledge production and bring parity to the global power dynamics of global knowledge production. The Open Access Movement, through the library publishing service, needs to broaden its focus from access to knowledge to full participation in knowledge creation in scholarly communication. Further, the movement must recapture its social justice and inclusivity imperatives in support of the equitable dissemination of Global South scholarship, including African scholarship. The inclusion of content for and by marginalized researchers is driven by the Ubuntu desire for an egalitarian society. The development of alternative scholarly communication platforms, such as the one being developed by UCT Libraries, provides opportunities for libraries and library partners to push back against a biased publishing system and support publications that might not otherwise have a voice: inclusivity and social justice must be at the epicenter of the dissemination of African scholarship.

Notes

1. Chan et al., "Budapest Open Access Initiative."

2. Subbiah Arunachalam, "Social Justice in Scholarly Publishing: Open Access Is the Only Way," *The American Journal of Bioethics* 17, no. 10 (2017): 15–17, https://doi.org/10.1080/15265161.2017.1366194; George Aulisio, "Open Access Publishing and Social Justice: Scranton's Perspectives," *Jesuit Higher Education: A Journal* 3, no. 2 (2014): 55–73.

3. Africa is divided into fifty-four culturally heterogeneous and politically differentiated countries which are distinct in terms of their pattern of capital accumulation, their degree of industrialization and commercialization, and their rates of literacy and urbanization. Fifty percent of the continent's gross national product is generated by only three countries; namely South Africa, Egypt, and Nigeria. These uneven patterns of growth are also evident within countries. The average literacy rate is 61 percent, one of the lowest in the world. This low literacy rate contributes to the continent's slow development and the high rate of poverty. See Fouad Makki, "Post-Colonial Africa and the World Economy: The Long Waves of Uneven Development," *Journal of World-Systems Research* 21, no. 1 (2015): 124–146, https://doi.org/10.5195/JWSR.2015.546; UNESCO, "Fact Sheet Sub-Saharan Africa Strong Foundations: Early Childhood Care and Education," accessed May 13, 2019, https://en.unesco.org/gem-report/sites/gem-report/files/fact_sheet_ssa.pdf.

4. "Diamond" refers to an open-access system in which there is neither cost to the reader nor the author.

5. Charlotte Roh, "Library Publishing and Diversity Values: Changing Scholarly Publishing through Policy and Scholarly Communication Education," *College & Research Libraries News* 77, no. 2 (2016): 83, https://doi.org/10.5860/crln.77.2.9446.

6. John Rawls, "Justice as Fairness," *The Philosophical Review* 67, no. 2 (1958): 164–194, https://doi.org/10.2307/2182612.

7. Stefanie Buck and Maura L. Valentino, "OER and Social Justice: A Colloquium at Oregon State University," *Journal of Librarianship and Scholarly Communication* 6, no. 2 (2018): 2231, https://doi.org/10.7710/2162-3309.2231; David Miller, *Principles of Social Justice* (Cambridge, MA: Harvard University Press, 1999).

8. Nikos Koutras, "Open Access: A Means for Social Justice and Greater Social Cohesion," *Seattle Journal for Social Justice* 16, no. 1 (2017): 105–134.

9. David Golumbia, "Marxism and Open Access in the Humanities: Turning Academic Labor against Itself," *Workplace: A Journal for Academic Labor*, no. 28 (2016), https://doi.org/10.14288/workplace.v0i28.186213.

10. Jacintha Ellers, Thomas W. Crowther, and Jeffrey A. Harvey, "Gold Open Access Publishing in Mega-Journals: Developing Countries Pay the Price of Western Premium Academic Output," *Journal of Scholarly Publishing* 49, no. 1 (2017): 89–102, https://doi.org/10.3138/jsp.49.1.89; Karen Shashok, "Can Scientists and Their Institutions Become Their Own Open Access Publishers?," *arXiv:1701.02461*, January 10, 2017, http://arxiv.org/abs/1701.02461; Jean-Claude Guédon, "Open Access: Toward the Internet of the Mind," Budapest Open Access Initiative, 2017, https://www.budapestopenaccessinitiative.org/open-access-toward-the-internet-of-the-mind.

11. K. Chaplin, "The Ubuntu Spirit in African Communities" (The South African Ubuntu Foundation and the Amy Biehl Foundation, 2006).

12. Reggie Raju, "From Green to Gold to Diamond: Open Access's Return to Social Justice" (IFLA WLIC, Kuala Lumpur, Malaysia, 2018), http://library.ifla.org/2220/.

13. Although, for the complexities of this argument, see Peter Suber, "The Taxpayer Argument for Open Access," *SPARC Open Access Newsletter*, no. 65 (September 4, 2003), http://dash.harvard.edu/handle/1/4725013.

14. Sarah Crissinger, "A Critical Take on OER Practices: Interrogating Commercialization, Colonialism, and Content," *In the Library with the Lead Pipe* (blog), October 21, 2015, http://www.inthelibrarywiththeleadpipe.org/2015/a-critical-take-on-oer-practices-interrogating-commercialization-colonialism-and-content.

15. Ingrid Burkett, "Beyond the 'Information Rich and Poor': Futures Understandings of Inequality in Globalising Informational Economies," *Futures* 32, no. 7 (2000): 679–694, https://doi.org/10.1016/S0016-3287(00)00016-1.

16. Elisa Bonaccorso et al., "Bottlenecks in the Open-Access System: Voices from Around the Globe," *Journal of Librarianship and Scholarly Communication* 2, no. 2 (2014): eP1126, https://doi.org/10.7710/2162-3309.1126.

17. Roh, "Library Publishing and Diversity Values."

18. Bonaccorso et al., "Bottlenecks in the Open-Access System."

19. Erin C. McKiernan, "Imagining the 'Open' University: Sharing Scholarship to Improve Research and Education," *PLOS Biology* 15, no. 10 (2017): 6, https://doi.org/10.1371/journal.pbio.1002614.

20. Reggie Raju, Jaya Raju, and Jill Claassen, "Open Scholarship Practices Reshaping South Africa's Scholarly Publishing Roadmap," *Publications* 3, no. 4 (2015): 263–284, https://doi.org/10.3390/publications3040263.

21. Karin Wulf and Alice Meadows, "Seven Things Every Researcher Should Know About Scholarly Publishing," The Scholarly Kitchen, March 21, 2016, https://scholarlykitchen.sspnet.org/2016/03/21/seven-things-every-researcher-should-know-about-scholarly-publishing/.

22. Raju, "From Green to Gold to Diamond."

4 Can Open Scholarly Practices Redress Epistemic Injustice?

Denisse Albornoz, Angela Okune, and Leslie Chan

Nearly two decades after the Budapest Open Access Initiative (2002) was drafted, the early optimism that the Internet would transform the structural inequities in scholarly communications may need to be tempered, as Thomas Mboa Nkoudou has also hinted at in this book. One of the aspirations of the Open Access Movement was to make visible the knowledge produced in the Global South,[1] which was perceived to have been rendered invisible by the Global North's publishing and academic system.[2] It was also widely assumed that once open access to global research was enabled, the gap between rich and poor institutions would narrow and a more inclusive and equitable system of knowledge production and sharing would emerge.[3]

However, there is growing evidence that open research practices or "openness"—when decontextualized from their historical, political, and socioeconomic roots—rather than narrowing gaps, can amplify the over-representation of knowledge produced by Northern actors and institutions and further the exclusion of knowledge produced by marginalized groups. In other words, open systems may potentially replicate the very values and power imbalances that the movement initially sought to challenge.[4] This has left scholars and activists wondering about the extent to which "openness," while necessary, is sufficient for tackling inequalities in global academic knowledge production. Among the many arguments supporting this thesis in this chapter, we focus on those that allude to how open research practices may replicate epistemic injustices—a concept that refers to the devaluing of someone's knowledge or capacity as a knower—particularly with regard to knowers and knowledge stemming from the Global South.[5] We ask: What might epistemic injustice look like in an open system, and can openness promote epistemic justice?

We ground our argument in the experiences of the Open and Collaborative Science in Development Network (OCSDNet), a research network composed of scientists, development practitioners and community activists from Latin America, Africa, the Middle East, and Asia, with the goal of investigating how and whether an open approach to science and knowledge making could contribute to sustainable development.[6] Central to the network's project was the concept of situated openness,[7] which posits that "openness" needs to be contextualized in its particular history and environment to determine who benefits or who is at risk in an "open" system.[8] Drawing from concepts developed by decolonial and feminist scholars that explore the power dimensions of knowledge production,[9] and the work of development scholar John Gaventa on power analysis, we elaborate on how "situated openness" is a critical reflective process for identifying and assessing how different forms of epistemic injustice are deeply embedded in the current global knowledge production system.[10]

In the first section of the chapter, we describe how the current scholarly communication system builds and sustains notions of "expertise" and "ignorance" that amplify preexisting power asymmetries between social actors. In the second section, we turn to case studies of OCSDNet's Projet Science Ouverte Haïti Afrique, Open Science in Francophone Africa and Haiti (SOHA), Natural Justice in South Africa, and environmental researchers in Latin America, to address this question and provide further insight into what epistemic injustice might look like in three diverse contexts. We conclude that the first step toward building an open system that promotes epistemic justice is to identify strategies to reduce epistemic harms that result from uncritical open practices. This would include assessing who is absent in the design of open scholarly systems, exercising "responsible agency" by being cognizant of the histories from which diverse voices emerge, and attempting to build infrastructures differently: nurturing relationships of mutual negotiation, and imagining openness as a more radical practice.[11]

Structural and Epistemic Injustice in Scholarly Communication

Feminist science scholars have long challenged positivist approaches to knowledge production that see knowledge making as an objective or neutral process. They have argued that knowledge is an important building block of power relations, or in the words of Patricia Hill Collins, "a vitally important part of the social relations of domination and resistance."[12] In this view, knowledge making is always shaped by the identities, social practices, social locations, and sociopolitical experiences of those who produce it and share it.[13] As a result, there are several risks and constraints in how groups interpret each other's knowledge when they hold differentiated power due to their social locations, values, and beliefs.[14] In this system, the knowledge of those who exist at the intersections of multiple layers of privilege—for example, an Anglo-American man from a prestigious American university—is often afforded higher epistemic value and thus considered to be more legitimate, valid, truthful, and universal.[15] Meanwhile, the knowledge of those who sit at multiple layers of oppression—for example, women of color, indigenous people, rural, and blue-collar workers with no access to formal education—is often considered to be false, less credible, folk knowledge, opinionated, or unworthy of consideration,[16] creating strong divides between those who are considered "experts" and those who are considered "ignorant."[17]

The scholarly communication system plays a fundamental role in constructing these notions of expertise and ignorance through several technical, social, and financial mechanisms. Some of the elements that foreground the institutional nature of what is rendered valid knowledge in a particular academic context include: the growing role of commercial publishers in building infrastructures and technical standards on which scholarship depends,[18] the promotion of criteria and "academic literacies" to determine quality and intellectual authority[19] and the ongoing dominance of the English language as part of a "rhetoric of excellence" in academia, among others.[20] Even though the diversity of the world is comprised of, echoing Boaventura de Sousa Santos, "distinct modes of being, thinking and feeling," this diversity remains largely absent from the theories, concepts, and infrastructures developed and employed in the academic world.[21] Feminist scholar Iris Marion Young referred to these mechanisms of exclusion as "conditions of structural injustice" that, when aligned in a particular way, put large groups of people under a systematic threat of domination or deprivation.[22] In the particular case of scholarly communications, the combination of these hidden practices builds an epistemological hierarchy that puts knowledge conforming to the norms and standards at the top, while deeming irrelevant or erasing the knowledges that do not.

Epistemic injustice also refers to the devaluing of someone's knowledge or capacity as a knower by eroding their credibility, legitimacy, and access to social resources to share new concepts through institutionalized means, such as books, articles, and journals.[23] According to decolonial scholars, the construction of ignorance or of "epistemically disadvantaged identities" silences and dehumanizes entire intellectual traditions, cultures and communities; most notably, those from the Global South.[24] "It is not simply facts, events, practices, or technologies that are rendered not known, but individuals and groups who are rendered 'not knowers,'" wrote philosopher Nancy Tuana.[25] By isolating epistemic communities from credibility and legitimacy, this system also deprives them of their right to participate in research and knowledge-making processes that, as Arjun Appadurai explained, "systematically increase that stock of knowledge which they consider most vital to their survival as human beings and to their claims as citizens."[26]

Can Open Scholarly Practices Redress Epistemic Injustice?

Concerned with the emerging effects of open scholarly systems and practices, OCSDNet undertook two years of research in collaboration with academics and grassroots communities from the Global South to address issues of power and inequality in open science. When analysing OCSDNet project team reflections, we discovered that different communities are willing to share their knowledge depending on how it will impact their well-being.[27] Drawing from three OCSDNet case studies from South Africa, Colombia, Costa Rica, and countries in Francophone Africa, we reflect on how openness as a goal may not be the means to redress epistemic injustice in scholarly communication. Rather, these examples show how a careful negotiation of the degrees and conditions around openness can allow for the ideation of community-based mechanisms to address different forms of epistemic injustice.

The research team based in South Africa (consisting of representatives from Natural Justice—a legal-research NGO in Cape Town—and academics from South Africa and the United States) developed a research partnership with Indigenous South African communities. The initial objective was to understand and potentially "open up" local knowledge that could be important for understanding the impact of climate change throughout the region and that could potentially help South Africans to learn from generations of indigenous expertise in dealing with harsh climatic conditions. However, as the team began to approach communities, the well-intentioned desire to foreground indigenous knowledge and bring "global" awareness to its existence by "opening it up" for the benefit of outsiders was met with great resistance due to the long history of research on the San communities and their experiences of research as an exploitive endeavor.[28] "Openness" in this context was seen as a tool that enabled nonlocal researchers to yet again benefit from San knowledge without necessarily addressing local community interests or challenges.[29]

This example highlights how a desire to bring further attention to "marginalized knowledges" in the Global South under the "open knowledge-sharing" banner was not viewed by the holders of such knowledges as radical practice but rather as a new name for a century-old practice of colonial knowledge extraction from Africa.[30] In response to this critique, the research team facilitated a process in which research partners questioned exploitative research relations in the project, claimed their right to refuse to share knowledge, and created frameworks to center indigenous sovereignty and indigenous ways of thinking.[31] In collaboration with San indigenous researchers, the team developed a set of tools including a flexible community-researcher contract and a guide to protect and promote indigenous peoples' rights in academic research processes that enable communities to negotiate—on (theoretically) more equal terms—with researchers and knowledge profiteers with whom they might interact in the future.[32]

An OCSDNet research team conducting research in Latin America faced a similar challenge. This project used a participatory methodology to facilitate knowledge exchange between academic researchers and rural farmers from Colombia and Costa Rica, with the objective of improving decision-making and governance mechanisms regarding biodiversity and climate change impact. The objective was to create conditions under which both academics and farmers could share their expertise with one another on equitable terms to design effective climate change adaptation strategies. This project is situated in a context of ongoing tension surrounding whose knowledge counts in defining biodiversity management and governance in Latin America. Postcolonial scholar Arturo Escobar's work highlights how "biodiversity" in itself is a complex historically produced discourse with several definitions among a diverse network of stakeholders. Despite new attention being paid to traditional knowledge, "the conventional scientific disciplines continue to dominate the overall approach" at the policy level.[33]

In this context, the research team found that, for rural farmers, "opening up their knowledge" was part of a larger aspiration for the recognition and appreciation of their ancestral and indigenous knowledge(s). The project therefore began to take openness not as a set of practices or technologies to follow, but rather, as a "state of mind or attitude" to be adopted primarily by individuals, and as a "methodology" to collaborate and work between diverse communities. Colombian researcher Hector Botero, who conducted similar projects in the area, has asserted that this "meeting of two worlds" can challenge the preexisting epistemological hierarchy of both groups, as long as actors who hold traditional knowledge get to define the priorities and conditions under which scientific knowledge is used to advance the project, and not the other way around.[34] The Latin America project lead Josique Lorenzo concluded that "research [needs to] begin and end with community problems, rather than with scientific problems."[35]

As a third case, OCSDNet's Projet SOHA consisted of a network collaboration across a number of Francophone West African countries and Haiti that were focused on raising awareness about the epistemic injustices that many university students in the region encounter over the course of their studies.[36] Along with some of the more obvious technical limitations for accessing academic knowledge (such as a lack of internet connectivity, computers, electricity, etc.), the project noted that some institutions tend to subscribe to and replicate the same norms surrounding "legitimate" knowledge creation as found in many Northern institutions: from the continued dominance of colonial languages to a heavy reliance on a canon and "standards of excellence" originating from centers in the Global North.[37] In doing so, these institutions were structurally delegitimizing forms of knowledge that strayed from these norms—such as the use of oral traditions, perspectives drawn from indigenous worldviews, and alternative forms of publishing. Furthermore, the team contended that these forms of epistemic injustices "reduce the ability of students to deploy the full potential of their intellectual skills, their knowledge and their scientific research capacity to serve sustainable local development of their community or country."[38] The intention of Projet SOHA was therefore to foster openness as a "culture of science aimed at the creation of locally relevant, freely accessible and reusable knowledge by empowered and confident researchers using not only epistemologies from the North, but all kinds of epistemologies and methods."[39] From their work, they found that young Haitian and West African scholars are keen to play a key role in establishing a culture of science and learning that is inclusive of a diversity of worldviews and intent on solving complex, local development issues.

In the studies briefly described above, these communities did not necessarily consider the open sharing of knowledge to be beneficial unless the root structures of epistemological injustice were also addressed. At the same time, they illustrate how each community attempted to reclaim the concept of openness as an opportunity to redress aspects of the historic epistemic injustice they have faced. In the first case, openness was redefined as a process to facilitate the equitable negotiation between actors with unequal levels of power. The second case highlights how openness came to be seen as a cultural shift to level the playing field between scientific and traditional knowledge. And in the third case, openness was reinterpreted as fostering a more plural and diverse knowledge-sharing system.

Even though the knowledge of all three epistemic communities has been previously "devalued" in the global scholarly system, the strategies devised by the projects did not seek legitimization through conventional academic norms and standards. Rather, they opted to assert their agency by determining the degree of openness that made sense for their particular context, and by identifying individual social and cultural mechanisms through which they could acquire the visibility, recognition, and protection of their ways of knowing. The dilemma these cases now pose revolves around how we can create systems in which we may open up and simultaneously protect the knowledge of vulnerable populations. How can we call for diversity and epistemic inclusion in open practices in and beyond academia, while ensuring that we establish safeguards and governance structures that honor these boundaries?

Openness in Pursuit of Epistemic Justice

Drawing on Boaventura de Santos's famous call to action: "the struggle for global justice includes the search for epistemic justice," and the related call that "political resistance needs to be premised upon epistemological resistance," we believe that a more just open scholarly communications system needs to aspire toward epistemic justice, in particular for those who are suffering under unjust sociopolitical and economic structures.[40] Decolonial scholars have long called for epistemic diversity in science and development, arguing for alternatives to "northern Epistemologies" and systems that allow for intercultural dialogues and an "ecology of knowledge(s)" that nurtures curiosity, appreciation, and respect for diverse ways of knowing the world.[41]

In this sense, the infrastructures we build and the practices we enable need to intentionally include voices, worldviews, and epistemologies that have been historically excluded from the system. While there is no one-size-fits-all approach toward achieving epistemic justice, we believe open research practices do hold promises for reducing historical and contemporary harms inflicted through the academic production system. Based on the cases and concepts elaborated in this chapter, we offer four recommendations to engage in more reflexive, critical, and just modes of working in open research.

The first recommendation is for those who hold power in the Global North to recognize and assume their positions within systems of privilege and oppression in order to exercise what philosopher José Medina calls, "responsible agency."[42] This exercise of introspection prods us to reflect on how we are implicated in producing epistemic harms in the open projects we promote, facilitate, and design. Through responsible agency, following Medina's logic, we can develop the habit of recognizing the social locations of those who are involved in the project, the histories and trajectories from which their voices emerge, the presuppositions and commitments attached to their knowledge—and more importantly, how their histories may intersect with the trajectory of our own voices. Such reflection also involves perhaps the hardest task of all: identifying the silos, absences, or silences in knowledge making that are covered by April M. Hathcock in this volume; asking who is missing from the conversation, and querying how this system inhibits the participation of a particular individual or of communities who are persistently excluded from it.[43] This is what de Sousa Santos calls practicing the sociology of absences: "whatever does not exist in our society is often actively produced as non-existent and we have to look into that reality."[44]

The second recommendation is to challenge technical standards, norms, and infrastructures that perpetuate epistemic injustice. To begin to disrupt such a system requires activists and scholars to move beyond challenging the visible barriers of the knowledge production system, notably paywalls and licensing, to question who has the ability to set agendas, standards, and norms; to make decisions and the conditions of participation; and ultimately, to control how knowledge infrastructures are built. As Gaventa noted: "without addressing power's invisible dimensions, greater participation may appear as increased inclusion and agency in knowledge production, but may in reality be just a more popular echo—a playing back—of the dominant values, knowledge, and messages of the status quo."[45] In the same vein, when openness is simply grafted atop existing technology and power structures, the powerful are further empowered, and the dominant epistemologies are further reproduced. Those in positions of privilege must be wary of a centralization of knowledge and instead explore how we might encourage a polyphony of perspectives and infrastructures that center other knowledges as well.[46] The challenges ahead include encouraging and enabling such diversity while simultaneously finding channels for scholarly communities and infrastructures to speak to each other and not to exist in siloed isolation.

The third recommendation is to build and learn from infrastructures that actively seek to redress these injustices. Various groups are already experimenting in this regard. For example, the Platform for Experimental Collaborative Ethnography (PECE) leverages explanatory pluralism and interpretive differences, the expectation that different researchers will develop alternative understandings of the same object or event.[47] By design, PECE encourages the creation and assembling of multiple interpretations, hypotheses, and theories in the firm belief that such explorations are necessary for the complex conditions that we seek to understand. You can see this in the platform's ability to allow multiple users to annotate the same works and in the explicit use of analytic questions for these different users to answer together. In this way, PECE turns difference—different artifacts, different annotations from diverse researchers, different and sometimes conflicting explanatory paradigms—into insight.[48]

Another digital anthropological platform, Mukurtu, addresses the "decoloniz[ation] of archival practices and modes of access"[49] through the observation of indigenous sensibilities, knowledge practices, and interdictions for the circulation of cultural materials.[50] Calling into question Creative Commons (CC) licenses as the accepted best practice standard, the project has generated a set of "Traditional Knowledge" (TK) labels that describe permissions and restrictions for cultural artifacts according to users' profiles and "cultural protocols."[51]

And finally, the fourth recommendation is to imagine openness as a radical practice that aspires to liberation and freedom from structural oppression. Historian Robin Kelley studied alternative visions of freedom held by various black radical movements that offered a way to "see beyond our immediate ordeals" to "transcend bitterness and cynicism and embrace love, hope and an all-encompassing dream of freedom, especially in rough times."⁵² Kelley argued that the most radical ideas grow out of concrete intellectual engagement with the roots of inequality and the problems of aggrieved populations confronting systems of oppression. For example, the Combahee River Collective Statement, a Black feminist declaration, not only reflects on their struggles, victories, and losses, crises and openings, but also dares to imagine what survival and liberation may look like.⁵³

Drawing on Kelley's work, we call for those working in public scholarship and open movements to engage in the hard work of reflecting on our values and reorganizing social life through political engagement, community involvement, education, debate, and dreaming. Instead of seeking to develop agreement and consensus around universal standards and technologies of "openness," time and space is necessary for policy makers, scholar activists, and concerned community members to develop collaborative imaginaries for more just and equitable knowledge infrastructures. Dismantling the old is just half the battle; the other half begins with attempting to imagine futures that are radically different from the present.⁵⁴

Notes

1. We align with decolonial scholars such as Boaventura de Sousa Santos, Jean and John Comaroff, Walter Mignolo, Anne Mahler, Maria Lugones, Arturo Escobar, and Raewyn Connell, among others, who consider the "Global South" a sociopolitical and epistemic space that extends beyond geographical lines and represents those who are at a disadvantage due to unjust sociopolitical and economic structures (such as capitalism, patriarchy, postcolonialism, and others) regardless of where they are placed in the world.

2. Laura Czerniewicz, "Inequitable Power Dynamics of Global Knowledge Production and Exchange Must Be Confronted Head On," *LSE Impact Blog* (blog), April 29, 2013, https://blogs.lse.ac.uk/impactofsocialsciences/2013/04/29/redrawing-the-map-from-access-to-participation/.

3. Leslie Chan and Sely Costa, "Participation in the Global Knowledge Commons: Challenges and Opportunities for Research Dissemination in Developing Countries," *New Library World* 106, no. 3/4 (2005): 141–163, https://doi.org/10.1108/03074800510587354.

4. Francis Nyamnjoh, "Institutional Review: Open Access and Open Knowledge Production Processes: Lessons from CODESRIA," *South African Journal of Information and Communication*, no. 10 (2010): 67–72, https://doi.org/10.23962/10539/19772; Stuart Lawson, "Open Access Policy in the UK: From Neoliberalism to the Commons," (Doctoral thesis, Birkbeck, University of London, 2019), https://ethos.bl.uk

/OrderDetails.do?uin=uk.bl.ethos.774255; Samuel Moore, "A Genealogy of Open Access: Negotiations between Openness and Access to Research," *Revue Française Des Sciences de l'information et de La Communication*, no. 11 (2017), https://doi.org/10.4000/rfsic.3220.

5. Miranda Fricker, "Forum on Miranda Fricker's Epistemic Injustice: Power and the Ethics of Knowing," *THEORIA: An International Journal for Theory, History and Foundations of Science* 23, no. 1 (2008): 69–71.

6. Leslie Chan et al., eds., *Contextualizing Openness: Situating Open Science* (Ottawa: University of Ottawa Press, 2019).

7. This concept was developed by researchers Laura Foster, Cath Traynor, and the Natural Justice team as part of their research with OCSDNet. The concept was also incorporated into the Open and Collaborative Science Manifesto, developed by OCSDNet and published in 2017.

8. Chan et al., *Contextualizing Openness*.

9. Marìa Lugones, "Toward a Decolonial Feminism," *Hypatia* 25, no. 4 (2010): 742–759, https://doi.org/10.1111/j.1527-2001.2010.01137.x; Chandra Talpade Mohanty, *Feminism without Borders: Decolonizing Theory, Practicing Solidarity* (Durham, NC: Duke University Press, 2003); Boaventura de Sousa Santos, ed., *Another Knowledge Is Possible: Beyond Northern Epistemologies* (London: Verso, 2008); Safiya Umoja Noble, "A Future for Intersectional Black Feminist Technology Studies," *Scholar & Feminist Online* 13, no. 3 (2016): 1–8; Virginia Eubanks, *Automating Inequality: How High-Tech Tools Profile, Police, and Punish the Poor* (New York: St. Martin's Press, 2017); Anne Pollock and Banu Subramaniam, "Resisting Power, Retooling Justice: Promises of Feminist Postcolonial Technosciences," *Science, Technology, & Human Values* 41, no. 6 (2016): 951–966, https://doi.org/10.1177/0162243916657879.

10. John Gaventa, "Finding the Spaces for Change: A Power Analysis," *IDS Bulletin* 37, no. 6 (2006): 23–33, https://doi.org/10.1111/j.1759-5436.2006.tb00320.x; John Gaventa, "12 Levels, Spaces and Forms of Power," in *Power in World Politics*, ed. Felix Berenskoetter and Michael J. Williams (London: Routledge, 2007), 204–224.

11. José Medina, "Whose Meanings? Resignifying Voices and Their Social Locations," *The Journal of Speculative Philosophy* 22, no. 2 (2008): 92–105.

12. Patricia Hill Collins, "Black Feminist Thought in the Matrix of Domination," in *Black Feminist Thought: Knowledge, Consciousness, and the Politics of Empowerment* (Boston: Unwin Hyman, 1990), 221.

13. Donna Haraway, "Situated Knowledges: The Science Question in Feminism and the Privilege of Partial Perspective," *Feminist Studies* 14, no. 3 (1988): 575–599, https://doi.org/10.2307/3178066; Sandra G. Harding, *Objectivity and Diversity: Another Logic of Scientific Research* (Chicago: University of Chicago Press, 2015).

14. Kimberlé Crenshaw, "Demarginalizing the Intersection of Race and Sex: A Black Feminist Critique of Antidiscrimination Doctrine," *University of Chicago Legal Forum*, no. 1 (1989): 139–167, https://doi.org/10.4324/9780429500480-5; Medina, "Whose Meanings?"

15. Merrill B. Hintikka and Sandra G. Harding, eds., *Discovering Reality: Feminist Perspectives on Epistemology, Metaphysics, Methodology, and Philosophy of Science* (Dordrecht: Reidel, 1983).

16. Boaventura de Sousa Santos, "Epistemologies of the South and the Future," *From the European South*, no. 1 (2016): 17–29; José-Manuel Barreto, "Epistemologies of the South and Human Rights: Santos and the Quest for Global and Cognitive Justice," *Indiana Journal of Global Legal Studies* 21, no. 2 (2014): 395–422, https://doi.org/10.2979/indjglolegstu.21.2.395; Miranda Fricker, "Epistemic Justice as a Condition of Political Freedom?," *Synthese* 190, no. 7 (2013): 1317–1332.

17. E. Summerson Carr, "Enactments of Expertise," *Annual Review of Anthropology* 39, no. 1 (2010): 17–32, https://doi.org/10.1146/annurev.anthro.012809.104948; H. M. Collins and Robert Evans, "The Third Wave of Science Studies: Studies of Expertise and Experience," *Social Studies of Science* 32, no. 2 (2002): 235–296, https://doi.org/10.1177/0306312702032002003.

18. Vincent Larivière, Stefanie Haustein, and Philippe Mongeon, "The Oligopoly of Academic Publishers in the Digital Era," *PLOS ONE* 10, no. 6 (2015): e0127502, https://doi.org/10.1371/journal.pone.0127502; Ernesto Priego et al., "Scholarly Publishing, Freedom of Information and Academic Self-Determination: The UNAM-Elsevier Case," *Authorea*, 2017, https://doi.org/10.22541/au.151160332.22737207; Alejandro Posada and George Chen, "Inequality in Knowledge Production: The Integration of Academic Infrastructure by Big Publishers" (22nd International Conference on Electronic Publishing, OpenEdition Press, 2018), https://doi.org/10.4000/proceedings.elpub.2018.30.

19. A. Suresh Canagarajah, *A Geopolitics of Academic Writing* (Pittsburgh, PA: University of Pittsburgh Press, 2002); David R. Russell et al., "Exploring Notions of Genre in 'Academic Literacies' and 'Writing Across the Curriculum': Approaches Across Countries and Contexts," in *Genre in a Changing World*, ed. Charles Bazerman, Adair Bonini, and Débora Figueiredo (Fort Collins, CO: WAC Clearinghouse/Parlor Press, 2009), 459–491, http://wac.colostate.edu/books/genre/chapter20.pdf; Joel Windle, "Hidden Features in Global Knowledge Production: (Re)Positioning Theory and Practice in Academic Writing," *Revista Brasileira de Linguística Aplicada* 17, no. 2 (2017): 355–378, https://doi.org/10.1590/1984-6398201610966.

20. Witold Kieńć, "Authors from The Periphery Countries Choose Open Access More Often," *Learned Publishing* 30, no. 2 (2017): 125–131, https://doi.org/10.1002/leap.1093; Mark Graham, Stefano De Sabbata, and Matthew A. Zook, "Towards a Study of Information Geographies: (Im)Mutable Augmentations and a Mapping of the Geographies of Information," *Geo: Geography and Environment* 2, no. 1 (2015):

88–105, https://doi.org/10.1002/geo2.8; Domenico Fiormonte and Ernesto Priego, "Knowledge Monopolies and Global Academic Publishing," *The Winnower*, August 24, 2016, https://doi.org/10.15200/winn.147220.00404.

21. de Sousa Santos, "Epistemologies of the South and the Future," 20.

22. Iris Marion Young, "Responsibility and Global Justice: A Social Connection Model," *Social Philosophy and Policy* 23, no. 1 (2006): 102, https://doi.org/10.1017/S0265052506060043.

23. Fricker, "Forum on Miranda Fricker's Epistemic Injustice"; Fricker, "Epistemic Justice as a Condition of Political Freedom?"

24. Nancy Tuana, "The Speculum of Ignorance: The Women's Health Movement and Epistemologies of Ignorance," *Hypatia* 21, no. 3 (2006): 13, https://doi.org/10.1111/j.1527-2001.2006.tb01110.x.

25. Tuana, "The Speculum of Ignorance," 13.

26. Arjun Appadurai, "The Right to Research," *Globalisation, Societies and Education* 4, no. 2 (2006): 168, https://doi.org/10.1080/14767720600750696.

27. Rebecca Hillyer et al., "Framing a Situated and Inclusive Open Science: Emerging Lessons from the Open and Collaborative Science in Development Network," in *Expanding Perspectives on Open Science: Communities, Cultures and Diversity in Concepts and Practices*, ed. Leslie Chan and Fernando Loizides (Amsterdam: IOS Press, 2017), 18–33, https://doi.org10.3233/978-1-61499-769-6-18; Chan et al., *Contextualizing Openness*.

28. We use the term "San" here, but would like to acknowledge and flag the ongoing debates over the terms of reference for the groups: San, Jun/oansi, "bushmen," "hunter-gatherers," BaSarwa, among others. For example, in Namibia, Jun/oansi call themselves "bushmen" when speaking Afrikaans, but otherwise call themselves Jun/oansi.

29. Dani Nabudale, "Research, Activism, and Knowledge Production," in *Engaging Contradictions: Theory, Politics, and Methods of Activist Scholarship*, ed. Charles Hale (Berkeley: University of California Press, 2008).

30. Paulin J. Hountondji, "Le Savoir Mondialise: Desequilibres et Enjeux Actuels" (La mondialisation vue d'Afrique, Université de Nantes/Maison des Sciences de l'Homme Guépin, 2001).

31. Eve Tuck and K. Wayne Yang, "R-Words: Refusing Research," in *Humanizing Research: Decolonizing Qualitative Inquiry with Youth and Communities* (London: SAGE, 2014), 223–248; Linda Tuhiwai Smith, *Decolonizing Methodologies: Research and Indigenous Peoples* (London: Zed Books, 2012).

32. Cath Traynor, Laura Foster, and Tobias Schonwetter, "Tensions Related to Openness in Researching Indigenous Peoples' Knowledge Systems and Intellectual Property Rights," in *Contextualizing Openness: Situating Open Science*, ed. Leslie Chan et al.

(Ottawa: University of Ottawa Press, 2019), 223–36, https://www.idrc.ca/en/book/contextualizing-openness-situating-open-science.

33. Arturo Escobar, "Whose Knowledge, Whose Nature? Biodiversity, Conservation, and the Political Ecology of Social Movements," *Journal of Political Ecology* 5, no. 1 (1998): 55, https://doi.org/10.2458/v5i1.21397.

34. Hector Botero, "The Meeting of Two Worlds: Combining Traditional and Scientific Knowledge," *OCSDNet* (blog), October 31, 2015, https://ocsdnet.org/the-meeting-of-two-worlds-combining-traditional-and-scientific-knowledge/.

35. Josique Lorenzo, John Mario Rodriguez, and Viviana Benavides, "On Openness and Motivation: Insights from a Pilot Project in Latin America," in *Contextualizing Openness: Situating Open Science*, ed. Leslie Chan et al. (Ottawa: University of Ottawa Press, 2019), 87–106, https://www.idrc.ca/en/book/contextualizing-openness-situating-open-science.

36. "Projet SOHA." This project referred to epistemic injustice as cognitive injustice.

37. Raewyn Connell, "Southern Theory and World Universities," *Higher Education Research & Development* 36, no. 1 (2017): 4–15, https://doi.org/10.1080/07294360.2017.1252311; Fredua-Kwarteng, "The Case for Developmental Universities."

38. Florence Piron et al., "Toward African and Haitian Universities in Service to Sustainable Local Development: The Contribution of Fair Open Science," in *Contextualizing Openness: Situating Open Science*, ed. Leslie Chan et al. (Ottawa: University of Ottawa Press, 2019), 311–331, https://www.idrc.ca/en/book/contextualizing-openness-situating-open-science.

39. Piron et al., "Toward African and Haitian Universities in Service to Sustainable Local Development."

40. See Barreto, "Epistemologies of the South and Human Rights"; Boaventura de Sousa Santos, "Introducción: Las Epistemologías Del Sur," in *Formas-Otras: Saber, Nombrar, Narrar, Hacer*, ed. Fundación CIDOB (España: CIDOB, 2011), 11–12.

41. Barreto, "Epistemologies of the South and Human Rights."

42. Medina, "Whose Meanings?"

43. Kristie Dotson, "Tracking Epistemic Violence, Tracking Practices of Silencing," *Hypatia* 26, no. 2 (2011): 236–257, https://doi.org/10.1111/j.1527-2001.2011.01177.x.

44. de Sousa Santos, "Epistemologies of the South and the Future," 21.

45. Gaventa, "12 Levels, Spaces and Forms of Power."

46. Arturo Escobar, *Designs for the Pluriverse: Radical Interdependence, Autonomy, and the Making of Worlds*, New Ecologies for the Twenty-First Century (Durham, NC: Duke University Press, 2018).

47. Evelyn Fox Keller, *Making Sense of Life: Explaining Biological Development with Models, Metaphors, and Machines* (Cambridge, MA: Harvard University Press, 2003).

48. Mike Fortun, Kim Fortun, and George E. Marcus, "Computers in/and Anthropology: The Poetics and Politics of Digitization," in *The Routledge Companion to Digital Ethnography*, ed. Larissa Hjorth et al. (London: Routledge, 2017), 11–20, https://doi.org/10.4324/9781315673974.

49. Kimberly Christen, "Tribal Archives, Traditional Knowledge, and Local Contexts: Why the 's' Matters," *Journal of Western Archives* 6, no. 1 (2015): 3, https://digitalcommons.usu.edu/westernarchives/vol6/iss1/3.

50. Luis Felipe Rosado Murillo, "What Does 'Open Data' Mean for Ethnographic Research?: Multimodal Anthropologies," *American Anthropologist* 120, no. 3 (2018): 577–582, https://doi.org/10.1111/aman.13088.

51. Christen, "Tribal Archives, Traditional Knowledge, and Local Contexts."

52. Robin D. G Kelley, *Freedom Dreams: The Black Radical Imagination* (Boston: Beacon Press, 2002), x.

53. The Combahee River Collective, "A Black Feminist Statement," in *The Second Wave: A Reader in Feminist Theory*, ed. Linda J. Nicholson (New York: Routledge, 1997), 63–70.

54. Escobar, Designs for the Pluriverse.

II Epistemologies

5 When the Law Advances Access to Learning: Locke and the Origins of Modern Copyright

John Willinsky

Let me begin with the singular historical fact that constitutes this chapter's endpoint.[1] On April 5, 1710, after nearly two decades of political wrangling over the reinstatement of some form of book licensing in Great Britain, to replace the granting of publisher monopolies in exchange for state censorship, the British Parliament passed the Statute of Anne 1710. Its extended title begins, "An Act for the Encouragement of Learning ..." And therein lies my tale. One of the things that makes this act remarkable is how much of that "encouragement" the bill contained. Another is that the act successfully launched the modern era of copyright law. For the first time, a legislative body recognized that the author of a work possessed rights over its reproduction, if for a limited term of up to 28 years. Yet the story I set out below is about how, in the decades preceding the act's passage, learning came to play the role that it did in initiating the age of copyright. The encouragement of learning was not the whole of the impetus for this new law, but the part that it played is surely worth pausing over today in light of the great turmoil and promise currently surrounding new models of scholarly publishing.

How is it, one might well ask, that learning held such a place in the introduction of modern copyright law, when the law today offers it so little encouragement to pursue what researchers, funders, librarians, and publishers now agree is learning's optimal state for the digital era—namely, "open access"? What the law supports is the selling of exclusive access to journals by subscription. This is the economic model that continues to dominate the circulation of this work and is proving a great roadblock to the transition to open access. One reason for that is how a growing proportion of these subscription journals are held by Elsevier and four other big corporate publishers who have been able to wring from them, with the support of copyright monopolies, a profit margin that exceeds those of most other businesses.[2]

Even as these publishers are encouraged by the law to wrest a greater share of research expenditures away from the academic community, the move to open access by authors, research funders, and scholarly publishers (including Elsevier for a small proportion of its titles) has resulted in roughly half of the current research articles being made freely available.[3] To be half open, however, is still to be in a state of flux. In 2018 and 2019, journal subscription negotiations with Elsevier and other publishers broke down in a number of countries; readers and researchers continue to turn to the pirated troves of research in Sci-Hub, just as fair use disputes over scholarly works continue to end up in the courts.[4] What success open access has achieved in all of this is largely the result of what amounts to copyright workarounds. For example, authors and journals use Creative Commons licenses to grant rights to users that the law does not. Funding agencies enter into a contract with grantees, as part of open-access mandates, that prevents them from, in effect, fully exercising their copyright. Given that the law is doing little enough to encourage learning in the digital era, grounds exist for revisiting learning's role in the origins of modern copyright. Think of it as a first step in considering how the law might once again encourage this form of learning.

In response to this question of how learning first became central to the origins of modern copyright, the philosopher John Locke will be our guide. In the 1690s, Locke's earnest lobbying on learning's behalf contributed to the lead up to the Statute of Anne 1710, which, as he died in 1704, he did not live, alas, to see pass. Amid late seventeenth-century debates over regulation of printing, Locke served as something of a public defender of scholarly interests. Yet before setting out the case that he made, I need to acknowledge that some historians take the act's seeming emphasis on learning to be nothing more than "window dressing," as John Feather puts it, with the good that it did learning, if any, "difficult to quantify."[5] The statute "ensured," in his estimation, "the continued dominance of English publishing by a few London firms."[6] While I do not doubt that the leading firms retained their market share, the proof of the substantial protection that the Statute of Anne 1710 afforded learning against commercial interests is found, as I will go on to show, in the ongoing political actions—and not without some success—by which printers and booksellers sought to curtail these protective measures.

In this, I follow the lead of Ronan Deazley, who, in contrast to Feather, holds that with this act, "Parliament focused upon the author's utility in society in the encouragement and advancement of learning," thereby upholding "pre-eminence of the common good" as copyright's organizing principle.[7] Still, Deazley also allows that "Parliament bowed to the lobbying of the book trade in passing the Statute of Anne."[8] I seek to establish how there was another source of forceful lobbying at work on Parliament, and that Locke offers a model, in this one instance, of an activist scholar who might well inspire efforts today in the face of relentless industry lobbying and market dominance.

Locke's contribution to the formation of early copyright law is also worth considering for what it can teach about his influential natural law theory of property. Locke made property a matter of human rights under natural law. Those rights extended, he held, to the individual's right of consent in democratic governance. This was in stark contrast, Locke insisted, to the authority that kings presumed to have over property and individuals through a divine right.

To consider his argument for property rights, in *Two Treatises of Government* (published anonymously in 1689), he posits a world that in its original state is given in common to humankind. Allowing that individuals have a right in themselves, they are able to acquire from the commons that which they labor over. Their acquisitions are subject to natural constraints, *to ensure that there is "enough, and as good, left in common for others" and that holding such property did not lead to its spoilage or waste*.[9] Locke's theory of property continues to be a major influence in the field of intellectual property jurisprudence.[10] Yet few of those considering his theory look to how he applied it to the Parliamentary proposals he made on the regulation of printing. I contend that his theory of property informs his legislative suggestions, particularly around balancing authors' ownership rights with the distinctive access and use rights that facilitate scholarship that were to find a place in the Statute of Anne 1710.

Locke's Lobbying

On January 2, 1693, Locke appears to have initiated his attempt to influence Parliament with a letter to his longstanding friend Edward Clarke, who was then serving as the Whig Member of Parliament from Taunton. The letter expresses Locke's concerns about the current state of the book trade. At the time, Parliament was considering renewing once more the 30-year-old Licensing of the Press Act of 1662, which was itself a continuation of state press regulation dating back to policies first instituted by Henry VIII in

1538.[11] The 1662 Act enabled the Stationers' Company, which was the guild representing London's leading printers and booksellers, to grant its members perpetual monopolies for titles and whole genres in exchange for the press's cooperation in executing state censorship of the press. The Act's full title, after all, was "An Act for Preventing the Frequent Abuses in Printing Seditious Treasonable and Unlicensed Books and Pamphlets and for Regulating of Printing and Printing Presses." It restricted printing to London, York, and, in recognition of the universities' historic rights, Oxford and Cambridge.[12] The Whig opposition to Charles II, however, regarded this licensing of censorship as another instance of Restoration overreach on the part of the reinstated monarchy (although book licensing had persisted through Cromwell's interregnum). Parliament allowed the Press Act to lapse in 1679, only to later renew it in 1685 for seven years, after Charles's controversial (which is to say Catholic) brother, James II, took the throne. The Act also survived the Glorious Revolution of 1688, which deposed James and placed William III and Mary on the throne. Following the passing of the Bill of Rights in 1689, the Whigs increasingly sought to put an end to press regulation as a regrettable carryover from the *ancien régime*.

In his 1693 letter to Clarke, Locke asked his friend to consider the damage done to learning by the Stationers' Company book monopolies granted by the Press Act of 1662. In particular, Locke addresses in his letter the effects of the broad monopolies granted in perpetuity to printers and booksellers by the Stationers' Company, under the terms of the Press Act. Such monopolies made it nearly impossible to undertake improved editions or import such editions of classical authors:

> I wish you would have some care of Book buyers as well as all of Book sellers, and the Company of Stationers who haveing got a Patent for all or most of the Ancient Latin Authors (by what right or pretence I know not) claime the text to be their and soe will not suffer fairer and more correct Editions than any thing they print here or with new Comments to be imported ... whereby these most usefull books are excessively dear to schollers.[13]

Locke's letter to Clarke was too little too late. The Press Act was renewed in March 1693.[14] It was only extended this time, however, for two years, indicating Parliament's lack of enthusiasm for book licensing, despite the case made for it by the Stationers' Company. The limited-terms renewal appears to have given Locke hope, as he continued his campaign against any further renewal of the act. To prevent that from happening, he worked not only with Clarke, but involved, in what he referred to as "the Colledg" (college), both John Freke, a lawyer and Whig lobbyist, and John Somers, who held the parliamentary post of lord keeper of the great seal and who was a member of the Privy Council.[15]

In 1694, Clarke was appointed to the House of Commons committee to review those laws that were about to expire, the 1662 Press Act among them. To assist Clarke in preventing the renewal, Locke prepared a memorandum for his friend which begins by sounding the familiar trumpet of a free press: "I know not why a man should not have liberty to print what ever he would speake."[16] To require that a license to print a work be obtained in advance was like "gagging a man for fear he should talk heresy or sedition."[17] All that was required, he proposed, was that the printer or author be clearly identified in the book to ensure that someone will "be answerable for" any legal transgressions.[18] As things stood, "by this act England loses in general," and as he puts it, "Scholars in particular are ground [down] and nobody gets [anything] but a lazy ignorant Company of Stationers. To say no worse of them. But anything rather than let mother church be disturbed in her opinion or impositions, by any bold voice from the press."[19] For Locke, the issues of freedom of speech and of scholarly inquiry were closely aligned in ways that, if both are supported, would benefit Britain as a whole.

Locke then moved into what mattered to him at least as much as press freedom, which was the current "restraint of printing the classic authors."[20] He asked with a touch of sarcasm about the value of such restraint: "Does [it in] any way prevent the printing of seditious and treasonable pamphlets, which is the title and pretense of this act?"[21] More than a decade before, Locke had been party to such sedition in print, escaping with his life to Holland in 1683.[22] More to our point, Locke was also indignant over how poorly the Stationers' Company served learning: "Scholars cannot but at excessive rates have the fair and correct editions of these books and the comments [commentaries] on them printed beyond [the] seas"; they are left with "scandalously illprinted" local editions, given the lack of competition amid the perpetual monopolies.[23] To illustrate, Locke referred to an imported edition of "Tully's Works" (Marcus Tullius Cicero), which he found to be "a very fine edition, with new corrections made by Gronovius, who takes the pains to compare that which was thought the best edition"; the work was "seized and kept a good while in [the Company's] custody," before it was sold with the booksellers "demanding 6s. 8d. per book."[24] The problem is that, broadly stated, the crown enabled the Stationers' Company to grant patents on whole bodies of work, such as classical authors, which a printer could exercise without end or limit.

Locke's overarching concern for scholars' rights to access such works led him to a backhanded commendation of the current act's requirement that a free copy of each new book be sent to "the public libraries of both universities."[25] This university-access policy originated in Britain with the 1610 agreement that Oxford patron Thomas Bodley secured from the Stationers' Company to supply the university library, which Bodley was in the process of restoring, with a copy of each book printed. The deed that Bodley drew up reads that the Stationers' Company of London "out of zeale to the advancement of good learning ... granted to the University of Oxford, for ever, one copy of every new book in quires that they might borrow or copy any book deposited, for reprinting."[26] This deposit requirement had been included in the 1662 Press Act, although Locke complains that it "will be found to be mightily if not wholly neglected" by the Stationers' Company, "however keenly it might otherwise support the act."[27] From my perspective, the book deposit stipulation, as it applied to the "public" or university libraries at Oxford and Cambridge, demonstrates how commerce sponsors, even as it stands apart from, the commons of learning. It is another instance of Locke's theory of property in which authors, printers, and booksellers have a right to the fruits of their labor, "at least where there is *enough, and as good, left in common for others.*"[28] The public library of the university was that commons, when it came to the properties of learning.

As part of Locke's concern for his balance of rights, he objected to the perpetual monopolies granted to the Stationers' Company. In its place, he recommended limits to *the ability to purchase or sell rights in a work*: "it may be reasonable to limit" the property of "those [printers and booksellers] who purchase copies from authors that live now and write," he states in his Licensing Act memo, "to a certain number of years after the death of the author or the first printing of the book as suppose 50 or 70 years."[29] This would encourage the publication of new editions of older works, in contrast to the current situation in which "the Company of Stationers have a monopoly of all the classic authors."[30] Locke also objected to restrictions on the importing of books into Britain. This was a point that his friend Clarke made to the House of Lords in Lockean terms by pointing out that, for book importers, restrictions and delays meant that "part of his Stock lie dead; or the Books, if wet, may rot and perish."³¹ Under Locke's natural law, whoever allowed property to spoil was claiming "more than his share, and [it] belongs to others," as he put in the famous chapter on property in *Two Treatises*.³²

What Locke ultimately bemoans in his memo on the Press Act of 1662 is that it is "so manifest an invasion on the trade, liberty, and property of the subject" that it places under siege what he sees to be the intellectual property rights of the learned.³³ As Locke saw it, access to this literature must be facilitated for scholars rather than impeded by unfair trade practices such as perpetual monopolies and book blockades: "That any person or company should have patents for the sole printing of ancient authors" he concludes in the memo, "is very unreasonable and injurious to learning."³⁴

In 1695, not long after Locke's memo, Clarke began to work with fellow legislator Robert Harley, Earl of Oxford, on a "Bill for the Better Regulating of Printing and Printing Presses." Their proposed bill had the virtue of exempting from state licensing books that dealt with science, arts, and heraldry. It made no reference to a number of previously granted privileges, including the Stationers' Company monopolies and the universities' printing rights.³⁵ Locke was not involved in Clarke and Harley's initial drafting of the new bill, but they sent him a copy of it and he soon proposed amendments. Although a number of Locke's suggestions for the bill have been lost, what remains in his papers makes clear that he had come by this point to recognize the importance of instantiating the authors' intellectual property rights. He proposes to Clarke that the new bill "secure the author's property in his copy" for a limited time.³⁶ This property in a work could be safeguarded, he suggests, by a registration process: upon printing, a book was first to be deposited *"for the use of the publique librarys of the said Universities,"* after which the bill "shall vest a privileg in the Author ... for __ years from the first edition."³⁷ This time, the exact number of years of a limited monopoly was left up to Parliament.

While Locke argues for the authors' intellectual property rights, the registration process he recommends could also be said to protect the rights of learning. He makes the authors' limited privileges dependent on depositing the work in the public libraries of the universities for the use of scholars. Authors are to be encouraged with an eye to the use of their work by the learned. In a similar spirit, Locke also proposed that authors should retain a right over subsequent editions of their work. At the time of the bill's drafting, he was likely revising the third editions of both *An Essay*

Concerning Human Understanding (1689) and *Two Treatises*, which may well have instilled in him a sense that the author has the ultimate sense of responsibility for, and interest in, correcting and improving a work with each new edition, even as the ultimate beneficiaries are the works' readers.

Still, Clarke and Harley's "Better Regulating of Printing" bill ran into the vehement objections of the Stationers' Company, which sought a straightforward renewal of the Licensing Act of 1662. The Company's representatives protested that the reforms proposed by Clarke and Harley were "wanting as to the Security of [our] Property."[38] This was a fair enough estimation of Clarke, Harley, and Locke's intent to eliminate monopoly privileges. Drawing on Locke's points over the potential loss to learning, Clarke responded to the Company's stand by circulating objections to its unfair and illogical trade practices.

Although the "Better Regulating of Printing" bill was not to attract the votes it needed and died on the floor of the Commons in 1695, Clarke and others had effectively sown the seeds of doubt about the Press Act of 1662, and that same year both the House of Commons and the House of Lords voted not to renew the act. It expired on May 3, 1695, putting an end to well over a century of press censorship, permanent monopolies, and a generally corrupted state of press regulation. The great nineteenth-century historian and politician Thomas Babington Macaulay declared that the act's expiry meant nothing less than that "English literature was emancipated, and emancipated for ever, from the control of the government."[39] Locke's part in the defeat of the Licensing Act led his biographer, Maurice Cranston, to praise his subject's political realism: "Unlike Milton, who called for liberty in the name of liberty, Locke was content to ask for liberty in the name of trade, and unlike Milton, he achieved his end."[40] For my part, I think Cranston sells Locke short on the degree to which he pursued the liberty of the press in order to advance learning, even if he also found cause in how monopolies damage the book trade.

Piracy's Interlude

Immediately following the expiry of print licensing in 1695, upstart printers and booksellers flooded the streets of London with an inventive array of broadsides and gazettes, cheap pirated editions of books and magazines, and scandalous and obscene pamphlets.[41] The statesman Sir William Trumbull wrote in a letter at the time that "since the Act for Printing Expired London swarmes with seditious Pamphletts."[42] By 1709, there were as many as eighteen London newspapers, including the first daily. Well before that, existing libel and blasphemy laws were applied to transgressive publications through arrests and warrants, much as Locke had held was preferable to press censorship. New laws were also added, such as the 1698 "Act for the More Effectual Suppressing of Blasphemy and Prophaneness."[43] The Stationers' Company denounced, with increasing rancor and outrage, a market flooded with cheap reprints of its titles. Since the 1680s, printers of such works were accused of *piracy*.[44] It was, in fact, a free market in print materials. And the Stationers' Company did not fail to return to Parliament in search of remedy, only to find reintroducing press regulation an uphill battle.

Following the Licensing Act's expiry in 1695, the Company promoted one unsuccessful parliamentary bill after another, while petitions were also submitted to no avail by the Church of England, Oxford University, and groups of journeymen printers.[45] In 1704 (the year of Locke's death), after the Company sponsored the introduction into Parliament of a "Bill to Restrain the Licentiousness of the Press" to no avail, it decided on another tactic. It embraced the language of learning, having earlier opposed its advocates in the form of Locke and before that Milton, with his 1644 *Areopagitica*.[46] The theme had just been revitalized by the novelist, pamphleteer, and journalist Daniel Defoe in his 1704 *Essay on the Regulation of the Press*. The book was full of praise for the French King Louis XIV for the "Encouragement" he had "given to Learning" through the liberty of the press in France, contending that the English "License of the Press" was not consistent with "the Encouragement due to Learning."[47]

Beginning in 1706, three anonymous petitions were presented before Parliament, likely with the Stationers' Company support, starting with the one-page *Reasons Humbly Offer'd for a Bill for the Encouragement of Learning, and the Improvement of Printing* (1706).[48] This petition opens with a concern for the "Many Learned Men [who] have been at great Pains and Expence in Composing and Writing of Books" and takes a Lockean stance on the author's "undoubted Right to the Copy of his own Book, as being a Product of his own Labor." The petition reflects the concern that "Learned Men will be wholly Discouraged from Propagating the most useful Parts of Knowledge," given how easily their work could be pirated without state oversight. The petition closes with what was to become the requisite image of the bereft author's widow who, in the case "of the late Arch-Bishop Tillotson," might have been generously provided for by "Booksellers" were it not for the print piracy of an unregulated era.

This petition may have been among the dozen such petitions, proposals, and bills that had failed since 1695, but this one managed to gain some purchase. A further iteration, combining authors' natural rights to their work and the public good of learning, was drafted and introduced into Parliament on January 11, 1710. It was entitled the "Bill for the Encouragement of Learning, and for the Securing of Property of Copies of Books to the Rightful Owners thereof." It refers to "Books and Writings" as "the undoubted Property" of authors, with such property regarded as "the Product of their Learning and Labor," with labor being the key to Locke's theory of property.[49] This was soon struck from the bill, so that an author's earned right of ownership is left implicit. It is not what is being legislated. As such, ownership is left to natural and common law, while the act determines that from such ownership, authors have a right to a limited-term monopoly to encourage their contribution to learning.

Statute of Anne 1710

The statute that was passed on April 5, 1710, begins "An Act for the Encouragement of Learning by Vesting the Copies of Printed Books in the Authors or Purchasers of such Copies, during the Times therein mentioned." Note how the act's title no longer sets out the encouragement of learning *and* the securing of property rights as two distinct purposes. Rather, it makes the encouragement of learning the very principle behind granting such property rights. And the switch from "securing" to "vesting" suggests that the act is not about pinning down a right but about placing a right-to-copy in the hands of authors for a limited term.[50]

The act opens with the Stationers' Company's complaint that "printers, booksellers, and other persons have of late frequently taken the liberty of printing ... books and other writings, without the consent of the authors or proprietors of such books and writings," which leads "too often to the ruin of them and their families."[51] Authors are characterized as "learned men" who strive to "compose and write useful books."[52] Thus, the author (or assignee) "shall have the sole liberty of printing and reprinting such book and books for the term of 14 years." The statute requires that books "before such publication, be entered in the register book of the Company of Stationers, in such manner as hath been usual."[53] What had been usual was the granting of a monopoly right in perpetuity, compared to what was now to be a 14-year term limit for the monopoly rights. Such rights were regarded as a temporary "encouragement" or incentive, intended to ward off "ruin" while inspiring authors to prepare additional useful books.

Of the roughly ten provisions that follow in the statute, four set out the distinctive rights associated with learning, as I see it, or "the public interest," as William Cornish frames them.[54] Two of these measures spoke directly to Locke's earlier concerns. The first addresses the price of learned books: "The Vice-Chancellors of the Two Universities ... the Rector of the College of *Edinburgh* ... have hereby full Power and Authority ... to Limit and Settle the Price of every such Printed Book ... as to them shall seem Just and Reasonable."[55] This power to roll back book prices, which the House of Commons introduced into the act, was also granted to the archbishop and other officials, but was of particular value for faculty and students in the context of the university.[56] This price-control clause was repealed only a few decades later by an "Act for prohibiting the Importation of Books" passed in 1739, which was clearly a bill much more to the Stationers' Company liking.[57]

The second new measure in favor of learning, and also a point advocated by Locke, makes it clear that with the reinstatement of print regulation, nothing in the act "shall be construed to extend to prohibit the importation, vending, or selling of any books in Greek, Latin, or any other foreign language printed beyond the seas."[58] This right was somewhat qualified by the 1739 act cited in the previous paragraph, which forbade importing books that had already been published in Great Britain.[59] While this revision was clearly directed against piracy, it kept open a channel for learned books published abroad, even as it potentially restricted the import of new editions of the classics, which was also among Locke's concerns.

The other two measures in support of learning were brought forward, in an enhanced form, from the Licensing Act of 1662. One was a reinstatement of the book deposit policy. It required printers to provide "Copies of each Book ... upon the best Paper" to a wider range of university and college libraries: "The Royal Library, the Libraries of the Universities of Oxford and Cambridge, the Libraries of the Four Universities in Scotland, the Library of Sion College in London, and the Library commonly called the Library belonging to the Faculty of Advocates at Edinburgh."[60] Where the Licensing Act set aside three copies for learning, the Statute of Anne 1710 increased the number to nine on the best paper. Extending this provision to all British universities serves as an excellent reminder of how fully the law expressed a public faith in these institutions' contribution to, at a minimum, the composing and writing of useful books. Although it took more than a century, the book trade also succeeded in reigning in this measure, by having six of the university libraries eliminated in the 1836 Copyright Act.[61] Still, *legal book deposit* was to grow into a common legislative requirement throughout the world.[62]

The final measure in the statute declares that nothing herein should "prejudice or confirm any right that the said universities" had "to the printing or reprinting any book or copy already printed, or hereafter to be printed."[63] The universities' rights had historically included Bibles and almanacs by which they cross-subsidized scholarly publications—often by leasing out these rights—although not without numerous legal disputes with the Stationers' Company.[64] Much as with the libraries and legal deposit, university presses were recognized as standing apart from the common book trade and worth protecting as such.

The Statute of Anne 1710 only refers to learned men and their "useful books" in the opening paragraph. After that, it identifies as its subject the "author of any book" and the "proprietors of such books and writings," which is to say the booksellers and printers to whom authors commonly sold their work, as well as to "other person or persons" to whom such rights were assigned. It is this aspect that the act reflects, as Mark Rose suggests, "the emergent ideology of the market," as putting an end to a "monopolistic system of privilege" among a select set of printers and booksellers.[65] The Stationers' Company, having thrived under the old system of privilege, was fully prepared to compete in a book market based on authors' rights to exercise short-term monopolies of 14 years that could be renewed once (which the booksellers succeeded in having lengthened over time). Still, an act that further opened the book market and introduced an age of copyright also granted distinct privileges of access to learning; that is, the law would now offer people a right to fairly priced books, imported books, books on library shelves, new and better editions from abroad, and books printed at university presses.

Still, it needs to be made clear that the guild members of the Stationers' Company were undoubtedly the principal financial beneficiaries of the act. Yet it did not put an end to print piracy, given that the act did not, for example, extend to Ireland.[66] At the same time, the Company's members continued to act for decades on a number of their older (perpetual) monopolies, at least until the courts, in *Donaldson v Becket*, put an end to their assumed rights in 1774.[67] The following year, the British Parliament further intervened in the book market, again on the side of learning, by passing a "Bill for enabling the Two Universities to hold in Perpetuity the Copy Right in books, for the advancement of useful Learning, and other purposes of Education, within the said Universities."[68] A decade or so later, the Statute of Anne inspired a similarly spirited intellectual property clause in the U.S. Constitution in 1788 that empowers Congress to pass laws "to promote the Progress of Science and useful Arts, by securing for limited Times to Authors and Inventors the exclusive Right to their respective Writings and Discoveries."[69] This concept of copyright as a legal vesting of limited-term rights in the author was to spread slowly around the world, if not without much controversy, complaint, and piracy, amid the ongoing negotiations of international trade bodies and national adoptions of more recent legal elements, such as "fair use," that bear on research and education.[70]

It is impossible to know how much credit Locke is owed in his lobbying for learning in the formation of modern copyright law. Yet he provides a clear instance, with backing from Milton, Defoe, and others, of how learning was a reference point in articulating the public good that underwrites intellectual property rights. The resulting Statute of Anne 1710 managed to bring into a legislative order the interests and rights of authors, scholars (also as authors), printers, and booksellers. If printers and booksellers were the ones who profited, authors and scholars had their rights advanced. Three centuries later, amid the emergence of the digital era, a new order of scholarly publishing is struggling to form, caught once more between powerful commercial forces and the distinctive interests of opening up a global commons for learning.

Much as Locke did earlier, scholars and research librarians are speaking out and lobbying today in favor of increased access to needed works and resources. And much as happened with the Statute of Anne 1710, I am cognizant of Kathy Bowrey and Natalie Fowell's caution that "faith in any enduring legal truth residing in copyright law to resist commodification is ill-founded and politically naïve."[71] What Locke worked toward was placing some legislative limits on the (inevitable) commodification of scholarly works. This is a special application, if self-interested on his and my part, of his theory of property, in which the appropriation of property "does not lessen but increase the common stock of [hu]mankind."[72]

The Statute of Anne created what was, in effect, a special intellectual property class for works of learning. This eighteenth-century legal reform of book regulation is worth reconsidering today. Much of its original protection has been lost and few legal limits exist today on publisher pricing and profits in the field of scholarly publishing. At the same time, the law has yet to offer ways of encouraging the degree of access and openness that many are finding to be the great promise of the digital era for learning. At the very least, the history of the Statute of Anne 1710 should incite academics and librarians to speak up in defense of legal rights that encourage learning. They should support the effective lobbying work for open learning and science carried on by organizations such as the Scholarly Publishing and Academic Resource Coalition (SPARC).[73] We must, once again, find the advantages for learning among the play of commercial interests, knowing that this was nothing less than the original intent of copyright law and is no less worthy a goal today.

Notes

1. An earlier version of this chapter appeared in the journal *KULA: Knowledge Creation, Dissemination, and Preservation Studies* 1, no. 1 (2017) under the author's copyright, and grows out of material initially explored in *The Intellectual Properties of Learning: A Prehistory from Saint Jerome to John Locke* (Chicago: University of Chicago Press, 2017).

2. Vincent Larivière, Stefanie Haustein, and Philippe Mongeon, "The Oligopoly of Academic Publishers in the Digital Era," *PLOS ONE* 10, no. 6 (2015): e0127502, https://doi.org/10.1371/journal.pone.0127502.

3. Hamid R. Jamali and Majid Nabavi, "Open Access and Sources of Full-Text Articles in Google Scholar in Different Subject Fields," *Scientometrics* 105, no. 3 (2015): 1635–1651, https://doi.org/10.1007/s11192-015-1642-2; Éric Archambault et al., "Proportion of Open Access Papers Published in Peer-Reviewed Journals at the European and World Levels—1996–2013" (Science-Metrix), accessed April 28, 2019, http://science-metrix.com/sites/default/files/science-metrix/publications/d_1.8_sm_ec_dg-rtd_proportion_oa_1996-2013_v11p.pdf.

4. Holly Else, "Dutch Publishing Giant Cuts off Researchers in Germany and Sweden," *Nature* 559 (2018): 454, https://doi.org/10.1038/d41586-018-05754-1; Michael Hiltzik, "In Act of Brinkmanship, a Big Publisher Cuts Off UC's Access to

Its Academic Journals," Los Angeles Times, July 11, 2019, https://www.latimes.com/business/hiltzik/la-fi-uc-elsevier-20190711-story.html; John Bohannon, "Who's Downloading Pirated Papers? Everyone," Science, April 25, 2016, https://www.sciencemag.org/news/2016/04/whos-downloading-pirated-papers-everyone; Nicholas Kaster, "Copyright Case: Cambridge University Press v. Albert, USA," Kluwer Copyright Blog, October 30, 2018, http://copyrightblog.kluweriplaw.com/2018/10/30/usa-cambridge-university-press-v-albert-united-states-court-appeals-eleventh-circuit-no-16-15726-19-october-2018/.

5. John Feather, "The Book Trade in Politics: The Making of the Copyright Act of 1710," Publishing History 8 (1980): 20, 35.

6. Feather, "The Book Trade in Politics," 37.

7. Ronan Deazley, "The Myth of Copyright at Common Law," The Cambridge Law Journal 62, no. 1 (2003): 108, 133.

8. Ronan Deazley, "What's New About the Statute of Anne? Or Six Observations in Search of an Act," in Global Copyright: Three Hundred Years Since the Statute of Anne, from 1709 to Cyberspace, ed. Lionel Bently, Uma Suthersanen, and Paul Torresmans (Cheltenham, UK: Edward Elgar Publishing, 2010), 45, https://doi.org/10.4337/9781849806428.00010.

9. John Locke, Two Treatises of Government, ed. Peter Laslett (Cambridge: Cambridge University Press, 1988), 2.27.

10. Joris Deene's work exemplifies the common scholarly assumption regarding Locke's contribution to copyright law: "The criterion of intellectual effort as a basis for human appropriation of one's own creation has its origins in John Locke's Labor Theory as Described in the Second Treatise of Government (1690): 'Every Man has a Property in his own Person … The Labor of his Body, and the Work of his Hands, we may say, are properly his.'" Joris Deene, "The Influence of the Statute of Anne on Belgian Copyright Law," in Global Copyright: Three Hundred Years Since the Statute of Anne, from 1709 to Cyberspace, ed. Lionel Bently, Uma Suthersanen, and Paul Torresmans (Cheltenham, UK: Edward Elgar Publishing, 2010), 141, https://doi.org/10.4337/9781849806428.00017; on Locke's continuing influence on intellectual property jurisprudence, see, for example, Robert P. Merges, Justifying Intellectual Property (Cambridge, MA: Harvard University Press, 2011), 31–67.

11. Henry VIII issued a proclamation on November 16, 1538, requiring that books receive "his maiesties special licence," in light of "wronge teachynge and naughtye printed bokes." Quoted in Alfred W. Pollard, "The Regulation of the Book Trade in the Sixteenth Century," The Library 7, no. 25 (1916): 22–23, https://doi.org/10.1093/library/s3-VII.25.18.

12. Raymond Astbury reports that during the 1690s, the universities entered into an agreement with the Stationers' Company not to compete on the sales of English

Stock-books, which included cheap editions of schoolbooks, psalm-books, and almanacs, further reflecting the universities' struggle to find the right trade-off of privileges to make a go of scholarly publishing. Raymond Astbury, "The Renewal of the Licensing Act in 1693 and Its Lapse in 1695," *The Library* 33, no. 4 (1978): 296–322, https://doi.org/10.1093/library/s5-XXXIII.4.296.

13. John Locke, *The Correspondence of John Locke*, ed. Esmond Samuel de Beer, vol. 4 (Oxford: Oxford University Press, 1976), 614–615.

14. In the House of Lords, 11 dissenting Peers issued a statement of protest against the act, as it "subjects all Learning and true Information to the arbitrary Will and Pleasure of a mercenary, and, perhaps ignorant, Licenser, destroys the Properties of Authors in their Copies; and sets up many Monopolies." "Because the Following Provisos Were Not Admitted," *Journal of the House of Lords* 12 (March 8, 1693): 163.

15. Locke, *The Correspondence of John Locke*, 4:288–289.

16. John Locke, "Liberty of the Press (1694–5)," in *Locke: Political Essays*, ed. Mark Goldie (Cambridge: Cambridge University Press, 1997), 331, https://doi.org/10.1017/CBO9780511810251.

17. Locke, "Liberty of the Press," 331.

18. Locke, "Liberty of the Press," 331.

19. Locke, "Liberty of the Press," 335.

20. Locke, "Liberty of the Press," 334.

21. Locke, "Liberty of the Press," 334.

22. Locke was at the time something of a hired pen for the late Lord Shaftesbury, who was behind the profligate pamphlet attacks on Charles II that marked the Exclusion Crisis (mounted against Charles's Catholic brother's claim to the throne). King Charles II saw to the expulsion of Locke from his faculty position at Oxford's Christ Church. After returning from political exile to Britain in 1689, Locke lived as an independent scholar on an annuity he'd arranged with Lord Shaftesbury— derived from slave-trade gains, despite his championing of (English) human rights— while residing with another patron, Damaris Cudworth; R. S. Woolhouse, *Locke: A Biography* (Cambridge: Cambridge University Press, 2007), 197–216.

23. Locke, "Liberty of the Press," 332.

24. Locke, "Liberty of the Press," 332–333.

25. Locke, "Liberty of the Press," 336.

26. Quoted in I. G. Philip, *The Bodleian Library in the Seventeenth and Eighteenth Centuries, 1980–1981* (Oxford: Oxford University Press, 1983), 27. Ian Philip calculates that this deposit system originally brought in about 20 percent of what was being

published in 1615–1616, 28; the idea, which came from Bodley's librarian Thomas James, may have been inspired by François I's Montpellier Ordinance of 1537 requiring (if seldom honored) the placing of books in the French king's library before they were sold. Robert C. Barrington Partridge, "The History of the Legal Deposit of Books throughout the British Empire" (Honours Diploma, Library Association, 1938), 18.

27. Locke, "Liberty of the Press," 336.

28. Locke, *Two Treatises of Government*, 2.27.

29. Locke, "Liberty of the Press," 337; Joseph Loewenstein judges that Locke's "opposition to perpetual copyright is one of the most consequential aspects of Locke's critique of the licensing bill," while pointing out that it was inspired by the "limited-term privilege" of "the old institution of the patent." Joseph Loewenstein, *The Author's Due: Printing and the Prehistory of Copyright* (Chicago: University of Chicago Press, 2002), 230.

30. Locke, "Liberty of the Press," 332.

31. "Commons Reasons for Disagreeing to the Clause for Reviving the Printing Act," *Journal of the House of Lords* 15 (1695): 546.

32. Locke, *Two Treatises of Government*, 2.31.

33. Locke, "Liberty of the Press," 336.

34. Locke continues: "Tis very absurd and ridiculous that anyone now living should pretend to have a property in or a power to dispose of the property of any copies or writings of authors who lived before printing was known and used in Europe." Locke, "Liberty of the Press," 337.

35. Among those calling for a renewal of the Licensing Act was John Wallis, book licenser and professor of geometry at Oxford, who warned that the university's loss of privileges in printing profitable books would leave it unable to subsidize costly scholarly works (a refrain heard from university presses today). Astbury, "The Renewal of the Licensing Act in 1693 and Its Lapse in 1695," 322.

36. Locke, *The Correspondence of John Locke*, 4:795.

37. Locke, *The Correspondence of John Locke*, 4:796.

38. Quoted in Astbury, "The Renewal of the Licensing Act in 1693 and Its Lapse in 1695," 312.

39. Thomas Babington Macaulay, *The History of England, from the Accession of James II*, vol. 4 (Philadelphia, PA: Butler, 1856), 337.

40. Maurice William Cranston, *John Locke, a Biography* (Oxford: Oxford University Press, 1957), 387; Astbury: "Clearly, the Commons' objections owed much to Locke's Memorandum of 1694, even though his expressions of animosity towards Court and

Church as the leading champions of preprinting censorship were expunged." Astbury, "The Renewal of the Licensing Act in 1693 and Its Lapse in 1695," 315; Deazley notes that "the parallels between Locke's commentary and those reasons presented by the Commons to the Lords for refusing to renew the 1662 Act are striking." Ronan Deazley, *On the Origin of the Right to Copy: Charting the Movement of Copyright Law in Eighteenth-Century Britain (1695–1775)* (Oxford: Hart Publishing, 2004), 4.

41. Deazley, *On the Origin of the Right to Copy*, 11.

42. Quoted in Astbury, "The Renewal of the Licensing Act in 1693 and Its Lapse in 1695," 317.

43. Geoff Kemp, "The 'End of Censorship' and the Politics of Toleration, from Locke to Sacheverell," *Parliamentary History* 31, no. 1 (2012): 26–27, https://doi.org/10.1111/j.1750-0206.2011.00282.x.

44. Adrian Johns, *Piracy: The Intellectual Property Wars from Gutenberg to Gates* (Chicago: University of Chicago Press, 2011), 41; On the origins of the term piracy, John Fell refers, in a 1674 letter, to the Stationers' Company as "land-pirats" for treading on the university's "propertie in Printing," quoted in Adrian Johns, *The Nature of the Book* (Urbana, IL: University of Chicago Press, 1998), 344. The Oxford English Dictionary credits J. Mennes' *Recreattion for Geniuses Head-peeces* (1654) with the first use of piracy in this sense.

45. Feather, "The Book Trade in Politics," 21–24.

46. John Milton, "Areopagitica," in *Milton's Prose Writings*, ed. K. M. Burton (London: Dent, 1958), 149.

47. Daniel Defoe, *An Essay on the Regulation of the Press* (London, 1704), 9, 11; Rose reviews Defoe's extensive writings as a journalist on this theme during this period, commenting at one point on Defoe's Lockean conception of authorship. Mark Rose, *Authors and Owners: The Invention of Copyright* (Cambridge, MA: Harvard University Press, 1993), 38.

48. Lionel Bently and Martin Kretschmer, eds., "Reasons Humbly Offer'd for the Bill for the Encouragement of Learning, London (1706)," in *Primary Sources on Copyright (1450–1900)*, 2008, http://www.copyrighthistory.org/cam/index.php.

49. Cited by Ronan Deazley, "Commentary on the Statute of Anne 1710," in *Primary Sources on Copyright (1450–1900)*, ed. Lionel Bently and Martin Kretschmer, 2008, http://www.copyrighthistory.org/cam/index.php.

50. "The Statute of Anne; April 10, 1710," The Avalon Project, 2008, http://avalon.law.yale.edu/18th_century/anne_1710.asp.

51. Feather establishes the degree to which the Stationers' Company influenced the final wording of the statute: the Company did bear the expenses associated with

seeing the statute through Parliament, although it was not allowed to change the term limit on copyright. Feather, "The Book Trade in Politics," 36.

52. This language dates back to the Company's 1706 petition, which begins, "Whereas many Learned Men have been at great Pains and Expense …" While any author was to a degree learned in early eighteenth-century Britain, the Company had in this earlier petition referred to "a Gentleman [who] has spent the greatest Part of his Time and Fortune in a Liberal Education." Bently and Kretschmer, "Reasons Humbly Offer'd for the Bill for the Encouragement of Learning, London (1706)," 706.

53. "The Statute of Anne; April 10, 1710."

54. William Cornish, "The Statute of Anne 1709–10: Its Historical Setting," in *Global Copyright: Three Hundred Years Since the Statute of Anne, from 1709 to Cyberspace*, ed. Lionel Bently, Uma Suthersanen, and Paul Torresmans (Cheltenham, UK: Edward Elgar Publishing, 2010), 23–24, https://doi.org/10.4337/9781849806428.00009.

55. "The Statute of Anne; April 10, 1710."

56. Harry Ransom, *The First Copyright Statute, an Essay on "An Act for the Encouragement of Learning," 1710* (Austin: University of Texas Press, 1956), 101–102.

57. George Ticknor Curtis, ed., "An Act for Prohibiting the Importation of Books Reprinted Abroad … (1739)," in *A Treatise on the Law of Copyright* (London: Maxwell & Sons, 1847), 11–14; Harry Ransom notes that "the regulation had not been effective" without elaborating further. Ransom, *The First Copyright Statute*, 107, n. 13. Still, in its original conception, it attests to a parliamentary interest in protecting access to learned works, as well as to how the Stationers' Company had to give leeway to learning, if only temporarily in this case.

58. "The Statute of Anne; April 10, 1710."

59. Eaton Sylvester Drone, *A Treatise on the Law of Property in Intellectual Productions in Great Britain and the United States: Embracing Copyright in Works of Literature and Art, and Playright in Dramatic and Musical Compositions* (Boston: Little, Brown, 1879), 468.

60. "The Statute of Anne; April 10, 1710."

61. Catherine Seville, "The Statute of Anne: Rhetoric and Reception in the Nineteenth Century," *Houston Law Review* 47 (2011): 840.

62. Richard Bell, "Legal Deposit in Britain (Part 1)," *Law Librarian* 8, no. 1 (1977): 5–8. For the most recent in this lineage, see Paul Gooding, Melissa Terras, and Linda Berube, "Towards User-Centric Evaluation of UK Non-Print Legal Deposit: A Digital Library Futures White Paper," Research Reports or Papers, May 21, 2019, http://elegaldeposit.org.

63. "The Statute of Anne; April 10, 1710."

64. Ian Gadd, ed., *The History of Oxford University Press: Volume I: Beginnings to 1780*, (Oxford: Oxford University Press, 2013).

65. Rose, *Authors and Owners*, 33–34.

66. Ransom, *The First Copyright Statute*, 195.

67. See Rose on the works of Milton and Shakespeare continuing to be subject to perpetual monopolies. Rose, *Authors and Owners*, 77; and Deazley, "The Myth of Copyright at Common Law" on the myth of a perpetual common law copyright to which *Donaldson v Becket* put an end.

68. "Bill for Enabling the Two Universities to Hold in Perpetuity the Copy Right in Books, for the Advancement of Useful Learning, and Other Purposes of Education, within the Said Universities," in *House of Lords Parchment Collection* (Manuscript List, 1714–1814, 1775).

69. United States of America, "U.S. Constitution: Article 1 Section 8," The U.S. Constitution Online, 2010, http://www.usconstitution.net/xconst_A1Sec8.html?ModPage speed=noscript; As Oren Bracha put it: "When, in the late eighteenth century, Americans created their first copyright regime—first through state enactments and then by the federal 1790 Copyright Act—they used the British Statute of Anne as their doctrinal blueprint. Despite a few changes and omissions, the degree of similarity on the level of basic concepts, structure, and text between the 1790 Copyright Act and the 1710 British statute is remarkable." Oren Bracha, "The Statute of Anne: An American Mythology," *Houston Law Review* 47, no. 4 (2010): 877–878.

70. Duncan Matthews, *Globalising Intellectual Property Rights: The TRIPs Agreement* (London: Routledge, 2003).

71. Kathy Bowrey and Natalie Fowell, "Digging up Fragments and Building IP Franchises," *The Sydney Law Review* 31, no. 2 (2009): 209.

72. Locke, *Two Treatises of Government*, 2.37.

73. Elliott Shore and Heather Joseph, "Positive Changes for SPARC's Operating Structure," SPARC, June 17, 2014, https://sparcopen.org/news/2014/positive-changes-for-sparcs-operating-structure/.

6 How Does a Format Make a Public?

Robin de Mourat, Donato Ricci, and Bruno Latour

"Journal," "monograph," "conference proceedings." These are just a few names of formats that evoke the institutions and practices of the academic world. On the one hand, they summon a shared framework for thinking, reading, and writing; connecting specific institutions, infrastructures, and activities. On the other hand, they contain diverse and differentiated expectations depending upon disciplines, countries, and schools of thoughts. Moreover, if we compare them with the contemporary objects to which they relate, a certain cognitive dissonance may arise. Is an "academic journal" still a "journal" when it is less and less affected by its periodicity, and more and more distributed and manipulated at the level of granularity of its articles or citations? Is the expression "conference proceedings" still relevant when it stands for the online publication of audio or video recordings? What is an "academic book" when this expression designates artefacts spanning from collections of diverse fragments and excerpts found on the web, to e-reader oriented .epub compositions? If one acknowledges that the materiality of an academic text significantly affects the communication functions and practices attached to it, these displacements between names and experiences take on some significance. Names are far more stable than the actual practices and purposes that they imply. How, then, to qualify these displacements and the persistence of a format's names? How do they affect the formation of scholarly communities in contemporary open and transdisciplinary collectives? How does a format make a public?

The format of an artefact generally refers to its *size* and *shape*, but also to its layout and technical structure. The term encompasses both measurement and organization. Format materiality should be understood from a technological as well as from an experiential perspective, where both dimensions are inextricably intertwined. While the format of an artefact designates a set of characteristics, it also *orients* and *conditions* certain modalities of reading, writing, arguing, reflecting, and speculating. Indeed, the format of a given artefact is also the outcome of "a whole range of decisions that affect the look, feel, experience, and workings of a medium" to which this artefact belongs, as Jonathan Sterne puts it, the expression of certain assumptions and constraints affecting its producers.[1] In that sense, it is the expression of a boundary between production and experience.

However, if "format"—in its singular form—designates the material organization, practical frame, and productive background of a given artefact, the "formats"—the word in its plural form, allowing to situate *a format among others*—refers to a different process that is attached to a set of relations embedded within specific contexts. In this sense, formats can be seen as genres associated with a set of cultural techniques and sociotechnological assemblages, not understood as a predefined category, but rather as a contingent, fleeting, local, and collective dynamic; an institutional process of recognition instantiated in discourse.

Formats, then, are involved within *processes of recognition* in the sense that they relate to an operation by which a given experience or object becomes *affiliated* with previous experiences or objects, or with a broader identified category. This process implies that elements act as announcements, signals, and references, in order to set "horizons of expectations" that provide reference coordinates for interpreting a specific instance.

Formats are *institutional*, as they set positions and functions within a given collective. Formats are what are recognized by a certain type of audience, but they are also that which *organize* the whole range of practices and actors that constitute a publishing environment. We follow here publishing's definition developed by Rachel Malik as "a set of historical processes and practices—composition, editing, design and illustration, production, marketing and promotion, and distribution—and a set of relations with various other institutions—commercial, legal, educational, political, cultural, and, perhaps, above all, other media."[2] We stress here the fact that the *recognition* process of a format among others is not only a process happening "in the mind" of readers of writers, away from materialities and technical aspects of publishing, but rather an actual agent for organizing a broad range of material practices, including technologies and material setups allowing for a certain format to be *recognized* but also *acknowledged*.

Formats are, however, also *discursive*, as the recognition process of a format arises within an environment in which it gets its name. Following Siles's work on the format of the "blog," we understand formats as the result of local and dynamic processes of stabilization implying technological apparatuses and cultural practices.[3] It is, however, important to remark that if formats are identified by their naming, working in an institutional fashion, this does not necessarily mean that all individual representations and practices driven by this name totally align or that the definition of what the name recovers is clearly defined.

Therefore, formats stand for a certain play between difference and repetition, a paradoxical process of stabilization whose outcome, the "crystallization" of some practices into a specific name, can then act as a volatile agent of destabilization when this name is reused and related to more and more heterogeneous instances. The survival of long-lived academic formats—as these names that continue to be in use within academic environments—despite the diversity of the individual formats they designate, is certainly the expression of such a dynamics of stabilization, allowing some academic institutions—the Library, the Academic Journal, the University Press, and so on—to persist until today. They also persist as a certain set of local conventions for authors, readers, and reviewers to know what to expect from each other, how the format should deliver upon the expectations placed upon it, and how to maintain a cohesion among all the sociotechnological assemblages that run through scholarly communications. Formats play a great part in building horizons for writing, reading, and publishing practices associated with academic research in specific environments and disciplines. We will now focus on situations where these horizons become blurred and challenged by new collective environments and intellectual projects.

AIME: Making a Format for Transdisciplinary Publics

A substantial challenge for contemporary academic publishing can be seen in transdisciplinary, open humanities projects that seek to gather variegated communities of scholars around a shared inquiry or object. To that extent, several initiatives within the academy have experimented with new forms of publishing that reframe the way academic arguments are materialized and how they can be manipulated and encountered by hybrid and transdisciplinary collectives. Whether it be through the reinvestments of prior academic genres such as journals or lexicons, or repurposing of previously private research tools as public and open-access spaces, these experiments actively play with scholarly formats to gather collectives of concerned participants in new ways. Among these experiments stands our project *An Inquiry into Modes of Existence* (*AIME*).

AIME is a philosophical investigation that aims at learning "how to compose a common world" by redefining what should be understood under the adjective "modern" when describing contemporary society. To that extent, the project proposes a conceptual and empirical account of various "modes of existence" that can only be detected when they clash with one another in specific and localized empirical courses of actions.

The purpose of *AIME* was to gather a collection of empirical accounts that could help to outline a set of modes of existence. The project was initiated by Bruno Latour, who asked other scholars and stakeholders to enrich, expand, and criticize his initial propositions. The project therefore consisted in transforming an individual argument into a collective endeavor involving an active public capable of grasping the subtle nuances of the various modes of existences.[4]

The project's challenge lay in the gathering of a *public*, constituted of scholars from various disciplines and backgrounds, but also incorporating practitioners, able to act as representatives of that for which they cared; for example, lawyers for the mode of *law*, priests for the mode of *religion*, artists for the mode of *fiction*, and so forth. The next step was to encourage them to contribute in a constructive way to the elaboration of a new, collective account of the modes of existence. Working with such a range of participants meant that the project needed to accommodate a diversity of backgrounds, skills (in close reading, digital literacy, composition, and oral discussion, for instance), and motives for contributing, whether they be advancing personal scholarly questions, defending an issue about which they care, receiving academic recognition, or simply satisfying their intellectual curiosity.

For these purposes, the *AIME* team—comprised of humanities scholars, designers, and engineers—has developed an *infrastructure* that aims to provide an underpinning for the various readers of the project, but that also involves some of them in the project's documentation and amendment, transforming their status from *readers* to *contributors*. To achieve this, the project was designed as a *distributed collection* of different *editions* that were dependent on each other, as shown in figure 6.1. These editions of the inquiry were as different as: a printed document, a website attached to several digital interfaces to the project, and a varying set of workshops and exhibitions. While they all revolve around the same shared purpose, the documents featured by these editions only partially overlap, and the activities they support are radically different—from bookish reading to slide-based digital composition, from oral document-based discussions to online collective writing—not forgetting exhibition-based thought experiments. Even though the editions were diverse and disparate, they were not developed in isolation. Grounded in Latour's edited notes, we established a database to feed both web interfaces of the project. In turn, the web interfaces were used as stimuli for physical meetings, and vice versa. In sum, despite the diversity of editions, the *AIME* ecosystem is built atop a complex set of infrastructural relations. Hence, the notes of Bruno Latour have supported the web edition's database as an empirical *mise en scène* of the *AIME* argument. The database has supported the web applications of the project to provide an empirical experience of the inquiry. The web application has

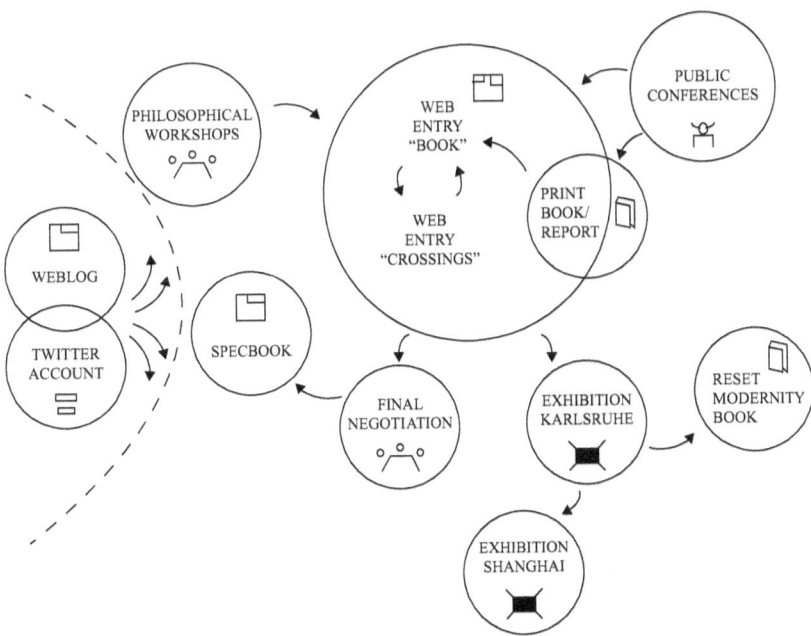

Figure 6.1
Schematic representation of the editions of the *AIME* ecosystem.

supported the contribution process, being used in physical meetings, which were in turn used to fill the database. The *ecosystem* of *AIME*, therefore, has been built as an interrelated set of dependences that could not be sketched in a linear way. This ecosystem as a whole was meant to act as an *infrastructure* for the inquiry itself, understood as a set of connected systems supporting the collection of empirical accounts.

While the *AIME* ecosystem was built as an *infrastructure*, it is nonetheless its *format* that has been experienced by its publics, for readers only encountered the project through one of its diverse outlets. The editions never appeared simultaneously to the public, both because they were not published synchronously but also because each new reader enters the project through a chance encounter with one of the editions and then discovers the others progressively, while situating each of these encounters within their preexisting cultures, practices and expectations. How, then, did the *format* of *AIME* act on the public engagement with the project itself?

How Horizons of Practice Shape Publics

We conducted a systematic review of feedback that described (and critiqued) the organizational and material infrastructures of the *AIME* project. This allowed us to grasp, to some extent, the contours and internal geography of the *public* constituted by *AIME*. In particular, the names used to describe the format of the project—"what it is"—played an important role in the phenomena of alignment and displacement, reinforcement and critique, gathering and antagonizing, observed through our review of the project editions' reception, and usage. Indeed, we observed the different names used to describe the project's setup and analyzed them with respect to the effects these names produced on the project's engagement. For the sake of this chapter, we will set aside more recurring projects' names—a "book" and a "website"—that would demand an extended analysis, and rather focus on three more specific of these diverse names: a "philosophy book," a "blog," and an "encyclopedic" format.

AIME "*is a philosophy book.*" Despite being continuously labeled as an "interim report" in our project team's vocabulary, the output was published by bodies recognized for providing that genre of artefacts (Harvard University Press and La Découverte for the respective English and French versions, for instance), and has been called as such by most of the reviews.[5]

Moreover, the digital edition points to a space explicitly labeled as "book," while not fitting with the experience expected from what is commonly associated with this name (the codex, for instance), whether it would be print or even electronic—a complex and highly interactive four-column interface; the print edition, on its side, lacks or betrays what one could expect from the format of a "philosophy book," because features such as footnotes or references are not presented within it, but are included in the digital edition. Despite repeated announcements of this fact, as well as notes in the peritextual forewords, within the core of the text, and in the project's blog or public presentations, we observed that many reviews (including from subscribers to the mailing list of the project!) did not take into account the form of the digital editions, and some critiqued the lack of textual apparatus and empirical evidence—while it was abundantly available online. These misalignments produced unexpected interpretations of the very content of the report.

AIME "is a blog." This label was assigned to one of the openly accessible formats in several ways: as an oppositional stance about the way coinquirers' contributions were specified in their roles (contributions to content rather than comments), as a comparison anchor for assessing the features of the project as more or less innovative, and eventually as an actual part of *AIME*'s vocabulary for describing one of the editions of the setup (*AIME*'s official blog).

AIME "is encyclopedic." Interestingly, the project was called such on several occasions, although this appellation was not used within the team's own internal vocabulary. Further, in contrast to the other examples quoted above, it was used as an adjective, rather than as a clear nominative label. When looking at these designations, it is clear that some commentators associate *AIME* with an encyclopedia from the systematic nature of Bruno Latour's proposition of modes of existence. That said, others seem to home in on the presence of controlled vocabulary—strongly signaled in typographic design, and in the open web edition's layout—to qualify the project as encyclopedic. This presupposition provoked claims and critiques; for instance, about the absence of some topics from the book, and a precise inquiry about the approach to language performed by the project itself. Interestingly, and adjacent to the strict "encyclopedic" naming of the project, old and new formats of the encyclopedia collide in this movement of association as the collective nature of *AIME* has also prompted its association with Wikipedia. As a result, the project has been approached by communities of persons interested in wiki technologies, who in return asked about the absence of some features and the dissonance with a wiki's traditional editorial projects in the *AIME* project.

The labels used in published reviews of the project are just a subset of clues that point to a broader set of recognitions that we have witnessed in oral exchanges and interviews around the *AIME* project. Through a series of displacements and comparisons, the project was understood, interpreted, and used in a variety of ways by the actors gathered around it. The distributed strategy of *AIME* has clearly produced a variety of sticking points that were understood in the framework of specific recognition processes, successfully assembling around the project a diversity of actors coming from different backgrounds and having entered into the collective from a variety of its instances. The result of this aggregation process has fostered, among other outcomes, a total of 134 contributions and 61 unique contributors to the web editions, and a "specbook" collectively written by a group constituted both of Latour's familiar collaborators and of new participants encountered through the project. However, the distributed, open strategy of *AIME* and the peculiarity of its different editions has also generated a wide range of expectations and requirements about the methodology and infrastructure of *AIME*, taking advantage or disadvantage of these in order to develop specific sense-making practices. If *AIME* is not relatable to any previous way of conducting and staging a philosophical inquiry, its constitutive editions have been. The *formats* of *AIME*, therefore, jointly produced plural *horizons of practices* where a collective adventure could take place relying on the *infrastructure* of the project. These horizons had both an influence on the composition of the public—who got *in* and who did not—and on its conduct, shaping practices and attitudes in a variety of ways.

How does a *format* make a *public*? In an academic context where, as Andrew Murphie has put it, "ecological contaminations between all forms of publishing are rife, so that publishing is now a kind of 'chaosmos,'" *AIME*'s experience has taught us that distributed and open publishing strategies foster a complex tension between aggregation—pulling heterogeneous members into the collective—and participation—developing common practices and endeavors.[6] The distributed collections of various editions implied by multimodal strategies of inquiry foster a play of repetition and difference in which the *format* of a project—as the set of points of encounters with its constitutive *infrastructure*—yields the *recognition of formats among others* that gather new participants into the research collective; doing so, the latter bring with them diverging *horizons of practices* that concur to drive the actual appropriation, transformation, and opening of the infrastructure.[7] If not always easy to handle, the displacements and divergent perspectives on the project not only succeeded in bringing a wide range of different scholars and practitioners into the debate, but also in fostering unexpected perspectives and fueling rich discussions around the project's issues. If format—singular—acts at the boundary of production and experience, formats—plural—are essential to understanding the way in which this boundary is traversed by the heterogeneous public of transdisciplinary scholarly projects.

The contemporary environments of scholarly publishing are constituted *de facto* by a set of places, organizations, technologies, and forms that vastly overflow the geography traditionally covered by dedicated institutions such as publishers and libraries, and their related models of practice and positions in academic worlds. This implies radical changes for these dedicated institutions themselves, as a rich literature in bibliographic and information sciences has shown. Nonetheless, one can also wonder how these new geographies will continue to transform the way *researchers* conduct and envision their work. As we have shown through the account of the *AIME* project, the role of publishing-related activities continually evolves beyond traditional functions of research dissemination to transform the very core of their activity. First, this transformation operates on a methodological plane: instead of practicing publishing as a way to present achieved results or even to test intermediary hypothesis, format-led research enables publishing activities to genuinely act as research methodologies, because they center upon encounters of concerned individuals within a meaningful infrastructure to put a specific issue to work. Second, this evolution deals with an aesthetic and *design*-related transformation: how can the thoughtful and patient deployment of a research process into complex "postdigital" settings affect, refine, and transform its research questions? How then should we understand the nature of the *arguments* being built in these processes, and find ways to account for them in subsequent works? There is here a *thingness* at work in the research processes that marks an unprecedented role for *materiality* and its related design processes in sense-making practices. Third, this transformation deals with the political and organizational definition of what can be called a *research collective* today: how to take advantage of the aggregating power of open and proteiform formats yielded by multimodal publishing strategies? This question acts at the same time as a promise for renewed research collective formations, and as a challenge—if not a radical questioning—for institutions, in a context where formats make publics, set expectations, and orient sense-making practices as much as well-defined organizations.

Notes

1. Jonathan Sterne, *MP3: The Meaning of a Format* (Durham, NC: Duke University Press, 2012), 7.

2. Rachel Malik, "Horizons of the Publishable: Publishing in/as Literary Studies," *ELH* 75, no. 3 (2008): 709, https://doi.org/10.1353/elh.0.0016.

3. Ignacio Siles, "From Online Filter to Web Format: Articulating Materiality and Meaning in the Early History of Blogs," *Social Studies of Science* 41, no. 5 (2011): 737–758, https://doi.org/10.1177/0306312711420190.

4. The notion of public is understood in this chapter in Dewey's particular sense of a collective constituted of "all those who are affected by the indirect consequences of transactions to such an extent that it is deemed necessary to have those consequences systematically cared for" in the frame of a specific issue, as opposed to a more general understanding of the notion. John Dewey, *The Public and Its Problems: An Essay in Political Inquiry* (University Park: Pennsylvania State University Press, 1927), 15.

5. Bruno Latour, *An Inquiry into Modes of Existence* (Cambridge, MA: Harvard University Press, 2013).

6. Andrew Murphie, "Ghosted Publics—the 'Unacknowledged Collective' in the Contemporary Transformation of the Circulation of Ideas," in *The Mag.Net Reader 3—Processual Publishing. Actual Gestures*, ed. Alessandro Ludovico and Nat Muller (London: Open Mute Press, 2008), 105, http://www.andrewmurphie.org/docs/Ghosted_Publics_Murphe.pdf.

7. For a more specific development into the relation of the AIME project to openness, see Donato Ricci et al., "Clues. Anomalies. Understanding. Detecting Underlying Assumptions and Expected Practices in the Digital Humanities through the AIME Project," in *Designing Interactive Hypermedia Systems*, ed. Everardo Reyes-Garcia and Nasreddine Bouhaï (Oxford: John Wiley & Sons, 2017), 185–211, https://doi.org/10.1002/9781119388272.ch6.

7 Peer Review: Readers in the Making of Scholarly Knowledge

David Pontille and Didier Torny

Who exactly assesses manuscripts submitted to journals? What are the actual conditions under which peer review is performed? How do different instances of judgment precisely coordinate with one another? To answer these questions, we consider peer review as a set of "technologies," following Shapin and Schaffer, who showed that the experimental practice took shape in the seventeenth century, based on three technologies that were intimately linked in the production of scholarly knowledge.[1] Indeed, instead of considering manuscript evaluation as a technology set in stone, in earlier work we have shown that different eras, disciplines, and journals have had their own particular arrangements from which the main historical and contemporary criticisms have arisen.[2] For journal peer review is at the heart of two conflicting horizons: on the one hand, the validation of manuscripts is seen as a collective reproducible process performed to assert scientific statements; on the other hand, the dissemination of articles is considered as a means to spur scientific discussion, to raise controversies, and to challenge a state of knowledge. For example, the sharing of new results with audiences far removed from the scientific collectives that produced them was considered as sufficiently problematic by Franz J. Ingelfinger, chief editor of the *New England Journal of Medicine*, systematically to refuse to publish articles presenting results previously exposed elsewhere, notably in the general press.[3] Symmetrically, the delays resulting from validation procedures have often been criticized as unacceptable barriers to the dissemination of knowledge, and from the 1990s onward these led numerous actors to organize the circulation of working papers and preprints.[4] This discordancy is resolved in the concrete set of technologies of journal peer review, which define the arrangements between dissemination and validation. If there never was such a thing as "traditional peer review," defined as a set of unified practices, reading has always been at the heart of manuscript evaluation. Hence, *who* reads, *when*, and *to what purposes* are key to understanding the shape of peer review.

Peer Review as Reading

Throughout the history of peer review, the three judging instances (editors-in-chief, editorial committees, outside reviewers) that have gradually emerged were the first readers of submitted manuscripts.[5] Their respective importance and the way in which their readings are coordinated may be subject to local conventions at a journal, disciplinary, or historical level. They are also marked by profound divergences due to distinct issues in manuscript evaluation. The "space of possibilities" within which these readings are conducted is a subject for public debate that leads to the invention of labels and the stabilization of categories, and to the elaboration of procedural and moral norms. For example, on the respective anonymity of authors and referees, four labels have been coined since the 1980s (see table 7.1).

These spaces of possibility currently coexist in each discipline, being attached to different scientific and moral values, pertaining to the responsibility of reviewers, objectivity of judgements, transparency of process, and equity toward authors.[6] The different possibilities here show that Merton's "organized skepticism"[7] and the agonistic nature of the production of scientific facts described by Latour and Woolgar are, indeed, not self-evident.[8]

The contemporary moment is characterized by reflexive readings of peer-review technologies: manuscript evaluation has itself become an object of

Table 7.1

Anonymity and identification labels in manuscript peer review

	Reviewers	
Authors	Anonymized	Identified
Anonymized	Double blind	Blind review
Identified	Single blind	Open review

Source: David Pontille and Didier Torny, "The Blind Shall See! The Question of Anonymity in Journal Peer Review," Ada 4 (2014), https://doi.org/10.7264/N3542KVW.

systematic scientific investigation.⁹ Authors, manuscripts, reviewers, journals, and readers have been scrupulously examined for their qualities and competencies, as well as for their "biases," faults, or even unacceptable behavior. This trend has risen with the pioneering work of Peters and Ceci, who resubmitted to journals articles that they had already published, simply replacing the names of the authors and their institutions with fictitious names and making minor changes to the texts.¹⁰ Much to their surprise, almost all of the manuscripts were rejected, and, three exceptions aside, without any accusation of plagiarism. Thirty-eight years later, hundreds of studies on manuscript evaluation are now available, while the tradition of putting journals to the test with duplicate or fake papers still thrives.¹¹ The diverse arrangements of manuscript evaluation are thus themselves systematically subjected to evaluation procedures.

Peer review in the twenty-first century can also be distinguished by a growing trend: the empowerment of "ordinary" readers as new key judging instances. If editors and reviewers produce judgments, it is through a reading within a very specific framework, as it is confined to restricted interaction, essentially via written correspondence, which aims at authorizing the dissemination of manuscripts-become-articles.¹² Other forms of reading accompany publications and participate in their evaluation, independently of their initial validation. This is particularly the case through citation, commenting, sharing, and examining, which have existed for a long time but are now being more and more treated as integral technologies of open peer review, through new arrangements between dissemination and validation.¹³

Citing Articles

With the popularization of bibliometric tools, citation counting has become a central element of journal and article evaluation. The implementation of these tools nevertheless required a series of operations on articles themselves. First, the identification of citations meant that one had to homogenize forms of referencing and isolate the references.¹⁴ From among all the texts they have read, readers thus choose those which they believe to be of essential value so as to refer specifically to them in their own manuscripts. Second, the tools made it necessary to blur the difference between reference and citation: the act of referencing relates to a given author, whereas a citation is a new and perhaps calculable property of the source text. According to Wouters, this reversal radically modified referencing practices and literally created a new "citation culture."[15] Under this condition, academic readers have become citers from the 1970s on, adding their voices to the already-published article and to the journal which validated it.

This citing activity pertains to journals (e.g., impact factor, eigenfactor), to articles (e.g., article-level metrics), to authors (e.g., h-index), or even to entire disciplines (e.g., half-life index) and institutions (e.g., a score for all international rankings). Using citation aggregation tools, it is possible equitably to assess all citers or else to introduce weighting tools relating to time span, to the reputation of the outlet, to their centrality, and so on. Highly disparate forms of intertextuality are rendered commensurable: the measured or radical criticism of a thought or result, integration within a scientific tradition, reliance on a standardized method described elsewhere, existence of data for a literary journal or meta-study, simple recopying of sources referenced elsewhere or self-promotion.[16] Citation thus points toward two complementary horizons of reading: science as a system for accumulating knowledge via a referencing operation, and research as a necessary discussion of this same knowledge through criticism and commentary.

Commenting Texts

Readers can be given a more formal place as commenters, in this view of publication as explicitly dialogical or polyphonic. Traditionally, before an article was published, comments were mainly directed toward the editor-in-chief or the editorial committee. Through open review, commenters enter into a dialogue with the authors and thus open up a space for direct confrontation.

Prior to the emergence of electronic spaces for discussion, at least two journals explicitly made prepublication commentaries the very principle behind their manuscript evaluation policy: *Current Anthropology* (CA) created in 1960 and *Behavioral and Brain Sciences* (B&BS) founded in 1978. Rather than gathering the opinions of just a few outside reviewers, they systematically contacted them in large numbers in an attempt to have the greatest possible diversity of judgments. Yet, unlike numerous other journals, where disagreements on manuscripts were seen as a problem, in this case they were considered to be "creative."[17]

The publication of commentaries alongside the articles themselves has existed for some time and is not a new phenomenon: "special issues" or "reports" in which a series of articles are brought together around a given theme to feed off one another after a short presentation. Similarly, the long-standing practice of a commentary followed by the author's response is common. CA and B&BS employed sophisticated versions of this technology, later known as open commentary: once a manuscript had been accepted, they invited dozens of new researchers to comment upon it, and then gave the author(s) the opportunity to provide a short response to the comments.

Finally, proposals have been made to revamp the traditional role of post-publication commenters. For a long time, these commenters acted in two elementary forms: by referring to the original article or by sending a letter to the editor. As from the 1990s, the emergence of electronic publications was seen as something that would revolutionize "post-publication peer review" (PPPR), by allowing comments and criticisms to be added to the document itself.[18] However, the experiments of open commentary in PPPR have been disappointing for traditional (e.g., *Nature*) and new (e.g., *PLOS ONE*) electronic journals, as few readers seem to be willing to participate in such a technology "if [their] comments serve no identifiable purpose."[19]

Sharing Papers

The readers mentioned so far have been peers of the authors of the original manuscript in a very restrictive sense: either their reading leads to a text of an equivalent nature, or it leads to a text published in the same outlet as the article. Until recently, readers other than citers and commenters remained very much in the shadows. Yet library users, students in classes, and colleagues in seminars, as just a few examples, also ascribe value to articles; for instance, through annotation.[20] But two major changes have rendered part of these forms of reading valuable.

The existence of articles in electronic form has made their readers more visible. People who access an "HTML" page or who download a "PDF" file are now taken into account, whereas in the past it was only the distribution of journals and texts, mostly through libraries, which allowed one to assess potential readership. By inventorying and aggregating the audience in this way, it is possible to assign readers the capacity to evaluate articles. Labels such as "highly accessed" or "most downloaded," frequently used on journal websites, make it possible to distinguish certain articles. The creation of online academic social networks (e.g., ResearchGate, Academia .edu) has trivialized this figure of the public, not only by counting "academic users," but also by naming them and offering contact. Researchers now take part in the dissemination of their own articles and are thus better able to grasp the extent and diversity of their audiences.[21]

At the same time, other devices make visible the sharing of articles. First of all, it is online bibliographic tools (e.g., CiteULike, Mendeley, Zotero) that objectify the readers and taggers who introduce references and attached documents into their bibliographic databases. Without being citers themselves, these readers select publications by sharing lists of references, the pertinence of which is notified by the use of "tags." These reader-taggers are also embedded in the use of hyperlinks within "generalist" social networks (e.g., Facebook, Twitter), by alerting others to interesting articles, or by briefly commenting on their content. These different channels for dissemination and sharing have been the object of numerous works that aimed to determine whether or not they were a means of evaluating articles compared to their citations.[22] They have also been reworked by advocates of "article-level metrics." The measurements of these different channels are now aggregated and considered to be a representation of a work's multiple uses and audiences. For its advocates, the resulting "total impact" is the true value of a article's importance shown through its dissemination. Here the readers, tracked by number and diversity, revalidate articles in the place of the judging instances historically qualified to do so.

Examining Documents

This movement is even more significant in that these tools are applied not only to published articles but also to documents which have not been validated through journal peer review. Indeed, after the establishment of the *arXiv* high-energy physics repository at the beginning of the 1990s, many scientific milieus and institutions acquired repository servers to host working papers.[23] Ideally, these manuscripts are preliminary versions submitted for criticism and comments by specialist groups that are notified of the submissions. The resulting exchanges are managed by the system, which archives the different versions produced. So readers do not simply exercise their judgment on validated articles, but also produce a collective evaluation of manuscripts. This flow of electronic manuscripts feeds the enthusiasm of the most visionary who, since the 1990s, have been announcing the approaching end of validation by journals' traditional judging instances.[24] Nevertheless, new technologies have been built on these archives, such as "overlay journals," in which available manuscripts are later validated by reading peers.[25] New journals have reembodied the old scholarly communication values of rapidity and open scientific discussion, by offering a publishing space to working papers, such as *PeerJ*, or by publishing manuscripts first, then inviting commenters to undertake peer review and pushing authors to publish revised versions of their texts, such as *F1000Research*.

With a view to dissemination, advocates of readers as a judging instance tend to downplay the importance of prior validation. While the validation process sorts manuscripts in a binary fashion (accepted or rejected), such advocates contend that varied forms of dissemination instead encourage permanent discussion and argument along a text's entire trajectory. In this perspective, articles remain "alive" after publication and are therefore always subject not only to various reader appropriations, but also to public evaluations, which can reverse their initial validation. The PubPeer website, which offers anonymized readers the opportunity to discuss the validity of experiments and to ask authors to answer their questions, is a good example of this kind of PPPR. The discussions occurring on this platform regularly result in the debunking of faked and manipulated images from many high-profile articles, which leads to corrections and even retractions of the publications by the journals themselves.

Conclusion

Driven by a constant process of specialization, the extension of judging instances to readers may appear as a reallocation of expertise, empowering a growing number of people in the name of distributed knowledge.[26] In an ongoing context of revelations of massive scientific fraud, which often implicates editorial processes and journals themselves, the dereliction inherent to judging instances prior to publication has transformed the mass of readers into a vital resource for unearthing error and fraud.[27] As in other domains where public expertise used to be exclusively held by a few professionals, crowdsourcing has become a collective gatekeeper for science publishing. Thus, peerdom shall be reshaped, as lay readers have now full access to a large part of the scientific literature and have become valued audiences as quantified end users of published articles.[28]

If open science has become a motto, it encompasses two different visions for journal peer review. The first one, which includes open identities, takes place within the academic closet, where the dissemination of manuscripts is made possible by small discourse collectives that shape consensual facts.[29] This vision is supported by the validation processes designed by Robert Boyle, one of the founders of the Royal Society, who thought that disputes about scientific facts needed a specific and limited "social space" in order to be solved.[30] By contrast, following Thomas Hobbes's Leviathan conception of sovereignty, the second vision urges a multiplication of points of view. The disentanglement of peer evaluation cuts through the ability given to readers to comment on published articles, produce social media metrics through the sharing of documents, and observe the whole evaluation process of each manuscript.[31] In this vision, scholarly communication relies on a plurality of instances that generate a continuous process of judgment. The first vision has been at the heart of the scientific article as a genre, and a key component of the scientific journal as the most important channel for scholarly communication.[32] Whether journals remain central in the second vision has yet to be determined.[33]

Notes

1. Steven Shapin and Simon Schaffer, *Leviathan and the Air-Pump: Hobbes, Boyle, and the Experimental Life* (Princeton, NJ: Princeton University Press, 1985).

2. David Pontille and Didier Torny, "From Manuscript Evaluation to Article Valuation: The Changing Technologies of Journal Peer Review," *Human Studies* 38, no. 1 (2015): 57–79, https://doi.org/10.1007/s10746-014-9335-z.

3. Franz J. Ingelfinger, "Definition of Sole Contribution," *New England Journal of Medicine* 281, no. 12 (1969): 676–677, https://doi.org/10.1056/NEJM196909182811208; see also Arnold S. Relman, "The Ingelfinger Rule," *New England Journal of Medicine* 305, no. 14 (1981): 824–826, https://doi.org/10.1056/NEJM198110013051408.

4. Herbert Van de Sompel and Carl Lagoze, "The Santa Fe Convention of the Open Archives Initiative," *D-Lib Magazine* 6, no. 2 (2000), https://doi.org/10.1045/february2000-vandesompel-oai.

5. Aileen Fyfe and Noah Moxham, "Making Public Ahead of Print: Meetings and Publications at the Royal Society, 1752–1892," *Notes and Records: The Royal Society Journal of the History of Science* 70, no. 4 (2016): 361–379, https://doi.org/10.1098/rsnr.2016.0030.

6. Mark Ware, "Peer Review in Scholarly Journals: Perspective of the Scholarly Community—Results from an International Study," *Information Services & Use* 28 (2008): 109–112, https://doi.org/10.3233/ISU-2008-0568.

7. R. K. Merton, "Science and Technology in a Democratic Order," *Journal of Legal and Political Sociology* 1 (1942): 115–126.

8. Bruno Latour and Steve Woolgar, *Laboratory Life: The Construction of Scientific Facts* (Beverly Hills, CA: SAGE, 1979).

9. Juan Miguel Campanario, "Peer Review for Journals as It Stands Today—Part 1," *Science Communication* 19, no. 3 (1998): 181–211, https://doi.org/10.1177/1075547098019003002.

10. Douglas P. Peters and Stephen J. Ceci, "Peer-Review Practices of Psychological Journals: The Fate of Published Articles, Submitted Again," *Behavioral and Brain Sciences* 5, no. 2 (1982): 187–195, https://doi.org/10.1017/S0140525X00011183.

11. Daryl E. Chubin and Edward J. Hackett, *Peerless Science: Peer Review and U.S. Science Policy*, SUNY Series in Science, Technology, and Society (Albany, NY: State University of New York Press, 1990); Bruce W. Speck, ed., *Publication Peer Review: An Annotated Bibliography* (Westport, CT: Greenwood Press, 1993); Ann C. Weller, "Editorial Peer Review: Its Strengths and Weaknesses," *Journal of the Medical Library Association* 90, no. 1 (2002): 115; Jonathan P. Tennant et al., "A Multi-Disciplinary Perspective on Emergent and Future Innovations in Peer Review," *F1000Research* 6 (2017): 1151, https://doi.org/10.12688/f1000research.12037.3; John Bohannon, "Who's Afraid of Peer Review?," *Science* 342, no. 6154 (2013): 60–65, https://doi.org/10.1126/science.342.6154.60; on the last of these, see also Amy Buckland et al., "On the Mark? Responses to a Sting," *Journal of Librarianship and Scholarly Communication* 2, no. 1 (2013), https://doi.org/10.7710/2162-3309.1116.

12. Stefan Hirschauer, "Editorial Judgments: A Praxeology of 'Voting' in Peer Review," *Social Studies of Science* 40, no. 1 (2010): 71–103, https://doi.org/10.1177/0306312709335405.

13. Tony Ross-Hellauer, "What Is Open Peer Review? A Systematic Review," *F1000Research* 6 (2017): 588, https://doi.org/10.12688/f1000research.11369.2.

14. Charles Bazerman, *Shaping Written Knowledge: The Genre and Activity of the Experimental Article in Science* (Madison, WI: University of Wisconsin Press, 1988).

15. Paul Franciscus Wouters, "The Citation Culture" (PhD dissertation, University of Amsterdam, 1999).

16. Martin G. Erikson and Peter Erlandson, "A Taxonomy of Motives to Cite," *Social Studies of Science* 44, no. 4 (2014): 625–637, https://doi.org/10.1177/0306312714522871.

17. Stevan Harnad, "Creative Disagreement," *The Sciences* 19 (1979): 18–20.

18. F. W. Lancaster, "Attitudes in Academia toward Feasibility and Desirability of Networked Scholarly Publishing," *Library Trends* 43, no. 4 (1995): 741–752.

19. Kathleen Fitzpatrick, *Planned Obsolescence: Publishing, Technology, and the Future of the Academy* (New York: New York University Press, 2011), 26.

20. Meegan Kennedy, "Open Annotation and Close Reading the Victorian Text: Using Hypothes.Is with Students," *Journal of Victorian Culture* 21, no. 4 (2016): 550–558, https://doi.org/10.1080/13555502.2016.1233905.

21. Richard Van Noorden, "Online Collaboration: Scientists and the Social Network," *Nature News* 512, no. 7513 (2014): 126, https://doi.org/10.1038/512126a.

22. Jason Priem and Kaitlin Light Costello, "How and Why Scholars Cite on Twitter," *Proceedings of the American Society for Information Science and Technology* 47, no. 1 (2010): 1–4, https://doi.org/10.1002/meet.14504701201; Gunther Eysenbach, "Can Tweets Predict Citations? Metrics of Social Impact Based on Twitter and Correlation with Traditional Metrics of Scientific Impact," *Journal of Medical Internet Research* 13, no. 4 (2011): e123, https://doi.org/10.2196/jmir.2012.

23. Ingemar Bohlin, "Communication Regimes in Competition: The Current Transition in Scholarly Communication Seen through the Lens of the Sociology of Technology," *Social Studies of Science* 34, no. 3 (2004): 365–391, https://doi.org/10.1177/0306312704041522; Kristrún Gunnarsdóttir, "Scientific Journal Publications: On the Role of Electronic Preprint Exchange in the Distribution of Scientific Literature," *Social Studies of Science* 35, no. 4 (2005): 549–579, https://doi.org/10.1177/0306312705052358.

24. Stevan Harnad, "Post-Gutenberg Galaxy: The Fourth Revolution in the Means of Production of Knowledge," *Public Access-Computer Systems Review* 2, no. 1 (1991): 39–53.

25. Arthur P. Smith, "The Journal as an Overlay on Preprint Databases," *Learned Publishing* 13, no. 1 (2000): 43–48, https://doi.org/10.1087/09531510050145542.

26. For more on the difficulties of this model, see John Holmwood's chapter in this book.

27. David Pontille and Didier Torny, "Behind the Scenes of Scientific Articles: Defining Categories of Fraud and Regulating Cases," *Revue d'Épidémiologie et de Santé Publique* 60, no. 4 (2012): 247–253; Sara Schroter et al., "What Errors Do Peer Reviewers Detect, and Does Training Improve Their Ability to Detect Them?," *Journal of the Royal Society of Medicine* 101, no. 10 (2008): 507–514, https://doi.org/10.1258/jrsm.2008.080062.

28. Archambault et al., "Proportion of Open Access Papers Published in Peer-Reviewed Journals at the European and World Levels—1996-2013."

29. Ross-Hellauer, "What Is Open Peer Review?"

30. Shapin and Schaffer, *Leviathan and the Air-Pump*.

31. Paul Wouters, Zohreh Zahedi, and Rodrigo Costas, "Social Media Metrics for New Research Evaluation," in *Springer Handbook of Science and Technology Indicators*, ed. Wolfgang Glanzel et al. (Berlin: Springer International Publishing, 2019).

32. Alex Csiszar, *The Scientific Journal: Authorship and the Politics of Knowledge in the Nineteenth Century* (Chicago: University of Chicago Press, 2018).

33. Tennant et al., "A Multi-Disciplinary Perspective on Emergent and Future Innovations in Peer Review."

8 The Making of Empirical Knowledge: Recipes, Craft, and Scholarly Communication

Pamela H. Smith, Tianna Helena Uchacz, Naomi Rosenkranz, and Claire Conklin Sabel

The making of empirical knowledge is, broadly speaking, regarded today as the result of research carried out by social and natural scientists, while the arts and humanities are considered to employ a different type of methodology, form a separate realm of inquiry, and produce insights that are sometimes complementary, but not equivalent, to objective facts. Yet, the empirical techniques of experiment and observation employed in the natural sciences have their origins both in the creative labors of Renaissance artists' workshops and in the empirical methods pioneered by Renaissance humanists and historians.[1] At the beginning of the Scientific Revolution in the sixteenth century, the craft workshop was understood to make knowledge about nature, as artisans codified material processes in technical recipes and "how-to" texts. The earliest European scientific societies avidly collected technical recipes from craftspeople in order to study and advance natural knowledge. Over the course of the seventeenth century, collaboration and experimentation that had taken place within the craft workshop became integrated into the practices of the natural sciences. However, in the eighteenth and nineteenth centuries, when the new sciences cohered as distinct disciplines, these shared origins became obscured, and since then, the divisions between the natural sciences and the arts and humanities have grown ever wider. Studying the premodern workshop provides an opportunity to bridge the modern communities of artists, historians, and scientists by fostering scholarly communication and collaboration around materials and the techniques of engaging with the material world.

As one of several "case-study" pieces in this volume, this essay first discusses the genre of how-to texts as a platform for a new type of communication of knowledge in the past as well as their role in the development of the massive infrastructure that we know today as "modern science." It then turns to document a large collaborative research and pedagogical initiative, the *Making and Knowing Project*, which explores historical and methodological intersections between artistic making and scientific knowing. The Project examines the structure of the "technical recipe book" or "how-to text" as a type of sociotechnical system that played a central role in the reconfiguring of older systems of knowledge about nature. In order to undertake this research, the Project has constructed a physical and virtual infrastructure for collaborative scholarship and pedagogy, and for interdisciplinary, open scholarly communication. In doing so, the Project is itself employing new technologies to reconfigure one of these historical how-to texts for new uses and as a platform for dissemination and collaboration. This essay thus deals with an important development in the history of scholarly communication; introduces a project that is dedicated both to understanding this development and to creating a platform for disseminating the knowledge it has created and the methods it has developed; and finally, makes a case for experimentation with material practices as an important site for open scholarly communication in the future.

The *Making and Knowing Project* explores the complex of scholarly practices and infrastructure by means of sharp focus on a well-defined object of research that is investigated using techniques from the laboratory, art studio, museum, and archive. From 2014 through 2020, the Project created a digital critical edition of an intriguing anonymous sixteenth-century artisanal and technical manuscript now held in the Bibliothèque nationale de France, Ms. Fr. 640. To achieve this, the Project brought together a network of over 400 collaborators in the humanities, arts, and natural sciences at institutions worldwide to undertake interdisciplinary research, teaching, and knowledge exchange on this manuscript. Thus, both the process of creating this digital critical edition as well as the resulting product (i.e., the digital critical edition) together compose the platform for the collaboration and dissemination referenced above.[2]

The Project's collaborative approach, combining text-, object-, and laboratory-based research with digital humanities tools, challenges the separation of pedagogy from original research and the division between scientific and humanistic inquiry. It brings to the fore methodological consideration of historical evidence and, like other recent collaborative humanities projects, indicates the important strengths of large-scale collaborative research in historical and humanities scholarship. The *Making and Knowing Project* also considers how training in the hands-on skills of material and technical literacy as well as in emergent digital and open-access technologies can transform the practice of historical research by reinforcing the value of differently encoded forms of knowledge.

The Early Modern How-to Text as a Platform for Knowledge-Making and Dissemination: BnF Ms. Fr. 640

In the last decades of the sixteenth century, an anonymous French-speaking craftsperson, most likely from the region of Toulouse, took the unusual step of setting down on paper techniques for a number of processes that we would now classify as belonging to the fine arts, crafts, and technology: drawing instruction; pigment application; dyeing; coloring of metal, wax, and wood; imitation gem production; metal and cannon casting; tree grafting; land surveying; preservation of animals, plants, and foodstuffs; distillation of acids; and much more. The resulting manuscript, now housed in France's Bibliothèque nationale as Ms. Fr. 640, is a unique communicative record of practices that gives rare insight into craft and artistic techniques, daily life, and material and intellectual understandings of the natural world in the sixteenth century. Above all, the manuscript demonstrates the common origins of artistic and scientific experimentation and innovation in the workshops of early modern Europe (ca. 1350–1700). This document is an early example of knowledge (or research) communication.

Ms. Fr. 640's compilation of artisanal techniques, recipes, and experimental notes produced by an experienced practitioner appeared at a pivotal moment in the growth of a new mode of gaining knowledge which we now call "empiricism" and "natural science." The fact that a practitioner recorded these technical procedures at all was part of a seminal development in early modern European history starting around 1400, when craftspeople increasingly began to write down their embodied knowledge in "how-to texts." As new communities of readers and writers grew, these treatises were imitated and disseminated by entrepreneurial printers to a diverse audience, helping to foster a culture that valued practical knowledge. These how-to books thus became a form of conveying both practical and scholarly activity as well as collaboration, exchange, and communication.

Scholars have long identified the period from 1400 to 1600 as one in which attitudes toward nature profoundly changed. New theories, practices, and materials brought renewed attention to the exploration of nature and to representing it in novel ways, whether through lifelike images and objects, mathematical models, or measuring instruments. Changing attitudes were accompanied by an explosion of printed information that codified and disseminated new kinds of learning to newly literate audiences. Ms. Fr. 640 represents the intersection of two essential developments behind this larger shift in intellectual and material production: the turn to writing down, communicating, and making explicit knowledge that had previously been tacit, embodied, and possessed by skilled craftspeople who learned by making things rather than by reading texts; and the move away from reliance on classical textual authorities toward methodical experimentation with natural materials and the refining of techniques and processes through firsthand experience. These developments occurred as a result of many converging factors—including the growing literacy of artisans and other urban populations, the rivalry among artists for patronage at the increasingly powerful territorial courts, and the important role that art and technology played in maintaining the power of these courts. They produced a new genre of "how-to" texts that included individual recipes, specialized treatises, and comprehensive compilations of procedures. These texts—although not "open access" in the same sense as we use when writing of our own digital age—nonetheless lay bare the knowledge of the artisan, mediating between lived experience and the written word. This "communicative event," in which practical knowledge came to be set down and disseminated in a new genre of texts, set off a crucial and thoroughgoing reconfiguration of the realms of scholarly knowledge and action, as the natural sciences began their long ascent to their present status as arbiters of method and authority among the disciplines. Certainly, the contemporary focus in the digital space on the open dissemination of new forms of practice-based research—frequently across novel media—has a far longer history than is often acknowledged.

Indeed, recent scholarship on artisans' knowledge, a domain to which Ms. Fr. 640 belongs, has profound implications for the history of science and culture, as it reconsiders the relationship between exploring ideas and exploring materials to produce new knowledge. In preindustrial societies, the workshop produced knowledge as authoritative and powerful as that of today's scientific laboratory, but the knowledge-making processes of the workshop privileged objects over words. Craftspeople expressed their knowledge largely in the mastery of techniques and in the objects of their art, but scarcely in writing until the fifteenth century. Ms. Fr. 640 and similar how-to manuscripts are rare evidence from this moment when craft became literate. This manuscript offers unusual insight into daily life and how natural materials and art objects were made, collected, appreciated, and circulated in a period of burgeoning production and consumption. Its detailed information about plants, animals, and the raw materials of nature provides an exceptional view into attitudes toward the natural world at the dawn of the "new experimental philosophy" out of which modern science developed. The manuscript is unique for recording its author's immediate, self-reflexive, and iterative notes on various processes for making objects and investigating material properties. It shows the methodical experimentation of the workshop and the ways in which craft was understood as a tool for the investigation of nature. This experimentation would be developed into a self-conscious epistemology and incorporated into the natural sciences as they were institutionalized over the course of the seventeenth through twentieth centuries, first in scientific societies and then in research universities.

The *Making and Knowing Project* as a Platform for Knowledge Creation and Exchange

From the Project's inception in 2014, ongoing work toward the full transcription of Ms. Fr. 640's French text, English translation, and the research generated around the manuscript became a platform, or an infrastructure of sorts, for hundreds of scholars and students to take part in active research and extend the Project's work to their own scholarship and teaching. Moreover, Ms. Fr. 640 is proving to be an important source of evidence across a number of disciplines, from technical art history to literary scholarship to the history of daily life. The publication of the annotated transcription and English translation of Ms. Fr. 640 as a scholarly edition has made accessible an important primary source that significantly enhances the existing body of early modern technical writing and allows readers to understand and analyze the actions of craft making as the creation of empirically tested knowledge about the natural world. As the Project's initial research and dissemination has already shown, Ms. Fr. 640 will engage readers, whether researchers, students, or broader publics, in a new approach to exploring historical texts, one which emphasizes the importance of the material conditions, interpretations, and outcomes that emerge when the written word is realized through investigations into materials in the laboratory. The manuscript codifies procedures that were not meant to be reproduced solely through the act of reading but were rather an invitation to imitate and experiment; the research that it communicates mediates the embodiment of this craft knowledge. The critical edition, in turn, through its critical commentary and accompanying videos and visual resources, invites its audiences not only to read and analyze the text but also to explore and investigate the materials and processes detailed within it.

The Digital Critical Edition of BnF Ms. Fr. 640

Secrets of Craft and Nature in Renaissance France: A Digital Critical Edition and English Translation of BnF Ms. Fr. 640 (https://doi.org/10.7916/78yt-2v41), hosted by the Columbia University Libraries, makes this unique manuscript freely available to students, scholars, and the general public through open-access publication. It presents the text of the manuscript in French transcription and English translation for the first time and, through the *Making and Knowing Project*'s customized encoding, transforms the manuscript's text into a rich and manipulable dataset for advanced analysis, search queries, and visualization. Moreover, *Secrets of Craft and Nature* situates the manuscript's contents within the material and historical contexts in which they were produced. Users of the edition not only read the manuscript as a text but, through the laboratory reconstructions of its recipes, also experience it as a record of material practices. To facilitate this experiential engagement, the edition's critical apparatus harnesses the flexibility and interactivity of tools in the digital humanities in a dynamic, multifunctional, web-based application. It presents traditional archival and paleographic research on the manuscript alongside innovative material reconstructions and analyses of the techniques described in it. In this way, the open-access digital critical edition actually embodies many of the principles that are key to Ms. Fr. 640 itself.

The edition comprises an intuitive user-directed online format for the four versions of the manuscript: (1) high-definition facsimile images, (2) diplomatic (verbatim) French transcription, (3) normalized (slightly modernized) French transcription, and (4) English translation. The digital critical edition presents the option to view the versions of the manuscript as user-directed sets in comparison panes with links to the critical commentary (figure 8.1). The versions are also available as standalone downloadable

PDFs. Comprehensive digital encoding and markup transforms the manuscript text into a database of recipes, materials, and processes, which users can freely search and analyze. The digital critical edition has an extensive search function that allows users to easily find and collect information through various filters, and the raw data, openly available through GitHub, can also be used for further analysis and visualization with existing digital humanities tools. For example, a user can query the data to locate every instance of the material "gold," and then further refine search results by the process of "gilding" to determine what proportion of gold usage is related to gilding (figures 8.2–8.4). This database and robust search/concordance feature allows scholars, educators, and students to draw new connections among thematic focuses, specific materials, and much more from the manuscript's contents.

Whether the manuscript is browsed or searched, the user has the option to consult relevant features of the critical commentary in pop-out windows that illuminate specific aspects of the manuscript such as a word or a technique, or the historical and cultural context of its production (figure 8.1).

The edition's critical apparatus includes multimedia research essays that place techniques and materials described in Ms. Fr. 640 in their textual and historical contexts, editorial comments, a glossary of technical terms, and resources for further exploration. The multimedia essays combine traditional historical research and comparative material (for example, historical objects in museum collections produced using techniques described in the manuscript) with innovative recipe reconstructions. The essays include images, objects, graphic animations, videos, and first-person accounts of processes that cannot adequately be conveyed in traditional print formats. In addition to the research essays that explicate material and technical content, linguistic and paleographic essays also make transparent the editors' and translators' interventions and interpretive decisions. The entirety of the critical apparatus is produced through student-scholar teaching-research partnerships, described in detail below.

The *Making and Knowing Project*: Process and Pedagogy

The *Making and Knowing Project*'s fusion of pedagogy with a focused research program has proven to be a powerful research model. Indeed, it partially adapts the model of lab-based scientific research groups to the humanities

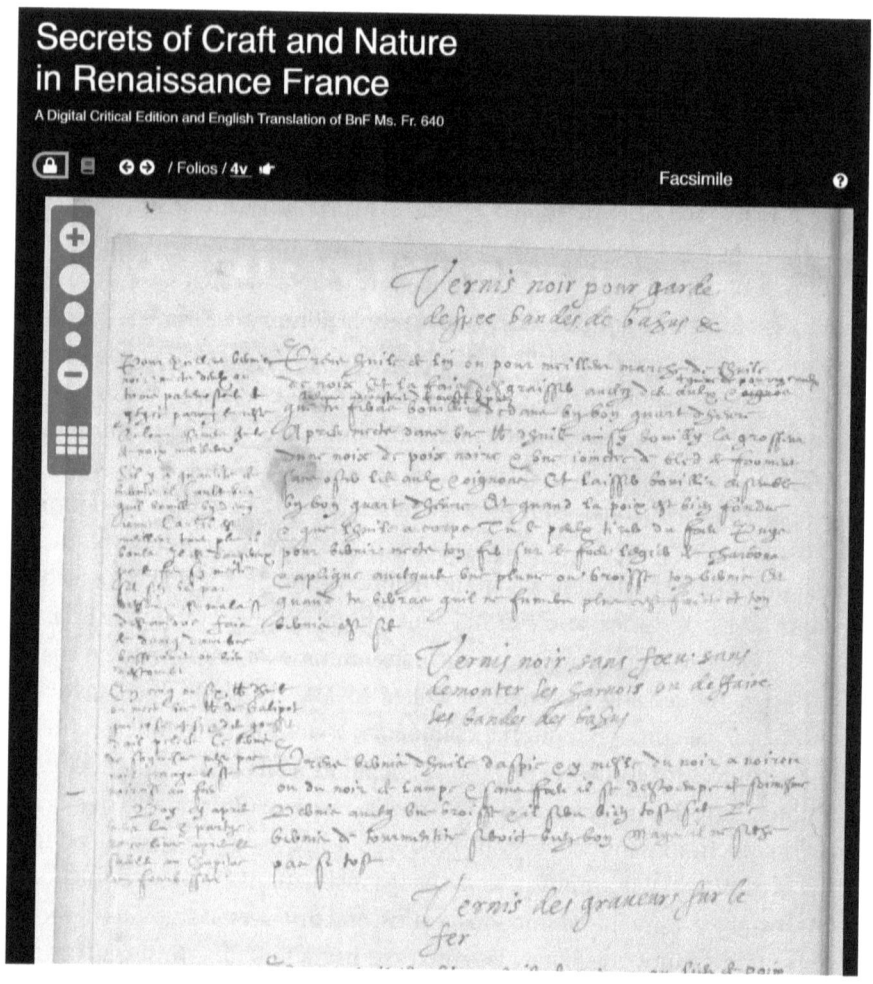

Figure 8.1
Dual-pane view of fol. 4v in the digital critical edition, showing user-directed text comparison panes with pop-out commentary (editorial note at lower left of right pane) and a dropdown research essay (marked with the flask icon) that explains and reconstructs the recipe.

and history, once more playing into the very traditions of scholarly communication and research seen in the how-to texts that are the Project's object of study. The creation of *Secrets of Craft and Nature* included a series of "expert crowdsourcing" workshops and regularly scheduled university courses that involved students, practitioners (such as sculptors and painters), scholars of

The Making of Empirical Knowledge

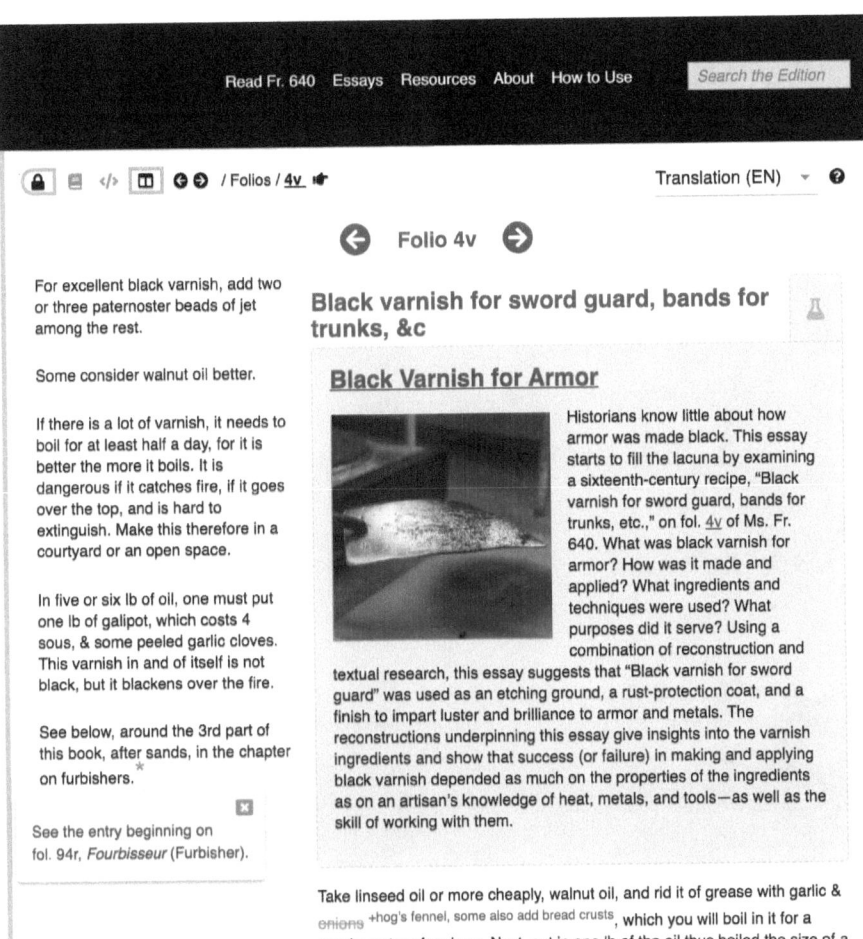

Figure 8.1 *(continued)*

the humanities and social sciences (history, art history, anthropology, and museum scholars), natural scientists (chemists, physicists, and conservation scientists), and specialists from the digital humanities and computer science (computer scientists, AR researchers, and librarians). The research process employs novel methodologies for history, such as large-scale collaboration in cross-disciplinary research groups, historical reconstructions of past techniques, and analysis and dissemination using new digital tools. The Project also provides a model for the preservation of, communication of, and

Summary: There are 643 unique words other than those in the stop list, there are 1631 words other than those in the stop list. There are 3474 words in total including the stop words.

Words	Counts		
	377	Apply	12
Silver	79	Good	10
Cast	33	Sand	10
Color	26	Image	9
Like	16	Work	8
Fine	14	Want	8
Make	14	Use	8
Casting	13	Gild	7
Leaf	12	Enamel	7

TAPoRware Tool Parameter Summary	
Tool name	Find Text -- Collocation (Plain)
Text source	translatedfolio.txt
Pattern	gold*
Context	word
Context length	5
Sorting	Co-ocurring words by frequency

Figure 8.2
TAPoRware collocation analysis for the term "gold*."

interaction with practice-based experiential knowledge by allowing readers to experience historical techniques through text, image, audio, and video.

The Project's creation of the edition consists of four interrelated and iteratively developed components, described in more detail below: (1) transcription, translation, and encoding of the manuscript; (2) critical commentary, including in-depth, multifaceted research of the manuscript's "recipes," notably by hands-on laboratory reconstructions; (3) working group meetings for critical review and oversight; and (4) digital development of the online environment of the edition. Each of the first five years of the Project focused on a single theme to draw together components of the manuscript and provide focus for analysis and activities: Moldmaking and Metalworking in 2014–2015; Colormaking in 2015–2016; Vernacular Natural History and Practical Optics, Perspective, and Mechanics in 2016–2017; Ephemeral Art in 2017–2018, and Making Prints and Other "Impressions" in 2018–2019.

11 co-occurrences found

To *gild* with **gold** color and tinsel Once you
imitates the basse-taille of **goldsmiths**, *gild* the whole glass
order to *gild* with matte **gold**, one has to pounce
so that the composition resembles **gold**. *Gild* the day after
gilding after with having applied **gold** color, but wait one
gild, and cut your **gold** with a knife near where
Gilding with ground **gold**: Take a coquille of gold
gild your animal with fine **gold**, as much homogenously
you can *gild* it with gold leaf, and set it
Removing **gold**: Gold as *gilding* goes away
Removing gold: **Gold** as *gilding* goes away if

TAPoRware Tool Parameter Summary	
Tool name	Find Text -- Co-ocurrence (Plain)
Text source	translatedfolio.txt
Primary pattern	gold*
Co-pattern	gild*
Context	word
Context length	5

Figure 8.3
TAPoRware co-occurrence analysis for the terms "gold*" and "gild*."

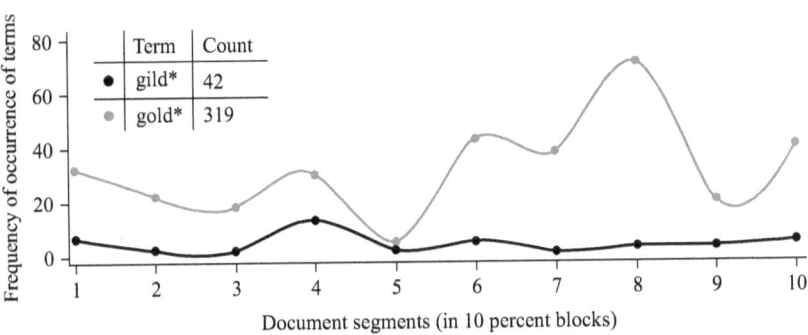

Term	Count
gild*	42
gold*	319

Figure 8.4
Voyant Tools graph showing distribution of terms "gold*" and "gild" across the manuscript.

The first stage of transcription and translation of the manuscript was carried out in a series of three-week paleography workshops that brought together both experts and graduate students. Every year from 2014 to 2018, approximately 15 to 20 graduate students gained skills in middle French script and textual analysis by transcribing, translating, and encoding the manuscript. These workshops resulted in a finalized, accurate, diplomatic transcription, a normalized transcription, and an English translation, all comprehensively marked-up in a custom XML tag set derived from the Text Encoding Initiative (TEI).

Collaborative editing took place via Google's free office software in Google Drive, which enabled the collective work on the manuscript text; multiple paleographers worked simultaneously on the same part of the text and saw edits in real time. Google Drive also crucially permitted all participants (including working group members and visiting experts) to write and view comments on any part of the shared documents. These comments facilitated the collective transcription, translation, and encoding work, and informed the critical apparatus as participants left questions, citations, external research, and most importantly notes about their decisions during all parts of the research and editing process. Throughout the years of Google Drive use, the Project discussed moving to the online software development and version control platform GitHub. While most parts of the Project are now managed there, because of the many collaborators and the limited timespan of grant funding, the Project chose not to manage all collaborative processes with Git.[3] The edition infrastructure and content, however, are now fully open-access, nonproprietary, and also adhere to the principles of minimal computing championed by the digital humanities community at Columbia University.[4]

The paleographers' transcription and translation formed the basis for hands-on laboratory research on the recipes carried out by laboratory seminar students in a course offered each fall and spring semester by Columbia's history department (*HIST GR8906: Craft & Science*). Laboratory research focused on understanding materials and processes by means of experimental reconstructions of selected recipes from the manuscript, in which the students comprehensively investigated historical materials, ingredients, processes, tools, and their associated terminology, availability, origin, and scientific significance. Reproducing the manuscript's technical recipes played a crucial role in deciphering this complex text and in understanding the changing

The Making of Empirical Knowledge

practices of creating, codifying, and transmitting knowledge about nature in early modern Europe. With oversight from course instructors and visiting "expert makers," the students integrated this research in multimedia essays that now form the historical and material commentary for the digital critical edition of the manuscript.[5]

Each year's focused research in paleography and laboratory activity culminated in the third component of the Project: annual working group meetings. Each meeting brought together about 20 expert scholars and practitioners with approximately 20 students from the year's two offerings of the lab seminar to discuss and critique the student-authored research essays. The meetings provided the necessary expert oversight of the digital critical edition and introduced rich new insights from the scholars' varied disciplines to inform the Project's research. In the same way, the year's laboratory research cycle informed the transcription and translation activities of the subsequent summer paleography workshops. The manuscript's often complex and/or technical descriptions required research of period- or technique-specific terms and materials, and the varied investigations of each component of the Project not only informed one another but also provided a more comprehensive understanding of the manuscript. The interpretation of the manuscript evolved continually in light of the material reconstructions of the lab seminar, the textual and lexical examinations of the paleography workshops, and the knowledge exchange of the working group meetings. This iterative approach is key to the design and methodologies of the *Making and Knowing Project*, because it integrates and enhances student research with critical scholarly consensus. The Project has come to see this approach as replicating the artisanal workshop in its apprenticeship-based learning models.

The final component of the Project was the transformation of the manuscript and the voluminous multimedia research and critical commentary into a public-facing digital environment. The Project is committed to ensuring the sustainability of the edition—an increasing problem in an open, digital age, as other chapters in this volume point out—and thus the functionality of the website and the data it represents were developed using the most durable formats that allow migration and conversion of all digital assets in response to changing technologies. Through the creation of the edition, the Project strives to encourage other digital humanities projects to consider technical debt and preservation considerations early in the development process. Like the other three components, the digital development followed the Project's methodologies of collaborative research, interdisciplinary knowledge exchange, and pedagogy. This approach began with the encoding and preparation of the text for digital presentation at the first paleography workshop in 2014, and evolved with the addition of new digital staff, collaborators, and course offerings in the digital humanities, including in 2017, when the Project developed and offered its first digital humanities seminar, *HIST GR8975: What Is a Book in the 21st Century?*, which introduced students both theoretically and practically to the concepts and tools relevant to the creation of a digital edition. The seminar equipped participating students with identifiable, measurable, and repurposable digital skills and simultaneously accomplished the research objectives of the Project by prototyping the minimal digital edition, a simplified early model of Ms. Fr. 640. The seminar also encouraged reflection on how the format of texts shapes the production of knowledge in historical and contemporary contexts, an issue also addressed by our collaboration with the Columbia Computer Graphics and User Interfaces Lab (CGUI). CGUI is developing an augmented reality (AR) toolset to complement the digital critical edition, which will enable communication of and interaction with practice-based experiential knowledge, allowing users to experience the process of historical techniques not only through the multimedia critical commentary but also through cutting-edge visualization technology. In many ways, this AR implementation is the perfect twenty-first-century, open counterpart to Ms. Fr. 640's own experimental systems of scholarly communication, once more bringing the "reader" back to the experiential and embodied forms of knowledge in the original manuscript.

This collaboration led to two additional pedagogical initiatives—the integration of historical data from the *Making and Knowing Project* into an existing computer science course in AR and a new advanced cross-listed digital humanities seminar, *HIST/ENGL/COMS GU4031 Transforming Texts: Textual Analysis, Literary Modeling, and Visualization*. The Project's textual, critical, and material data served as the basis for the experimentation with text representation and modes of digital communication by the digital seminars and collaborators, and allowed for the continued exploration of the digital critical edition as a flexible, customizable tool that responds to the needs of students, researchers, and the broader public.

The interrelation of research and pedagogical components proved to be an efficient method of realizing the Project's collective and iterative research design. Through each cycle, from paleography workshop through lab seminar to working group meeting to digital seminar and prototyping, new insights were gained, accumulating information and generating questions for the next phase in the cycle. The strength of the Project's collaborative research also derives from the fact that the participants not only come together from different disciplinary backgrounds but also possess varying degrees of expertise. Teaching and researching through collective workshops, in which experienced participants overseen by disciplinary experts work closely with novices, has fruitfully facilitated both the training of the novices and the consolidation of knowledge by the more experienced participants.

Dissemination of the *Making and Knowing Project* through a Teaching Platform

The innovative methodologies developed by the Project, partly modeled on the natural scientific research group, have the potential to be applied beyond the study of Ms. Fr. 640. The Project will continue to serve as an incubator of pedagogical and research methodologies and is presently working to go a step further to articulate them in a formal implementation guide: the "Making and Knowing Research and Teaching Companion." The Companion will offer a scalable model with resources that scholars, instructors, and students can use in their own research endeavors or in the classroom, at small or large scales. These resources will include standardized protocols, lesson plans, digital literacy competencies and modes of assessment, templates for research workflows and management, participant testimonials, reports on successful applications of techniques, description of methods and philosophy, and frequently asked questions. The Companion will not provide step-by-step instructions for recreating the *Making and Knowing Project*, but rather will form a resource for others to apply the Project's methodology to their own contexts and needs. It will be freely available on the Project's website and on that of the digital critical edition of Ms. Fr. 640 and will form a platform for dissemination and a demonstration of how experimentation with material practices can provide a site for scholarly communication in the future. The Companion will also ensure that the methodologies employed in the creation of *Secrets of Craft and Nature* are not lost behind the scholarly publication, but instead highlighted and disseminated within the scholarly community and beyond.

Among the most distinctive components of the Project is its exploration of hands-on reconstructions of historical techniques and processes as a form of historical evidence, as well as the integration of this method of inquiry into the classroom. The study of a text from both material and textual perspectives simultaneously—and the challenges of communicating such an approach within textual forms—encourages careful decipherment of terminology and processes in historical making practices. It provides a type of close reading that raises many questions that would otherwise go unasked, questions that often turn out to be crucial for insights into historical practices and attitudes toward the natural world, materials, and processes. Moreover, the challenges of reenacting the skilled material manipulations of an artisan provide valuable, experience-driven understanding of embodied forms of knowledge that cannot be accessed through conventional historical research and pedagogy. Learning skilled handwork, whether in workshop or laboratory, also proves valuable in itself for students and scholars: the process of trial, failure, replication, and extension in both hypothesis and experiment design, as well as the practice of close observation (both of one's fellow worker at the bench and of the material being experimented upon) not only inculcate manual skills but can also enhance cognitive abilities of observation and reflection.

In the process of reconstructing a historical procedure, a participant also gains literacy in and firsthand knowledge of techniques and materials that can only come from engagement with process. Some techniques wholly lost or indecipherable, such as the long-confounding "incuse reverse casting" described in Ms. Fr. 640 and reconstructed in the fall 2014 lab seminar, are only recoverable through the process of attempting to recreate them. These attempts often require repeated trials, improvisation, creative reinterpretation, integration of available complementary sources or information, and a responsive and adaptive approach to unexpected outcomes. This goes against the grain of much contemporary textual scholarly communication, reintegrating an openness to processes and objects into the research lifecycle.

The Project's deciphering of the manuscript's ruby glass recipe, for example, required not only multiple trials in response to unanticipated results but also the collective expertise of historians, material scientists, geochemists, glassblowers, artists, curators, and students. This demonstrates the Project's collaborative and interdisciplinary approach, which facilitates and relies on collective interaction and knowledge sharing among individuals of varying disciplinary backgrounds who offer unique perspectives, approaches, and skillsets. The range in skill levels forces participants to clearly articulate and communicate ideas, problems, and gaps in information, knowledge, and expertise toward the common goal of producing new and significant scholarship.

Additionally, the sharing of knowledge and expertise among Project staff, collaborators, and students mitigates gaps in skill or experience, frequently following an "apprenticeship" model, as each participant imparts knowledge and trains other Project participants in their specialization—whether as a visiting expert maker leading skill-building sessions (such as teaching lab seminar students how to incorporate pigment into binding media), or as returning paleography students mentoring and training newcomers in the requisite skills as well as the Project's methodologies and protocols.

These multidisciplinary, expertise-directed, and process-oriented practices undergird the Project's pedagogy-driven research. Pedagogy is an integral part of every component of the Project (transcription, translation, reconstruction, working groups, and digital development). By making all students active participants in and contributors to core research, the Project provides training and engagement unlike traditional undergraduate and graduate lecture and seminar courses. Following the precepts of project-based learning, the students' acquisition of skills by generating research content cements their newly gained understanding of both concepts and tools, and allows them to employ these skills and new ways of thinking in other courses, in their own research, and in their future careers.

The *Making and Knowing Project* has been a collaborative and interdisciplinary endeavor since its inception. This has necessitated physical and intellectual openness to allow disciplinary differences to permeate the undertaking. In all aspects of research and development, the creation of the digital critical edition has brought together scholars, researchers, practitioners, and students to interpret the text, to attempt to replicate and understand its recipes and procedures, and to participate in its representation in a digital environment. In conjunction with the Project's reciprocal, iterative design, this interdisciplinary approach presents a rich and efficient model for collaborative research. Each step of the Project is critically informed by the preceding steps and consequently informs the succeeding steps. The *Making and Knowing Project* Research and Teaching Companion will provide a flexible and adaptable resource for other nascent projects and will allow the Project's impact to expand beyond its own research focuses and timeline.

Results

At root, the Project asks what a book *was* in the sixteenth century, what a book is *for* in the twenty-first century, and what it can *do* for us. Until recently, the form of the book, as printed codex, was taken as a standard for the production and dissemination of knowledge. Current research on the early modern era has disrupted an overly simplified conception of the book, revealing that even in the age of Gutenberg, books were often collectively compiled and the idea of a single author with a proprietary right to the creative content of a text was the exception. Our assumptions that printed books superseded the inefficient and limited communication of manuscript culture have been discredited by a more sophisticated understanding of writing technologies. The medieval scriptorium did not end because of a new technology of "artificial writing"; print and manuscript coexisted well into the eighteenth century, and Ms. Fr. 640 is a testament to this longevity. Early modern knowledge was made through the circulation of many different forms of media (including letters, manuscripts, instruments, and objects—among them printed books). This proliferation of media was not entirely dissimilar to today's blogs, zines, websites, web projects, e-books, minimal online publishing (e.g., sx:archipelagos), digital databases and archives, online exhibits, streaming videos, and podcasts. The "printed book" as a monolithic concept—containing and conveying knowledge seamlessly from author to audience—seems increasingly inadequate to describe the products of the past, let alone where we are going in the present. However, in spite of the discrediting of this narrative, it continues to constrain scholarly and public conceptions of how knowledge is conveyed: we strive to imitate a "reading experience" on our digital humanities platforms. We "turn pages" on our devices. We view the text as if it were simply a sheet of paper, rather than metal, plastic, and liquid crystal; and we naively neglect to consider it as containing proprietary code that can be used to look back at its readers or potentially to censor text automatically.

Drawing upon a deep interest in what it means to make and communicate knowledge (a central concern of the history of science and technology), the *Making and Knowing Project* rethinks the book as a scholarly object for the twenty-first century from the perspective of the early modern world. To recapture this exciting and highly experimental moment in human history and to allow people today to access it more vividly, the scholars of the *Making and Knowing Project* aim to think creatively with the technologies available to us today. How can we effectively present historical content and analysis in ways that communicate the dynamic and multidimensional nature of texts, especially that of a how-to text? Through the iterative process described above, the *Making and Knowing Project* is disassembling the manuscript's assemblage of written and practiced activity by means of unusual methodologies and pedagogy-driven research, which includes historical laboratory reconstructions and new tools in the digital humanities. The Project's edition combines text- and object-based historical research with laboratory experimentation, computer science, digital humanities, visualization, and design research in order to communicate the results of its investigations in ways that are intellectually rigorous, methodologically innovative, and able to draw in new audiences and participants. One important outcome of the Project's disassembly and reassembly of Ms. Fr. 640 has been to demonstrate that disciplinary divides between science, art, craft, and the humanities can also be dismantled in the research and publication process.

Notes

1. Among numerous works, see the publications of Nancy Siraisi; in particular, Gianna Pomata and Nancy G. Siraisi, eds., *Historia: Empiricism and Erudition in Early Modern Europe*, Transformations (Cambridge, MA: The MIT Press, 2005), especially the introduction; and Gianna Pomata, "Praxis Historialis: The Uses of Historia in Early Modern Medicine," in *Historia: Empiricism and Erudition in Early Modern Europe*, ed. Gianna Pomata and Nancy G. Siraisi, Transformations (Cambridge, MA: The MIT Press, 2005), 105–146; of Pamela O. Long, especially, "Hydraulic Engineering and the Study of Antiquity: Rome, 1557–70," *Renaissance Quarterly* 61, no. 4 (2008): 1098–1138, https://doi.org/10.1353/ren.0.0320; and Pamela O. Long, *Artisan/Practitioners and the Rise of the New Sciences, 1400–1600* (Corvallis: Oregon State University Press, 2011); of Gianna Pomata, especially, "Observation Rising: Birth of an Epistemic Genre, ca. 1500–1650," in *Histories of Scientific Observation*, ed. Lorraine Daston and Elizabeth Lunbeck (Chicago: University of Chicago Press, 2011), 45–80; and of Pamela H. Smith, especially, *The Body of the Artisan* (Chicago: University of Chicago Press, 2004). See also the works of Deborah Harkness, Alexander Marr, and Cristiano Zanetti's, *Janello Torriani and the Spanish Empire: A Vitruvian Artisan at the*

Dawn of the Scientific Revolution, Nuncius Series: Studies and Sources in the Material and Visual History of Science, vol. 2 (Leiden: Brill, 2017).

2. The edition is openly accessible as the Making and Knowing Project, Pamela H. Smith, Naomi Rosenkranz, Tianna Helena Uchacz, Tillmann Taape, Clément Godbarge, Sophie Pitman, Jenny Boulboullé, Joel Klein, Donna Bilak, Marc Smith, and Terry Catapano, eds., *Secrets of Craft and Nature in Renaissance France: A Digital Critical Edition and English Translation of BnF Ms. Fr. 640* (New York: The Making and Knowing Project, 2020), https://doi.org/10.7916/78yt-2v41. For more information on the *Making and Knowing Project*, including a roster of team members, collaborators, and supporters, see http://www.makingandknowing.org/. The Project thanks the National Science Foundation, the National Endowment for the Humanities, the Henry Luce Foundation, the Science History Institute, the Gerda Henkel Foundation, the Gladys Krieble Delmas Foundation, the Florence Gould Foundation, the Maurice I. Parisier Foundation, and Howard and Natalie Shawn for support.

3. Git is a version-control system initially developed by Linus Torvalds for the collaborative work on his Linux operating system. GitHub is a third-party hosting platform, now owned by Microsoft, that plays home to thousands of projects that use the Git versioning system, allowing large-scale and international collaboration on these efforts. While Git was designed for software development, it can be used in any collaborative working setup where maintenance of versioning is desirable.

4. An example of this minimal computing approach is the Project's 2017 minimal edition: https://cu-mkp.github.io/2017-workshop-edition/. Our thanks to Terry Catapano for his contribution to this edition.

5. The *Making and Knowing Project* photo repository from the lab reconstruction experiments can be accessed at: https://www.flickr.com/photos/128418753@N06/albums.

III Publics and Politics

9 The Royal Society and the Noncommercial Circulation of Knowledge

Aileen Fyfe

Introduction

The history of learned society publishing reveals that the philanthropic desire to make scholarship widely available, and free to read and reuse, is a scholarly tradition far older than the current Open Access Movement.[1] The Royal Society of London is the publisher of the world's longest-running scholarly journal, the *Philosophical Transactions*. It was launched in 1665 as a private venture by Henry Oldenburg, secretary to the recently founded Society; and since 1752, has been owned by the Society. The *Transactions* has historically been a useful way for the Society to enhance its reputation, not simply through the selection of interesting papers for publication but also by ensuring that its volumes and papers were widely available to scholars in Britain and the learned world. This was done through an extensive program of noncommercial distribution of printed copies of the *Transactions* and its later sibling, the *Proceedings*; and by encouraging reprinting and reuse of the material appearing in those journals.

For over two hundred years, from around 1750 to 1950, the Royal Society was heavily and successfully committed to funding the wide circulation of scholarly knowledge. The judicious distribution of the Society's publications—as membership perks, gifts to important individuals and institutions, tokens of exchange with other publishing societies, and as offprints circulating in personal scholarly networks—was central to this aim; but so too was a permissive approach to copying, reprinting, and reuse.

The Society's journals did have some paid-for sales, but the majority of the printed copies of the Society's journals prior to ca. 1930 were accessible without the need for payment by the end users. I start by considering how, in the absence of any significant sales income, the substantial costs of producing and distributing scientific research in printed form were supported. The story reveals that there is a much longer history of using alternative sources of income to support the circulation of research than is usually assumed in discussions of open access.

Money

It has too often been assumed that scholarly publishing has been a lucrative commercial undertaking for over three centuries, and that open access would be an unprecedented transformation of a well-established business model. Such an assumption would be utterly mistaken.[2]

It is true that back in 1665, Henry Oldenburg had hoped that the *Philosophical Transactions* would find enough paying customers to augment his modest income; and it is true that since the 1950s, the Royal Society's publishing division has generated increasingly large surpluses (£3.6 million in 2015).[3] But for most of the period in between, the *Philosophical Transactions* and the *Proceedings* were seen as legitimate causes for expenditure, not as potential sources of income.

The Royal Society's archive clearly shows that, while Oldenburg did make a little money from the *Transactions*, he was probably the last person to do so for almost three hundred years. His immediate successors as editor bankrolled the *Transactions* from their own pockets. When the Society took over the ownership and management in 1752, its leaders did so in the knowledge that this would involve financially supporting the *Transactions*. Their stated aim was to issue the *Transactions* for "the sole use and benefit of the Society, and the Fellows thereof."[4]

The ways in which that intention to "benefit" was put into action meant that the level of support needed by the publications increased over time: from 1752, Fellows were entitled to claim free copies of the *Transactions* as a membership perquisite; and from the 1760s onwards, the Society used copies as gifts to individuals and institutions. It was only during the difficult economic times of the 1930s, when the cost of the Society's now extensive program of gifts and exchanges became unsupportable, that a series of radical cuts to its generosity was followed by an increase in copies sold. By the 1950s, the Society shifted to a commercial model, in which sales and subscriptions were both the main source of income, and the main mode of circulation.

How did the Society support its publications financially from the 1750s to the 1950s? For most of this period, publication finances were not separated from the Society's general finances: any income from sales was not earmarked as "publication income," and the publication expenditure was met from the Society's general sources of income. In broad terms, that means that the publications were supported in the eighteenth century by membership fees, with a little help from income from property and investments. In the nineteenth century, investment income became vastly more important than membership fees; and from the 1880s onwards, the Society's activities were also supported by grants and donations received from government, industry, and private individuals.

It is from the 1890s that we can see evidence of specific income streams to support publications. The growth in scientific research over the later nineteenth century had meant that the cost of supporting the publication of research papers was straining the resources of all learned societies, not just the Royal Society. In 1895, therefore, the Royal Society led an appeal on behalf of society publishers for a grant-in-aid of scientific publishing from the UK government.[5] The result was the creation of a fund administered by the Royal Society, using government money, to which learned societies could apply for support for their publications; each year, the Royal Society kept any balance remaining to support its own publications. The government grant was increased at various points over the first half of the twentieth century, but by the 1960s it was more usually used to support occasional book publications rather than research journals. The existence of this mechanism for government support of scientific publishing may explain why UK learned societies do not seem to have adopted the "page charges" used by certain US societies from the 1930s onwards.[6]

During the early twentieth century, therefore, the costs of producing and distributing printed scientific knowledge were being covered from a mix of income streams: the Society's investment portfolio; the annual grant from government (and, from 1925, an annual grant from Imperial Chemical Industries); and the income from modest sales. Together, this was (just about) enough to enable the Society to continue circulating so much research outside the commercial market.

1. A Membership Perk

The first of the ways in which Royal Society journals circulated noncommercially was as a membership perquisite. Fellows were entitled to claim a free copy of every volume of the *Transactions*, though they had to do this in person and within five years of publication. The requirement to collect in person protected the Society from postage costs, while the generous time-window assisted those who were only in London occasionally.

The copies for Fellows accounted for a large fraction of the print run. For instance, in the 1840s, the print run of *Transactions* was just 1,000, and there were over 700 Fellows (although only about two-thirds of them actually claimed their copies).[7] By 1947, Fellows could have their copies mailed to them, and this accounted for between 25 percent and 30 percent of the print runs of the several research journals then published by the Society.[8] Fellows were now asked to choose among the journals rather than receiving all of them.

With so many copies destined for the hands of privileged individuals, this may not seem particularly "open" to modern eyes. However, these personal copies were not necessarily as private as we might now imagine. Before the twentieth century, public or university libraries were scarce, and so personal libraries often became resources for the friends, colleagues, and local community of the owner. There are surviving accounts of eighteenth-century scholars consulting books in each other's libraries, and of nineteenth-century artisans gaining access to knowledge via the library of an employer, patron, or local minister. Further, after the death of their original owners, these personal copies typically entered the secondhand book trade. Thus, while it is difficult to quantify the use that may have been made of these out-of-commerce copies of the *Transactions*, we must not ignore them.

2. Institutional Gifts and Exchanges

The most striking way in which the Royal Society supported the circulation of knowledge was by using copies of its publications as tokens in gift exchange with other bodies. Some gifts were efforts to enhance the Society's prestige within Britain, such as regular donations to the King, the British Museum, and the universities of Oxford and Cambridge from the 1760s.[9] Others were attempts to spread the Society's reputation internationally, such as the gifts to the Royal Academies of the Sciences in Stockholm, Lisbon, Brussels, and Berlin. Sometimes, they acknowledged a gift received, and sometimes not.

The use of *Transactions* as a gift was relatively small in scale in the late eighteenth century, but by the 1840s, the Society was giving around 60 copies each year to learned societies, observatories, academies, and universities, as well as another 20 or 30 copies as gifts to individuals.[10] By the early twentieth century, there would be over 460 institutions receiving the Royal Society's publications.[11]

Within Britain, the beneficiaries included virtually all the universities and university colleges, as well as national scientific organizations (the National Physical Laboratory), metropolitan scientific societies, provincial societies (the Essex Field Club, Glasgow Natural History Society), and public libraries in Birmingham, Manchester, and Cardiff.

The increasingly long list of beneficiaries was due to the Society's expanding international ambitions over the later nineteenth century, which reflected Britain's expanding political and commercial influence. By 1908, over 70 percent of the gifts were going overseas. As the map in figure 9.1 shows,

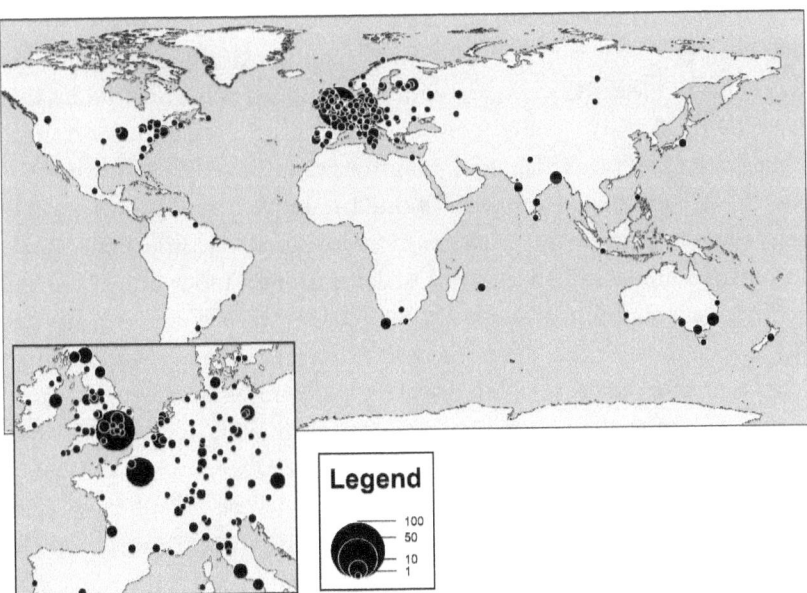

Figure 9.1
Location of institutions receiving free copies of Royal Society publications in 1908.

the majority of these went to European universities and scientific societies, but significant numbers also went to similar institutions in Canada, Australia, New Zealand, India, and South Africa, and to the US. A handful were sent even further afield—to the observatory at Rio de Janeiro, the university library at Caracas, the imperial university in Tokyo, and the bureau of science in Manila. The distribution pattern combines a commitment to scholarly sharing with cognate institutions anywhere in the world, with a paternalistic vision of the Royal Society's role in Britain and the wider world that included public libraries in Cardiff as well as those in Alexandria and the Cape colony.

This increasing generosity was one of the reasons why the Royal Society sought additional income streams to support its publication activities from the 1890s onwards. The cost of sending copies to more institutions, often at great distance, was exacerbated by the fact that the Society—like other organizations—was publishing more research papers. In the early nineteenth century, the Society had printed about 500 pages of *Transactions* each year; but by the 1930s, it issued about 4,000 pages of *Proceedings* as well as 900 pages of *Transactions*.

An analysis in the 1930s noted that, historically, the Society's main aim in granting gifts had been to get its own publications out in the world.[12] It did, however, often benefit by receiving reciprocal gifts of publications for its library. In the early twentieth century, almost 200 of the institutions that received the Society's publications did reciprocate. They formed an international system of exchanges amongst a group of scholarly institutions that both published research and hosted research libraries. This enabled the creation of (printed) repositories of international scientific publications in national academies and learned societies around the world. The Royal Society was a net funder of this system: a 1954 review revealed that the Royal Society spent £2,300 on the production and shipping of the printed journals it sent out, but only received £800 of journals in return.[13]

In addition to these exchanges, the Society gifted its journals to a substantial list of universities, research institutions, observatories, and public libraries that did not publish their own research journals but did have members or staff seeking access to research from elsewhere. However, in the 1930s, an analysis of the cost of this "free list" swiftly led to the removal of privileges from most foreign universities, research institutions, and libraries. All the universities in Britain and its former colonies were entitled to retain their place on the free list, and that included over 270 institutions.[14] But after a further review in 1954, universities were expected in future to buy the Society's publications, and only the Queen continued to get the *Transactions* for free.[15]

3. Offprints

Bound volumes were not the only ways in which the research printed in the *Transactions* and *Proceedings* circulated. The practice of allowing authors to acquire copies of their papers for circulation among their own friends, colleagues, and correspondents had been already well established by the 1780s.[16] In the days before photocopiers, these copies were valued as the only way to get a copy of the complete text—and tables, images, and formulae—without the labor of hand transcription. Authors sent them to their correspondents as soon as they were available; but they could also expect requests to arrive in the mail from researchers who wanted a personal copy.

These "separate copies" were, therefore, an important means for the circulation of individual articles in the age of print on paper; although, until it became standard practice to include full bibliographic details on the cover or in the header, their use could lead to misleading or inaccurate citations.[17]

The number and financing of separate copies varied over time. In the late eighteenth century, they were merely permitted—but not funded—by the Society: authors could pay for up to 100 copies of their article, directly from the printer.[18] By the start of the nineteenth century, the Society had begun to provide a certain number of copies to authors for free, with additional copies available at a charge; and by the 1840s, it was usually 100 copies for free.[19] This set the general pattern for the next century, although there were repeated attempts both to restrict free copies further and to restrict the number of additional copies that the authors could purchase.[20]

Separate copies facilitated certain forms of reuse, without the expense of recomposing type and hiring a printer, which would have been entailed by reprinting. Some researchers bound up a master set of their own papers, or used offprints received from others to create bespoke volumes on particular topics. Research institutions used the printed pages to create books out of the papers published by their staff. The scale of their requests for copies indicates that these were not just for internal use: in 1910, one author requested 500 additional copies for binding into his laboratory's "archives"; and in 1950, the Rothamsted Experimental Station sought 400 extra copies to be used in volumes of "memoirs" showcasing the agricultural research of its staff.[21]

Allowing the production and circulation of "separate copies"—and funding the production of a certain number of them—was another means of enabling access to the research papers published by the Royal Society. Like the institutional gifts and exchanges, it was of most benefit to active researchers who were either themselves, or through their institution, well-connected to other active researchers and institutions.

4. Copying, Reprinting, and Reuse

For readers outside the main scholarly research networks, it helped that the Society generally encouraged and enabled the copying, excerpting, reprinting, and summarizing of its research papers, rather than attempting to use copyright to restrict copying.[22] *Philosophical Transactions* itself, of course, is older than copyright, and it was not until the early nineteenth century that UK copyright protection was explicitly applied to periodicals as well as books. By that time, the Royal Society's approach to copying and reprinting was long established, and was based upon custom and courtesy, not legislation.

Throughout the nineteenth century, the Royal Society made generous dispensation to its authors to reuse their material. Authors who wished to reprint their articles were granted permission to do so. The Society also routinely granted permission to authors and their publishers to make use of the engraved metal plates (and later, wooden blocks) that carried the illustrations for their paper. The Society had paid for the images as part of the original publication in the *Transactions* or *Proceedings*, and it cost little or nothing to allow authors to reuse them; but it was a very significant cost saving to those who reused them. Permission to reuse images was also granted to certain third parties, such as the editor of *Nature*, to enable him to illustrate a report on a recent paper.[23]

The Society's willingness to allow third-party reuse of its material had been established in the early eighteenth century, when the Society gave permission to a series of editors, from 1703 onwards, who wished to produce an abridgement of the back volumes of *Transactions*. These abridgements were sufficiently commercially successful that there were more copies of the abridgements in circulation than of the original journal volumes. Despite the fact that the editors and printers of the abridgements made money, the Society made no effort to interfere, nor to secure a share of the proceeds.

Abridgements of back numbers did not give access to current research, however. Around 1800, this role was taken on by a new group of scientific journals, which carried reports of papers read at Royal Society meetings and summaries of published articles.[24] The Royal Society's own *Proceedings* began in the early 1830s with this function, though it later evolved into a research journal. As with the eighteenth-century abridgements, the Society generally enabled and encouraged the secondary reporting and excerpting of its research papers. In the early nineteenth century, editors depended upon the author circulating some of his separate copies; but by the 1890s, the Society had created a list of journal editors who should receive copies of new articles automatically.[25]

The one point on which the Society stood firm was the timing of any reporting and reprinting. Until the 1890s, all research published by the Royal Society had first been announced at one of its meetings; was then available as separate copies; and was eventually formally published in the volume of the *Transactions*.[26] This meant that there was a real possibility that the key facts of the paper—if not the full details—could circulate through scholarly networks well ahead of formal publication. Thus, well-connected journal editors might, either accidentally or intentionally, report or reprint *before* publication. In 1802, the then-president of the Society had been vehement in his rebuke to an offending journal editor, and this appears to have established the practices of courtesy that governed reporting and reprinting of Society papers for the rest of the century.[27] The Royal Society insisted on having the prestige and credit of being the point of first publication for new research, but after that moment it welcomed efforts to distribute, report, abstract, and index its published papers. It did not seek to use copyright legislation to constrain the circulation of knowledge, and in 1950, it would be the architect of the Fair Copying Declaration, in which over a hundred signatory publishers agreed to allow articles in their journals to be photocopied for the purposes of research and study. This resulted in equivalent provisions in the 1956 UK Copyright Act.[28]

Conclusion

In the late nineteenth and early twentieth centuries, Royal Society publications were not as easily accessible to global readers as open-access articles are now on the internet; but by the standards of the day, they were very widely available, and few end users had to pay. Until the 1950s, hundreds of copies of the Society's *Transactions* and *Proceedings* were being sent to organizations with libraries where they could be consulted by anyone with access rights to the library. Many university students and staff, and government researchers throughout Britain, Europe, North America and beyond, would have been able to get hold of Royal Society publications. It might involve a trip to a larger city or asking a favor from a colleague with membership in a society—but for individuals within the scholarly community, these publications could be obtained without any need to purchase them.

The Society's efforts were primarily directed toward those who were in some way part of a scholarly community. Copies were sent to public libraries in some of the large industrial cities, but the wider public was expected to learn about the contents of the Society's publications through third-party reporting, commenting, and reprinting. The argument that researchers should make their work publicly available, as a form of giving back to the taxpayers who funded them, is a far more recent development. Even when the Royal Society was presenting the argument for government funding of scientific publications in the 1890s, it focused on supporting the advance of scientific knowledge by aiding the circulation of knowledge among researchers.

By that time, the financial challenges of funding the Royal Society's increasingly ambitious, generous, and international vision for the circulation of printed knowledge were already apparent. For the next half-century, the Society struggled to find ways to keep this vision alive, slashing the provision of free and exchange copies, and seeking additional sources of external funding. In the world of print-on-paper publication, the Society's commitment to the noncommercial circulation of knowledge was ultimately defeated by scale.

It was during the rebuilding of the Society's publication practices after the Second World War that sales income came to be regarded as the preferred form of financial support for circulating knowledge. This is the same period in which a new group of commercially motivated firms moved into the publication of research journals and created a new business model based on the sale of journal subscriptions to international institutions. In the context of the early Cold War, when budgets for scientific research were generous, this strategy proved highly profitable.[29]

By the mid-1960s, the Royal Society's success in selling its journals to the cash-rich universities of the United States (and also to British universities who no longer received them as gifts) meant that it no longer struggled to cover the costs of publishing. Instead, the Society was beginning to see publishing as an income stream that might support the increased range of scientific, educational, and policy activities it wished to pursue.[30]

Royal Society leaders in the 1940s and 1950s had hoped for a technological revolution that would transform the circulation of what was then called "scientific information," making it faster and more accessible, and bringing costs back to a level sustainable by learned societies. But by the time that revolution arrived, the switch to a commercial model of knowledge circulation meant that new means of sharing research seemed a threat to income, rather than an opportunity. A 1993 committee worried that "we know how to give electronic journals away, but we have no idea how to sell them."[31] The same was true of the Society's initial response to open access, which a 2005 statement described, with a dubious grasp of history, as "the biggest change in the way that knowledge is exchanged since the invention of the peer-reviewed scientific journal 340 years ago."[32]

In 2006, the Society adopted a hybrid model of open access for its existing journals, and since then it has launched two new open access journals (initially supported by the Society's general publishing funds, but now using an article processing charge (APC) model). As at many learned societies, there is an ongoing tension between the desire to retain the useful income stream from publications (dating from the 1970s), and the (much older) desire to circulate knowledge widely.

Much like the Royal Society in 2005, the Open Access Movement's emphasis on making use of new communication technologies has failed to appreciate that we do not need to invent a new world of free-to-read access to scholarly knowledge. Rather, we are seeking to use that technology to revive a traditional and long-standing noncommercial ethos of scholarly publishing.

Notes

1. The research for this paper was supported by the UK Arts & Humanities Research Council, grant AH/K001841.

2. The following discussion is based on Aileen Fyfe, "Journals, Learned Societies and Money: *Philosophical Transactions*, ca. 1750–1900," *Notes and Records: The Royal Society Journal of the History of Science* 69, no. 3 (2015): 277–299, https://doi.org/10.1098/rsnr.2015.0032.

3. The Royal Society, "Trustees' Report and Financial Statements 2015–16," 2016, 111, note 3, https://royalsociety.org/-/media/about-us/governance/trustees-report-2015-2016.pdf?la=en-GB&hash=82396A1A10887287879D8F973D72A2B0.

4. The Royal Society, "Council Minutes," March 19, 1751, RS CMO/4.

5. Text of letter in The Royal Society, "Council Minutes," June 20, 1895, RS CMP/7.

6. Tom Scheiding, "Paying for Knowledge One Page at a Time: The Author Fee in Physics in Twentieth-Century America," *Historical Studies in the Natural Sciences* 39, no. 2 (2009): 219–247, https://doi.org/10.1525/hsns.2009.39.2.219; Marianne Noel, "La Construction de la Valeur Économique d'Une Revue en Chimie: Le Cas du *Journal of the American Chemical Society* (1879–2010)," *Revue Française des Sciences de l'Information et de la Communication*, no. 11 (2017), https://doi.org/10.4000/rfsic.3281.

7. Fellowship claims, from The Royal Society, "Undated Circulation Figures [before 12 Feb 1846]," n.d., RS CMB/86/A.

8. The Royal Society, "Distribution of Royal Society Publications 1947. Officers' Minutes," January 7, 1948, RS OM/2(48).

9. The Royal Society, "Council Minutes," June 25, 1761, RS CMO/4; The Royal Society, "Council Minutes," December 12, 1765, RS CMO/4.

10. See, for instance, list printed in *Proceedings of the Royal Society* (1838).

11. The 1908 list has 467 institutions, of which 260 were receiving the *Transactions*, and the rest the *Proceedings*. See *Year Book of the Royal Society of London* (London: Harrisons and Sons, 1908), 125–142.

12. The Royal Society, "Report of the Library Committee to Council," April 21, 1932, RS CMB/47/5.

13. The Royal Society, "Revision of the Lists of Exchanges and Gifts of the Royal Society's Publications," March 2, 1954, RS OM/14(54). There were 198 institutions on the exchange list at that point.

14. The Royal Society, "Revision of the Lists of Exchanges and Gifts."

15. The Royal Society, "Recommended Reductions in Exchanges and Gifts of the Royal Society's Publications," 1954, RS OM/16(54). An alternative incarnation of the "free list" emerged in the early twenty-first century, when the Society began to participate in the UN Programme for the Enhancement of Research Information, to make scientific journals more easily available to institutions in the developing world. The Royal Society, "Review of the Year," 2003, 9.

16. For example, see Charles Blagden to Erasmus Darwin, September 14, 1786, RS CB/2/34, Blagden Papers.

17. On Darwin's confusion, involving an offprint, see Alex Csiszar, "Seriality and the Search for Order: Scientific Print and Its Problems during the Late Nineteenth Century," *History of Science* 48, no. 3–4 (2010): 399–434, https://doi.org/10.1177/007327531004800306. The Royal Society offprints had carried the name of the *Transactions* since the start of the nineteenth century; the date was added in the late 1870s. See The Royal Society, "Council Minutes," March 21, 1878, RS CMP/5.

18. Blagden to Darwin, September 14, 1786.

19. This is apparent from The Royal Society, "Council Minutes," July 15, 1802, RS CMO/8.

20. The Royal Society, "Council Minutes," December 20, 1849, RS CMP/2.

21. On Rothamsted, see FC Bawden to Salisbury, "Application for Reduction in Charge for Reprints," December 7, 1950, RS OM/57(50).

22. For an extended discussion of the Royal Society's attitude to copyright, see Aileen Fyfe, Julie McDougall-Waters, and Noah Moxham, "Credit, Copyright, and the Circulation of Scientific Knowledge: The Royal Society in the Long Nineteenth Century," *Victorian Periodicals Review* 51, no. 4 (2018): 597–615, https://doi.org/10.1353/vpr.2018.0045.

23. For instance, William Herschel arranged to use RS plates for the reprint of his papers. See The Royal Society, "Council Minutes," June 22, 1797, RS CMO/8; and the Council Minutes for 20 March 1902 grant permission to several authors as well as to the editor of *Nature*. The Royal Society, "Council Minutes," March 20, 1902, RS CMP/8.

24. On the new journals, see Csiszar, *The Scientific Journal*, chapter 2.

25. "Notes on the Reading and Publication of Papers," in *Year Book of the Royal Society of London* (London: Harrisons and Sons, 1899), 88–89.

26. Aileen Fyfe and Noah Moxham, "Making Public Ahead of Print: Meetings and Publications at the Royal Society, 1752–1892," *Notes and Records: The Royal Society Journal of the History of Science* 70, no. 4 (2016): 361–379, https://doi.org/10.1098/rsnr.2016.0030.

27. This episode is discussed in Iain P. Watts, "'We Want No Authors': William Nicholson and the Contested Role of the Scientific Journal in Britain, 1797–1813," *The British Journal for the History of Science* 47, no. 3 (2014): 397–419, https://doi.org/10.1017/S0007087413000964.

28. Brad Sherman and Leanne Wiseman, "Fair Copy: Protecting Access to Scientific Information in Post-War Britain," *The Modern Law Review* 73, no. 2 (2010): 240–261.

29. Aileen Fyfe et al., "Untangling Academic Publishing: A History of the Relationship between Commercial Interests, Academic Prestige and the Circulation of Research" (Zenodo, May 25, 2017), https://doi.org/10.5281/zenodo.546100.

30. The Royal Society, "Special Meeting of Officers Minutes: 3. Review of the Society's Finances," January 26, 1973, xiv, RS OM/16(73).

31. The Royal Society, "Minutes of the Publications Management Committee," July 21, 1993, RS PMC/24(93).

32. The Royal Society, "Royal Society Position Statement on 'Open Access,'" November 24, 2005, https://web.archive.org/web/20060207171805/http://www.royalsoc.ac.uk/page.asp?id=3882.

10 The Political Histories of UK Public Libraries and Access to Knowledge

Stuart Lawson

To complement contemporary discussions on open access, this chapter considers public libraries as one element of the longer history of access to scholarly knowledge.[1] A historical perspective reveals that access to knowledge has undergone a long, slow process of change, related to social, technical, and political developments in printing, mass literacy, universities, and libraries. Until the advent of the digital technologies that enable the Open Access Movement, public access to the scholarly record required physical access to printed works. Public libraries helped facilitate this, fulfilling a vital role in extending access to scholarship beyond the academy. However, the complex power dynamics at play in the dissemination of ideas are visible in the creation of public libraries, through the role of philanthropy, Enlightenment notions of self-improvement, and the class politics of the Victorian era. This chapter examines these origins, with a focus on the UK, to reveal that current debates around the consequences of widening public access to scholarship—and how this expansion should be paid for—are nothing new. The liberal ideals underpinning librarianship in the nineteenth and twentieth centuries are still present in the digital era and exploring the biases and contradictions contained within public libraries' history may give us pause when considering the political context of scholarly publishing today.

Public Libraries and Expanding Access

For most of their history, libraries have existed to serve specific communities, although some were also open to members of the general public. The transition from a patchwork of community and membership libraries to what would be recognized today as a modern national public library service is well illustrated by examining the origins of public libraries in the UK, the country generally recognized as the first to legislate for a nationwide library service.[2] The term "public library" was used in Britain as early as the seventeenth century to describe libraries supported by a variety of funding models:[3] endowed libraries (founded by philanthropists), subscription libraries,[4] and institutional libraries. These models encompassed a diverse range of library types, from the institutional libraries of religious organizations through to cooperatively owned workers libraries. When public libraries in the modern sense—that is, publicly funded institutions for use by the whole community—were created, they built on this earlier legacy, in some cases very directly with the transfer of books and buildings.[5] The idea of public libraries as a network of institutions to serve an entire nation only became possible in the UK following the 1850 Public Libraries Act, which allowed town councils to establish libraries funded by raising local taxes.[6] Over the next century, the national network slowly came into being, with steady growth in the number of libraries, driven by further legislation such as the 1919 Public Libraries Act that extended library provision beyond urban centers to counties as well. The amount of funding that could be raised through taxation was limited, so many libraries relied on philanthropy from wealthy individuals to fund the acquisition of reading materials, with the steel magnate Andrew Carnegie taking a leading role in paying for the buildings themselves.[7] Library provision to all finally became a statutory obligation of local authorities with the 1964 Public Libraries and Museums Act.

Concurrently, working-class education had expanded greatly throughout the nineteenth century, and not only through state-sponsored channels: mutual improvement societies, cooperative societies, miners' libraries and mechanics' institutes all contributed to adult education. Formal higher education also underwent big changes in the same period: despite their medieval origins, modern universities were largely a product of the nineteenth century,[8] during which time new universities were created in Britain's civic centers.[9] By the mid-nineteenth century, education reforms meant that most adults were literate to some degree,[10] and details of the occupations of registered library users in the 1870s show that a majority were of the working classes.[11] The coupling of broadened access to education with public library provision resulted in a dramatic expansion of public appetite for access to scholarship. The professionalization of science around the turn of the twentieth century[12] also contributed to greater participation in scholarship beyond the traditional "gentleman-scholars" who had previously dominated science, although the requirement of a university education may have had a negative impact on self-trained working-class scientists.[13] Access to reference materials through public libraries played an important supporting role in all of this—at least in the cities—particularly in expanding access to women, who had often been excluded both from universities and from institutions designed for working men.[14]

A counter reading of the history of working-class education in the UK, though, shows a gradual shift of control out of the hands of the workers themselves and toward the governing classes. It began with working-class activists organizing among themselves, was solidified into institutions such as mechanics' institutes that were much more heavily reliant on middle-class patronage, and finally led to state control of education. While in some ways this was a victory, resulting in universal free education for all children regardless of class, it also diminished traditions of mutual support and self-organization in place of benevolent "care." This narrative is somewhat oversimplified—after all, self-educated intellectuals were always a minority within the working classes—but raises important issues around power relations that are discussed further below.[15] Public libraries were part of this process. The state-funded public library network that was becoming fairly comprehensive by the early twentieth century did offer greatly expanded opportunities for working-class people to access books, but at the cost of removing some of the agency[16] from the decision over what to purchase that was present in the small local libraries of a century earlier. This trade-off between access and agency has resonance with current debates surrounding the geopolitics of open access, especially regarding the relations between the Global North and South. Indeed, one specific model of funding open access, article processing charges (APCs), has been widely criticized as a form of "neocolonialism" that entrenches unequal power relations, fueling a disparity between those who can afford to publish using that model and those who cannot (for more on this, see Thomas Hervé Mboa Nkoudou's chapter in this volume).[17] The "missionary" aspect of the UK's early public library provision, whereby wealthy philanthropists bestowed gifts upon the poor, must be avoided in new open systems of knowledge dissemination by taking care to foster relationships of mutual cooperation.

Class, Colonialism, and Access

Libraries have often been idealized as "neutral" and classless, which obscures their political dimension.[18] Indeed, class relations were intrinsic to the public library movement that led to the original British legislation in 1850—enacted after campaigns by Liberal MPs William Ewart and Joseph Brotherton—with Victorian middle-class notions of social- and self-improvement a key driver in the idea of providing library facilities to all.[19] Public libraries were created with the aim of "bettering" the working classes; they were designed as cultural institutions that would shape public taste and foster "good citizenship."[20] It was thought by some advocates that providing free literature to workers would dull revolutionary tendencies and interest in radical socialism.[21] Conversely, Rose argues against this—that rather than instill bourgeois values, working-class education was a means for workers to break out of prescribed class roles.[22] If "economic inequality rested on inequality of education," then institutions designed to provide greater equity of access to knowledge were part of the egalitarian spirit of liberal reform.[23] Equity of access is seen as central to the purpose of public libraries, with McMenemy arguing that they "represent the ideal that everyone within society deserves the right to access materials for their educational, cultural and leisure benefit."[24]

Such ideals are emblematic of the liberal Enlightenment, so it is vital to remember the destructive legacy of colonialism and empire that coexists within this same tradition. Comparing the creation of public library services in the UK with the experience of some former colonial nations shows the imprint of this imperialist legacy and the fight against it. For instance, New Zealand had an incredibly high density of libraries within a few decades of European colonization but these were almost all subscription libraries rather than being municipally funded,[25] as were the British-introduced libraries in Malaysia until American organizations introduced free libraries in the 1950s.[26] The Dutch colonial administration in Indonesia created 2,500 public libraries to cement its authority through instilling its values.[27] While Britain was responsible for introducing modern public libraries to some countries,[28] it used a similar propagandist model to the Dutch in various African and Asian colonies.[29] In 1930s India, on the other hand, the influential library theorist Sirkazhi Ramamrita Ranganathan saw libraries as part of an anticolonial political project, "draw[ing] a link between open access to knowledge and the need for wider social transformation."[30] Although a scattering of public libraries already existed in various Indian cities,[31] these did not cover most of the population, and the movement to create a national network of public libraries (along with mass literacy and education) was grounded in the struggle against colonial rule.[32] These histories show a diverse global picture in terms of the political dynamics of introducing national public library systems, particularly in terms of their colonial origins, with lasting consequences for their future development.[33] Widening access to knowledge has been viewed as both emancipatory and, conversely, as a tool for indoctrination.[34] If public libraries are governed solely in the interests of governing classes rather than for ordinary citizens, their potential for facilitating a more equitable distribution of knowledge is diminished.

In this light, librarians act as both facilitators of access to information but also as gatekeepers, a dual role that highlights a tension within the profession's ethics.[35] In some ways, the need to mediate between library users and their materials has been reduced over time through both social and technological advances. For instance, the term "open access" was originally used to refer to print materials held on open shelves rather than in closed stacks, a practice which was unknown in the early days of public libraries;[36] and after being introduced in the US from the 1890s,[37] it only became widespread in the UK following the First World War.[38] To take a more recent example, if a library now provides an electronic version of a text then members of that library may be able to access it without physically going to the library. In both of these examples, library workers are still facilitating access but their role is less obvious to the end user and so the necessity of librarians' labor is obscured. Unfortunately, the fact that labor is often hidden has resulted in calls from the libertarian right to end public library services due to ill-conceived notions that librarians have already been automated out.

Open Access and Knowledge Politics

Public libraries have always had to be responsive to the political context of the time. For example, in England under New Labour (circa 1997–2010), social inclusion became an explicit part of library policy,[39] whereas the later 2010–2015 Conservative-Liberal coalition government cut local government spending to such an extent that many councils closed libraries in response.[40] Such an engagement with the policy direction of particular governments is also very clear with regard to open access. A central rationale for open access is that not all users (or potential users) of academic research are within the academy and research could have greater impact if results are made more widely available. The composition of publics outside of the academy varies at any given time, but includes teachers, further education students, retired academics, industry and entrepreneurs, refugees, and "para-academic" or contingent academic labor without a permanent faculty position (and for more on the composition of different publics, see Mourat, Ricci, and Latour in this book).[41] The UK government has made open access a priority in order to exploit the economic potential of these publics—especially startups and entrepreneurs. The notion that public libraries could provide scientific and technical knowledge in order to drive innovation and therefore stimulate economic growth is an old one. Although in the late nineteenth century public libraries' provision of technical literature was patchy,[42] by the First World War they were seen as supporting economic activity around scientific and technical progress, leading to the development of numerous commercial and technical libraries.[43]

A similar supporting role for public libraries was envisaged by David Willetts, the former Minister for Universities and Science (2010–2014), who initiated the UK's current national open-access policy direction. After 150 years of expanding access to knowledge through public libraries, using them to increase access to online research can be seen as a logical expansion and resulted in the UK's free access service, "Access to Research."[44] The scheme provides free access to online journal articles from public library computers. This is an exception to most UK open-access policy in that it focuses on end users rather than the supply side—that is, academia. It has so far not been a runaway success—figures from the initial 19-month pilot period of the service showed a wide variance in usage between different library authorities, with some seeing no usage at all, and the national total of 89,869 searches from 34,276 user sessions during the period translates as only 1,800 users per month.[45] Furthermore, the Access to Research scheme is taking place concurrently with an unprecedented level of budgetary cuts to public library provision in the UK, alongside ongoing commercialization and deprofessionalization, which threaten to reduce the ability of public libraries to function as a site of lifelong learning and civic engagement. From 2010–2016, 343 UK public libraries were closed, 174 were deprofessionalized by handing control over to community groups and volunteers, and 7,933 library staff (around 25 percent of the total) were made redundant.[46] Walk-in access to research is of no value to citizens whose library has been closed.

Conclusion

From the creation of public libraries, the expansion of higher education, to the global adoption of the internet, a shifting distribution of power has put more information in the hands of more people. Open access to research in the digital era is part of this longer history of access to knowledge. But if the decisions governing open-access policy are subject to whims of temporary administrations, then nothing is inevitable about the success or otherwise of open access—rights obtained after a long struggle can always be rolled back. Despite all the gains made so far,[47] not everyone has equal access to knowledge: money and social advantage are still barriers to accessing the results of scholarship, let alone participating in its creation. The extent of academic piracy highlights the uneven geographical distribution of access to research: pirate websites such as Sci-Hub and Library Genesis show great demand in countries where access is a significant problem, such as Indonesia and Iran.[48] This indicates that there is still much work to be done. Throughout history, progress in this area has often followed on the heels of grassroots or illicit activity. For example, although nineteenth-century public libraries resulted from top-down work of social reformers rather than bottom-up demand, they entered a world already containing a rich variety of autonomous working-class libraries. And piracy is often a precursor to the implementation of legal solutions.[49] By paying attention to the lessons of history, particularly its social and political dimensions, those of us who see open access as a progressive catalyst for social change can work toward the *kind* of open access we want to see.

Notes

1. For further information about the topics raised in this chapter, see the PhD thesis: Stuart Lawson, "Open Access Policy in the UK: From Neoliberalism to the Commons" (London: Birkbeck, University of London, 2019) https://ethos.bl.uk/OrderDetails.do?uin=uk.bl.ethos.774255.

2. To qualify this statement, it should be mentioned that the UK's initial legislation only allowed individual local authorities to raise taxes for public libraries, rather

than require them to do so. And legislation was also passed at a local level in the US around the same time, such as in New Hampshire in 1849 and Boston in 1852. Jesse H. Shera, *Foundations of The Public Library—The Origins Of The Public Library Movement In New England 1629–1855* (Chicago: University of Chicago Press, 1949), 165–188.

3. Thomas Kelly, *History of Public Libraries in Great Britain, 1845–1975* (London: Library Association Publishing, 1977), 3–4.

4. Subscription libraries lasted until the mid-twentieth century when they were finally supplanted by tax-funded libraries. Alistair Black, *The Public Library in Britain, 1914–2000* (London: The British Library, 2000), 115; Kelly, *History of Public Libraries*, 344.

5. Kelly, *History of Public Libraries*, 72–74.

6. The initial 1850 Act only applied to England and Wales but was soon extended to Scotland through additional legislation. See Kelly, *History of Public Libraries*, 20–22.

7. Kelly, *History of Public Libraries*, 115–137; David McMenemy, *The Public Library* (London: Facet Publishing, 2009), 27–30. Carnegie also funded libraries elsewhere, notably in the US.

8. Bill Readings, *The University in Ruins* (Cambridge, MA: Harvard University Press, 1996), 7; Walter Rüegg, "Themes: The French and German University Models," in *Universities in the Nineteenth and Early Twentieth Centuries (1800–1945)*, ed. Walter Rüegg, vol. 3 (Cambridge: Cambridge University Press, 2004), 5–6.

9. Stefan Collini, *What Are Universities For?* (London: Penguin, 2012), 27–28.

10. Kelly, *History of Public Libraries*, 18; In fact, there were fairly high levels of literacy much earlier than this—see Jonathan Rose, *The Intellectual Life of the British Working Classes*, 2nd ed. (New Haven, CT: Yale University Press, 2010)—but a national system of free primary education helped make this more consistent across different classes and regions.

11. Kelly, *History of Public Libraries*, 82–83.

12. James A. Secord, "Science, Technology and Mathematics," in *The Cambridge History of the Book in Britain*, ed. David McKitterick (Cambridge: Cambridge University Press, 2009), 443–474, https://doi.org/10.1017/CHOL9780521866248.014.

13. Rose, *The Intellectual Life*, 70–72.

14. Chris Baggs, "'The Whole Tragedy of Leisure in Penury': The South Wales Miners' Institute Libraries during the Great Depression," *Libraries & Culture* 39, no. 2 (2004): 120; Rose, *The Intellectual Life of the British Working Classes*, 18–20, 76–77.

15. Rose, *The Intellectual Life*, 236.

16. See Baggs, "'The Whole Tragedy of Leisure in Penury,'" for details of this process in action in the miners' libraries of south Wales.

17. Gerald Beasley, "Article Processing Charges: A New Route to Open Access?," in *Positioning and Power in Academic Publishing: Players, Agents and Agendas*, ed. Fernando Loizides and Birgit Schmidt (Amsterdam: IOS Press, 2016), 125–130, https://doi.org/10.3233/978-1-61499-649-1-125; Thomas Hervé Mboa Nkoudou, "The (Unconscious?) Neocolonial Face of Open Access" (Berlin, 2017); Florence Piron, "Postcolonial Open Access," in *Open Divide: Critical Studies on Open Access*, ed. Joachim Schöpfel and Ulrich Herb (Sacramento, CA: Library Juice Press, 2018), 117–126, https://corpus.ulaval.ca/jspui/handle/20.500.11794/16178.

18. John Pateman, "Public Libraries and Social Class," in *Open to All? The Public Library and Social Exclusion*, by Dave Muddiman et al. (London: Resource: The Council for Museums, Archives and Libraries, 2000), 26–42, http://eprints.rclis.org/6283/; Alison M. Lewis, "Introduction," in *Questioning Library Neutrality: Essays from Progressive Librarian*, ed. Alison M. Lewis (Duluth, MI: Library Juice Press, 2008), 1–4. See Pateman on class, and Lewis for a critique of library neutrality.

19. McMenemy, *The Public Library*, 24–25.

20. Black, *The Public Library in Britain*, 4.

21. Black, *The Public Library in Britain*, 25–27, 145–146.

22. Rose, *The Intellectual Life*, 23.

23. Rose, *The Intellectual Life*, 24.

24. McMenemy, *The Public Library*, xiii; See also IFLA, "IFLA/UNESCO Public Library Manifesto," 1994, https://www.ifla.org/publications/iflaunesco-public-library-manifesto-1994.

25. J. E. Traue, "The Public Library Explosion in Colonial New Zealand," *Libraries & the Cultural Record* 42, no. 2 (2007): 153.

26. C. Yu Priscilla, "History of Modern Librarianship in East Asia," *Library History* 24, no. 1 (2008): 65–67, https://doi.org/10.1179/174581608X295293; The US also played a similar role in Japan. Priscilla, "History of Modern Librarianship," 67–68.

27. Elizabeth B. Fitzpatrick, "The Public Library as Instrument of Colonialism: The Case of the Netherlands East Indies," *Libraries & the Cultural Record* 43, no. 3 (2008): 270–285. For more historical context, see also L. Sulistyo-Basuki, "The Rise and Growth of Libraries in Pre-War Indonesia," *Library History* 14, no. 1 (1998): 55–64, https://doi.org/10.1179/lib.1998.14.1.55.

28. For example, Ethiopia. See Sterling Joseph Coleman, "The British Council and Unesco in Ethiopia: A Comparison of Linear and Cyclical Patterns of Librarianship Development," *Library History* 21, no. 2 (2005): 121–130, https://doi.org/10.1179/002423005x44952; However, see also Rosenberg on the British colonial authority's lack of interest in setting up a national library service in Kenya. Diana Rosenberg,

"Imposing Libraries: The Establishment of National Public Library Services in Africa, with Particular Reference to Kenya," *Third World Libraries* 4, no. 1 (1993): 35–44.

29. Fitzpatrick, "The Public Library as Instrument of Colonialism."

30. George Roe, "Challenging the Control of Knowledge in Colonial India: Political Ideas in the Work of S. R. Ranganathan," *Library & Information History* 26, no. 1 (2010): 19, https://doi.org/10.1179/175834909X12593371068342.

31. Jashu Patel and Krishan Kumar, *Libraries and Librarianship in India* (Westport, CT: Greenwood Press, 2001), 2–14.

32. Roe, "Challenging the Control of Knowledge in Colonial India."

33. Jennifer Cram, "Colonialism and Libraries in Third World Africa," *The Australian Library Journal* 42, no. 1 (1993): 13–20, https://doi.org/10.1080/00049670.1993.10755621; Gabe Ignatow, "What Has Globalization Done to Developing Countries' Public Libraries?," *International Sociology* 26, no. 6 (2011): 746–68, https://doi.org/10.1177/0268580910393373; Adakole Ochai, "The Purpose of the Library in Colonial Tropical Africa: An Historical Survey," *International Library Review* 16, no. 3 (1984): 309–315, https://doi.org/10.1016/0020-7837(84)90007-4; Amusi Odi, "The Colonial Origins of Library Development in Africa: Some Reflections on Their Significance," *Libraries & Culture* 26, no. 4 (1991): 594–604; Kate Parry, "Libraries in Uganda: Not Just Linguistic Imperialism," *Libri* 61, no. 4 (2011): 328–337, https://doi.org/10.1515/libr.2011.027.

34. See Rose, *The Intellectual Life*, on the importance of paying attention to readers' own perceptions of the effect of reading and education, rather than relying entirely on theoretical exposition.

35. Adetoun A. Oyelude and Alice A. Bamigbola, "Libraries as the Gate: 'Ways' and 'Keepers' in the Knowledge Environment," *Library Hi Tech News* 29, no. 8 (2012): 7–10, https://doi.org/10.1108/07419051211287615.

36. Kelly, *History of Public Libraries*, 176–182.

37. Wayne Wiegand, *Part of Our Lives: A People's History of the American Public Library* (Oxford: Oxford University Press, 2015), 79–81.

38. Black, *The Public Library in Britain*, 52.

39. Department for Culture, Media and Sport, "Libraries for All: Social Inclusion in Public Libraries," 1999, https://webarchive.nationalarchives.gov.uk/+/http:/www.culture.gov.uk/images/publications/Social_Inclusion_PLibraries.pdf; McMenemy, *The Public Library*; Dave Muddiman et al., *Open to All? The Public Library and Social Exclusion*, ed. Dave Muddiman, vol. 1, Ove (London: Resource: The Council for Museums, Archives and Libraries, 2000), http://eprints.rclis.org/6283/. Muddiman et al. questioned the efficacy of this policy.

40. BBC, "Libraries 'Facing Greatest Crisis,'" March 29, 2016, sec. England, https://www.bbc.com/news/uk-england-35707956.

41. An often-overlooked point, but many refugees are university students or graduates. Jessica Magaziner, "The Importance of Higher Education for Syrian Refugees," *World Education News + Reviews*, December 7, 2015, https://wenr.wes.org/2015/12/the-importance-of-higher-education-for-syrian-refugees. With close to 1 percent of the global population now displaced—there are an estimated 65.3 million refugees out of a global population of 7.4 billion, i.e., 0.8 percent of people—access to education and research for refugees has become a major global issue. Sam Jones, "One in Every 113 People Forced to Flee, Says UN Refugee Agency," *The Guardian*, June 20, 2016, sec. Global development, https://www.theguardian.com/global-development/2016/jun/20/one-in-every-113-people-uprooted-war-persecution-says-un-refugee-agency; United Nations Refugee Agency, "Figures at a Glance," UNHCR, accessed April 29, 2019, https://www.unhcr.org/figures-at-a-glance.html.

42. Kelly, *History of Public Libraries*, 77–78.

43. Black, *The Public Library in Britain*, 13–14, 28–29; Kelly, *History of Public Libraries*, 243–244.

44. Sarah Faulder and Shinwha Cha, "Access to Research: The Experience of Implementing a Pilot in Public Libraries," *Learned Publishing* 27, no. 2 (2014): 85–92, https://doi.org/10.1087/20140202. The Access to Research site is available at http://www.accesstoresearch.org.uk/.

45. Shared Intelligence, "Access to Research: A Report to the Publishers Licensing Society and the Society of Chief Librarians," 2015, 15–19, https://www.pls.org.uk/media/199841/Access-to-Research-final-report-Oct-2015.pdf. The Shared Intelligence report treats this as successful, but 1,800 out of a population of 65 million is extremely low.

46. BBC, "Libraries 'Facing Greatest Crisis.'"

47. For data on the growth of open access, see Archambault et al., "Proportion of Open Access Papers Published in Peer-Reviewed Journals at the European and World Levels—1996–2013"; Rob Johnson, Anthony Watkinson, and Michael Mabe, *The STM Report: An Overview of Scientific and Scholarly Journal Publishing*, 5th ed. (The Hague: International Association of Scientific, Technical and Medical Publishers, 2018), https://www.stm-assoc.org/2018_10_04_STM_Report_2018.pdf.

48. See Bodó on "shadow libraries," the geographical distribution of their users, and the historical reasons why Russia is the center of much academic piracy. Balázs Bodó, "The Genesis of Library Genesis: The Birth of a Global Scholarly Shadow Library," in *Shadow Libraries: Access to Educational Materials in Global Higher Education*, ed. Joe Karaganis (Cambridge, MA: The MIT Press, 2018), 25–52; Balázs Bodó, "Library Genesis in Numbers: Mapping the Underground Flow of Knowledge," in

Shadow Libraries: Access to Educational Materials in Global Higher Education, ed. Joe Karaganis (Cambridge, MA: The MIT Press, 2018), 53–78. High-income nations do also have significant use of pirate websites though, as analysis of Sci-Hub usage data has made clear. John Bohannon, "Who's Downloading Pirated Papers? Everyone," *Science*, April 25, 2016, https://www.sciencemag.org/news/2016/04/whos-downloading-pirated-papers-everyone; Bastian Greshake, "Correlating the Sci-Hub Data with World Bank Indicators and Identifying Academic Use," *The Winnower* 3 (May 30, 2016), https://doi.org/10.15200/winn.146485.57797.

49. Adrian Johns, *Piracy: The Intellectual Property Wars from Gutenberg to Gates* (Chicago: University of Chicago Press, 2011).

11 Libraries and Their Publics in the United States

Maura A. Smale

Although it has been proclaimed from the rooftops for many years, the dire situation for US libraries of all kinds on the ground, as of 2020, cannot be overstated. Indeed, it is partially the budgetary and social position of American libraries that has driven the adoption of open access to date. In this chapter, I recapitulate what may be a familiar narrative, but one that nonetheless bears repeating.

The mission of libraries, albeit not historically singular, as Stuart Lawson has shown in their chapter in this volume, is at once simple and sweeping: to provide access to information, resources, and services, and to assist community members in their use. In his foundational 1931 book *The Five Laws of Library Science*, Sirkazhi Ramamrita Ranganathan asserted that "books are for use" and "every person his or her book." Ranganathan proposed that libraries are fundamental to education, and that education must be available for all.[1] I am a librarian and scholar at New York City College of Technology (City Tech) of the City University of New York (CUNY), the largest urban public university in the US. CUNY was established to offer affordable access to higher education for everyone in our diverse city—from students who have just graduated from secondary school to adults who are returning to complete a degree—and our libraries are an integral component of the university.

While I write from my experience in the US and at CUNY, libraries around the world, of all types and in all locations, aim to make information in all formats available for their communities. Public libraries arguably have the broadest remit, and typically serve all residents of a community. Librarians provide invaluable guidance to public library patrons seeking information for a wide range of reasons—from leisure to civic, career, or academic research. School librarians serve students in a variety of primary and secondary educational settings, and work with teachers and administrative staff in public and private schools to provide access to information and curricular materials that students need in their course of study. Academic libraries are used by the students, faculty, and staff of colleges and universities, in coursework and in research. Information literacy—encompassing critically evaluating and making use of information—is an important component of academic librarian work, as well.

Library Funding Is Cut while Demands for Access Increase

While providing access to and guidance about information across a variety of formats and a range of topics, interests, and levels is a core component of all libraries' missions, library funding is increasingly a concern. Public libraries are funded in part by tax monies, and over the past few decades their budgets have been in decline more often than not. Almost 50 percent of states in the US cut library funding between 2010 and 2012,[2] cuts that come at a time of heavy use, with a 2016 Pew Research Center survey reporting that "66% [of respondents] say the closing of their local public library would have a major impact on their community."[3] In the UK, more than 300 public libraries have closed in the past 10 years, with more closures possibly to come.[4] School libraries have sometimes been hardest hit in the US, with many publicly funded primary and secondary schools lacking a librarian or even a library.[5] Academic library budgets have also been flat or declining. In the US this is most concerning at public colleges and universities, many of which have suffered from a decrease in state funding beginning about 30 years ago,[6] though even some well-endowed private institutions have found it difficult to appropriately fund their libraries.[7]

The challenges of declines in library funding are multifaceted and somewhat dependent on broader societal factors that include disinvestment in services for the public good and increasing pressure toward privatization of education. However, there is no question that the economics of the scholarly communication system have had an impact on library budgets. Scholarly journal prices have increased at an unsustainable rate over the past 30 years, a trend typically referred to by librarians as the serials crisis. As has been widely reported by librarians, serials expenditures by Association of Research Libraries members increased 391 percent between 1986 and 2009, while monograph expenditures increased by only 77 percent during that time.[8] Prices for textbooks and other curricular materials for primary through postgraduate study have also increased unsustainably. The Student Public Interest Group in the US reports that college textbook prices have risen by 73 percent since 2006, with individual textbooks now priced as high as $400.[9] The requirements of the academic tenure and promotion process in higher education and curricular standards and practices in primary through higher education have enabled publishers to implement these drastic price increases for scholarly journals and course textbooks; increases that are generally not possible for traditional monograph publishers.

In academic libraries, especially, unchecked price increases throughout the scholarly communication system have had profound effects on the information, resources, and services that librarians can provide for their college and university communities. Many librarians have had to eliminate institutional subscriptions to scholarly journals or reduce their reliance on packages of journal titles by replacing them with individual subscriptions to the handful of journals that are most in need by their students, faculty, and staff. Some college and university libraries cannot afford to subscribe to the journals in which their faculty publish. Academic librarians have also reduced monograph purchases as more funds are devoted to maintaining journal subscriptions, which has contributed to the contraction of university presses and academic monograph publishing. This redistribution of funds is especially concerning for scholars in the humanities and social sciences, disciplines that traditionally rely more heavily on monographs than do those in the science, technology, engineering, and mathematics (STEM) fields. The tragic suicide in 2010 of Aaron Swartz, an activist who "faced federal charges of up to 35 years in prison" for illegally downloading scholarly articles from the JSTOR database at MIT, drew national attention to the serials crisis, and prices have only continued to increase since then.[10]

At the college where I work, we in the library strive to provide access to as much information for faculty and students to use in teaching and research as we can, though our collections budget cannot keep up with the increasing prices in scholarly publishing. Faculty do use interlibrary loan services to augment our library's collections, and employ workarounds that are in common use by researchers throughout the world: contacting article authors to request that they share a copy of their article, using social media to make similar requests of other academics, and visiting SciHub and other websites that make paywalled research freely available (sometimes in violation of copyright laws). Our library offers some textbooks on reserve loan for students, though they are only available for a short period of time, and we cannot purchase textbooks for every course or in sufficient quantity for all of our 17,000 students. Many City Tech students face challenges in affording housing, food, and tuition, and lack of access to scholarly research and curricular materials may not be their most significant difficulty. However, lack of access can impede students' success in their coursework and progress toward graduation, as it can hinder the research endeavors of our faculty.

Open Access and Open Educational Resources Increase Access

Open access and open educational resources increase the opportunities for all to use information and resources.

Some publishers have defended the barriers toward open access to scholarly research by asserting that the general public has no need for or interest in specialized research publications. This assertion is classist and misguided at best. The website *Who Needs Access? You Need Access!* collects testimonials from those who have benefited from open access to scholarly research.[11] Among the many examples is a study in which a researcher collaborated with a group of primary school children in England to examine honeybees, the results of which were then written up by the children and published in *Biology Letters*.[12] Caregivers for family members who have rare illnesses also use scientific research online. As one parent interviewed on the site notes, it can be challenging for doctors to keep up with the latest developments on uncommon diseases, and open access has enabled her to advocate for her child's care and to share information among her community of patient advocates.[13] Beyond its use for individuals and independent researchers, immediate open access to research results speeds discoveries in medical and other scientific disciplines.[14] Public access to humanities and social science research is also valuable; these disciplines enable us to understand and contextualize human history, social relations, and our place in the world, which is perhaps especially important in our current historical moment. It is clear that increased availability of scholarly research is a benefit to all in society and should not be restricted solely to those with an academic affiliation.

Much—though not all—scholarly research is publicly funded, and as such the results from and publication of that research should be available to the public. Tax monies fund research via grants from the government, which is then undertaken by faculty and staff at public universities. As Suber has noted, "tax money should be spent in the public interest, not to create intellectual property for the benefit of private publishers, who acquire it and profit from it without paying the authors or compensating the public treasury."[15] Open access can also help ameliorate funding inequities between public and private institutions by enabling access to information regardless of an institution's endowment or operating budget. For scholars and faculty at public institutions, who are typically required to research and publish as part of the tenure and promotion process, open access facilitates the academic research process regardless of the size and funding level of their academic libraries.

Open access can also be an alternative to expensive textbooks, as the open educational resources initiatives at institutions worldwide have shown. As in scholarly journal publishing, many textbook authors are faculty at institutions of higher education and, while they may have received royalties for writing textbooks, can be encouraged to convert their textbooks to open educational resources with compensation in time or funds from their institutions. Open educational resources initiatives are especially relevant for low-income college and university students and their families, as the cost of textbooks can be very high in addition to the cost of tuition. Primary and secondary schools in the US often provide textbooks to their students at no cost, and their expense means that textbooks may not be updated or replaced in a timely manner. Open access and open educational resources can help provide current, relevant scholarly materials to libraries and schools. As noted above, this is of special concern because the poorest students are often served by underfunded institutions; for example, at the public university where I work, 42.2 percent of students have an annual household income of less than $20,000.[16]

While open access and the scholarly communication system are most often discussed with reference to academic libraries, open access is highly relevant to public libraries as well. Public libraries also typically provide a wide range of information outside of academic research, and most have little to no budget available for scholarly materials. This is especially problematic given the broad mission of public libraries to serve entire communities. Community residents who may have had access to scholarly research while enrolled in college or university will typically lose it once they have left school. Increasing the opportunities for patrons at public libraries to use research information would help fill the gap for independent researchers without an affiliation to a higher education or research institution.

Open Access and Open Educational Resources Benefit Libraries and Their Publics

Open access to scholarly research and curricular materials is a sure benefit to libraries and their publics. Wide adoption of open-access publishing will allow our communities to read and use the results of scholarly research both within and outside of the bounds of an institutional affiliation, helping to dismantle information privilege and increasing equity so that libraries of all kinds can better serve their communities. As the International Federation of Library Associations and Institutions (IFLA) has asserted: "comprehensive open access to scholarly literature and research documentation is vital to the understanding of our world and to the identification of solutions to global challenges and particularly the reduction of information inequality."[17]

The affordances of digital publishing—which enable open access and open educational resources—can also increase accessibility for patrons with disabilities that may make reading a printed volume challenging. However, access to information online does not necessarily equate to universal access. Home broadband internet access varies in the US, with persistent gaps especially in some urban and rural areas, as does access to the internet via smartphone or other wifi-enabled devices; worldwide, there are many locations in which internet access is difficult or lacking.[18] Libraries are helping to bridge these gaps, and for many communities, access to the internet is an invaluable service provided by their libraries.

Librarians and libraries will continue to remain vital to their communities with the transition to open access publishing, as Ranganathan's fifth and final law—"the library is a growing organism"—suggests. Librarians have been important advocates for open access from the beginning, have been instrumental in its current successes, and will continue to be valuable partners in advocacy in the future.[19] Open access helps libraries fulfill their mission to their publics.

Notes

1. S. R. Ranganathan, *The Five Laws of Library Science* (London: The Madras Library Association, 1931), https://catalog.hathitrust.org/Record/001661182.

2. John Carlo Bertot et al., "Public Libraries and the Internet 2012: Key Findings, Recent Trends, and Future Challenges," *Public Library Quarterly* 31, no. 4 (2012): 303–325, https://doi.org/10.1080/01616846.2012.732479.

3. John B. Horrigan, "Libraries 2016," *Pew Research Center* (blog), September 9, 2016, https://www.pewinternet.org/2016/09/09/libraries-2016/.

4. Danuta Kean, "Library Closures 'Will Double Unless Immediate Action Is Taken,'" *The Guardian*, December 12, 2016, sec. Books, https://www.theguardian.com/books/2016/dec/12/library-closures-will-double-unless-immediate-action-is-taken.

5. Fernanda Santos, "Schools Eliminating Librarians as Budgets Shrink," *The New York Times*, June 24, 2011, sec. N.Y. / Region, https://www.nytimes.com/2011/06/25/nyregion/schools-eliminating-librarians-as-budgets-shrink.html.

6. Karin Fischer and Jack Stripling, "An Era of Neglect," *The Chronicle of Higher Education*, March 2, 2014, https://www.chronicle.com/article/An-Era-of-Neglect/145045.

7. Ian Sample, "Harvard University Says It Can't Afford Journal Publishers' Prices," *The Guardian*, April 24, 2012, http://www.theguardian.com/science/2012/apr/24/harvard-university-journal-publishers-prices.

8. Martha Kyrillidou and Shaneka Morris, "Monograph and Serial Expenditures in ARL Libraries, 1986–2009," in *ARL Statistics 2008–2009* (Washington, DC: Association of College and Research Libraries, 2011), https://publications.arl.org/ARL-Statistics-2008-2009/11?ajax.

9. Ethan Senack, "Student Group Releases New Report on Textbook Prices," US PIRG, February 3, 2016, https://uspirg.org/news/usp/student-group-releases-new-report-textbook-prices.

10. Benjamin Hockenberry, "The Guerilla Open Access Manifesto: Aaron Swartz, Open Access and the Sharing Imperative," *Lavery Library Faculty/Staff Publications*, November 21, 2013, 1.

11. "Who Needs Access? You Need Access!," accessed April 21, 2016, https://whoneedsaccess.org/.

12. P. S. Blackawton et al., "Blackawton Bees," *Biology Letters* 7, no. 2 (2011): 168–172, https://doi.org/10.1098/rsbl.2010.1056.

13. Mike Taylor, "Christy Collins, Mother and M-CM Patient Advocate," *Who Needs Access? You Need Access!* (blog), April 26, 2012, https://whoneedsaccess.org/2012/04/26/christy-collins-mother-and-m-cm-patient-advocate/.

14. Peter Suber, "The Taxpayer Argument for Open Access," *SPARC Open Access Newsletter*, no. 65 (September 4, 2003), http://dash.harvard.edu/handle/1/4725013.

15. Suber, "The Taxpayer Argument for Open Access."

16. City University of New York, "A Profile of Undergraduates at CUNY Senior and Community Colleges: Fall 2017," 2018, http://www2.cuny.edu/wp-content/uploads/sites/4/page-assets/about/administration/offices/oira/institutional/data/current-student-data-book-by-subject/ug_student_profile_f17.pdf.

17. International Federation of Library Associations and Institutions, "IFLA Statement on Open Access to Scholarly Literature and Research Documentation," 2003, https://www.ifla.org/publications/ifla-statement-on-open-access-to-scholarly-literature-and-research-documentation.

18. Lee Rainie, "Digital Divides—Feeding America," *Pew Research Center* (blog), February 9, 2017, https://www.pewinternet.org/2017/02/09/digital-divides-feeding-america/.

19. Hockenberry, "The Guerilla Open Access Manifesto."

12 Open Access, "Publicity," and Democratic Knowledge

John Holmwood

Barack Obama's stunning election victory in 2008 was the culmination of a campaign that was energized by social media networks, especially Facebook. Commentators hailed the new president's "virtual network of citizens."[1] As the 2016 presidential campaign began, it initially looked as if Bernie Sanders's bid for the Democratic nomination was following similar lines. However, as events unfolded it emerged that the impact of social media belonged to Donald Trump, to the "alt.Right" and a populist and nativist reaction against civil rights and equalities of opportunity.

In a short space of time, social media had moved from being a powerful means of social and political expression and democratic participation to something altogether darker. Whereas, in the first phase, communication on Facebook shared among "friends" was seen as extending networks of persuasion and influence, now "mining" of Facebook likes reveals psychological "traits" that could be targeted by well-funded political campaigns designed to get reluctant voters to the polls. "Authoritarian personalities," it seemed, could be directly addressed with messages that were specifically designed to offset their (relative) alienation from the political process.[2] Thus, a little known data analytics company, Cambridge Analytica, emerged as having provided a data base of "sympathizers" to the Trump campaign, as well as to the leave campaign for the British referendum on the European Union.[3]

Social media were no longer hailed simply as bringing about greater openness, but also manipulation. They were no longer a way of providing greater access to information necessary for informed decision-making but could also be a way of mobilizing "fake" information that could undermine expert knowledge. Everyone would be their own expert in a "post-truth" era. In fact, with everyone an expert, no one could be, and knowledge claims become reduced to expressions of "interests"—for example, those of "elites," or "ordinary people." "People like us" also became a rallying call, one which has recently received academic respectability in arguments by Kaufmann and Goodhardt that "racial self-interest"—people like us—should not be understood as racism, even where it represents the voice of the (relatively) privileged and is directed against others.[4]

Some of these issues have been taken up by Steve Fuller in his recent book, *Post-Truth: Knowledge as a Power Game*.[5] The idea of post-truth (or perhaps, more correctly, of multiple—competing and irresolvable—truths) has been widely seen as a consequence of the post-modern turn associated with late capitalism.[6] Put very simply, Fuller endorses the idea of post-truth as the logical conclusion of the arguments of the sociology of science and its deconstruction of philosophical attempts at demarcation—reason from emotion, knowledge from belief, and so on. For him, there is little to be gained from lamenting the situation and everything to be gained from joining the game. Post-truth, for Fuller, is nothing less than a consequence of the "democratization" of knowledge, especially in the context of social media and the internet where information and counterinformation is readily available. Fuller describes the new game in terms taken from Vilfredo Pareto's theory of the circulation of elites, where "establishment lions" represent organized power, patronage, and conformity, which is disrupted from time to time by "innovator/ speculator foxes." Professional organizations, journals, peer review, PhDs, doctoral programs, and so forth, are how a "monopoly" on knowledge claims is maintained and reproduced. The academy needs to get with the new game.

In this short chapter, I want to address these issues through an indirect route, albeit with the UK—more properly, England—and its universities as an exemplar of a new "knowledge regime" with potentially wider significance (depending on the extent to which its audit and other policies are diffused).[7] I don't think that the changing role of social media can be understood independently of changes in wider social structures of opinion formation and it is the latter that will be my focus. The problem, I will suggest, is less to do with how social media function and much more to do with separate changes to the social structures of expertise associated with neoliberalism.[8] For example, "fake news" has an older sibling, "rumor," which had previously been argued to provide some positive sociological functions, generating solidarity in moments of great anxiety or uncertainty.[9] However, "rumor" was stabilized and neutralized by "trusted" sources, frequently

Open Access, "Publicity," and Democratic Knowledge 183

associated with major institutions like those of public broadcasting and universities.

What has changed, I will suggest, is less that social media operating in the context of wider neoliberal public policies have put those institutions under challenge, and more that neoliberal policies have undermined their social role. I will illustrate my argument in the case of universities. I will begin from their status as institutions of the public sphere, as developed by Habermas in his groundbreaking study of early bourgeois civil society. In his introduction, McCarthy describes the public sphere as, "a sphere between civil society and the state, in which critical public discussion of matters of general interest ... [came to be] ... institutionally guaranteed."[10] What is significant about this definition is that it stresses processes of opinion formation separately from mechanisms of political representation through institutions of the state. At the same time, it situates them between political representation and the other activities of members of society expressed through private associations, including the market exchanges of emerging capitalism. The public sphere, then, is distinct from both the market and the state. It is the space in which the university operates.[11]

As an institution of the public sphere, the university has multiple functions, giving rise to Clark Kerr's description of it as a "multiversity."[12] Among these functions is its service to what the North American sociologist Talcott Parsons called the "citizenship complex" of modern societies.[13] Whereas the university had previously served the reproduction of elite culture—that is, a restricted public sphere—Parsons suggested that this was changed by developments in wider society (what he called the societal community): "The principle of equality has broken through to a new level of pervasiveness and generality. A societal community as basically composed of equals seems to be the 'end of the line' in the long process of undermining the legitimacy of ... older, more particularistic ascriptive bases of membership."[14]

Parsons was conscious that the modern university resembled the modern corporation in terms of its scale. However, he rather neatly reversed the argument to suggest that it was the modern corporation that was becoming like the university in so far as "associational" (or collegial) modes of management followed from the separation of ownership from control. Managers were increasingly called upon to have a "political" role reconciling the different claims upon the organization, as a short-term orientation to profits was transcended.[15] In this way, management took on some of the characteristics of a profession, including being credentialized within university business schools. Parsons was writing before the neoliberal return to shareholder value as the governing principle of the corporation.

The university is also responsible for what Parsons calls the "cognitive complex" within modern societies; that is, the knowledge associated with an emergent knowledge society. However, that knowledge is at the service of the values that underpin the citizenship complex of the public sphere. While "professions" are the "outward" face of the knowledge society and its demand for specialized expertise, the university is increasingly the guarantor of the knowledge base of that expertise and its development through research. However, on this analysis, the professions do not represent a self-interest derived from their monopoly of warranted knowledge, but a public interest, organized under democratic values of a society of equals. In contrast, under neoliberalism, private interests aggregated through the market have become the definition of the public interest, while claims of public benefits realized through the public funding of higher education are represented as an ideological cover for the sectional interests of faculty (operating as a profession).

The characteristic of knowledge production in the modern university is that it should be produced through dialogue and collegiality, obeying norms of what Habermas calls communicative rationality.[16] Although the knowledge produced can be marketized through various kinds of application, the point is that it is, at its core, produced in a process unconstrained by the market or direct political power. To the extent that it is so constrained, then, its status as public knowledge is reduced to instrumental interests or political authority.

It is precisely the broader values of openness to criticism and revision that make universities and their academics particularly vulnerable to the claims of open access. The high cost of journal subscriptions and the limited access to university libraries, as much as the technical language of academic discourse, has served to restrict the extension of the ideals of communicative rationality. In this context, free open access represents a means of realizing those ideals, constituting the academy as a free, open-access, virtual library.

It is here that we can see the role of a different development of open access alongside private proprietary claims. In the UK, the driver of open access was less a democratic imperative than an economic imperative.[17] How might university research be made available to small and medium businesses? How might open access encourage academic researchers to commercialize their research through claims to intellectual property rights, claims made more imperative by open access to their findings?

In this way, the creation of a new academic commons as the completion of the democratic function of the university has faced a new enclosure movement. Thus, open data access provides a new possibility of data mixing and proprietary algorithms outside the public sphere. Indeed, as we shall see, it gives rise to the possibility of ceding the evaluation of public services to private data analytic companies. This arises in the context where commercial companies—for example, pharmaceutical firms—have been reluctant to commit to the publicity of data, especially those of negative outcomes associated with clinical trials.[18] The use of commercial data analytics can now also take place within the academy itself, where data analytics companies offer data for the performance management of staff. In this way, collegiality is transformed into hierarchical management, where data-tracking points of performance are automatically generated by the ordinary activities of academic publishing, downloading, and citing. The audit regime of big data becomes inescapable at the same time as it becomes available to managers.

The wider context is the application of neoliberal policies to all public services, including universities themselves. This can be illustrated in policies for English higher education. The Jarrett Report of 1985 first introduced managerial practices from the private sector through the recommendation that departments should be treated as devolved cost centers. However, the search for market proxies has become more accentuated since the Browne Review and the various White Papers that have set out a new regulatory framework.[19] In effect, the only functions that are recognized for universities are the development of human capital and the enhancement of economic growth.

With regard to the first, it was proposed that since students were the beneficiaries of higher education, they should pay for their degrees through fees (supported by income-contingent loans). At the same time, for-profit providers would be allowed access to students with loans and would be allowed the title of university. In this way, single function, teaching-only, for-profit providers were allowed to compete with multifunction universities, potentially undermining the viability of those other functions in the name of competitive efficiency.

As far as research is concerned, the Government introduced the "impact agenda," where all publicly funded research should show a direct benefit for identifiable users. Whereas the logic of the teaching reforms was that *the beneficiary should pay*, the logic of the impact agenda is the opposite. There should be no publicly funded research without a beneficiary, *but the beneficiary should not pay*. It might be argued that the taxpayer is the ultimate beneficiary of economic growth, but this would require the latter to be inclusive. Neoliberal public policies, in contrast, are associated with widening inequalities.[20]

The impact agenda, for example, recommends that research should be coproduced with beneficiaries.[21] In consequence, it proposes that research should be aligned with the interests of those beneficiaries and modified in order better to realize them. The intention of the impact agenda was to speed up the commercialization of research, or the time from idea to income. However, it does allow the beneficiaries to be noncommercial. In principle, this suggests that research might also be directed toward democratic ends, even where the democratic functions of universities are demoted. However, this misses the significance of wider changes to the public sphere.

Neoliberal policies have also encouraged public authorities to become commissioners of services rather than direct providers. The providers of public services are increasingly for-profit companies and charities. The latter, for their part, are also recommended to coprovide services together with for-profit companies. For example, academy schools are frequently set up as charities with back-office services provided by for-profit companies and consultancies. In this context, the putative "public good," or "social justice" focus of charities becomes attenuated, at just the moment that coproduction becomes a requirement of the impact agenda.

Michael Barber (member of the Browne Review,[22] former chief education adviser at Pearson, and now designated head of the new regulatory body, the Office for Students) regards these arrangements as following on from the disruptive effects of new technology, which are "unbundling" organizations.[23] This unbundling includes not only the separation of teaching from research within universities, but also the creation of new research bodies and private consultancies outside universities, all seeking access to public funding and all potential agents within the coproduction of research.

This changing nature of civil society is well expressed in a report for the National Coalition for Independent Action:

> the force of entering the welfare market, increasingly as bid candy, has had disastrous consequences for voluntary services and their ability to respond to community needs. The capitulation by many in the voluntary sector, including its national and local leadership bodies, to these government agendas has done

much damage to the ability of voluntary organisations to work with and represent the interests of individuals and communities under pressure. Privatisation and co-option into the market is driving down the conditions of staff working in voluntary services, diminishing their role in advocacy and jeopardising the safety of people using such services.[24]

In effect, the impact agenda requires academics to align their research with private interests, rather than a general public interest. For the most part, academics have acceded to the wider environment that has eroded academic freedom and nonutilitarian claims about the public value of research. For example, the UK Academy of Social Sciences sponsored a Campaign for the Social Sciences, which lobbied MPs at the time of the 2015 general election. However, the value of social science it promoted was its benefit to policymakers and commercial organizations seeking to understand different aspects of the public's resistance to their endeavors.[25] It will be recalled that this was an election in which the Conservative Party manifesto committed a Conservative government to holding a referendum on leaving the European Union, yet there was no mention of social science research facilitating public debate.

In Donald Trump's campaign for the presidency (and his conduct of office since) and the campaigns for the UK to leave the European Union, expertise was disparaged as self-interested and social media used to promote fake news, much to the dismay of many commentators; perhaps, especially, academics. Yet I have suggested that the attachment of expertise to interests has been a gradual process within the academy as neoliberal policies for higher education have been promoted. As Chris Newfield argues, the university has been privatized, where neoliberalism favors the market over professionalism, regarding the latter as a monopolistic producer interest.[26]

Yet acceding to a neoliberal project for universities—"putting the student-consumer at the heart of the system"—opens the university to a wider neoliberal project. The neoliberal preference for markets also involves the representation of professional organization as a monopolistic producer interest. This is precisely what Fuller sets out in the justification of post-truth. He calls post-truth a consequence of democratization, but he conflates self-determination within the market and democracy. We can understand the conflation by going back to an older sociological (pragmatist) understanding of democracy in terms of "publics" and discursive processes of decision-making. The wider project of neoliberalism is to displace publics with markets, and thus the displacement of democracy itself by the market.

Little wonder that a "hollowed out" public sphere is vulnerable to populism. And part of the hollowing out of the public sphere is the privatization of the public university. In the history of reflection on the nature of the university, the figure of Kant reigns large—the faculty of philosophy, for him, was emblematic of the university's relation to truth. Without irony, Fuller suggests that the emblem of the university in the age of post-truth is the business school, writing, "if any part of the university deserves to carry the torch for anti-expertism, it is business schools."[27]

It is associational relations of civil society that provide a defense against populism at the same time that neoliberalism requires populism as its supplement. Thus, Donald Trump promotes corporate interests in the name of populism; while in the UK, a hard neoliberal Brexit is promoted in the name of "taking back control." The problem at hand is not that of the potentially malign role of social media, but of a broken public sphere. I began this article with a brief discussion of David Goodhardt. He has coined the terms "somewhere" and "nowhere" to characterize a new political division between those rooted in place (and nation) and those who represent unrooted elite values.[28] This makes it difficult to understand how a populism grounded in the former can be made to serve corporate interests. However, his distinction echoes an older one put forward by the sociologist Alvin Gouldner, in order to understand the new "associational" corporation, that of "cosmopolitans" and "locals."[29] The former were those with professional expertise deriving from outside the corporation, while "locals" were those whose careers depended on the corporation. The latter were integrated with the hierarchy of the corporation and suspicious of the former. In this context, academics are the quintessential "cosmopolitans," but we are increasingly under pressure to be "locals" (acting to sustain our corporate "brand").

The new populist "localism" is one that subverts "cosmopolitanism." However, it is not "elites" that are its target but public values, including those of the university and its functions of critique. It is in the latter context that open access now functions to provide data for private companies providing managerial consultancy to a new polity run as an exercise in public relations.

Notes

1. Soumitra Dutta and Matthew Fraser, "Barack Obama and the Facebook Election," *US News & World Report*, November 19, 2008, https://www.usnews.com/opinion/articles/2008/11/19/barack-obama-and-the-facebook-election.

2. See Ronald F. Inglehart and Pippa Norris, "Trump, Brexit, and the Rise of Populism: Economic Have-Nots and Cultural Backlash," SSRN Scholarly Paper (Rochester, NY: Social Science Research Network, July 29, 2016), https://papers.ssrn.com/abstract=2818659.

3. See Hannes Grassegger and Mikael Krogerus, "The Data That Turned the World Upside Down," *Vice* (blog), January 28, 2017, https://www.vice.com/en_us/article/mg9vvn/how-our-likes-helped-trump-win. It was less the ideology of Brexit that inspired the Trump campaign than the techniques of campaigning. Differences in the use of Facebook by the Obama campaign and by Cambridge Analytica have been analysed by Manuela Tobias, "Comparing Facebook Data Use by Obama, Cambridge Analytica," PolitFact, March 22, 2018, https://www.politifact.com/truth-o-meter/statements/2018/mar/22/meghan-mccain/comparing-facebook-data-use-obama-cambridge-analyt/. The differences turn on the consent protocols, where the Obama campaign told potential subscribers what data and how their data would be used, whereas Cambridge Analytica did not.

4. See Eric Kaufmann, "'Racial Self-Interest' Is Not Racism," *Policy Exchange* (blog), 2017, https://policyexchange.org.uk/publication/racial-self-interest-is-not-racism/. For further discussion, see, John Holmwood, "Claiming Whiteness," *Ethnicities* 20, no. 1, 2020.

5. Steve Fuller, *Post-Truth: Knowledge as a Power Game* (New York: Anthem Press, 2018).

6. Fredric Jameson, *Postmodernism, or, The Cultural Logic of Late Capitalism* (London: Verso, 1991).

7. Higher education is a devolved responsibility in the UK and recent reforms to higher education have applied most comprehensively to England, although those associated with research are more wide-ranging.

8. For present purposes, neoliberalism will be defined as a political commitment to private property, markets, and deregulation. In this context, it represents a form of political ideology governing public policy. Its hegemonic role is consistent with criticisms of economists and their expertise.

9. Dan E. Miller, "Rumor: An Examination of Some Stereotypes," *Symbolic Interaction* 28, no. 4 (2005): 505–519, https://doi.org/10.1525/si.2005.28.4.505.

10. Thomas McCarthy, "Introduction," in *The Structural Transformation of the Public Sphere: An Inquiry into a Category of Bourgeois Society*, by Jürgen Habermas (Cambridge, MA: The MIT Press, 1989), xi.

11. For a detailed elaboration of these arguments, see John Holmwood, "The University, Democracy and the Public Sphere," *British Journal of Sociology of Education* 38, no. 7 (2017): 927–942, https://doi.org/10.1080/01425692.2016.1220286.

12. Clark Kerr, *The Uses of the University* (Cambridge, MA: Harvard University Press, 2001).

13. Talcott Parsons, *The System of Modern Societies*, Foundations of Modern Sociology Series (Englewood Cliffs, NJ: Prentice-Hall, 1971).

14. Parsons, *The System of Modern Societies*, 119.

15. Howard Brick, *Transcending Capitalism: Visions of a New Society in Modern American Thought* (Ithaca, NY: Cornell University Press, 2006).

16. Jürgen Habermas, *The Theory of Communicative Action*, trans. Thomas McCarthy, vol. 2. (Cambridge: Polity, 1987).

17. Working Group on Expanding Access to Published Research Findings ("Finch Group"), "Accessibility, Sustainability, Excellence: How to Expand Access to Research Publications."

18. See, for example, Vasee S. Moorthy et al., "Rationale for WHO's New Position Calling for Prompt Reporting and Public Disclosure of Interventional Clinical Trial Results," *PLOS Medicine* 12, no. 4 (2015): e1001819, https://doi.org/10.1371/journal.pmed.1001819.

19. See Edmund John Philip Browne, "Securing a Sustainable Future for Higher Education: An Independent Review of Higher Education Funding and Student Finance," Department for Business, Innovation and Skills, 2010, https://www.gov.uk/government/publications/the-browne-report-higher-education-funding-and-student-finance; Department for Business, Innovation and Skills, "Students at the Heart of the System.," 2011, https://assets.publishing.service.gov.uk/government/uploads/system/uploads/attachment_data/file/31384/11-944-higher-education-students-at-heart-of-system.pdf; Department for Business, Innovation and Skills, "Success as a Knowledge Economy: Teaching Excellence, Social Mobility and Student Choice," 2016, https://assets.publishing.service.gov.uk/government/uploads/system/uploads/attachment_data/file/523396/bis-16-265-success-as-a-knowledge-economy.pdf.

20. In its advocacy for inclusive growth, the Organisation for Economic Co-operation and Development (OECD), for example, argues that, "Inclusive growth is economic growth that creates opportunity for all segments of the population and distributes the dividends of increased prosperity, both in monetary and non-monetary terms, fairly across society. In many countries, people have not seen their incomes rise for years. The gap between rich and poor has widened, with those at the top capturing the 'lion's share' of growth." See OECD, "Inclusive Growth," accessed May 10, 2019, http://www.oecd.org/inclusive-growth/#inequality-puts-our-world-at-risk.

21. See Research Councils UK, "Pathways to Impact," n.d., http://www.rcuk.ac.uk/innovation/impacts/.

22. Alternatively known as the Independent Review of Higher Education Funding and Student Finance, chaired by Lord Browne of Madingley, the former chief executive of BP. This review considered and determined the future direction of higher education funding in England. See note 19.

23. Michael Barber, Katelyn Donnelly, and Saad Rizvi, "An Avalanche Is Coming: Higher Education and the Revolution Ahead" (Institute for Public Policy Research, 2013), https://s3.amazonaws.com/avalanche-assets/avalanche-is-coming_Mar2013_10432.pdf.

24. Penny Waterhouse, "Homes for Local Radical Action: The Position and Role of Local Umbrella Groups" (National Coalition for Independent Action, Inquiry into the Future of Voluntary Services, June 2014), 2, http://www.independentaction.net/wp-content/uploads/sites/8/2014/08/Role-of-local-umbrella-groups-final.pdf.

25. Campaign for Social Science, "The Business of People: The Significance of Social Science over the Next Decade" (SAGE, 2015), https://campaignforsocialscience.org.uk/businessofpeople/. Among its statements are, "Advancing and applying science depends on profits, policies, markets, organisations and attitudes" (from the executive summary); "The study of public values and attitudes is vital, too, especially when innovation prompts uncertainties and concerns, as with genetically modified crops or shale gas extraction" (page 6); and "without a better grasp of people, technological advances may be frustrated, or blocked, and fail to realise their potential" (page 5).

26. Christopher Newfield, *The Great Mistake: How We Wrecked Public Universities and How We Can Fix Them* (Baltimore, MD: Johns Hopkins University Press, 2016). For discussion of the parallels with the UK, see John Holmwood, "Inegalitarian Populism and the University: British Reflections on Newfield's *The Great Mistake: How We Wrecked Public Universities and How We Can Fix Them*," *British Journal of Sociology*, 69, no. 2 (2018).

27. Fuller, *Post-Truth*, 22.

28. David Goodhart, *The Road to Somewhere: The Populist Revolt and the Future of Politics* (London: Hurst & Company, 2017).

29. Alvin W. Gouldner, "Cosmopolitans and Locals: Toward an Analysis of Latent Social Roles," *Administrative Science Quarterly* 2, no. 3 (1957): 281, https://doi.org/10.2307/2391000.

IV Archives and Preservation

13   Libraries, Museums, and Archives as Speculative Knowledge Infrastructure

Bethany Nowviskie

Two basic tenets of Afrofuturism have shaped my understanding of digital libraries, archives, and museums as twenty-first-century knowledge infrastructure. The first is a question; the second, a set of twinned assertions. The alarming geopolitical and environmental inflection points at which we currently find ourselves demand—more clearly than ever—that we answer the *question* in the affirmative, and that we actively encode Afrofuturist *assertions* from the surface to the bones of our digital libraries: from the deep structures in which we store, deliver, protect, and preserve cultural and scientific data; to the ontologies and metadata systems through which we produce information and organize, rationalize, and seek to make it interoperable; to those platforms and interfaces for discovery, contemplation, analysis, and storytelling that must be forevermore inextricably algorithmic and humane—predicated on decisions, understandings, and ethical, empathetic engagement with communities understood both locally and "at scale": communities large and small; present, past, and yet to come. It is in this light that I present five spectra along which digital cultural heritage and open science platform-builders must more consciously and collaboratively design enabling knowledge infrastructure, if we mean to use information technology to meet present social challenges and future global and personal responsibilities.

A Question and Two Assertions

In a 1994 *Flame Wars* essay, cyberculture critic Mark Dery both coined the term "Afrofuturism" and posed a question at the heart of the speculative art, music, fiction, poetry, fashion, and design that meet in this rich and longstanding nexus of Black diasporic aesthetics and inquiry. The question is this: "Can a community whose past has been deliberately rubbed out, and whose energies have subsequently been consumed by the search for legible traces of its history, imagine possible futures?"[1] Afrofuturism's answer to the question has been a defiant yes, but victims and descendants of the transatlantic slave trade are not the only communities marginalized by archival absence and who have been subject—in our inherited systems of knowledge representation as well as in their digital manifestations and evolutions—to problems of structural misrepresentation, exploitation, thwarted agency, and neglect.

Our responsibility as stewards of sources and scholarship, and as designers of cultural heritage infrastructure that serves the broadest cause of social justice and the public good is not merely to address that first, daunting task (the provision of "legible traces" of the past through more broadly accessible special collections, archives, and archaeological, environmental, and genetic datasets) but to enable the independent production, by our varied and often marginalized constituencies, of community-driven, future-oriented *speculative collections*. By this I mean not merely visions for change and social uplift, as crucial as those may be, but also wholly new ontologies and epistemologies: inventive archival assemblages, structures, or re/presentations of human experience and understanding. Can new knowledge representation systems challenge Western, progressive, and neoliberal notions of time as an arrow and regularly ticking clock? Can they counter the limiting sense our digital library and museum interfaces too often give, of archives as incontrovertible evidence—the suggestion, reinforced by design, that the present state of human affairs is the inevitable and singularly logical result of the accumulated data of the past; that our repositories primarily look backward to flat facts, not forward to imaginative, generative, alternate futures or slantwise through branching, looping time?[2]

Two assertions by Afrofuturist thinkers may usefully direct our response to contemporary challenges and opportunities in digital library interface and systems design.[3] The first is jazz saxophonist Shabaka Hutchings's distillation of the core message of musician and performer Sun Ra: the deceptively simple idea that the fundamental marker of liberty is found in a people's ability to build knowledge infrastructure: "the fact that communities that have agency [are] able to form their own philosophical structures"—in other words, not just to receive and use information within epistemological bounds defined by those in authority (whether they be scholars and teachers, legislators and corporate overlords, or librarians and technologists), but instead actively to shape knowledge at its springs and on its surfaces, for purposes of safeguarding, discovery, delivery, argument, and understanding.[4] The second is theorist and artist Kodwo Eshun's conception of historical, archival, and archaeological sources—including intangible cultural heritage, such as language and song—as functional and generative, active technologies in themselves. Eshun understands the objects of cultural heritage not as static content, merely to be received, but as still-running code or tools that hum with potential. Our historical repositories contain active instruments and artefacts ripe for *scratchadelia*: traces of the past intended to be *used anew and transformed even as they are played back*—just as surely as a scratch artist makes productive dissonance from a phonograph record.[5]

How might Eshun's technological reframing of the longstanding historiographical concept of a "usable past," Hutchings's location of liberation and community agency in the capacity not merely to access information but to create independent philosophical infrastructure, and Dery's summation of the speculative goals of Afrofuturism become informing principles for the next generation of digital library, museum, and archives builders? What considerations must be taken up, if we mean to attempt an implementation of these ideas in the form of access, storage, and preservation mechanisms, ontologies and knowledge representation systems, and platforms for discovery, (counter)narrative, and display?

Five Spectra for Twenty-First-Century Knowledge Design

I offer here a nonexclusive list of questions and concerns for future-oriented and liberatory digital library design, figured as spectra along which responsible creators of user interfaces and open-access infrastructures might more consciously and actively position their work. In no case are the ends of a spectrum self-cancelling notions; in other words, we may usefully imagine malleable systems that open themselves to multiple, simultaneous applications and axial orientations. The most fruitful outcome of any design exercise considering digital knowledge spectra like these would be increased awareness of the implications of such concerns on individuals and communities: the possibilities they welcome and foreclose; the dangers they forestall and fail to see; their fundamental generosities and parsimony.

Enlightenment versus Afrofuturist Structurings

Popular and even scholarly imagination of library organizational schemes rests in an Enlightenment-era crystallization of singular, dominant understandings: the best that a rational society accepts and knows. It is no accident that we appeal to "authority files" in creating interoperable metadata and often find it simplest to conceive of and share information in stemmatic, parent-child relationships and tabular form. But new possibilities for locating intersections and melding of multiple taxonomies and inheritances—alternate logical systems and naming schemes—through approaches leveraging linked open data and topic modeling bring us closer than ever to enabling an Afrofuturist vision of actualized community agency in the formation of digital knowledge infrastructure. This is fundamental liberty that would reach its fullest expression in the creation of grassroots, independent, broadly accessible, machine-readable philosophical framings, beholden to no one. We might invest in such a thing. However, in an era of climate data denial, derogated scientific and scholarly expertise, rising white supremacy, and so-called fake news, as John Holmwood covers elsewhere in this volume, is it not also our responsibility to construct libraries that reflect and prop up those structures for knowledge sharing, truth-seeking, and enlightened liberalism that the academy has long evolved and optimized, namely the forms and methods of our sciences and disciplines?[6] If so, how can indigenous knowledge and resistant or subaltern premises also be made central to digital library design? How might we honor and elevate grassroots, marginalized viewpoints structurally, without providing platforms that simultaneously open themselves to political disinformation campaigns and to ideologies of violence and oppression?

Historico-Evidentiary versus Speculative Orientation

Similarly, prototyping exercises that address the basic *temporal* and *evidentiary* alignment of our libraries could help us produce improved discovery interfaces and richer platforms for argument, storytelling, and display. Present designs more often suggest the primacy of singular, retrospective and historical orientations, and too few afford users the opportunity to create and share multiple speculative or futurist arrangements and understandings. The fundamental questions are these: do our digital libraries present their contents as fact, or as fodder for interpretation? Do they adequately indicate gaps and absences, and allow for their exploration as a force? Do they allow us to look backwards *and* ahead?

To answer these questions in the form of prototype designs requires us to delve beyond the interface layer in digital knowledge infrastructure and into the fundamental nature of our archives. Wendy Duff and Verne Harris, in seeking a new basis for archival description, argue against positioning "archives and records within the numbing strictures of record keeping ... which posit 'the record' as cocooned in a timebound layering of meaning, and reduce description to the work of capturing and polishing the cocoon." Instead, they call for "a liberatory [descriptive] standard ... posit[ing] the record as always in the process of being made, the record opening out of the future. Such a standard would not seek to affirm the keeping of something already made ... [but rather] open-ended making and re-making."[7] In considering the orientation of our libraries toward digital objects as evidence, we should also heed Anne Gilliland and Michelle Caswell's call for increased attention to the "archival imaginary": those absent (perhaps missing, destroyed, merely theorized or wished-for) documents that traverse aporia and offer "counterbalances and sometimes resistance to dominant legal, bureaucratic, historical and forensic notions of evidence that ... fall short in explaining the capacity of records and archives" to move us. Designing for such imaginaries would counter "strands of archival theory and practice [that] maintain an un-reflexive preoccupation with the actual, the instantiated, the accessible and the deployable—that is, with records that have ... evidentiary capacity." How might "differing imagined trajectories of the future" emerge from records both present in and absent from the past?[8]

Assessment versus the Incommensurate

These questions lead us to the hyper-measured condition of contemporary digital libraries. Comprised of counting machines and situated in the neoliberal academy, how could our digital knowledge platforms and systems be otherwise? And indeed, thoughtfully designed and well-supported metrics can help us to refine those systems and suit them better to the people who must inhabit them. Their collection is also a necessary, pragmatic response to straightened circumstances. In the face of information abundance, increasing service demands, and limited financial and staffing capacity, assessment measures are instruments through which open-access advocates and cultural heritage professionals can make the case for resources and show where they are wisely applied.[9] Measurement is not going away. The challenge for systems and interface designers is to build in ways that enable *humane and ethical quantification* of behaviors and objects that are by nature deeply ambiguous and even ineffable. These include users' complex interactions with digital cultural data and those instantiations themselves: both digitized and born-digital information—records that are continually remediated as they are delivered or displayed. Both the (non-self-identical) objects of study in digital libraries and the experiences we wish to promote with/in them are fundamentally fungible, organic, fluid, and incommensurate, one with another.[10]

Transparency versus Surveillance

Patron records have emerged, through the latter half of the twentieth century and most sharply in the United States after the passage of the 2001 USA PATRIOT Act, as among the most closely guarded and assiduously expunged datasets librarians hold. So must twenty-first-century digital knowledge infrastructure design keep privacy concerns paramount.[11] Even as we come to understand technologies of sharing and surveillance as a single Janus-faced beast, it is our legal and ethical obligation to create mechanisms by which we can uphold core library values and protect users' rights to read, explore, and assemble information unobserved. Our designs must also respect individual and community agency in determining whether historical or contemporary cultural records should be open to access and display in the first place—ideally fostering and encouraging local intellectual control.[12] But an added challenge is to shield while also opening up—ensuring that digital library infrastructure can contribute to salutary watchdog and sunlight initiatives, meant to promote transparency, accountability, and openness in government and corporate archives—and while balancing cultural and individual rights to privacy against the commons and the public good. What interface designs can serve to make these deep structural decisions and commitments apparent?

Local versus Global Granularities

The fundamental paradox of the Anthropocene is that we must henceforth hold local unpredictability and planetary-scale inevitability simultaneously in mind—and come to understand humankind as both infinitesimally small and fragile, and as a grim, global prime mover.[13] How do our digital library systems help us to bridge that conceptual gap, so crucial to fashioning futures that use both scientific data and empathetic understanding to their fullest extent? We require design experimentation, at all levels of our open knowledge infrastructure, that addresses the relationship of big-data processing to small-data interpretation—that understands broad, systemic thinking and local application or inquiry as part of a unified endeavor, and that can help us identify trends even as we explicate edge cases and tell the stories of exceptional experience. Can our platforms for discovery more clearly link small narratives to massive datasets? Can we design tools that help users understand visualization not as an impartial algorithmic result but as a dialogic process, an act of interpretation (one of many possible acts) that will always, necessarily, be shaped by the unique course of its own creation?

* * *

These are only five among many possible vectors for design thinking that might more fully open twenty-first-century knowledge infrastructure to broader community ownership, richer scholarly application, and more creative, speculative ends. Conceptual frameworks that differ from Afrofuturism might usefully direct experimentation and prototyping in alternate ways. Indeed, the responsibilities of designers of digital libraries, museums, archives, and data repositories—like the sample spectra I present here—stretch out across a wide expanse, reaching backward into histories we have yet to tell and forward to each future we may craft.

Notes

1. Mark Dery, "Black to the Future: Interviews with Samuel R. Delany, Greg Tate, and Tricia Rose," in *Flame Wars: The Discourse of Cyberculture*, ed. Mark Dery (Durham, NC: Duke University Press, 1994), 180, https://doi.org/10.1215/9780822396765-010.

2. See Deborah A. Thomas, "Time and the Otherwise: Plantations, Garrisons and Being Human in the Caribbean," *Anthropological Theory* 16, no. 2–3 (2016): 177–200, https://doi.org/10.1177/1463499616636269; and the work of Rasheedah Phillips on Quantum Black Futurism (Rasheedah Phillips, "Future," in *Keywords for Radicals: The Contested Vocabulary of Late Capitalist Struggle*, ed. Kelly Fritsch, Clare O'Connor, and A. K. Thompson [Oakland, CA: AK Press, 2016], 167–174); and as described by Hyunjee Kim in "An Afrofuturist Community Center Targets Gentrification,"

Hyperallergic, June 23, 2016, https://hyperallergic.com/307013/an-afrofuturist-comm
unity-center-targets-gentrification/. These issues are taken up in more depth here:
Bethany Nowviskie, "Speculative Collections," *Bethany Nowviskie* (blog), October
27, 2016, http://nowviskie.org/2016/speculative-collections/; they are informed by
my own early design experimentation on the Temporal Modeling Project: Bethany
Nowviskie, "Speculative Computing: Instruments for Interpretive Scholarship" (PhD
diss., University of Virginia, 2004), http://search.lib.virginia.edu/catalog/7h149q13w;
and described in the "Temporal Modeling" section of Johanna Drucker and Bethany
Nowviskie, "Speculative Computing: Aesthetic Provocations in Humanities Computing," in *A Companion to Digital Humanities*, ed. Susan Schreibman, Ray Siemens, and
John Unsworth (Oxford: John Wiley & Sons, 2007), 431–447, https://doi.org/10.1002
/9780470999875.ch29.

3. Here and throughout, when I refer to "digital library" design, I mean to encompass fundamental design problems pertaining—despite their rich differences, readily acknowledged—to digital libraries, archives, museums and galleries, thematic
research collections, and open repositories of data and the products of scholarship.

4. Shabaka Hutchings, "Journey Through Jazz (an Interview by Stewart Smith),"
Red Bull Academy Music Daily, April 4, 2016, https://daily.redbullmusicacademy
.com/2016/04/shabaka-hutchings. Hutchings references Kodwo Eshun, Sun Ra, and
John Akomfrah's 1996 documentary "The Last Angel of History," all discussed here:
Bethany Nowviskie, "Everywhere, Every When," *Bethany Nowviskie* (blog), April 29,
2016, http://nowviskie.org/2016/everywhere-every-when/.

5. See Kodwo Eshun, "Further Considerations on Afrofuturism," *CR: The New Centennial Review* 3, no. 2 (2003): 287–302, https://doi.org/10.1353/ncr.2003.0021; and
Kodwo Eshun, *More Brilliant Than the Sun: Adventures in Sonic Fiction* (London: Quartet Books, 1998); Laurent Fintoni, "A Brief History of Scratching," *FACT Magazine:
Music News, New Music.* (blog), September 24, 2015, https://www.factmag.com/2015
/09/24/a-brief-history-of-scratching/.

6. On this subject, see Chad Wellmon, *Organizing Enlightenment: Information Overload and the Invention of the Modern Research University* (Baltimore, MD: Johns Hopkins University Press, 2015).

7. Wendy M. Duff and Verne Harris, "Stories and Names: Archival Description as
Narrating Records and Constructing Meanings," *Archival Science* 2, no. 3 (2002):
263–285, https://doi.org/10.1007/BF02435625.

8. Anne J. Gilliland and Michelle Caswell, "Records and Their Imaginaries: Imagining
the Impossible, Making Possible the Imagined," *Archival Science* 16, no. 1 (2016):
53–75, https://doi.org/10.1007/s10502-015-9259-z. See also Michelle Caswell, "Inventing New Archival Imaginaries: Theoretical Foundations for Identity-Based Community Archives," in *Identity Palimpsests: Archiving Ethnicity in the U.S. and Canada*, ed.
Dominique Daniel and Amalia S. Levi (Sacramento, CA: Litwin Books, 2014), 35–56.

9. Among grassroots initiatives in this sphere is the Digital Library Federation's Assessment Interest Group (the DLF-AIG), which includes a team focused on the "cultural assessment" of digital libraries and archives: Digital Library Federation, "Digital Library Assessment," *DLF* (blog), 2018, https://www.diglib.org/groups/assessment/.

10. See Jerome McGann, "Imagining What You Don't Know: The Theoretical Goals of The Rossetti Archive," Institute for Advanced Technology in the Humanities, University of Virginia, 1997, http://www2.iath.virginia.edu/jjm2f/old/chum.html; and Jerome McGann, "Marking Texts of Many Dimensions," in *A New Companion to Digital Humanities*, ed. Susan Schreibman, Ray Siemens, and John Unsworth (Oxford: John Wiley & Sons, 2015), 358–376, https://doi.org/10.1002/9781118680605.ch25.

11. Joan Starr, "Libraries and National Security: An Historical Review," *First Monday* 9, no. 12 (2004), https://doi.org/10.5210/fm.v9i12.1198.

12. An excellent example here is the work of Kimberly Christen on the Mukurtu CMS: Mukurtu, "About," accessed May 1, 2019, http://mukurtu.org/about/. See also her "Tribal Archives, Traditional Knowledge, and Local Contexts."

13. This is an idea I take up at greater length in "Digital Humanities in the Anthropocene," *Digital Scholarship in the Humanities* 30, no. suppl_1 (2015): i4–i15, https://doi.org/10.1093/llc/fqv015.

14 Preserving the Past for the Future: Whose Past? Everyone's Future

April M. Hathcock

History is important. Accurate, inclusive history is absolutely vital. In an era of "fake news" and "alternative facts," the importance of preserving and providing access to the scholarly record goes beyond a passing responsibility to preserve and maintain the status quo.[1] In fact, accurately preserving the past is an essential component of creating and disseminating scholarship, even in the "open" era. The creation of the scholarly record goes beyond documenting knowledge creation for the moment. It is a means of tracking the ways in which knowledge has been created and shared across generations.[2] Thus, natural questions when looking at the scholarly record for any group or time period are: *Whose record is documented here? What is present? What is missing? Where are there gaps in the knowledge record?* When only mainstream, dominant scholarship is prioritized and preserved, the record becomes skewed in such a way as to render invisible the important work being done by those at the margins.

It is crucial, however, for an empowered, informed citizenry that the scholarship of the past and present be preserved in an open and inclusive way. As librarian Rebecca Hankins notes, "Providing a population access to information and history that is inclusive, broad, and diverse gives a sense of agency to all citizens."[3] This work necessitates a two-pronged approach, looking both to secure a more inclusive view of knowledge creation from the past and to create a more inclusive survey of today's scholarship for the future. Adopting theory and methods from archivists, librarians, and other information professionals, we can address gaps in the scholarly record in a way that provides a more inclusive and accurate view of knowledge at any given moment in knowledge history. Thus, in identifying and filling the gaps in the records of our past and present, we can ensure that we are preserving material produced at the margins of society, begin to embrace scholarship more fully as an open, inclusive conversation, and in so doing, change our scholarly and cultural values for the better.

Preservation at the Margins

Any examination of the gaps in the scholarly record must begin with a conscientious and reflective examination of the ways in which the biases and oppressions of broader society become recreated in the dissemination and preservation of knowledge. As archivist Rodney G. S. Carter notes, these "archival silences" in the record are rooted in systems of power and oppression; those from the dominant perspective are more likely to be over-represented in the record, while those from the margins are relegated to the silent and forgotten annals of time.[4] Moreover, these silences of the past and present adversely affect the quality and completeness of scholarly work now and moving forward. For instance, archivist Kate Theimer notes, regarding the use of available text corpora for digital humanities scholars, that "the materials that have been digitized and marked-up serve as a kind of 'corpus' for this group of scholars. It is this corpus that is incomplete, and for the foreseeable future always will be."[5]

A concrete example of the ways in which archival silences affect current and future scholarship lies in the work of digital humanist Nicole Brown and her fellow researchers. In their research, applying the principles of Black feminist thought to digital humanities methodologies, Brown et al. discovered a marked discrepancy in the number of available texts relating to the Black experience and culture.[6] Specifically, of the more than 13 million texts housed in the HathiTrust corpora, fewer than 25,000 were classified under the subject heading "African American."[7] That's less than 0.002 percent of the texts in Hathi. Certainly, HathiTrust is widely recognized as a valuable source of scholarship and has done exceptional work in helping to preserve and make available the scholarly record. Nonetheless, this discrepancy makes clear that even within the realm of openness, systemic marginalization continues to play a significant role.

Another concrete example of archival silence in the scholarly record involves the work of archivist Rebecka Sheffield. In her research on archival documentation of lesbian, gay, bisexual, transgender, queer/questioning, intersex, asexual/aromantic, plus community (LGBTQIA+) history,

Sheffield describes the haphazard and serendipitous way in which early LGBTQIA+ history has been collected and preserved, and even that has been done almost exclusively by and among activist communities.[8] Sheffield notes that much of what is known about LGBTQIA+ history often begins with the Stonewall riots of 1969 because they constituted an event that was deemed of significant importance to the broader mainstream community.[9] However, LGBTQIA+ resistance to discrimination and struggle for liberation had existed long before that.

Sheffield discusses the importance of scholars and information professionals working conscientiously to help steward and preserve these stories that run the risk of being lost at the margins. Rather than referring to them as "untold" or "silent" histories, she adopts archivist Rabia Gibbs's term "unexplored histories" to refer to these materials as works that have full existence and importance, even if they have largely been ignored by mainstream scholarship.[10] Sheffield also highlights the importance of these histories being stewarded rather than owned or even necessarily collected by the mainstream. Citing cultural theorist Roderick Ferguson, she writes, "just because a university preserves unexplored history does not mean that it is ready to acknowledge or confront any of the structural inequalities that exist in order to create the conditions in which that history remains unexplored to begin with. Preservation of unexplored history cannot take place if systems of power are also preserved."[11]

The question thus remains: if structural inequalities create these archival silences and gaps in the scholarly record, then what can we do to prevent them going forward?

Scholarship as Open, Inclusive Conversation

One way to help ensure a more inclusive scholarly record, both from the past and within the present, is to approach scholarship as an open, inclusive conversation. The Association of College and Research Libraries has recently adopted "Scholarship as Conversation" as one of the foundational threshold concepts for information literacy in higher education. Librarians are encouraged to teach new researchers that the scholarly record is built through an iterative process and that so-called "experts understand that a given issue may be characterized by several competing perspectives as part of an ongoing conversation in which information users and creators come together and negotiate meaning."[12]

This may be the aspirational goal of those engaged in teaching information literacy, but it is far from the nature of traditional scholarship today. The traditional mode of scholarly communication—with a limited selection of materials on a limited selection of topics published by a limited selection of gatekeepers and housed behind paywalls accessible only to a limited selection of researchers and users—constitutes a closed conversation at best, an extended monologue at worst. It is not the "scholarship as conversation" that we envision when we talk aspirationally about the function of scholarly discourse. It is not discourse at all.

Pursuing openness and inclusion, however, allows for scholarship to take place as a real conversation—a conversation that is not only open in access but also open in scope of ideas and topics, and open in participation in terms of the voices represented, including those voices that are normally relegated to the margins. This type of open and inclusive scholarship demands that scholarly discourse be more than an echo chamber, in which the same articles and ideas are preserved and reused well into the future. Open and inclusive scholarship allows for previously silenced voices and discussions to be heard and for those discussions to be preserved for the future.

In a primary way, creating open and inclusive scholarship as conversation means opening up the research process beyond the realm of the final research output or product. In other words, going beyond the Western mode of knowledge creation that must always result in a written, published book or article, to different, decolonized ways of thinking and knowing; ways that involve collaboration, self-reflection, and slow, purposeful methodology and theorizing. In their article "For Slow Scholarship," geographers Alison Mountz et al.[13] provide an important reflection on slow, conversational scholarship that goes beyond the current "counting culture" of modern-day neoliberal research institutions. As Mountz et al. note, "overzealous production of research for audit damages the production of research that actually makes a difference."[14]

Another way to create a more open and inclusive scholarly record—thereby bringing marginalized voices into the conversation of scholarship—is by opening scholarly discourse up beyond the researcher. Open, inclusive scholarship necessitates disrupting the town-versus-gown divide and bringing voices from outside the ivory tower into scholarly discourse. Too often, nonacademics are seen as not being intellectuals and are not included in scholarly communication except as subjects of study.[15] With the principles of openness and inclusivity, it is possible to bring more marginalized voices from outside of academia into scholarly conversations and thereby benefit from their direct knowledge and experience. In this way, the conversation of scholarship can go beyond the researcher to incorporate and preserve the voices of the researched.

This focus on open, inclusive scholarly discourse ties closely with shifts in archival theory pushing for more "post-custodial" approaches to the collection and maintenance of research collections. As touched upon by István Rév in his chapter, archival scholars Ricardo Punzalan and Michelle Caswell describe this reinterpretation of archival concepts as a shift in the ways information professionals deal with the issue of provenance:

> [In the archival world], provenance has been recast as a dynamic concept that includes not only the initial creators of the records, who might be agents of a dominant colonial or oppressive institution, but more importantly the subjects of the records themselves, the archivists who processed those records, and the various instantiations of their interpretation and use by researchers.[16]

Thus, among information professionals, the conversation of scholarship surrounding primary source material is being opened to include not only the voices of the researcher, but the perspectives of the community creators and even the material curators. These additional voices are becoming more centered in scholarly discourse and being preserved to provide a more inclusive record for the future.

Empowering and Involving Marginalized Communities

One of the keys to preserving a more inclusive scholarly record for the future lies in empowering and involving marginalized communities in the creation and preservation of scholarship. This essentially involves broadening the spectrum of what is meant by "scholarship" to include decolonized ways of knowing and knowledge creation. Again, the work in the archival field is instructive here, as archivists such as Caswell, Alda Allina Megoni, and Noah Geraci demonstrate in their work on community archives as sites for "representational belonging."[17] Too often, as has been seen, the intellectual work from marginalized communities remains in the margins and becomes relegated to the forgotten discard heaps of the scholarly record. However, by empowering these communities to respond "to being symbolically annihilated by mainstream repositories" by developing "independent, identity-based community archives [and knowledge collections]," they can preserve their own voices to be heard throughout future generations of scholars.[18]

A number of groups have begun facilitating this kind of representational work by putting the power of the researcher into the hands of the traditionally researched. For example, the content management system Mukurtu and its partner project Local Contexts provide infrastructure for indigenous communities to collaborate with local cultural institutions to digitally preserve and share their cultural and intellectual heritage in ways that are meaningful for their unique communities.[19] Mukurtu provides the online platform for the preservation and sharing of indigenous cultural and intellectual materials, and Local Contexts, a digital licensing and labeling process for traditional knowledge, allows communities to protect their intellectual property and restrict access to their materials in ways appropriate to their cultural norms.[20] Rather than leaving indigenous heritage to be lost to future community members or scholars, or worse, allowing that heritage to be exploited by colonizing institutions for research by outsiders, Mukurtu and Local Contexts provide power and agency to indigenous communities wishing to preserve and share the objects of their knowledge creation.

Another effort in this vein is Documenting the Now, a community-based platform for collecting, using, and preserving born-digital social media content.[21] Developed in the wake of the #BlackLivesMatter movement, which arose following the police killings of unarmed Black people throughout the United States, Documenting the Now couples a user-friendly interface with strong ethical standards for documenting community reactions to such tragic historical events.[22] The intention of the platform and its community is simple: to provide a counternarrative to the official government, police, and media reports of tragic events happening in marginalized neighborhoods across the US and around the world. By placing the power for developing, sharing, and preserving their narratives in the hands of the members of the community, these marginalized voices can ensure that their ways of knowing and seeing the world do not become silenced.

Changing Values

Through efforts like Documenting the Now, Mukurtu, and Local Contexts, the scholarly record is beginning to expand to include more marginalized perspectives and sources of knowledge creation. This work helps to ensure that efforts to preserve the past for the future involve preserving *everyone's* past for *everyone's* future. However, it is not enough. In order truly to ensure a more complete and inclusive scholarly record, we must change our scholarly criteria for determining what is of value for creating, sharing, and preserving in the realm of knowledge creation. Nonetheless, it is important to note, these preservation decisions are made not only on the basis of intellectual value but also on the basis of economic value.[23] The preservation of material culture, including scholarly works, requires funding and human labor—finite resources that will only ever be spent on that which meets certain criteria for priority. Essentially, that which is valued is that which is preserved, so we must critically examine our values if we wish to make meaningful change to the ways we preserve the past and present for the future.

A critical step in transforming scholarly values lies in diversifying those who serve as gatekeepers to knowledge creation and sharing. It is important to incorporate more diverse voices to break out of the current echo chamber of scholarship. We need more diverse perspectives among scholars doing the actual labor of research and writing; we need more diverse perspectives among reviewers who determine what scholarship is worthy of publication and what is not; we need more diverse perspectives among publishers packaging this research and making it available; and finally we need more diverse perspectives among librarians who are organizing and curating this material and making it discoverable to researchers. As librarian Charlotte Roh notes, we need "to push back against these biased systems and support publications that might not otherwise have a voice."[24] Likewise, Mountz et al. provide crucial advice:

> We should take time to seek out unfamiliar names that may be attached to high quality, original work, names we do not recognize because they have been mapped as marginal to the field by gendered, racialized, classed, heteronormative, and ableist power relations. We can recognize the value of collective authorship, mentorship, collaboration, community building, and activist work in the germination and sharing of ideas.[25]

As we work to preserve the past and present for the future, we need to do so with an intentional aim toward creating a more inclusive record of knowledge creation using a more inclusive method of knowledge sharing and preservation. We must, as librarian Melissa Adler encourages, "bear in mind that the power to establish ... what counts as knowledge operates through reiteration and citation, but also through exclusion. In fact, power relies on the things it excludes, producing absences and silences through acts of refusal, concealment, exclusion, or restriction."[26] To preserve a true vision of our scholarly past for the future, we must challenge our current values and power structures and work to ensure that all voices are heard throughout the ages.

Notes

1. Grace Githaiga, "Fake News: A Threat to Digital Inclusion," *Media Development* 65, no. 1 (2019): 35–38. For more on this, see also John Holmwood's chapter in this volume. Eric Bradner, "Conway: Trump White House Offered 'Alternative Facts' on Crowd Size," CNN, January 23, 2017, https://www.cnn.com/2017/01/22/politics/kellyanne-conway-alternative-facts/index.html.

2. Historian Anthony Grafton describes it thus: "No apparatus can prevent all mistakes or eliminate all disagreements. … Nonetheless, the culturally contingent and eminently fallible footnote offers the only guarantee we have that statements about the past derive from identifiable sources." Anthony Grafton, *The Footnote: A Curious History* (Cambridge, MA: Harvard University Press, 1999). I would further argue that careful attention must be paid to *what* is preserved in order to furnish a broad range of "identifiable sources," comprising multiple and differing voices and perspectives.

3. Rebecca Hankins, "Racial Realism: An African American Muslim Woman in the Field," in *Where Are All the Librarians of Color? The Experiences of People of Color in Academia*, ed. Rebecca Hankins and Miguel Juárez (Sacramento, CA: Library Juice Press, 2015), 212, http://hdl.handle.net/1969.1/156069.

4. Rodney G. S. Carter, "Of Things Said and Unsaid: Power, Archival Silences, and Power in Silence," *Archivaria* 61 (2006): 217–218.

5. Kate Theimer, "Two Meanings of 'Archival Silences' and Their Implications," *ArchivesNext* (blog), March 27, 2012.

6. Nicole M. Brown et al., "Mechanized Margin to Digitized Center: Black Feminism's Contributions to Combatting Erasure within the Digital Humanities," *International Journal of Humanities and Arts Computing* 10, no. 1 (2016): 110–125, https://doi.org/10.3366/ijhac.2016.0163.

7. Brown et al., "Mechanized Margin to Digitized Center."

8. Rebecka T. Sheffield, "More than Acid-Free Folders: Extending the Concept of Preservation to Include the Stewardship of Unexplored Histories," *Library Trends* 64, no. 3 (2016): 574–575, https://doi.org/10.1353/lib.2016.0001.

9. The Stonewall riots took place over two days in June 1969 when NYC police attempted to "take over" Stonewall Inn, a gay bar in Greenwich Village. Bar patrons overpowered the police and resisted their attempts at violent abuse of power.

10. Sheffield, "More than Acid-Free Folders," 573–574; Rabia Gibbs, "The Heart of the Matter: The Developmental History of African American Archives," *The American Archivist* 75, no. 1 (2012): 196, https://doi.org/10.17723/aarc.75.1.n1612w0214242080.

11. Sheffield, "More than Acid-Free Folders," 580; Roderick A. Ferguson, *The Reorder of Things: The University and Its Pedagogies of Minority Difference*, Difference Incorporated (Minneapolis: University of Minnesota Press, 2012).

12. Association of College & Research Libraries (ACRL), "Scholarship as Conversation," Text, Framework for Information Literacy for Higher Education, February 9, 2015, http://www.ala.org/acrl/standards/ilframework#conversation.

13. Alison Mountz et al., "For Slow Scholarship: A Feminist Politics of Resistance through Collective Action in the Neoliberal University," *ACME: An International E-Journal for Critical Geographies* 14, no. 4 (2015): 1244.

14. Mountz et al., "For Slow Scholarship," 1241.

15. Philosopher Paolo Virno refers to the concept of "mass intellectuality," based on the Marxist ideas of knowledge as labor, and distinguishes between this and a "labour aristocracy" centered on "scientific erudition," Joss Winn, "Mass Intellectuality," *Josswinn.Org* (blog), June 4, 2014, https://josswinn.org/2014/06/04/mass-intellectuality/; See also Joss Winn and Richard Hall, eds., *Mass Intellectuality and Democratic Leadership in Higher Education* (London: Bloomsbury, 2017).

16. Ricardo L. Punzalan and Michelle Caswell, "Critical Directions for Archival Approaches to Social Justice," *The Library Quarterly* 86, no. 1 (2016): 29, https://doi.org/10.1086/684145.

17. Michelle Caswell, Alda Allina Migoni, and Noah Geraci, "Representation, Symbolic Annihilation, and the Emotional Potentials of Community Archives" (Gender and Sexuality in Information Science Symposium, Simon Fraser University, Vancouver, BC, 2016).

18. Caswell, Migoni, and Geraci, "Representation."

19. Mukurtu, "About"; Local Contexts, "About," accessed May 1, 2019, http://localcontexts.org/about/.

20. Mukurtu, "About"; Local Contexts, "About."

21. DocNow, "About," Documenting the Now, accessed May 1, 2019, https://www.docnow.io/.

22. DocNow, https://www.docnow.io/.

23. James Currall and Peter McKinney, "Investing in Value: A Perspective on Digital Preservation," *D-Lib Magazine* 12, no. 4 (2006), https://doi.org/10.1045/april2006-mckinney.

24. Charlotte Roh, "Library Publishing and Diversity Values: Changing Scholarly Publishing through Policy and Scholarly Communication Education," *College & Research Libraries News* 77, no. 2 (2016): 82–85, https://doi.org/10.5860/crln.77.2.9446.

25. Mountz et al., "For Slow Scholarship," 1250.

26. Melissa Adler, "Classification along the Color Line: Excavating Racism in the Stacks," *Journal of Critical Library and Information Studies* 1, no. 1 (2017): 24, https://doi.org/10.24242/jclis.v1i1.17.

15 Is There a Text in These Data? The Digital Humanities and Preserving the Evidence

Dorothea Salo

The "digital humanities" umbrella shelters scholars curious about novel computer-mediated analysands—software, computer games, works of digital art and literature, social media, online-only forms such as the video supercut, and so forth—as well as scholars applying computational analysis methods to text, image, sound, and video corpora both small and unimaginably large.[1] Nearly all of these scholars discover that fitting their work and its associated evidence into the humanities' present print-centered scholarly communication system—is there a readable, reviewable, (print-)publishable, citable, immutable, preservable *text* in these data?—carries serious challenges. Until the humanities consciously break the hegemony and path dependency of print, digital humanists will remain alienated from the rest of the humanities, preventing the humanities from adopting open processes such as data sharing and open-access publishing. In turn, this harms the reach and sustainability of the humanities as a whole.

How Digital Humanities Changes Humanities Evidence and Its Stewardship

Humanist scholarship relies on a reliable past of carefully preserved cultural materials, reluctant though humanists often are to acknowledge those who do preservation work.[2] Accumulating evidence (not to say "research data," as many humanists find that phrase unintelligible with respect to their own work) is a key task of humanist inquiry, obligatory for responsible publication, since humanist scholarly communication assumes that a scholar may at any time reexamine the evidence adduced by an earlier scholar. Moreover, in recent years many disciplines have strategically embraced data sharing and open data not only to advance work in the field, but to explain the field to external agents and even to bring such actors into the disciplinary space, as with various "citizen science" initiatives such as Galaxy Zoo. As István Rév notes elsewhere in this volume, obviously evidence cannot always persist or be open to all; wars destroy art; performances not recorded are lost to time; archives contain much sensitive material inappropriate for public dissemination. Yet much analogue evidence is so straightforward to adduce, and so many analogue analysis techniques are wholly contained within the skull of the humanist scholar, that the assumption that past evidence must be available to future scholars tends to go unnoticed.

Digital-humanist modes of research such as the various forms of corpus analysis, however, add significant complexity to the adducing of evidence:[3] What is the corpus? When and how was it collected? What does (and doesn't) it contain? How has it been processed, both prior to and during the research? Should the corpus change or disappear, or the analysis tools become unusable due to technological change, subsequent scholars may reasonably suspect analysis error, bugs in analysis software, or (most troublingly) actual skullduggery to "prove" a point, and those scholars may therefore find themselves wholly unable to check or build on prior scholars' work, a significant hindrance to progress in humanities knowledge.[4]

Unfortunately, digital objects and digital tools are notoriously prone to change or disappearance without warning or trace; this has already been noticed as a scholarly communication problem in the guise of "reference rot."[5] Some digital humanists are fortunate enough to conduct research on digital objects already under responsible stewardship, such as collections of digitized materials or born-digital art from well-run libraries, archives, and museums. For other digital humanists, though, particularly though not exclusively those who build or curate their own digital artefact collections, data disappearance is a daily reality in the absence of significant preservation effort.[6] The World Wide Web, for example, is one object of humanist study, social media another; both resemble Heraclitus's ever-changing river, with the added drawbacks of extreme growth and rapid decay.

Addressing one too-common shibboleth immediately: caring for digital materials, known as "digital preservation" to its practitioners, is not as impossible as it is sometimes portrayed by people who have never done it.[7] Most born-digital and digitized cultural objects are indeed preservable, given appropriate forethought, infrastructure, staff, budget, and a favorable legal situation—not coincidentally, the identical prerequisites necessary for preservation of analogue cultural objects. Most digital preservation problems, then, are not strictly technological problems, but organizational priority, local infrastructure, and funding problems.[8] One additional vital question not to be ignored, of course, is when digital objects worthy of study can be preserved without doing violence to their creators; scholars of social media, for example, must ethically consider the social vulnerability of many contributors when deciding whether and how to preserve and make accessible collected postings.[9]

A related shibboleth does have considerable truth to it: digital objects and collections thereof rarely reach a clear point of completion or immutability.[10] Print publication, in contrast, is predicated on completion; even revision and reissuance of books are easy to conceive as discrete, bounded projects in time and materials. Print publishers' self-concept and workflows therefore do not easily fit digital-object collection and refinement practices that may never actually end.[11]

Providing open access to preserved materials relevant to humanities research adds additional considerations, often complex and difficult ones. Copyright, of course, looms large, as digitization and digital preservation inherently require making copies. The often-noted cultural abyss into which much twentieth-century culture has fallen owes its existence to unwillingness to incur copyright liability.[12] As April M. Hathcock notes in her chapter, cultural appropriation and colonialism may also block access, as members of the originating cultures object to artefacts of their cultural practices and memories being exploited by outsiders.[13] A related issue with some online collections, from social media to digitized zines, is the unwanted extra attention, even exposure, that open access creates, as Rév also gestures towards.[14]

Print-centered monograph publishers, especially though not exclusively in the humanities, tend to have little internal capacity for digital preservation and zero intent to build any. (Contrast this with science journal publishers, many of which are beginning to consider the preservation and availability of data underlying published papers crucial to those papers' credibility. Science journal publishers also participate in electronic journal preservation networks such as (C)LOCKSS, Portico, and European national-library efforts.) Such monograph publishers have therefore essentially declared outside their purview the preservation of the digital scholarly evidence underlying the digital humanities texts they publish, likely because preservation of analogue evidence was never their problem and they have not come to grips with how digital methods and analysands change the landscape of humanities evidence. Those publishers who do consider digital preservation part of their operations (for example, those who participate in HighWire Press and similar operations) plan to preserve their own publications only, not the evidence on which those publications rest. Looking to these publishers for digital preservation capacity, then, seems ill-advised.

As for scholarly societies, while the Modern Language Association is taking cautious steps toward digital infrastructure (for example, the MLA's *Humanities Commons* effort, described more fully in Kathleen Fitzpatrick's chapter), which might eventually mean infrastructure for the preservation of digital humanities evidence, most humanities societies have adopted the same out-of-scope stance toward digital preservation as print monograph publishers.

What evidence preservation options remain, and how viable are they? Commercially available storage services such as Dropbox, even when humanists can afford them, are not an acceptable alternative for the long-term preservation of digital scholarship and scholarly evidence. They and the data they hold are vulnerable to buyouts, legal proceedings, poor technology and business management, and complete shutdowns; moreover, they operate on a fee-for-service basis, such that whenever the money stops coming in—as when a scholar retires or passes away—the data are destroyed.[15] One or two independent nonprofit organizations, such as the Internet Archive, operate reasonably trustworthy digital preservation infrastructure at substantial scale, but many humanists' collections of digital objects fall outside such organizations' missions and policies. Law can also be a formidable barrier to preserving and openly sharing twentieth- and twenty-first-century analysands; digital artefacts stored in the United States may be vulnerable to takedown demands under the Digital Millennium Copyright Act, and those stored in Europe that include living identifiable people may be vulnerable to takedown demands under a patchwork of European right-to-be-forgotten laws, 2018's General Data Protection Regulation not least.

Libraries, archives, and museums, major repositories of analogue humanist evidence, are very unevenly prepared and funded to take on the work of preserving digital evidence, leaving many digital humanists with nowhere to turn to preserve their evidence collections.[16] Preservation-related disparities among libraries particularly are of long standing due to historically uneven assignment of responsibility for preservation of analogue materials. For the most part, only academic libraries at research-intensive institutions consider long-term print preservation within their mission, for example.[17] Other academic libraries, outside whatever special collections they have, design and arrange their collections for immediate use and discard unused or outdated volumes accordingly—at dark of night if necessary, to avoid humanist faculty who appear to believe physical shelf space infinite and all printed codices of infinite value—without considering the larger scholarly record.[18] Public libraries may have small unique local history collections (often in the form of physical "vertical files"), but these typically represent the whole of their commitment to preservation.

This pattern of preservation capacity disparity only intensifies with respect to digital preservation, with the added wrinkle that even libraries at research-intensive institutions do not always consider digital preservation a priority,[19] often scared off from doing so by the immense scale of the human and financial investment required[20] or unable to overcome internal staff resistance.[21] The startlingly few research libraries and library consortia that have bravely waded in find that they "continue to struggle to find scalable approaches to offering open, shared, sustainable scholarly infrastructure," especially in "the data publishing and research data management space where institution-focused approaches to capturing and curating data may be hindering our ability to grow adoption by our researchers."[22] Worse yet, hardly any libraries in teaching-focused institutions have built the sort of flexible, large-capacity, scholar-centric preservation infrastructure and associated staff necessary to solve the problem of preserving and usefully presenting the broad variety of evidence their local digital humanists may collect.

Such services as are fairly commonly (though far from universally) available across academic libraries—institutional repositories, perhaps digitized local collections on a platform such as ContentDM or Omeka—occasionally work well enough, but they are technologically insufficient to present many humanists' evidence collections usefully, which (quite reasonably) discourages humanists from using them to help safeguard those collections.[23] Moreover, some libraries' policies around which content is acceptable to add to these platforms exclude digital humanists' evidence collections. Institutional repository software also tends to share with print publishers an unshakable but often-wrong notion of digital-object and digital-collection fixity and finality.

Central campus IT never has an adequate digital preservation solution, rarely if ever considering digital preservation part of its mission. The central problem is that digital preservation goes far beyond mere provisioning of digital *storage*, just as analogue conservation and preservation require far more than mere shelf space. Assessment, technical and descriptive metadata, access controls (that may change over time), file format management, geographic replication, intellectual property management, human subjects ethics, financial planning, organizational management, and disaster planning may all form part of a digital object's lifecycle.[24] IT departments that only understand storage and backup cannot be trusted with digital preservation on their own and must be approached about it with caution and clarity;[25] one need only examine the disappearance of digital records from two entire gubernatorial administrations in Maine to understand the dangers of uncritical trust.[26] Campus IT departments in particular commonly make three classic digital preservation errors: assuming that only tenured or tenure-track faculty (not graduate students, visitors, or adjuncts) have digital objects to preserve; considering storage and backup the whole of the problem (as Maine's IT department unfortunately did); and (like for-profit cloud-storage companies) deciding on perpetual-payment business models that discard digital objects as soon as money stops coming in to preserve them.[27]

In the presence of insufficient or even nonexistent support from the campus library and campus IT, then, digital humanists' challenge of securing digital preservation for the products they create and the evidence they collect often reduces to a problem of voice and numbers. Most institutions investing anything at all in the digital humanities have only one to a mere handful of digital humanists on the faculty. These paltry few face the Sisyphean task of successfully persuading their library, campus IT organization, and campus administrators to allocate significant money and staff toward digital preservation. Such an appeal typically only happens in the first place if digital humanists are already lucky enough to have access to basic computing and support, which is often not the case.[28] Digital humanists find themselves countered, not to say opposed, in their efforts to secure support and funding by a much greater number of faculty humanists not identifying with the digital humanities, who think of libraries only as print-book purveyors[29] and believe products of digital culture barely or not at all worth preserving,[30] parallel to historic reactions to the advent in the West of printed codices (as opposed to scribed manuscripts), photography, film, television, and comics/graphic novels.

The considerable up-front expense and effort involved in bootstrapping, never mind sustaining and growing, a digital preservation program only worsens digital humanists' persuasion challenge. Grant funding, project-based as it generally is, is not well suited to solving longer-term sustainability and infrastructural problems.[31] In fact, many grant-funded digital humanities projects wholly disappear not long after the grant money runs out.[32] The National Endowment for the Humanities' (NEH) Office of Digital Humanities has tried to create some digital preservation impetus by creating an analogue to the National Science Foundation's data management plan requirement for grant applications[33] but neither holds applicants to any plan quality standards nor assesses post-grant outcomes. Institutions and libraries not already implementing digital preservation infrastructure—which is nearly all of them—have to date ignored the NEH's provocation.

Whether humanists can preserve their collections of digital evidence for future scrutiny, then, depends neither on the intrinsic quality or usefulness of the collection nor on the eminence of the scholars or their research work, but on local campus priorities. Research institutions are much more likely to have appropriate technical and legal infrastructure, digital librarians, and archivists, and funding earmarked for preservation of locally grown digital materials than are teaching-focused institutions. Not even research institutions can universally be relied upon, however, and when they can, they focus exclusively on the work of their own local faculty. Efforts to redress these and similar disparities via collective infrastructure planning have thus far failed in the US, though Project Bamboo's dissolution at least taught some valuable lessons,[34] and several European countries and Australia have managed better. Until the patchwork, sparse availability of digital preservation capacity is addressed, however, the present text-bound scholarly communication system cannot guarantee digital humanists' ability to retrace their steps and to build on prior work—an ability taken for granted by other humanists due to the analogue preservation efforts of archives, museums, and research libraries.

How Humanities Publication Practices Enforce Text Hegemony

The present system of humanist scholarly communication relies on print monographs, mostly print journals, and their publishers. With the sometime exception of performing and visual artists, humanists publish *texts*, a form forced on them by publishers who publish little or nothing else, and tenure and promotion systems that value little or nothing else.[35] Unless and until this situation changes, the humanities not only do not but *cannot* welcome or support digital humanities scholars. Shutting down novel humanities methods as well as humanities study of digital analysands is no way to ensure a generative future for the humanities.

Not only do many humanists still insist on print publication of text, they insist that not just any print publisher will do, requiring publication through a highly circumscribed set of market-based actors: often though not always corporate, often though not always for-profit or required to recover some or all costs from sales.[36] Much though many humanities publishers such as university presses try to remain mission-driven, their mission alone cannot keep them in operation, especially as operational subsidies from institutions dry up;[37] they must have a steady flow of author manuscripts and sold books. This imperative, alongside near-unshakable humanist notions of prestige, creates a collective intellectual and process monopoly fenced in by copyright law and tenure and promotion systems.[38] What chance has digital dissemination of scholarship, much less open access, against a system so deeply entrenched? Yet without digital dissemination and open access, how do the humanities avoid writing themselves into a remote inaccessible powerless corner? Already, print runs for humanities monographs have sunk to the dozens from the thousands.[39]

Because of the insistence on print publication by humanities internal career processes, the *digital* humanities have been unable to step away from print; a handful of respected digital-only journals such as *Digital Humanities Quarterly* aside. Not a few tenure-track digital humanists shoulder the doubled research burden of writing a print monograph or a set of journal articles over and above their digital humanities research output solely because of books' and articles' intelligibility as research products to tenure and promotion committees.[40] Digital humanists' nontextual research products, which may be software code, digitized or born-digital artefact collections, websites, or novel analysis methods or workflows, are usually not even printable, if printable at all, without loss of function. Print publishers therefore rarely know what to do with these non-texts, save reject them outright or reduce them to clumsy approximations such as "case studies."

Unable or unwilling to expand their genre and form horizons, senior humanist scholars reproduce print's hegemony for future generations by demanding that their graduate students' dissertations adhere to print-friendly research projects and publishing modalities. In several humanities fields, the main question hanging over a dissertation is whether it can be "turned into a [print] book" on which to found a tenure-track academic career. This prevents digital humanities dissertators from choosing a digital form in which to present their research even when digital forms best suit the work.[41] Moreover, much dubiously sourced folklore claims a negative impact of open dissertation dissemination on future publishability;[42] many dissertation advisors, and even entire scholarly societies such as the American Historical Association, therefore advise dissertators against making their dissertations openly accessible.[43] This has slowed the adoption of open access not only in the humanities, but across academe altogether, as open dissemination of dissertations at several higher education institutions are delayed or even halted due to objections from humanists.[44]

It is hard to blame senior scholars for enforcing print hegemony, however, when those responsible for hiring, tenure, and promotion decisions in the humanities and at the institutional level freeze like deer in headlights when deprived of simplistic text-based achievement heuristics of the "publish one or two print monographs with reputable presses" ilk.[45] Both peer reviewers and tenure committees complain incessantly of inability to judge and value non-texts.[46] The Modern Language Association's (MLA) response, Guidelines for Evaluating Work in Digital Humanities and Digital Media, far from improving matters, is a stark demand that digital humanists make non-texts intelligible to colleagues still textually bound.[47] These guidelines explicitly invite evaluation committees to dump the work of intelligibility onto digital humanists, abandoning any responsibility to learn about digital humanities research and its products. For example, the first requirement listed for committees is to "delineate and communicate responsibility"— not the committees' own responsibility to learn to read and assess their digital-humanist colleagues' non-text forms, but the *digital humanists'* responsibility to shoehorn their work into some form intelligible to the committee. Moreover, committees must "engage qualified reviewers," a curious and dismaying admission that many humanists are unqualified to review non-text digital forms, presumably because humanities disciplines do not require that humanists learn to read or appreciate them. Digital humanists themselves must, per these guidelines, "ask about evaluation and support," which for textual forms is taken for granted. They must also "negotiate and document [their] role in the non-text product"—also taken for granted with print forms, despite the resulting lamentable erasure of print production labor[48]—and, in a remarkable example of text forcing its way back into the not wholly textual, "document and explain [their] work." Sometimes all this extra explanatory work accomplishes nothing, as a committee reallocates digital humanities work to "service" instead of research.[49]

Why is it invariably digital humanists' burden to explain their non-text research output, rather than their colleagues' responsibility to learn to understand it and the research modes that produce it? Surely a set of disciplines that (per the MLA's mission statement) "facilitates scholarly inquiry in and across periods, geographic sites, genres, languages, and disciplines in higher education that focus on communication, aesthetic production and reception, translation, and interpretation" should be better prepared to cope with more forms and media than print alone?

Conclusion

Publisher intransigence, library unpreparedness, and unshakable humanist allegiance to print forms of research communication distort scholarly communication systems in ways that disadvantage digital humanists and prevent migration to opener and likely more sustainable digital modes of publication and dissemination. This, in turn, isolates and disadvantages the humanities both within and outside the academy. Exactly how the humanities in general and the digital humanities specifically will break out of this untenable box remains unclear. Until they do, however, the monograph crisis will intensify, digital humanists will continue fleeing the academy for fairer, greener pastures, and the humanities will impoverish their own future.

Notes

1. My thanks to Martin Paul Eve for his interest in the idea behind this piece, to Margaret Smith for advice, and to the anonymous peer reviewers for their helpful suggestions and comments. Remaining errors and infelicities are of course mine.

2. Michelle Caswell, "'The Archive' Is Not an Archives: On Acknowledging the Intellectual Contributions of Archival Studies," *Reconstruction: Studies in Contemporary Culture* 16, no. 1 (2016), https://escholarship.org/uc/item/7bn4v1fk.

3. Alex H. Poole, "Now Is the Future Now? The Urgency of Digital Curation in the Digital Humanities," *Digital Humanities Quarterly* 7, no. 2 (2013).

4. For more on this, see Nan Z. Da, "The Computational Case against Computational Literary Studies," *Critical Inquiry* 45, no. 3 (2019): 601–639, https://doi.org/10.1086/702594.

5. Mia Massicotte and Kathleen Botter, "Reference Rot in the Repository: A Case Study of Electronic Theses and Dissertations (ETDs) in an Academic Library," *Information Technology and Libraries* 36, no. 1 (2017): 11–28, https://doi.org/10.6017/ital.v36i1.9598.

6. Trevor Muñoz and Allen Renear, "Issues in Humanities Data Curation" (Humanities Data Curation Summit, Palo Alto, CA, 2010), http://cirss.ischool.illinois.edu/paloalto/whitepaper/.

7. Such as Vinton Gray Cerf, "On Digital Preservation" (Heidelberg Laureate Forum, Heidelberg, 2013), https://www.heidelberg-laureate-forum.org/laureate/vinton-gray-cerf.html.

8. Blue Ribbon Task Force on Sustainable Digital Preservation and Access, "Sustaining the Digital Investment: Issues and Challenges of Economically Sustainable Digital Preservation," December 2008, http://brtf.sdsc.edu/biblio/BRTF_Interim_Report.pdf.

9. Steven Bingo, "Of Provenance and Privacy: Using Contextual Integrity to Define Third-Party Privacy," *The American Archivist* 74, no. 2 (2011): 506–521, https://doi.org/10.17723/aarc.74.2.55132839256116n4.

10. Matthew G. Kirschenbaum, "Done: Finishing Projects in the Digital Humanities," *Digital Humanities Quarterly* 3, no. 2 (2009), http://www.digitalhumanities.org/dhq/vol/3/2/000037/000037.html.

11. Trevor Muñoz, "Data Curation as Publishing for the Digital Humanities," *Journal of Digital Humanities* 2, no. 3 (2013), http://journalofdigitalhumanities.org/2-3/data-curation-as-publishing-for-the-digital-humanities/.

12. Julia Fallon and Pablo Uceda Gomez, "The Missing Decades: The 20th Century Black Hole in Europeana," Europeana Pro, November 13, 2015, https://pro.europeana.eu/post/the-missing-decades-the-20th-century-black-hole-in-europeana.

13. Amy E. Earhart, "Do We Trust the University? Digital Humanities Collaborations with Historically Exploited Cultural Communities," in *Bodies of Information: Intersectional Feminism and Digital Humanities*, ed. Elizabeth Losh and Jacqueline Wernimont (Minneapolis: University of Minnesota Press, 2018), 369–390.

14. Tara Robertson, "Not All Information Wants to Be Free: The Case Study of On Our Backs," in *Applying Library Values to Emerging Technology: Tips and Techniques for Advancing within Your Mission*, ed. Kelly Tilton and Peter Fernandez (Washington, DC: Association of College and Research Libraries, 2018), 225–239.

15. Jon Brodkin, "Kim Dotcom: Megaupload Data in Europe Wiped out by Hosting Company," Ars Technica, June 19, 2013, https://arstechnica.com/tech-policy/2013/06/kim-dotcom-megaupload-data-in-europe-wiped-out-by-hosting-company/.

16. Malina Thiede, "Preservation in Practice: A Survey of New York City Digital Humanities Researchers—In the Library with the Lead Pipe," *In the Library with the Lead Pipe* (blog), May 17, 2017, http://inthelibrarywiththeleadpipe.org/2017/preservation-in-practice-a-survey-of-new-york-city-digital-humanities-researchers/.

17. Deanna Marcum, "Due Diligence and Stewardship in a Time of Change and Uncertainty" (New York: Ithaka S+R, April 26, 2016), https://doi.org/10.18665/sr.278232.

18. Lizanne Payne, "Winning the Space Race," American Libraries Magazine, September 23, 2014, https://americanlibrariesmagazine.org/2014/09/23/winning-the-space-race/.

19. Gail McMillan, Matt Schultz, and Katherine Skinner, "Digital Preservation, SPEC Kit 325" (Association of Research Libraries, 2011), https://publications.arl.org/Digital-Preservation-SPEC-Kit-325/.

20. Jennifer Howard, "Born Digital, Projects Need Attention to Survive," *The Chronicle of Higher Education*, January 6, 2014, https://www.chronicle.com/article/Born-Digital-Projects-Need/143799.

21. Dorothea Salo, "How to Scuttle a Scholarly Communication Initiative," *Journal of Librarianship and Scholarly Communication* 1, no. 4 (2013), https://doi.org/10.7710/2162-3309.1075.

22. John Chodacki, "Community-Owned Data Publishing Infrastructure," *UC3: California Digital Library* (blog), October 24, 2018, https://uc3.cdlib.org/2018/10/24/community-owned-data-publishing-infrastructure/.

23. Dorothea Salo, "Innkeeper at the Roach Motel," *Library Trends* 57, no. 2 (2008): 98–123, https://doi.org/10.1353/lib.0.0031.

24. Alexander Ball, "Review of Data Management Lifecycle Models," February 13, 2012, https://researchportal.bath.ac.uk/en/publications/review-of-data-management-lifecycle-models.

25. Scott Prater, "How to Talk to IT about Digital Preservation," *Journal of Archival Organization* 14, no. 1–2 (2017): 90–101, https://doi.org/10.1080/15332748.2018.1528827.

26. Colin Woodward, "Huge Number of Maine Public Records Have Likely Been Destroyed," *Press Herald* (blog), December 30, 2018, https://www.pressherald.com/2018/12/30/huge-number-of-maine-public-records-have-likely-been-destroyed/.

27. See, for example, "Bucky Backup Archive" at https://it.wisc.edu/services/backup-bucky-backup/ which commits all these errors in addition to inappropriately pretending to be a genuine digital archive.

28. Janet Broughton and Gregory A. Jackson, "Bamboo Planning Project: An Arts and Humanities Planning Project to Develop Shared Technology Services for Research," January 16, 2008, https://wikihub.berkeley.edu/display/pbamboo/Proposals+to+the+Andrew+W+Mellon+Foundation.

29. Christine Wolff, Alisa Rod, and Roger Schonfeld, "Ithaka S+R US Faculty Survey 2015" (New York: Ithaka S+R, April 4, 2016), https://doi.org/10.18665/sr.277685.

30. Nicholson Baker, *Double Fold: Libraries and the Assault on Paper* (New York: Random House, 2002).

31. Miriam Posner, "Money and Time," *Miriam Posner's Blog*, March 13, 2016, http://miriamposner.com/blog/money-and-time/.

32. Broughton and Jackson, "Bamboo Planning Project"; Quinn Dombrowski, "What Ever Happened to Project Bamboo?," *Literary and Linguistic Computing* 29, no. 3 (2014): 326–339, https://doi.org/10.1093/llc/fqu026.

33. National Endowment for the Humanities, "Data Management Plans for NEH Office of Digital Humanities Proposals and Awards," 2017.

34. Dombrowski, "What Ever Happened to Project Bamboo?"

35. Stacy Konkiel, "Approaches to Creating 'Humane' Research Evaluation Metrics for the Humanities," *Insights: The UKSG Journal* 31 (2018), https://doi.org/10.1629/uksg.445.

36. Geoffrey Crossick, "Monographs and Open Access: A Report for the Higher Education Funding Council for England," Higher Education Funding Council for England, 2015, https://dera.ioe.ac.uk/21921/.

37. Roger C. Schonfeld, "A Taxonomy of University Presses Today," 2017, http://www.sr.ithaka.org/blog/a-taxonomy-of-university-presses-today/.

38. Donald A. Barclay, "Academic Print Books Are Dying: What's the Future?," *The Conversation* (blog), November 10, 2015, https://theconversation.com/academic-print-books-are-dying-whats-the-future-46248.

39. Carl Straumsheim, "Amid Declining Book Sales, University Presses Search for New Ways to Measure Success," Inside Higher Ed, August 1, 2016, https://www.insidehighered.com/news/2016/08/01/amid-declining-book-sales-university-presses-search-new-ways-measure-success; although Crossick, "Monographs and Open Access: A Report for the Higher Education Funding Council for England" comes to a different conclusion.

40. Sydni Dunn, "Digital Humanists: If You Want Tenure, Do Double the Work," Vitae, January 5, 2014, https://chroniclevitae.com/news/249-digital-humanists-if-you-want-tenure-do-double-the-work.

41. Denise Troll Covey, "Opening the Dissertation: Overcoming Cultural Calcification and Agoraphobia," *TripleC: Communication, Capitalism & Critique* 11, no. 2 (2013): 543–557, https://doi.org/10.31269/triplec.v11i2.522.

42. Jill Cirasella and Polly Thistlethwaite, "Open Access and the Graduate Author: A Dissertation Anxiety Manual," in *Open Access and the Future of Scholarly*

Communication: Policy and Infrastructure, ed. Kevin L. Smith and Katherine A. Dickson (Lanham, MD: Rowman & Littlefield, 2016), 203–224.

43. American Historical Association, "Statement on Policies Regarding the Embargoing of Completed History PhD Dissertations," Perspectives on History, July 22, 2013, https://www.historians.org/publications-and-directories/perspectives-on-history/summer-2013/american-historical-association-statement-on-policies-regarding-the-embargoing-of-completed-history-phd-dissertations.

44. Andrea L. Foster, "U. of Iowa Reverses New Policy That Would Have Made Nearly All Theses Freely Available Online," *The Chronicle of Higher Education*, March 18, 2008, https://www.chronicle.com/article/Students-Protect-Their-Novels/601.

45. Matthew McAdam, "Deans Care About Books," Infernal Machine, March 5, 2018, https://hedgehogreview.com/blog/infernal-machine/posts/deans-care-about-books.

46. For examples, see the cluster of articles in "Profession," MLA Journals, 2011, https://www.mlajournals.org/toc/prof/2011/1.

47. Modern Language Association of America, "Guidelines for Evaluating Work in Digital Humanities and Digital …," Modern Language Association, 2012, https://www.mla.org/About-Us/Governance/Committees/Committee-Listings/Professional-Issues/Committee-on-Information-Technology/Guidelines-for-Evaluating-Work-in-Digital-Humanities-and-Digital-Media.

48. Kathleen Fitzpatrick, *Planned Obsolescence: Publishing, Technology, and the Future of the Academy*, New York: New York University Press, 2011, 57–60.

49. Sean Takats, "A Digital Humanities Tenure Case, Part 2: Letters and Committees," *The Quintessence of Ham* (blog), February 7, 2013, http://quintessenceofham.org/2013/02/07/a-digital-humanities-tenure-case-part-2-letters-and-committees/.

16 Accessing the Past, or Should Archives Provide Open Access?

István Rév

The Archive, as we knew it for a long time, seemed to consist of static repositories based on a read-only paradigm.[1] Once documents were accessioned and processed, described and entered into finding aids, they were usually expected to remain dormant, except when read, consulted by the researcher. In recent decades the situation has changed: the Archive is now considered to be key to the understanding of an individual or a collective past, of future memory, of private and official secrets that provide explanations for either historical or quotidian—but nonetheless important— events.[2] Thus, archives became targets for openness, to shed light on the darkness of the depths of depositories, to reveal secrets, to gain access to the documents in custody of these solid, locked, dusty, unhealthy institutions. The public, instead of waiting for the researcher to find the relevant documents in the cellar, demanded immediate, free, digital access to all documents that are deemed important.

When, in December 2001, we invited a dozen or so scholars to a meeting— out of which came the Budapest Open Access Initiative (BOAI), one of the founding documents of the Open Access Movement—we were convinced that not only scholarly reports, the transactions of the learned societies, but also documents stored in the archives should become freely and openly accessible. In hindsight, it was a naïve and mistaken expectation.

* * *

Open and free access to documents is now conventionally understood as the right to have unimpeded access to documents with political, historical, or cultural significance for either the relevant community or the individual citizen concerned. The assumption is that the public has or should have the right to gain access to the information contained in documents that are produced with direct or indirect public funding, that are legally no longer constrained by acceptable national security and secrecy provisions, are free of intellectual property or copyright restrictions, and that do not disproportionately harm the privacy of specific, nameable corporations or private individuals. Open data initiatives, providing free access to public or nonsensitive information, are now treated as a natural part of the widening concept of basic human rights. On the basis of this interpretation of rights, secrecy provisions, intellectual property and copyright restrictions, and archival laws and rules began to be disputed and challenged.

As part of such efforts to achieve openness, access, and transparency, legislatures have been urged to pass freedom of information acts, to change archival laws, and to make publicly available historical documents (especially documents of recent reprehensible government actions or incriminating documents of overturned repressive regimes). The public, often in the wake of regime change, wants to know not only what has happened, but also the specific legally or morally unjustifiable acts of named individuals. The publics in Argentina, Chile, Columbia, South Africa, Germany, Poland, and Russia demanded openness and public access to documents of the overthrown regimes. Archival or legal concerns about privacy, the informational rights of either implicated individuals, or third parties—individuals whose names were recorded in the documents, but who did not play any incriminating role in the events described in the sources—were treated by the public mostly as alibis for keeping the shameful acts of the past locked up in the dark.

In the course of the first decades of the twenty-first century, the situation of archives and archival documents has, thus, radically changed. The assumption cannot be made any more that there is a clear, strictly definable distinction between public and private information. As a growing body of empirical research shows:

> The degree to which information is thought to be accessible does not drive judgments about the appropriateness of accessing that information. ... The immediate source of information matters to the perceived appropriateness of the data flows, even for information contained in public records. ... Considering the respondents' strong judgments about the appropriate uses of information, the term "public data" may be not only inaccurate, but also misleading. The term "public" is often conflated with "not private" thereby leading policy makers to believe that individuals have no privacy concerns or expectations around the access and use of these public records. However, our study suggests the opposite. The data

presented shows that individuals have deep concerns about who should have access to public records data and how it should be used.³

The relative value of information, its contextual meaning and sensitivity, are perceived differently in the open digital era and can have dramatically different consequences than under a previous information regime. The meaning, value, and significance of the documents in the care of the archive could undergo radical changes, depending on changes in the historical, political, and cultural context. For instance, until the dawn of the twenty-first century, one's gender was considered a nonsensitive item of public information, contained in every birth certificate. No longer: in a growing number of countries, individuals have the possibility and the right to choose their gender and to decide to keep that information (and identity) private or public. On the other hand, in some countries, one's sexual orientation, once a highly sensitive private item of information, has ceased to be a personal matter.

Around 1989, at the time of the political changes in Eastern and Central Europe, the archives of the former secret services were treated as depositories of denunciations, the repositories of lies, the material evidence of collaboration. Legislatures and archivists had to weigh the possible harm the accessibility of the obvious lies might cause to the individuals concerned, on the one hand, and the right of the public to get to know the real, until then secret, face of the previous regimes. In radical illiberal states, among them Russia, Poland, and Hungary, so called institutes of "remembrance and national memory," the official agents of historical revisionism, now use these records as reliable historical documents, giving credit to the allegations of the informers in order to denounce historical actors, former members of the democratic oppositions, and present adversaries. Sensitive documents, including medical records, information about past forcible psychiatric treatment (an often-used tool to isolate, lock up, and compromise the adversaries of the autocratic regimes) are now customarily made available to the public as information of genuine "public interest."

The change of the cultural milieu can lead to retroactive redescriptions of the past that, in turn, change the status of archival documents, and thus the way archivists and historians should handle them. Des Browne, the UK Secretary of State for Defence, announced in September 2006:

> The Government [plans] to seek parliamentary approval for a statutory pardon for service personnel executed for a range of disciplinary offences during the First World War. ... Although this is a difficult issue it is right to recognize the exceptional

circumstances that gave rise to these executions and to show compassion to the families who have had to live with the associated stigma over the years. ...

Rather than naming individuals, the amendment will pardon all those executed following conviction by court martial for a range of offences likely to have been strongly influenced by the stresses associated with this terrible war; this will include desertion, cowardice, mutiny and comparable offences committed during the period of hostilities from 4 August 1914 to 11 November 1918. Over 300 individuals from the UK, her dominions and colonies were executed under the 1881 Army Act. We will also seek pardons for those similarly executed under the provisions of the 1911 Indian Army Act. ...[4]

The philosopher Ian Hacking, when commenting on a draft of the bill, a decade before it was finally passed by the British Parliament, asserted that "the author of the private member's bill states that today the men would be judged to be suffering from post-traumatic stress disorder and to be in need of psychiatric help not execution."[5] The new bill changed the status of both the dead and also the documents related to them: for about ninety years they had been treated as traitors and/or deserters, the documents of their story as part of military history, including legal documents of court martial procedures. As the law redescribed them as sick persons, victims of post-traumatic shock syndrome, the related documents should be treated (at least in part) as medical records, sensitive medical information, and handled as such in the archive. Different jurisdictions treat protected health information differently, providing privacy protection even for the dead for a varying period, sometimes well beyond the 50 years mandated under the Health Insurance Portability and Accountability Act (HIPAA) Privacy Rule in the US.

As Hacking pointed out, the private member's bill had changed not only the status of the dead, but the status and perception of the surviving relatives, and the public at large. In the course of the Great War, court-martialed soldiers were described, treated, and stigmatized as traitors, and most probably the wider public saw them as such. Following the war, after the first literary reflections, such as Erich Maria Remarque's *All Quiet on the Western Front* (adapted to an Academy Award-winning film in 1930), Hemingway's *A Farewell to Arms* or Charles Yale Harrison's *Generals Die in Bed*, became available, the perception could have changed, and the executed soldiers might have turned into conscientious objectors, pacifists, who did the only thing one could expect of sane and courageous people. The law passed finally in 2006 in the British Parliament twisted the story one more time, and medicalized the conscientious objectors into sick individuals, who were not in

Accessing the Past, or Should Archives Provide Open Access?

charge of their fate, whom the surviving relatives could not remember with a certain pride, but in the best case, with melancholy compassion. This is an instance of retroactive intervention in the past.

In 2012 a historian was confronted with a similar problem, although from the opposite angle of the private member's bill. Sydney Halpern was conducting research on federally funded human hepatitis experiments that ran in the US between 1942 and 1972:

> In the process, she has turned up names of many experimental subjects. Halpern had no intention of naming the vast majority of them, especially the mentally disabled and prisoners since they are now considered vulnerable populations. ... Her problem was ... what to do with the conscientious objectors during World War II who freely agreed to participate in experiments on hepatitis as an option for alternative service: "The COs weren't just research subjects. They were also historical actors making a statement. They were speaking through their actions ... I think it's a mistake to apply a no-names convention without considering the situation of particular subjects. Leaving COs nameless robs them of a voice in the narrative—it silences them, and they wanted to be heard."[6]

* * *

In 2013, my archive, the Open Society Archives, one of the largest repositories of grave violations of human rights, received a letter from a Rwandan woman who was living in the US. Fearing deportation based on an archival description on our website, she demanded that her name be erased from the online finding aid. As part of our human-rights related film collection, our archive holds a copy of a short BBC documentary, *Rwanda, Master Conform*, directed by a British journalist, Lindsey Hilsum, who lived in Rwanda during the first weeks of the genocide.[7] She decided to return to Rwanda to investigate the fate of the people she once knew. The film features interviews with former acquaintances, some of them in an internment camp, among them a woman, who tells the reporter in French—subtitled in English—that she had been accused of having taken part in the genocide. The detailed archival description included both the names of the interviewees and a short summary of the interviews. The film was shown on the BBC. In the letter demanding the erasure of her name, the woman claimed that although she told the reporter that she had been accused of genocide, she was innocent, but now in danger of deportation from the US.

We knew that only a tiny minority of the perpetrators had been identified in Rwanda. We also knew that people with questionable pasts managed to receive entry visas to the US, among them another woman who had received permission to enter the US; but when it was discovered that the Rwanda Gacaca Courts had convicted her for human rights violations in absentia, the US authorities deported this second woman back to Kigali in November 2011. Still, after careful consideration, the Archive decided to remove this woman's name from the description because archives, although custodians of information about the past, are not legal authorities, and thus cannot—when describing documents—judge or implicate individuals.

This was an unusual case: it was the subject herself, answering a question from the filmmaker, who stated that she had been accused of genocide. As Judge Posner of the United States Court of Appeals for the Seventh Circuit stated in a ruling in 1993, it is not easy to "bury the past" by claiming invasion of privacy when information comes from the public record.[8]

According to the UK's Rehabilitation of Offenders Act (1974), some, mostly relatively minor, criminal convictions can be ignored after a defined rehabilitation period.[9] Serious crimes, though, punished with over four years in prison—even according to the 2014 amendment of the Act—cannot be considered "spent," and thus cannot be erased from the records.

This Rehabilitation of Offenders Act has been considered one of the precursors of the so-called and now-prevalent "right to be forgotten." From the early 2000s, activists of strict privacy protection have been arguing for the "right to be forgotten" to be treated as a basic human right. Advocates of free speech, on the other hand, have reason to fear that a broad interpretation of the right might lead to suppression of free speech and to a widening censorship of the internet. In 2014, the Court of Justice of the European Union decided in one of its rulings that "if, following a search made on the basis of a person's name, the list of results displays a link to a web page which contains information on the person in question, that data subject may approach the operator directly and, where the operator does not grant his request, bring the matter before the competent authorities in order to obtain, under certain conditions, the removal of that link from the list of results."[10] Although the ruling invoked respect for private and family life, besides the requirements of protecting personal data, the decision of the court was widely interpreted as upholding the right to be forgotten, even without explicit reference to this right.

Indeed, according to the General Data Protection Regulation (GDPR) adopted by the European Union (and enforced since May 25, 2018), "data subjects" have the right to request erasure of personal data related to them on certain defined grounds. The "right of erasure" is similar to but more limited than the right to be forgotten:

> Personal data must be erased immediately where ... the data subject has withdrawn his consent and there is no other legal ground for processing, the data subject has objected and there are no overriding legitimate grounds for the processing. ... The controller is therefore on the one hand automatically subject to statutory erasure obligations, and must, on the other hand, comply with the data subject's right to erasure. In addition, the right to be forgotten is found in Art. 17(2) of the GDPR.
>
> The right to be forgotten is not unreservedly guaranteed. It is limited especially when colliding with the right of freedom of expression and information. Other exceptions are if the processing of data which is subject to an erasure request is necessary to comply with legal obligations, for archiving purposes in the public interest, scientific or historical research purposes or statistical purposes or for the defence of legal claims.[11]

Between May 2014 (the ruling of the Court of Justice in a case against Google) and March 2019, Google received more than 3 million erasure requests, and decided to remove 780,265 search results from its search engine.[12]

Based on the precedent established by the 2014 ruling of the Court of Justice of the European Union, a case is now pending in front of the Court in Luxembourg. In this case, the French data regulator is seeking to extend the right of state authorities to request so-called data controllers, such as Google, to erase information deemed unacceptable for state authorities. Extending the applicability and interpretation of the 2014 ruling, so as to include state actors, might have far-reaching consequences for freedom of information. Thomas Hughes, the executive director of Article 19, an NGO that monitors free speech, claimed that

> This case could see the right to be forgotten threatening global free speech. European data regulators should not be allowed to decide what internet users around the world find when they use a search engine. The [court] must limit the scope of the right to be forgotten in order to protect the right of internet users around the world to access information online. ... If European regulators can tell Google to remove all references to a website, then it will be only a matter of time before countries like China, Russia and Saudi Arabia start to do the same. The [ECJ] should protect freedom of expression, not set a global precedent for censorship.[13]

* * *

The GDPR contains provisions related to archives, and provides certain exemptions and derogations in cases of personal data processed for archiving purposes.[14] Still, as far their freely and globally available digitized documents are concerned, archives should be considered data controllers, for according to the definition of "data controller" under Article 4 of the Regulation: "controller means the natural or legal person, public authority, agency or other body which, alone or jointly with others, determines the purposes and means of the processing of personal data."[15]

Archives exist not only for collecting, storing, and preserving documents but also in order to make the documents available, retrievable, and usable for all those who—for whatever reason—decide to study, consult or scrutinize the documents deposited in the archive. Archives should thus provide retrievable access to the documents they keep. However, the way the documents can be accessed makes an important difference of type, rather than just of degree. Electronic copies of documents accessible on the website of the archive become available without control to the public at large, for anyone, without the mediation of a known (re)searcher, who could and should bear ethical and moral—not just legal—responsibility for the way personal data are made public in (print or electronic) publication. While it is in the public interest that (historically, socially, economically, legally, and so forth) relevant information—even that containing named, identifiable individuals—should become available, it is also in the public interest that archives should retain their status as trusted institutions.

Trust depends not only on the respect *des fonds*, the guarded and provable authenticity and integrity of the documents in the archival collection, but on the demonstrated care with which the archive also handles sensitive personal information. Records of the same provenance should not be mixed with documents of a different provenance, since without the context in which records were created, the original intention or meaning of the records would, supposedly, be lost. As Anne J. Gilliland-Swetland puts it: "the principle of provenance has two components: records of the same provenance should not be mixed with those of a different provenance, and the archivist should maintain the original order in which the records were created and kept. The latter is referred to as the principle of original order."[16] Trust springs from the assumption that the archive preserves the authentic documents, guarding their integrity, and would not "deaccession" or destroy them. It comes from an understanding that the archive makes such items retrievable but would not mishandle sensitive personal information either; that it would handle them in a legally and ethically foreseeable way.

In the spirit of its responsibility to the public, the Archive should make the documents, unrestricted by the donor, but containing sensitive personal information related to third parties and nonpublic figures, available on their premises, while exercising great care and discretion when making personal information openly and freely available on its websites. Archives are expected to engage in a never-ending balancing act between their responsibility to the public, which has the right to know, and to private individuals, who have the right to be protected.

My archive has two large Russian collections that demonstrate this dilemma: the so-called Red Archive of official reports by Soviet party and government sources, and the "Samizdat Archive," containing unofficial, underground documents produced by generations of anti-Soviet opposition. Documents in the "Red Archive" mention the name of a Russian psychiatrist, who, in the official sources "having betrayed his country," defected from the Soviet Union in order to live in the West. The name of the same person surfaced in samizdat publications, as one of those who had been engaged in the forcible psychiatric treatment of members of the opposition, and who having arrived in London as a self-styled critic of Soviet psychiatry, was offered a position at the famous Tavistock Clinic.

As it is the obligation of the Archive to preserve the integrity of the documents, it is unimaginable to redact the name in either of the collections. Whenever a researcher wants to consult one or both sources, the archive does not anonymize the documents. Being neither able nor inclined to judge the authenticity of the claim in any of the documents, the Archive does not and should not take a stand in the truthfulness of the sources.

Indeed, since we are the custodians of one of the largest propaganda archives in the world[17] our repository is obviously full of unsubstantiated claims, *ad hominem* accusations, and blatant lies about identifiable private citizens, not just public figures. The Cold War was fought with mutual lies and fantasies, the fabrications are the authentic sources of the times, as the title of a collection of essays on Cold War science says: *How Reason Almost Lost Its Mind.*[18] In lies there lies the truth.

The Archive is also the repository of forensic documents, testimonials, witness reports, the sources of which—victims, witnesses, accidental observers—could suffer retribution, even grave physical harm, were their identities made public. As we are an archive of both recent history and recent violations of human rights, tens of thousands of people implicated in the documents under our care are still alive, among them victims and witnesses of mass rapes of Bosnian women or mass atrocities during the Balkan war in the 1990s. The Archive is obliged to protect not only the informational rights of private citizens but also the complete anonymity of legal and forensic sources.

There are in fact whole groups of archival documents in our repository, such as the antemortem questionnaires used in the course of the exhumation and identification of the victims of the Srebrenica massacre, that it would be ethically improper to make public, even in an anonymized form. Relatives can consult the documents, and researchers the anonymized sources—that contain sensitive personal information—but out of respect for the victims of the tragedy and their relatives, it would be unacceptable to make even the redacted documents public, or to upload them to the public web.

* * *

The authority of the archive as an institution traditionally rests on trust in the authenticity and integrity of the documents housed inside the walls of the archive, as well as trust in the integrity of the archivists, the custodians of the documents. From 1840 onward, the notion of archival integrity has been based on and connected to the principle of the chain of custody, the chronological documentation of the movement of the records, and the principle of provenance, which stipulates that records that originate from a common source are kept together, if not physically, at least intellectually with the help of the archival finding aids, in order to prove and to substantiate the authenticity and integrity of the records.

The archive, however, in the course of its daily routine of professional archival work endangers the authenticity and integrity of the documents; the archive could not exist without harming the integrity of the documents that it keeps. The institution that is supposed to guard the privacy and the information rights of people, especially of private persons, whose names and acts are recorded in the sources, contributes every single day to the violation of these rights.

Even in traditional archives, documents did not remain completely unaltered. Keepers of the archives, minor officials, monks, scribes, learned antiquarians copied, rescribed, translated, and annotated the documents. The Library of Alexandria, one of the first known archives—in Ptolemaic Alexandria, the librarian, "the guardian of the books" was considered to

Accessing the Past, or Should Archives Provide Open Access?

be the "keeper of the archives"—contained tens of thousands of papyrus scrolls, a large number of which were confiscated from the ships in the harbor of the city and copied in the library, after which the copy was given back to the owner. In the course of copying the original, the text was frequently altered, involuntarily, as a mistake of the scribbler, or consciously in order to "improve" the original. The archivists or philologists ("the lovers of words") of the Ptolemaic museum were engaged in conserving, "rectifying," restoring a past (corpus) that had, supposedly, become altered, distorted, contaminated, or corrupted. In the words of the philologist Daniel Heller-Roazen, the practice, the guiding consideration, the figure of the library (of Alexandria), the notion of the library and the archive, demonstrates and stands for the understanding "of history as catastrophe."[19] The ongoing daily activity of the Archive is a heroic attempt to preserve or restore the presumed "the original," and to prevent the worst from happening: the flood, fire, invasion of mice or worms, sudden technological changes, digital decay, and so on, that make retrieval impossible.

Libraries and archives have been set up in order to collect under one roof, and thus preserve, otherwise dispersed texts: to prevent the disappearance and destruction of important records. The materiality of the documents has always been highly vulnerable: the majority of the papyrus scrolls of the Library of Alexandria most probably would have disappeared even without the fire that allegedly destroyed the library. Papyri survive more than two or three hundred years only in exceptional climatic circumstances, and even then, bugs and mice might finish off what the climate left intact. Papyri, like other manuscripts, had to be copied in order to be preserved, the corrected documents then often became reattributed, and named individuals in the copied documents reappear in new contexts with the possibility of their deeds being redescribed, thus posing new concerns for privacy.

Archives have never been completely immune from the suspicion of having forged documents in the interests of the archives, external authorities, or private individuals. Monastic archives in the West started with massive selective remembrance, by discarding documents deemed contrary to the interests of the monastery, or by producing fake documents to strengthen the spiritual, legal, or economic standing of the house. The forgeries implicated benefactors, legal heirs, dead or still alive, and their past deeds. Revisiting and rectifying the past was a double process of creation and destruction. In most cases, the original documents were destroyed in order to cover the traces of alterations. The archive of the Abbey of St. Denis, which reaches "back to the dawn of institutional archival formation, was systematically pillaged and destroyed [already in the eleventh century] in order to build from its fragments a more useful and appropriate past," to make alternative interpretations inaccessible.[20]

As the documents in the archive have always been prone to both material and textual deterioration, they had to be moved, reshelved, reboxed, transcribed, altered, reattributed and, in consequence, recontextualized. With the emergence of digitization, however, dangers to authenticity and privacy became more pervasive. Digitization might affect the text and its readability as the yet far-from-perfect optical character recognition software cannot faithfully recognize the printed text, the manuscript or longhand. My archive has contracted unemployed Cambodians to fix digitized and OCR-ed text collections, but the nonnative, though highly conscientious, English readers came up with versions that barely resemble the originals.

Digitized information is always in movement: from one server to another, from one format to another, uploaded to the cloud and then copied, and stored on multiple servers. Cloud architectures necessitate the replication of data, which are in constant, automated movement from one location to another, without the consent or the knowledge of the administrator, the data specialist or the archivist.[21] Multiple storage locations increase the leakage of data, which could become public even without the malicious efforts of unfriendly hackers.

Archivists working in a digital environment are confronted, then, with the so-called Collingridge dilemma, named after the British academic, David Collingridge, who came to the conclusion that "when change is easy, the need for it cannot be foreseen; when the need for change is apparent, change has become expensive, difficult and time consuming."[22] Archivists are not able to foresee the impact of technological changes on issues related to privacy. Had they been able to understand the future implications at the time when the new technologies were introduced, before they became embedded and widely distributed, there would then still have been a chance to take into consideration such concerns, and to modify the technology or its parameters. By the time the full impact of the new technology became apparent, however, it was too late: there are now strong corporate and/or political forces with vested interests in the insistence on keeping such profitable technologies, even when they have obvious high social costs.

Accessing the Past, or Should Archives Provide Open Access?

Digitized archival documents could be connected to the holdings of other archives that store specialized data, placing the original documents and their subjects in a new and completely different frame. Descriptive documents can now be related to sensor or geospatial data, radio-frequency identification, social data to images obtained from surveillance cameras, and data originating from the Internet of Things. Billions of individuals voluntarily provide, share, and transmit data that finally end up on the servers of a few big data companies, state or private surveillance organizations. Relating and connecting archived records, and data coming from different—historical, social, commercial, surveillance—repositories, results in a deep layer of recursivity: the collectors or keepers of the original records are not able to predict where the aggregation of the data might lead. For, "when analysts can draw rules from the data of a small cohort of consenting individuals that generalize to an entire population, consent loses its practical import."[23] Indeed, information related to specific individuals that seems harmless from the perspective of the Archive, "may implicate others who happen to share ... observable traits that correlate with the traits disclosed."[24]

* * *

Archives are institutions entrusted with the task of collecting and preserving records, even when recognizing that preservation and conservation endangers the very documents that the archive was meant to save for posterity. Archives are responsible for protecting the privacy and information rights of those mentioned and implicated in the documents; however, the archival workflow itself undermines the safeguards that are supposed to provide privacy protection. For a historian, some of the most important data are (or used to be until recently) the set of proper names, names of individuals, connected to certain events, since "sentences containing proper names can be used to make identity statements which convey factual and not merely linguistic information," as the philosopher of language John Searle stated.[25]

In a specific and limited sense, there is no difference between the natural sciences and the historical profession: both require experiments that can be repeated and then checked, verified, confirmed, or falsified using the same data.

Since the end of the 1960s, when Searle wrote his essay, the situation has changed: in the contemporary world, aggregated sets of metadata, including geospatial information, provide factual information on the basis of which identity claims—even without mentioning the name—could be made. Still, "the thread of Ariadne that leads the researcher through the archival labyrinth is the same thread that distinguishes one individual from another in all societies known to us: the name."[26]

While, for data companies, specific information and traits are more important than proper names because personal identities can be reconstructed from cross-referenced data without knowing the name of the user (for Google, the personal name is just noise), historians go back to the archives, sources, and documents to find and check the names in order to analyze them one more time in a new context. Proper names are rigid designators (that is, in every possible world they designate the same person). If, in the effort to protect personal data privacy, archivists were to start erasing names, anonymizing documents, they would prevent historians from practicing their profession.

* * *

Archives are thus trusted custodians, appointed by the present on behalf of future generations, but functioning in such a way that fulfilling one part of their mandate—protecting privacy—would force the archive to delete larger and larger parts of its collection; to limit the period of data retention, to prevent connections between metadata sets, and in this way to make the work of the researchers more difficult and complex, or even impossible. Archives are trafficking in sensitive, dangerous material. Newly available digital technology, the ease and carelessness of voluntary, individual data production, the willingness of individuals to sell themselves by offering their data free to huge, nontransparent, data monopoly companies, in the business of targeted advertising or data mining ("if something is free it must be you that is being sold")[27] makes the archived material highly explosive. Surveillance and intelligence organizations, and obviously commercial data companies, are able—and willing—to collect all the data digitally produced by anyone, including archives. Although millions, even billions of individuals are voluntarily willing to share with the wider public even sensitive personal information on social networking sites, this does not absolve archives from their responsibilities as institutions of trust. Individuals with information kept in the archives have the right to expect trusted institutions to handle their information according to widely shared public norms, despite the private practices of the same individuals. Even in the midst of rapid technological change, archives cannot disregard the norms that distinguish everyday practices from the responsibilities of trusted institutions. In order to guard the remaining and ever-shrinking authority and integrity of the institution, archives cannot open up all their secrets to the public at large on their websites. Public archives, or archives serving the public, should serve the interest of the citizens, both as members of the community and as private individuals.

Helen Nissenbaum, the American media scholar and privacy expert, is an advocate of the Principle of Respect for Context.[28] The Principle was included in the Obama administration's 2012 Privacy Bill of Rights as its third principle. That Bill of Rights, however, interpreted context specificity in a very limited way: with the naïve expectation that "companies will collect, use, and disclose personal data in ways that are consistent with the context in which consumers provide the data."[29] When consumers, companies, or archives make data openly available today, the future trajectory of the data remains unknown, and thus future contextual integrity cannot be guaranteed. As we are witnessing now, when consenting to disclosure of personal data we do not know the possible consequences of our consent: we cannot foresee the possible impact of interrelated media; we do not know in what ways data and attributes collected from others would disclose additional sensitive data about ourselves; or how a limited quantity of information would be amplified by the connected data sources.

Issues of privacy, according to the notion of contextual integrity, are not private, but social matters. In their practices, the Archive should consider both the interests and the preferences of all the affected parties, which include the public, present and future researchers, and nonpublic figures whose sensitive data the documents contain, and the archivists' control. Individuals have differing expectations about how their private data will be handled depending on the context: our expectations and behaviors at airport security are different from those we expect from a professional archive. Public interest archives are in the business of serving the public good by sustaining ethical, political, and scholarly principles, even when these principles might conflict with each other. Archives should be aware that they are expected to promote complex contextual functions, even when the different functions (promoting and enabling research, protecting sensitive information, transmitting historical knowledge but protecting the personal dignity of individuals) might be in competition with each other. Archives, where they exist as not-for-profit institutions, are in the position to experiment with and demonstrate to commercial companies trafficking in data, context-specific substantive norms that constrain what information websites can collect, with whom they can share it, and under what conditions it can be shared.[30]

In *De Doctrina Christiana* Augustine wrote: "Because it is shameful [*flagitiose*] to strip the body naked at a banquet among the drunken and licentious, it does not follow that it is shameful [*flagitium*] to be naked in the baths. ..." As the historian Carlo Ginzburg noted: "Augustine carefully traced a distinction between criminal *facinus* and shameful *flagitium*, the latter a sphere which, he insisted, had to be evaluated according to circumstances. We must, therefore, consider carefully what is suitable to times and places and persons, and not rashly charge men with sins [*flagitia*]."[31] Since privacy is a complex non-private issue, archives should think twice and act in a careful, differentiated way, taking the needs of context specificity into consideration before making archival documents openly accessible. This has been an issue for all of history, ever since we kept archives, but it is an especially complicated quandary in our open, digital era, when even public information, when placed, analyzed, aggregated, and used in a new context for previously unforeseen purposes, can have sometimes seriously harmful private consequences.

Notes

1. I here and throughout use the capitalized form of Archive to refer to the idealized instantiation, rather than any concrete, actually existing space.

2. See: Aleida Assmann, "Canon and Archive," in *Media and Cultural Memory*, ed. Astrid Erll and Ansgar Nünning (Berlin: Walter de Gruyter, 2008), 97–108, https://kops.uni-konstanz.de/handle/123456789/13382; Anthea Josias, "Toward an Understanding of Archives as a Feature of Collective Memory," *Archival Science* 11, no. 1 (2011): 95–112, https://doi.org/10.1007/s10502-011-9136-3; Marianne Hirsch and Leo Spitzer, "The Witness in the Archive: Holocaust Studies/Memory Studies," *Memory Studies* 2, no. 2 (2009): 151–170, https://doi.org/10.1177/1750698008102050; Michelle Caswell, "Khmer Rouge Archives: Accountability, Truth, and Memory in Cambodia," *Archival Science* 10, no. 1 (2010): 25–44, https://doi.org/10.1007/s10502-010-9114-1; Ann Laura Stoler, *Along the Archival Grain: Epistemic Anxieties and Colonial Common Sense* (Princeton, NJ: Princeton University Press, 2009); Diana Taylor, *The Archive and the Repertoire: Performing Cultural Memory in the Americas* (Durham, NC: Duke University Press, 2003).

3. Kirsten Martin and Helen Nissenbaum, "Privacy Interests in Public Records: An Empirical Investigation," *Harvard Journal of Law & Technology* 31, no. 1 (2017): 116, 141.

4. Des Browne, "House of Commons Hansard Ministerial Statement," UK Parliament, September 18, 2006, https://publications.parliament.uk/pa/cm200506/cmhansrd/vo060918/wmstext/60918m0187.htm.

5. Ian Hacking, *Rewriting the Soul: Multiple Personality and the Sciences of Memory* (Princeton, NJ: Princeton University Press, 1998), 241.

6. Susan C. Lawrence, *Privacy and the Past: Research, Law, Archives, Ethics* (New Brunswick, NJ: Rutgers University Press, 2016), 107–108.

7. Lindsey Hilsum, "Rwanda, Master Conform" (BBC, October 30, 1996), Box 374, Videocassette RW038, International Monitor Institute. Rwanda Videotapes and Audiotapes, David M. Rubenstein Rare Book & Manuscript Library, Duke Universities.

8. Quoted by Lawrence, *Privacy and the Past*, 59.

9. "Rehabilitation of Offenders Act 1974," The National Archives Legislation, 1974, https://www.legislation.gov.uk/ukpga/1974/53.

10. Court of Justice of the European Union, "Judgment in Case C-131/12 Google Spain SL, Google Inc. v Agencia Española de Protección de Datos, Mario Costeja González," May 13, 2014.

11. Intersoft Consulting, "Right to Be Forgotten," *General Data Protection Regulation (GDPR)* (blog), accessed April 29, 2019, https://gdpr-info.eu/issues/right-to-be-forgotten/.

12. Google, "Search Removals under European Privacy Law," Google Transparency Report, 2019, https://transparencyreport.google.com/eu-privacy/overview.

13. Owen Bowcott, "'Right to Be Forgotten' Could Threaten Global Free Speech, Say NGOs," *The Guardian*, September 9, 2018, sec. Technology, https://www.theguardian.com/technology/2018/sep/09/right-to-be-forgotten-could-threaten-global-free-speech-say-ngos.

14. See, among other provisions: Under Article 9: 1. "Processing of personal data revealing racial or ethnic origin, political opinions, religious or philosophical beliefs, or trade union membership, and the processing of genetic data, biometric data for the purpose of uniquely identifying a natural person, data concerning health or data concerning a natural person's sex life or sexual orientation shall be prohibited. 2. Paragraph 1 shall not apply if one of the following applies : ... (j) processing is necessary for archiving purposes in the public interest, scientific or historical research purposes or statistical purposes ... Article 89: Safeguards and derogations relating to processing for archiving purposes in the public interest, scientific or historical research purposes or statistical purposes ..." The European Parliament, "Regulation (EU) 2016/679 of The European Parliament and of The Council," European Union Law, April 27, 2016, https://eur-lex.europa.eu/legal-content/EN/TXT/HTML/?uri=CELEX:02016R0679-20160504.

15. The European Parliament, "Regulation (EU) 2016/679."

16. Anne J. Gilliland-Swetland, "Enduring Paradigm, New Opportunities: The Value of the Archival Perspective in the Digital Environment" (CLIR, 2000), 12.

17. We house the former archive of the Research Institute of Radio Free Europe/Radio Liberty, perhaps the most important propaganda organization in the Cold War era, and also the propaganda materials of the former Communist countries.

18. Paul Erickson et al., *How Reason Almost Lost Its Mind: The Strange Career of Cold War Rationality* (Chicago: University of Chicago Press, 2015).

19. See Daniel Heller-Roazen, "Tradition's Destruction: On the Library of Alexandria," *October* 100 (2002): 133–153.

20. Patrick J. Geary, *Phantoms of Remembrance: Memory and Oblivion at the End of the First Millennium* (Princeton, NJ: Princeton University Press, 1996), 107.

21. Copying entire digital collections seems to be a reasonable foresight today. The LOCKSS (Lots of Copies Keep Stuff Safe) Program at the Stanford University Library developed and provides open source tools for libraries and archives to copy, and thus to preserve their content. COAR, the Confederation of Open Access Repositories keeps multiple copies of the collections of its members. The Internet Archive, based in San Francisco—as its storage is in constant danger of destruction, since the Archive sits literally on top of the San Andreas Fault—set up a mirror site in the new Library of Alexandria. Following the November 2016 US election, the Internet Archive, which held, as of October, 2016, 273 billion webpages from over 510 billion web objects, and grows by over 500 million webpages a week, taking up 15 petabytes of storage, decided to move its backup data to Canada, in order "to keep the Archive free, accessible and reader private." Brewster Kahle, "Help Us Keep the Archive Free, Accessible, and Reader Private," *Internet Archive Blogs*, November 29, 2016, https://blog.archive.org/2016/11/29/help-us-keep-the-archive-free-accessible-and-private/. See also Tung-Hui Hu, *A Prehistory of the Cloud* (Cambridge, MA: The MIT Press, 2015) for a set of theoretical provocations around cloud infrastructures.

22. David Collingridge, *The Social Control of Technology* (New York: St. Martin's Press, 1980), 11.

23. Solon Barocas and Helen Nissenbaum, "Big Data's End Run around Procedural Privacy Protections," *Communications of the ACM* 57, no. 11 (2014): 32, https://doi.org/10.1145/2668897.

24. Barocas and Nissenbaum, "Big Data's End Run," 32.

25. John R. Searle, *Speech Acts: An Essay in the Philosophy of Language* (Cambridge: Cambridge University Press, 1969), 165.

26. Carlo Ginzburg and Carlo Poni, "The Name and the Game: Unequal Exchange and the Historiographic Marketplace," in *Microhistory and the Lost Peoples of Europe*,

ed. Edward Muir and Guido Ruggiero (Baltimore, MD: Johns Hopkins University Press, 1991), 5.

27. Tim Worstall, "Facebook Is Free Therefore It Is You Getting Sold," Forbes, November 10, 2012, https://www.forbes.com/sites/timworstall/2012/11/10/facebook-is-free-therefore-it-is-you-getting-sold/.

28. See Helen Nissenbaum, *Privacy in Context: Technology, Policy, and the Integrity of Social Life* (Stanford, CA: Stanford University Press, 2009).

29. Quoted in Helen Nissenbaum, "Respecting Context to Protect Privacy: Why Meaning Matters," *Science and Engineering Ethics* 24, no. 3 (2018): 834, https://doi.org/10.1007/s11948-015-9674-9.

30. See Helen Nissenbaum, "A Contextual Approach to Privacy Online," *Daedalus* 140, no. 4 (2011): 32.

31. Quoted in Carlo Ginzburg, "The Bond of Shame," in *Passionen. Objekte—Schauplätze—Denkstile*, ed. Corina Caduff, Anne-Kathrin Reulecke, and Ulrike Vedder (Munich: Wilhelm Fink, 2010), 24, http://publikationen.ub.uni-frankfurt.de/frontdoor/index/index/year/2017/docId/44333.

V Infrastructures and Platforms

17 Infrastructural Experiments and the Politics of Open Access

Jonathan Gray

How can digital technologies make research publicly available?[1] Available for whom, and to what end? Many definitions and declarations of open access argue for the removal of "price and permission barriers."[2] For example, the widely cited Budapest Open Access Initiative suggests that open access entails:

> free availability on the public internet, permitting any users to read, download, copy, distribute, print, search, or link to the full texts of these articles, crawl them for indexing, pass them as data to software, or use them for any other lawful purpose, *without financial, legal, or technical barriers other than those inseparable from gaining access to the internet itself* [emphasis added].[3]

Such barrier-removal talk might be taken as a sign that open access advances a "negative" conception of openness focusing on the removal of constraints, rather than more substantive "positive" conceptions of who and what open-access research is for and the conditions under which it might thrive.[4] A closer look suggests, perhaps unsurprisingly, that there are many ways in which open access is mobilized, advocated, and practiced in the service of a range of different kinds of social, cultural, political, and economic values and visions of the future.[5]

As a contribution toward the study of the digital cultures, practices, and politics of open access, this chapter explores how scholarly communication infrastructures reflect, enact, and configure different ways of making research public. Such infrastructures are not simply neutral vehicles for the dissemination and communication of research. They are both substantive objects of social and cultural research and can serve as sites of public experimentation.[6] Infrastructures shape who and what is assembled around research, as well as what is attended to. They play a concrete role in organizing and enabling different forms of knowledge, value, meaning, sociality, participation, and publicity around scholarly communication—including both "formal" outputs (e.g., books, articles) and "informal" spaces and channels within, across, and beyond research fields.[7]

Previous research on knowledge and information infrastructures suggests how we might study the "ways in which our social, cultural and political values are braided into the wires, coded into the applications and built into the databases which are so much a part of our daily lives."[8] This includes through strategies of "infrastructural inversion" to bring the social, cultural and political background work involved in infrastructures into the foreground for analysis, critique, and intervention.[9] Rather than thinking of infrastructures as "thing[s] stripped from use," it has been suggested that they can be seen in terms of "relations."[10] In the case of infrastructures for open-access research, this can include ensembles of documents, software systems, metadata standards, editorial boards, and web technologies. Other scholars have suggested that for very large infrastructures that develop across multiple systems, sites and settings, it may be more appropriate to consider how they "grow" rather than just how they are "designed."[11]

Infrastructures associated with open scholarly communication may also be characterized by their potential to multiply and organize relations through digital technologies in specific ways. As such, their study may be informed by recent research in fields such as science and technology studies, (new) media studies, internet studies, platform studies, digital culture, and digital sociology. Drawing on approaches from these fields, rather than focusing on how such infrastructures can bring research to "the public," we can instead examine the sociotechnical arrangements for "making things public" and assembling different "publics."[12] As well as making research available, scholarly communication infrastructures are involved in making many different types of objects and activities commensurable, comparable, and quantifiable, whether for the purposes of research assessment, performance management, resource allocation, or otherwise.[13]

It might be argued that established systems for publishing, organizing, and valuing scholarly work can become so ingrained as to constitute a kind of "infrastructural *a priori*," providing conditions for recognition, legibility, and relationality. Previous studies examine how researchers respond to frictions by remaining loyal to such infrastructures or by exiting in search of alternatives.[14] There also remains a degree of "interpretive flexibility," and the extent to which infrastructures shape and are shaped by users and their practices remains an open and empirical question.[15]

Infrastructural Experiments and the Politics of Open Access

In what follows I shall explore "infrastructural experiments," which can be understood to make different aspects of the politics of open access and scholarly communication visible and actionable. Rather than focusing simply on optimizing systems through feedback loops or composing new improved ones that will recede into the background, such experiments may serve to facilitate collective inquiry into who and what research is for, as well as "infrastructural imagination" about how it may be organized differently.[16] Infrastructures may thus serve as experimental "sites and devices for intervention in the 'composition of the world,'"[17] as well as "where multiple agents meet, engage, and produce new worlds."[18]

Below I discuss several examples of infrastructural experiments grouped around four areas: (1) "who has access?"; (2) "what counts?"; (3) "what matters?"; and (4) "how are relations reconfigured?" They are intended to be taken as illustrative rather than exhaustive, overlapping rather than mutually exclusive.

1. Who Has Access?

The Open Access Button (openaccessbutton.org) started as a project to "track the impact of paywalls and help you get access to the research you need."[19] It began as an advocacy device to "make this invisible problem visible" by serving to "show the global effects of research paywalls" and to "help change the system."[20] While ethnographic studies on infrastructures have suggested how they may become "visible upon breakdown,"[21] it is arguably not the infrastructural failure of paywalls that is at issue (sure, they limit and monetize access by design) but rather their malalignment with the interests and concerns of those who come to them.[22] The button gathers and materializes a public without access.

The button may thus be understood as a form of "infrastructural activism," in order to articulate access issues and to mobilize support for openness in scholarly communication. It does so by recording a variety of interactions across space and time, which can then be documented, aggregated, counted, and displayed. As the creators put it: "We wanted to change the experience of hitting a paywall, and transform it from this disempowering denial of access into an explicit call to action."[23] The Open Access Button thus served as a sociotechnical device to make individual incidents of encountering paywalls experienceable and visible as cases of a broader systemic "paywall injustice" and being "denied access,"[24] as well as facilitating associated processes of commensuration and quantification of what the project calls "blocks" ("any instance [when] an individual can't access a resource they want"). The datafication of paywall injustice means that the button can also be understood in relation to recent practices of "statactivism" and "data activism."[25]

As well as making access issues collectively visible, the button invited users to document their circumstances and aspirations: "Tell your story—why were you blocked? What were you trying to do at the time?" The project uses a browser extension to draw attention to underrecognized alternatives to accessing articles, including self-archived (or "green open access") versions in institutional repositories, subject-based archives, aggregators, and other sources. It facilitates and records requests for access to researchers, contending that "a request system for science should be open, community-owned infrastructure that's free to use, citable, effective, safe, and just."[26] To this end, the project uses GitHub to facilitate involvement in the project, including discussion, ideas, and project management, as well as software development.

There are other mechanisms offering alternative access routes to paywalled research, including through legal aggregators (e.g., Unpaywall, Kopernio) as well as "pirate" sites such as Sci-Hub.[27] There are also other request buttons.[28] What is distinctive about the Open Access Button as an infrastructural experiment, though, is that it not only facilitates access and requests, but also documents and datafies access issues, assembling a public in order to challenge and problematize existing infrastructures and mobilize around alternatives.

2. What Counts?

There are also infrastructural experiments around what is recognized and counted as research work and research outputs, and the different forms that these can take. Many institutions and infrastructures prioritize the recognition of historically contingent, highly conventionalized forms of knowledge production such as the monograph and the peer-reviewed article.[29] Infrastructures can thus support and enact different social and cultural practices of recognition, legitimation, and classification, or "sorting things out."[30]

For example, the Zenodo project based at CERN functions as a "catch-all repository" to support the sharing of "all research outputs" from "all fields

Infrastructural Experiments and the Politics of Open Access

of research," "all over the world."[31] Notably, this includes nontraditional outputs such as: "posters, presentations, datasets, images (figures, plots, drawings, diagrams, photos), software, videos/audio and interactive materials such as lessons." By providing digital object identifiers (DOIs) to all materials, Zenodo aims to make many different kinds of work easier to discover, cite, and institutionally recognize. It deliberately remains receptive to all kinds of digital objects and "does not impose any requirements on format, size, access restrictions or license." At the same time, it seeks institutional recognition for these activities through its close association with the EU-funded "Open Access Infrastructure for Research in Europe" (OpenAIRE) initiative, as well as through collaborations with national funders, ministries, and institutions across Europe, the United States and Australia.

In a similar vein, the Research Ideas and Outcomes (RIO) journal publishes "all outputs of the research cycle,"[32] and the Figshare project carries the tagline "credit for *all* your research"[33] (emphasis in original), thus aspiring to surface and recognize different aspects of research work which may traditionally be overlooked. The nonprofit ORCID project that provides "persistent digital identifiers" for researchers may also be considered a site of "ontological experimentation," insofar as its forums and discussion channels do not only resolve but also open up discussions about the articulation, definition, and conventionalization of entities and relations involved in research, including around the recording and disambiguation of names (and different cultural naming practices), what counts as an affiliation (e.g., professional associations as well as universities?), what counts as a country (e.g., Kosovo?) and what should be included as "work categories" (e.g., blog posts, field work, oceanographic cruises, policy reports, media interviews, podcasts, software, maps, sheet music, performances, infographics, teaching materials).

There are also infrastructural experiments in recognizing and supporting existing and emerging forms of scholarly work. For example, Publons (publons.com) provides public recognition for peer reviewing and Depsy (depsy.org) for research software development. There are also a growing variety of projects to support, credential, and legitimate evolving, hybrid, interactive, dynamic, multimodal, and collaborative research formats and outputs—from living books to collective authorship models.[34]

3. What Matters?

Infrastructural experiments may serve to explore not only what scholarly communication is and what counts, but also what matters and what is considered valuable. Many of these serve as responses to dominant forms of quantifying, valuing, measuring, assessing, and metrifying research, such as journal impact factors, and measures such as the h-index and the i10-index. Recent work in the sociology of quantification suggests how we may attend to the reactive and performative effects of such practices, and their capacities not only to represent but also to intervene in social life.[35]

One prominent response to established scientometric measures is "altmetrics," or alternative metrics, which explore other ways of measuring the value of research publications beyond metrics based on citation counts. They are positioned as a way to "expand our view of what impact looks like, but also of what's making the impact," partly as a response to the fact that "expressions of scholarship are becoming more diverse."[36] This includes by exploring the use of web and social media data in order to look at the life of research publications outside of formal channels and referencing practices. Alternative ways of appraising value and measuring attention based on web and social media data are included in journals alongside other measures. As well as provided aggregated counts, altmetrics may look at the character of not just counts, but also the character of mentions, asking "how and why?" as well as "how many?"[37]

For example, ImpactStory Profiles (profiles.impactstory.org) provide a range of different analytical functions and "badges" for researchers—including for achievements such as "Hot Streak" (the degree of ongoing online discussion around a publication); "Global South" (recognizing the percentage of online engagement that comes from countries in the south); and "Wikitastic" (the number of Wikipedia articles which cite a researcher's publications). The inclusion of ironic metrics such as "Rickroll" (being tweeted by a person named Richard and punning on the internet meme in which users posted a catchy Rick Astley pop song to unsuspecting victims), suggests that metrics can be arbitrary, contingent, and an area of ongoing experimentation, rather than taken at face value. Web and social media data can enable different ways of valuing and measuring research and approaching its role in society, and can not only resolve but also raise questions about what matters.

Other initiatives emphasize that measurement practices should be informed by the different societal settings in which research is accounted for.

For example, the Leiden Manifesto argues that quantitative valuation should support qualitative assessment; that research should be considered in relation to (potentially diverse) goals of institutions, fields and researchers; that there should be processes for involving researchers in evaluation processes; and that assessment practices may be required for different fields.[38] It also argues for recognition of the reactive and performative effects of indicators, as well as the dangers of "misplaced concreteness" through the reification of measurements. In a similar vein, the San Francisco Declaration on Research Assessment (DORA) suggests caution in how journal-based metrics are used, arguing that they should not be taken "as a surrogate measure of the quality of individual research articles, to assess an individual scientist's contributions, or in hiring, promotion, and funding decisions."[39]

In considering how metrics are attuned to the interests of diverse actors and publics, ongoing infrastructural experiments about what matters may benefit from recent research on the social and cultural study of valuation (see, e.g., the *Valuation Studies* journal), as well as "inventive methods," "critical analytics," and "situational analytics."[40]

4. How Are Relations Reconfigured?

Following the abovementioned shift from the "general public" to attending to the material formation of specific publics,[41] infrastructures can also be considered as sites for experimentation in reassembling and reconfiguring relations between different actors around research. Just as it has been argued in relation to transparency initiatives, infrastructures do not only facilitate access to preexisting publics, they can also gather their own.[42] Research infrastructures may thus become sites of very different kinds of public involvement and material participation, opening up the processes of scholarly communication not only to nonacademic publics, but also advertisers, data flows, startups, algorithms, and activists.

For example, one recent development is the rise of the "platform" as a way of configuring and organizing relations around research.[43] In the emerging field of "platform studies" this has been considered both in terms of the "discursive positioning" of platforms,[44] as well as their material-technical and computational affordances.[45] Platforms are said to organize actors and relations between them to accommodate different economic models such as multisided markets (e.g., between users, publishers, advertisers). In the case of Facebook, this is described in terms of the "double logic" of decentralizing platform features and recentralizing platform-ready data.[46] Such economic models may shape (but do not determine) user practices and the forms of mediation that platforms afford.

Though their economic models and material organization may differ, platforms and services such as Academia.edu, ResearchGate, Mendeley, and Google Scholar aim to organize and monetize relations in and across research communities to suit their respective business models, whether through transactional metadata, advertising, or user fees.[47] Researchers have raised questions about whether these forms of organization are suitable in the context of research.[48] As well as dedicated platforms, other kinds of social media platforms (such as Twitter) have become entangled in scholarly communication systems, leading to not only the platformization of infrastructures, but also the infrastructuralization of platforms.[49] This also has the consequence that the online dissemination of scholarly research may become entangled with digital advertising markets, trending algorithms, and digital cultures associated with platforms—a development that is implicitly encouraged and credentialed through altmetrics for social media shares.

A range of alternative projects have arisen in response and parallel to such platforms. ScholarlyHub (scholarlyhub.org) is mobilizing resources and support for a "truly open-access repository, publishing service, and scholarly social networking site," which is "run by scholars, for scholars." Projects such as PubPeer (pubpeer.com) and Hypothesis (hypothes.is) aim to support online interaction, discussion, and annotation around research material through browser extensions and databases. The Directory of Open Access Journals (doaj.org), provides a "community-curated online directory" (with an API to facilitate reuse) in order to index open-access material and provide alternative search and query facilities, and has been positioned as a potential mechanism to address inequities not only in access, but also in knowledge production with respect to the Global South.[50]

Conclusion

In this chapter I have explored how scholarly communication infrastructures may constitute both an object of research and a site of experimentation to explore questions of who has access, what counts, what matters, and how relations are organized. The examples suggest how infrastructural work may be brought into the foreground not only to enact dominant regimes of quantification, valuation, and interactivity, but also to question them and to explore alternatives. Drawing on infrastructure studies, these reflect and enact specific social and cultural practices of classification and organization. Infrastructural experiments may serve not only to optimize existing systems, but also to interrogate their operations, to better understand their specificities and limitations, and broaden involvement around them. This task will surely become even more vital as the plurality and variety of actors involved in scholarly communication increases, from platform companies to third-party analytics services, text-mining bots, citizen scientists, digital knowledge cultures, research start-ups, relevance algorithms, and artificial intelligence projects, along with all of their attendant imaginaries, economic models, practices, and publics.

Notes

1. I'm grateful to Liliana Bounegru, Geoffrey Bowker, Timothy Weil Elfenbein, Jean Christophe Plantin, and three reviewers invited by MIT Press for their careful readings and thoughtful responses to this chapter.

2. Peter Suber, *Open Access*, Essential Knowledge Series (Cambridge, MA: The MIT Press, 2012), http://bit.ly/oa-book; Martin Paul Eve, *Open Access and the Humanities: Contexts, Controversies and the Future* (Cambridge: Cambridge University Press, 2014), https://doi.org/10.1017/CBO9781316161012.

3. Leslie Chan et al., "Budapest Open Access Initiative" February 14, 2002, http://www.soros.org/openaccess/read.shtml.

4. By way of analogy with Isaiah Berlin's distinction in Isaiah Berlin, *Four Essays on Liberty* (Oxford: Oxford University Press, 1969).

5. See, for example Nathaniel Tkacz, "From Open Source to Open Government: A Critique of Open Politics," *Ephemera: Theory and Politics in Organization* 12, no. 4 (2012): 386–405; Eve, *Open Access and the Humanities*; Janneke Adema and Samuel A. Moore, "Collectivity and Collaboration: Imagining New Forms of Communality to Create Resilience in Scholar-Led Publishing," *Insights: The UKSG Journal* 31 (2018), https://doi.org/10.1629/uksg.399.

6. Here I draw on recent research in science and technology studies that explores not only scientific experimentation in settings of laboratories and controlled environments, but also broader practices and cultures of public experimentation in society. See, for example, J. Lezaun, Noortje Marres, and M. Tironi, "Experiments in Participation," in *Handbook of Science and Technology Studies*, ed. U. Felt et al., vol. 4 (Cambridge, MA: The MIT Press, 2017), 195–222; and Noortje Marres, "Why Political Ontology Must Be Experimentalized: On Eco-Show Homes as Devices of

Participation," *Social Studies of Science* 43, no. 3 (2013): 417–443, https://doi.org/10.1177/0306312712475255.

7. For more on "formal" and "informal" channels of scholarly communication see, e.g., Sally Morris et al., *The Handbook of Journal Publishing* (Cambridge: Cambridge University Press, 2013), https://doi.org/10.1017/CBO9781139107860.

8. Geoffrey Bowker, "The Infrastructural Imagination," in *Information Infrastructure(s): Boundaries, Ecologies, Multiplicity*, ed. Alessandro Mongili and Giuseppina Pellegrino (Cambridge: Cambridge Scholars Publishing, 2014), xii–xiii.

9. Geoffrey C. Bowker and Susan Leigh Star, *Sorting Things out: Classification and Its Consequences*, Inside Technology (Cambridge, MA: The MIT Press, 1999).

10. Susan Leigh Star and Karen Ruhleder, "Steps Toward an Ecology of Infrastructure: Design and Access for Large Information Spaces," *Information Systems Research* 7, no. 1 (1996): 111–134, https://doi.org/10.1287/isre.7.1.111.

11. Steven J. Jackson et al., "Understanding Infrastructure: History, Heuristics and Cyberinfrastructure Policy," *First Monday* 12, no. 6 (2007), https://doi.org/10.5210/fm.v12i6.1904.

12. See Bruno Latour and Peter Weibel, eds., *Making Things Public: Atmospheres of Democracy* (Cambridge, MA: The MIT Press, 2005); Noortje Marres, "The Issues Deserve More Credit: Pragmatist Contributions to the Study of Public Involvement in Controversy," *Social Studies of Science* 37, no. 5 (2007): 759–780, https://doi.org/10.1177/0306312706077367.

13. Wendy Nelson Espeland and Mitchell L. Stevens, "Commensuration as a Social Process," *Annual Review of Sociology* 24, no. 1 (1998): 313–343, https://doi.org/10.1146/annurev.soc.24.1.313; Wendy Nelson Espeland and Mitchell L. Stevens, "A Sociology of Quantification," *European Journal of Sociology* 49, no. 3 (2008): 401–436, https://doi.org/10.1017/S0003975609000150.

14. Carl Lagoze et al., "Should I Stay or Should I Go? Alternative Infrastructures in Scholarly Publishing," *International Journal of Communication* 9 (2015): 1052–1071.

15. Wiebe E. Bijker, Thomas Parke Hughes, and Trevor Pinch, eds., *The Social Construction of Technological Systems: New Directions in the Sociology and History of Technology* (Cambridge, MA: The MIT Press, 2012).

16. Bowker, "The Infrastructural Imagination."

17. Noortje Marres, *Material Participation* (Basingstoke, UK: Palgrave Macmillan, 2015), 130.

18. Casper Bruun Jensen and Atsuro Morita, "Infrastructures as Ontological Experiments," *Engaging Science, Technology, and Society* 1 (2015): 85, https://doi.org/10.17351/ests2015.21.

19. Joseph McArthur et al., "Open Access Button," 2013, https://web.archive.org/web/20131206130920/https://www.openaccessbutton.org/.

20. Ibid.

21. Susan Leigh Star, "The Ethnography of Infrastructure," *American Behavioral Scientist* 43, no. 3 (1999): 382, https://doi.org/10.1177/00027649921955326.

22. Jonathan Gray, Carolin Gerlitz, and Liliana Bounegru, "Data Infrastructure Literacy," *Big Data & Society* 5, no. 2 (2018), https://doi.org/10.1177/2053951718786316.

23. David Carroll and Joseph McArthur, "New Apps Find Free Access to Scientific and Scholarly Research," Open Access Button, October 21, 2014, https://openaccessbutton.org/livelaunch.

24. David Carroll and Joseph McArthur, "The Open Access Button: It's Time We Capture Individual Moments of Paywall Injustice and Turn Them into Positive Change," *LSE Impact Blog*, September 2, 2013, https://blogs.lse.ac.uk/impactofsocialsciences/2013/09/02/the-open-access-button-carroll-mcarthur/.

25. Isabelle Bruno, Emmanuel Didier, and Tommaso Vitale, "Statactivism: Forms of Action between Disclosure and Affirmation," *PARTECIPAZIONE E CONFLITTO* 7, no. 2 (2014): 198-220-220; Stefania Milan and Lonneke van der Velden, "The Alternative Epistemologies of Data Activism," *Digital Culture & Society* 2, no. 2 (2016), https://doi.org/10.14361/dcs-2016-0205.

26. "About," Open Access Button, accessed June 4, 2019, https://openaccessbutton.org/about.

27. John Bohannon, "Who's Downloading Pirated Papers? Everyone," *Science*, April 25, 2016, https://www.sciencemag.org/news/2016/04/whos-downloading-pirated-papers-everyone.

28. Arthur Sale et al., "Open Access Mandates and the 'Fair Dealing' Button," *arXiv:1002.3074*, February 16, 2010, http://arxiv.org/abs/1002.3074.

29. See, for example, chapters by Fyfe; Pontille and Torny; and Mourat, Ricci, and Latour in this volume.

30. Bowker and Star, *Sorting Things Out*.

31. "Zenodo—Research. Shared," Zenodo, accessed June 4, 2019, https://zenodo.org/.

32. "Research Ideas and Outcomes," RIO, accessed June 4, 2019, https://riojournal.com/; Daniel Mietchen, Ross Mounce, and Lyubomir Penev, "Publishing the Research Process," *Research Ideas and Outcomes* 1 (2015): e7547, https://doi.org/10.3897/rio.1.e7547.

33. Figshare, "Credit for All Your Research," figshare, accessed June 4, 2019, https://figshare.com/.

34. Janneke Adema and Samuel A. Moore, "Collectivity and Collaboration: Imagining New Forms of Communality to Create Resilience in Scholar-Led Publishing," *Insights: The UKSG Journal* 31 (2018), https://doi.org/10.1629/uksg.399.

35. Wendy Nelson Espeland and Michael Sauder, "Rankings and Reactivity: How Public Measures Recreate Social Worlds," *American Journal of Sociology* 113, no. 1 (2007): 1–40, https://doi.org/10.1086/517897.

36. Jason Priem, Dario Taraborelli, and Cameron Neylon, "Altmetrics: A Manifesto," October 26, 2010, http://altmetrics.org/manifesto/.

37. Priem, Taraborelli, and Neylon, "Altmetrics."

38. Diana Hicks et al., "Bibliometrics: The Leiden Manifesto for Research Metrics," *Nature* 520, no. 7548 (2015): 429–431, https://doi.org/10.1038/520429a.

39. "San Francisco Declaration on Research Assessment: Putting Science into the Assessment of Research" (San Francisco), accessed February 18, 2016, http://www.ascb.org/files/SFDeclarationFINAL.pdf.

40. Celia Lury and Nina Wakeford, eds., *Inventive Methods: The Happening of the Social*, Culture, Economy, and the Social (London: Routledge, 2012); Richard Rogers, "Otherwise Engaged: Social Media from Vanity Metrics to Critical Analytics," *International Journal of Communication* 12 (2018): 450–472; Noortje Marres, "For a Situational Analytics: An Interpretative Methodology for the Study of Situations in Computational Settings" (under review).

41. Marres, "The Issues Deserve More Credit."

42. Andrew Barry, "Transparency as a Political Device," in *Débordements: Mélanges Offerts à Michel Callon*, ed. Madeleine Akrich et al., Sciences Sociales (Paris: Presses des Mines, 2013), 21–39, http://books.openedition.org/pressesmines/721.

43. For further discussion on this see Penny Andrews's chapter in this volume, as well as Lagoze et al., "Should I Stay or Should I Go?"; Jean-Christophe Plantin et al., "Infrastructure Studies Meet Platform Studies in the Age of Google and Facebook," *New Media & Society* 20, no. 1 (2018): 293–310, https://doi.org/10.1177/1461444816661553.

44. Tarleton Gillespie, "The Politics of 'Platforms,'" *New Media & Society* 12, no. 3 (2010): 347–364, https://doi.org/10.1177/1461444809342738.

45. Anne Helmond, "The Platformization of the Web: Making Web Data Platform Ready," *Social Media + Society* 1, no. 2 (2015): 205630511560308, https://doi.org/10.1177/2056305115603080; Jean-Christophe Plantin, Carl Lagoze, and Paul N Edwards, "Re-Integrating Scholarly Infrastructure: The Ambiguous Role of Data Sharing Platforms," *Big Data & Society* 5, no. 1 (2018), https://doi.org/10.1177/2053951718756683.

46. Plantin, Lagoze, and Edwards, "Re-Integrating Scholarly Infrastructure."

47. See the chapters by Eileen Joy and Kathleen Fitzpatrick in this volume.

48. Janneke Adema, "Don't Give Your Labour To Academia.Edu, Use It To Strengthen The Academic Commons," *Open Reflections* (blog), April 7, 2016, https://openreflections.wordpress.com/2016/04/07/dont-give-your-labour-to-academia-edu-use-it-to-strengthen-the-academic-commons/; Gary Hall, "Does Academia.Edu Mean Open Access Is Becoming Irrelevant?," *Media Gifts* (blog), October 18, 2015, http://www.garyhall.info/journal/2015/10/18/does-academiaedu-mean-open-access-is-becoming-irrelevant.html.

49. Plantin et al., "Infrastructure Studies Meet Platform Studies in the Age of Google and Facebook."

50. Florence Piron, "Open Access in the Francophone Global South: Between Collective Empowerment and Neocolonialism," *News Service* (blog), February 14, 2018, https://blog.doaj.org/2018/02/14/open-access-in-the-francophone-global-south-between-collective-empowerment-and-neocolonialism/.

18   The Platformization of Open

Penny C. S. Andrews

As Jonathan Gray has suggested in the previous chapter in this book, any attempt to understand the emergence of platforms and platformization in "open" needs to take a multifaceted approach. As van Dijck makes plain, ownership, technology, governance, business models, content, and users/usage are all part of the picture.[1] In this chapter, "open" will be used as an umbrella term to cover various forms of open practice (open access, open data, open knowledge, open source, open science, open government, open research, and so on) in order to be able to speak to the broader issues in the knowledge space than concentrating on open access or open science, in isolation, would allow.

Historically, in platform studies (the field of studies of digital media focused on the underlying computer systems supporting creative work), a platform was defined as a computing system on which other services could be built.[2] The system could consist of hardware, software, or both.[3] Here the focus was on the relationships between hardware and software design of platforms and the creative content produced on or for those platforms, predominantly video games, virtual worlds, and experiments in art, literature, and music. In Business and Management Studies, the concept was defined slightly differently: an internal platform is here seen as "a set of assets organized in a common structure from which a company can efficiently develop and produce a stream of derivative products" and an external platform is a similar structure that allows third parties to build products or services on top.[4] This external platform idea was borrowed by other writers to describe the potential for different approaches to government,[5] libraries,[6] and others.

As the study of platforms as a concept has reemerged as a current topic, Tarleton Gillespie of Microsoft Research New England draws attention to the ambiguity of the word "platform" and the way it is used in architecture, figurative speech, politics, and computing, as well as business, to the point where now it is used to mean any computational service, but particularly social networking services and "open" tools and services.[7] The term "platform," as defined today in a digital context, now includes giving people and companies "a platform" in the figurative and political sense, as well as the infrastructure through which they can sell products and services, share data and content, express themselves, and connect with other people. What were once termed "Web 2.0," "new media," and "apps," have been amalgamated into a single, less quickly outdated term: platform.

Alongside the development of new platforms, organizations have been undergoing a process of what has been dubbed "platformization"—which also has multiple definitions. In business, it is generally used to describe a company transitioning from a business selling products to one managing direct transactions between two or more actors[8] in a platform-mediated network; for example, Amazon's evolution from directly selling products to enabling third-party sellers to use its platform and logistics network.[9] In media and communications, the term is increasingly being used to describe the process of making the data on the web compatible with social media platforms and their extension into external web and app contexts.[10]

It can be argued that research-sharing infrastructures and open tools and services are engaging with all these senses of platforms and platformization, with academic social networking services being seen as "reputational platforms" and mediating both connections between researchers and the sharing of research outputs, processes, and information.[11] The biggest players in academic publishing and scholarly communication are also building suites of products based on data sharing and acting as intermediaries between libraries, universities, researchers, and the public—and platforms rarely have open and transparent governance.[12] Anyone who controls access to data, including these academic publishers, can also remove that data as it suits them.[13] This chapter therefore takes a pluralist approach to definitions of these contested terms. When platformization is used as a description of the process of what is happening to research-sharing infrastructures, all of the above meanings are considered.

Platformization can also be a route to (positive and negative) disruption of markets, and monopolization/oligopolization. Consider the example of platformization in the form of the platform economy, otherwise known as the "gig economy." The best-known examples, Airbnb and Uber, have

The Platformization of Open

disrupted the hotel and taxi industries respectively, while being funded by venture capital connected to political power. They dominate their domains, with only the similarly financed Lyft (in some markets) proving any real challenge to Uber. Third-party services have emerged that build on the success of these platforms, such as UrbanBellhop for Airbnb hosts, and Uber has experimented with adding other products such as Uber Eats (food delivery) and UberRUSH (same day courier service) to their platform. Platforms in open include both new and existing tools and services, and platformization as the transformation of legacy academic publishers. As I will go on to discuss, the disruptive effects and funding models of these platforms are often not so different from the lifestyle brands of the platform economy.

Platforms are not a new concept for open. It could be argued that *arXiv*, PubMed, and other long-standing subject repositories for open content fit the definition of platforms,[14] albeit without social features such as commenting or following/friending other users observed in more recently established academic social platforms.[15] Tools such as software development platform GitHub have a long history in academia, open-source software, and scholarly communication. However, the more disruptive elements of platforms have entered the open domain in the past 10 years, including many for-profit, publisher-acquired and venture capital (VC) funded entities. GitHub itself (before its acquisition by Microsoft) shared VC investors[16] with less scholar-friendly technologies such as the union-rejecting Kickstarter and is not an open source or not-for-profit platform.[17] Popular service ResearchGate has similar issues, sharing investors with Uber. Likewise, Academia.edu (VC-funded), Mendeley (VC-funded until bought by Elsevier), SSRN (independently run until bought by Elsevier) and bepress (independently run until bought by Elsevier) were all focused on community building and prosocial behavior and were acquired for their data-mining and full scholarly lifecycle integration potential. The political and economic infrastructure supporting open is not always known to users or even important to them. This is why users are often surprised when a platform is shut down or acquired by a bigger player—if they realize it at all.

One approach to developing new services for open practices has been the platformizing, digitizing, and scaling of existing tools and practices such as reference and paper management, lab notebooks, collaborative databases, and the sharing of research outputs. It is easy to see how in principle these platforms offer value as a more efficient way of doing what is already done.

Another approach can make claims to solving user problems, serving new communities, and bringing innovation to scholarly communication—a useful form of disruption. Some platforms go further, in a form of "technosolutionism," looking to remove friction and add technology to every process to make it more efficient.[18] There has been proliferation of metric products (including "alternative"/attention metrics, digital badges, writing platforms, and add-ons to the academic publishing process (e.g., Publons)) that are either produced or acquired by the biggest publishers and aggregators. Much of this dubious innovation, for profit, excludes features and disciplines not considered by a less than diverse group of developers and shuts out workflows and output types that are not easy to standardize and metricize.[19]

The final form of platformization in open is scholar-owned, hosted and/or run platforms (Open Library of the Humanities, *SocArxiv*, *Humanities Commons*) with different funding models and using different technological solutions and partners. For example, the Open Library of the Humanities (OLH) has developed its own scholarly platform in Janeway, which was used at the time of writing for their website and limited journals, but also partner with Ubiquity Press as a platform for most OLH content.[20] Some funding and governance models in this form of platformization are more stable and sustainable than others. While some sort of start-up funding will usually be needed, relying on grant funding from a handful of big foundations rather than contribution from members can be a risky proposition. Funders tend to fund proof of concept and early development, but not 10 or 20 years of implementation or the staffing costs involved.

Against this commercial imperative, the principles of platform cooperativism pose an alternative, encouraging a values-driven approach that could lead to greater sustainability. The seven cooperative principles, also adopted by platform cooperativism are:

1. Voluntary and open membership
2. Democratic member control
3. Member economic participation
4. Autonomy and independence
5. Education, training, and information
6. Cooperation among cooperatives
7. Concern for community[21]

The Platformization of Open

The principles are supported by two sets of values:

Cooperative values

- self-help
- self-responsibility
- democracy
- equality
- equity
- solidarity

Ethical values

- honesty
- openness
- social responsibility
- caring for others[22]

These values and principles would seem to accord with those of many scholars, librarians, and educators involved in open, especially when aspects such as economic participation are considered at the institutional rather than personal level. The values of for-profit publishers and platforms are much more geared toward competition than community and equitable participation in the scholarly commons. For example, RELX (Elsevier's parent group) had "Winning" as a corporate value in 2017.[23] However, it is not unknown for cooperatives to behave as though they are typical businesses—for example, OCLC, a library cooperative, has been critiqued for its "corporate greed."[24] Even nonprofit, scholar-founded platforms such as *arXiv* do not allow for voluntary and truly open participation, requiring proof of membership of the academic/disciplinary community.[25] ResearchGate replicates this gatekeeping activity by requiring an institutional email address. Yet Academia.edu breaks with this tradition by allowing anyone to join and upload/download content, as do some of the other for-profit services.

The principles of freedom to contribute and freedom to be read are aspects that more "responsible" not-for-profit open platforms need to consider, even if the founders of those platforms may initially struggle with the idea of a cooperative-based commons where every participant has ownership. Srnicek argues that as platforms scale, they transform from innovative enablers into stifling gatekeepers.[26] Emerging open tools often copy behaviors of platforms in other domains, by ignoring the legal constraints that hamper institutional services and allowing the unauthorized upload of copyrighted material (e.g., ResearchGate).[27] Safe Harbor agreements protect intermediaries from liability in copyright claims,[28] which is why Facebook and Google continue to argue that they are not media companies/publishers and absorb the relatively small penalties incurred when they break the rules.[29] The platforms developed or acquired by legacy publishers are supported by their parent companies' government lobbying power[30] and influence in higher education, which is not so far from the regulatory entrepreneurship practiced by many technology companies to bend the law and common practice to their will.[31]

Recently, there have been calls by librarians and academics for scholars to delete their accounts on the for-profit platforms Academia.edu and ResearchGate.[32] But assuming a gatekeeper position by policing copyright and embargoes for legacy publishers[33] or insisting that particular platforms are not open enough, may form part of paid scholarly communication roles, but this is not necessarily a helpful direction for librarians and open activists to take.[34] Telling other researchers they are wrong does not make more content or data open and it does not convince the majority of researchers and other users of available research outputs who prioritize "satisficing"—taking a course of action that satisfies their minimum requirements—over optimization of their practices.[35] It can be all too glib to criticize scholars for using for-profit platforms or to talk about the "Uberfication" of the university as a full-time academic librarian or white male full professor on a secure contract. The choice to avoid self-branding and the biggest, most visible social networking services is one that can most comfortably be made by those not fighting for a permanent, full-time academic post while working several precarious, fractional jobs.

Scholarly communication platforms with a social networking element, which includes most commercial services in open, play the same game as Facebook, Google, Snapchat and other big companies in their commodification of participatory media and prosocial sharing. They profit (whether or not that is reinvested) from the long-established sharing behaviors within academic communities, now transferred to the internet. Most of the value in the platforms is actively provided or what Smith calls passively "leaked" by the users—content, network effects, relationships, actions, data, metadata.[36] Users in most cases cannot retrieve and consolidate their own data via Open APIs—the platform owners are the ones who can monetize user behavior via new products and metrics or the valuation of a tool at the time of acquisition.

The Platformization of Open

It is important not to ignore the role of vertical integration and acquisition as platformization strategies. The "Fourth Industrial Revolution" or 4IR concerns the financialization of data, via pipelines and workflows or control of the data sources themselves.[37] To succeed under contemporary capital, "platform capitalism" or no, means being abreast of trends inside and outside a sector and being agile enough to transform businesses before they are left behind. In open, two large corporations have done very well out of responding to 4IR, and not just when it comes to their scholarly communication segments.

RELX, Elsevier's parent company, has divested itself of print magazines and acquired and developed products around legal technology, predictive policing, risk management and scoring, and health education; and most importantly, they are data brokers and data service providers for a range of sectors. This datacentric change in focus is reflected in the hugely profitable Elsevier academic publishing and services segment of the business. First, their spokespeople talked of a move from products to services, acquiring businesses that enhanced their service offerings, and now RELX markets itself as an "information and analytics" group—analytics meaning data products and services.[38] Elsevier's academic segment does both parts of this and fits well with the wider company strategy. Central to this segment's model is Pure, its "enterprise research management solution that aggregates an organization's research information from numerous internal and external sources into a single platform."[39] RELX has a start-up incubator to help find new acquisitions and the group has a venture capital arm that invests in Palantir, Peter Thiel's software company, controversial for its involvement in deportations in the US, military intelligence, surveillance of US citizens, and other privacy-invasive work in the public and private sectors.

Elsevier and other RELX group acquisitions show a clear desire to capture multiple workflows from end to end in various sectors. In academia, they have products covering the full researcher workflow, an assessment workflow for administration, ranking hiring and research assessment exercises and access to enough data flows via the various parts of RELX and all the Elsevier products to produce new metrics, prediction tools, and other products regularly—as befits a data broker. They do not have to own the data, only control the pipeline and flows of data. RELX is embedded in other areas of higher education, such as the UK USS academic pension scheme investments, university league tables, and more.

While Elsevier is the most obvious example of platformization, oligopolization, and data control in this space, especially with the company's connections to others in the group, it is not alone in scholarly communication and, therefore, open. Clarivate Analytics, the company formed when the intellectual property and services part of Thomson Reuters was sold off to venture capital firms, has been acquiring additional emerging platforms and occupies a similar "workflow capture" space. Digital Science, part of the same Holtzbrinck group as legacy publishing giants Springer Nature, portrays a researcher-friendly image, but its own website talks about products across the researcher workflow, and while its offering is not as integrated as that of Elsevier, that looks like the company's eventual intention. Deals for piloting workflow packages from these single and barely interoperable suppliers are being signed by universities at a high administrative level.[40] What Elsevier calls "interoperable" actually means *intra*operable within its own suite of products. The signing of these workflow deals—for example, Digital Science at the University of Sheffield and Elsevier at the University of Manchester—has ramifications for higher education, particularly in countries like the UK, which traditionally used open-source software and library staff to run their open access and research data management services.

Finally, it is worth addressing the role of funders in the platformization of open. At the smaller end of the scale, a project-based approach to developing new services around open in institutions, a lack of funding for technical expertise in libraries, and poor user-experience design of in-house and open-source systems made it easier for decision-makers to outsource their infrastructure needs to commercial platforms—especially as most universities in the UK, in particular, operate as though they are in competition, leading to replication of staffing and services. This is a simplification of the problem but covers some of the issues. Large funders such as the Wellcome and Gates Foundations have invested heavily in commercial as well as not-for-profit open platforms, ResearchGate and F1000 being notable examples. F1000, a for-profit company privately owned by a serial entrepreneur and multimillionaire, is seeking to be the main provider of mega-journal and preprint platforms for various funders and institutions. The UK research councils chose to fund the payment of article processing charges (APCs) to legacy publishers to achieve Open Access rather than prioritizing funding for the staffing of institutional repositories or scholar-led no-APC options like the Open Library of the Humanities, and it remains to be seen whether initiatives such as Plan S will help with supporting this human infrastructure or just add to their burden. Projects such as the Joint Roadmap for Open Science Tools (JROST) offer a little more hope, as creators and those who currently host their content are involved and not just funders and technologists.

Funder requirements (with consequences) have been the only successful instrument so far for ensuring researcher compliance with open-access and open-data mandates. The question remains though: is a sector that is reliant on venture capital plus large funders plus the public sector a mixed economy, or a platformized accident waiting to happen? Full stakeholder involvement is required in finding a solution, and researchers must not be outweighed by the views of proxy groups such as learned societies, whose statements reflect their connections to big publishers and their need for income to carry out their work.

Notes

1. Jose van Dijck, "Disassembling Platforms, Reassembling Sociality," in *The Culture of Connectivity: A Critical History of Social Media* (Oxford: Oxford University Press, 2013), 24–44, https://doi.org/10.1093/acprof:oso/9780199970773.001.0001.

2. Bobby Schweizer, "Platforms," in *The Routledge Companion to Video Game Studies*, ed. Mark J. P. Wolf and Bernard Perron (Abingdon, UK: Routledge, 2010), 41–48, https://doi.org/10.4324/9780203114261.

3. Ian Bogost and Nick Montfort, "Platform Studies: Frequently Questioned Answers," *Digital Arts and Culture*, December 12–15 (2009): 1–6.

4. Annabelle Gawer, "Bridging Differing Perspectives on Technological Platforms: Toward an Integrative Framework," *Research Policy* 43, no. 7 (2014): 1239–1249, https://doi.org/10.1016/j.respol.2014.03.006.

5. Tim O'Reilly, "Government as a Platform," *Innovations: Technology, Governance, Globalization* 6, no. 1 (2011): 13–40, https://doi.org/10.1162/INOV_a_00056.

6. David Weinberger, "Library as Platform," *Library Journal*, September 4, 2012, https://lj.libraryjournal.com/2012/09/future-of-libraries/by-david-weinberger/.

7. Tarleton Gillespie, "Platforms Intervene," *Social Media + Society* 1, no. 1 (2015): 205630511558047, https://doi.org/10.1177/2056305115580479.

8. Elizabeth Altman and Mary Tripsas, "Product-to-Platform Transitions: Organizational Identity Implications," in *The Oxford Handbook of Creativity, Innovation, and Entrepreneurship*, ed. Christina Shalley, Michael A. Hitt, and Jing Zhou (Oxford: Oxford University Press, 2015), https://doi.org/10.1093/oxfordhb/9780199927678.013.0032.

9. Thomas R. Eisenmann, Geoffrey Parker, and Marshall W. Van Alstyne, "Opening Platforms: How, When and Why?," *SSRN Electronic Journal*, 2008, 1–27, https://doi.org/10.2139/ssrn.1264012.

10. Anne Helmond, "The Platformization of the Web: Making Web Data Platform Ready," *Social Media + Society* 1, no. 2 (2015): 205630511560308. https://doi.org/10.1177/2056305115603080.

11. Hamid R. Jamali, David Nicholas, and Eti Herman, "Scholarly Reputation in the Digital Age and the Role of Emerging Platforms and Mechanisms," *Research Evaluation* 25, no. 1 (2016): 37–49, https://doi.org/10.1093/reseval/rvv032.

12. Wilma Clark et al., "Digital Platforms and Narrative Exchange: Hidden Constraints, Emerging Agency," *New Media & Society* 17, no. 6 (2015): 919–938, https://doi.org/10.1177/1461444813518579; Pia Mancini and Farida Vis, "How Do Digital Platforms Shape Our Lives?," World Economic Forum, 2015, https://www.weforum.org/agenda/2015/10/how-do-digital-platforms-shape-our-lives/.

13. L. DeNardis and A. M. Hackl, "Internet Governance *by* Social Media Platforms," *Telecommunications Policy* 39, no. 9 (2015): 761–770, https://doi.org/10.1016/j.telpol.2015.04.003; Frank Pasquale, "Platform Neutrality: Enhancing Freedom of Expression in Spheres of Private Power," *Theoretical Inquiries in Law* 17 (2016): 487–514; Martin Weller, *The Battle For Open: How Openness Won and Why It Doesn't Feel Like Victory* (London: Ubiquity Press, 2014), https://doi.org/10.5334/bam; Mike Zajko, "The Copyright Surveillance Industry," *Media and Communication* 3, no. 2 (2015): 42, https://doi.org/10.17645/mac.v3i2.270.

14. Xuemei Li, Mike Thelwall, and Kayvan Kousha, "The Role of arXiv, RePEc, SSRN and PMC in Formal Scholarly Communication," *Aslib Journal of Information Management* 67, no. 6 (2015): 614–635, https://doi.org/10.1108/AJIM-03-2015-0049; Oya Y. Rieger, "arXiv User Survey Report," arXiv Wiki, 2016, https://confluence.cornell.edu/display/arxivpub/arXiv+User+Survey+Report.

15. Angelika Bullinger et al., "Towards Research Collaboration—a Taxonomy of Social Research Network Sites," *AMCIS 2010 Proceedings*, August 1, 2010, http://aisel.aisnet.org/amcis2010/92.

16. Gerrit De Vynck, "Josh Kushner's Thrive Capital Strikes Gold in GitHub Deal," *Bloomberg*, June 5, 2018, https://www.bloomberg.com/news/articles/2018-06-05/josh-kushner-s-thrive-capital-strikes-gold-in-github-deal.

17. Bijan Stephen, "Kickstarter Will Not Voluntarily Recognize Its Employee Union," The Verge, May 15, 2019, https://www.theverge.com/2019/5/15/18627052/kickstarter-union-nlrb-election.

18. Evgeny Morozov, *To Save Everything, Click Here: Technology, Solutionism and the Urge to Fix Problems That Don't Exist* (London: Allen Lane, 2013).

19. Amy Brand, Albert Greco, and Robert Wharton, "Demographics and Education of Scholarly Publishing Professionals" (Figshare, 2015), https://doi.org/10.6084/m9.figshare.1424476.v2; Sasha Costanza-Chock, "Design Justice: Towards an Intersectional Feminist Framework for Design Theory and Practice," SSRN Scholarly Paper (Rochester, NY: Social Science Research Network, June 3, 2018), https://papers.ssrn.com/abstract=3189696; Brand, Greco, and Wharton, "Demographics of Scholarly Publishing and Communication Professionals."

20. Martin Paul Eve and Andy Byers, "Janeway: A Scholarly Communications Platform," *Insights* 31 (2018), https://doi.org/10.1629/uksg.396.

21. ICA, "What Is a Cooperative?," 1995, https://www.ica.coop/en/what-co-operative-0; Trevor Scholz, "Platform Cooperativism: Challenging the Corporate Sharing Economy," 2016, http://www.rosalux-nyc.org/platform-cooperativism-2/.

22. ICA, "What Is a Cooperative?"

23. RELX Group, "Governance," 2017, https://www.relx.com/corporate-responsibility/being-a-responsible-business/governance.

24. Barbara Fister, "Liberating Knowledge: A Librarian's Manifesto for Change," *Thought & Action* (Fall 2010): 83–90.

25. Sophie Ritson, "'Crackpots' and 'Active Researchers': The Controversy over Links between arXiv and the Scientific Blogosphere," *Social Studies of Science* 46, no. 4 (2016): 607–628, https://doi.org/10.1177/0306312716647508.

26. Nick Srnicek, *Platform Capitalism*, Theory Redux (Cambridge: Polity, 2017).

27. Hamid R. Jamali, "Copyright Compliance and Infringement in ResearchGate Full-Text Journal Articles," *Scientometrics* 112, no. 1 (2017): 241–254, https://doi.org/10.1007/s11192-017-2291-4.

28. Ian Brown and Christopher T. Marsden, *Regulating Code: Good Governance and Better Regulation in the Information Age*, Information Revolution and Global Politics (Cambridge, MA: The MIT Press, 2013).

29. Frank Pasquale, *The Black Box Society: The Secret Algorithms That Control Money and Information* (Cambridge, MA: Harvard University Press, 2015).

30. Martin Paul Eve, "Transcript of Meeting between Elsevier and the Minister for Higher Education in the UK, Jo Johnson," *Martin Paul Eve* (blog), May 4, 2016, https://eve.gd/2016/05/04/what-elsevier-and-the-minister-for-higher-education-in-the-uk-jo-johnson-met-about/.

31. Elizabeth Pollman and Jordan M. Barry, "Regulatory Entrepreneurship," SSRN Scholarly Paper (Rochester, NY: Social Science Research Network, March 3, 2016), https://papers.ssrn.com/abstract=2741987.

32. D. Bond, "RELX Buys Bepress to Boost Academic Publishing," August 8, 2017, https://amp.ft.com/content/c6f6c594-7787-11e7-a3e8-60495fe6ca71; Guy Geltner, "On Leaving Academia.Edu," November 23, 2015, https://f.hypotheses.org/wp-content/blogs.dir/1137/files/2015/12/On-leaving-Academia.pdf; Mita Williams, "Why I Think Faculty and Librarians Should Not Host Their Work on Academic.Edu or Researchgate.Com," November 20, 2015, http://librarian.newjackalmanac.ca/2015/11/why-i-think-faculty-and-librarians.html.

33. Penelope C. S. Andrews, "An Investigation into Changes to Institutional Repositories Following the Publication of the Finch Report in July 2012 and Subsequent Developments in UK Funder and Government Policies and Guidance" (MSc Digital Library Management, The University of Sheffield, 2014); Pablo de Castro, Kathleen Shearer, and Friedrich Summann, "The Gradual Merging of Repository and CRIS Solutions to Meet Institutional Research Information Management Requirements," *Procedia Computer Science*, 12th International Conference on Current Research Information Systems, CRIS 2014, 33 (2014): 39–46, https://doi.org/10.1016/j.procs.2014.06.007.

34. Kathleen Fitzpatrick, "Academia, Not Edu," *Planned Obsolescence* (blog), October 26, 2015, http://www.plannedobsolescence.net/academia-not-edu/; Katie Fortney and Justin Gonder, "A Social Networking Site Is Not an Open Access Repository," *Office of Scholarly Communication* (blog), December 1, 2015, http://osc.universityofcalifornia.edu/2015/12/a-social-networking-site-is-not-an-open-access-repository/.

35. Jackson et al., "Understanding Infrastructure: History, Heuristics and Cyberinfrastructure Policy," *First Monday* 12, no. 6 (2007), https://doi.org/10.5210/fm.v12i6.1904; Jere Odell, "How Many Repositories Do We Need?," 2016, http://www.ulib.iupui.edu/digitalscholarship/blog/how-many.

36. Gavin J. D. Smith, "Surveillance, Data and Embodiment: On the Work of Being Watched," *Body & Society* 22, no. 2 (2016): 108–139, https://doi.org/10.1177/1357034X15623622.

37. Klaus Schwab, *The Fourth Industrial Revolution* (New York: Crown Business, 2017).

38. Bond, "RELX Buys Bepress to Boost Academic Publishing."

39. Elsevier, "Pure and Simple: A Modular Research Information System," April 12, 2017.

40. Stephane Berghmans et al., "Open Data: The Researcher Perspective—Survey and Case Studies," *Mendeley Data* 1 (April 4, 2017), https://doi.org/10.17632/bwrnfb4bvh.1; Figshare, "Mission Statement & Core Beliefs," figshare, accessed May 20, 2019, https://knowledge.figshare.com/articles/item/mission-statement-and-core-beliefs; Alan Hyndman, "New Funding Information on Figshare Items," Figshare, November 12, 2018, https://figshare.com/blog/New_funding_information_on_Figshare_items/446.

19 Reading Scholarship Digitally

Martin Paul Eve

Scholarship, Labor Power, and Proliferation

In the present moment of 2020, more scholarship and research is published every year than it would be possible to read in a lifetime. The open-access mega-journal *PLOS ONE*, for example, publishes 20,000 papers per year alone.[1] This is not necessarily a bad thing; it may be that high volumes of publication are beneficial to the scientific endeavor and that this volume represents a healthy global research ecosystem. Such a volume does, though, pose a serious challenge for the contemporary researcher, even when one is speaking only of a single, subdisciplinary field.

Namely, the difficulty faced by the contemporary researcher is as follows: how is it possible to keep up to date with the most recent research and scholarship, amid competing demands for time in the saturated life of an academic? How, with a scarce volume of labor time, is it possible to know that one has read all of the most recent and relevant research and scholarship?

The problems of this environment of proliferation are abundantly clear already in academic hiring panels, although the digital solutions that I here pose will not solve this particular case.[2] Faced with hundreds of candidates per post, it becomes near-impossible for panel members to *read* all of the scholarship before them. In the humanities, the prospect of reading 200 monographs to appoint to a junior lectureship is simply beyond the realm of possibility. In the sciences, one could say the same of journal articles or conference proceedings.

It is from this challenge that proxy measures such as the notorious journal impact factor (JIF) sprung. These aggregate and insensitive measures of citation statistics were designed to assign quantitative value to specific venues. In other words, they moved from the evaluation of the specific article to an evaluation of a scarcity correlation in the container. For, if it can be presumed that only one in 200 papers is admitted to a journal, then that publication outlet can act as a perfect correlation for the scarcity that faces the hiring panel, with 200 applicants for a single job. Since JIF is premised on a scarcity—as it is calculated as citations against volume—this scarcity becomes important.

The problem is that such aggregation to the journal level is deeply flawed on several levels. For one, Brembs et al. have recently contended that the JIF correlates most closely with retractions.[3] For another, such scoring restricts academic choice and freedom in publication venue; if academics and their managers believe that certain journals will be used in their evaluation before hiring, promotion, and tenure committees, they will flock to publish only in such venues and will feel a pressure *not* to publish elsewhere. This can create a set of additional market problems for library budgets in the ever more restricted and almost monopolistic situation that has fueled the serials crisis since the 1980s.[4] Such methods of evaluation are also problematic in their aggregation since every "top" journal has published bad research and every "poor" journal could, in theory, contain brilliant articles.

To avoid these negative situations, the San Francisco Declaration on Research Assessment (DORA) was born, whereby institutional signatories agree to avoid the use of JIF-like proxy measures for their appointment panels.[5] This goes some way toward resolving the unintended consequences of the JIF, but it doesn't then answer the more fundamental question of what lies beneath the development of this measure: how can we know how to spend our reading time, without actually reading the work itself?

One suggestion for how we might fix this is to move to a mode of assessment where candidates for hiring present a research narrative in which they outline the impact, outcomes, and overall arch of their research, referring to a couple of key outputs, to which a hiring panel might turn and read in detail (the kind of "ImpactStory" approach). This sounds good in principle, even with the entirely valid concerns about the Impact agenda in the UK. (In the UK context, "impact" refers to demonstrable behavioral change in response to research and it is measured as part of the Research Excellence Framework (REF). This is controversial because it places an emphasis on translational, rather than early-stage, research. It also seems to demand that research change the world, rather than people's understandings, which can be hard in the humanities and social sciences—although in the 2014 REF, these disciplines fared well nonetheless in impact assessments.) It reinforces the importance of understanding why we do research and what the work told us, while also moving away from relying solely on the prestige of the venue in which the work appeared.

The problem with this is the onus it puts on candidates. Applying for academic jobs is arduous, unpaid work, with only a slim chance of a payoff. The dilemma then becomes: in implementing initiatives such as DORA through displacing the burden onto researchers/applicants to narrativize their work, the academy achieves some good. It is good that researchers should think more broadly about their work and how they can articulate this to a wide audience. This also gives those with a more quirky, non-prestige-based track record a better chance of employment in academia (at least in theory).

On the other hand, this approach asks candidates to take on more work, in order to spare the work of hiring panels (who are employed members of staff). If candidates have disabilities, (child)care responsibilities, or a host of other life circumstances, this method once more privileges those who can afford to put the most time into a gamble on an academic job. My conclusion from this thinking is that we need new ways to search and appraise scholarship.

Such an approach would not especially help with the problems of evaluation into which I have delved in this introduction; the assessment of the importance and quality of research work without recourse to crude metrics remains a difficult task. But it could help with the rigor of research and scholarship, which frequently does not and cannot cite the secondary literature comprehensively, since discovery has become so hard in an age of open abundance. In other words, while evaluative circumstances are among those where the demands on our reading time are most clear, this is only really a reflection of a broader problem in the general research environment, with which a range of computational approaches could assist.

Distant Reading Methodologies

This problem of abundant material and scarce time is not distinct to scholarship. In the fields of history and English, for instance, various digital methods have been born under the name of "distant reading" to attempt to solve this problem of insufficient reading labor-power.[6] In the sociological study of social media and the web, the computational solution would be called "text mining." JSTOR Labs has also recently released an example platform that allows for the digital close and distant reading of scholarly material within their database and has been thinking about alternative digital approaches to the monograph.[7] The fundamental premise of such methods, though, is to use digital techniques to scan through hundreds of thousands of papers, articles, or books, and to bring pertinent work or aspects to the attention of the operator.

One prominent group of scientists who are already embedded in such a culture is the Murray-Rust research group at Cambridge University. In 2014, Peter Murray-Rust, a crystallographer by background, was awarded a Shuttleworth Fellowship for his work on a suite of tools for the extraction of facts from the scientific literature: the ContentMine.[8] Working strictly within the bounds of the law—yet exploiting the exemption that facts cannot be placed under copyright, only their expression can—this nonetheless has the potential to revolutionize how we search academic literature at scale.[9]

For Murray-Rust, the benefits of mining the scholarly literature can be summarized as follows:[10]

- Comprehensive coverage of the secondary literature. At present, in all disciplines, work can go unnoticed or uncited, causing problems of repeated work and duplicated argument. A system that could comprehensively search the scholarly literature would avoid this.
- Comprehensive coverage within a paper. Scholars often read only parts of a work, for time, rather than reading the whole piece. This problem could be mitigated by a system such as that proposed by Murray-Rust that would summarize the entire argument of a paper and ensure coverage of the complete work.
- Aggregation and interdomain analytics. The example that Murray-Rust gives here is the fact that we are currently poor at cross-referencing information. For instance, consider the question: "What pesticides are used in what countries where Zika virus is endemic and mosquito control is common?" This is hard for a person to answer, but relatively easy to aggregate computationally when one has related documents.
- Semantically rich entity tags. Connecting terms that are used in the literature to other sources has the potential to greatly accelerate the research process in many domains.

Murray-Rust believes that his activities in mining the scholarly literature in this way are covered by the Hargreaves amendments to UK copyright law in 2014, which cover his development of the software, but he cannot be utterly sure. Indeed, a lot of time at the ContentMine project is clearly dedicated to ensuring the legality of what they do, the majority of which is due to the fact that the copyright to most research material is owned by publishers.[11]

This is also complicated by Technical Protection Measures (TPM) and Digital Rights Management systems, which more publishers are now employing atop research and scholarship. The purpose of these mechanisms is to ensure that the works cannot be put into general circulation. The problem is that TPMs make it impossible to use such papers with any custom software without breaking the law. Indeed, while it is technically trivial to circumvent some of these systems, there are also hefty criminal penalties for so doing. In the EU, this is specified by EU Directive 2001/29/EC and in the US by the Digital Millennium Copyright Act (DMCA). As an example of a nation-specific implementation of these legal frameworks, the UK has Section S296ZE of the Copyright, Designs and Patents Act. This section allows a researcher to appeal a rightsholder's TPMs where the use is noncommercial research. This involves asking a publisher to voluntarily provide a copy that can be used in such a way and, if they will not, then contacting the Secretary of State to ask for a directive to yield a way of benefiting from the copyright exemption for noncommercial academic research purposes.[12] As of 2014, there had been no successful challenges under this legislation.[13]

Machine Learning and Research Literature Classification

On top of the above, a further promising area that has yet to be explored is whether machine learning approaches could provide a future way by which to bring relevant research and scholarly literature to the attention of researchers. As with their biological counterparts, artificial neural networks consist of groups of interrelated processing units, called neurons, that connect together in order to solve problems. For instance, character-based recurrent neural networks are particularly good at generating sentences and words on a probabilistic basis, once trained on a suitable reference corpus.[14]

One of the tasks for which such software systems—and other forms of machine learning—are well-suited is classificatory problems. Given a known corpus subdivided into groups of desirability, accuracy, or general interest (from "not interested," through to "highly relevant"), one could easily envisage a system that could provide an appraisal on behalf of researchers when fed a new paper or book. One could also imagine the classification of works based on their intersecting bibliographies ("show me works that sit at the center of the citation networks of all these other works"), methodological principles, or any other taxonomographic feature by which scholarship could be clustered.

There are, of course, challenges with such a method. Artificial neural networks tend to replicate existing structures of value. This has even led, in fields of natural language processing, to racist and sexist networks because, unfortunately, these are structural phenomena of our societies at large.[15]

If using machine learning to classify scholarship for personal reading preference, then, the danger is that we simply replicate a list of the works that a scholar would have read anyway; a filter bubble. Instead, we need ways to inject the *unexpected* and *fortuitous* into such systems so that we can still have the experience of chance advancing thought and research, without affecting the classificatory measures too adversely. (Although it is also worth noting that what researchers call serendipity is often actually the result of library classification procedures that bring works into parataxis.) On the other hand, such a system would bring with it the long-sought-after promise of relevant material for reading, reducing the burdening effects of abundance upon the contemporary researcher.

Tempered Possibilities

Such futurological technologies as those upon which I have here speculated are not far off in technical terms; these are no impossible science fiction or utopian dreams, at least in one sense. However, in social and legal terms, we remain some way from such visions. For the ability of these technologies to reach fruition at a viable scale depends upon *access to research works*. There are several routes by which this could become possible. Each of these ways is equally difficult to achieve but some are more desirable than others:

- Total centralization of all research article publication under a large corporate entity. This would allow that corporate entity to develop such systems as those to which I have here gestured. It would also, though, be hugely monopolistic and commercially dangerous.

- A compact between academic publishers to deposit all of their works in centralized repositories upon which mining operations can be performed.
- Total open access to the research literature.

Clearly, despite the promise of amplifying our labor time by reading scholarship with computers, we still have some way to go.

Notes

1. Alison McCook, "PLOS ONE Has Faced a Decline in Submissions—Why? New Editor Speaks," Retraction Watch, March 15, 2017, http://retractionwatch.com/2017/03/15/plos-one-faced-decline-submissions-new-editor-speaks/.

2. For more on this, see Martin Paul Eve, "Scarcity and Abundance," in *The Bloomsbury Handbook of Electronic Literature* (London: Bloomsbury Academic, 2017).

3. Björn Brembs, Katherine Button, and Marcus Munafò, "Deep Impact: Unintended Consequences of Journal Rank," *Frontiers in Human Neuroscience* 7 (2013): 291, https://doi.org/10.3389/fnhum.2013.00291.

4. For a selection of sources on these subjects, see Association of Research Libraries, "ARL Statistics 2009–2011"; George Monbiot, "Academic Publishers Make Murdoch Look like a Socialist," *The Guardian*, August 29, 2011, sec. Comment is free, http://www.guardian.co.uk/commentisfree/2011/aug/29/academic-publishers-murdoch-socialist; Eve, *Open Access and the Humanities: Contexts, Controversies and the Future*, chap. 2; Larivière, Haustein, and Mongeon, "The Oligopoly of Academic Publishers in the Digital Era."

5. "San Francisco Declaration on Research Assessment: Putting Science into the Assessment of Research."

6. For just a selection of such work, see Franco Moretti, *Graphs, Maps, Trees: Abstract Models for Literary History* (London: Verso, 2007); Franco Moretti, "The Slaughterhouse of Literature," *MLQ: Modern Language Quarterly* 61, no. 1 (2000): 207–227; Franco Moretti, *Distant Reading* (London: Verso, 2013); Matthew L. Jockers, *Macroanalysis: Digital Methods and Literary History* (Urbana: University of Illinois Press, 2013); Ted Underwood, "A Genealogy of Distant Reading," *Digital Humanities Quarterly* 11, no. 2 (2017), http://www.digitalhumanities.org/dhq/vol/11/2/000317/000317.html; Andrew Piper, *Enumerations: Data and Literary Study* (Chicago: University of Chicago Press, 2018); Ted Underwood, *Distant Horizons: Digital Evidence and Literary Change* (Chicago: University of Chicago Press, 2019); Martin Paul Eve, *Close Reading With Computers: Textual Scholarship, Computational Formalism, and David Mitchell's* Cloud Atlas (Stanford, CA: Stanford University Press, 2019).

7. JSTOR Labs, "Text Analyzer Beta," 2017, https://www.jstor.org/analyze; Laura Brown et al., "Reimagining the Digital Monograph: Design Thinking to Build New

Tools for Researchers" (JSTOR Labs, 2017), https://hcommons.org/deposits/item/hc:14411/.

8. Note that Murray-Rust uses the term "content mining" instead of the legal terms "text and data mining," because he believes that it has broader connotations for where we might find useful information among multimedia forms, even if these are all, already, technically "data." See Peter Murray-Rust, "What Is TextAndData/ContentMining?," *Petermr's Blog*, July 11, 2017, https://blogs.ch.cam.ac.uk/pmr/2017/07/11/what-is-textanddatacontentmining/.

9. Tom Arrow, Jenny Molloy, and Peter Murray-Rust, "A Day in the Life of a Content Miner and Team," *Insights: The UKSG Journal* 29, no. 2 (2016): 208–211, https://doi.org/10.1629/uksg.310.

10. These bullet points are all taken from Murray-Rust, "What Is TextAndData/ContentMining?" sometimes with the same wording or example questions.

11. Peter Murray-Rust, "Sci-Hub and Legal Aspects of ContentMining 4/n," *Petermr's Blog*, May 6, 2016, https://blogs.ch.cam.ac.uk/pmr/2016/05/06/sci-hub-and-legal-aspects-of-contentmining/.

12. I write more on this in Martin Paul Eve, "Close Reading with Computers: Genre Signals, Parts of Speech, and David Mitchell's *Cloud Atlas*," *SubStance* 46, no. 3 (2017): 76–104.

13. Government of the United Kingdom, "Complaints to Secretary of State under s.296ZE under the Copyright, Designs and Patents Act 1988," August 15, 2014, https://www.gov.uk/government/publications/complaints-to-secretary-of-state-under-s296ze-under-the-copyright-designs-and-patents-act-1988.

14. For more, see Martin Paul Eve, "The Great Automatic Grammatizator: Writing, Labour, Computers," *Critical Quarterly* 59, no. 3 (2017): 39–54.

15. Tolga Bolukbasi et al., "Man Is to Computer Programmer as Woman Is to Homemaker? Debiasing Word Embeddings," *arXiv:1607.06520*, July 21, 2016, http://arxiv.org/abs/1607.06520; Aylin Caliskan, Joanna J. Bryson, and Arvind Narayanan, "Semantics Derived Automatically from Language Corpora Contain Human-like Biases," *Science* 356, no. 6334 (2017): 183–186, https://doi.org/10.1126/science.aal4230; Safiya Umoja Noble, *Algorithms of Oppression: How Search Engines Reinforce Racism* (New York: New York University Press, 2018).

20 Toward Linked Open Data for Latin America

Arianna Becerril-García and Eduardo Aguado-López

Scholarly communication is perhaps *the* phase in the research life cycle that has most seized the opportunity to broaden inclusion through the use of information technologies. Open access has promoted free and unrestricted access to scientific content, especially, driven by mandates, when it has been publicly funded. OA holds out the promise of a global scientific dialogue that would allow for a more inclusive, global research ecosystem.

Globalization has indeed become the ultimate goal in scientific practice, in which the circulation of knowledge generated in all regions is expected to have worldwide visibility. Often, this goal of global visibility has been equated with journals' presences in "mainstream" databases such as Web of Science (WoS) or Scopus. Those outside the Global North are encouraged to publish in journals indexed by these databases if their contributions are to have international visibility (although this is not guaranteed), but also so that these publications are viewed as high quality.[1]

Latin America, as with many other developing regions, has historically faced a lack of visibility and recognition for the science that it generates. This is mainly due to the scarce presence of Latin American journals in the aforementioned mainstream databases, which has led to the marginalization of research produced in the region.

Indeed, only 276 Latin American journals are indexed by WoS and 795 by Scopus, whereas in Redalyc there are 1,111. Figure 20.1 shows a Venn diagram with the journal sets' distribution among Redalyc, WoS, and Scopus. Further, a deeper analysis shows that most of the few indexed journals hold very low quartile positions. This distorted representation is not spread evenly between the disciplines. For instance, the social sciences and humanities (SSH) are particularly poorly represented. Only 90 social science and humanities journals from this region are indexed by WoS and 361 by Scopus. However, Redalyc indexes 555 journals from those areas (see figures 20.1 and 20.2).

This paradigm of valuation and communication presents a conundrum for the regional context. That is: there is low representation of Latin American research output in the legitimated knowledge circulation channels for the Global North, even though this region is possessed of an extremely robust ecosystem of science communication—and a system that is natively open and scholar-owned at that. Indeed, Latin American scholarly journals are led, owned, and financed by academic institutions. As covered in other chapters in this volume, each academic institution is part of an informal cooperative system that is neither formalized nor made explicit. Each institution supports journals that are managed by their own faculty members and the content of these journals is available to everyone. Where an institution is publicly funded, public budgets from local or national governments are used to support these publications. In this way, each institution's investment in journals mutually benefits all other institutions. This kind of

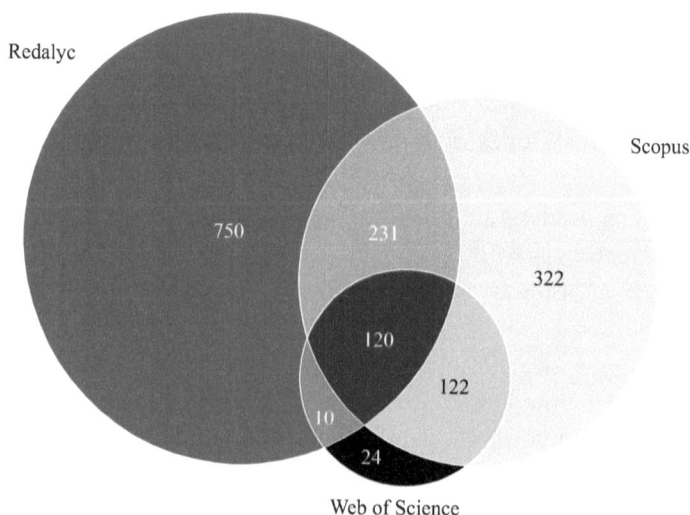

Figure 20.1
Latin American journals indexed by Redalyc, Scopus, and WoS.
Data sources: Redalyc database (2018), Scopus Source Title (2018), Source Publication List for Web of Science: Science Citation Index Expanded (2017), Social Sciences Citation Index (2017), Arts & Humanities Citation Index (2017).

informal cooperative was already operational before the term "open access" was even coined.

This Latin American ecosystem is composed of several layers. The base level is supported by hundreds of "university presses" with journals published electronically using software such as Open Journal Systems. Then, in an upper layer, platforms such as CLACSO, Redalyc, SciELO, and Latindex provide a set of added value features. Latindex's job, for instance, is to keep a well-organized directory of quality journals published in the region. CLACSO has contributed strongly to the Open Access Movement with promotion of and contents for the social sciences. Redalyc provides journals with mechanisms to increase their visibility, services of interoperability, search engine optimization, metrics, usage tracking, and more recently, technology to procure XML typesetting under the JATS (Journal Article Tag Suite) standard, then transformed automatically to PDF, HTML, and EPUB file formats of articles.[2]

Latin America has relied upon open access as its path to inclusion in a more participatory worldwide scholarly system. Originally, with the OA initiatives and declarations, a counterweight was sought to reduce the

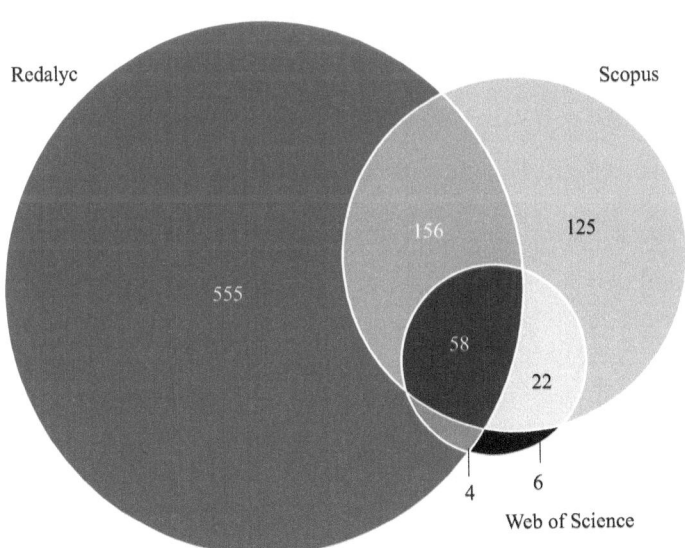

Figure 20.2
Latin American Social Sciences and Humanities Journals Indexed by Redalyc, Scopus, and WoS.

asymmetries generated by the primary communication, collaboration, and dissemination channels in the Global North. As noted by Marin, Petralia and Stubrin, and Banerjee, Babini, and Aguado, OA is viewed as the best option to promote a democratic and inclusive development and has proven results in increasing the international visibility of research.[3]

Yet, this has been shown to be an overly optimistic stance. For although, as highlighted by Babini, open access is the standard in Latin America, this openness has not broken the inertial dependencies of traditional legitimation circuits.[4] Thus, the exclusion, asymmetry, and gaps remain.

Further, this regional OA landscape is threatened by commercial open-access strategies from the Global North, which put at risk of rupture the Latin American OA nonprofit ecosystem while proposing to move to a new circumstance of exclusion: from "paying to read" to "paying to publish" (the APC-based OA model).

Hence, openness is not enough. It remains imperative also to modify systems of research assessment and to find more effective methods of communicating the knowledge generated in different regions, disciplinary fields, and languages. As Beigel suggests, it is not about giving the voices from the South a space in the channels where the North is established, but to question the very foundations of supposedly "universal" academic recognition and find ways to implement a non-hegemonic transnational dialogue.[5]

There are multiple approaches to achieving this. One strategy in Latin America is gambling upon reaching visibility within existing legitimized channels by adopting questionable research assessment practices, such as the use of the impact factor. This is the approach adopted by the SciELO Citation Index. Conversely, others such as Redalyc and CLACSO seek to integrate the region's developments, experience, and the academic model in order to minimize costs and join forces to guarantee the sustainability of OA and to maintain the academic-owned nature of dissemination and production of knowledge. This is being done through a recently launched, initiative called AmeliCA (Open Knowledge for Latin America and the Global South), which is supported by UNESCO and dozens of universities throughout the region.[6]

Technology for Visibility, Discoverability, and Internationalization

Some of the questions that arise when trying to build a more neutral, equitable, and inclusive space for scholarly communications include: are technologies capable of contributing to this? What might be the roles of semantic technologies, artificial intelligence techniques, ontological engineering, natural language processing, machine learning, and other advancements? We believe that there is a future role for technological innovations to contribute to a more integrated knowledge ecosystem and here go on to describe the semantic technologies that could help, without adopting a wholesale techno-solutionist perspective.

Certainly, interoperability is an important area in which technological developments have already been applied. The concept of interoperability arose from the need to exchange information across different applications and organizations with diverse data sources. What, though, if interoperability principles could be applied to scholarly communication in terms of the interchange of research results across geographical regions, disciplines, or even languages? Research published online—particularly when it is openly accessible—has the potential to join a giant mass of knowledge where visibility and discoverability are achieved intrinsically. A researcher from any place could retrieve any informational input needed to do his or her job and, eventually, his or her results would rejoin this database. Everything starts, though, with data structuring.

On the web, scholarly resources have been structured by the Open Archives Initiative Protocol for Metadata Harvesting (OAI-PMH) for interoperability purposes. In turn, this has contributed to the visibility of contents because metadata can be automatically distributed to libraries, universities, portals, and aggregators in ways that facilitate retrieval and consumption.

The data model specified by OAI-PMH provides a basic semantic level for understanding the nature of described resources, but only at an identification level. This is insufficient fully to capitalize on all textual elements, including citation data, figures, mathematical expressions, tables, supplementary material, and more.

Having scholarly resources structured at the element level goes well beyond OAI-PMH capabilities. This is an area where eXtensible Markup Language (XML) plays a major role, since it provides a set of simple rules and a uniform method to describe and exchange structured data, separated from the format in which the information is presented. XML—of which JATS is a schema—enables the structuring of full texts of scholarly resources and brings them a greater potential for readability and indexing, which favors their capacity to be discovered. It also, as Martin Paul Eve outlines in his chapter, facilitates potential future machine-reading possibilities for ingesting the scholarly corpus.

As Abel Packer points out elsewhere in this book, SciELO has promoted the use of XML since 2012 but began its full-scale adoption across all of its journals as of 2015. Health sciences journals began to adopt it as of 2014.[7] Meanwhile, Redalyc started to adopt XML in 2015 with a strategy based on the empowerment of scholarly publishers, providing tools and knowledge to make XML tagging a sustainable process.[8] Currently, approximately 90 percent of journals indexed by Redalyc publish their content in XML JATS.

While the implementation of XML in journals carries great potential, there is a deeper and more relational level of granularity at which information could be disseminated. Every piece of information that comprises a text from a journal article or from any other scholarly content could be understood, interpreted, and linked into a "knowledge cloud."

There are many barriers to such a global system, though. As noted by Ora Lassila, although everything on the web is machine-readable, it is not machine-comprehensible.[9] For instance, the information content of scholarly outputs could be represented as connections of informational elements where the structure, formed by nodes and connections, expresses knowledge. That form of structuration, though, goes far beyond the capabilities of XML, whose data model is a tree. Indeed, we would argue that a far better data model for knowledge representation is a graph, as provided by RDF (a resource description framework).

Thus, we argue, a transition needs to be made from a machine-readable to machine-comprehensible paradigm with respect to scholarly information resources: a transition from XML to RDF.

Leveraging Semantic Technologies to Achieve a Global Research Dialogue

The "HowOpenIsIt?®" Open Access Spectrum guide provides a scale for machine readability of OA content that includes, as a maximum level of openness, a notion of semantics that has not yet been achieved by Latin American journals.[10] RDF, the technology that would enable this, is an abstract model, a way to break down knowledge into discrete pieces.[11] And, indeed, there are two different purposes behind XML and RDF that should be understood for a future semantic scholarly context. This boils down to the use cases: for those who wish to query documents (XML) and those who wish to extract the "meaning" in some form and query that (RDF).[12]

Minimal structuring and semantics are integral to the web as it currently exists, in the form of hypertext. The essential feature of hypertext is the nonlinearity of content production by the authors and of content perception and navigation by users.[13] Indeed, from even minimal semantics have arisen amazing results. What, though, if web pages had more semantics?[14] Semantics, the process of communicating enough meaning to result in an action, has great potential to enable scholarly resources to join the so-called Web of Data.[15]

Semantic technologies discover relationships that exist among resources and then represent those relationships via some form of metadata, making it easier to develop reusable techniques for querying, exploring, and using the underlying data.[16] Using this semantic web, software can process content, reason with it, combine it, and perform deductions logically to solve problems automatically.

We, the authors of this chapter, have previously applied semantic technologies to structured scholarly resources. The results consist of a semantic model for selective knowledge discovery dubbed "OntoOAI" a semantic application that enables the processing of data structured with OAI-PMH, the application of ontologies in the description and verification of the knowledge obtained from OAI-PMH resources, and inference-testing mechanisms on the resultant dataset.[17]

OntoOAI was executed using a combination of three sources of information: Redalyc, the institutional repository of Roskilde University (RUDAR), and DBpedia. This data integration was possible through two ontologies: Dublin Core and Friend of a Friend (FOAF). OntoOAI processed 395,940 items resulting in 7.9 million triplets, which correspond to granular pieces (for instance, 60,354 triplets of author names; 1.6 million triplets of topics; 394,775 triplets of dates, and more).

It should be noted that given the identified associations between resources, it is possible to take advantage of graphs, hierarchical, or other net visualizations that allow users to explore and browse information following relations at different levels, which adds value for discoverability purposes.

OntoOAI's application verified the feasibility and benefits of using semantic technologies to achieve selective knowledge discovery while also showing some of the limitations of using OAI-PMH data for this purpose (among which is the lack of both URIs and full-text structuration). The latter would enable a journal article (or another scholarly resource) to be broken down into pieces that individually would form nodes in a graph whose relations among them are represented as edges and together they might be expressed in an ontology. RDF based on JATS could also work to achieve that task (see figure 20.3). Indeed, if this lack of URIs and RDF availability are overcome by Latin American scholarly resources, all this information could be part of the Linked Open Data (LOD) Cloud.[18] This would mean that every piece of information published by scholarly journals in Latin

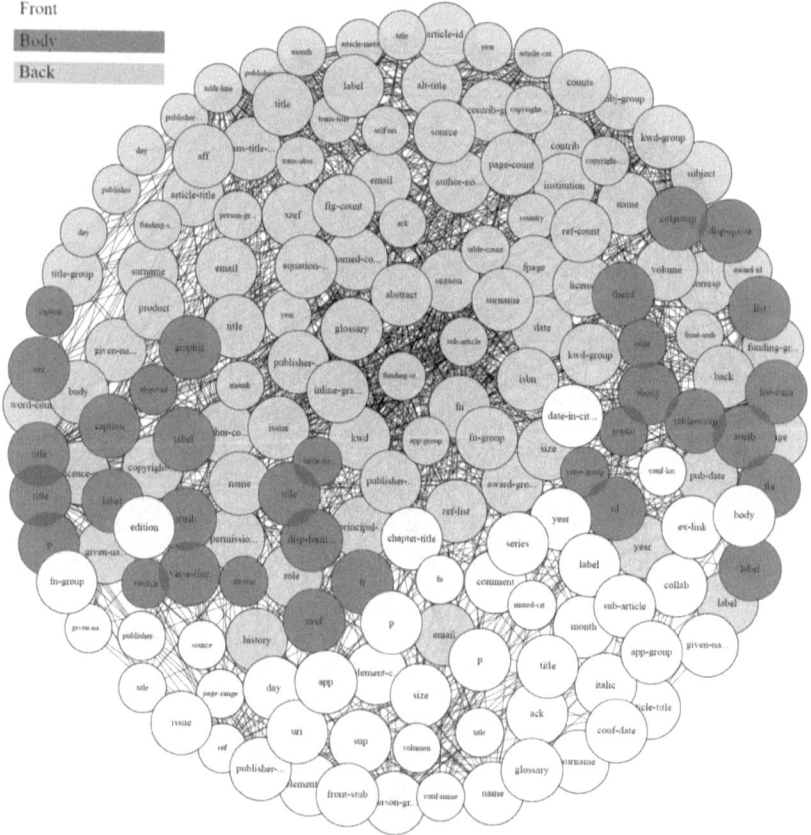

Figure 20.3
Knowledge representation of a journal article (RDF derived from JATS XML) based on the representation of the Linked Open Data Cloud.

America could be linked to all data provided by all other LOD sources (see figure 20.4). Had we such semantic markups within our systems of scholarly communications, novel mechanisms of knowledge discovery could be developed to query, extract, infer, and retrieve information in such a way that usability and applicability of knowledge generated in Latin America—and other regions—could be improved, and that published knowledge *per se* could reach visibility, discoverability, and internationalization, all provided by the inherent composition of it in the knowledge structure. Thus, traditional circuits of scholarly communication, the ones legitimated by current research assessment strategies, could be left behind. Information could speak by itself in benefit of a global science communication.

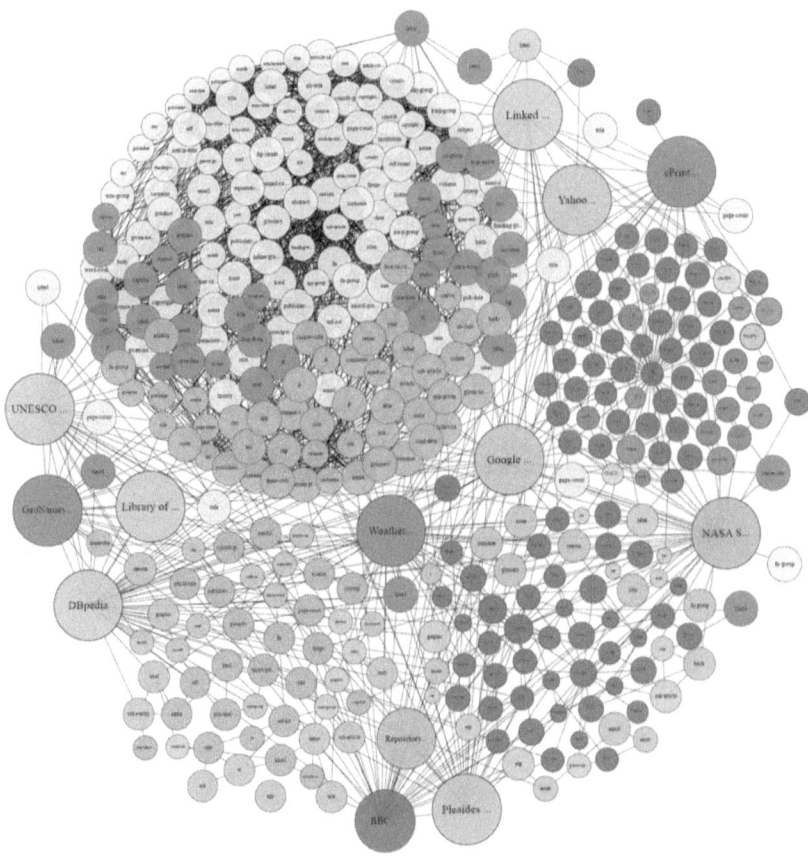

Figure 20.4
Journal articles as part of the Linked Open Data Cloud.

Certainly, many will see this technological solution as overly optimistic. After all, most difficult problems have social, rather than technological, answers. Yet we believe in the potentially liberatory powers of information technologies.

Notes

1. Eduardo Aguado-López, Arianna Becerril-García, and Sheila Godínez-Larios, "Colaboración Internacional en Las Ciencias Sociales y Humanidades: Inclusión, Participación e Integración," *Convergencia Revista de Ciencias Sociales*, no. 75 (2017): 16, https://doi.org/10.29101/crcs.v0i75.4227.

2. JATS, the international standard ANSI/NISO Z39.96–2015, defines a set of XML elements and attributes that describe content and metadata of journal articles, aimed to provide a common format in which journal content can be exchanged. National Information Standards Organization, "JATS: Journal Article Tag Suite, Version 1.1," 2015.

3. Anabel Marin, Sergio Petralia, and Lilia Stubrin, "Evaluating the Impact of Open Access Initiatives within the Academia and Beyond," in *Made in Latin America: Open Access, Scholarly Journals, and Regional Innovations*, ed. Juan Pablo Alperin and Gustavo Fischman (Ciudad Autónoma de Buenos Aires: CLACSO, 2015), 75–102, http://biblioteca.clacso.edu.ar/clacso/se/20150921045253/MadeInLatinAmerica.pdf; Dominique Babini, Eduardo Aguado López, and Indrajit Banerjee, "Tesis a Favor de La Consolidación Del Acceso Abierto Como Una Alternativa de Democratización de La Ciencia En América Latina," in *Acceso Abierto*, by Peter Suber (México: Universidad Autónoma del Estado de México, 2015), 13–48.

4. Dominique Babini, "Voices from the Global South on Open Access in the Social Sciences," in *Open Access Perspectives in the Humanities and Social Sciences* (London: London School of Economics, 2013), 15, https://blogs.lse.ac.uk/impactofsocialsciences/files/2013/10/Open-Access-HSS-eCollection.pdf.

5. Fernanda Beigel, "El Nuevo Carácter de la Dependencia Intelectual," *Cuestiones de Sociología* 14 (2016): 9, http://hdl.handle.net/10915/54650.

6. Redalyc, CLACSO, and UNESCO, "AmeliCA—Conocimiento abierto para América Latina y el sur Global," 2019, http://www.amelica.org/; see also "AmeliCA vs Plan S: Same Target, Two Different Strategies to Achieve Open Access.—AmeliCA," accessed May 1, 2019, http://www.amelica.org/en/index.php/2019/01/10/amelica-vs-plan-s-mismo-objetivo-dos-estrategias-distintas-para-lograr-el-acceso-abierto/.

7. SciELO, "¿Porqué XML?," *SciELO En Perspectiva* (blog), April 4, 2014, https://blog.scielo.org/es/2014/04/04/porque-xml/.

8. Eduardo Aguado-López, Arianna Becerril-García, and Salvador Chávez-Ávila, "Conectando al Sur Con La Ciencia Global: El Nuevo Modelo de Publicación en

ALyC, No Comercial, Colaborativo y Sustentable," 2016, 8–10, https://blogredalyc.files.wordpress.com/2016/08/redalycnuevomodelopublicacion2016-11.pdf.

9. Ora Lassila, "Web Metadata: A Matter of Semantics," *IEEE Internet Computing* 2, no. 4 (1998): 1, https://doi.org/10.1109/4236.707688.

10. Scholarly Publishing, Academic Resources Coalition, Public Library of Science, and Open Access Scholarly Publishers Association, "HowOpenisit?," Public Library of Science, 2014, https://www.plos.org/files/HowOpenIsIt_English.pdf.

11. Joshua Tauberer, *What Is RDF and What Is It Good For?* (2014; repr., Github, 2008), https://github.com/JoshData/rdfabout.

12. Tim Berners-Lee, "Why RDF Is More Than XML," W3C, September 1998, https://www.w3.org/DesignIssues/RDF-XML.html.

13. Gerti Kappel et al., "An Introduction to Web Engineering," in *Web Engineering: The Discipline of Systematic Development of Web Applications*, ed. Gerti Kappel (Hoboken, NJ: John Wiley & Sons, 2003), 11.

14. Steve Bratt, "Semantic Web, and Other Technologies to Watch," W3C, January 2007, https://www.w3.org/2007/Talks/0130-sb-W3CTechSemWeb/#(1).

15. Toby Segaran, Colin Evans, and Jamie Taylor, *Programming the Semantic Web* (Sebastopol, CA: O'Reilly Media, 2009), 3.

16. Oswald Campesato and Kevin Nilson, *Web 2.0 Fundamentals: With AJAX, Development Tools, and Mobile Platforms* (Sudbury, MA: Jones & Bartlett Learning, 2010), 33; Segaran, Evans, and Taylor, *Programming the Semantic Web*, 37.

17. Arianna Becerril-García and Eduardo Aguado-López, "A Semantic Model for Selective Knowledge Discovery over OAI-PMH Structured Resources," *Information* 9, no. 6 (2018): 4–12, https://doi.org/10.3390/info9060144; Arianna Becerril-García, Rafael Lozano Espinosa, and José Martín Molina Espinosa, "Semantic Approach to Context-Aware Resource Discovery over Scholarly Content Structured with OAI-PMH," *Computación y Sistemas* 20, no. 1 (2016): 131–135, https://doi.org/10.13053/cys-20-1-2189; Arianna Becerril-García, Rafael Lozano Espinosa, and José Martín Molina Espinosa, "Modelo Para Consultas Semánticas Sensibles al Contexto Sobre Recursos Educativos Estructurados con OAI-PMH" (Encuentro Nacional de Ciencias de la Computación, ENC 2014, Oaxaca, Mexico, 2014), 1–4.

18. The Linked Open Data Cloud is available at https://lod-cloud.net.

21 The Pasts, Presents, and Futures of SciELO

Abel L. Packer

Launched in 1998, the Scientific Electronic Library Online (SciELO), of which I am the director, has made important contributions to the research and democratization of scientific knowledge. It has done so through a not-for-profit network of over 1,000 journals and by emphasizing the academic, cultural, and social relevance of scholarly communications. These journals are housed within university departments and faculties, in other research institutions, at scientific societies and professional associations, all spread across 16 countries, including Latin America and the Caribbean, Portugal, Spain, and South Africa.

The network is dispersed; as an average, most institutions in the SciELO Network publish fewer than two indexed journals. This poses challenges for sustainability. Indeed, when SciELO was founded, most of these journals were barely breaking even. There were only a limited number of subscriptions to their print editions, their presence was known only to small and insular research communities, and they held low or no international visibility. These titles were also ignored by the indexes of the Institute for Scientific Information (ISI, now Clarivate Analytics), which were emerging in the eyes of authors, research authorities, journal publishers, and editors as the favored—albeit flawed—benchmark list of high-quality journals. In part, SciELO emerged in order to mitigate this situation through the adoption of digital open-access publishing, indexing, and dissemination, at scale.

Since that time, SciELO has managed to position itself as a benchmark of quality journals and has commensurately elevated the status of Latin American publications in proportion to its scientific production. It has been followed by other regional open-access initiatives such as *La Referencia*, a regional network of open-access repositories, and Redalyc, a centralized aggregator of journals, both of which are more thoroughly detailed in Dominique Babini's chapter.

In 2018, SciELO celebrated its twentieth birthday by hosting a public forum of SciELO Network authorities, journal editors, and scholarly communication editors. Culminating in the "20 Years of SciELO" week event, with over 700 participants, the network also took this opportunity to revisit the future goals for the platform. In particular, representatives of the national collections agreed to update the "common action lines" for the platform, in order to advance our journals' professionalization, internationalization, and sustainability for the next five years, with an emphasis on the transition to broader paradigms of open science.[1] This paints a bright picture for the future of SciELO and we expect the network to continue for many years to come. In this chapter, though, I will revisit the determinant forces that shaped the creation and development of SciELO and will project how these renovated forces can drive the future of the platform.[2]

Building a Common Publishing Model

SciELO is a program based on international cooperation, in which nations work together to adopt common technical standards for academic publishing. This cooperation manifests in the form of a common "meta-publisher"; that is, a virtual space that aggregates journal publications into a single location. From its very outset, SciELO was conceived as an open-access model, seeking to gain economies of scale, to adopt best editorial practices, and to maximize interoperability, visibility, and credibility. The model thrives on a balance between improving the capacities and qualifications of journals while respecting the independence of their editorial policies, missions, and research-community profiles.

Initial planning of the publishing model took place over a one-year pilot, beginning in February 1997 and formally launching in March 1998. The pilot model consisted of a partnership between the São Paulo Research Foundation (FAPESP) under Professor Rogerio Meneghini and the Latin America and Caribbean Center on Health Sciences Information of the Pan American Health Organization at the regional office of the World Health Organization (BIREME/PAHO/WHO) under my leadership. The initial relationship between FAPESP and BIREME was brokered by the Brazilian Association of Scientific Editors (ABEC), a tripartite relationship which bestowed on the model an authoritative status in research advancement and scientific information management. The pilot selected 10 leading journals from Brazil, which were already indexed by ISI or MEDLINE, spanning the scientific disciplines.

One of the most sought-after outcomes from this early pilot was the development of a trustworthy bibliometric database. In line with other leading research agencies in Latin America in the late 1990s, FAPESP was already running a program to support journals published by institutions from the State of São Paulo, which is responsible for nearly half of all Brazilian research articles and one quarter of Latin America's output. At that time, journals requesting financial support were mapped to a predefined ranking of journals in Brazil based on "academic relevance," defined by scientific committees from each discipline. There was also a similar program and ranking system to fund journals at the national level run by the Brazilian National Council for Scientific and Technological Development (CNPq). SciELO was designed to improve this extant situation, in which rankings were established without any bibliometric indicators due to the limited coverage of the bibliographic indexes and lack of existing performance metrics.

BIREME's expertise in scientific information management—derived from its regional technical cooperation through the Latin American and Caribbean network of health science libraries—made it an ideal partner for the development of this database. Indeed, BIREME's background in this space came from its provision of multilingual access to health science literature using the United States' National Library of Medicine (NLM) MEDLINE database and its regional complement, the Latin American and Caribbean Health Sciences Literature (LILACS). BIREME was also one of the five Medical Literature Analysis and Retrieval System (MEDLARS) centers that the NLM promoted in the late 1960s to disseminate the MEDLINE database. Through these projects and others, BIREME acquired substantial expertise in the operation of bibliographic databases in multilingual contexts with accessible and affordable methodologies and technologies. In the late 1990s, for example, it developed the Virtual Health Library (VHL) as its platform for web-based international cooperation to maximize access to health science information, a strategy that was aligned with UNESCO's Information for ALL Program.[3]

SciELO was initially conceived by BIREME as an associated network of the VHL. Thus, the creation of SciELO is also rooted in cooperation with the United Nations and with North America. For instance, a key collaboration between BIREME and UNESCO was the development of the public-domain

ISIS database software—used for information retrieval—which was widely used by libraries in developing regions and is still today a key component of SciELO's operating platform.

From these common goals—also sanctioned by the Information Department of the Chilean National Council for Scientific and Technological Research (CONICYT), and a workshop held in in March 1998 in São Paulo—SciELO was born. The launch was signaled by a special issue of *Ciência da Informação* and the first article describing the SciELO publishing model was published in Portuguese and translated and published in Spanish.[4] Early international dissemination of the SciELO project and model took place at the 1998 and 1999 workshops and conferences on electronic publishing in science organized by the International Council for Science (ICSU) and UNESCO.[5] Shortly thereafter, SciELO's importance for developing regions was highlighted in *Nature* in 2002 and in *Science* in 2009.[6]

After SciELO's launch in Brazil and Chile, the platform expanded rapidly, both in geographical scope and in subject coverage. For instance, the model was adopted over the next 11 years by 12 other Latin American and Caribbean countries, as well as Portugal, Spain, and South Africa. In terms of subject areas, in 2000 we launched the SciELO Public Health collection, specifically for health-related journals. These changes also led to some reallocations of roles. SciELO Brazil, for instance, now acts as the secretariat for the network and is responsible for communications, network meeting organization, and the management, maintenance and development of the methodological and technological work packages, training, and guidance for establishing new collections. Since 2010, BIREME, by contrast, has restricted its operation to the coordination of SciELO Public Health.

As part of its expansion, SciELO also developed a set of simple protocols for establishing new collections. Each new collection must be led and funded by a nationally recognized research and technology organization, beginning with a three-month "pilot collection" of three to five journals operating in an intranet setting. This is followed by an open web operation under the label of an "in-development collection" for approximately six to eight months. Finally, when all requirements are in place, the collection moves to certified status (which can be revoked if the quality standards drop). While the network is open to thematic collections, so far only the public health collection has taken this option. A tentative plan to operate a social sciences collection with selected articles from SciELO journals translated into English did not materialize due to the lack of resources and complexities around the quality control of translations. Joining the SciELO Network, of course, remains a voluntary decision at both the national and journal levels. The status of the network, as of 2018, is shown in figures 21.1 and 21.2.

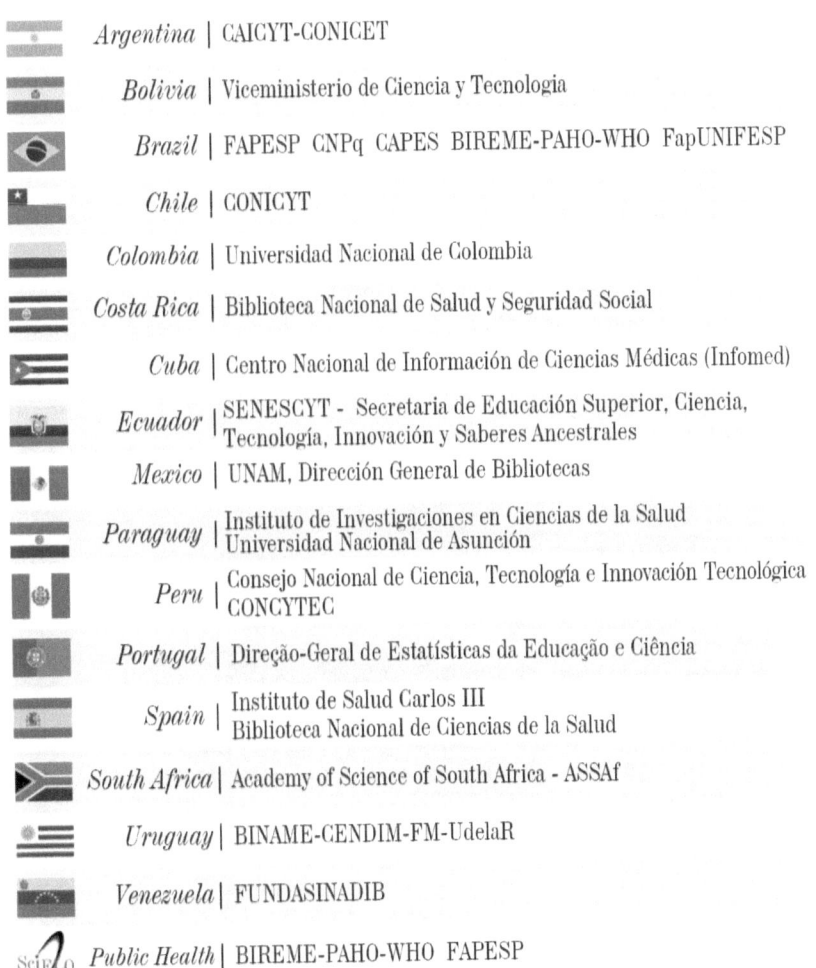

	Argentina	CAICYT-CONICET
	Bolivia	Viceministerio de Ciencia y Tecnologia
	Brazil	FAPESP CNPq CAPES BIREME-PAHO-WHO FapUNIFESP
	Chile	CONICYT
	Colombia	Universidad Nacional de Colombia
	Costa Rica	Biblioteca Nacional de Salud y Seguridad Social
	Cuba	Centro Nacional de Información de Ciencias Médicas (Infomed)
	Ecuador	SENESCYT - Secretaria de Educación Superior, Ciencia, Tecnología, Innovación y Saberes Ancestrales
	Mexico	UNAM, Dirección General de Bibliotecas
	Paraguay	Instituto de Investigaciones en Ciencias de la Salud Universidad Nacional de Asunción
	Peru	Consejo Nacional de Ciencia, Tecnología e Innovación Tecnológica CONCYTEC
	Portugal	Direção-Geral de Estatísticas da Educação e Ciência
	Spain	Instituto de Salud Carlos III Biblioteca Nacional de Ciencias de la Salud
	South Africa	Academy of Science of South Africa - ASSAf
	Uruguay	BINAME-CENDIM-FM-UdelaR
	Venezuela	FUNDASINADIB
	Public Health	BIREME-PAHO-WHO FAPESP

Figure 21.1
SciELO Network collections.

Distribution of SciELO Network collections by year of starting, type of collection, number of journals indexed, total of articles, May 2019							
Year started	#	Collections		Journals Indexed			Documents
		Collection	Status[1]	All[2]	Active[3]	Certified[4]	
1998	1	Brazil	C	372	298	298	386,617
	2	Chile	C	121	107	107	64,632
2000	3	Costa Rica	C	42	37	37	9,832
	4	Public Health[5]	C	20	18	18	42,727
	5	Cuba	C	77	67	67	33,478
2001	6	Spain	C	60	43	43	38,237
	7	Venezuela	C	60	37	37	18,971
2003	8	Mexico	C	214	127	127	66,295
	9	Argentina	C	150	107	107	39,872
	10	Colombia	C	236	227	227	72,031
2004	11	Peru	C	31	31	31	9,618
	12	Portugal	C	68	46	46	18,745
2005	13	Uruguay	C	25	21	21	4,667
2006	14	Social Sciences[6]	I	33	33	33	665
	15	West Indian	I	1	1	1	1,307
2007	16	Paraguay	D	15	14	14	2,310
2009	17	Bolivia	C	27	23	23	4,758
	18	South Africa	C	78	76	76	28,104
Total Network				1595	1268	1247	824,159
1 - C=Certified; D=in Development; I=Interrupted							
2 - All journals indexed: actives, excluded, name changed or publication interrupted							
3 - Journals being published regularly							
4 - Journals from collections that comply with SciELO standards							
5 - Includes 12 journals and 23,394 articles already indexed in national collections							
6 - Includes 23 journals and 523 articles already indexed by national collections							

Figure 21.2
Distribution of SciELO Network collections by start year, status, number of journals indexed, total of articles (May 2019).

Documenting the Evolution of the SciELO Program and Network

The growth and evolution of SciELO can be seen in the distributions of the annual total number of journals (figure 21.3) and documents indexed by the network of national collections (figure 21.4).[7] For journals, one distribution accumulates all indexed journals and another only those that remained active (for there are many reasons why journals may be discontinued: noncompliance with indexing criteria, interruption of publication, a turn to for-profit publishing, and at the journal's decision). The annual growth of the active journals was 21 percent per year over 20 years, starting with 26 journals in 1998 and ending with 1,270 in 2018. The number of journals indexed tends to stabilize toward a core in each collection, resulting in overall decreasing growth, well expressed by the annual growth for successive quinquennials: 40 percent, 26 percent, 16 percent, 7 percent (figure 21.5). The current SciELO Network has reached a stable level of 51,000 newly published documents per year, 90 percent of which are articles and reviews. The documents are physically hosted on nationally operated servers but conceptually they are integrated within the SciELO common virtual space. In fact, the metadata of the newly input documents are physically uploaded weekly by the national collections into the network repository. With over 800,000 documents, the SciELO Network repositories serve a daily average of over 1,000,000 HTML and PDF articles, using COUNTER-compliant

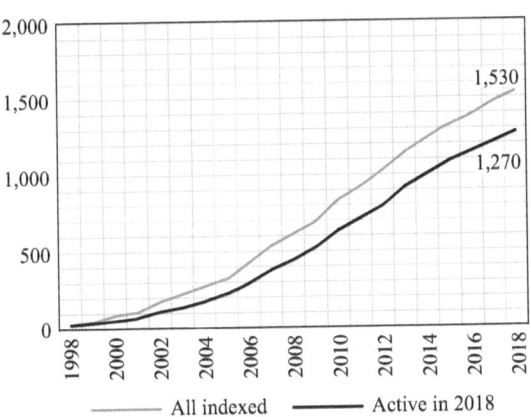

Figure 21.3
Yearly increase in SciELO Network journals.

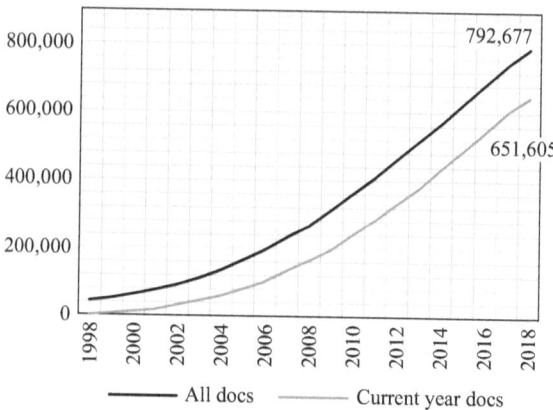

Figure 21.4
Yearly increase in SciELO Network articles.

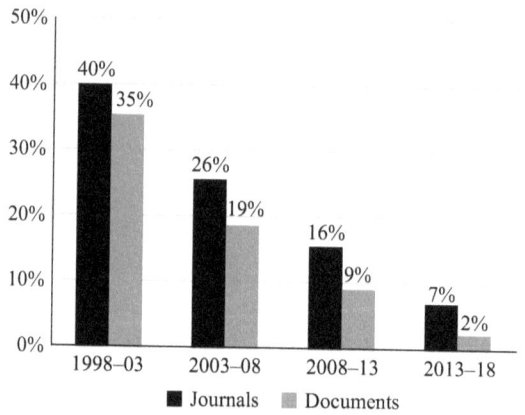

Figure 21.5
SciELO Network quinquennial rate of growth.

metrics (a standard for measuring article hits in a way that doesn't count duplicates).

SciELO's collections span a variety of subjects and editorial policies. There is no predefined pattern, priority, or privilege with respect to the composition of the collections. Multilingualism is also an inherent characteristic of research communication in the SciELO Publishing Model.[8] Indeed, figure 21.6 evidences the diversity of the composition of the SciELO national collections in terms of the distribution of number of journals and documents published in 2017 by major knowledge areas, language, authorship affiliation, and citations per article from inside and outside the SciELO Network. As can be seen, Brazil is responsible for about 40 percent of the contents, followed by Colombia, Mexico, and Chile. Together these four countries publish about 70 percent of the documents. Paraguay is not included in the table because it is not yet a certified collection. About 12 percent of the documents are not identified as communicating research, which is the case with opinion editorials, obituaries, and so forth. Brazil publishes an average of 71 such articles per journal per year while all other collections publish an average of 30 articles.

With respect to thematic areas: health sciences, human sciences, and applied social sciences comprise 67 percent of the articles. The presence of other disciplinary spaces is limited, reflecting the general scope of the research communicated by nationally published journals. Exceptions here include agricultural topics, covering 17 percent of articles from Brazil and reflecting the importance of this area within the country's economy. Further, biological sciences have a prominent profile in Costa Rica and South Africa, with 17 percent and 27 percent of their articles, respectively. Spain's collection is restricted to health sciences, which also comprises more than 50 percent of the output from Cuba, Peru, Uruguay, and Venezuela. Multidisciplinary categories include journals with three or more thematic areas assigned. Except for South Africa's and Brazil's collections, non-English articles prevail in more than two-thirds of the articles of 12 collections and in more than 90 percent of seven collections. SciELO Brazil journals, which traditionally faced a limited global reach due to their Portuguese native language, made a huge effort to increase the number of English articles, achieving 70 percent in 2017 and planning to reach 80 percent in the coming three to five years.

With respect to the proportion of foreign authorship (that is, authors from outside the nation hosting the journal) and global reach, the selected countries in figure 21.6 had valid data for at least 85 percent of the articles. For different reasons, Brazil and Cuba publish predominantly national authors, while Chile and Costa Rica have a foreign author on more than 50 percent of their articles.[9] In addition to the language of publication and authorship, the source of the citations the research received is an indicator of degree of globalization. Taking the Web of Science (WoS) ALL Database as the source because it covers all SciELO journals, figure 21.6 shows for the documents published in 2015 by each collection the distribution of the citations per document received from SciELO Network journals and from all WoS ALL Database journals up to May 2019. Overall, there is a threefold increase when moving from SciELO to WoS ALL Database, always taking into consideration that the actual citation values per collection depend on the distribution of thematic areas, language of publication, and authorship affiliation. Brazil's and Chile's multithematic collections perform better in citations per document in both contexts. In terms of presence in international commercial bibliometric indexes, figure 21.6 also shows the

Country	Composition							Major Thematic Areas				
	Journals	% Journals / total	Docs	% Docs / total	Citable docs	% Citable docs / docs	Articles / journal	Agriculture	Applied social sciences	Biological sciences	Engineering	Exact and earth
Argentina	124	10%	3,438	5.9%	2,905	84%	23	8%	17%	15%	2%	4%
Bolivia	17	1%	175	0.3%	137	78%	8	4%	23%	8%	6%	9%
Brazil	291	23%	22,593	39.1%	20,566	91%	71	17%	7%	9%	8%	3%
Chile	104	8%	4,457	7.7%	3,895	87%	37	9%	18%	14%	9%	9%
Colombia	227	18%	6,929	12.0%	6,095	88%	27	8%	22%	5%	11%	5%
Costa Rica	34	3%	1,020	1.8%	917	90%	27	8%	25%	17%	9%	3%
Cuba	64	5%	3,298	5.7%	2,902	88%	45	10%	13%	2%	9%	3%
Ecuador	13	1%	276	0.5%	257	93%	20	0%	37%	0%	39%	14%
Mexico	169	13%	6,101	10.6%	5,020	82%	30	10%	29%	13%	7%	7%
Peru	29	2%	1,171	2.0%	979	84%	34	9%	8%	13%	0%	4%
Portugal	46	4%	1,799	3.1%	1,524	85%	33	9%	40%	0%	2%	2%
South Africa	74	6%	3,262	5.6%	2,979	91%	40	7%	11%	27%	9%	9%
Spain	42	3%	2,488	4.3%	2,016	81%	48	0%	0%	0%	0%	0%
Uruguay	22	2%	593	1.0%	404	68%	18	0%	29%	7%	0%	0%
Venezuela	14	1%	194	0.3%	174	90%	12	17%	3%	13%	18%	0%
Total	1,268	100%	57,794	100%	50,770	88%	40	11%	14%	10%	7%	4%

Figure 21.6
SciELO Network collections coverage by major thematic areas and global visibility given by proportion of English articles and foreign authors, citations per document received in WoS ALL Database and presence in Scopus and SJR.

presence of SciELO Network in the 2019 edition of Scopus, which offers incomplete but elaborate journal coverage. SciELO Bolivia and Ecuador are not in Scopus and SciELO Venezuela is not considered because it is not updated. About half of the SciELO journals are indexed and about 70 percent are above the twenty-fifth percentile of Scimago Journal Ranking (SJR), with SciELO South Africa and Brazil journals above 91 percent and 87 percent respectively (this could be due to language factors as these latter two nations, as noted, publish predominantly in English).

						Global Visibility					
						WoS citations/doc received			Scopus indexing		
Health sciences	Human sciences	Linguistic, literature and arts	Multidisciplinary	Articles in English	Articles author's abroad affiliation	From SciELO journals	From WoS ALL database journals	Increase	% Journals indexed	% Journals SJR Q1, Q2 or Q3	Country
29%	34%	3%	0%	7%	–	0.23	0.69	3.01	30%	41%	Argentina
22%	19%	0%	16%	6%	–	0.08	0.19	2.31	–	–	Bolivia
40%	18%	3%	3%	70%	24%	0.85	2.68	3.15	73%	87%	Brazil
30%	22%	7%	1%	26%	52%	0.56	1.76	3.11	75%	72%	Chile
24%	24%	3%	6%	25%	39%	0.40	0.91	2.28	35%	69%	Colombia
24%	17%	7%	8%	16%	61%	0.22	0.72	3.29	9%	67%	Costa Rica
62%	6%	0%	2%	3%	21%	0.20	0.33	1.63	30%	5%	Cuba
11%	0%	9%	0%	7%	48%	0.00	0.00	0.00	–	–	Ecuador
18%	21%	1%	6%	20%	36%	0.34	1.09	3.19	45%	62%	Mexico
61%	20%	2%	0%	6%	–	0.36	0.77	2.16	28%	25%	Peru
37%	20%	4%	4%	23%	–	0.22	0.60	2.74	35%	31%	Portugal
28%	30%	5%	8%	94%	–	0.36	1.35	3.75	58%	91%	South Africa
100%	0%	0%	0%	34%	33%	0.57	2.02	3.52	86%	58%	Spain
54%	26%	3%	0%	2%	48%	0.18	0.39	2.11	5%	0%	Uruguay
59%	6%	0%	0%	6%	–	–	–	–	–	–	Venezuela
37%	20%	3%	4%	42%	31%	0.55	1.69	3.06	49%	69%	Total

SciELO, Open Access, and Technology

The SciELO model and platform have brought technological innovations to the production of its included journals. The most important of these was the pioneering adoption of open access as inherent to online publishing, which happened four years before the Budapest Declaration. Three main conditions made this possible.

First, SciELO's successful implementation as a pilot project embraced the innate characteristics of the web and developed a common methodological and technological solution to index, publish, and disseminate journals online with minimal or no costs for the institutions responsible and with no interference with the paper-based publication. Thus, SciELO was created as a public platform using the ISIS public domain software developed by UNESCO and BIREME to run collections of journals allowing anyone access to journal content. In 1997, very few journals had access to online publication and those that had were mostly restricted to PDF files. Indeed, this intervention was so early that full-text databases and HTML web publication were perceived as radical innovations and faced strong resistance. Second, most of the quality journals targeted by SciELO were nonprofit with subscription fees intended to recover only the costs of publication. However, journals with many subscriptions, particularly in the social sciences, resisted open access and took a long time to embrace this model. Third, as stated before, the institutional authority given by FAPESP and BIREME was essential. Worthy of mention is that the new publishing model succeeded in national contexts unused to innovations because SciELO became a quality seal.

A key facet of the successful implementation of the SciELO publishing model was to build a qualified indexing function. The purpose was to supplement the role played by indexes in the US, which were not properly covering the journals of Brazil and many other countries. This was partially because of the publishing characteristics of these journals—such as scattered publication of journals, multilingual publication, research subjects or schools of thought distant from the scope or inclinations of the indexes. It was also, though, due to the lack of lobbying capacity to influence bibliographic indexes compared to that of commercial publishers. The emergence of SciELO as an international index of quality journals represented a breakthrough for national scholarly publishing, overcoming existing restrictions, and the lack of information and capacity faced by public and institutional policies to govern the advancement of journals. For although Google Scholar and other emergent indexes do not, technically, differentiate results by national source, the way in which research communicated by noncommercial publishers, particularly from developing regions, is consistently undervalued—as shown by many other chapters in this book—puts the lie to the myth of an a-national meritocracy.

To return to open access, though, taking open access as an inherent condition of a web publishing model was a programmatic and political decision by SciELO, made to enhance the relevance of the research communicated by quality journals, to maximize that research's visibility under the broad concept and belief in scientific knowledge as a public good, and as a determinant of academic, social, cultural, and technological development. In terms of open-access operation, SciELO evolved to formally adopt the Creative Commons Attribution License (CC BY) as the standard license, thus contributing to universal nonrestricted, continued access to updated, qualified, and relevant scientific information and knowledge. This was adopted, in particular, to minimize the so-called know-do gap (in which research is not translated from its theoretical groundings) that affects developing countries through the implementation of research, but also to improve the local flow of scientific information and to maximize the capacity for action of evidence-based public policies and services, continued improvement of research and education, support for professional practices, and a public library to inform citizens.[10]

Integral to the evolution of SciELO's dissemination power is the platform's compliance with bibliographic standards, which were progressively applied to the entire full text using XML semantic markup elements.[11] The first version of SciELO's implementation restricted SGML markup to the identification of the article's front bibliographic reference elements, the back-matter bibliographic references, and the beginning and end of full-text paragraphs. Since 2015, however, SciELO has implemented the Journal Article Tag Suite (JATS) standard through the SciELO Publishing Schema, which is updated every six months. The idea here is to work progressively toward all bibliographic elements being controlled by multilingual dictionaries to assure text quality and improve interoperability. The pace of adoption of new methodologies and technologies across the network is determined by the coordinators of the national collections according to their own specific conditions and priorities. In complex cases, such as the adoption of JATS in 2015, it is expected to take five or more years to cover all journals.

The most important challenge SciELO and similar journals face, however, lies in governmental and institutional policies that have prioritized a simplistic use of crude metrics, such as the journal impact factor, as proxies for the value of research. Similar barriers are imposed by universities whose research policies are driven by university rankings. Sadly, there are plenty of studies that have shown that research published by nonetheless high-quality, nationally published journals receives fewer citations than commercially high-"impact" journals; a phenomenon that is not properly addressed by the algorithms that calculate impact.[12] For example, a lack of international collaboration lessens impact (used in a broader sense) of research oriented to local problems, which are better investigated by nationally affiliated researchers. In the same vein, non-English articles are restricted to domestic or regional citations.

The Collective Building of the Present and Future of SciELO

SciELO's foundations of governance and operation have remained essentially constant from its inception. Principles of decentralization, disintermediation, and networking—key web-inherent attributes—drive the governance, implementation, and operation of the SciELO Program in order to maximize inclusion, academic autonomy, and widespread development of capacities and infrastructures as the basis for autonomous national policies on scholarly communication with global interoperability. The entire flow of research communication is technologically aligned with scholarly communication standards and best practices. Under these principles, SciELO features a well-established modus operandi that encompasses all network collections and individual journals covering different subjects and a variety of editorial policies. SciELO collections have the implicit objective of promoting quality journals within an inclusive vision of bibliodiversity.

SciELO's development is conducted with no formal bilateral or multilateral signed documents at the level of the network of collections and within national collections. The SciELO Network and its common virtual space are voluntary, and collectively built and developed by both the national collections and their individual journals. They are driven by three main agreed lines of action covering the next five years. The first line of action is professionalization. This line aims for the production of state-of-the-art journals for the sake of improving research capacity and democratization of scientific knowledge. The internationalization line seeks an appropriate balance of the presence of national- and foreign-qualified researchers as editors, peer reviewers, and authors, as well as publication in the English language in order to maximize the proactive presence in the international flow of scientific information. The third line of action seeks the strengthening of operational and financial sustainability of the journals as a commitment to the research community. The ultimate objective is to increase credibility and competitive positioning to induct journals as proactive participants in the global flow of scientific information.

The transition to open science as a fully open workflow is the programmatic plan for the future of SciELO.[13] Following national and international advancements in open-science implementation, the three lines of action for SciELO journals are enriched, in the first place, by the acceleration of research communication, which requires the widening of the publishing flow to include preprints, and the continuous publication of individual manuscripts as soon as they are approved. Secondly, the exhaustive citation and deposition of all data, software source code, and any material or content that underlies articles will be required to be available in certified repositories to ease their reuse, and particularly the reproduction of the research process and results. Finally, the strengthening of transparency and progressive opening of the peer review process, players, and decisions.

These lines of action, embedded within the open-science practices listed above, project a renewed future for the SciELO Program, with journals focusing their role progressively on the validation of research. Open science broadens the research communication spectrum via the use of preprints and data repository servers, so journals are being moved from their traditional role to become part of an interconnected complex system of information sources and communication vehicles. It is also expected that the comprehensive nature of open science will contribute to enhancing the evaluation of SciELO and similar journals by national research agencies and institutions beyond the simplistic adoption of rankings. The richness of open science and the related complexities do represent threats to journals, but they open also new opportunities to enhance their role in the future of scholarly communications: an approach to which the SciELO Program is committed.

Notes

1. SciELO, "Priority Lines of Action," SciELO 20, August 17, 2018, https://www.scielo20.org/redescielo/wp-content/uploads/sites/2/2018/09/L%C3%ADneas-prioritaris-de-acci%C3%B3n-2019-2023_en.pdf.

2. For a more thorough list of works about SciELO, see SciELO, "Bibliography about SciELO," SciELO, accessed June 2, 2019, https://scielo.org/en/about-scielo/bibliography-about-scielo/; see also Dennis F. Shaw, eds., *Proceedings of the Second ICSU-UNESCO International Conference on Electronic Publishing in Science: Held in Association with CODATA, IFLA, ICSTI & STM Publishers at UNESCO House, Paris 20–23 February, 2001* (Oxford: ICSU Press, 2001).

3. Abel L. Packer and Elenice de Castro, *Virtual Health Library* (São Paulo: Latin American and Caribbean Center on Health Sciences Information, BIREME, 1998), http://red.bvsalud.org/modelo-bvs/wp-content/uploads/sites/3/2016/11/Virtual-Health-Library-The-book.pdf.

4. Instituto Brasileiro de Informação em Ciência e Tecnologia, "Ciência Da Informação," SciELO, 1998, http://www.scielo.br/scielo.php?script=sci_issuetoc&pid=0100-196519980002&lng=es&nrm=iso; Abel L. Packer, Irati Antonio, and Vera Sílvia Marão Beraquet, "Rumo à Publicação Eletrônica," *Ciência Da Informação* 27, no. 2 (1998): 107–108, https://doi.org/10.1590/S0100-19651998000200002; Abel L. Packer et al., "SciELO: Una Metodología Para la Publicación Electrónica," *Revista Española de Salud Pública* 75, no. 4 (2001): 291–312, https://doi.org/10.1590/S1135-57272001000400004.

5. Abel L. Packer, "SciELO—Scientific Electronic Library Online" (Proceedings of ICSU Press Workshop on Economics, Real Costs and Benefits of Electronic Publishing in Science—A Technical Study, Keble College, University of Oxford, 1998), http://web.archive.org/web/19991007150424/http://www.bodley.ox.ac.uk/icsu/packerppr.htm; Abel L. Packer, "The SciELO Project Initiative for Latin America and Caribbean" (AAAS/UNESCO/ICSU Workshop on Developing Practices and Standards for Electronic Publishing in Science, UNESCO HQ, Paris, 1998), http://web.archive.org/web/20000919121422/http://www.aaas.org/spp/dspp/sfrl/projects/epub/ses1/Packer.htm; Abel L. Packer, "The SciELO Model for Electronic Publishing and Measuring of Usage and Impact of Latin American and Caribbean Scientific Journals" (Second ICSU/UNESCO International Conference on Electronic Publishing in Science, UNESCO HQ, Paris, 2001) http://eos.wdcb.ru/eps2/eps02016/eps02016.pdf.

6. Wladimir J. Alonso and Esteban Fernández-Juricic, "Regional Network Raises Profile of Local Journals," *Nature* 415, no. 6871 (2002): 471, https://doi.org/10.1038/415471c; Wieland Gevers, "Globalizing Science Publishing," *Science* 325, no. 5943 (2009): 920, https://doi.org/10.1126/science.1178378.

7. The term "documents" refers to all types of text published, while "articles" and "reviews" apply to research-related communications. Documents include articles and reviews in addition to editorial and other non-peer-reviewed texts.

8. Rogerio Meneghini and Abel L. Packer, "Is There Science Beyond English? Initiatives to Increase the Quality and Visibility of Non-English Publications Might Help to Break Down Language Barriers in Scientific Communication," *EMBO Reports* 8, no. 2 (2007): 112–116, https://doi.org/10.1038/sj.embor.7400906.

9. In the case of Cuba, this is due mainly to the political embargo that has been affecting all aspects of the country and that reflects limited international interoperability and cooperation. In the case of Brazil, one reason is the native Portuguese language that until recently predominated in the communication of research by many journals. This naturally limited submissions by non-Portuguese native-language researchers. With the internationalization promoted by SciELO, English became the main language used by most of the journals, which is easing the submission of manuscripts by foreign authors, so there is an increasing proportion of foreign authors.

10. Sally Theobald et al., "Implementation Research: New Imperatives and Opportunities in Global Health," *The Lancet* 392, no. 10160 (2018): 2214–2228, https://doi.org/10.1016/S0140-6736(18)32205-0.

11. Markup costs are rolled into the overall costs to produce a journal. It is carried out in different ways by national collections. Most of the national collections demand that journals send the articles in XML and PDF, so each journal has its own devolved mechanism for marking up articles. Due to the complexity involved in marking up according to the SciELO Publishing Schema (JATS implementation), many journals now employ third parties to undertake this work. There are also cases where journals have in-house mark-up solutions. In a few cases the national coordinators undertake the mark-up.

12. Vincent Larivière and Yves Gingras, "The Impact Factor's Matthew Effect: A Natural Experiment in Bibliometrics," *Journal of the American Society for Information Science and Technology* 61, no. 2 (2010): 424–427, https://doi.org/10.1002/asi.21232.

13. SciELO, "Priority Lines of Action."

VI Global Communities

22 Not Self-Indulgence, but Self-Preservation: Open Access and the Ethics of Care

Eileen A. Joy

> Caring for myself is not self-indulgence, it is self-preservation and that is an act of political warfare.
> —Audre Lorde[1]

How might certain forms of academic publishing—especially scholar-led, community-owned, open-access platforms, and presses—enable better forms of institutional life conducive to personal flourishing and the increase of public knowledge (and to lubricating the important connection between the two), especially at a time when the University is swarming with managerial technocrats invested in privatizing and outsourcing higher education, students are saddled with staggering levels of debt, and the casualization of academic labor is at an all-time high?[2] This question feels particularly acute at a time when the University is more than neck-deep in accelerating the quantification of long-entrenched (and toxic) forms of research and career gatekeeping, and thus the Academy no longer feels like a hospitable place within which to practice what some call "academic freedom."[3] There is perhaps no concept that is less debatable among faculty-researchers than academic freedom, yet I've personally seen so little of it in actual practice (even when "secured" by tenure—in the US context, at least), partly because of the myriad ways in which scholars are coerced (subtly and otherwise) to follow certain methodologies of thought and to seek particular, peer-approved modes and outlets for the dissemination of their work, outside of which it is believed only bad or mediocre scholarship could result. And thus, there isn't much academic freedom in the precise place where it is cherished and argued for as a high ethical good.

I nevertheless consider academic freedom to be the most vital, and elusive, element of academic life. But there is no absolute right to academic freedom (that would be sheltered, in the US context, under the First Amendment), even when supposedly affirmed by judicial decisions in the US such as *Cary v. Board of Education*, which held that tenured secondary school teachers had the right to determine the subject matter taught in their classrooms, but at the same time "determined their [First Amendment] constitutional rights were waived under the terms of a collective bargaining agreement ... between the Aurora Education Association ... and the school district."[4] It is also important to note that the US Supreme Court has never recognized "academic freedom" as an independent constitutional right, and according to W. Stuart Stuller, despite "tributes" to "academic freedom" in many cases, "the courts are remarkably consistent in their unwillingness to give analytical shape to the rhetoric of academic freedom."[5] The US Constitution guarantees freedom of speech, but legal guarantees do not ensure that everyone, everywhere, has equal access to the expression of that right. Which is why we need to understand that "academic freedom" is more of a practice of care (for ourselves and others) at which we have to work vigilantly every day and thus one of the most important tasks of the University today should be to make room for ideas to merely emerge—to foster spaces within which researchers might have more freedom than currently exists to experiment and to pursue in their work their desires, unencumbered by professional anxieties over whether or not those desires are legitimated in advance by what particular fields have already deemed as "proper" to themselves. Rather than regulating thought, we should be working harder to create the hospitable conditions for its emergence. This will entail an attention to and care for the importance of individual scholarly desires, which of necessity come before community, and yet rely on community for their articulation (which articulation is the very foundation of communication in general).[6] Under continual assault and threat by protocols and checkpoints for tenure, for promotion, and for professional affirmation and advancement in general, we have lost sight in the Humanities of the important meaningfulness of singularity and self-expression, in our work and in our relationships, and this is an issue that raises ethical questions regarding how we care for others' ability to self-express.[7] And the business-as-usual of academic publishing plays no little part in hampering our capabilities for such.

Here is where I have some hope that the Open Access Movement could be one possible route for positive change and renewal. First and foremost, we need to take back into the University (under Academic Affairs + Libraries) as many of the means of the production of academic publishing as possible, and we need to do so in ways that reenergize the Demos of the Academy;[8] we need to reject any and all forms of the privatization of our intellectual work (or at least enable "leaking" by any means necessary[9]); and we also need to make space and shelter for new forms of intellectual and bodily life, and for fostering the well-being of intellection, in ourselves and in others. We need also to pay better attention to the fact that how our work is published is just as important as the content of what we write. As Gary Hall asks, how can we "operate in a manner that is different not just from the neoliberal model of the entrepreneurial academic associated with corporate social networks such as Facebook and LinkedIn, but also from the traditional liberal humanist model that comes replete with clichéd, ready-made (some would even say cowardly) ideas of proprietorial authorship, the book, originality, fixity, and the finished object"?[10] To begin, we need to understand that each of us bears a special responsibility for enabling styles and modes of scholarship and cultural systems that would "give priority to the protection, the maximum use, and the enjoyment of the one resource that is almost equally distributed among all people: personal energy under personal control."[11]

Open access (OA) still has many hurdles to cross, in terms of its sustainability and evasion of commercial capture, but we are thankfully beginning to move beyond debates over the so-called integrity, prestige, and authority of OA publications.[12] In the UK and much of Europe, OA is not only fast becoming the norm,[13] but is even government-mandated: if you don't publish, or deposit your publications, in OA venues—venues, moreover, that have adopted all of the "best practices" of editorial review, metadata management, and the like—then your work might not "count" in the evaluation of your research, such as in the UK's REF, or Research Excellence Framework, which is the national system for assessing the quality of research in UK universities.[14] Unfortunately, nothing like this broad governmental support exists in the US context.[15] Nevertheless, researchers have responded globally to the Knowledge Economy (heavily leveraged by commercial-conglomerate interests) by agitating for governmental and institutional policies that would support OA, designing knowledge-sharing platforms (such as *arXiv*), building new publishing platforms (such as the Open Library of Humanities), and even establishing digital "pirate" and "shadow" libraries (such as aaaaarg.fail and Sci-Hub) that have proved sustaining to the increasing ranks of deinstitutionalized scholars, even as they have also been under siege by corporate litigators seeking to protect copyrights.[16] Within the US context, although many institutions now have OA policies of one sort or another (such as mandates for self-archiving preprints of published journal articles),[17] the University of California system has led the way in promoting what they have called "transformative" pathways to open access. In 2013, the system-wide UC Academic Senate adopted an OA policy mandate, which was strengthened by a further directive from UC's Office of the President in 2015, which requires the deposit of published work (where allowed by publishers) in open university repositories.[18] More recently, in 2018, UC's Council of University Librarians (CoUL) released a Pathways to Open Access "toolkit" that describes and analyzes "the many approaches and strategies for advancing the large-scale transition to OA, and identifies possible next action steps for UC system-wide investment and experimentation."[19] In October of the same year, UC Libraries hosted a working forum in Berkeley, "Choosing Pathways to Open Access," which was "designed to enable North American library and consortium leaders and key academic stakeholders to engage in action-focused deliberations about redirecting subscription and other funds toward sustainable open access (OA) publishing."[20] In addition, UC Libraries also severed ties with Elsevier in 2019 by deciding not to renew its bulk subscription to Elsevier journals because, under Elsevier's proposed contract renewal, "the publisher would capture significant new revenue on top of the university's current multimillion-dollar subscription while significantly diminishing UC's rights to Elsevier content," and also because UC Libraries wanted default OA publication for all UC-corresponding authored articles in Elsevier journals, with no increase in total payments made by UC to Elsevier.[21]

UC Press has also served as somewhat of a leader in OA publishing by launching a platform for OA monographs in the Humanities and Social Sciences and an OA mega-journal in Science (Luminos and Collabra, respectively), but they are dependent upon author-pay schemes (in the case of Luminos, anywhere from $5,000 to $7,500 per book[22]), which in the Humanities is simply untenable, and administrators and librarians on individual UC campuses have struggled to aid UC researchers who want to publish with these platforms. While scientists have access to bigger pots of money to support publication charges, humanists simply do not. This is a troubling issue with respect to the ability of humanists to embrace OA venues for their work. In this scenario, the democracy of thought is threatened.

The term "democracy" does not often enter into conversations around the subject of OA publishing, but alongside Derrida's idea of a "university without condition," where it is the Humanities' singular purpose to ensure the "right to say everything, whether it be under the heading of fiction and the experimentation of knowledge, and the right to say it publicly, to publish it,"[23] I believe it is the unique purview of scholarly communications to insist upon the centrality of the "right to say everything" relative to modes of publication. This is why it is also important to understand the vital connection between free speech (and "academic freedom") and the fact that democracy, in the words of Janneke Adema and Gary Hall, is "not an established reality," but rather "a permanent struggle for democratization," and in which struggle, I would add, some OA publishers could have an important role to play in always clearing ground for more (and different sorts of) speech to emerge, which speech opens up more horizons for a Democracy-to-come.[24] Any version of OA that does not begin with this emphasis has lost sight of the vital relationship between access to modes of publication and academic freedom. This is also why having for-profit actors (and also university presses that are forced, more and more, to justify their "bottom line") in this landscape potentially warps what should be the nurturing and capaciously curatorial role of the academic publisher because, regardless of claims to the contrary, editorial and marketing decisions are always closely correlated, whereas it ought to be the role of the public research university—and by extension, of its platforms for disseminating research results—not to regulate and officiate thought, while also subjecting its potential publication to market conditions,[25] but rather to create the hospitable open conditions for its creative emergence, in whatever form(s) it might take.

Let me pause, then, to sum up what I see as the ways in which the OA movement (and the cooption of such by various forces) represents desires and values that are not always compatible with and can even be antithetical to each other, while also explaining why I feel OA publishers (especially within the scholar-led, nonprofit sphere) should be taking up this state of affairs as a primary cause of action. First, there is the governmental rationale to make publicly funded research accessible to the public(s) who fund it, which also entails centralized systems of data management sometimes requiring unhealthy alliances between public institutions, nonprofit service agencies, and for-profit corporations. Second, there is the for-profit business imperative to capitalize upon the governmental rationale in ways that allow commercial publishers to continue charging exorbitant rates for subscription journals while also taking cash up front to make selective content in these journals more accessible ("double-dipping"), and as always, continuing to shore up obscene profit margins.[26] And then there is the more anarchic-ethical imperative to make the means of the possibility of publishing work more possible, and to pose no barriers to authors or readers. The imperative here is to diversify the voices that "count" within the University and to disrupt conventional paradigms of thought. Can these various forces work together to enhance the long-term sustainability of a more open Knowledge Commons? The answer, decidedly, is no, primarily because the mission of for-profit companies will never line up with the values of public research institutions. It may be possible for the governmental and the anarchic-ethical forces to work together, but there will be tough hurdles to cross in terms of how the primary stakeholders in OA (researchers, publishers, university administrators, librarians, knowledge managers, and so forth) define what the values and outputs of scholarly communications should be, and how those definitions won't always be compatible.

Consider the Mellon-funded study undertaken by the University of California–Davis and the California Digital Library to investigate whether it would be possible for large North American research institutions to sustain a model of OA that depended upon article processing charges (APCs).[27] In a survey of researchers that accompanied the study, scientists indicated they were invested in OA, and also in publishing outlets with high impact factors and good citation metrics, whereas humanists were primarily concerned with prestige, with publishing their work in journals of a certain, significant reputation. In the same study, it was suggested that it might be possible to "flip" library collections budgets from journals subscriptions to APCs, with the understanding that the burden of these fees would have to be shared by researchers, granting agencies, and libraries, such that publishers would be forced to make APCs more affordable, because researchers would help to apply "multiplayer" "market pressure" to publishers' OA fee schedules (especially when their institutions make clear that they cannot supply the entire fee from one source only). This would turn researchers into "speculators," which is frankly obscene.[28] And we would still be allowing corporations that have proven to be bad actors with respect to the mission of public research libraries to profit from the dissemination of our research (the report is agnostic with respect to for-profit versus nonprofit publishers), and I think we need to seriously understand how untenable this situation is, not just financially, but ethically.

If, as humanists, we embrace and put into practice certain values in our research and teaching—such as openness, pluralism, constructive dissensus, freedom of thought, equity, decoloniality, and the like—then shouldn't we be mindful of the ways in which the practices of the dissemination of our research may be at odds with these values? Shouldn't we be paying better attention to the modes of production of our work, especially with an eye toward not just moving away from for-profit publishing platforms, but also helping to promote a more rowdily diverse set of voices seeking to amplify and diversify what "counts" as the University? If we care so much about "prestige," we might remind ourselves that the word derives from the Latin *praestigium* ("illusion" or "trick") and only later came to mean "glamor" and, eventually, something that is worthy of "admiration," With the advent of "impact factors," tracked and calculated by for-profit companies, and the long-running obsession with "excellence" as a calculable commodity of higher education, the gamification of "prestige" has come full circle.[29]

One group that is working toward maximizing processes of radical democratization within the OA landscape is the Radical OA Collective, a consortium of scholar-led, nonprofit OA presses and platforms that is motivated by a desire to reconceptualize academic publishing as a techne of "care of the self"—of individuals, and of individual projects, that are the indivisible units of any legitimate democracy (which again, is always a struggle for democratization, and never an established reality). Further, the Collective wants to provide alternatives to the legacy model of commercial publishers and many of its members' projects diverge significantly from the importance that is generally attached in mainstream OA debates to the development of centralized (one-size-fits-all) platforms, publication fees, and sustainable business models. For the Collective, the main issue concerns scholarly communication—not business models.[30] One important outcome of the Collective's work has been the formation of ScholarLed, a consortium of five OA presses specializing in books in the Humanities and Social Sciences, which opposes "the monopolisation of OA book publishing by commercial publishers and for-profit intermediaries" and is dedicated to working on opening up "a more diverse, scholar-led, community-owned, and not-for-profit publishing ecosystem" that they believe is "crucial for the cultivation of more creative modes and forms of scholarship and their open dissemination and preservation as public knowledge." While ScholarLed recognizes "the entangled mesh of players and providers (for- and not-for-profit) that are essential for scholarly communications to flourish and be accessible to the widest possible readership," they are also concerned "to build infrastructure for smaller-scale OA book publishers that would prioritise the needs of the creative research community and the values of public research institutions against the for-profit entities who seek to privatise (and also homogenize) knowledge."[31]

For me personally, and especially through my work with punctum books, the Radical OA Collective, and ScholarLed, there is an urgency to rewire the definition of OA such that, in addition to making works broadly available to readers without barriers to access, OA publishers must also stop chasing markers for "prestige," "authority," "quality control," and the like, in order to devise more radically open pathways for access to publication for authors who otherwise might not find a publisher, either because their work does not fit within a readily recognizable current disciplinary paradigm or because they want to experiment with forms and styles of academic writing, and so on. It's a question of personal freedom and how the publisher should strive to be an agent of both sustenance (care) and productive transformation. Ultimately, we need to move away from an author-pay system (which harms democracy as well as limits diversity) to more richly hybrid funding models in which all of the vested partners—government, universities (including libraries), granting agencies, and also readers and other end users (which include faculty, students, and the larger public)—play a role as financial supporters.[32] This will also entail taking back from commercial publishers the full reins of the means of production of academic publishing and reinventing the academic press as a critical arm of both the research and teaching mission of the University. There is likely no possible stemming of the tide of neoliberal capital's narrow-minded imaginary and hyper-accelerated technologized infrastructures, but for me this also means that the task for the Humanities now is to think harder about how to repurpose these infrastructures in order unleash new, more capacious imaginaries and organs of dissemination for those imaginaries. I have no faith whatsoever that we could accomplish this at a large scale. But I (ridiculously) insist on the necessity of trying to live up to values that the University professes to profess. And on smaller scales, here and there, some of us will continue our work to improve the general weather conditions for a more Open Commons.

Notes

1. Audre Lorde, "A Burst of Light: Living with Cancer," in *A Burst of Light and Other Essays* (London: Sheba Feminist Publishers, 1988), 130.

2. See, e.g., Maximillian Alvarez, "Contingent No More," *The Baffler*, May 3, 2017, https://thebaffler.com/the-poverty-of-theory/contingent-no-more; L. O. Aranye Fradenburg, *Staying Alive: A Survival Manual for the Liberal Arts*, ed. Eileen A. Joy (Brooklyn, NY: punctum books, 2013), https://punctumbooks.com/titles/staying-alive/; Gary Hall, *The Uberfication of the University* (Minneapolis: University of Minnesota Press, 2016); Christopher Newfield, *The Great Mistake: How We Wrecked Public Universities and How We Can Fix Them* (Baltimore, MD: Johns Hopkins University Press, 2016).

3. Bill Readings, *The University in Ruins* (Cambridge, MA: Harvard University Press, 1996), never ceases to be instructive on this point. On the intensity of the metrification of scholarly communications and the concerns over whether or not "humanist" metrics are possible or desirable for measuring the "impact" of scholarship in the humanities, see Martina Franzen, Eileen Joy, and Christopher Long, *Humane Metrics/Metrics Noir* (Coventry, UK: Post Office Press/meson press, 2018), https://hcommons.org/deposits/item/hc:19823/. See also Stacy Konkiel, "Approaches to Creating 'Humane' Research Evaluation Metrics for the Humanities," *Insights: The UKSG Journal* 31 (2018), https://doi.org/10.1629/uksg.445.

4. See United States Court of Appeals, 598 F.2d 535, *Cary v. Board of Education of Adams* (December 31, 1969), for details of the original case as well as its 1978 appeal.

5. Laurence H. Tribe, *American Constitutional Law*, 2nd ed. (St. Paul, MN: West Academic Publishing, 1988), 1812–1813n32; W. Stuart Stuller, "High School Academic Freedom: The Evolution of a Fish Out of Water," *Nebraska Law Review* 77, no. 2 (1998): 302.

6. My thinking here stems from Jean-Luc Nancy's argument that "behind the theme of the individual, but [also] beyond it, lurks the question of singularity. ... What is their singular necessity in the sharing that divides and that puts into communication bodies, voices and writings in general and in totality?" Jean-Luc Nancy, *The Inoperative Community*, ed. Peter Connor, trans. Peter Connor et al. (Minneapolis: University of Minnesota Press, 1991), 6.

7. On the importance of self-expression to human flourishing, see Owen J. Flanagan, *Self-Expressions: Mind, Morals, and the Meaning of Life* (Oxford: Oxford University Press, 1996).

8. See Wendy Brown, *Undoing the Demos: Neoliberalism's Stealth Revolution* (New York: Zone Books, 2015). Brown has defined neoliberalism as "as a governing rationality through which everything is 'economized' and in a very specific way: human beings become market actors and nothing but, every field of activity is seen as a market, and every entity (whether public or private, whether person, business, or

state) is governed as a firm"; quoted in Timothy Shenk, "What Exactly Is Neoliberalism?," *Dissent Magazine* (blog), April 2, 2015, https://www.dissentmagazine.org/blog/booked-3-what-exactly-is-neoliberalism-wendy-brown-undoing-the-demos.

9. I give a nod here to the political urgency of leaking information inspired by the work of Alexandria Lockett, whose 2013 PhD dissertation eloquently defends hacktivism as an urgently ethical project, not only in information cultures but also in noncomputing contexts such as contemporary African American literature, where to practice what Lockett calls "leak literacy" means that, despite state-sponsored forms of suppression, some systems are capable, when "leaking," of enabling transformative and progressive change, as well as resistance to a surveillance culture. Alexandria Lockett, "Leaked: A Grammar of Information in Surveillance Cultures" (PhD diss., Pennsylvania State University, 2013).

10. Gary Hall, *Pirate Philosophy: For a Digital Posthumanities* (Cambridge, MA: The MIT Press, 2016), xiv.

11. Ivan Illich, *Tools for Conviviality* (New York: Harper and Row, 1973); quoted in Mark Seem, "Introduction," in *Anti-Oedipus: Capitalism and Schizophrenia*, by Gilles Deleuze and Félix Guattari, trans. Robert Hurley, Mark Seem, and Helen R. Lane (Minneapolis: University of Minnesota Press, 1983), xxiv.

12. Lamentably, there are still some who voice concern over the quality and authority of OA. As Martin Paul Eve has pointed out, "prestige barriers (hiring, promotion, simple reputation)" have made the majority of academics "reliant upon a narrow set of conventional publishers," and there is, further, "a persisting belief in ... open access meaning a dip in quality control/peer review." Martin Paul Eve, "Four Implementation Questions about Open Access and Monographs," *Martin Paul Eve* (blog), January 3, 2017, https://eve.gd/2017/01/03/four-implementation-questions-about-open-access-and-monographs/.

13. It should be noted here that, while my focus in this chapter is primarily upon open-access publishing contexts in the US, UK, and Europe, that other regions, such as Latin America, have long been leaders in this area, such as with the establishment of SciELO (Scientific Electronic Library Online) in Brazil in 1997. In addition to the chapters in this volume devoted to this topic, see Sergio Minniti, Valeria Santoro, and Simone Belli, "Mapping the Development of Open Access in Latin America and Caribbean Countries: An Analysis of Web of Science Core Collection and SciELO Citation Index (2005–2017)," *Scientometrics* 117, no. 3 (2018): 1905–1930, https://doi.org/10.1007/s11192-018-2950-0. See also Juan Pablo Alperin, "The Public Impact of Latin America's Approach to Open Access" (PhD diss., Stanford, 2015), https://purl.stanford.edu/jr256tk1194.

14. According to the 2016 Consultation on the Second Research Excellence Framework, "journal articles and conference proceedings accepted for publication from 1 April 2016 need to have been deposited in an institutional or subject repository."

Higher Education Funding Council for England, "Consultation on the Second Research Excellence Framework," Higher Education Funding Council for England, 2016. In a recent news release from UKRI (UK Research and Innovation), it was stated that "sixty-one per cent of research outputs known to be in scope for the REF 2021 are meeting open access deposit, discovery and access requirements." Research England, "Over 80% of Research Outputs Meet Requirements of REF 2021 Open Access Policy," UK Research and Innovation, June 14, 2018, https://re.ukri.org/news-events-publications/news/oa-report-130618/.

15. One notable exception is the Obama administration's 2013 policy memorandum directing federal agencies with more than $100 million in research and development expenditures "to develop plans to make the results of federally funded [scientific] research freely available to the public—generally within one year of publication." John P. Holdren, "Memorandum for the Heads of Executive Departments and Agencies: Increasing Access to the Results of Federally Funded Scientific Research," whitehouse.gov, February 22, 2013, https://obamawhitehouse.archives.gov/sites/default/files/microsites/ostp/ostp_public_access_memo_2013.pdf. This directive did not, unfortunately, extend to agencies such as the National Endowment for the Humanities, which has done very little on behalf of OA initiatives.

16. On the history of OA as an advocacy movement, see Peter Suber, "Timeline," Open Access Directory, accessed May 31, 2019, http://oad.simmons.edu/oadwiki/Timeline. On digital "pirate" libraries and their successes and travails, see Bohannon, "Who's Downloading Pirated Papers?" and Quirin Schiermeier, "US Court Grants Elsevier Millions in Damages from Sci-Hub," *Nature News*, June 22, 2017, https://doi.org/10.1038/nature.2017.22196.

17. See Stevan Harnad, "ROARMAP," accessed July 25, 2014, http://roarmap.eprints.org/.

18. Office of Scholarly Communication, University of California, "UC Open Access Policies," *Office of Scholarly Communication* (blog), accessed May 31, 2019, https://osc.universityofcalifornia.edu/open-access-at-uc/open-access-policy/.

19. UC Council of University Librarians, "Pathways to Open Access," February 27, 2018, https://libraries.universityofcalifornia.edu/content/uc-libraries-release-pathways-oa-analysis.

20. "Choosing Pathways to OA," accessed May 31, 2019, https://cp2oa18.com/.

21. Ivy Anderson et al., "Open Statement: Why UC Cut Ties with Elsevier," UC Berkeley Library News, March 20, 2019, https://news.lib.berkeley.edu/uc-elsevier-statement.

22. University of California Press, "Luminos FAQ," Luminos OA, accessed May 31, 2019, https://www.luminosoa.org/site/faqs/#author-faqs-open-access.

23. Jacques Derrida, "The Future of the Profession or the University without Condition (Thanks to the 'Humanities,' What Could Take Place Tomorrow)," in *Jacques*

Derrida and the Humanities: A Critical Reader, ed. Tom Cohen (Cambridge: Cambridge University Press, 2001), 26.

24. See Janneke Adema and Gary Hall, "The Political Nature of the Book: On Artists' Books and Radical Open Access," *New Formations*, no. 78 (2013): 34, https://doi.org/10.3898/NewF.78.07.2013. On democracy-to-come, see Jacques Derrida, *Rogues: Two Essays on Reason*, trans. Pascale-Anne Brault and Michael Naas (Stanford, CA: Stanford University Press, 2005), chaps. 3, 8.

25. Typical questions asked of peer reviewers by both traditional university presses and also commercial-conglomerate academic publishers include "in what sorts of university courses might this book be adopted?," "what other titles exist now that this book would be in competition with?," "are there any new trends in scholarship in this area that the author has overlooked?," "has this book adequately addressed the state of the field in X, Y, or Z areas?," and so on.

26. See Martin Paul Eve, "On Open-Access Books and 'Double Dipping'," *Martin Paul Eve* (blog), January 31, 2015, https://eve.gd/2015/01/31/on-open-access-books-and-double-dipping/, and Mike Taylor, "Academic Publishers Have Become the Enemies of Science," *The Guardian*, January 16, 2012, sec. Science, https://www.theguardian.com/science/2012/jan/16/academic-publishers-enemies-science.

27. University of California Libraries, "Pay It Forward: Investigating a Sustainable Model of Open Access Article Processing Charges for Large North American Research Institutions," IATUL—International Association of University Libraries, June 30, 2016, https://www.iatul.org/about/news/pay-it-forward-investigating-sustainable-model-open-access-article-processing-charges.

28. On the idea that researchers can help "flip" library budgets to OA by becoming "more thoughtful consumers when publishing their research," see University of California Libraries, "Pay It Forward," 98–99. To be clear, the authors of this report do not recommend this strategy as desirable; they simply indicate that if libraries were to engage in "flipping" at a large scale, such "multiplayer" pressure would likely have to come into play.

29. See Samuel Moore et al., "Excellence R Us: University Research and the Fetishisation of Excellence," *Palgrave Communications* 3 (2017), https://doi.org/10.1057/palcomms.2016.105.

30. For more on the Radical OA Collective, see Radical Open Access Collective, "About the Collective," Radical Open Access Collective, accessed May 31, 2019, https://radicaloa.disruptivemedia.org.uk/about/. The OA press that I co-direct with Vincent W. J. van Gerven Oei, punctum books, is a founding member of the Collective.

31. See ScholarLed, "Open Infrastructure Development," ScholarLed, accessed May 31, 2019, https://scholarled.org/#infrastructure, and Lucy Barnes, "ScholarLed Collaboration: A Powerful Engine to Grow Open Access Publishing," *LSE Impact Blog*, October

26, 2018, https://blogs.lse.ac.uk/impactofsocialsciences/2018/10/26/scholarled-collaboration-a-powerful-engine-to-grow-open-access-publishing/.

32. Punctum has experimented with multiple business models in the OA books landscape, and has ultimately settled on a hybrid approach that combines: (a) consortial library funding (https://punctumbooks.com/supporting-library-membership-program/); (b) sales of print books; (c) revolving individual reader support (https://punctumbooks.com/membership-account/membership-levels/); and (d) an institutional partnership: as of January 2020, UC Santa Barbara (UCSB) Library and Punctum are in a three-year pilot partnership to test a no-fees OA book publishing model that privileges cooperative knowledge- and expertise-sharing between communities of professional-public academic practice (https://www.library.ucsb.edu/punctum-books-ucsb-library-partnership).

23 Toward a Global Open-Access Scholarly Communications System: A Developing Region Perspective

Dominique Babini

When looking at international research and policy agendas concerned with important sustainable development issues—climate change, hunger and poverty reduction, ensuring health and education services, reducing inequalities, strengthening democratic institutions, sustaining economic growth, among others—it strikes us at the Latin American Council of Social Sciences (CLACSO), a network of more than 700 research institutions in 52 countries, that the development of an inclusive and participatory global open-access scholarly communications system is not given priority. We consider this to be a grave oversight.[1]

After two decades developing collaborative, publicly funded, scholar-led open-access initiatives, with no commercial outsourcing, Latin America is now being invited, together with other developing regions, to join or give an opinion on proposals to accelerate the transition to open-access scholarly communications where article processing charges (APCs) have an important role (OA2020, Plan S). From the perspective of a developing region, these proposals carry a risk of replicating, albeit this time from within open access and with APCs, the traditional international scholarly communications system built in past decades. Such a system would be concentrated upon "mainstream" journals and their evaluative indicators, managed by commercial partners with growing profit margins covered by research funding, with poor diversity and representation from developing regions, and with negative impact upon the evaluative cultures of those developing regions.[2]

Should an increasingly few international commercial publishers, whose exorbitant profits have been among the reasons for the Open Access Movement itself, act as important partners in building the future of open access? In the developing world, where resources for research are extremely scarce, is it not also an ethical issue that research money is being used to support a for-profit industry with margins of more than 30 percent?

In this context, and around its seventieth anniversary year, it is worth remembering the Universal Declaration of Human Rights (1948). This declaration advanced the right to access and benefit from scientific discovery, as well as the right to participate in scientific advances; and both these rights should be taken into consideration when discussing the future of open-access scholarly communications and open science, in an international context.[3] Indeed, as Czerniewicz puts it, "the open access movement needs to broaden its focus from access to knowledge to full participation in knowledge creation."[4] Access needs to cut both ways.

For we live in times of international research and of global development agendas. An example is the United Nations Sustainable Development Goals signed by nations worldwide.[5] Research cooperation in support of these international goals would benefit from an international open-access scholarly communications and evaluation system that is more inclusive of a diversity of voices, formats, and contents from less privileged institutions and countries.

Openness provides opportunities for innovation in scholar-led collaboration and cooperation.[6] Indeed, cooperative and collaborative open-access publishing initiatives present in developed regions are challenging commercial solutions with a diversity of nonprofit platforms for journals, as well as repositories and platforms. In fact, we believe it is important to foster "bibliodiversity and innovation without involving the exclusive transfer of journal subscription monies to APC payments," as stated in the recent Jussieu Call for Open Science and Bibliodiversity.[7]

In the case of developing regions, there are many examples that can provide inspiration along these lines. In Africa these include African Journals Online (AJOL), SciELO South Africa, and a growing number of repositories. In Asia, there are JOL collections of journals in several countries and also a growing number of repositories and repository networking solutions. And in Latin America, whose experience will be described in this chapter, there is the most advanced open-access system of scholarly communications in the world based on percentage of research publications available through publicly funded, collaborative, scholar-led initiatives.[8]

From the perspective of a developing region, accelerating a global transition to openly accessible scholarly communications presents greater possibilities for inclusivity and diversity if it provides public infrastructure and an opportunity to collaborate and cooperate with publicly funded, community-led initiatives. We further advocate for government agreements for joint negotiations with big publishers under new terms concerning reasonable prices for open-access article/book processing charges. Waivers of such fees are not our favored solution for less privileged institutions and countries because in the long term, they often become a mere sales promotion strategy.

The examples to which I turn in the remainder of this chapter demonstrate how different open-access scholarly communications have evolved in a developing region—Latin America—and illustrate how a scholar-led transition to global open access that is more inclusive and participatory is possible.

Open Access in Latin America: Scholar-Led and Publicly Funded

Latin America has led the way in the development of scholar-led, open-access scholarly communications. The main drivers toward open access in Latin America have been public universities and government organizations, with no outsourcing to commercial publishers, as described in the Global Open Access Portal (UNESCO-GOAP).[9] This is in part due to the lack of interest by commercial publishers in the Latin American and Caribbean (LAC) region.[10] However, it is mainly due to strong publicly funded, scholar-led initiatives that have helped journals in the region improve quality, make the transition to open access without APCs, and provide initial open-access indicators. Regional government agreements and national open-access policies have also spurred the development of repositories, which are the required venue to comply with open-access policies and legislation approved in several countries.

Open-Access Journals from Latin America: Regional Directory, Publishing Platforms, and Indexing Services

One of the main research universities in Latin America, the National Autonomous University of Mexico (UNAM/Universidad Nacional Autónoma de México), has developed several regional databases of journals published in Iberoamerican countries. One of the main services is "Latindex (Online Regional Information System for Scientific Journals from Latin America, the Caribbean, Spain and Portugal)," which started in 1998 as the Latindex Directory, providing basic information about journals in the region. In 2002 it complemented the directory with both the Latindex Catalog to identify quality journals within the region, and the Latindex Portal of Portals (*Latindex Portal de Portales*), a discovery facility to search full texts within regional open-access journal portals from Iberoamerican countries.

SciELO—the Scientific Electronic Library Online—by contrast, is a cooperative publishing system for peer-reviewed, open-access journals.[11] It was started in Brazil in 1997 for health journals, by the Latin American and Caribbean Center on Health Sciences Information (BIREME). It was supported initially by the publicly funded São Paulo Research Foundation (FAPESP) and later also by the Brazilian National Council for Scientific and Technological Development (CNPq) and the Brazilian federal government agency Coordenação de Aperfeiçoamento de Pessoal de Nível Superior (CAPES). Today, SciELO has 1,285 active open-access, peer-reviewed journals published in all disciplines by universities and other scholarly institutions from 15 Iberoamerican countries and from South Africa. Countries have developed their own SciELO national collections, which are run in many cases by science policy institutions. Fewer than 5 percent of journals in SciELO charge APCs. Bibliometric indicators are provided at publication, collection, and citation levels. Since 2014, citations are provided by SciELO Citation Index, a partnership of SciELO with Clarivate and it is expected that "the inclusion of SciELO CI into WoS [Web of Science] should, in the short to mid-term, improve compliance with international editing norms and governance structures."[12] The SciELO-Clarivate alliance for SciELO Citation Index has raised concerns, among others, as to whether initiatives such as SciELO should "be investing in support for open infrastructure instead of enriching private businesses."[13]

Another public university in Latin America, The Autonomous University of Mexico State (UAEM/Universidad Autónoma del Estado de México), started an initiative in 2002 called Redalyc (Red de Revistas Científicas de América Latina y el Caribe, España y Portugal). This is a publishing system for peer-reviewed, open-access journals from Latin America, the Caribbean, Spain, and Portugal, in collaboration initially with editors of social science journals. Today, Redalyc has 1,294 active open-access, peer-reviewed journals published across all disciplines by universities and other scholarly institutions from 16 Iberoamerican countries. Again, fewer than 5 percent of these journals charge APCs, and recently Redalyc has decided not to accept journals that charge APCs. Thousands of authors have created profiles in Redalyc, linked to ORCID when available. Bibliometric and scientometric indicators are provided at publication, institution, country, and discipline levels. As a reply to an invitation from Redalyc, 500 journals in their publishing and indexing platform have signed the DORA declaration, which recommends that publishers reduce their emphasis on the journal impact factor as a promotional tool, and instead make available a range of article-level metrics to encourage a shift toward assessment based on the scientific content of an article rather than publication metrics of the journal in which it was published.[14]

Concerned about restrictions on research budgets in Latin America and the need to ensure scholar-led, collaborative open access in the region, rather than alliances with commercial publishing and indexing services, Redalyc together with CLACSO, UNESCO, and a group of universities and institutions with research and development programs concerning open-access publishing and indicators, started a new system in 2018: AmeliCA-Open Knowledge (AmeliCA-Conocimiento Abierto). AmeliCA works to further develop a scholar-led, decentralized collaborative initiative for research and development of open-access scholarly communications and open-access indicators, with no commercial outsourcing and no APCs.

The Latin American open-access initiatives described here work in complement to international traditional services, enriching them with local and regional contents that are necessary if we want to move toward more inclusive and participatory scholarly communications systems. A recent study compared the coverage of journals, by country and topic, from Latin America and the Caribbean included in SciELO, Redalyc and Scopus during the years 2005 through 2009, and the results showed that the three sources are complementary.[15]

Another study in the core collection indexes of the Web of Science (WoS) and the SciELO Citation Index, which was integrated into the larger WoS platform in 2014, concluded that SciELO CI integrates a system of scientific knowledge that otherwise remains invisible in the mainstream journals contained in WoS.[16]

Repositories in Latin America: Institutional, National, Regional, and Subject Repositories

Open-access national legislation that mandates deposit of state-funded research results in open-access digital repositories was approved in Argentina and Peru in 2013; in Mexico in 2014; and a bill was introduced in Congress in Brazil in 2007 and reintroduced in 2011.

According to the Directory of Open Access Repositories (OpenDOAR), 528 digital repositories have been developed in the region.[17] Complementing approved national legislations, nine Latin American science and technology public agencies (Argentina, Brazil, Colombia, Costa Rica, Chile, Ecuador, El Salvador, Mexico, and Perú) agreed in 2012 to develop in each country a national system of repositories to coordinate funding, training, and national and regional cooperation. These agencies also started, with the initial support of the Interamerican Development Bank, a Latin American Federated Network of Institutional Repositories of Scientific Publications, known simply as *La Referencia*, which has central offices in Chile but a rotating presidency among the national participants. *La Referencia* boosts interoperability agreements in the region and its regional harvester has 1,431,703 full-text, peer-reviewed articles, theses, and research reports. At the international level, *La Referencia* follows OpenAIRE interoperability guidelines, and is an active member of the Confederation of Open Access Repositories (COAR), working together with the participation of repositories worldwide toward an international network of repositories, and functionality for next-generation repositories.[18]

Latin America has also a historical tradition of participating in cooperative subject information systems with national focal points, usually located in research or government institutions, and coordinated by regional research and policy organizations. These cooperative information systems, which started in the 1990s, have evolved from providing online open access to bibliographic information to full-text availability of all kinds of contents (journal articles, reports, books, documents, theses, multimedia). The leading concept is "sharing a little so that all can have more," as expressed on the webpage of the Alliance of Agricultural Information Services (SIDALC).[19] These regional subject repositories in Latin America have been developed extensively in agriculture, health, and social sciences—disciplines where local information is vital for research, professional, and productive activities, and for informing policies and international cooperation.

As a further example, the Virtual Health Library (VHL) is sponsored by the Pan American Health Organization (PAHO) for management of health information and knowledge in the Latin American and Caribbean region. Developed and operated by BIREME—working in a decentralized mode with national focal points in institutions related to research, education, and health services—more than 400,000 full text are openly available through this resource.

Finally, CLACSO's social science digital repository (Red de Bibliotecas Virtuales de Ciencias Sociales) provides open access to a collection of 930 peer-reviewed social science and humanities journals, managed by Redalyc (387,018 full texts). Collections from CLACSO members include journals, books, working documents, research reports, theses, and multimedia (103,000 full texts).

Declarations on Open Access in Latin America

Given its strong support for open access, it will come as little surprise that Latin America has issued several regional declarations in support of OA—the Salvador Declaration on Open Access: The Developing World Perspective, in 2005; CLACSO's declaration on open access to knowledge managed as a commons by the scholarly community, in 2015; and the declaration of Mexico in favor of the Latin American noncommercial open-access ecosystem, in 2017.[20]

In relation to APCs, the consortium of government offices making centralized national purchases of international journals, in their First Consortium Assembly in 2017, has agreed that an open-access expansion policy through payment of APCs is "impossible to undertake from a financial point of view for the participant countries" and recommends that institutions not create grants to pay for APCs.[21]

Evaluation Systems in Developing Regions

As Laura Czerniewicz (2015), professor at the University of Cape Town, notes:

> Researchers in the Global South are caught in a double bind. They are rewarded for publishing in "international" journals in several ways: through promotions and often even financially. But development imperatives, government policies and their own interests pressurize them to undertake research that is relevant to pressing social and related problems which may not be appealing or even "academic" enough to interest the international journals.[22]

After 20 years of improving the quality of journals and developing successful open-access initiatives in Latin America, a region with "a long tradition of research but a low record of impact of this research,"[23] the evaluation systems need review because they still reward the impact factor of the "mainstream" journals where research is published, confusing excellence or prestige with quality (to use Vessuri, Guédon, and Cetto's terms).[24]

Further, as Vasen notes, "while the political discourse promotes a model of researcher committed to knowledge transfer and mobilization activities, academic evaluation practices encourage a classic academic profile."[25] The use of the impact factor and citation indicators contributes to tenure, promotion, and economic compensation in the region, as well as the position of the universities and countries in rankings.

Disappointingly, Latin America is not applying the recommendations from DORA and, with very few exceptions, is not considering the new open-access indicators being provided for quality journals from developing regions; for example, in Latin America by SciELO and Redalyc,[26] even if there is "a high equivalence between the criteria used by the national systems of evaluation of scientific publications in Latin American countries and the characteristics required by SciELO, Redalyc, and Latindex for indexing journals in their databases."[27] More research is needed in the region to better understand the hold of Global North–imposed metrics.

These quality open-access journals are used by researchers (30 percent), but also by other publics such as students (50 percent), and individuals interested for professional or personal reasons (20 percent), according to a study on the public impact of Latin America's approach to open access.[28] They thus contribute to the transition toward open education and open-science information needs in a significant way.

Conclusion

Successful development and growth of scholar-led and publicly funded open access in Latin America and other developing and developed regions, gives hope to the possibility of building a global transition to open access that will be more inclusive, sustainable, and diverse with respect to knowledge produced in developed and developing countries; a relevant goal for international conversations in science and global sustainable development agendas. We seek to avoid, as mentioned in the introduction to this chapter, the risk of repeating—this time from within open access and with APCs—the traditional international scholarly communications system built in past decades, concentrated in "mainstream" journals of the Global North and their evaluative indicators, managed by commercial partners with unusually high profit margins, paid out of scarce research money, with poor diversity and low participation from less privileged institutions and countries, and with negative impacts from their evaluation systems.

Notes

1. The author thanks Martin Paul Eve for his valuable comments and contributions to improve this chapter.

2. Larivière, Haustein, and Mongeon, "The Oligopoly of Academic Publishers in the Digital Era," https://doi.org/10.1371/journal.pone.0127502.

3. Mikel Mancisidor, "El Derecho Humano a La Ciencia: Un Viejo Derecho Con Un Gran Futuro," *Anuario de Derechos Humanos*, no. 13 (2017): 211–221, https://doi.org/10.5354/0718-2279.2017.46887.

4. Laura Czerniewicz, "This Map of the World's Scientific Research Is Disturbingly Unequal," Quartz, July 11, 2015, https://qz.com/449405/this-map-of-the-worlds-scientific-research-is-disturbingly-unequal/.

5. United Nations, "Sustainable Development Goals," UNDP, accessed May 12, 2019, https://www.undp.org/content/undp/en/home/sustainable-development-goals.html.

6. Martin Paul Eve and John Willinsky, "Open Access in Humanities and Social Sciences: Visions for the Future of Publishing," *College and Research Libraries News* 76 (2015): 88–91.

7. Bibliothèque Scientifique Numérique, or Digital Scientific Library, "Jussieu Call for Open Science and Bibliodiversity," 2018, https://jussieucall.org/jussieu-call/.

8. Juan Pablo Alperin, "The Public Impact of Latin America's Approach to Open Access" (PhD diss., Stanford University, 2015), https://purl.stanford.edu/jr256tk1194.

9. United Nations, "Overview of OA in Latin America and the Caribbean," United Nations Educational, Scientific and Cultural Organization, accessed May 12, 2019, http://www.unesco.org/new/en/communication-and-information/portals-and-platforms/goap/access-by-region/latin-america-and-the-caribbean/.

10. Hebe Vessuri, Jean-Claude Guédon, and Ana María Cetto, "Excellence or Quality? Impact of the Current Competition Regime on Science and Scientific Publishing in Latin America and Its Implications for Development," *Current Sociology* 62, no. 5 (2014): 647–665, https://doi.org/10.1177/0011392113512839.

11. Again, see Abel Packer's chapter in this volume.

12. Gabriel Vélez-Cuartas, Diana Lucio-Arias, and Loet Leydesdorff, "Regional and Global Science: Publications from Latin America and the Caribbean in the SciELO

Citation Index and the Web of Science," *El Profesional de La Información* 25, no. 1 (2016): 45, https://doi.org/10.3145/epi.2016.ene.05.

13. Leslie Chan, "SciELO, Open Infrastructure and Independence," *SciELO in Perspective* (blog), September 3, 2018, https://blog.scielo.org/en/2018/09/03/scielo-open-infrastructure-and-independence/.

14. "San Francisco Declaration on Research Assessment: Putting Science into the Assessment of Research," http://www.ascb.org/files/SFDeclarationFINAL.pdf.

15. Sandra Edith Miguel, "Revistas y Producción Científica de América Latina y el Caribe: Su Visibilidad en SciELO, RedALyC y SCOPUS" 34, no. 2 (2011): 187–199. http://www.memoria.fahce.unlp.edu.ar/art_revistas/pr.6384/pr.6384.pdf.

16. Vélez-Cuartas, Lucio-Arias, and Leydesdorff, "Regional and Global Science."

17. "Browse by Country and Region," Directory of Open Access Repositories, accessed September 16, 2019, https://v2.sherpa.ac.uk/view/repository_by_country/019.html.

18. "OpenAIRE Guidelines Documentation," OpenAIRE, accessed September 23, 2019, https://guidelines.openaire.eu/en/latest/.

19. SIDALC, "About," Alliance of Agricultural Information and Documentation Services of the Americas, accessed May 12, 2019, http://www.sidalc.net/en/aboutsidalc.

20. "Salvador Declaration on Open Access: The Developing World Perspective," International Seminar on Open Access for Developing Countries, 2005, http://www.icml9.org/meetings/openaccess/public/documents/declaration.htm; CLACSO, "Declaration on Open Access to Knowledge Managed as a Commons by the Scholarly Community," 2015, https://www.clacso.org.ar/conferencia2015/documentos/asamblea/declaraciones/CLACSO-Declaration-on-open-access-to-knowledge-managed-as-a-commons-by-the-scholarly-community.pdf; Latindex-Redalyc-CLACSO-Ibict, "Joint Declaration by Latindex-Redalyc-CLACSO-Ibict on the Use Of CC BY-NC-SA License to Guarantee Protection of Academic and Scientific Open Access Output," 2017, http://www.accesoabiertoalyc.org/declaracion-mexico-en/.

21. First Consortium Assembly from Ibero-America and The Caribbean, "Declarations," September 1, 2017, http://reuniondeconsorcios.conricyt.mx/index.php/primera-reunion/declaraciones/?lang=en.

22. Czerniewicz, "This Map of the World's Scientific Research Is Disturbingly Unequal."

23. Anabel Marin, Sergio Petralia, and Lilia Stubrin, "Evaluating the Impact of Open Access Initiatives within the Academia and Beyond," in *Made in Latin America: Open Access, Scholarly Journals, and Regional Innovations*, ed. Juan Pablo Alperin and Gustavo Fischman (Ciudad Autónoma de Buenos Aires: CLACSO, 2015), 75–102, http://biblioteca.clacso.edu.ar/clacso/se/20150921045253/MadeInLatinAmerica.pdf.

24. Vessuri, Guédon, and Cetto, "Excellence or Quality?"

25. Federico Vasen, "The 'Ivory Tower' as Safe Bet: Science Policies and Research Evaluation in Mexico," *Education Policy Analysis Archives* 26, no. 96 (2018): 1–27, https://doi.org/10.14507/epaa.26.3594.

26. Juan Pablo Alperin, Dominique Saugy de Babini, and Gustavo Fischman, *Open Access Indicators and Scholarly Communications in Latin America* (Ciudad Autónoma de Buenos Aires: CLACSO, 2014), http://biblioteca.clacso.edu.ar/clacso/se/20140917054406/OpenAccess.pdf.

27. Keyla Mafalda de Oliveira Amorin et al., "Evaluation Systems of Scientific Journals in Latin America," in *Made in Latin America: Open Access, Scholarly Journals, and Regional Innovations*, ed. Juan Pablo Alperin and Gustavo Fischman (Ciudad Autónoma de Buenos Aires: CLACSO, 2015), 61–74, http://biblioteca.clacso.edu.ar/clacso/se/20150921045253/MadeInLatinAmerica.pdf.

28. Alperin, "The Public Impact of Latin America's Approach to Open Access."

24 Learned Societies, Humanities Publishing, and Scholarly Communication in the UK

Jane Winters

As documented by Aileen Fyfe's chapter in this book, *Philosophical Transactions*, described as "the world's first and longest-running scientific journal," was published in 1665, five years after the establishment of the Royal Society, which first licensed and then owned the title.[1] The communication and advancement of research through publication was deemed central to the Society's role from the outset. More than 350 years later, scholarly communication remains vitally important to the work, the standing, and increasingly the economic viability of learned societies and subject organizations across the sciences, humanities, and social sciences. Access at reduced or no charge to society publications—whether journals, edited texts or monographs—is viewed as one of the key benefits of society membership for individual researchers.[2] Most learned society websites have a prominent publications section, and special membership areas leave no doubt that this is an activity to be valued. These publications serve multiple, reinforcing purposes. They might be signifiers of belonging, either as an owner or a contributor; enticements to pay an annual member subscription; showcases for both the society and the discipline; sites of argumentation; forums for innovation, or conversely protest against change; or a means of subsidizing other society activity.

For most of the twentieth century there has been no need to question or perhaps really even to think about the role of the learned society as publisher, or these days more often publishing partner. However, in the last two decades the assumptions and "certainties" that underpinned this model have begun to be challenged by the development of the web, and by the demand for broader open access to what might once have been viewed as privileged knowledge that the web has both encouraged and enabled. And this challenge is a multifaceted one. It is perhaps most immediately an economic problem; this was certainly the concern that dominated early discussions about the impact of open-access mandates on learned societies. As the money to be earned from scholarly publishing, especially in partnership with the large commercial entities that positioned themselves as "society publishers," increased, so too did the dependence on income from this source. Organizations representing the humanities never enjoyed the publishing bonanza from which many of their counterparts in the sciences benefited, but the sums involved were sufficiently large to encourage what with hindsight begins to look like overreliance on a single source of income. The apparently sudden threat to this ecosystem posed by open access in particular caused, and continues to cause, great concern.[3] If the income from publications was largely to be lost—and this was often the lens through which open access was viewed—how would a learned society continue to fund its work, to pay its staff, to stay in business? The initial alarm receded, but I suspect only because green open access came to be accommodated with relatively little disruption to the dominant subscription models.[4]

More interesting, and ultimately perhaps more difficult to address, are the cultural implications of these changes. Scholarly publishing is inextricably entangled with our understandings of academic rigor, reputation, and authority. There are explicit and implicit hierarchies, often impenetrable to those just embarking on their university careers, which center in particular on university presses and on the journals published in the name of learned societies. These hierarchies are in large part self-imposed, and consequently all the more persistent. In the UK, the 2014 Research Excellence Framework (REF)[5] FAQs may include a very clear statement that "No sub-panel will make any use of journal Impact Factors, rankings, lists or the perceived standing of publishers in assessing the quality of research outputs,"[6] but it is very difficult to persuade researchers, much less REF administrators in their universities, that this is really true. In general, scholars are liable to assume that judgments about quality will be made according to the criteria that they use themselves, where the publisher or journal becomes a proxy for quality and open access can become shorthand for "less rigorously peer reviewed." In this context, learned societies become guardians of an established brand, with their imprimatur guaranteeing quality. There is little incentive to initiate change, and indeed preservation of the status quo may be viewed as an important responsibility for those involved in academic publishing. To do otherwise is to risk unmooring research from any markers of quality and value. At a time of ever-increasing publication,[7] the argument that we need precisely these robust and well-trusted systems in place to help filter out the noise can seem very attractive indeed.

Change, however, is happening regardless, and it is incumbent on learned societies to mediate new developments in scholarly publishing, and in the broader culture of the academy, for their subject and disciplinary communities, as they have done so successfully in the past. There is an opportunity for bodies of this kind to offer different services for researchers, and to explore new ways of providing and articulating value. What are learned societies for in the early twenty-first century? Which communities do they serve, particularly as so many of them are registered charities with an obligation to look beyond their members and fellows? Scholarly communication can, and in my view should, remain at the heart of their activity, but it is possible to think imaginatively about everything that this might encompass.

The arguments against radical change are often financial ones. Learned societies do need to remain financially sound if they are to achieve anything at all, but this is not to say that the economics of their publishing programs should remain unscrutinized. Does it still make sense to derive substantial income from journals which are paid for at least twice over from membership fees and university library subscriptions, for example? And where this is the case, it becomes difficult to argue that access to publications is what is really driving society membership. There is another kind of value on offer here, which retains its attraction despite the open availability of a society's published outputs. Learned societies which are tackling head on the problems facing their disciplines, influencing policy so that it works for their professional cultures and practices, and helping researchers to investigate and benefit from new ways of communicating research stand a very good chance not just of surviving, but of thriving. They can begin to shape the future of academic publishing.

This is particularly the case with regard to open-access monograph publishing. Thanks to the consultation on the second REF published in December 2016, we know that the open access mandate that currently applies to journal articles and conference proceedings in the UK will be extended to books for the third REF in the mid-2020s.[8] We do not yet know, however, what a fully open-access landscape for monographs might look like. But we do have between five and 10 years to think about what will most effectively serve the humanities, where book-based disciplines still predominate, and to experiment with new ways of publishing books.[9] Experimentation can be unsettling, for established and new researchers alike, and at a time of rapid change it can be exceptionally difficult to navigate a "safe" course. And there is undoubtedly risk involved in digital publishing. There is no commonly accepted business model for publishing open-access books, but there is already a degree of experimentation. Notable examples include Knowledge Unlatched, punctum books, Open Humanities Press, Open Book Publishers and OpenEdition, among others.[10] In the coming years, many more different approaches will be adopted, and many new initiatives will spring up. Some will be led by publishers, some by libraries, some by scholars themselves—and some of them will inevitably fail. This is not the future that an author wants for their first book, even if open access will allow it to survive the demise of its publisher in multiple forms and places. You want your first book to be part of a growing portfolio of related titles that show how it complements and advances research in your chosen field. That is one reason for the continuing significance of book series, which are about more than ease of marketing. There will be anxiety about open-access books, some of it justified, some of it the result of misinformation, but all of it needing to be addressed—and that is where learned societies come in.

One interesting early intervention is that of the Royal Historical Society (RHS), which has taken the decision to close its long-running monograph series, Studies in History, and to launch a fresh open-access alternative, New Historical Perspectives. The series is aimed at early career researchers, within 10 years of completing the PhD, and is designed to make open access an option of first choice rather than last resort. With even the lowest book processing charges currently costing an author around £5,000 (approximately $6,600), and fee waiver schemes likely to be heavily oversubscribed, publishing an open-access book seems simply out of the question for many humanities researchers. Developing a scheme that covers this cost, as part of the RHS's service for its subject community, makes open access possible.[11] There are still arguments to be made about authority, value, and the importance of impact and reach, but the initial, and often insurmountable, financial hurdle is overcome. The books, which will be published through the relaunched University of London Press, will take the familiar form of the PDF, supplemented by print-on-demand and ePub versions. There is not yet much in the way of digital experimentation. The goal is rather to embed open access within the publishing practices of early career historians, and this necessitates a degree of caution. There is nevertheless innovation: in the partnership with a small university publisher and other learned societies; in the openness to a broad definition of the book, which includes not just monographs and edited collections but shorter works of 30,000–40,000 words; and in a peer review process that allows authors to workshop their book with leading researchers in their field. Once the series and the publishing platform are more established, there will be options to play with form, to incorporate data and other digital objects in the open-access book, and finally to think beyond the PDF. All of this becomes easier, and less frightening for researchers, if digital-first publication has been normalized within a discipline through the involvement and sponsorship of learned societies.

This is, of course, just a single example, in a single discipline. It might work for history, where the monograph continues to dominate the academic publishing environment and to determine career progression, but not be quite right for philosophy or classics. Other humanities disciplines will have more or less differing concerns and imperatives. The point is not the type of activity, but the fact that learned societies are beginning to seize the opportunity to rethink the ways in which they can support and develop scholarly communication. They can, as in this instance, provide financial assistance and new publishing opportunities. But they might equally seek to influence the use of bibliometrics to measure quality, provide guidance around ethical publishing practices, address questions of diversity at all stages of the publishing process, work together to explore the possible evolutions of peer review, or discuss how best to deal with research outputs of all kinds that have multiple authors. These are developments which are already affecting humanities researchers, but which they may have little or no capacity to influence. Their learned societies can speak for them and help to deliver change that builds on the best humanities practice. If bibliometrics are to become one measure for judging the quality of research, for example, then it is vital both that humanities citation is fully understood, and that robust data is collected for the full range of publications. If research in the digital humanities tends to produce more books and journal articles with multiple authors, then the roles of the various authors need to be explored and mechanisms established for recognizing their unique contributions. If altmetrics are to play a role in evaluation processes, the forums in which humanities researchers share their findings online and the networks that they use to engage with their colleagues and the wider public need to be investigated.

Learned societies can, if they choose, play an important role in the reshaping of scholarly communication for the twenty-first century. It may well be vital for their own survival that they do so. They do not, however, have to act alone. Many learned societies in the humanities are very small indeed and have to marshal and prioritize their limited resources carefully. They often draw heavily on the work of volunteer officers, who have their own paying jobs to keep them occupied and cannot afford to take on even more commitments. In this environment, consultation and collaboration become key. A group of learned societies working together is much better placed to influence policy, develop infrastructure, and effect change. Publishers' humanities catalogues, after all, have always accommodated a range of humanities disciplines and found common ground between them. The benefits of sharing knowledge and expertise not just within small consortia but with the sector as a whole—of extending the principles behind open-access publication beyond the research outputs themselves to include the methods by which they are published—would also be enormous. Commercial publishers have a clear imperative to keep private those aspects of their work that give them an advantage over their rivals. This need not be the case where publishers are learned societies, or libraries, or universities. There is room for many business models, for many ways of publishing, and for many kinds of publisher. Equally, there is space for many and varied forms of publication. Some of this activity will remain on a purely commercial footing, some will be conducted on a not-for-profit basis, and some may never cover its costs but be viewed rather as an investment in organizational reputation. It is a time to experiment, and it would be a missed opportunity for learned societies not to rise to the challenge.

Notes

1. Julie McDougall-Waters, Aileen Fyfe, and Noah Moxham, Philosophical Transactions: *350 Years of Publishing at the Royal Society (1665–2015)* (London: The Royal Society, 2014).

2. It is not, however, the service that is most valued by members of learned societies. Mary Waltham, for example, notes that "Numerous surveys show that the primary reason for being a member of a society is for the opportunities that membership brings for conferences, networking and collaboration." Mary Waltham, "What Do Society and Association Members Really Want?," *Learned Publishing* 21, no. 1 (2008): 7–14, https://doi.org/10.1087/095315108X247294. I owe this reference to one of the anonymous reviewers for this book.

3. The "threat" was not, of course, a sudden one, but humanities researchers in the UK were undoubtedly taken by surprise by the open-access mandates that emerged first from Research Councils UK (RCUK) and then the Higher Education Funding Council for England (HEFCE).

4. In Europe, the announcement of "Plan S" in September 2018 raised the alarm once again. Ninth among the 10 principles of Plan S is the statement that "The 'hybrid' model of publishing is not compliant" with the view of open access set out by the European Commission and a number of other national research funders, including UK Research and Innovation (UKRI). It is precisely this hybrid model of journal publishing, offering a mixture of subscription-based and open access, that minimized the disruption experienced by publishers (but did not deliver a full open-access publishing landscape). cOAlition S, "Plan S," Plan S and cOAlition S, 2018, https://www.coalition-s.org/.

5. The Research Excellence Framework is "the system for assessing the quality of research in UK higher education institutions." Higher Education Funding Council for England, "REF 2021," Research Excellence Framework, 2019, https://www.ref.ac.uk.

6. Higher Education Funding Council for England, "FAQs—REF 2021," Research Excellence Framework, 2019, https://www.ref.ac.uk/faqs/.

7. Geoffrey Crossick, "Monographs and Open Access: A Report for the Higher Education Funding Council for England," 21–22, noted, for example, that "the decline in monograph publishing turns out to be a myth," citing an almost 100 percent increase in the number of monographs published annually by four major publishers between 2004 and 2013.

8. Higher Education Funding Council for England, "Consultation on the Second Research Excellence Framework," 2. "In the long term … we want to see the benefits that open access has brought to journal articles extended to other research outputs, including monographs. We therefore intend to move towards an open-access requirement for monographs in the exercise that follows the next REF (expected in the mid-2020s)."

9. Even Plan S, with its original ambitious target of 2020 for most kinds of publication, acknowledged that "the timeline to achieve Open Access for monographs and books may be longer than 1 January 2020," and this has indeed turned out to be the case. cOAlition S, "Plan S."

10. I am grateful to Martin Paul Eve for his advice on this list.

11. The series is also supported by the Economic History Society and the Past and Present Society, and published in association with the Institute of Historical Research, University of London.

25   Not All Networks: Toward Open, Sustainable Research Communities

Kathleen Fitzpatrick

The May 2016 purchase of the Social Science Research Network (SSRN) by the Anglo-Dutch publishing megacompany Elsevier created a firestorm among researchers and others interested in open-access scholarly communication, who worried about what would become of the network and its data—and not without reason. The acquisition of such a well-established research-sharing network by a major commercial publisher not only presented the possibility that the company would seek to close down access to the network's store of research papers or that it would mine them for other forms of saleable data, but also, alongside their prior acquisition of Mendeley, seemed to indicate that Elsevier sought to vertically integrate the entirety of the research workflow (an indication intensified by the patent the company recently obtained for an online peer review process).[1] The publisher, unsurprisingly, argued that such integration would bring benefits to authors, enabling them to move fluidly from research to drafting to journal submission, but many researchers expressed concern about what such all-encompassing lock-in might do to their community, and not least to the values that the community espoused.[2] This concern was borne out two months later, when SSRN users began reporting that shared materials perceived not to be in compliance with a newly imposed copyright transfer policy were being removed.[3] The Authors Alliance responded by asking whether it might be time for authors to leave SSRN, and other groups, including the Association of Research Libraries, picked up the charge.[4]

This is only one among many recent calls imploring researchers to abandon the apparently free and open networks on which they have come to rely. Earlier in 2016, the Twitter hashtag #DeleteAcademiaEdu urged scholars to close down their accounts on the popular scholarly social network in response to the network's suggestion that it might charge scholars for recommendations, a move that felt to many uncomfortably like a type of academic payola.[5] In each of these cases, many researchers were prompted to seek alternatives to their accustomed community spaces when the specter of monetization appeared, revealing a discomfort with the intrusion of commercial enterprises into academic workflows. As Paolo Mangiafico has pointed out, however, this focus on the role that capitalism should or shouldn't play in scholarly communication runs the risk of obscuring a larger, more important point: that companies providing the platforms supporting these research communities did not share the researchers' values, and that it might be a fruitful moment for scholars to consider switching over to services provided by organizations whose interests more closely mapped to their own.[6]

Mangiafico pointed toward institutional repositories and other services provided by academic libraries as key examples, but even there value-alignment remains a potentially slippery matter. That slipperiness became all too clear in August 2017, when Elsevier purchased bepress, a company that contracted with many academic libraries to provide institutional repository and open-access publishing services.[7] Though bepress had been founded by academics eighteen years earlier, and though it continues to describe its mission as serving academia, the company's amenability to being acquired by a mega-corporation that many hold responsible for the dire state of library budgets sent shockwaves through the sector.[8] These concerns resulted later in the year in a concerted effort by many libraries to seek or develop bepress alternatives, including a session at the December membership meeting of the Coalition for Networked Information entitled "beprexit: Rethinking Repository Services in a Changing Scholarly Communication Landscape."[9] Academic institutions are thus similarly being called upon to consider the importance of value alignment with their vendors; only through such value alignment can scholars and their institutions become reasonably confident that the platforms supporting their research communities will develop and evolve appropriately with them.

All of this is to say that these crises of conscience that have visited online research communities have at long last highlighted for the scholarly communication landscape a situation that's been visible in other sectors of social media for a while: when it comes to networks, openness is a virtue, but other determinants matter as much or more. Put another way: there is open, and then there is open, and while the difference may seem semantic, it is anything but. SSRN and Academia.edu have long been open, in the sense that any interested user can create a free account, connect with other users, share work, and so forth; bepress's products remain open, in the sense that they support libraries in openly disseminating the scholarship produced on their campuses. None of these services are open, however, in the deeper sense of providing user understanding of and input into their business and sustainability models; none are focused on interoperability with other systems in the research infrastructure or in sharing research data with other entities, except as it might provide a source of revenue; none are in any sufficient sense in dialogue with or connected to the research community. SSRN and Academia.edu may permit any scholar to contribute their work to the platform, and bepress may help libraries create spaces for open sharing of scholarly work, but scholars and libraries in the end have precious little control over the platforms on which they rely.

Boiling the SSRN/Academia.edu situation down to "if you're not paying, you're the product being sold" gets at something important for scholars to consider—a crucial caveat emptor about the business models we inadvertently support and their potential ramifications for our research workflows—but it's nonetheless a vast oversimplification. There have long been more possible models available for research services than user-pays or user-gets-datamined-and/or-sold-to-advertisers. Perhaps most significant among them is the collective funding model provided by membership organizations such as learned and professional societies. These societies, since the Royal Society of London, have been founded for the express purpose of fostering and facilitating communication amongst their members, and between those members and the broader intellectual world.[10] Early in their histories, that communication took the form of letters circulated to the membership and meetings at which member work was presented and discussed. Over time, these practices formalized into the journals and conferences with which we are familiar today. While different societies have maintained different membership policies and requirements, and thus are not "open" in the sense espoused by many web-based social platforms—in which anyone can participate without cost—they are ideally open in our other sense: governed by their members, as collectives working in the interest of their members.

While I strongly believe that the latter sense of openness is far more important than the former, the challenge presented by the current moment both in internet-based scholarly communication and in the increasingly precarious academic economic environment is nonetheless finding a way to support and sustain both kinds of openness. How can we create research communities online that invite everyone to participate, that are transparent about their governance and community-oriented in their values, and that remain both technologically and fiscally sustainable?

This is, I would argue, one of the places in which the progress that scholarly communication has made toward open access has gotten tangled up in priorities that do not reflect the actual goals of the scholarly community. The Budapest Open Access Initiative defined its goals in a frequently cited statement:

> By "open access" to this literature, we mean its free availability on the public internet, permitting any users to read, download, copy, distribute, print, search, or link to the full texts of these articles, crawl them for indexing, pass them as data to software, or use them for any other lawful purpose, without financial, legal, or technical barriers other than those inseparable from gaining access to the internet itself. The only constraint on reproduction and distribution, and the only role for copyright in this domain, should be to give authors control over the integrity of their work and the right to be properly acknowledged and cited.[11]

This is an expansive definition, and a profoundly idealistic one, and yet one that presents a couple of problems: first, it made it possible for many to read "free availability on the public internet" and go no further; the real impact of open access's openness lies further down in the definition, in the ways that the products of scholarly research can be built upon and reused, and yet that goal winds up a bit easy to overlook. The second issue follows from this, and represents a problem at the very heart of much of what has happened since: by focusing our attention on "access," and in particular on the elimination of "financial, legal, or technical barriers" to the consumption of the products of scholarly research, we wind up restricting ourselves to affecting the ability of end users to see the stuff we create. It's crucial that such consumer access be made as open and seamless as possible, but in focusing on that end of things we don't address concerns about what we're creating, or how we're creating it. And this is how we end up with an increasingly pervasive system of ostensibly open-access publishing that relies on the simple substitution of article-processing charges—which is to say, author-side fees—for the revenue previously produced through sales and subscriptions. Nothing about the system itself changes—and in fact, the existing formats, venues, and publishers further entrench themselves as the only viable, trustworthy options. The sole substantive shift that this model of "open" brings about is that the inequities move from the consumer side of the equation to the producer side, raising the possibility that only researchers in grant-rich fields, or at institutions with substantial research support, will be able to afford to disseminate the work they produce.

If our goals are not just to make the work being produced by well-funded researchers, in well-supported fields, or at well-heeled institutions, openly available on the internet, but rather to facilitate open communication among all researchers, within all fields, across all institutions, in ways that promote not just the free consumption of the work that's already being done but that support and facilitate the production of more new kinds of exciting work, from more areas of the research environment, than ever before—if we genuinely espouse these more expansive goals, then what we need is not just ways to make existing publications available without charge, but instead an entirely new, open, community-oriented, sustainable research infrastructure. What we need is a model of collective, cooperative, sustainable support for open platforms; an architecture that makes those platforms' data not just available but interoperable, shareable, reusable; and an ethic that makes commitment to those platforms and the organizations that provide them an important element of professional belonging.

These are the goals that the Modern Language Association had in mind as the organization set about building *Humanities Commons*, a developing network that is sponsored by a group of scholarly societies but that is both open to participation from any researcher or practitioner who wants to create a profile and share work with the community, and mission-driven, committed to the needs and interests of that community. *Humanities Commons* is our effort, first and foremost, to leverage the collectives represented by scholarly societies on behalf of the common good.[12]

The MLA launched a social network called *MLA Commons* in 2013 to provide its more than 25,000 members worldwide with a platform for communication and collaboration, both to extend year-round the kinds of conversations that take place at the organization's annual meetings and to provide means for members to share their scholarly work with one another.[13] *MLA Commons* supports a wide range of member interactions, including public and private group discussions, web-based publishing, collaborative document authoring, and more. Members can create CV-like profiles linking to their work on the *Commons* and across the web. And they can deposit their work—preprints, datasets, presentations, syllabi, you name it—to *CORE*, the repository integrated into the *Commons*, and share that work with the *Commons* groups to which they belong.[14] *MLA Commons* helped foster new kinds of online scholarly interaction amongst MLA members, but it quickly became apparent that those members, who work in increasingly interdisciplinary ways, want a space for active collaboration that allows for connections across fields.

In order to create those interdisciplinary linkages, the *MLA Commons* team first undertook a planning process and then, in December 2016, launched a pilot project designed to connect multiple scholarly societies.[15] So while *Humanities Commons* invites any interested researcher or practitioner in the humanities to create a free account, regardless of their institutional affiliation, employment status, society memberships, or any other determining factor, members of participating societies receive additional access to those societies' resources and the ability to take part in those societies' conversations. Faculty members in Slavic literature, who are members of both the MLA and ASEEES, can create accounts on *Humanities Commons* that give access to *MLA Commons* and *ASEEES Commons*. Their profiles on the network appear on all three sites, and the academic interests they list there connect them to others across the network with those same interests. They can deposit work in *CORE* and share it with the groups to which they belong; that work is linked from their profile, and they can track the impact that it has within the field by aggregating information about how the work is downloaded, cited, and used. They can start an individual blog, or participate in a group blog, or contribute to an experimental publication housed anywhere within the sites to which they have access.

Crucially, however, it's not just tenure-track researchers, or researchers whose societies are already part of the network, who benefit from *Humanities Commons*. Graduate students in history, for instance, can create accounts on *Humanities Commons*, despite the fact that their scholarly society isn't yet participating in the federation. They won't be able to participate in discussions on the sites where they are not members, but they can deposit and share work with the larger *Humanities Commons* community. And our hope is that their active participation, and the active participation of their colleagues, will draw their scholarly societies to join the federation—to come where their members already are, draw them into more active participation in society business, and support the open interdisciplinary work their members want to do.

Reaching full sustainability for *Humanities Commons*, which we hope to accomplish within five years, will require the support of many scholarly organizations and institutions, as the network must gradually shift from grant-based support to a funding model based largely on annual fees paid into a common fund by participating groups. Based on the experiences of projects like *arXiv*, we expect that we'll need to be prepared to do some fundraising as well, in order not just to support the existing infrastructure but also the ongoing development, maintenance, technical support, and member facilitation that the network will require. But fundraising on its own cannot create the community buy-in that a network like *Humanities Commons* requires. For that, the community itself must feel ownership of the network, and so we are developing a governance model that will grant both participating organizations and individual members a voice in setting the network's future directions.

That is perhaps the most crucial aspect of the openness of *Humanities Commons*: not just that anyone can create an account, free of charge, and not just that the broader public can access the material shared there, but that the network is and will remain not-for-profit, that it will be sustained and governed by scholars themselves. We hope that the network's members will encourage their professional organizations to participate, and then support those organizations that do this work on their behalf. In this way, we are drawing on the strengths that membership organizations have long possessed: their mission and their values align in their focus on and support from their members. In building *Humanities Commons*, we are not just building a new infrastructure for the open distribution of new kinds of scholarly work, nor just developing a new platform for new kinds of research communities, but helping to foster a new intellectual economy, a collectivist network that scholars both support and lead. It is that alignment between economics and values that will ensure that the open research communities we develop today remain open and vibrant tomorrow.

Notes

1. See Mike Masnick, "Disappointing: Elsevier Buys Open Access Academic Pre-Publisher SSRN," Techdirt, May 17, 2016, https://www.techdirt.com/articles/20160517/13513134465/disappointing-elsevier-buys-open-access-academic-pre-publisher-ssrn

.shtml; Chris Kelty, "It's the Data, Stupid: What Elsevier's Purchase of SSRN Also Means," *Savage Minds* (blog), May 18, 2016, https://savageminds.org/2016/05/18/its-the-data-stupid-what-elseviers-purchase-of-ssrn-also-means/; Cameron Neylon, "Canaries in the Elsevier Mine: What to Watch for at SSRN," *Science in the Open* (blog), June 7, 2016, http://cameronneylon.net/blog/canaries-in-the-elsevier-mine-what-to-watch-for-at-ssrn/; see also Goldie Blumenstyk, "Elsevier's New Patent for Online Peer Review Throws a Scare Into Open-Source Advocates," *The Chronicle of Higher Education*, September 1, 2016, https://www.chronicle.com/article/Elsevier-s-New-Patent-for/237656.

2. Gregg Gordon, "SSRN—the Leading Social Science and Humanities Repository and Online Community—Joins Elsevier," Elsevier Connect, May 17, 2016, https://www.elsevier.com/connect/ssrn-the-leading-social-science-and-humanities-repository-and-online-community-joins-elsevier.

3. Howard Wasserman, "SSRN Postings and Copyright," *PrawfsBlawg* (blog), July 15, 2016, https://prawfsblawg.blogs.com/prawfsblawg/2016/07/ssrn-postings-and-copyright.html.

4. Authors Alliance, "Is It Time for Authors to Leave SSRN?," *Authors Alliance* (blog), July 17, 2016, https://www.authorsalliance.org/2016/07/17/is-it-time-for-authors-to-leave-ssrn/; Krista Cox, "Moving from SSRN to SocArXiv," ARL Policy Notes, July 22, 2016, http://policynotes.arl.org/?p=1403.

5. See https://twitter.com/hashtag/DeleteAcademiaEdu, but also Corinne Ruff, "Scholars Criticize Academia.Edu Proposal to Charge Authors for Recommendations," *The Chronicle of Higher Education*, January 29, 2016, https://www.chronicle.com/article/Scholars-Criticize/235102.

6. Paolo Mangiafico, "Should You #DeleteAcademiaEdu?," *Scholarly Communications @ Duke* (blog), January 29, 2016, https://blogs.library.duke.edu/scholcomm/2016/01/29/should-you-deleteacademiaedu/.

7. Elsevier, "Elsevier Acquires Bepress, a Leading Service Provider Used by Academic Institutions to Showcase Their Research," Elsevier, August 2, 2017, https://www.elsevier.com/about/press-releases/corporate/elsevier-acquires-bepress,-a-leading-service-provider-used-by-academic-institutions-to-showcase-their-research.

8. On the bepress mission, see bepress, "About," *Bepress* (blog), accessed May 23, 2019, https://www.bepress.com/about/; on library responses, see Lindsay McKenzie, "Elsevier Makes Move into Institutional Repositories with Acquisition of Bepress," Inside Higher Ed, August 3, 2017, https://www.insidehighered.com/news/2017/08/03/elsevier-makes-move-institutional-repositories-acquisition-bepress; as well as Roger C. Schonfeld, "Reflections on 'Elsevier Acquires Bepress,'" *Ithaka S+R* (blog), August 7, 2017, https://sr.ithaka.org/blog/reflections-on-elsevier-acquires-bepress/.

9. See Coalition for Networked Information, "CNI Fall 2017 Membership Meeting Schedule," CNI: Coalition for Networked Information, August 30, 2017, https://www

.cni.org/events/membership-meetings/past-meetings/fall-2017/schedule-f17; see also "Operation Beprexit," Operation beprexit, accessed May 23, 2019, https://beprexit.wordpress.com/.

10. On the history of the Royal Society and its role in scholarly communication, see Aileen Fyfe's chapter in this volume.

11. Leslie Chan et al., "Budapest Open Access Initiative," February 14, 2002, http://www.soros.org/openaccess/read.shtml.

12. A note on the use of "our" here, and the second-person plural in what follows: I was director of scholarly communication at the MLA during the planning and launch of *MLA Commons* and *Humanities Commons*, and though I am no longer employed by the organization, I remain project director of *Humanities Commons*. "We" and "us" should thus be understood to refer to the *Commons* team rather than to the MLA.

13. *MLA Commons* was developed with support from the Andrew W. Mellon Foundation and is built on the CUNY Graduate Center's open-source Commons In A Box platform.

14. *CORE* was developed with support from the National Endowment for the Humanities and in partnership with the Center for Digital Research and Scholarship at the Columbia University libraries. *CORE* is a Fedora/Solr repository for which we developed a WordPress-based front end for deposit, markup, discovery, and sharing. *CORE* thus brings together a library-quality repository (adhering to commonly accepted metadata standards, employing digital object identifiers, and so on) with a social network, with the result that work is not simply put into the repository and forgotten, but actively shared and used. In the next phase of development, we will focus on making *CORE* interoperable with institutional repositories and other key research services.

15. Both the planning and the pilot stages of this project have been generously supported by the Andrew W. Mellon Foundation. Our partners in this project are the Association for Jewish Studies; the Association for Slavic, East European, and Eurasian Studies; and the College Art Association.

Conclusion

Martin Paul Eve and Jonathan Gray

Open access does not exist in technological isolation from the political and social contexts in which it was conceived and under which it is being implemented. Across the spans of colonial legacies and globalization, knowledge frameworks, ideas of publics and audience, notions of archives and (digital) preservation, infrastructures and platforms, and communities, the contributors to this volume have demonstrated that there are complex political, philosophical, and pragmatic implications for opening research work and other forms through digital technologies. Hence, while those seeking to implement the ever-growing number of funder- and institution-driven OA mandates hope for easily transmissible messaging of communicable truths, the reality—in both theory and practice—is very different.

A good example of this can be seen in Stuart Lawson's chapter. This is because a traditional rationale for the transformation of academic libraries in the twenty-first century has been to argue that open access is aligned with the long-standing goal of libraries to provide information to anyone who desires it. Clearly, such an argument has persuasive rhetorical force. However, if one pierces the historical veneer, as does Lawson, then this argument falters somewhat. For the idealized prehistory of libraries to which we often gesture turns out to be less than solid. Conversely, though, as Aileen Fyfe has demonstrated, anyone who argues that learned society publishing has always been a source of revenue for such entities and that this sits at odds with broader public dissemination have a different challenge now to answer. Many truths about open access are more inconvenient than we might like.

Furthermore, while arguments for open access have often been premised, in the Global North, on equitable worldwide access to research, this conversation has too often been unidirectional. As Packer and others have demonstrated, the Global South is (or developing countries are[1]) rich with long-standing and successful open-access initiatives from which the Global North consistently refuses to learn. Instead, openness is mischaracterized as a silver bullet for all the ills and iniquities of the unequal global academic publishing landscape. Until we dismantle the prestige-economy scaffold on which the edifice of academic publishing is hung, the North-to-South export of elite open access and its associated cost-concentrating business models will continue to have dire consequences, as Thomas Hervé Mboa Nkoudou has ably demonstrated.

It is also clear that the underlying digital infrastructures on which open access is based come with both opportunities and threats to conventional notions of scholarship. Radical experiments in format (Robin de Mourat, Donato Ricci, and Bruno Latour's chapter as well as that by Pamela H. Smith, Tianna Helena Uchacz, Naomi Rosenkranz, and Claire Conklin Sabel) lead to changes in the underlying assumptions around, for instance, digital preservation (Dorothea Salo and April Hathcock), as just one example. Of course, as Salo points out, the difficulties are not primarily technological; they are economic. However, the imbalances of scarcity introduced twofold by the digitization of scholarship and the mass expansion of higher education and concomitant research output create socioeconomic problems. These are introduced, partially, by digital technologies, infrastructures, and platforms, as Penny Andrews and Jonathan Gray, in particular, point out.

These changes to the economics of research production extend well beyond publishers. As the last section of this book demonstrated—in the work of Eileen A. Joy, Jane Winters, and Kathleen Fitzpatrick, among others—the interconnectedness of learned societies with publishing practices (and revenue streams) poses fundamental questions about the way our disciplinary communities construct themselves. There is a cascading "domino effect" from changes to the (political) economics of research publishing that some would deem catastrophic, while others see it as an opportunity to rethink our practices.

Of course, there is also scope to rethink publishing practices based on the successful initiatives that have paved the way. Be that in SciELO (Abel Packer), in linked open data (Arianna Becerril-García and Eduardo Aguado-López), from organizational structures such as CLACSO (Dominique Babini), and from text-mining initiatives (Martin Paul Eve), there is far too much of a tendency—perhaps particularly among those in the Global North—to reinvent the wheel when it comes to the design of fresh infrastructures. Even as we know that there is nothing new under the sun, a greater culture of adaptation and dialogue might de-duplicate efforts and foster greater international communication in the dissemination of research work. There are often commensurately old(er) technologies to go alongside our university traditions than might be believed.

Ultimately, though, in a world of shifting certainties for scholarly communications, the drive toward open access looks set only to continue. As we write, we are, for instance, on the cusp of the implementation of the major, if contentious, pan-global open-access initiative, "Plan S." However, critics have railed that such a declaration, coming from within Europe, has insufficiently contextualized its own creation and implementation, say in the light of South American initiatives.[2] In other words, understandings drawn from a diverse set of geographic locations and histories are *important* for policymakers, for publishers, for academics, and for funders. Without such understandings, we become trapped in repetitive loops, reinventing wheels, and lacking that most fundamental of activities for scholarly communication: communication itself. The chapters in this volume indicate how scholarly communication is both a substantive object of study, deserving of critical reflection and exploration from a wide variety of disciplinary perspectives, as well as an important area of intervention and experimentation to shape that which in turn shapes who and what we are, what we do, what is recognized and valued, and who is involved. Thereby we might make space to challenge, to recompose, and to participate in how research and inquiry unfolds and is given life in the world.

Notes

1. As ever, please see the terminological note at the start of this book. The SciELO project does not favor the term "Global South," and we have had to negotiate such language with care.

2. Humberto Debat and Dominique Babini, "Plan S: Take Latin America's Long Experience on Board," *Nature* 573 (2019): 495, https://doi.org/10.1038/d41586-019-02857-1.

Bibliography

Adema, Janneke. "Don't Give Your Labour to Academia.Edu, Use It to Strengthen the Academic Commons." *Open Reflections* (blog), April 7, 2016. https://openreflections.wordpress.com/2016/04/07/dont-give-your-labour-to-academia-edu-use-it-to-strengthen-the-academic-commons/.

Adema, Janneke, and Gary Hall. "The Political Nature of the Book: On Artists' Books and Radical Open Access." *New Formations*, no. 78 (2013): 138–156. https://doi.org/10.3898/NewF.78.07.2013.

Adema, Janneke, and Samuel A. Moore. "Collectivity and Collaboration: Imagining New Forms of Communality to Create Resilience in Scholar-Led Publishing." *Insights: The UKSG Journal* 31 (2018). https://doi.org/10.1629/uksg.399.

Adler, Melissa. "Classification Along the Color Line: Excavating Racism in the Stacks." *Journal of Critical Library and Information Studies* 1, no. 1 (2017): 1–32. https://doi.org/10.24242/jclis.v1i1.17.

Aguado-López, Eduardo, Arianna Becerril-García, and Salvador Chávez-Ávila. "Conectando al Sur Con La Ciencia Global. El Nuevo Modelo de Publicación en ALyC, No Comercial, Colaborativo y Sustentable," 2016. https://blogredalyc.files.wordpress.com/2016/08/redalycnuevomodelopublicacion2016-11.pdf.

Aguado-López, Eduardo, Arianna Becerril-García, and Sheila Godínez-Larios. "Colaboración Internacional en Las Ciencias Sociales y Humanidades: Inclusión, Participación e Integración." *Convergencia Revista de Ciencias Sociales*, no. 75 (2017): 13. https://doi.org/10.29101/crcs.v0i75.4227.

Alonso, Wladimir J., and Esteban Fernández-Juricic. "Regional Network Raises Profile of Local Journals." *Nature* 415, no. 6871 (2002): 471. https://doi.org/10.1038/415471c.

Alperin, Juan Pablo. "The Public Impact of Latin America's Approach to Open Access." PhD diss., Stanford University, 2015. https://purl.stanford.edu/jr256tk1194.

Alperin, Juan Pablo, Dominique Saugy de Babini, and Gustavo Fischman. *Open Access Indicators and Scholarly Communications in Latin America*. Ciudad Autónoma de Buenos Aires: CLACSO, 2014. http://biblioteca.clacso.edu.ar/clacso/se/20140917054406/OpenAccess.pdf.

Altman, Elizabeth, and Mary Tripsas. "Product-to-Platform Transitions: Organizational Identity Implications." In *The Oxford Handbook of Creativity, Innovation, and Entrepreneurship*, edited by Christina Shalley, Michael A. Hitt, and Jing Zhou. Oxford: Oxford University Press, 2015. https://doi.org/10.1093/oxfordhb/9780199927678.013.0032.

Alvarez, Maximillian. "Contingent No More." *The Baffler*, May 3, 2017. https://thebaffler.com/the-poverty-of-theory/contingent-no-more.

"AmeliCA vs Plan S: Same Target, Two Different Strategies to Achieve Open Access.—AmeliCA." Accessed May 1, 2019. http://www.amelica.org/en/index.php/2019/01/10/amelica-vs-plan-s-mismo-objetivo-dos-estrategias-distintas-para-lograr-el-acceso-abierto/.

American Association of University Professors. "Background Facts on Contingent Faculty Positions." AAUP. Accessed May 14, 2019. https://www.aaup.org/issues/contingency/background-facts.

American Historical Association. "Statement on Policies Regarding the Embargoing of Completed History PhD Dissertations." Perspectives on History, July 22, 2013. https://www.historians.org/publications-and-directories/perspectives-on-history/summer-2013/american-historical-association-statement-on-policies-regarding-the-embargoing-of-completed-history-phd-dissertations.

Anderson, Ivy, Jeffrey Mackie-Mason, Günter Waibel, Richard A. Schneider, Dennis J. Ventry Jr., and Mihoko Hosoi. "Open Statement: Why UC Cut Ties with Elsevier." UC Berkeley Library News, March 20, 2019. https://news.lib.berkeley.edu/uc-elsevier-statement.

Andrews, Penelope CS. "An Investigation into Changes to Institutional Repositories Following the Publication of the Finch Report in July 2012 and Subsequent Developments in UK Funder and Government Policies and Guidance." MSc Digital Library Management, The University of Sheffield, 2014.

Appadurai, Arjun. "The Right to Research." *Globalisation, Societies and Education* 4, no. 2 (2006): 167–177. https://doi.org/10.1080/14767720600750696.

Archambault, Éric, Didier Amyot, Philippe Deschamps, Aurore Nicol, Françoise Provencher, Lise Rebout, and Guillaume Roberge. "Proportion of Open Access Papers Published in Peer-Reviewed Journals at the European and World Levels—1996–2013." Science-Metrix. Accessed April 28, 2019. http://science-metrix.com/sites/default/files/science-metrix/publications/d_1.8_sm_ec_dg-rtd_proportion_oa_1996-2013_v11p.pdf.

Arrow, Tom, Jenny Molloy, and Peter Murray-Rust. "A Day in the Life of a Content Miner and Team." *Insights: The UKSG Journal* 29, no. 2 (2016): 208–211. https://doi.org/10.1629/uksg.310.

Arunachalam, Subbiah. "Social Justice in Scholarly Publishing: Open Access Is the Only Way." *The American Journal of Bioethics* 17, no. 10 (2017): 15–17. https://doi.org/10.1080/15265161.2017.1366194.

Assmann, Aleida. "Canon and Archive." In *Media and Cultural Memory*, edited by Astrid Erll and Ansgar Nünning, 97–108. Berlin: Walter de Gruyter, 2008. https://kops.uni-konstanz.de/handle/123456789/13382.

Association of College & Research Libraries (ACRL). "Scholarship as Conversation." Text. Framework for Information Literacy for Higher Education, February 9, 2015. http://www.ala.org/acrl/standards/ilframework#conversation.

Association of Research Libraries. "ARL Statistics 2009–2011," 2014. https://www.arl.org/arl-statistics-survey-statistical-trends/.

Astbury, Raymond. "The Renewal of the Licensing Act in 1693 and Its Lapse in 1695." *The Library* 33, no. 4 (1978): 296–322. https://doi.org/10.1093/library/s5-XXXIII.4.296.

Atkinson-Bonasio, Alice. "Gender Balance in Research: New Analytical Report Reveals Uneven Progress." Elsevier Connect, 2017. https://www.elsevier.com/connect/gender-balance-in-research-new-analytical-report-reveals-uneven-progress.

Aulisio, George. "Open Access Publishing and Social Justice: Scranton's Perspectives." *Jesuit Higher Education: A Journal* 3, no. 2 (2014): 55–73.

Authors Alliance. "Is It Time for Authors to Leave SSRN?" *Authors Alliance* (blog), July 17, 2016. https://www.authorsalliance.org/2016/07/17/is-it-time-for-authors-to-leave-ssrn/.

The Avalon Project. "The Statute of Anne; April 10, 1710," 2008. http://avalon.law.yale.edu/18th_century/anne_1710.asp.

Babini, Dominique. "Voices from the Global South on Open Access in the Social Sciences." In *Open Access Perspectives in the Humanities and Social Sciences*, 15–16. London: London School of Economics, 2013. https://blogs.lse.ac.uk/impactofsocialsciences/files/2013/10/Open-Access-HSS-eCollection.pdf.

Babini, Dominique, Eduardo Aguado López, and Indrajit Banerjee. "Tesis a Favor de La Consolidación Del Acceso Abierto Como Una Alternativa de Democratización de La Ciencia En América Latina." In *Acceso Abierto*, by Peter Suber, 13–48. México: Universidad Autónoma del Estado de México, 2015.

Baggs, Chris. "'The Whole Tragedy of Leisure in Penury': The South Wales Miners' Institute Libraries during the Great Depression." *Libraries & Culture* 39, no. 2 (2004): 115–136.

Baker, Nicholson. *Double Fold: Libraries and the Assault on Paper*. New York: Random House, 2002.

Ball, Alexander. "Review of Data Management Lifecycle Models," February 13, 2012. https://researchportal.bath.ac.uk/en/publications/review-of-data-management-lifecycle-models.

Barber, Michael, Katelyn Donnelly, and Saad Rizvi. "An Avalanche Is Coming: Higher Education and the Revolution Ahead." Institute for Public Policy Research, 2013. https://s3.amazonaws.com/avalanche-assets/avalanche-is-coming_Mar2013_10432.pdf.

Barclay, Donald A. "Academic Print Books Are Dying. What's the Future?" *The Conversation* (blog), November 10, 2015. https://theconversation.com/academic-print-books-are-dying-whats-the-future-46248.

Barnes, Lucy. "ScholarLed Collaboration: A Powerful Engine to Grow Open Access Publishing." *LSE Impact Blog*, October 26, 2018. https://blogs.lse.ac.uk/impactofsocialsciences/2018/10/26/scholarled-collaboration-a-powerful-engine-to-grow-open-access-publishing/.

Barocas, Solon, and Helen Nissenbaum. "Big Data's End Run around Procedural Privacy Protections." *Communications of the ACM* 57, no. 11 (2014): 31–33. https://doi.org/10.1145/2668897.

Barreto, José-Manuel. "Epistemologies of the South and Human Rights: Santos and the Quest for Global and Cognitive Justice." *Indiana Journal of Global Legal Studies* 21, no. 2 (2014): 395–422. https://doi.org/10.2979/indjglolegstu.21.2.395.

Barry, Andrew. "Transparency as a Political Device." In *Débordements: Mélanges Offerts à Michel Callon*, edited by Madeleine Akrich, Yannick Barthe, Fabian Muniesa, and Philippe Mustar, 21–39. Sciences Sociales. Paris: Presses des Mines, 2013. http://books.openedition.org/pressesmines/721.

Bawden, F. C. Letter to Salisbury. "Application for Reduction in Charge for Reprints," December 7, 1950. RS OM/57(50).

Bazerman, Charles. *Shaping Written Knowledge: The Genre and Activity of the Experimental Article in Science*. Madison, WI: University of Wisconsin Press, 1988.

BBC. "Libraries 'Facing Greatest Crisis,'" March 29, 2016, sec. England. https://www.bbc.com/news/uk-england-35707956.

Beall, Jeffrey. "Is SciELO a Publication Favela?" *Emerald City Journal*, July 30, 2015. https://www.emeraldcityjournal.com/2015/07/is-scielo-a-publication-favela/.

Beall, Jeffrey. "The Open-Access Movement Is Not Really about Open Access." *TripleC: Communication, Capitalism & Critique. Open Access Journal for a Global Sustainable Information Society* 11, no. 2 (2013): 589–597.

Beall, Jeffrey. "Predatory Publishers Are Corrupting Open Access." *Nature News* 489, no. 7415 (2012): 179. https://doi.org/10.1038/489179a.

Bibliography

"Because the Following Provisos Were Not Admitted." *Journal of the House of Lords* 12 (March 8, 1693).

Becerril-García, Arianna, and Eduardo Aguado-López. "A Semantic Model for Selective Knowledge Discovery over OAI-PMH Structured Resources." *Information* 9, no. 6 (2018): 144. https://doi.org/10.3390/info9060144.

Becerril-García, Arianna, Rafael Lozano Espinosa, and José Martín Molina Espinosa. "Modelo Para Consultas Semánticas Sensibles al Contexto Sobre Recursos Educativos Estructurados con OAI-PMH," 1–15. Oaxaca, Mexico, 2014.

Becerril-García, Arianna, Rafael Lozano Espinosa, and José Martín Molina Espinosa. "Semantic Approach to Context-Aware Resource Discovery over Scholarly Content Structured with OAI-PMH." *Computación y Sistemas* 20, no. 1 (2016). https://doi.org/10.13053/cys-20-1-2189.

Beigel, Fernanda. "El Nuevo Carácter de la Dependencia Intelectual." *Cuestiones de Sociología* 14 (2016). http://hdl.handle.net/10915/54650.

Bell, Richard. "Legal Deposit in Britain (Part 1)." *Law Librarian* 8, no. 1 (1977): 5–8.

Bently, Lionel, and Martin Kretschmer, eds. "Reasons Humbly Offer'd for the Bill for the Encouragement of Learning, London (1706)." In *Primary Sources on Copyright (1450–1900)*, n.d. http://www.copyrighthistory.org/cam/index.php.

Bepress. "About." *Bepress* (blog). Accessed May 23, 2019. https://www.bepress.com/about/.

Berghmans, Stephane, Helena Cousijn, Gemma Deakin, Ingeborg Meijer, Adrian Mulligan, Andrew Plume, Sarah de Rijcke, et al. "Open Data: The Researcher Perspective—Survey and Case Studies." *Mendeley Data* 1 (April 4, 2017). https://doi.org/10.17632/bwrnfb4bvh.1.

"Berlin Declaration on Open Access to Knowledge in the Sciences and Humanities," October 22, 2003. https://openaccess.mpg.de/Berlin-Declaration.

Berlin, Isaiah. *Four Essays on Liberty*. Oxford: Oxford University Press, 1969.

Berners-Lee, Tim. "Why RDF Is More than XML." W3C, September 1998. https://www.w3.org/DesignIssues/RDF-XML.html.

Bertot, John Carlo, Ursula Gorham, Paul T. Jaeger, and Natalie Greene Taylor. "Public Libraries and the Internet 2012: Key Findings, Recent Trends, and Future Challenges." *Public Library Quarterly* 31, no. 4 (2012): 303–325. https://doi.org/10.1080/01616846.2012.732479.

Bibliothèque Scientifique Numérique, or Digital Scientific Library. "Jussieu Call for Open Science and Bibliodiversity," 2018. https://jussieucall.org/jussieu-call/.

Bijker, Wiebe E., Thomas Parke Hughes, and Trevor Pinch, eds. *The Social Construction of Technological Systems: New Directions in the Sociology and History of Technology.* Cambridge, MA: The MIT Press, 2012.

"Bill for Enabling the Two Universities to Hold in Perpetuity the Copy Right in Books, for the Advancement of Useful Learning, and Other Purposes of Education, within the Said Universities." In *House of Lords Parchment Collection.* Manuscript List, 1714–1814, 1775.

Bingo, Steven. "Of Provenance and Privacy: Using Contextual Integrity to Define Third-Party Privacy." *The American Archivist* 74, no. 2 (2011): 506–521. https://doi.org/10.17723/aarc.74.2.55132839256116n4.

Black, Alistair. *The Public Library in Britain, 1914–2000.* London: The British Library, 2000.

Blackawton, P. S., Airzee S., Allen A., Baker S., Berrow A., Blair C., Churchill M., et al. "Blackawton Bees." *Biology Letters* 7, no. 2 (2011): 168–172. https://doi.org/10.1098/rsbl.2010.1056.

Blagden, Charles. Letter to Erasmus Darwin, September 14, 1786. RS CB/2/34. Blagden Papers.

Blue Ribbon Task Force on Sustainable Digital Preservation and Access. "Sustaining the Digital Investment: Issues and Challenges of Economically Sustainable Digital Preservation," December 2008. http://brtf.sdsc.edu/biblio/BRTF_Interim_Report.pdf.

Blumenstyk, Goldie. "Elsevier's New Patent for Online Peer Review Throws a Scare into Open-Source Advocates." *The Chronicle of Higher Education*, September 1, 2016. https://www.chronicle.com/article/Elsevier-s-New-Patent-for/237656.

Bodó, Balázs. "The Genesis of Library Genesis: The Birth of a Global Scholarly Shadow Library." In *Shadow Libraries: Access to Educational Materials in Global Higher Education*, edited by Joe Karaganis, 25–52. Cambridge, MA: The MIT Press, 2018.

Bodó, Balázs. "Library Genesis in Numbers: Mapping the Underground Flow of Knowledge." In *Shadow Libraries: Access to Educational Materials in Global Higher Education*, edited by Joe Karaganis, 53–78. Cambridge, MA: The MIT Press, 2018.

Bogost, Ian, and Nick Montfort. "Platform Studies: Frequently Questioned Answers." *Digital Arts and Culture* 12–15 (2009): 1–6.

Bohannon, John. "Who's Afraid of Peer Review?" *Science* 342, no. 6154 (2013): 60–65. https://doi.org/10.1126/science.342.6154.60.

Bohannon, John. "Who's Downloading Pirated Papers? Everyone." *Science*, April 25, 2016. https://www.sciencemag.org/news/2016/04/whos-downloading-pirated-papers-everyone.

Bohlin, Ingemar. "Communication Regimes in Competition: The Current Transition in Scholarly Communication Seen through the Lens of the Sociology of Technology." *Social Studies of Science* 34, no. 3 (2004): 365–391. https://doi.org/10.1177/0306312704041522.

Bolukbasi, Tolga, Kai-Wei Chang, James Zou, Venkatesh Saligrama, and Adam Kalai. "Man Is to Computer Programmer as Woman Is to Homemaker? Debiasing Word Embeddings." *arXiv:1607.06520*, July 21, 2016. http://arxiv.org/abs/1607.06520.

Bonaccorso, Elisa, Reneta Bozhankova, Carlos Cadena, Veronika Čapská, Laura Czerniewicz, Ada Emmett, Folorunso Oludayo, et al. "Bottlenecks in the Open-Access System: Voices from Around the Globe." *Journal of Librarianship and Scholarly Communication* 2, no. 2 (2014): eP1126. https://doi.org/10.7710/2162-3309.1126.

Bond, D. "RELX Buys Bepress to Boost Academic Publishing," August 8, 2017. https://amp.ft.com/content/c6f6c594-7787-11e7-a3e8-60495fe6ca71.

Botero, Hector. "The Meeting of Two Worlds: Combining Traditional and Scientific Knowledge." *OCSDNet* (blog), October 31, 2015. https://ocsdnet.org/the-meeting-of-two-worlds-combining-traditional-and-scientific-knowledge/.

Bowcott, Owen. "'Right to Be Forgotten' Could Threaten Global Free Speech, Say NGOs." *The Guardian*, September 9, 2018, sec. Technology. https://www.theguardian.com/technology/2018/sep/09/right-to-be-forgotten-could-threaten-global-free-speech-say-ngos.

Bowker, Geoffrey. "The Infrastructural Imagination." In *Information Infrastructure(s): Boundaries, Ecologies, Multiplicity*, edited by Alessandro Mongili and Giuseppina Pellegrino, xii–xiii. Cambridge: Cambridge Scholars Publishing, 2014.

Bowker, Geoffrey C., and Susan Leigh Star. *Sorting Things out: Classification and Its Consequences*. Inside Technology. Cambridge, MA: The MIT Press, 1999.

Bowrey, Kathy, and Natalie Fowell. "Digging up Fragments and Building IP Franchises." *The Sydney Law Review* 31, no. 2 (2009): 185–210.

Bracha, Oren. "The Statute of Anne: An American Mythology." *Houston Law Review* 47, no. 4 (2010): 877–918.

Bradner, Eric. "Conway: Trump White House Offered 'Alternative Facts' on Crowd Size." CNN, January 23, 2017. https://www.cnn.com/2017/01/22/politics/kellyanne-conway-alternative-facts/index.html.

Brand, Amy, Albert Greco, and Robert Wharton. "Demographics and Education of Scholarly Publishing Professionals." Figshare, 2015. https://doi.org/10.6084/m9.figshare.1424476.v2.

Bratt, Steve. "Semantic Web, and Other Technologies to Watch." W3C, January 2007. https://www.w3.org/2007/Talks/0130-sb-W3CTechSemWeb/#(1).

Brembs, Björn, Katherine Button, and Marcus Munafò. "Deep Impact: Unintended Consequences of Journal Rank." *Frontiers in Human Neuroscience* 7 (2013): 291. https://doi.org/10.3389/fnhum.2013.00291.

Bremmer, Jan. "Scapegoat Rituals in Ancient Greece." *Harvard Studies in Classical Philology* 87 (1983): 299. https://doi.org/10.2307/311262.

Brick, Howard. *Transcending Capitalism: Visions of a New Society in Modern American Thought*. Ithaca, NY: Cornell University Press, 2006.

Brodkin, Jon. "Kim Dotcom: Megaupload Data in Europe Wiped out by Hosting Company." Ars Technica, June 19, 2013. https://arstechnica.com/tech-policy/2013/06/kim-dotcom-megaupload-data-in-europe-wiped-out-by-hosting-company/.

Broughton, Janet, and Gregory A. Jackson. "Bamboo Planning Project: An Arts and Humanities Planning Project to Develop Shared Technology Services for Research," January 16, 2008. https://wikihub.berkeley.edu/display/pbamboo/Proposals+to+the+Andrew+W+Mellon+Foundation.

Brown, Ian, and Christopher T. Marsden. *Regulating Code: Good Governance and Better Regulation in the Information Age*. Information Revolution and Global Politics. Cambridge, MA: The MIT Press, 2013.

Brown, Laura, Alex Humphreys, Matt Loy, Ron Snyder, and Christina Spencer. "Reimagining the Digital Monograph: Design Thinking to Build New Tools for Researchers." JSTOR Labs, 2017. https://hcommons.org/deposits/item/hc:14411/.

Brown, Nicole M., Ruby Mendenhall, Michael L. Black, Mark Van Moer, Assata Zerai, and Karen Flynn. "Mechanized Margin to Digitized Center: Black Feminism's Contributions to Combatting Erasure within the Digital Humanities." *International Journal of Humanities and Arts Computing* 10, no. 1 (2016): 110–125. https://doi.org/10.3366/ijhac.2016.0163.

Brown, Wendy. *Undoing the Demos: Neoliberalism's Stealth Revolution*. New York: Zone Books, 2015.

Browne, Des. "House of Commons Hansard Ministerial Statement." UK Parliament, September 18, 2006. https://publications.parliament.uk/pa/cm200506/cmhansrd/vo060918/wmstext/60918m0187.htm.

Browne, Edmund John Philip. "Securing a Sustainable Future for Higher Education: An Independent Review of Higher Education Funding and Student Finance." Department for Business, Innovation and Skills, 2010. https://www.gov.uk/government/publications/the-browne-report-higher-education-funding-and-student-finance.

Bruno, Isabelle, Emmanuel Didier, and Tommaso Vitale. "Statactivism: Forms of Action between Disclosure and Affirmation." *PARTECIPAZIONE E CONFLITTO* 7, no. 2 (2014): 198–220.

Bibliography

Buck, Stefanie, and Maura L. Valentino. "OER and Social Justice: A Colloquium at Oregon State University." *Journal of Librarianship and Scholarly Communication* 6, no. 2 (2018): 2231. https://doi.org/10.7710/2162-3309.2231.

Buckland, Amy, Martin Paul Eve, Graham Steel, Jennifer Gardy, and Dorothea Salo. "On the Mark? Responses to a Sting." *Journal of Librarianship and Scholarly Communication* 2, no. 1 (2013). https://doi.org/10.7710/2162-3309.1116.

Bullinger, Angelika, Stefan Hallerstede, Uta Renken, Jens-Hendrik Soeldner, and Kathrin Moeslein. "Towards Research Collaboration—a Taxonomy of Social Research Network Sites." *AMCIS 2010 Proceedings*, August 1, 2010. http://aisel.aisnet.org/amcis 2010/92.

Burkett, Ingrid. "Beyond the 'Information Rich and Poor': Futures Understandings of Inequality in Globalising Informational Economies." *Futures* 32, no. 7 (2000): 679–694. https://doi.org/10.1016/S0016-3287(00)00016-1.

Butler, Declan. "Investigating Journals: The Dark Side of Publishing." *Nature* 495, no. 7442 (2013): 433–435. https://doi.org/10.1038/495433a.

Caliskan, Aylin, Joanna J. Bryson, and Arvind Narayanan. "Semantics Derived Automatically from Language Corpora Contain Human-like Biases." *Science* 356, no. 6334 (2017): 183–186. https://doi.org/10.1126/science.aal4230.

Campaign for Social Science. "The Business of People: The Significance of Social Science over the Next Decade." SAGE, 2015. https://campaignforsocialscience.org.uk/businessofpeople/.

Campanario, Juan Miguel. "Peer Review for Journals as It Stands Today—Part 1." *Science Communication* 19, no. 3 (1998): 181–211. https://doi.org/10.1177/107554709 8019003002.

Campesato, Oswald, and Kevin Nilson. *Web 2.0 Fundamentals: With AJAX, Development Tools, and Mobile Platforms*. Sudbury, MA: Jones & Bartlett Learning, 2010.

Canagarajah, A. Suresh. *A Geopolitics of Academic Writing*. Pittsburgh, PA: University of Pittsburgh Press, 2002.

Carr, E. Summerson. "Enactments of Expertise." *Annual Review of Anthropology* 39, no. 1 (2010): 17–32. https://doi.org/10.1146/annurev.anthro.012809.104948.

Carroll, David, and Joseph McArthur. "New Apps Find Free Access to Scientific and Scholarly Research." Open Access Button, October 21, 2014. https://openaccessbutton.org/livelaunch.

Carroll, David, and Joseph McArthur. "The Open Access Button: It's Time We Capture Individual Moments of Paywall Injustice and Turn Them into Positive Change." *LSE Impact Blog*, September 2, 2013. https://blogs.lse.ac.uk/impactofsocialsciences/2013/09/02/the-open-access-button-carroll-mcarthur/.

Carter, Rodney G. S. "Of Things Said and Unsaid: Power, Archival Silences, and Power in Silence." *Archivaria* 61 (2006): 215–233.

Castro, Pablo de, Kathleen Shearer, and Friedrich Summann. "The Gradual Merging of Repository and CRIS Solutions to Meet Institutional Research Information Management Requirements." *Procedia Computer Science*, 12th International Conference on Current Research Information Systems, CRIS 2014, 33 (2014): 39–46. https://doi.org/10.1016/j.procs.2014.06.007.

Caswell, Michelle. "'The Archive' Is Not an Archives: On Acknowledging the Intellectual Contributions of Archival Studies." *Reconstruction: Studies in Contemporary Culture* 16, no. 1 (2016). https://escholarship.org/uc/item/7bn4v1fk.

Caswell, Michelle. "Inventing New Archival Imaginaries: Theoretical Foundations for Identity-Based Community Archives." In *Identity Palimpsests: Archiving Ethnicity in the U.S. and Canada*, edited by Dominique Daniel and Amalia S. Levi, 35–56. Sacramento, CA: Litwin Books, 2014.

Caswell, Michelle. "Khmer Rouge Archives: Accountability, Truth, and Memory in Cambodia." *Archival Science* 10, no. 1 (2010): 25–44. https://doi.org/10.1007/s10502-010-9114-1.

Caswell, Michelle, Alda Allina Migoni, and Noah Geraci. "Representation, Symbolic Annihilation, and the Emotional Potentials of Community Archives." Simon Fraser University, Vancouver, BC, 2016.

Cerf, Vinton Gray. "On Digital Preservation." Heidelberg Laureate Forum. Heidelberg, 2013. https://www.heidelberg-laureate-forum.org/laureate/vinton-gray-cerf.html.

Chan, Leslie. "Asymmetry and Inequality as a Challenge for Open Access—an Interview with Leslie Chan, (Interview by Joachim Schöpfel)." In *Open Divide: Critical Studies on Open Access*, edited by Ulrich Herb and Joachim Schöpfel, 169–182. Sacramento, CA: Library Juice Press, 2018.

Chan, Leslie. "SciELO, Open Infrastructure and Independence." *SciELO in Perspective* (blog), September 3, 2018. https://blog.scielo.org/en/2018/09/03/scielo-open-infrastructure-and-independence/.

Chan, Leslie, and Sely Costa. "Participation in the Global Knowledge Commons: Challenges and Opportunities for Research Dissemination in Developing Countries." *New Library World* 106, no. 3/4 (2005): 141–163. https://doi.org/10.1108/03074800510587354.

Chan, Leslie, Darius Cuplinskas, Michael Eisen, Fred Friend, Yana Genova, Jean-Claude Guédon, Melissa Hagemann, et al. "Budapest Open Access Initiative," February 14, 2002. http://www.soros.org/openaccess/read.shtml.

Bibliography

Chan, Leslie, Barbara Kirsop, and Subbiah Arunachalam. "Towards Open and Equitable Access to Research and Knowledge for Development." *PLOS Medicine* 8, no. 3 (2011): e1001016. https://doi.org/10.1371/journal.pmed.1001016.

Chan, Leslie, Angela Okune, Becky Hillyer, Denisse Albornoz, and Alejandro Posada, eds. *Contextualizing Openness: Situating Open Science*. Ottawa, ON: University of Ottawa Press, 2019.

Chaplin, K. "The Ubuntu Spirit in African Communities." The South African Ubuntu Foundation and the Amy Biehl Foundation, 2006.

Chodacki, John. "Community-Owned Data Publishing Infrastructure." *UC3: California Digital Library* (blog), October 24, 2018. https://uc3.cdlib.org/2018/10/24/community-owned-data-publishing-infrastructure/.

"Choosing Pathways to OA." Accessed May 31, 2019. https://cp2oa18.com/.

Christen, Kimberly. "Tribal Archives, Traditional Knowledge, and Local Contexts: Why the 's' Matters." *Journal of Western Archives* 6, no. 1 (2015). https://digitalcommons.usu.edu/westernarchives/vol6/iss1/3.

Christensen, Clayton M. *The Innovator's Dilemma: When New Technologies Cause Great Firms to Fail*. The Management of Innovation and Change Series. Boston: Harvard Business School Press, 1997.

Chubin, Daryl E., and Edward J. Hackett. *Peerless Science: Peer Review and U.S. Science Policy*. SUNY Series in Science, Technology, and Society. Albany, NY: State University of New York Press, 1990.

Cirasella, Jill, and Polly Thistlethwaite. "Open Access and the Graduate Author: A Dissertation Anxiety Manual." In *Open Access and the Future of Scholarly Communication: Policy and Infrastructure*, edited by Kevin L. Smith and Katherine A. Dickson, 203–224. Lanham, MD: Rowman & Littlefield, 2016.

City University of New York. "A Profile of Undergraduates at CUNY Senior and Community Colleges: Fall 2017," 2018. http://www2.cuny.edu/wp-content/uploads/sites/4/page-assets/about/administration/offices/oira/institutional/data/current-student-data-book-by-subject/ug_student_profile_f17.pdf.

CLACSO. "Declaration on Open Access to Knowledge Managed as a Commons by the Scholarly Community," 2015. https://www.clacso.org.ar/conferencia2015/documentos/asamblea/declaraciones/CLACSO-Declaration-on-open-access-to-knowledge-managed-as-a-commons-by-the-scholarly-community.pdf.

Clark, Wilma, Nick Couldry, Richard MacDonald, and Hilde C Stephansen. "Digital Platforms and Narrative Exchange: Hidden Constraints, Emerging Agency." *New Media & Society* 17, no. 6 (2015): 919–938. https://doi.org/10.1177/1461444813518579.

Coalition for Networked Information. "CNI Fall 2017 Membership Meeting Schedule." CNI: Coalition for Networked Information, August 30, 2017. https://www.cni.org/events/membership-meetings/past-meetings/fall-2017/schedule-f17.

cOAlition S. "Plan S." Plan S and cOAlition S, 2018. https://www.coalition-s.org/.

Cochran, Angela, Sara McNamara, Ann Michael, Mady Tissenbaum, Alice Meadows, and Lauren Kane. "Mind the Gap: Addressing the Need for More Women Leaders in Scholarly Publishing." Arlington, VA, 2015. https://youtu.be/sDS0lWz7lNU.

Coleman, Sterling Joseph. "The British Council and Unesco in Ethiopia: A Comparison of Linear and Cyclical Patterns of Librarianship Development." *Library History* 21, no. 2 (2005): 121–130. https://doi.org/10.1179/002423005x44952.

Collingridge, David. *The Social Control of Technology*. New York: St. Martin's Press, 1980.

Collini, Stefan. *What Are Universities For?* London: Penguin, 2012.

Collins, H. M., and Robert Evans. "The Third Wave of Science Studies: Studies of Expertise and Experience." *Social Studies of Science* 32, no. 2 (2002): 235–296. https://doi.org/10.1177/0306312702032002003.

Collins, Patricia Hill. "Black Feminist Thought in the Matrix of Domination." In *Black Feminist Thought: Knowledge, Consciousness, and the Politics of Empowerment*, 221–238. Boston: Unwin Hyman, 1990.

The Combahee River Collective. "A Black Feminist Statement." In *The Second Wave: A Reader in Feminist Theory*, edited by Linda J. Nicholson, 63–70. New York: Routledge, 1997.

"Commons Reasons for Disagreeing to the Clause for Reviving the Printing Act." *Journal of the House of Lords* 15 (1695): 546.

Connell, Raewyn. "Southern Theory and World Universities." *Higher Education Research & Development* 36, no. 1 (2017): 4–15. https://doi.org/10.1080/07294360.2017.1252311.

Connell, Raewyn. "Using Southern Theory: Decolonizing Social Thought in Theory, Research and Application." *Planning Theory* 13, no. 2 (2014): 210–23. https://doi.org/10.1177/1473095213499216.

Cooperative Children's Book Center, School of Education, University of Wisconsin–Madison. "Publishing Statistics on Children's Books about People of Color and First/Native Nations and by People of Color and First/Native Nations Authors and Illustrators," 2019. https://ccbc.education.wisc.edu/books/pcstats.asp.

Cornish, William. "The Statute of Anne 1709–10: Its Historical Setting." In *Global Copyright: Three Hundred Years Since the Statute of Anne, from 1709 to Cyberspace*, edited by Lionel Bently, Uma Suthersanen, and Paul Torresmans, 14–25. Cheltenham, UK: Edward Elgar Publishing, 2010. https://doi.org/10.4337/9781849806428.00009.

Costanza-Chock, Sasha. "Design Justice: Towards an Intersectional Feminist Framework for Design Theory and Practice." SSRN Scholarly Paper. Rochester, NY: Social Science Research Network, June 3, 2018. https://papers.ssrn.com/abstract=3189696.

Cottom, Tressie McMillan. *Lower Ed: The Troubling Rise of for-Profit Colleges in the New Economy*. New York: The New Press, 2018.

Court of Justice of the European Union. "Judgment in Case C-131/12 Google Spain SL, Google Inc. v Agencia Española de Protección de Datos, Mario Costeja González," May 13, 2014.

Cox, Krista. "Moving from SSRN to SocArXiv." ARL Policy Notes, July 22, 2016. http://policynotes.arl.org/?p=1403.

Cram, Jennifer. "Colonialism and Libraries in Third World Africa." *The Australian Library Journal* 42, no. 1 (1993): 13–20. https://doi.org/10.1080/00049670.1993.10755621.

Cranston, Maurice William. *John Locke, a Biography*. Oxford: Oxford University Press, 1957.

Creative Commons. "Case Law," 2013. http://wiki.creativecommons.org/Case_Law.

Crenshaw, Kimberlé. "Demarginalizing the Intersection of Race and Sex: A Black Feminist Critique of Antidiscrimination Doctrine." *University of Chicago Legal Forum*, no. 1 (1989): 139–167. https://doi.org/10.4324/9780429500480-5.

Crissinger, Sarah. "A Critical Take on OER Practices: Interrogating Commercialization, Colonialism, and Content." *In the Library with the Lead Pipe* (blog), October 21, 2015. http://www.inthelibrarywiththeleadpipe.org/2015/a-critical-take-on-oer-practices-interrogating-commercialization-colonialism-and-content.

Crossick, Geoffrey. "Monographs and Open Access: A Report for the Higher Education Funding Council for England." Higher Education Funding Council for England, 2015. https://dera.ioe.ac.uk/21921/.

Csiszar, Alex. *The Scientific Journal: Authorship and the Politics of Knowledge in the Nineteenth Century*. Chicago: University of Chicago Press, 2018.

Csiszar, Alex. "Seriality and the Search for Order: Scientific Print and Its Problems during the Late Nineteenth Century." *History of Science* 48, no. 3–4 (2010): 399–434. https://doi.org/10.1177/007327531004800306.

Currall, James, and Peter McKinney. "Investing in Value: A Perspective on Digital Preservation." *D-Lib Magazine* 12, no. 4 (2006). https://doi.org/10.1045/april2006-mckinney.

Curtis, George Ticknor, ed. "An Act for Prohibiting the Importation of Books Reprinted Abroad … (1739)." In *A Treatise on the Law of Copyright*, 11–14. London: Maxwell & Sons, 1847.

Czerniewicz, Laura. "Inequitable Power Dynamics of Global Knowledge Production and Exchange Must Be Confronted Head On." *LSE Impact Blog*, April 29, 2013. https://blogs.lse.ac.uk/impactofsocialsciences/2013/04/29/redrawing-the-map-from-access-to-participation/.

Czerniewicz, Laura. "This Map of the World's Scientific Research Is Disturbingly Unequal." *Quartz*, July 11, 2015. https://qz.com/449405/this-map-of-the-worlds-scientific-research-is-disturbingly-unequal/.

Da, Nan Z. "The Computational Case against Computational Literary Studies." *Critical Inquiry* 45, no. 3 (2019): 601–639. https://doi.org/10.1086/702594.

Dahlmann, Simone, and Ursula Huws. "Sunset in the West: Outsourcing Editorial Work from the UK to India—a Case Study of the Impact on Workers." *Work Organisation, Labour & Globalisation* 1, no. 1 (2007): 59–75.

Das, Jishnu, Quy-Toan Do, Karen Shaines, and Sowmya Srikant. "U.S. and Them: The Geography of Academic Research." *Journal of Development Economics* 105 (2013): 112–130. https://doi.org/10.1016/j.jdeveco.2013.07.010.

DasGupta, Ria. "Connecting Diversity Programs in Higher Education to the Legacy of HRE." San Francisco, CA, 2017.

Davies, William. *The Limits of Neoliberalism: Authority, Sovereignty and the Logic of Competition*. Thousand Oaks, CA: SAGE, 2014.

Deazley, Ronan. "Commentary on the Statute of Anne 1710." In *Primary Sources on Copyright (1450–1900)*, edited by Lionel Bently and Martin Kretschmer, 2008. http://www.copyrighthistory.org/cam/index.php.

Deazley, Ronan. "The Myth of Copyright at Common Law." *The Cambridge Law Journal* 62, no. 1 (2003): 106–133.

Deazley, Ronan. *On the Origin of the Right to Copy: Charting the Movement of Copyright Law in Eighteenth-Century Britain (1695–1775)*. Oxford: Hart Publishing, 2004.

Deazley, Ronan. "What's New about the Statute of Anne? Or Six Observations in Search of an Act." In *Global Copyright: Three Hundred Years Since the Statute of Anne, from 1709 to Cyberspace*, edited by Lionel Bently, Uma Suthersanen, and Paul Torresmans, 26–33. Cheltenham, UK: Edward Elgar Publishing, 2010. https://doi.org/10.4337/9781849806428.00010.

Debat, Humberto, and Dominique Babini. "Plan S: Take Latin America's Long Experience on Board." *Nature* 573 (2019): 495. https://doi.org/10.1038/d41586-019-02857-1.

Deene, Joris. "The Influence of the Statute of Anne on Belgian Copyright Law." In *Global Copyright: Three Hundred Years Since the Statute of Anne, from 1709 to Cyberspace*, edited by Lionel Bently, Uma Suthersanen, and Paul Torresmans, 136–143. Cheltenham, UK: Edward Elgar Publishing, 2010. https://doi.org/10.4337/9781849806428.00017.

Defoe, Daniel. *An Essay on the Regulation of the Press*. London, 1704.

DeNardis, L., and A. M. Hackl. "Internet Governance *by* Social Media Platforms." *Telecommunications Policy* 39, no. 9 (2015): 761–770. https://doi.org/10.1016/j.telpol.2015.04.003.

Department for Business, Innovation and Skills. "Students at the Heart of the System," 2011. https://assets.publishing.service.gov.uk/government/uploads/system/uploads/attachment_data/file/31384/11-944-higher-education-students-at-heart-of-system.pdf.

Department for Business, Innovation and Skills. "Success as a Knowledge Economy: Teaching Excellence, Social Mobility and Student Choice," 2016. https://assets.publishing.service.gov.uk/government/uploads/system/uploads/attachment_data/file/523396/bis-16-265-success-as-a-knowledge-economy.pdf.

Department for Culture, Media and Sport. "Libraries for All: Social Inclusion in Public Libraries," 1999. https://webarchive.nationalarchives.gov.uk/+/http:/www.culture.gov.uk/images/publications/Social_Inclusion_PLibraries.pdf.

Derrida, Jacques. "The Future of the Profession or the University Without Condition (Thanks to the 'Humanities,' What Could Take Place Tomorrow)." In *Jacques Derrida and the Humanities: A Critical Reader*, edited by Tom Cohen, 24–57. Cambridge: Cambridge University Press, 2001.

Derrida, Jacques. "Plato's Pharmacy." In *Dissemination*, translated by Barbara Johnson, 67–186. London: Continuum, 2004.

Derrida, Jacques. *Rogues: Two Essays on Reason*. Translated by Pascale-Anne Brault and Michael Naas. Stanford, CA: Stanford University Press, 2005.

Dery, Mark. "Black to the Future: Interviews with Samuel R. Delany, Greg Tate, and Tricia Rose." In *Flame Wars: The Discourse of Cyberculture*, edited by Mark Dery, 179–222. Durham, NC: Duke University Press, 1994. https://doi.org/10.1215/9780822396765-010.

de Sousa Santos, Boaventura. "Epistemologies of the South and the Future." *From the European South*, no. 1 (2016): 17–29.

de Sousa Santos, Boaventura. "Introducción: Las Epistemologías Del Sur." In *Formas-Otras: Saber, Nombrar, Narrar, Hacer*, edited by Fundación CIDOB, 11–12. España: CIDOB, 2011.

de Sousa Santos, Boaventura, ed. *Another Knowledge Is Possible: Beyond Northern Epistemologies*. London: Verso, 2008.

de Sousa Santos, Boaventura, ed. *Cognitive Justice in a Global World: Prudent Knowledges for a Decent Life*. Lanham, MD: Lexington Books, 2007.

De Vynck, Gerrit. "Josh Kushner's Thrive Capital Strikes Gold in GitHub Deal." *Bloomberg*, June 5, 2018. https://www.bloomberg.com/news/articles/2018-06-05/josh-kushner-s-thrive-capital-strikes-gold-in-github-deal.

Dewey, John. *The Public and Its Problems: An Essay in Political Inquiry*. University Park: Pennsylvania State University Press, 1927.

Digital Library Federation. "Digital Library Assessment." *DLF* (blog), 2018. https://www.diglib.org/groups/assessment/.

Dijck, Jose van. "Disassembling Platforms, Reassembling Sociality." In *The Culture of Connectivity: A Critical History of Social Media*, 24–44. Oxford: Oxford University Press, 2013. https://doi.org/10.1093/acprof:oso/9780199970773.001.0001.

Directory of Open Access Journals. "Journals by Publication Charges." Accessed January 20, 2014. https://www.doaj.org/.

Directory of Open Access Repositories. "Browse by Country and Region." Accessed September 16, 2019. https://v2.sherpa.ac.uk/view/repository_by_country/019.html.

DocNow. "About." Documenting the Now. Accessed May 1, 2019. https://www.docnow.io/.

Dombrowski, Quinn. "What Ever Happened to Project Bamboo?" *Literary and Linguistic Computing* 29, no. 3 (2014): 326–339. https://doi.org/10.1093/llc/fqu026.

Dotson, Kristie. "Tracking Epistemic Violence, Tracking Practices of Silencing." *Hypatia* 26, no. 2 (2011): 236–257. https://doi.org/10.1111/j.1527-2001.2011.01177.x.

Drone, Eaton Sylvester. *A Treatise on the Law of Property in Intellectual Productions in Great Britain and the United States: Embracing Copyright in Works of Literature and Art, and Playright in Dramatic and Musical Compositions*. Boston: Little, Brown, 1879.

Drucker, Johanna, and Bethany Nowviskie. "Speculative Computing: Aesthetic Provocations in Humanities Computing." In *A Companion to Digital Humanities*, edited by Susan Schreibman, Ray Siemens, and John Unsworth, 431–447. Oxford: John Wiley & Sons, Ltd, 2007. https://doi.org/10.1002/9780470999875.ch29.

Duff, Wendy M., and Verne Harris. "Stories and Names: Archival Description as Narrating Records and Constructing Meanings." *Archival Science* 2, no. 3 (2002): 263–285. https://doi.org/10.1007/BF02435625.

Dunn, Sydni. "Digital Humanists: If You Want Tenure, Do Double the Work." Vitae, January 5, 2014. https://chroniclevitae.com/news/249-digital-humanists-if-you-want-tenure-do-double-the-work.

Dutta, Soumitra, and Matthew Fraser. "Barack Obama and the Facebook Election." US News & World Report, November 19, 2008. https://www.usnews.com/opinion/articles/2008/11/19/barack-obama-and-the-facebook-election.

Earhart, Amy E. "Do We Trust the University? Digital Humanities Collaborations with Historically Exploited Cultural Communities." In *Bodies of Information: Intersectional Feminism and Digital Humanities*, edited by Elizabeth Losh and Jacqueline Wernimont, 369–390. Minneapolis: University of Minnesota Press, 2018.

Eisenmann, Thomas R., Geoffrey Parker, and Marshall W. Van Alstyne. "Opening Platforms: How, When and Why?" *SSRN Electronic Journal*, 2008, 1–27. https://doi.org/10.2139/ssrn.1264012.

Ellers, Jacintha, Thomas W. Crowther, and Jeffrey A. Harvey. "Gold Open Access Publishing in Mega-Journals: Developing Countries Pay the Price of Western Premium Academic Output." *Journal of Scholarly Publishing* 49, no. 1 (2017): 89–102. https://doi.org/10.3138/jsp.49.1.89.

Else, Holly. "Dutch Publishing Giant Cuts off Researchers in Germany and Sweden." *Nature* 559 (2018): 454. https://doi.org/10.1038/d41586-018-05754-1.

Elsevier. "Elsevier Acquires Bepress, a Leading Service Provider Used by Academic Institutions to Showcase Their Research." Elsevier, August 2, 2017. https://www.elsevier.com/about/press-releases/corporate/elsevier-acquires-bepress,-a-leading-service-provider-used-by-academic-institutions-to-showcase-their-research.

Elsevier. "Pricing," 2018. https://www.elsevier.com/about/our-business/policies/pricing#Dipping.

Elsevier. "Pure and Simple: A Modular Research Information System," April 12, 2017.

Erickson, Paul, Judy L Klein, Lorraine Daston, Rebecca Lemov, Thomas Sturm, and Michael D Gordin. *How Reason Almost Lost Its Mind: The Strange Career of Cold War Rationality*. Chicago: University of Chicago Press, 2015.

Erikson, Martin G., and Peter Erlandson. "A Taxonomy of Motives to Cite." *Social Studies of Science* 44, no. 4 (2014): 625–637. https://doi.org/10.1177/0306312714522871.

Escobar, Arturo. *Designs for the Pluriverse: Radical Interdependence, Autonomy, and the Making of Worlds*. New Ecologies for the Twenty-First Century. Durham, NC: Duke University Press, 2018.

Escobar, Arturo. "Whose Knowledge, Whose Nature? Biodiversity, Conservation, and the Political Ecology of Social Movements." *Journal of Political Ecology* 5, no. 1 (1998): 53–82. https://doi.org/10.2458/v5i1.21397.

Eshun, Kodwo. "Further Considerations on Afrofuturism." *CR: The New Centennial Review* 3, no. 2 (2003): 287–302. https://doi.org/10.1353/ncr.2003.0021.

Eshun, Kodwo. *More Brilliant Than the Sun: Adventures in Sonic Fiction.* London: Quartet Books, 1998.

Espeland, Wendy Nelson, and Michael Sauder. "Rankings and Reactivity: How Public Measures Recreate Social Worlds." *American Journal of Sociology* 113, no. 1 (2007): 1–40. https://doi.org/10.1086/517897.

Espeland, Wendy Nelson, and Mitchell L. Stevens. "Commensuration as a Social Process." *Annual Review of Sociology* 24, no. 1 (1998): 313–343. https://doi.org/10.1146/annurev.soc.24.1.313.

Espeland, Wendy Nelson, and Mitchell L. Stevens. "A Sociology of Quantification." *European Journal of Sociology* 49, no. 3 (2008): 401–436. https://doi.org/10.1017/S0003975609000150.

Eubanks, Virginia. *Automating Inequality: How High-Tech Tools Profile, Police, and Punish the Poor.* New York: St. Martin's Press, 2017.

European Commission. "Open Innovation, Open Science, Open to the World—A Vision for Europe." Text. Digital Single Market—European Commission, May 30, 2016. https://ec.europa.eu/digital-single-market/en/news/open-innovation-open-science-open-world-vision-europe.

European Parliament. "Regulation (EU) 2016/679 of The European Parliament and of The Council." European Union Law, April 27, 2016. https://eur-lex.europa.eu/legal-content/EN/TXT/HTML/?uri=CELEX:02016R0679-20160504.

Eve, Martin Paul. "Close Reading with Computers: Genre Signals, Parts of Speech, and David Mitchell's *Cloud Atlas.*" *SubStance* 46, no. 3 (2017): 76–104.

Eve, Martin Paul. *Close Reading with Computers: Textual Scholarship, Computational Formalism, and David Mitchell's* Cloud Atlas. Stanford, CA: Stanford University Press, 2019.

Eve, Martin Paul. "Four Implementation Questions about Open Access and Monographs." *Martin Paul Eve* (blog), January 3, 2017. https://eve.gd/2017/01/03/four-implementation-questions-about-open-access-and-monographs/.

Eve, Martin Paul. "The Great Automatic Grammatizator: Writing, Labour, Computers." *Critical Quarterly* 59, no. 3 (2017): 39–54.

Eve, Martin Paul. "On Open-Access Books and 'Double Dipping.'" *Martin Paul Eve* (blog), January 31, 2015. https://eve.gd/2015/01/31/on-open-access-books-and-double-dipping/.

Eve, Martin Paul. *Open Access and the Humanities: Contexts, Controversies and the Future.* Cambridge: Cambridge University Press, 2014. https://doi.org/10.1017/CBO9781316161012.

Eve, Martin Paul. "Open Publication, Digital Abundance, and Scarce Labour." *Journal of Scholarly Publishing* 49, no. 1 (2017): 26–40. https://doi.org/10.3138/jsp.49.1.26.

Eve, Martin Paul. "Scarcity and Abundance." In *The Bloomsbury Handbook of Electronic Literature*. London: Bloomsbury Academic, 2017.

Eve, Martin Paul. "Transcript of Meeting between Elsevier and the Minister for Higher Education in the UK, Jo Johnson." *Martin Paul Eve* (blog), May 4, 2016. https://eve.gd/2016/05/04/what-elsevier-and-the-minister-for-higher-education-in-the-uk-jo-johnson-met-about/.

Eve, Martin Paul, and Andy Byers. "Janeway: A Scholarly Communications Platform." *Insights* 31 (2018). https://doi.org/10.1629/uksg.396.

Eve, Martin Paul, Kitty Inglis, David Prosser, Lara Speicher, and Graham Stone. "Cost Estimates of an Open Access Mandate for Monographs in the UK's Third Research Excellence Framework." *Insights: The UKSG Journal* 30, no. 3 (2017). https://doi.org/10.1629/uksg.392.

Eve, Martin Paul, and Ernesto Priego. "Who Is Actually Harmed by Predatory Publishers?" *TripleC: Communication, Capitalism & Critique. Open Access Journal for a Global Sustainable Information Society* 15, no. 2 (2017): 755–770. https://doi.org/10.31269/triplec.v15i2.867.

Eve, Martin Paul, and John Willinsky. "Open Access in Humanities and Social Sciences: Visions for the Future of Publishing." *College and Research Libraries News* 76 (2015): 88–91.

Eysenbach, Gunther. "Can Tweets Predict Citations? Metrics of Social Impact Based on Twitter and Correlation with Traditional Metrics of Scientific Impact." *Journal of Medical Internet Research* 13, no. 4 (2011): e123. https://doi.org/10.2196/jmir.2012.

Fallon, Julia, and Pablo Uceda Gomez. "The Missing Decades: The 20th Century Black Hole in Europeana." Europeana Pro, November 13, 2015. https://pro.europeana.eu/post/the-missing-decades-the-20th-century-black-hole-in-europeana.

Faulder, Sarah, and Shinwha Cha. "Access to Research: The Experience of Implementing a Pilot in Public Libraries." *Learned Publishing* 27, no. 2 (2014): 85–92. https://doi.org/10.1087/20140202.

Feather, John. "The Book Trade in Politics: The Making of the Copyright Act of 1710." *Publishing History* 8 (1980): 19–44.

Ferguson, Roderick A. *The Reorder of Things: The University and Its Pedagogies of Minority Difference*. Difference Incorporated. Minneapolis: University of Minnesota Press, 2012.

Figshare. "Credit for All Your Research." figshare. Accessed June 4, 2019. https://figshare.com/.

Figshare. "Mission Statement & Core Beliefs." figshare. Accessed May 20, 2019. https://knowledge.figshare.com/articles/item/mission-statement-and-core-beliefs.

Fintoni, Laurent. "A Brief History of Scratching." *FACT Magazine: Music News, New Music* (blog), September 24, 2015. https://www.factmag.com/2015/09/24/a-brief-history-of-scratching/.

Fiormonte, Domenico, and Ernesto Priego. "Knowledge Monopolies and Global Academic Publishing." *The Winnower*, August 24, 2016. https://doi.org/10.15200/winn.147220.00404.

First Consortium Assembly from Ibero-America and The Caribbean. "Declarations," September 1, 2017. http://reuniondeconsorcios.conricyt.mx/index.php/primera-reunion/declaraciones/?lang=en.

Fischer, Karin, and Jack Stripling. "An Era of Neglect." *The Chronicle of Higher Education*, March 2, 2014. https://www.chronicle.com/article/An-Era-of-Neglect/145045.

Fish, Stanley. *Is There a Text in This Class? The Authority of Interpretive Communities*. Cambridge, MA: Harvard University Press, 1990.

Fister, Barbara. "Liberating Knowledge: A Librarian's Manifesto for Change." *Thought & Action*, Fall 2010, 83–90.

Fitzpatrick, Elizabeth B. "The Public Library as Instrument of Colonialism: The Case of the Netherlands East Indies." *Libraries & the Cultural Record* 43, no. 3 (2008): 270–285.

Fitzpatrick, Kathleen. "Academia, Not Edu." *Planned Obsolescence* (blog), October 26, 2015. http://www.plannedobsolescence.net/academia-not-edu/.

Fitzpatrick, Kathleen. *Planned Obsolescence: Publishing, Technology, and the Future of the Academy*. New York: New York University Press, 2011.

Flanagan, Owen J. *Self Expressions: Mind, Morals, and the Meaning of Life*. Oxford: Oxford University Press, 1996.

Fortney, Katie, and Justin Gonder. "A Social Networking Site Is Not an Open Access Repository." *Office of Scholarly Communication* (blog), December 1, 2015. http://osc.universityofcalifornia.edu/2015/12/a-social-networking-site-is-not-an-open-access-repository/.

Fortun, Mike, Kim Fortun, and George E. Marcus. "Computers in/and Anthropology: The Poetics and Politics of Digitization." In *The Routledge Companion to Digital Ethnography*, edited by Larissa Hjorth, Heather Horst, Anne Galloway, and Genevieve Bell, 11–20. London: Routledge, 2017. https://doi.org/10.4324/9781315673974.

Foster, Andrea L. "U. of Iowa Reverses New Policy That Would Have Made Nearly All Theses Freely Available Online." *The Chronicle of Higher Education*, March 18, 2008. https://www.chronicle.com/article/Students-Protect-Their-Novels/601.

Fradenburg, L. O. Aranye. *Staying Alive*. Edited by Eileen A. Joy. Brooklyn, NY: punctum books, 2013. https://punctumbooks.com/titles/staying-alive/.

Franzen, Martina, Eileen Joy, and Chris Long. *Humane Metrics/Metrics Noir.* Coventry, UK: Post Office Press / meson press, 2018. https://hcommons.org/deposits/item/hc:19823/.

Franzoni, Chiara, Giuseppe Scellato, and Paula Stephan. "Changing Incentives to Publish." *Science* 333, no. 6043 (August 5, 2011): 702–703. https://doi.org/10.1126/science.1197286.

Fredua-Kwarteng, Eric. "The Case for Developmental Universities." *University World News,* October 30, 2015. https://www.universityworldnews.com/post.php?story=20151028020047530.

Fricker, Miranda. "Epistemic Justice as a Condition of Political Freedom?" *Synthese* 190, no. 7 (2013): 1317–1332.

Fricker, Miranda. "Forum on Miranda Fricker's Epistemic Injustice: Power and the Ethics of Knowing." *THEORIA. An International Journal for Theory, History and Foundations of Science* 23, no. 1 (2008): 69–71.

Fuller, Steve. *Post-Truth: Knowledge as a Power Game.* New York: Anthem Press, 2018.

Fyfe, Aileen. "Journals, Learned Societies and Money: *Philosophical Transactions,* ca. 1750–1900." *Notes and Records: The Royal Society Journal of the History of Science* 69, no. 3 (2015): 277–299. https://doi.org/10.1098/rsnr.2015.0032.

Fyfe, Aileen, Kelly Coate, Stephen Curry, Stuart Lawson, Noah Moxham, and Camilla Mørk Røstvik. "Untangling Academic Publishing: A History of the Relationship between Commercial Interests, Academic Prestige and the Circulation of Research." Zenodo, May 25, 2017. https://doi.org/10.5281/zenodo.546100.

Fyfe, Aileen, Julie McDougall-Waters, and Noah Moxham. "Credit, Copyright, and the Circulation of Scientific Knowledge: The Royal Society in the Long Nineteenth Century." *Victorian Periodicals Review* 51, no. 4 (2018): 597–615. https://doi.org/10.1353/vpr.2018.0045.

Fyfe, Aileen, and Noah Moxham. "Making Public Ahead of Print: Meetings and Publications at the Royal Society, 1752–1892." *Notes and Records: The Royal Society Journal of the History of Science* 70, no. 4 (2016): 361–379. https://doi.org/10.1098/rsnr.2016.0030.

Gadd, Ian, ed. *The History of Oxford University Press: Volume I: Beginnings to 1780.* Oxford: Oxford University Press, 2013.

Gaventa, John. "Finding the Spaces for Change: A Power Analysis." *IDS Bulletin* 37, no. 6 (2006): 23–33. https://doi.org/10.1111/j.1759-5436.2006.tb00320.x.

Gaventa, John. "12 Levels, Spaces and Forms of Power." In *Power in World Politics,* edited by Felix Berenskoetter and Michael J. Williams, 204–224. London: Routledge, 2007.

Gawer, Annabelle. "Bridging Differing Perspectives on Technological Platforms: Toward an Integrative Framework." *Research Policy* 43, no. 7 (2014): 1239–1249. https://doi.org/10.1016/j.respol.2014.03.006.

Geary, Patrick J. *Phantoms of Remembrance: Memory and Oblivion at the End of the First Millennium*. Princeton, NJ: Princeton University Press, 1996.

Geltner, Guy. "On Leaving Academia.Edu," November 23, 2015. https://f.hypotheses.org/wp-content/blogs.dir/1137/files/2015/12/On-leaving-Academia.pdf.

"Gender Pay Gaps across the Book Trade Reported by Majority of Larger Businesses: Book Businesses Mostly Unflattered by Compulsory Disclosure of Gender Pay Gap Data." *The Bookseller*, no. 5795 (April 6, 2018): 6–9.

Gerald, Beasley. "Article Processing Charges: A New Route to Open Access?" In *Positioning and Power in Academic Publishing: Players, Agents and Agendas*, edited by Fernando Loizides and Birgit Schmidt, 125–130. Amsterdam: IOS Press, 2016. https://doi.org/10.3233/978-1-61499-649-1-125.

Gevers, Wieland. "Globalizing Science Publishing." *Science* 325, no. 5943 (2009): 920. https://doi.org/10.1126/science.1178378.

Gibbs, Rabia. "The Heart of the Matter: The Developmental History of African American Archives." *The American Archivist* 75, no. 1 (2012): 195–204. https://doi.org/10.17723/aarc.75.1.n1612w0214242080.

Gillespie, Tarleton. "Platforms Intervene." *Social Media + Society* 1, no. 1 (2015): 205630511558047. https://doi.org/10.1177/2056305115580479.

Gillespie, Tarleton. "The Politics of 'Platforms.'" *New Media & Society* 12, no. 3 (2010): 347–364. https://doi.org/10.1177/1461444809342738.

Gilliland, Anne J., and Michelle Caswell. "Records and Their Imaginaries: Imagining the Impossible, Making Possible the Imagined." *Archival Science* 16, no. 1 (2016): 53–75. https://doi.org/10.1007/s10502-015-9259-z.

Gilliland-Swetland, Anne J. "Enduring Paradigm, New Opportunities: The Value of the Archival Perspective in the Digital Environment." CLIR, 2000.

Ginzburg, Carlo. "The Bond of Shame." In *Passionen. Objekte—Schauplätze—Denkstile*, edited by Corina Caduff, Anne-Kathrin Reulecke, and Ulrike Vedder, 19–26. Munich: Wilhelm Fink, 2010. http://publikationen.ub.uni-frankfurt.de/frontdoor/index/index/year/2017/docId/44333.

Ginzburg, Carlo, and Carlo Poni. "The Name and the Game: Unequal Exchange and the Historiographic Marketplace." In *Microhistory and the Lost Peoples of Europe*, edited by Edward Muir and Guido Ruggiero, 1–10. Baltimore, MD: Johns Hopkins University Press, 1991.

Githaiga, Grace. "Fake News: A Threat to Digital Inclusion." *Media Development* 65, no. 1 (2019): 35–38.

Golumbia, David. "Marxism and Open Access in the Humanities: Turning Academic Labor against Itself." *Workplace: A Journal for Academic Labor*, no. 28 (2016). https://doi.org/10.14288/workplace.v0i28.186213.

Goodhart, David. *The Road to Somewhere: The Populist Revolt and the Future of Politics*. London: Hurst & Company, 2017.

Gooding, Paul, Melissa Terras, and Linda Berube. "Towards User-Centric Evaluation of UK Non-Print Legal Deposit: A Digital Library Futures White Paper." Research Reports or Papers, May 21, 2019. http://elegaldeposit.org.

Google. "Search Removals under European Privacy Law." Google Transparency Report, 2019. https://transparencyreport.google.com/eu-privacy/overview.

Gordon, Gregg. "SSRN—the Leading Social Science and Humanities Repository and Online Community—Joins Elsevier." Elsevier Connect, May 17, 2016. https://www.elsevier.com/connect/ssrn-the-leading-social-science-and-humanities-repository-and-online-community-joins-elsevier.

Gouldner, Alvin W. "Cosmopolitans and Locals: Toward an Analysis of Latent Social Roles." *Administrative Science Quarterly* 2, no. 3 (1957): 281. https://doi.org/10.2307/2391000.

Government of the United Kingdom. "Complaints to Secretary of State under s.296ZE under the Copyright, Designs and Patents Act 1988," August 15, 2014. https://www.gov.uk/government/publications/complaints-to-secretary-of-state-under-s296ze-under-the-copyright-designs-and-patents-act-1988.

Grafton, Anthony. *The Footnote: A Curious History*. Cambridge, MA: Harvard University Press, 1999.

Graham, Mark, Stefano De Sabbata, and Matthew A. Zook. "Towards a Study of Information Geographies: (Im)Mutable Augmentations and a Mapping of the Geographies of Information: Towards a Study of Information Geographies." *Geo: Geography and Environment* 2, no. 1 (2015): 88–105. https://doi.org/10.1002/geo2.8.

Grassegger, Hannes, and Mikael Krogerus. "The Data That Turned the World Upside Down." *Vice* (blog), January 28, 2017. https://www.vice.com/en_us/article/mg9vvn/how-our-likes-helped-trump-win.

Gray, Eve. "Bridging the North-South Divide in Scholarly Communication: Threats and Opportunities in the Digital Era at the South-Eastern Frontier: The Impact of Higher Education Policy on African Research Publication," 2006. http://www.policy.hu/gray/docs/ASC_Codesria_conference_paper.doc.

Gray, Jonathan, Carolin Gerlitz, and Liliana Bounegru. "Data Infrastructure Literacy." *Big Data & Society* 5, no. 2 (2018). https://doi.org/10.1177/2053951718786316.

Greco, Albert N., Robert M. Wharton, and Amy Brand. "Demographics of Scholarly Publishing and Communication Professionals: Demographics of Publishing Professionals." *Learned Publishing* 29, no. 2 (2016): 97–101. https://doi.org/10.1002/leap.1017.

Greshake, Bastian. "Correlating the Sci-Hub Data with World Bank Indicators and Identifying Academic Use." *The Winnower* 3 (May 30, 2016). https://doi.org/10.15200/winn.146485.57797.

Guédon, Jean-Claude. "Open Access: Toward the Internet of the Mind." Budapest Open Access Initiative, 2017. https://www.budapestopenaccessinitiative.org/open-access-toward-the-internet-of-the-mind.

Guédon, Jean-Claude, and Alain Loute. "L'Histoire de la Forme Revue au Prisme de L'Histoire de la «Grande Conversation Scientifique»." *Cahiers du GRM. publiés par le Groupe de Recherches Matérialistes—Association*, no. 12 (2017). https://doi.org/10.4000/grm.912.

Gunnarsdóttir, Kristrún. "Scientific Journal Publications: On the Role of Electronic Preprint Exchange in the Distribution of Scientific Literature." *Social Studies of Science* 35, no. 4 (2005): 549–579. https://doi.org/10.1177/0306312705052358.

Habermas, Jürgen. *The Theory of Communicative Action*. Translated by Thomas McCarthy. Vol. 2. Cambridge: Polity, 1987.

Hacking, Ian. *Rewriting the Soul: Multiple Personality and the Sciences of Memory*. Princeton, NJ: Princeton University Press, 1998.

Haider, Jutta. "Openness as Tool for Acceleration and Measurement: Reflections on Problem Representations Underpinning Open Access and Open Science." In *Open Divide: Critical Studies on Open Access*, edited by Ulrich Herb and Joachim Schöpfel, 17–30. Sacramento, CA: Library Juice Press, 2018.

Hall, Gary. "Does Academia.Edu Mean Open Access Is Becoming Irrelevant?" *Media Gifts* (blog), October 18, 2015. http://www.garyhall.info/journal/2015/10/18/does-academiaedu-mean-open-access-is-becoming-irrelevant.html.

Hall, Gary. *Pirate Philosophy: For a Digital Posthumanities*. Cambridge, MA: The MIT Press, 2016.

Hall, Gary. "Should This Be the Last Thing You Read on Academia.Edu?" *Academia.Edu*, 2017. https://www.academia.edu/16959788/Should_This_Be_the_Last_Thing_You_Read_on_Academia.edu.

Hall, Gary. *The Uberfication of the University*. Minneapolis: University of Minnesota Press, 2016.

Hall, Richard. *The Alienated Academic: The Struggle for Autonomy Inside the University*. London: Palgrave, 2018. https://doi.org/10.1007/978-3-319-94304-6.

Hammill, Faye, and Hannah McGregor. "Bundling, Reprinting, and Reframing: Serial Practices Across Borders." *Journal of Modern Periodical Studies* 9, no. 1 (2019): 76–100.

Hankins, Rebecca. "Racial Realism: An African American Muslim Woman in the Field." In *Where Are All the Librarians of Color? The Experiences of People of Color in Academia*, edited by Rebecca Hankins and Miguel Juárez, 209–219. Sacramento, CA: Library Juice Press, 2015. http://hdl.handle.net/1969.1/156069.

Haraway, Donna. "Situated Knowledges: The Science Question in Feminism and the Privilege of Partial Perspective." *Feminist Studies* 14, no. 3 (1988): 575–599. https://doi.org/10.2307/3178066.

Harding, Sandra G. *Objectivity and Diversity: Another Logic of Scientific Research*. Chicago: University of Chicago Press, 2015.

Harnad, Stevan. "Creative Disagreement." *The Sciences* 19 (1979): 18–20.

Harnad, Stevan. "Post-Gutenberg Galaxy: The Fourth Revolution in the Means of Production of Knowledge." *Public Access-Computer Systems Review* 2, no. 1 (1991): 39–53.

Harnad, Stevan. "ROARMAP." Accessed July 25, 2014. http://roarmap.eprints.org/.

Heller-Roazen, Daniel. "Tradition's Destruction: On the Library of Alexandria." *October* 100 (2002): 133–153.

Helmond, Anne. "The Platformization of the Web: Making Web Data Platform Ready." *Social Media + Society* 1, no. 2 (2015): 205630511560308. https://doi.org/10.1177/2056305115603080.

Herb, Ulrich. "Open Access and Symbolic Gift Giving." In *Open Divide: Critical Studies on Open Access*, edited by Joachim Schöpfel and Ulrich Herb, 69–81. Sacramento, CA: Library Juice Press, 2018. https://doi.org/10.5281/zenodo.1206377.

Hesse, Tom. "A Journal's Apology Prompts Soul-Searching Over Racial Gatekeeping in Academe." *The Chronicle of Higher Education*, April 21, 2017. https://www.chronicle.com/article/A-Journal-s-Apology-Prompts/239852.

Hicks, Diana, Paul Wouters, Ludo Waltman, Sarah de Rijcke, and Ismael Rafols. "Bibliometrics: The Leiden Manifesto for Research Metrics." *Nature* 520, no. 7548 (2015): 429–431. https://doi.org/10.1038/520429a.

Higher Education Funding Council for England. "Consultation on the Second Research Excellence Framework." Higher Education Funding Council for England, 2016.

Higher Education Funding Council for England. "FAQs—REF 2021." Research Excellence Framework, 2019. https://www.ref.ac.uk/faqs/.

Higher Education Funding Council for England. "REF 2021." Research Excellence Framework, 2019. https://www.ref.ac.uk.

Hillyer, Rebecca, Alejandro Posada, Denisse Albornoz, Leslie Chan, and Angela Okune. "Framing a Situated and Inclusive Open Science: Emerging Lessons from the Open and Collaborative Science in Development Network." In *Expanding Perspectives on Open Science: Communities, Cultures and Diversity in Concepts and Practices*, edited by Leslie Chan and Fernando Loizides, 18–33. Amsterdam: IOS Press, 2017. https://doi.org/10.3233/978-1-61499-769-6-18.

Hilsum, Lindsey. "Rwanda, Master Conform." BBC, October 30, 1996. Box 374, Videocassette RW038. International Monitor Institute. Rwanda Videotapes and Audiotapes, David M. Rubenstein Rare Book & Manuscript Library, Duke Universities.

Hiltzik, Michael. "In Act of Brinkmanship, a Big Publisher Cuts Off UC's Access to When the Law Advances Access to Learning Its Academic Journals." *Los Angeles Times*, July 11, 2019. https://www.latimes.com/business/hiltzik/la-fi-uc-elsevier-20190711-story.html.

Hintikka, Merrill B., and Sandra G. Harding, eds. *Discovering Reality: Feminist Perspectives on Epistemology, Metaphysics, Methodology, and Philosophy of Science*. Dordrecht: Reidel, 1983.

Hirsch, Marianne, and Leo Spitzer. "The Witness in the Archive: Holocaust Studies/Memory Studies." *Memory Studies* 2, no. 2 (2009): 151–170. https://doi.org/10.1177/1750698008102050.

Hirschauer, Stefan. "Editorial Judgments: A Praxeology of 'Voting' in Peer Review." *Social Studies of Science* 40, no. 1 (2010): 71–103. https://doi.org/10.1177/0306312709335405.

Hockenberry, Benjamin. "The Guerilla Open Access Manifesto: Aaron Swartz, Open Access and the Sharing Imperative." *Lavery Library Faculty/Staff Publications*, November 21, 2013, 1–7.

Holdren, John P. "Memorandum for the Heads of Executive Departments and Agencies: Increasing Access to the Results of Federally Funded Scientific Research." whitehouse.gov, February 22, 2013. https://obamawhitehouse.archives.gov/sites/default/files/microsites/ostp/ostp_public_access_memo_2013.pdf.

Holmwood, John. "Claiming Whiteness." *Ethnicities* 20, no. 1 (2020).

Holmwood, John. "Inegalitarian Populism and the University: British Reflections on Newfield's *The Great Mistake: How We Wrecked Public Universities and How We Can Fix Them*." *British Journal of Sociology* 69, no. 2 (2018).

Holmwood, John. "Markets versus Dialogue: The Debate over Open Access Ignores Competing Philosophies of Openness." *Impact of Social Sciences* (blog), October 21, 2013. http://blogs.lse.ac.uk/impactofsocialsciences/2013/10/21/markets-versus-dialogue/.

Holmwood, John. "The University, Democracy and the Public Sphere." *British Journal of Sociology of Education* 38, no. 7 (2017): 927–942. https://doi.org/10.1080/01425692.2016.1220286.

Horrigan, John B. "Libraries 2016." *Pew Research Center* (blog), September 9, 2016. https://www.pewinternet.org/2016/09/09/libraries-2016/.

Horton, Richard. "Medical Journals: Evidence of Bias against the Diseases of Poverty." *The Lancet* 361, no. 9359 (2003): 712–713. https://doi.org/10.1016/S0140-6736(03)12665-7.

Hountondji, Paulin J. "Le Savoir Mondialise: Desequilibres et Enjeux Actuels." Université de Nantes/Maison des Sciences de l'Homme Guépin, 2001.

Howard, Jennifer. "Born Digital, Projects Need Attention to Survive." *The Chronicle of Higher Education*, January 6, 2014. https://www.chronicle.com/article/Born-Digital-Projects-Need/143799.

Hu, Tung-Hui. *A Prehistory of the Cloud*. Cambridge, MA: The MIT Press, 2015.

Huggett, Sarah. "Cash Puts Publishing Ethics at Risk in China: Impact Factors." *Nature* 490, no. 7420 (2012): 342. https://doi.org/10.1038/490342c.

Hutchings, Shabaka. "Journey through Jazz (an Interview by Stewart Smith)." Red Bull Academy Music Daily, April 4, 2016. https://daily.redbullmusicacademy.com/2016/04/shabaka-hutchings.

Hyndman, Alan. "New Funding Information on Figshare Items." Figshare, November 12, 2018. https://figshare.com/blog/New_funding_information_on_Figshare_items/446.

ICA. "What Is a Cooperative?," 1995. https://www.ica.coop/en/what-co-operative-0.

ICSU-UNESCO International Conference on Electronic Publishing in Science, and Dennis F. Shaw, eds. *Proceedings of the Second ICSU-UNESCO International Conference on Electronic Publishing in Science: Held in Association with CODATA, IFLA, ICSTI & STM Publishers at UNESCO House, Paris 20–23 February, 2001*. Oxford: ICSU Press, 2001.

IFLA. "IFLA Statement on Open Access to Scholarly Literature and Research Documentation," 2003. https://www.ifla.org/publications/ifla-statement-on-open-access-to-scholarly-literature-and-research-documentation.

IFLA. "IFLA/UNESCO Public Library Manifesto," 1994. https://www.ifla.org/publications/iflaunesco-public-library-manifesto-1994.

Ignatow, Gabe. "What Has Globalization Done to Developing Countries' Public Libraries?" *International Sociology* 26, no. 6 (2011): 746–768. https://doi.org/10.1177/0268580910393373.

Illich, Ivan. *Tools for Conviviality*. New York: Harper and Row, 1973.

Inefuku, Harrison W. "Globalization, Open Access, and the Democratization of Knowledge." *Educause Review* 52 (August 2017): 62–63.

Inefuku, Harrison W., and Charlotte Roh. "Agents of Diversity and Social Justice: Librarians and Scholarly Communication." In *Open Access and the Future of Scholarly Communication: Policy and Infrastructure*, edited by Kevin L. Smith and Katherine A. Dickson, 107–128. Lanham, MD: Rowman & Littlefield, 2016. https://repository.usfca.edu/librarian/8.

Ingelfinger, Franz J. "Definition of Sole Contribution." *New England Journal of Medicine* 281, no. 12 (1969): 676–677. https://doi.org/10.1056/NEJM196909182811208.

Inglehart, Ronald F., and Pippa Norris. "Trump, Brexit, and the Rise of Populism: Economic Have-Nots and Cultural Backlash." SSRN Scholarly Paper. Rochester, NY: Social Science Research Network, July 29, 2016. https://papers.ssrn.com/abstract=2818659.

Instituto Brasileiro de Informação em Ciência e Tecnologia. "Ciência Da Informação." SciELO, 1998. http://www.scielo.br/scielo.php?script=sci_issuetoc&pid=0100-196519980002&lng=es&nrm=iso.

International Seminar on Open Access for Developing Countries. "Salvador Declaration on Open Access: The Developing World Perspective," 2005. http://www.icml9.org/meetings/openaccess/public/documents/declaration.htm.

Intersoft Consulting. "Right to Be Forgotten." *General Data Protection Regulation (GDPR)* (blog). Accessed April 29, 2019. https://gdpr-info.eu/issues/right-to-be-forgotten/.

Jackson, Steven J., Paul N. Edwards, Geoffrey C. Bowker, and Cory P. Knobel. "Understanding Infrastructure: History, Heuristics and Cyberinfrastructure Policy." *First Monday* 12, no. 6 (2007). https://doi.org/10.5210/fm.v12i6.1904.

Jamali, Hamid R. "Copyright Compliance and Infringement in ResearchGate Full-Text Journal Articles." *Scientometrics* 112, no. 1 (2017): 241–254. https://doi.org/10.1007/s11192-017-2291-4.

Jamali, Hamid R., and Majid Nabavi. "Open Access and Sources of Full-Text Articles in Google Scholar in Different Subject Fields." *Scientometrics* 105, no. 3 (2015): 1635–1651. https://doi.org/10.1007/s11192-015-1642-2.

Jamali, Hamid R., David Nicholas, and Eti Herman. "Scholarly Reputation in the Digital Age and the Role of Emerging Platforms and Mechanisms." *Research Evaluation* 25, no. 1 (2016): 37–49. https://doi.org/10.1093/reseval/rvv032.

Jameson, Fredric. *Postmodernism, or, The Cultural Logic of Late Capitalism*. London: Verso, 1991.

Jensen, Casper Bruun, and Atsuro Morita. "Infrastructures as Ontological Experiments." *Engaging Science, Technology, and Society* 1 (2015): 81–87. https://doi.org/10.17351/ests2015.21.

Jiménez-Contreras, Evaristo, Emilio Delgado López-Cózar, Rafael Ruiz-Pérez, and Víctor M. Fernández. "Impact-Factor Rewards Affect Spanish Research." *Nature* 417, no. 6892 (2002): 898. https://doi.org/10.1038/417898b.

Jockers, Matthew L. *Macroanalysis: Digital Methods and Literary History*. Urbana: University of Illinois Press, 2013.

Johns, Adrian. *The Nature of the Book*. Urbana, IL: University of Chicago Press, 1998.

Johns, Adrian. *Piracy: The Intellectual Property Wars from Gutenberg to Gates*. Chicago: University of Chicago Press, 2011.

Johnson, Rob, Anthony Watkinson, and Michael Mabe. *The STM Report: An Overview of Scientific and Scholarly Journal Publishing*. 5th ed. The Hague: International Association of Scientific, Technical and Medical Publishers, 2018. https://www.stm-assoc.org/2018_10_04_STM_Report_2018.pdf.

Jones, Sam. "One in Every 113 People Forced to Flee, Says UN Refugee Agency." *The Guardian*, June 20, 2016, sec. Global development. https://www.theguardian.com/global-development/2016/jun/20/one-in-every-113-people-uprooted-war-persecution-says-un-refugee-agency.

Josias, Anthea. "Toward an Understanding of Archives as a Feature of Collective Memory." *Archival Science* 11, no. 1 (2011): 95–112. https://doi.org/10.1007/s10502-011-9136-3.

JSTOR Labs. "Text Analyzer Beta," 2017. https://www.jstor.org/analyze.

Kahle, Brewster. "Help Us Keep the Archive Free, Accessible, and Reader Private." *Internet Archive Blogs* (blog), November 29, 2016. https://blog.archive.org/2016/11/29/help-us-keep-the-archive-free-accessible-and-private/.

Kappel, Gerti, Birgit Pröll, Siegfried Reich, and Werner Retschitzegger. "An Introduction to Web Engineering." In *Web Engineering: The Discipline of Systematic Development of Web Applications*, edited by Gerti Kappel, 1–22. Hoboken, NJ: John Wiley & Sons, 2003.

Kaster, Nicholas. "Copyright Case: Cambridge University Press v. Albert, USA." Kluwer Copyright Blog, October 30, 2018. http://copyrightblog.kluweriplaw.com/2018/10/30/usa-cambridge-university-press-v-albert-united-states-court-appeals-eleventh-circuit-no-16-15726-19-october-2018/.

Kaufmann, Eric. "'Racial Self-Interest' Is Not Racism." *Policy Exchange* (blog), 2017. https://policyexchange.org.uk/publication/racial-self-interest-is-not-racism/.

Kean, Danuta. "Library Closures 'Will Double Unless Immediate Action Is Taken.'" *The Guardian*, December 12, 2016, sec. Books. https://www.theguardian.com/books/2016/dec/12/library-closures-will-double-unless-immediate-action-is-taken.

Keller, Evelyn Fox. *Making Sense of Life: Explaining Biological Development with Models, Metaphors, and Machines*. Cambridge, MA: Harvard University Press, 2003.

Kelley, Robin D. G. *Freedom Dreams: The Black Radical Imagination.* Boston: Beacon Press, 2002.

Kelly, Thomas. *History of Public Libraries in Great Britain, 1845–1975.* London: Library Association Publishing, 1977.

Kelty, Chris. "It's the Data, Stupid: What Elsevier's Purchase of SSRN Also Means." *Savage Minds* (blog), May 18, 2016. https://savageminds.org/2016/05/18/its-the-data-stupid-what-elseviers-purchase-of-ssrn-also-means/.

Kember, Sarah. "Opening Out from Open Access: Writing and Publishing in Response to Neoliberalism." *Ada New Media* (blog), April 21, 2014. https://adanewmedia.org/2014/04/issue4-kember/.

Kemp, Geoff. "The 'End of Censorship' and the Politics of Toleration, from Locke to Sacheverell." *Parliamentary History* 31, no. 1 (2012): 47–68. https://doi.org/10.1111/j.1750-0206.2011.00282.x.

Kennedy, Meegan. "Open Annotation and Close Reading the Victorian Text: Using Hypothes.Is with Students." *Journal of Victorian Culture* 21, no. 4 (2016): 550–558. https://doi.org/10.1080/13555502.2016.1233905.

Kerr, Clark. *The Uses of the University.* Cambridge, MA: Harvard University Press, 2001.

Kieńć, Witold. "Authors from The Periphery Countries Choose Open Access More Often." *Learned Publishing* 30, no. 2 (2017): 125–131. https://doi.org/10.1002/leap.1093.

Kim, Hyunjee Nicole. "An Afrofuturist Community Center Targets Gentrification." *Hyperallergic*, June 23, 2016. https://hyperallergic.com/307013/an-afrofuturist-community-center-targets-gentrification/.

Kirschenbaum, Matthew G. "Done: Finishing Projects in the Digital Humanities." *Digital Humanities Quarterly* 3, no. 2 (2009). http://www.digitalhumanities.org/dhq/vol/3/2/000037/000037.html.

Konkiel, Stacy. "Approaches to Creating 'Humane' Research Evaluation Metrics for the Humanities." *Insights: The UKSG Journal* 31 (2018). https://doi.org/10.1629/uksg.445.

Koutras, Nikos. "Open Access: A Means for Social Justice and Greater Social Cohesion." *Seattle Journal for Social Justice* 16, no. 1 (2017): 105–134.

Krabbe, Julia Suárez. "Introduction: Coloniality of Knowledge and Epistemologies of Transformation." *KULT. Postkolonial Temaserie* 6 (2009): 1–10.

Kyrillidou, Martha, and Shaneka Morris. "Monograph and Serial Expenditures in ARL Libraries, 1986–2009." In *ARL Statistics 2008–2009.* Washington, DC: Association of College and Research Libraries, 2011. https://publications.arl.org/ARL-Statistics-2008-2009/11?ajax.

Lagoze, Carl, Paul Edwards, Christian Sandvig, and Jean-Christophe Plantin. "Should I Stay or Should I Go? Alternative Infrastructures in Scholarly Publishing." *International Journal of Communication* 9 (2015): 1052–1071.

Lancaster, F W. "Attitudes in Academia toward Feasibility and Desirability of Networked Scholarly Publishing." *Library Trends* 43, no. 4 (1995): 741–752.

Larivière, Vincent, and Yves Gingras. "The Impact Factor's Matthew Effect: A Natural Experiment in Bibliometrics." *Journal of the American Society for Information Science and Technology* 61, no. 2 (2010): 424–427. https://doi.org/10.1002/asi.21232.

Larivière, Vincent, Stefanie Haustein, and Philippe Mongeon. "The Oligopoly of Academic Publishers in the Digital Era." *PLOS ONE* 10, no. 6 (2015): e0127502. https://doi.org/10.1371/journal.pone.0127502.

Larivière, Vincent, Chaoqun Ni, Yves Gingras, Blaise Cronin, and Cassidy R. Sugimoto. "Bibliometrics: Global Gender Disparities in Science." *Nature* 504, no. 7479 (2013): 211–213. https://doi.org/10.1038/504211a.

Lassila, Ora. "Web Metadata: A Matter of Semantics." *IEEE Internet Computing* 2, no. 4 (1998): 30–37. https://doi.org/10.1109/4236.707688.

Latindex-Redalyc-CLACSO-Ibict. "Joint Declaration by Latindex-Redalyc-CLACSO-Ibict on the Use of CC BY-NC-SA License to Guarantee Protection of Academic and Scientific Open Access Output," 2017. http://www.accesoabiertoalyc.org/declaracion-mexico-en/.

Latour, Bruno. *An Inquiry into Modes of Existence*. Cambridge, MA: Harvard University Press, 2013.

Latour, Bruno, and Peter Weibel, eds. *Making Things Public: Atmospheres of Democracy*. Cambridge, MA: The MIT Press, 2005.

Latour, Bruno, and Steve Woolgar. *Laboratory Life: The Construction of Scientific Facts*. Beverly Hills, CA: SAGE, 1979.

Lawrence, Susan C. *Privacy and the Past: Research, Law, Archives, Ethics*. New Brunswick, NJ: Rutgers University Press, 2016.

Lawson, Stuart. "Open Access Policy in the UK: From Neoliberalism to the Commons." Doctoral thesis, Birkbeck, University of London, 2019. https://ethos.bl.uk/OrderDetails.do?uin=uk.bl.ethos.774255.

Lerback, Jory, and Brooks Hanson. "Journals Invite Too Few Women to Referee." *Nature* 541, no. 7638 (2017): 455–457. https://doi.org/10.1038/541455a.

Lewis, Alison M. "Introduction." In *Questioning Library Neutrality: Essays from Progressive Librarian*, edited by Alison M. Lewis, 1–4. Duluth, MI: Library Juice Press, 2008.

Lezaun, J., Noortje Marres, and M. Tironi. "Experiments in Participation." In *Handbook of Science and Technology Studies*, edited by U. Felt, R. Fouche, C. Miller, and E. Smith-Doer, 4: 195–222. Cambridge, MA: The MIT Press, 2017.

Li, Xuemei, Mike Thelwall, and Kayvan Kousha. "The Role of arXiv, RePEc, SSRN and PMC in Formal Scholarly Communication." *Aslib Journal of Information Management* 67, no. 6 (2015): 614–435. https://doi.org/10.1108/AJIM-03-2015-0049.

Local Contexts. "About." Accessed May 1, 2019. http://localcontexts.org/about/.

Locke, John. "Liberty of the Press (1694–5)." In *Locke: Political Essays*, edited by Mark Goldie, 329–338. Cambridge: Cambridge University Press, 1997. https://doi.org/10.1017/CBO9780511810251.

Locke, John. *The Correspondence of John Locke*. Edited by Esmond Samuel de Beer. Vol. 4. Oxford: Oxford University Press, 1976.

Locke, John. *Two Treatises of Government*. Edited by Peter Laslett. Cambridge: Cambridge University Press, 1988.

Lockett, Alexandria. "Leaked: A Grammar of Information in Surveillance Cultures." PhD diss., Pennsylvania State University, 2013.

Loewenstein, Joseph. *The Author's Due: Printing and the Prehistory of Copyright*. Chicago: University of Chicago Press, 2002.

Long, Pamela O. *Artisan/Practitioners and the Rise of the New Sciences, 1400–1600*. Corvallis: Oregon State University Press, 2011.

Long, Pamela O. "Hydraulic Engineering and the Study of Antiquity: Rome, 1557–70." *Renaissance Quarterly* 61, no. 4 (2008): 1098–1138. https://doi.org/10.1353/ren.0.0320.

Lorde, Audre. "A Burst of Light: Living with Cancer." In *A Burst of Light and Other Essays*, 49–134. London: Sheba Feminist Publishers, 1988.

Lorenzo, Josique, John Mario Rodriguez, and Viviana Benavides. "On Openness and Motivation: Insights from a Pilot Project in Latin America." In *Contextualizing Openness: Situating Open Science*, edited by Leslie Chan, Angela Okune, Becky Hillyer, Denisse Albornoz, and Alejandro Posada, 87–106. Ottawa, ON: University of Ottawa Press, 2019. https://www.idrc.ca/en/book/contextualizing-openness-situating-open-science.

Low, Jason, Sarah Park Dahlen, and Nicole Catlin. "Where Is the Diversity in Publishing? The 2015 Diversity Baseline Survey Results." *The Open Book Blog*, January 26, 2016. https://blog.leeandlow.com/2016/01/26/where-is-the-diversity-in-publishing-the-2015-diversity-baseline-survey-results/.

Lugones, Marìa. "Toward a Decolonial Feminism." *Hypatia* 25, no. 4 (2010): 742–759. https://doi.org/10.1111/j.1527-2001.2010.01137.x.

Lury, Celia, and Nina Wakeford, eds. *Inventive Methods: The Happening of the Social.* Culture, Economy, and the Social. London: Routledge, 2012.

Macaulay, Thomas Babington. *The History of England, from the Accession of James II.* Vol. 4. Philadelphia, PA: Butler, 1856.

Mackenthun, Gesa. "Coloniality of Knowledge." Institut für Anglistik/Amerikanistik—Universität Rostock, April 19, 2016. https://www.iaa.uni-rostock.de/forschung/laufende-forschungsprojekte/american-antiquities-prof-mackenthun/project/theories/coloniality-of-knowledge/.

Magaziner, Jessica. "The Importance of Higher Education for Syrian Refugees." *World Education News + Reviews*, December 7, 2015. https://wenr.wes.org/2015/12/the-importance-of-higher-education-for-syrian-refugees.

Making and Knowing Project. Pamela H. Smith, Naomi Rosenkranz, Tianna Helena Uchacz, Tillmann Taape, Clement Godbarge, Sophie Pitman, Jenny Boulboulle, Joel Klein, Donna Bilak, Marc Smith, and Terry Catapano, eds. *Secrets of Craft and Nature in Renaissance France: A Digital Critical Edition and English Translation of BnF Ms. Fr. 640.* New York: The Making and Knowing Project, 2020. https://doi.org/10.7916/78yt-2v41.

Makki, Fouad. "Post-Colonial Africa and the World Economy: The Long Waves of Uneven Development." *Journal of World-Systems Research* 21, no. 1 (2015): 124–146. https://doi.org/10.5195/JWSR.2015.546.

Malik, Rachel. "Horizons of the Publishable: Publishing in/as Literary Studies." *ELH* 75, no. 3 (2008): 707–735. https://doi.org/10.1353/elh.0.0016.

Mancini, Pia, and Farida Vis. "How Do Digital Platforms Shape Our Lives?" World Economic Forum, 2015. https://www.weforum.org/agenda/2015/10/how-do-digital-platforms-shape-our-lives/.

Mancisidor, Mikel. "El Derecho Humano a La Ciencia: Un Viejo Derecho Con Un Gran Futuro." *Anuario de Derechos Humanos*, no. 13 (2017): 211–221. https://doi.org/10.5354/0718-2279.2017.46887.

Mandler, Peter. "Open Access: A Perspective from the Humanities." *Insights: The UKSG Journal* 27, no. 2 (2014): 166–170. https://doi.org/10.1629/2048-7754.89.

Mandler, Peter. "Open Access for the Humanities: Not for Funders, Scientists or Publishers." *Journal of Victorian Culture* 18, no. 4 (2013): 551–557. https://doi.org/10.1080/13555502.2013.865981.

Mangiafico, Paolo. "Should You #DeleteAcademiaEdu?" *Scholarly Communications @ Duke* (blog), January 29, 2016. https://blogs.library.duke.edu/scholcomm/2016/01/29/should-you-deleteacademiaedu/.

Marcum, Deanna. "Due Diligence and Stewardship in a Time of Change and Uncertainty." New York: Ithaka S+R, April 26, 2016. https://doi.org/10.18665/sr.278232.

Marin, Anabel, Sergio Petralia, and Lilia Stubrin. "Evaluating the Impact of Open Access Initiatives within the Academia and Beyond." In *Made in Latin America: Open Access, Scholarly Journals, and Regional Innovations*, edited by Juan Pablo Alperin and Gustavo Fischman, 75–102. Ciudad Autónoma de Buenos Aires: CLACSO, 2015. http://biblioteca.clacso.edu.ar/clacso/se/20150921045253/MadeInLatinAmerica.pdf.

Maron, Nancy, Rebecca Kennison, Paul Bracke, Nathan Hall, Isaac Gilman, Kara Malenfant, Charlotte Roh, and Yasmeen Shorish. "Open and Equitable Scholarly Communications: Creating a More Inclusive Future." Chicago: Association of College and Research Libraries, 2019. https://doi.org/10.5860/acrl.1.

Marres, Noortje. "The Issues Deserve More Credit: Pragmatist Contributions to the Study of Public Involvement in Controversy." *Social Studies of Science* 37, no. 5 (2007): 759–780. https://doi.org/10.1177/0306312706077367.

Marres, Noortje. *Material Participation*. Basingstoke, UK: Palgrave Macmillan, 2015.

Marres, Noortje. "Why Political Ontology Must Be Experimentalized: On Eco-Show Homes as Devices of Participation." *Social Studies of Science* 43, no. 3 (2013): 417–443. https://doi.org/10.1177/0306312712475255.

Martin, Kirsten, and Helen Nissenbaum. "Privacy Interests in Public Records: An Empirical Investigation." *Harvard Journal of Law & Technology* 31, no. 1 (2017): 33.

Masnick, Mike. "Disappointing: Elsevier Buys Open Access Academic Pre-Publisher SSRN." Techdirt, May 17, 2016. https://www.techdirt.com/articles/20160517/13513134465/disappointing-elsevier-buys-open-access-academic-pre-publisher-ssrn.shtml.

Massicotte, Mia, and Kathleen Botter. "Reference Rot in the Repository: A Case Study of Electronic Theses and Dissertations (ETDs) in an Academic Library." *Information Technology and Libraries* 36, no. 1 (2017): 11–28. https://doi.org/10.6017/ital.v36i1.9598.

Matthews, Duncan. *Globalising Intellectual Property Rights: The TRIPs Agreement*. London: Routledge, 2003.

Max Planck Digital Library. "Roadmap." *Open Access 2020* (blog), 2017. https://oa2020.org/.

Mboa Nkoudou, Thomas Hervé. "Le Web et la production scientifique africaine: visibilité réelle ou inhibée?" *Projet SOHA* (blog), June 18, 2016. https://www.projetsoha.org/?p=1357.

Mboa Nkoudou, Thomas Hervé. "The (Unconscious?) Neocolonial Face of Open Access." Berlin, 2017. https://www.youtube.com/watch?v=-HSOzoSLHL0.

McAdam, Matthew. "Deans Care About Books." Infernal Machine, March 5, 2018. https://hedgehogreview.com/blog/infernal-machine/posts/deans-care-about-books.

McArthur, Joseph, David Carroll, Nicholas Ng, Andy Lulham, Florian Rathgeber, Jez Cope, Alf Eaton, et al. "Open Access Button," 2013. https://web.archive.org/web/20131206130920/https://www.openaccessbutton.org/.

McCarthy, Thomas. "Introduction." In *The Structural Transformation of the Public Sphere: An Inquiry into a Category of Bourgeois Society*, edited by Jürgen Habermas, xi. Cambridge, MA: The MIT Press, 1989.

McCook, Alison. "PLOS ONE Has Faced a Decline in Submissions—Why? New Editor Speaks." Retraction Watch, March 15, 2017. http://retractionwatch.com/2017/03/15/plos-one-faced-decline-submissions-new-editor-speaks/.

McDougall-Waters, Julie, Aileen Fyfe, and Noah Moxham. Philosophical Transactions: *350 Years of Publishing at the Royal Society (1665–2015)*. London: The Royal Society, 2014.

McGann, Jerome. "Imagining What You Don't Know: The Theoretical Goals of The Rossetti Archive." Institute for Advanced Technology in the Humanities, University of Virginia, 1997. http://www2.iath.virginia.edu/jjm2f/old/chum.html.

McGann, Jerome. "Marking Texts of Many Dimensions." In *A New Companion to Digital Humanities*, edited by Susan Schreibman, Ray Siemens, and John Unsworth, 358–376. Oxford: John Wiley & Sons, 2015. https://doi.org/10.1002/9781118680605.ch25.

McGregor, Hannah. "Remediation as Reading: Digitising The Western Home Monthly." *Archives and Manuscripts* 42, no. 3 (2014): 248–257. https://doi.org/10.1080/01576895.2014.958864.

McKenzie, Lindsay. "Elsevier Makes Move into Institutional Repositories with Acquisition of Bepress." Inside Higher Ed, August 3, 2017. https://www.insidehighered.com/news/2017/08/03/elsevier-makes-move-institutional-repositories-acquisition-bepress.

McKiernan, Erin C. "Imagining the 'Open' University: Sharing Scholarship to Improve Research and Education." *PLOS Biology* 15, no. 10 (2017): e1002614. https://doi.org/10.1371/journal.pbio.1002614.

McMenemy, David. *The Public Library*. London: Facet Publishing, 2009.

McMillan, Gail, Matt Schultz, and Katherine Skinner. "Digital Preservation, SPEC Kit 325." Association of Research Libraries, 2011. https://publications.arl.org/Digital-Preservation-SPEC-Kit-325/.

Medina, José. "Whose Meanings? Resignifying Voices and Their Social Locations." *Journal of Speculative Philosophy* 22, no. 2 (2008): 92–105.

Meneghini, Rogerio, and Abel L. Packer. "Is There Science Beyond English? Initiatives to Increase the Quality and Visibility of Non-English Publications Might Help to Break Down Language Barriers in Scientific Communication." *EMBO Reports* 8, no. 2 (2007): 112–116. https://doi.org/10.1038/sj.embor.7400906.

Merges, Robert P. *Justifying Intellectual Property*. Cambridge, MA: Harvard University Press, 2011.

Merton, R.K. "Science and Technology in a Democratic Order." *Journal of Legal and Political Sociology* 1 (1942): 115–126.

Mietchen, Daniel, Ross Mounce, and Lyubomir Penev. "Publishing the Research Process." *Research Ideas and Outcomes* 1 (2015): e7547. https://doi.org/10.3897/rio.1.e7547.

Miguel, Sandra Edith. "Revistas y Producción Científica de América Latina y el Caribe: Su Visibilidad en SciELO, RedALyC y SCOPUS" 34, no. 2 (2011): 187–199. http://www.memoria.fahce.unlp.edu.ar/art_revistas/pr.6384/pr.6384.pdf

Milan, Stefania, and Lonneke van der Velden. "The Alternative Epistemologies of Data Activism." *Digital Culture & Society* 2, no. 2 (2016). https://doi.org/10.14361/dcs-2016-0205.

Miller, Dan E. "Rumor: An Examination of Some Stereotypes." *Symbolic Interaction* 28, no. 4 (2005): 505–519. https://doi.org/10.1525/si.2005.28.4.505.

Miller, David. *Principles of Social Justice*. Cambridge, MA: Harvard University Press, 1999.

Miller, Elise. "The People, the Money, the Books: Inside Stanford University Press." *The Stanford Daily* (blog), June 5, 2019. https://www.stanforddaily.com/2019/06/05/the-people-the-money-the-books-inside-stanford-university-press/.

Milliot, Jim. "The PW Publishing Industry Salary Survey 2015: A Younger Workforce, Still Predominantly White." Publishers Weekly, October 16, 2015. https://www.publishersweekly.com/pw/by-topic/industry-news/publisher-news/article/68405-publishing-industry-salary-survey-2015-a-younger-workforce-still-predominantly-white.html.

Milton, John. "Areopagitica." In *Milton's Prose Writings*, edited by K. M. Burton, 145–185. London: Dent, 1958.

Minniti, Sergio, Valeria Santoro, and Simone Belli. "Mapping the Development of Open Access in Latin America and Caribbean Countries. An Analysis of Web of Science Core Collection and SciELO Citation Index (2005–2017)." *Scientometrics* 117, no. 3 (2018): 1905–1930. https://doi.org/10.1007/s11192-018-2950-0.

MLA Journals. "Profession," 2011. https://www.mlajournals.org/toc/prof/2011/1.

Modern Language Association of America. "Guidelines for Evaluating Work in Digital Humanities and Digital ..." Modern Language Association, 2012. https://www.mla.org/About-Us/Governance/Committees/Committee-Listings/Professional-Issues/Committee-on-Information-Technology/Guidelines-for-Evaluating-Work-in-Digital-Humanities-and-Digital-Media.

Mohanty, Chandra Talpade. *Feminism without Borders: Decolonizing Theory, Practicing Solidarity*. Durham, NC: Duke University Press, 2003.

Monbiot, George. "Academic Publishers Make Murdoch Look like a Socialist." *The Guardian*, August 29, 2011, sec. Comment is free. http://www.guardian.co.uk/commentisfree/2011/aug/29/academic-publishers-murdoch-socialist.

Moody, Glyn. "German Court Says Creative Commons 'Non-Commercial' Licenses Must Be Purely for Personal Use." Techdirt, 2014. https://www.techdirt.com/articles/20140326/11405526695/german-court-says-creative-commons-non-commercial-licenses-must-be-purely-personal-use.shtml.

Moore, Samuel. "Common Struggles: Policy-Based vs. Scholar-Led Approaches to Open Access in the Humanities." Doctoral Thesis, King's College London, 2019. https://hcommons.org/deposits/item/hc:24135/.

Moore, Samuel. "A Genealogy of Open Access: Negotiations between Openness and Access to Research." *Revue Française Des Sciences de l'information et de La Communication*, no. 11 (2017). https://doi.org/10.4000/rfsic.3220.

Moore, Samuel, Cameron Neylon, Martin Paul Eve, Daniel O'Donnell, and Damian Pattinson. "Excellence R Us: University Research and the Fetishisation of Excellence." *Palgrave Communications* 3 (2017). https://doi.org/10.1057/palcomms.2016.105.

Moorthy, Vasee S., Ghassan Karam, Kirsten S. Vannice, and Marie-Paule Kieny. "Rationale for WHO's New Position Calling for Prompt Reporting and Public Disclosure of Interventional Clinical Trial Results." *PLOS Medicine* 12, no. 4 (2015): e1001819. https://doi.org/10.1371/journal.pmed.1001819.

Moretti, Franco. *Distant Reading*. London: Verso, 2013.

Moretti, Franco. *Graphs, Maps, Trees: Abstract Models for Literary History*. London: Verso, 2007.

Moretti, Franco. "The Slaughterhouse of Literature." *MLQ: Modern Language Quarterly* 61, no. 1 (2000): 207–227.

Morozov, Evgeny. *To Save Everything, Click Here: Technology, Solutionism and the Urge to Fix Problems That Don't Exist*. London: Allen Lane, 2013.

Morris, Sally, Ed Barnas, Douglas LaFrenier, and Margaret Reich. *The Handbook of Journal Publishing*. Cambridge: Cambridge University Press, 2013. https://doi.org/10.1017/CBO9781139107860.

Morrish, Liz, and Helen Sauntson. *Academic Irregularities: Language and Neoloberalism in Higher Education*. New York: Routledge, 2020. https://doi.org/10.4324/9781315561592.

Morrison, Heather. "Elsevier 2009 $2 Billion Profits Could Fund Worldwide OA at $1,383 per Article." *The Imaginary Journal of Poetic Economics* (blog). Accessed January 21, 2013. http://poeticeconomics.blogspot.co.uk/2010/04/elsevier-2009-2-billion-profits-could.html.

Mountz, Alison, Anne Bonds, Becky Mansfield, Jenna Loyd, Jennifer Hyndman, Margaret Walton-Roberts, Ranu Basu, Risa Whitson, Roberta Hawkins, and Trina Hamilton. "For Slow Scholarship: A Feminist Politics of Resistance through Collective Action in the Neoliberal University." *ACME: An International E-Journal for Critical Geographies* 14, no. 4 (2015): 1253–1259.

Muddiman, Dave, Shiraz Durrani, Martin Dutch, Rebecca Linley, John Pateman, and John Vincent. *Open to All? The Public Library and Social Exclusion*. Edited by Dave Muddiman. Vol. 1, Ove. London: Resource: The Council for Museums, Archives and Libraries, 2000. http://eprints.rclis.org/6283/.

Mukurtu. "About." Accessed May 1, 2019. http://mukurtu.org/about/.

Muñoz, Trevor. "Data Curation as Publishing for the Digital Humanities." *Journal of Digital Humanities* 2, no. 3 (2013). http://journalofdigitalhumanities.org/2-3/data-curation-as-publishing-for-the-digital-humanities/.

Muñoz, Trevor, and Allen Renear. "Issues in Humanities Data Curation." Palo Alto, CA, 2010. http://cirss.ischool.illinois.edu/paloalto/whitepaper/.

Murillo, Luis Felipe Rosado. "What Does 'Open Data' Mean for Ethnographic Research?: Multimodal Anthropologies." *American Anthropologist* 120, no. 3 (2018): 577–582. https://doi.org/10.1111/aman.13088.

Murphie, Andrew. "Ghosted Publics—the 'Unacknowledged Collective' in the Contemporary Transformation of the Circulation of Ideas." In *The Mag.Net Reader 3—Processual Publishing. Actual Gestures*, edited by Alessandro Ludovico and Nat Muller, 102–110. London: Open Mute Press, 2008. http://www.andrewmurphie.org/docs/Ghosted_Publics_Murphe.pdf.

Murray-Rust, Peter. "Sci-Hub and Legal Aspects of ContentMining 4/n." *Petermr's Blog*, May 6, 2016. https://blogs.ch.cam.ac.uk/pmr/2016/05/06/sci-hub-and-legal-aspects-of-contentmining/.

Murray-Rust, Peter. "What Is TextAndData/ContentMining?" *Petermr's Blog*, July 11, 2017. https://blogs.ch.cam.ac.uk/pmr/2017/07/11/what-is-textanddatacontentmining/.

Mve Ondo, Bonaventure. "La Fracture Scientifique." *Présence Africaine* 175-176-177, no. 1 (2007): 585. https://doi.org/10.3917/presa.175.0585.

Nabudale, Dani. "Research, Activism, and Knowledge Production." In *Engaging Contradictions: Theory, Politics, and Methods of Activist Scholarship*, edited by Charles Hale. Berkeley, CA: University of California Press, 2008.

Nancy, Jean-Luc. *The Inoperative Community*. Edited by Peter Connor. Translated by Peter Connor, Lisa Garbus, Michael Holland, and Simona Sawhney. Minneapolis: University of Minnesota Press, 1991.

The National Archives Legislation. "Rehabilitation of Offenders Act 1974," 1974. https://www.legislation.gov.uk/ukpga/1974/53.

National Endowment for the Humanities. "Data Management Plans for NEH Office of Digital Humanities Proposals and Awards," 2017.

National Information Standards Organization. "JATS: Journal Article Tag Suite, Version 1.1," 2015.

Ndlovu-Gatsheni, Sabelo J. "The Dynamics of Epistemological Decolonisation in the 21st Century: Towards Epistemic Freedom." *Strategic Review for Southern Africa* 40, no. 1 (2018): 16–45.

Newfield, Christopher. *The Great Mistake: How We Wrecked Public Universities and How We Can Fix Them.* Baltimore, MD: Johns Hopkins University Press, 2016.

Neylon, Cameron. "Canaries in the Elsevier Mine: What to Watch for at SSRN." *Science in the Open* (blog), June 7, 2016. http://cameronneylon.net/blog/canaries-in-the-elsevier-mine-what-to-watch-for-at-ssrn/.

Nissenbaum, Helen. "A Contextual Approach to Privacy Online." *Daedalus* 140, no. 4 (2011): 32–48.

Nissenbaum, Helen. *Privacy in Context: Technology, Policy, and the Integrity of Social Life.* Stanford, CA: Stanford University Press, 2009.

Nissenbaum, Helen. "Respecting Context to Protect Privacy: Why Meaning Matters." *Science and Engineering Ethics* 24, no. 3 (2018): 831–852. https://doi.org/10.1007/s11948-015-9674-9.

Noble, Safiya Umoja. *Algorithms of Oppression: How Search Engines Reinforce Racism.* New York: New York University Press, 2018.

Noble, Safiya Umoja. "A Future for Intersectional Black Feminist Technology Studies." *Scholar & Feminist Online* 13, no. 3 (2016): 1–8.

Noble, Safiya Umoja. "Social Justice and Library Publishing." In *Library Publishing Forum.* Baltimore, MD, 2017. https://www.periscope.tv/w/1yNGaPXEjXbKj?t=1.

Noel, Marianne. "La Construction de la Valeur Économique d'Une Revue en Chimie. Le Cas du Journal of the American Chemical Society (1879–2010)." *Revue Française des Sciences de l'Information et de la Communication*, no. 11 (2017): 1879–2010. https://doi.org/10.4000/rfsic.3281.

"Notes on the Reading and Publication of Papers." In *Year Book of the Royal Society of London*, 88–89. London: Harrisons and Sons, 1899.

Nowviskie, Bethany. "Digital Humanities in the Anthropocene." *Digital Scholarship in the Humanities* 30, no. suppl_1 (2015): i4–15. https://doi.org/10.1093/llc/fqv015.

Nowviskie, Bethany. "Everywhere, Every When." *Bethany Nowviskie* (blog), April 29, 2016. http://nowviskie.org/2016/everywhere-every-when/.

Nowviskie, Bethany. "Speculative Collections." *Bethany Nowviskie* (blog), October 27, 2016. http://nowviskie.org/2016/speculative-collections/.

Nowviskie, Bethany. "Speculative Computing: Instruments for Interpretive Scholarship." PhD diss., University of Virginia, 2004. http://search.lib.virginia.edu/catalog/7h149q13w.

Nyamnjoh, Francis. "Institutional Review: Open Access and Open Knowledge Production Processes: Lessons from CODESRIA." *South African Journal of Information and Communication*, no. 10 (2010): 67–72. https://doi.org/10.23962/10539/19772.

Ochai, Adakole. "The Purpose of the Library in Colonial Tropical Africa: An Historical Survey." *International Library Review* 16, no. 3 (1984): 309–315. https://doi.org/10.1016/0020-7837(84)90007-4.

Odell, Jere. "How Many Repositories Do We Need?," 2016. http://www.ulib.iupui.edu/digitalscholarship/blog/how-many.

Odi, Amusi. "The Colonial Origins of Library Development in Africa: Some Reflections on Their Significance." *Libraries & Culture* 26, no. 4 (1991): 594–604.

OECD. "Inclusive Growth." Accessed May 10, 2019. http://www.oecd.org/inclusive-growth/#inequality-puts-our-world-at-risk.

Office of Scholarly Communication, University of California. "UC Open Access Policies." *Office of Scholarly Communication* (blog). Accessed May 31, 2019. https://osc.universityofcalifornia.edu/open-access-at-uc/open-access-policy/.

Oliveira Amorin, Keyla Mafalda de, Filipe Degani-Carneiro, Nathalia da Silva Ávila, and Glaucio José Marafon. "Evaluation Systems of Scientific Journals in Latin America." In *Made in Latin America: Open Access, Scholarly Journals, and Regional Innovations*, edited by Juan Pablo Alperin and Gustavo Fischman, 61–74. Ciudad Autónoma de Buenos Aires: CLACSO, 2015. http://biblioteca.clacso.edu.ar/clacso/se/20150921045253/MadeInLatinAmerica.pdf.

Open Access Button. "About." Accessed June 4, 2019. https://openaccessbutton.org/about.

OpenAIRE. "OpenAIRE Guidelines Documentation." Accessed September 23, 2019. https://guidelines.openaire.eu/en/latest/.

Operation beprexit. "Operation Beprexit." Accessed May 23, 2019. https://beprexit.wordpress.com/.

O'Reilly, Tim. "Government as a Platform." *Innovations: Technology, Governance, Globalization* 6, no. 1 (2011): 13–40. https://doi.org/10.1162/INOV_a_00056.

Oxford University Press. "About Us." Accessed May 14, 2019. https://global.oup.com/about/.

Oyelude, Adetoun A., and Alice A. Bamigbola. "Libraries as the Gate: 'Ways' and 'Keepers' in the Knowledge Environment." *Library Hi Tech News* 29, no. 8 (2012): 7–10. https://doi.org/10.1108/07419051211287615.

Packer, Abel L. "The SciELO Model for Electronic Publishing and Measuring of Usage and Impact of Latin American and Caribbean Scientific Journals." Second ICSU/UNESCO International Conference on Electronic Publishing in Science. UNESCO HQ, Paris, 2001. http://eos.wdcb.ru/eps2/eps02016/eps02016.pdf"eps02016/eps02016.pdf.

Packer, Abel L. "The SciELO Project Initiative for Latin America and Caribbean." AAAS/UNESCO/ICSU Workshop on Developing Practices and Standards for Electronic Publishing in Science. UNESCO HQ, Paris, 1998. http://web.archive.org/web/20000919121422/http://www.aaas.org/spp/dspp/sfrl/projects/epub/ses1/Packer.htm.

Packer, Abel L. "SciELO—Scientific Electronic Library Online." Proceedings of ICSU Press Workshop on Economics, Real Costs and Benefits of Electronic Publishing in Science—A Technical Study. Keble College, University of Oxford, 1998. http://web.archive.org/web/19991007150424/http://www.bodley.ox.ac.uk/icsu/packerppr.htm.

Packer, Abel L., Irati Antonio, and Vera Sílvia Marão Beraquet. "Rumo à Publicação Eletrônica." *Ciência Da Informação* 27, no. 2 (1998): 107–108. https://doi.org/10.1590/S0100-19651998000200002.

Packer, Abel L., Mariana Rocha Biojone, Irati Antonio, Roberta Mayumi Takenaka, Alberto Pedroso García, Asael Costa da Silva, Renato Toshiyuki Murasaki, Cristina Mylek, Odila Carvalho Reis, and Hálida Cristina Rocha F. Delbucio. "SciELO: Una Metodología Para la Publicación Electrónica." *Revista Española de Salud Pública* 75, no. 4 (2001): 291–312. https://doi.org/10.1590/S1135-57272001000400004.

Packer, Abel L., and Elenice de Castro. *Virtual Health Library*. Sao Paulo: Latin American and Caribbean Center on Health Sciences Information, BIREME, 1998. http://red.bvsalud.org/modelo-bvs/wp-content/uploads/sites/3/2016/11/Virtual-Health-Library-The-book.pdf.

Parry, Kate. "Libraries in Uganda: Not Just Linguistic Imperialism." *Libri* 61, no. 4 (2011): 328–337. https://doi.org/10.1515/libr.2011.027.

Parsons, Talcott. *The System of Modern Societies*. Foundations of Modern Sociology Series. Englewood Cliffs, NJ: Prentice-Hall, 1971.

Partridge, Robert C. Barrington. "The History of the Legal Deposit of Books throughout the British Empire." Honours Diploma, Library Association, 1938.

Pasquale, Frank. *The Black Box Society: The Secret Algorithms That Control Money and Information*. Cambridge, MA: Harvard University Press, 2015.

Pasquale, Frank. "Platform Neutrality: Enhancing Freedom of Expression in Spheres of Private Power." *Theoretical Inquiries in Law* 17 (2016): 487–514.

Patel, Jashu, and Krishan Kumar. *Libraries and Librarianship in India*. Westport, CT: Greenwood Press, 2001.

Pateman, John. "Public Libraries and Social Class." In *Open to All? The Public Library and Social Exclusion*, by Dave Muddiman, Shiraz Durrani, Martin Dutch, Rebecca Linley, John Pateman, John Vincent, and Dave Muddiman, 26–42. London: Resource: The Council for Museums, Archives and Libraries, 2000. http://eprints.rclis.org/6283/.

Payne, Lizanne. "Winning the Space Race." American Libraries Magazine, September 23, 2014. https://americanlibrariesmagazine.org/2014/09/23/winning-the-space-race/.

Peters, Douglas P., and Stephen J. Ceci. "Peer-Review Practices of Psychological Journals: The Fate of Published Articles, Submitted Again." *Behavioral and Brain Sciences* 5, no. 2 (1982): 187–195. https://doi.org/10.1017/S0140525X00011183.

Philip, I. G. *The Bodleian Library in the Seventeenth and Eighteenth Centuries*. 1980–1981. Oxford: Oxford University Press, 1983.

Phillips, Rasheedah. "Future." In *Keywords for Radicals: The Contested Vocabulary of Late Capitalist Struggle*, edited by Kelly Fritsch, Clare O'Connor, and A. K. Thompson, 167–174. Oakland, CA: AK Press, 2016.

Piper, Andrew. *Enumerations: Data and Literary Study*. Chicago: University of Chicago Press, 2018.

Piron, Florence. "Open Access in the Francophone Global South: Between Collective Empowerment and Neocolonialism." *News Service* (blog), February 14, 2018. https://blog.doaj.org/2018/02/14/open-access-in-the-francophone-global-south-between-collective-empowerment-and-neocolonialism/.

Piron, Florence. "Postcolonial Open Access." In *Open Divide: Critical Studies on Open Access*, edited by Joachim Schöpfel and Ulrich Herb, 117–126. Sacramento, CA: Library Juice Press, 2018. https://corpus.ulaval.ca/jspui/handle/20.500.11794/16178.

Piron, Florence, Antonin Benoît Diouf, Marie Sophie Dibounje Madiba, Thomas Hervé Mboa Nkoudou, Zoé Aubierge Ouangré, Djossè Roméo Tessy, Hamissou Rhissa Achaffert, Anderson Pierre, and Zakari Lire. "Le Libre Accès vu d'Afrique Francophone Subsaharienne." *Revue Française Des Sciences de l'information et de La Communication*, no. 11 (2017). https://doi.org/10.4000/rfsic.3292.

Piron, Florence, Thomas Hervé Mboa Nkoudou, Marie Sophie Dibounje Madiba, Judicaël Alladatin, Hamissou Rhissa Achaffert, and Anderson Pierre. "Toward African and Haitian Universities in Service to Sustainable Local Development: The Contribution of Fair Open Science." In *Contextualizing Openness: Situating Open Science*, edited by Leslie Chan, Angela Okune, Becky Hillyer, Denisse Albornoz, and Alejandro Posada, 311–331. Ottawa, ON: University of Ottawa Press, 2019. https://www.idrc.ca/en/book/contextualizing-openness-situating-open-science.

Piron, Florence, Samuel Régulus, Marie Sophie Dibounje Madiba, Thomas Hervé Mboa Nkoudou, Dany Rondeau, Marie-Claude Bernard, and Jean Jacques Demba.

Bibliography

Justice Cognitive, Libre Accès et Savoirs Locaux: Pour une Science Ouverte Juste, au Service du Développement Local Durable. Éditions science et bien commun, 2016. https://scienceetbiencommun.pressbooks.pub/justicecognitive1/.

Plantin, Jean-Christophe, Carl Lagoze, and Paul N. Edwards. "Re-Integrating Scholarly Infrastructure: The Ambiguous Role of Data Sharing Platforms." *Big Data & Society* 5, no. 1 (2018). https://doi.org/10.1177/2053951718756683.

Plantin, Jean-Christophe, Carl Lagoze, Paul N. Edwards, and Christian Sandvig. "Infrastructure Studies Meet Platform Studies in the Age of Google and Facebook." *New Media & Society* 20, no. 1 (2018): 293–310. https://doi.org/10.1177/1461444816661553.

Pollard, Alfred W. "The Regulation of the Book Trade in the Sixteenth Century." *The Library* 7, no. 25 (1916): 18–43. https://doi.org/10.1093/library/s3-VII.25.18.

Pollman, Elizabeth, and Jordan M. Barry. "Regulatory Entrepreneurship." SSRN Scholarly Paper. Rochester, NY: Social Science Research Network, March 3, 2016. https://papers.ssrn.com/abstract=2741987.

Pollock, Anne, and Banu Subramaniam. "Resisting Power, Retooling Justice: Promises of Feminist Postcolonial Technosciences." *Science, Technology, & Human Values* 41, no. 6 (2016): 951–966. https://doi.org/10.1177/0162243916657879.

Pomata, Gianna. "Observation Rising: Birth of an Epistemic Genre, ca. 1500–1650." In *Histories of Scientific Observation*, edited by Lorraine Daston and Elizabeth Lunbeck, 45–80. Chicago: University of Chicago Press, 2011.

Pomata, Gianna. "Praxis Historialis: The Uses of Historia in Early Modern Medicine." In *Historia: Empiricism and Erudition in Early Modern Europe*, edited by Gianna Pomata and Nancy G. Siraisi, 105–146. Transformations. Cambridge, MA: The MIT Press, 2005.

Pomata, Gianna, and Nancy G. Siraisi, eds. *Historia: Empiricism and Erudition in Early Modern Europe*. Transformations. Cambridge, MA: The MIT Press, 2005.

Pontille, David, and Didier Torny. "Behind the Scenes of Scientific Articles: Defining Categories of Fraud and Regulating Cases." *Revue d'Épidémiologie et de Santé Publique* 60, no. 4 (2012): 247–253.

Pontille, David, and Didier Torny. "The Blind Shall See! The Question of Anonymity in Journal Peer Review." *Ada: A Journal of Gender, New Media, and Technology* 4 (2014). https://doi.org/10.7264/N3542KVW.

Pontille, David, and Didier Torny. "From Manuscript Evaluation to Article Valuation: The Changing Technologies of Journal Peer Review." *Human Studies* 38, no. 1 (2015): 57–79. https://doi.org/10.1007/s10746-014-9335-z.

Poole, Alex H. "Now Is the Future Now? The Urgency of Digital Curation in the Digital Humanities." *Digital Humanities Quarterly* 7, no. 2 (2013).

Posada, Alejandro, and George Chen. "Inequality in Knowledge Production: The Integration of Academic Infrastructure by Big Publishers." OpenEdition Press, 2018. https://doi.org/10.4000/proceedings.elpub.2018.30.

Posner, Miriam. "Money and Time." *Miriam Posner's Blog*, March 13, 2016. http://miriamposner.com/blog/money-and-time/.

Prater, Scott. "How to Talk to IT about Digital Preservation." *Journal of Archival Organization* 14, no. 1–2 (2017): 90–101. https://doi.org/10.1080/15332748.2018.1528827.

Priego, Ernesto, Erin McKiernan, Alejandro Posada, Ricardo Hartley, Nuria Rodríguez Ortega, Domenico Fiormonte, Alex Gil, et al. "Scholarly Publishing, Freedom of Information and Academic Self-Determination: The UNAM-Elsevier Case." *Authorea*, 2017. https://doi.org/10.22541/au.151160332.22737207.

Priem, Jason, and Kaitlin Light Costello. "How and Why Scholars Cite on Twitter." *Proceedings of the American Society for Information Science and Technology* 47, no. 1 (2010): 1–4. https://doi.org/10.1002/meet.14504701201.

Priem, Jason, Dario Taraborelli, and Cameron Neylon. "Altmetrics: A Manifesto," October 26, 2010. http://altmetrics.org/manifesto/.

Priscilla, C. Yu. "History of Modern Librarianship in East Asia." *Library History* 24, no. 1 (2008): 64–77. https://doi.org/10.1179/174581608X295293.

Publons. "Global State of Peer Review," 2018. https://publons.com/static/Publons-Global-State-Of-Peer-Review-2018.pdf.

punctum books. "THREAD on What We Feel Is One of the Most Under-Attended Issues in the Academic Publishing Landscape: Author Compensation. How Can the World's Knowledge Increase When More than 70% of All Teaching Lines in the US Are Adjunctified & Many Post-PhD Scholars Have No Uni Employment?" Tweet. @*punctum_books* (blog), March 8, 2019. https://twitter.com/punctum_books/status/1104105017827643392.

Punzalan, Ricardo L., and Michelle Caswell. "Critical Directions for Archival Approaches to Social Justice." *The Library Quarterly* 86, no. 1 (2016): 25–42. https://doi.org/10.1086/684145.

Radical Open Access Collective. "About the Collective." Radical Open Access Collective. Accessed May 31, 2019. https://radicaloa.disruptivemedia.org.uk/about/.

Rainie, Lee. "Digital Divides—Feeding America." *Pew Research Center* (blog), February 9, 2017. https://www.pewinternet.org/2017/02/09/digital-divides-feeding-america/.

Raju, Reggie. "From Green to Gold to Diamond: Open Access's Return to Social Justice." Kuala Lumpur, Malaysia, 2018. http://library.ifla.org/2220/.

Raju, Reggie, Jaya Raju, and Jill Claassen. "Open Scholarship Practices Reshaping South Africa's Scholarly Publishing Roadmap." *Publications* 3, no. 4 (2015): 263–84. https://doi.org/10.3390/publications3040263.

Ranganathan, S. R. *The Five Laws of Library Science*. London: The Madras Library Association, 1931. https://catalog.hathitrust.org/Record/001661182.

Ransom, Harry. *The First Copyright Statute, an Essay on "An Act for the Encouragement of Learning," 1710*. Austin: University of Texas Press, 1956.

Rawls, John. "Justice as Fairness." *The Philosophical Review* 67, no. 2 (1958): 164–194. https://doi.org/10.2307/2182612.

Readings, Bill. *The University in Ruins*. Cambridge, MA: Harvard University Press, 1996.

Redalyc, CLACSO, and UNESCO. "AmeliCA—Conocimiento abierto para América Latina y el sur Global," 2019. http://www.amelica.org/.

Relman, Arnold S. "The Ingelfinger Rule." *New England Journal of Medicine* 305, no. 14 (1981): 824–826. https://doi.org/10.1056/NEJM198110013051408.

RELX Group. "Governance," 2017. https://www.relx.com/corporate-responsibility/being-a-responsible-business/governance.

Research Councils UK. "Pathways to Impact," n.d. http://www.rcuk.ac.uk/innovation/impacts/.

Research England. "Over 80% of Research Outputs Meet Requirements of REF 2021 Open Access Policy." UK Research and Innovation, June 14, 2018. https://re.ukri.org/news-events-publications/news/oa-report-130618/.

RIO. "Research Ideas and Outcomes." Accessed June 4, 2019. https://riojournal.com/.

Reuters. "Reed Elsevier Says to Exit Defence Industry Shows." *Reuters*, June 1, 2007. https://uk.reuters.com/article/uk-reedelsevier-defence-idUKL0135316020070601.

Ricci, Donato, Robin De Mourat, Christophe Leclercq, and Bruno Latour. "Clues. Anomalies. Understanding. Detecting Underlying Assumptions and Expected Practices in the Digital Humanities through the AIME Project." In *Designing Interactive Hypermedia Systems*, edited by Everardo Reyes-Garcia and Nasreddine Bouhaï, 185–211. Oxford: John Wiley & Sons, 2017. https://doi.org/10.1002/9781119388272.ch6.

Rieger, Oya Y. "arXiv User Survey Report." arXiv Wiki, 2016. https://confluence.cornell.edu/display/arxivpub/arXiv+User+Survey+Report.

Ritson, Sophie. "'Crackpots' and 'Active Researchers': The Controversy over Links between arXiv and the Scientific Blogosphere." *Social Studies of Science* 46, no. 4 (2016): 607–628. https://doi.org/10.1177/0306312716647508.

Robertson, Tara. "Not All Information Wants to Be Free: The Case Study of On Our Backs." In *Applying Library Values to Emerging Technology: Tips and Techniques for*

Advancing within Your Mission, edited by Kelly Tilton and Peter Fernandez, 225–239. Washington, DC: Association of College and Research Libraries, 2018.

Roe, George. "Challenging the Control of Knowledge in Colonial India: Political Ideas in the Work of S. R. Ranganathan." *Library & Information History* 26, no. 1 (2010): 18–32. https://doi.org/10.1179/175834909X12593371068342.

Rogers, Everett M. *Diffusion of Innovations*. New York: Simon and Schuster, 2003.

Rogers, Richard. "Otherwise Engaged: Social Media from Vanity Metrics to Critical Analytics." *International Journal of Communication* 12 (2018): 450–472.

Roh, Charlotte. "Library Publishing and Diversity Values: Changing Scholarly Publishing through Policy and Scholarly Communication Education." *College & Research Libraries News* 77, no. 2 (2016): 82–85. https://doi.org/10.5860/crln.77.2.9446.

Rose, Jonathan. *The Intellectual Life of the British Working Classes*. 2nd ed. New Haven, CT: Yale University Press, 2010.

Rose, Mark. *Authors and Owners: The Invention of Copyright*. Cambridge, MA: Harvard University Press, 1993.

Rosenberg, Diana. "Imposing Libraries: The Establishment of National Public Library Services in Africa, with Particular Reference to Kenya." *Third World Libraries* 4, no. 1 (1993): 35–44.

Ross-Hellauer, Tony. "What Is Open Peer Review? A Systematic Review." *F1000Research* 6 (2017): 588. https://doi.org/10.12688/f1000research.11369.2.

Røstvik, Camilla Mørk, and Aileen Fyfe. "Ladies, Gentlemen, and Scientific Publication at the Royal Society, 1945–1990." *Open Library of Humanities* 4, no. 1 (2018): 1–40. https://doi.org/10.16995/olh.265.

The Royal Society. "Council Minutes," March 19, 1751. RS CMO/4.

The Royal Society. "Council Minutes," June 25, 1761. RS CMO/4.

The Royal Society. "Council Minutes," December 12, 1765. RS CMO/4.

The Royal Society. "Council Minutes," June 22, 1797. RS CMO/8.

The Royal Society. "Council Minutes," July 15, 1802. RS CMO/8.

The Royal Society. "Council Minutes," December 20, 1849. RS CMP/2.

The Royal Society. "Council Minutes," March 21, 1878. RS CMP/5.

The Royal Society. "Council Minutes," June 20, 1895. RS CMP/7.

The Royal Society. "Council Minutes," March 20, 1902. RS CMP/8.

The Royal Society. "Distribution of Royal Society Publications 1947. Officers' Minutes," January 7, 1948. RS OM/2(48).

Bibliography

The Royal Society. "Minutes of the Publications Management Committee," July 21, 1993. RS PMC/24(93).

The Royal Society. "Recommended Reductions in Exchanges and Gifts of the Royal Society's Publications," 1954. RS OM/16(54).

The Royal Society. "Report of the Library Committee to Council," April 21, 1932. RS CMB/47/5.

The Royal Society. "Review of the Year," 2003.

The Royal Society. "Revision of the Lists of Exchanges and Gifts of the Royal Society's Publications," March 2, 1954. RS OM/14(54).

The Royal Society. "Royal Society Position Statement on 'Open Access'," November 24, 2005. https://web.archive.org/web/20060207171805/http://www.royalsoc.ac.uk/page.asp?id=3882.

The Royal Society. "Special Meeting of Officers Minutes: 3. Review of the Society's Finances," January 26, 1973. RS OM/16(73).

The Royal Society. "Trustees' Report and Financial Statements 2015–16," 2016. https://royalsociety.org/-/media/about-us/governance/trustees-report-2015-2016.pdf?la=en-GB&hash=82396A1A10887287879D8F973D72A2B0.

The Royal Society. "Undated Circulation Figures [before 12 Feb 1846]," n.d. RS CMB/86/A.

Rüegg, Walter. "Themes: The French and German University Models." In *Universities in the Nineteenth and Early Twentieth Centuries (1800–1945)*, edited by Walter Rüegg, Vol. 3. Cambridge: Cambridge University Press, 2004.

Ruff, Corinne. "Scholars Criticize Academia.Edu Proposal to Charge Authors for Recommendations." *The Chronicle of Higher Education*, January 29, 2016. https://www.chronicle.com/article/Scholars-Criticize/235102.

Russell, David R., Mary Lea, Jan Parker, Brian Street, and Tiane Donahue. "Exploring Notions of Genre in 'Academic Literacies' and 'Writing Across the Curriculum': Approaches Across Countries and Contexts." In *Genre in a Changing World*, edited by Charles Bazerman, Adair Bonini, and Débora Figueiredo, 459–491. Fort Collins, CO: WAC Clearinghouse/Parlor Press, 2009. http://wac.colostate.edu/books/genre/chapter20.pdf.

Sale, Arthur, Marc Couture, Eloy Rodrigues, Leslie Carr, and Stevan Harnad. "Open Access Mandates and the 'Fair Dealing' Button." *arXiv:1002.3074*, February 16, 2010. http://arxiv.org/abs/1002.3074.

Salo, Dorothea. "How to Scuttle a Scholarly-Communication Initiative." *Journal of Librarianship and Scholarly Communication* 1, no. 4 (2013). https://doi.org/10.7710/2162-3309.1075.

Salo, Dorothea. "Innkeeper at the Roach Motel." *Library Trends* 57, no. 2 (2008): 98–123. https://doi.org/10.1353/lib.0.0031.

Sample, Ian. "Harvard University Says It Can't Afford Journal Publishers' Prices." *The Guardian*, April 24, 2012. http://www.theguardian.com/science/2012/apr/24/harvard-university-journal-publishers-prices.

"San Francisco Declaration on Research Assessment: Putting Science into the Assessment of Research." San Francisco. Accessed February 18, 2016. http://www.ascb.org/files/SFDeclarationFINAL.pdf.

Santos, Fernanda. "Schools Eliminating Librarians as Budgets Shrink." *The New York Times*, June 24, 2011, sec. N.Y. / Region. https://www.nytimes.com/2011/06/25/nyregion/schools-eliminating-librarians-as-budgets-shrink.html.

Santos, Joana Vieira, and Paulo Nunes da Silva. "Issues with Publishing Abstracts in English: Challenges for Portuguese Linguists' Authorial Voices." *Publications* 4, no. 2 (2016). https://doi.org/10.3390/publications4020012.

Scheiding, Tom. "Paying for Knowledge One Page at a Time: The Author Fee in Physics in Twentieth-Century America." *Historical Studies in the Natural Sciences* 39, no. 2 (2009): 219–247. https://doi.org/10.1525/hsns.2009.39.2.219.

Schiermeier, Quirin. "US Court Grants Elsevier Millions in Damages from Sci-Hub." *Nature News*, June 22, 2017. https://doi.org/10.1038/nature.2017.22196.

ScholarLed. "Open Infrastructure Development." ScholarLed. Accessed May 31, 2019. https://scholarled.org/#infrastructure.

Scholarly Publishing, Academic Resources Coalition, Public Library of Science, and Open Access Scholarly Publishers Association. "HowOpenisit?" Public Library of Science, 2014. https://www.plos.org/files/HowOpenIsIt_English.pdf.

Scholz, Trevor. "Platform Cooperativism: Challenging the Corporate Sharing Economy," 2016. http://www.rosalux-nyc.org/platform-cooperativism-2/.

Schöneberg, Julia. "Decolonising Teaching Pedagogies—Convivial Reflections." *Convivial Thinking* (blog), August 14, 2018. https://www.convivialthinking.org/index.php/2018/08/14/decolonising-teaching-pedagogies-convivial-reflections/.

Schonfeld, Roger C. "Reflections on 'Elsevier Acquires Bepress.'" 2017. https://sr.ithaka.org/blog/reflections-on-elsevier-acquires-bepress/.

Schonfeld, Roger C. "A Taxonomy of University Presses Today," 2017. http://www.sr.ithaka.org/blog/a-taxonomy-of-university-presses-today/.

Schönfelder, Nina. "APCs—Mirroring the Impact Factor or Legacy of the Subscription-Based Model? Regression Analysis." *National Contact Point Open Access* (blog), January 21, 2019. https://oa2020-de.org/en/blog/2019/01/21/APCregressionanalysis/.

Bibliography

Schroter, Sara, Nick Black, Stephen Evans, Fiona Godlee, Lyda Osorio, and Richard Smith. "What Errors Do Peer Reviewers Detect, and Does Training Improve Their Ability to Detect Them?" *Journal of the Royal Society of Medicine* 101, no. 10 (2008): 507–514. https://doi.org/10.1258/jrsm.2008.080062.

Schwab, Klaus. *The Fourth Industrial Revolution*. New York: Crown Business, 2017.

Schweizer, Bobby. "Platforms." In *The Routledge Companion to Video Game Studies*, edited by Mark J. P. Wolf and Bernard Perron, 41–48. Abingdon, UK: Routledge, 2010. https://doi.org/10.4324/9780203114261.

SciELO. "Bibliography about SciELO." SciELO. Accessed June 2, 2019. https://www.scielo.org/en/about-scielo/bibliography-about-scielo/.

SciELO. "¿Porqué XML?" *SciELO En Perspectiva* (blog), April 4, 2014. https://blog.scielo.org/es/2014/04/04/porque-xml/.

SciELO. "Priority Lines of Action." SciELO 20, August 17, 2018. https://www.scielo20.org/redescielo/wp-content/uploads/sites/2/2018/09/L%C3%ADneas-prioritaris-de-acci%C3%B3n-2019-2023_en.pdf.

SciELO. "Rebuttal to the Blog Post 'Is SciELO a Publication Favela?' Authored by Jeffrey Beall." *SciELO in Perspective* (blog), August 25, 2015. http://blog.scielo.org/en/2015/08/25/rebuttal-to-the-blog-post-is-scielo-a-publication-favela-authored-by-jeffrey-beall/.

Science Ouverte Haïti Afrique. "Projet SOHA." Accessed June 1, 2019. https://www.scielo.org/en/about-scielo/bibliography-about-scielo/.

Searle, John R. *Speech Acts: An Essay in the Philosophy of Language*. Cambridge: Cambridge University Press, 1969.

Secord, James A. "Science, Technology and Mathematics." In *The Cambridge History of the Book in Britain*, edited by David McKitterick, 443–474. Cambridge: Cambridge University Press, 2009. https://doi.org/10.1017/CHOL9780521866248.014.

Seem, Mark. "Introduction." In *Anti-Oedipus: Capitalism and Schizophrenia*, by Gilles Deleuze and Félix Guattari, translated by Robert Hurley, Mark Seem, and Helen R. Lane. Minneapolis: University of Minnesota Press, 1983.

Segaran, Toby, Colin Evans, and Jamie Taylor. *Programming the Semantic Web*. Sebastopol, CA: O'Reilly Media, 2009.

Senack, Ethan. "Student Group Releases New Report on Textbook Prices." U.S. PIRG, February 3, 2016. https://uspirg.org/news/usp/student-group-releases-new-report-textbook-prices.

Severin, Anna, Matthias Egger, Martin Paul Eve, and Daniel Hürlimann. "Discipline-Specific Open Access Publishing Practices and Barriers to Change: An Evidence-Based Review." *F1000Research* 7 (2018): 1925. https://doi.org/10.12688/f1000research.17328.1.

Seville, Catherine. "The Statute of Anne: Rhetoric and Reception in the Nineteenth Century." *Houston Law Review* 47 (2011): 819–875.

Shapin, Steven, and Simon Schaffer. *Leviathan and the Air-Pump: Hobbes, Boyle, and the Experimental Life.* Princeton, NJ: Princeton University Press, 1985.

Shared Intelligence. "Access to Research: A Report to the Publishers Licensing Society and the Society of Chief Librarians," 2015. https://www.pls.org.uk/media/199841/Access-to-Research-final-report-Oct-2015.pdf.

Shashok, Karen. "Can Scientists and Their Institutions Become Their Own Open Access Publishers?" *arXiv:1701.02461*, January 10, 2017. http://arxiv.org/abs/1701.02461.

Sheffield, Rebecka T. "More than Acid-Free Folders: Extending the Concept of Preservation to Include the Stewardship of Unexplored Histories." *Library Trends* 64, no. 3 (2016): 572–584. https://doi.org/10.1353/lib.2016.0001.

Shenk, Timothy. "What Exactly Is Neoliberalism?" Dissent Magazine, April 2, 2015. https://www.dissentmagazine.org/blog/booked-3-what-exactly-is-neoliberalism-wendy-brown-undoing-the-demos.

Shera, Jesse H. *Foundations of The Public Library—The Origins of The Public Library Movement In New England 1629–1855.* Chicago: University of Chicago Press, 1949.

Sherman, Brad, and Leanne Wiseman. "Fair Copy: Protecting Access to Scientific Information in Post-War Britain." *Modern Law Review* 73, no. 2 (2010): 240–261.

Shore, Elliott, and Heather Joseph. "Positive Changes for SPARC's Operating Structure." SPARC, June 17, 2014. https://sparcopen.org/news/2014/positive-changes-for-sparcs-operating-structure/.

SIDALC. "About." Alliance of Agricultural Information and Documentation Services of the Americas. Accessed May 12, 2019. http://www.sidalc.net/en/aboutsidalc.

Siles, Ignacio. "From Online Filter to Web Format: Articulating Materiality and Meaning in the Early History of Blogs." *Social Studies of Science* 41, no. 5 (2011): 737–758. https://doi.org/10.1177/0306312711420190.

Smith, Arthur P. "The Journal as an Overlay on Preprint Databases." *Learned Publishing* 13, no. 1 (2000): 43–48. https://doi.org/10.1087/09531510050145542.

Smith, Gavin J. D. "Surveillance, Data and Embodiment: On the Work of Being Watched." *Body & Society* 22, no. 2 (2016): 108–139. https://doi.org/10.1177/1357034X15623622.

Smith, Kevin L., and Katherine A. Dickson, eds. *Open Access and the Future of Scholarly Communication: Implementation.* Creating the 21st-Century Academic Library 10. Lanham, MD: Rowman & Littlefield, 2017.

Smith, Linda Tuhiwai. *Decolonizing Methodologies: Research and Indigenous Peoples.* London: Zed Books, 2012.

Smith, Pamela H. *The Body of the Artisan*. Chicago: University of Chicago Press, 2004.

Speck, Bruce W., ed. *Publication Peer Review: An Annotated Bibliography*. Westport, CT: Greenwood Press, 1993.

SpringerNature. "Prospectus Dated April 25, 2018," 2018.

Srnicek, Nick. *Platform Capitalism*. Theory Redux. Cambridge: Polity, 2017.

Star, Susan Leigh. "The Ethnography of Infrastructure." *American Behavioral Scientist* 43, no. 3 (1999): 377–391. https://doi.org/10.1177/00027649921955326.

Star, Susan Leigh, and Karen Ruhleder. "Steps toward an Ecology of Infrastructure: Design and Access for Large Information Spaces." *Information Systems Research* 7, no. 1 (1996): 111–134. https://doi.org/10.1287/isre.7.1.111.

Starr, Joan. "Libraries and National Security: An Historical Review." *First Monday* 9, no. 12 (2004). https://doi.org/10.5210/fm.v9i12.1198.

Stephen, Bijan. "Kickstarter Will Not Voluntarily Recognize Its Employee Union." The Verge, May 15, 2019. https://www.theverge.com/2019/5/15/18627052/kickstarter-union-nlrb-election.

Sterne, Jonathan. *MP3: The Meaning of a Format*. Durham, NC: Duke University Press, 2012.

Stoler, Ann Laura. *Along the Archival Grain: Epistemic Anxieties and Colonial Common Sense*. Princeton, NJ: Princeton University Press, 2009.

Straumsheim, Carl. "Amid Declining Book Sales, University Presses Search for New Ways to Measure Success." Inside Higher Ed, August 1, 2016. https://www.insidehighered.com/news/2016/08/01/amid-declining-book-sales-university-presses-search-new-ways-measure-success.

Stuller, W. Stuart. "High School Academic Freedom: The Evolution of a Fish Out of Water." *Nebraska Law Review* 77, no. 2 (1998): 301–343.

Suber, Peter. *Open Access*. Essential Knowledge Series. Cambridge, MA: The MIT Press, 2012. http://bit.ly/oa-book.

Suber, Peter. Open Access When Authors Are Paid." *SPARC Open Access Newsletter*, no. 68 (December 2, 2003). http://dash.harvard.edu/handle/1/4552040.

Suber, Peter. "The Taxpayer Argument for Open Access." *SPARC Open Access Newsletter*, no. 65 (September 4, 2003). http://dash.harvard.edu/handle/1/4725013.

Suber, Peter. "Timeline." Open Access Directory. Accessed May 31, 2019. http://oad.simmons.edu/oadwiki/Timeline.

Suber, Peter, Patrick O. Brown, Diane Cabell, Aravinda Chakravarti, Barbara Cohen, Tony Delamothe, Michael Eisen, et al. "Bethesda Statement on Open Access Publishing," 2003. http://dash.harvard.edu/handle/1/4725199.

Sulistyo-Basuki, L. "The Rise and Growth of Libraries in Pre-War Indonesia." *Library History* 14, no. 1 (1998): 55–64. https://doi.org/10.1179/lib.1998.14.1.55.

Takats, Sean. "A Digital Humanities Tenure Case, Part 2: Letters and Committees." *The Quintessence of Ham* (blog), February 7, 2013. http://quintessenceofham.org/2013/02/07/a-digital-humanities-tenure-case-part-2-letters-and-committees/.

Tauberer, Joshua. *What Is RDF and What Is It Good For?* 2014. Reprint, Github, 2008. https://github.com/JoshData/rdfabout.

Taylor, Diana. *The Archive and the Repertoire: Performing Cultural Memory in the Americas*. Durham, NC: Duke University Press, 2003.

Taylor, Mike. "Academic Publishers Have Become the Enemies of Science." *The Guardian*, January 16, 2012, sec. Science. https://www.theguardian.com/science/2012/jan/16/academic-publishers-enemies-science.

Taylor, Mike. "Christy Collins, Mother and M-CM Patient Advocate." *Who Needs Access? You Need Access!* (blog), April 26, 2012. https://whoneedsaccess.org/2012/04/26/christy-collins-mother-and-m-cm-patient-advocate/.

Teixeira da Silva, Jaime A., and Panagiotis Tsigaris. "What Value Do Journal Whitelists and Blacklists Have in Academia?" *Journal of Academic Librarianship* 44, no. 6 (2018): 781–792. https://doi.org/10.1016/j.acalib.2018.09.017.

Tennant, Jonathan P., Jonathan M. Dugan, Daniel Graziotin, Damien C. Jacques, François Waldner, Daniel Mietchen, Yehia Elkhatib, et al. "A Multi-Disciplinary Perspective on Emergent and Future Innovations in Peer Review." *F1000Research* 6 (2017): 1151. https://doi.org/10.12688/f1000research.12037.3.

Theimer, Kate. "Two Meanings of 'Archival Silences' and Their Implications." *ArchivesNext* (blog), March 27, 2012.

Theobald, Sally, Neal Brandes, Margaret Gyapong, Sameh El-Saharty, Enola Proctor, Theresa Diaz, Samuel Wanji, et al. "Implementation Research: New Imperatives and Opportunities in Global Health." *The Lancet* 392, no. 10160 (2018): 2214–2228. https://doi.org/10.1016/S0140-6736(18)32205-0.

Thiede, Malina. "Preservation in Practice: A Survey of New York City Digital Humanities Researchers—In the Library with the Lead Pipe." *In the Library with the Lead Pipe* (blog), May 17, 2017. http://inthelibrarywiththeleadpipe.org/2017/preservation-in-practice-a-survey-of-new-york-city-digital-humanities-researchers/.

Thomas, Deborah A. "Time and the Otherwise: Plantations, Garrisons and Being Human in the Caribbean." *Anthropological Theory* 16, no. 2–3 (2016): 177–200. https://doi.org/10.1177/1463499616636269.

Tkacz, Nathaniel. "From Open Source to Open Government: A Critique of Open Politics." *Ephemera: Theory and Politics in Organization* 12, no. 4 (2012): 386–405.

Tlostanova, Madina V., and Walter D. Mignolo. *Learning to Unlearn: Decolonial Reflections from Eurasia and the Americas*. Columbus: Ohio State University Press, 2012.

Tobias, Manuela. "Comparing Facebook Data Use by Obama, Cambridge Analytica." PolitFact, March 22, 2018. https://www.politifact.com/truth-o-meter/statements/2018/mar/22/meghan-mccain/comparing-facebook-data-use-obama-cambridge-analyt/.

Toshkov, Dimiter. "The 'Global South' Is a Terrible Term. Don't Use It!" *RE-DESIGN* (blog), November 6, 2018. http://re-design.dimiter.eu/?p=969.

Traue, J. E. "The Public Library Explosion in Colonial New Zealand." *Libraries & the Cultural Record* 42, no. 2 (2007): 151–164.

Traynor, Cath, Laura Foster, and Tobias Schonwetter. "Tensions Related to Openness in Researching Indigenous Peoples' Knowledge Systems and Intellectual Property Rights." In *Contextualizing Openness: Situating Open Science*, edited by Leslie Chan, Angela Okune, Becky Hillyer, Denisse Albornoz, and Alejandro Posada, 223–236. Ottawa, ON: University of Ottawa Press, 2019. https://www.idrc.ca/en/book/contextualizing-openness-situating-open-science.

Tribe, Laurence H. *American Constitutional Law*. 2nd ed. St. Paul, MN: West Academic Publishing, 1988.

Troll Covey, Denise. "Opening the Dissertation: Overcoming Cultural Calcification and Agoraphobia." *TripleC: Communication, Capitalism & Critique* 11, no. 2 (2013): 543–557. https://doi.org/10.31269/triplec.v11i2.522.

Tuana, Nancy. "The Speculum of Ignorance: The Women's Health Movement and Epistemologies of Ignorance." *Hypatia* 21, no. 3 (2006): 1–19. https://doi.org/10.1111/j.1527-2001.2006.tb01110.x.

Tuck, Eve, and K. Wayne Yang. "R-Words: Refusing Research." In *Humanizing Research: Decolonizing Qualitative Inquiry with Youth and Communities*, 223–248. London: SAGE, 2014.

UC Council of University Librarians. "Pathways to Open Access," February 27, 2018. https://libraries.universityofcalifornia.edu/content/uc-libraries-release-pathways-oa-analysis.

Underwood, Ted. *Distant Horizons: Digital Evidence and Literary Change*. Chicago: University of Chicago Press, 2019.

Underwood, Ted. "A Genealogy of Distant Reading." *Digital Humanities Quarterly* 11, no. 2 (2017). http://www.digitalhumanities.org/dhq/vol/11/2/000317/000317.html.

UNESCO. "Fact Sheet Sub-Saharan Africa Strong Foundations: Early Childhood Care and Education." Accessed May 13, 2019. https://en.unesco.org/gem-report/sites/gem-report/files/fact_sheet_ssa.pdf.

United Nations. "Overview of OA in Latin America and the Caribbean." United Nations Educational, Scientific and Cultural Organization. Accessed May 12, 2019. http://www.unesco.org/new/en/communication-and-information/portals-and-platforms/goap/access-by-region/latin-america-and-the-caribbean/.

United Nations. "Sustainable Development Goals." UNDP. Accessed May 12, 2019. https://www.undp.org/content/undp/en/home/sustainable-development-goals.html.

United Nations Refugee Agency. "Figures at a Glance." UNHCR. Accessed April 29, 2019. https://www.unhcr.org/figures-at-a-glance.html.

United States Court of Appeals. 598 F.2d 535, Cary, et al. v. Board of Education of Adams-Arapahoe School District, et al. (December 31, 1969).

United States of America. "U.S. Constitution: Article 1 Section 8." The U.S. Constitution Online, 2010. http://www.usconstitution.net/xconst_A1Sec8.html?ModPagespeed=noscript.

University of California Libraries. "Pay It Forward: Investigating a Sustainable Model of Open Access Article Processing Charges for Large North American Research Institutions." IATUL—International Association of University Libraries, June 30, 2016. https://www.iatul.org/about/news/pay-it-forward-investigating-sustainable-model-open-access-article-processing-charges.

University of California Press. "Luminos FAQ." Luminos OA. Accessed May 31, 2019. https://www.luminosoa.org/site/faqs/#author-faqs-open-access.

Van de Sompel, Herbert, and Carl Lagoze. "The Santa Fe Convention of the Open Archives Initiative." *D-Lib Magazine* 6, no. 2 (2000). https://doi.org/10.1045/february2000-vandesompel-oai.

Van Noorden, Richard. "Online Collaboration: Scientists and the Social Network." *Nature News* 512, no. 7513 (2014): 126. https://doi.org/10.1038/512126a.

Vasen, Federico. "The 'Ivory Tower' as Safe Bet: Science Policies and Research Evaluation in Mexico." *Education Policy Analysis Archives* 26, no. 96 (2018): 1–27. https://doi.org/10.14507/epaa.26.3594.

Vélez-Cuartas, Gabriel, Diana Lucio-Arias, and Loet Leydesdorff. "Regional and Global Science: Publications from Latin America and the Caribbean in the SciELO Citation Index and the Web of Science." *El Profesional de La Información* 25, no. 1 (2016). https://doi.org/10.3145/epi.2016.ene.05.

Vessuri, Hebe, Jean-Claude Guédon, and Ana María Cetto. "Excellence or Quality? Impact of the Current Competition Regime on Science and Scientific Publishing in Latin America and Its Implications for Development." *Current Sociology* 62, no. 5 (2014): 647–665. https://doi.org/10.1177/0011392113512839.

Visvanathan, Shiv. "The Search for Cognitive Justice." India Seminar, 2009. http://www.india-seminar.com/2009/597/597_shiv_visvanathan.htm.

Wallerstein, Immanuel Maurice. *World-Systems Analysis: An Introduction*. Durham, NC: Duke University Press, 2004.

Waltham, Mary. "What Do Society and Association Members Really Want?" *Learned Publishing* 21, no. 1 (2008): 7–14. https://doi.org/10.1087/095315108X247294.

Ware, Mark. "Peer Review in Scholarly Journals: Perspective of the Scholarly Community—Results from an International Study." *Information Services & Use* 28 (2008): 109–112. https://doi.org/10.3233/ISU-2008-0568.

Wasserman, Howard. "SSRN Postings and Copyright." PrawfsBlawg, July 15, 2016. https://prawfsblawg.blogs.com/prawfsblawg/2016/07/ssrn-postings-and-copyright.html.

Waterhouse, Penny. "Homes for Local Radical Action: The Position and Role of Local Umbrella Groups." National Coalition for Independent Action, Inquiry into the Future of Voluntary Services, June 2014. http://www.independentaction.net/wp-content/uploads/sites/8/2014/08/Role-of-local-umbrella-groups-final.pdf.

Watts, Iain P. "'We Want No Authors': William Nicholson and the Contested Role of the Scientific Journal in Britain, 1797–1813." *The British Journal for the History of Science* 47, no. 3 (2014): 397–419. https://doi.org/10.1017/S0007087413000964.

Weinberger, David. "Library as Platform." Library Journal, September 4, 2012. https://lj.libraryjournal.com/2012/09/future-of-libraries/by-david-weinberger/.

Weller, Ann C. "Editorial Peer Review: Its Strengths and Weaknesses." *Journal of the Medical Library Association* 90, no. 1 (2002): 115.

Weller, Martin. *The Battle for Open: How Openness Won and Why It Doesn't Feel Like Victory*. London: Ubiquity Press, 2014. https://doi.org/10.5334/bam.

Wellmon, Chad. *Organizing Enlightenment: Information Overload and the Invention of the Modern Research University*. Baltimore, MD: Johns Hopkins University Press, 2015.

West, Jevin D., Jennifer Jacquet, Molly M. King, Shelley J. Correll, and Carl T. Bergstrom. "The Role of Gender in Scholarly Authorship." *PLOS ONE* 8, no. 7 (2013): e66212. https://doi.org/10.1371/journal.pone.0066212.

"Who Needs Access? You Need Access!" Accessed April 21, 2016. https://whoneedsaccess.org/.

Whyte, Kyle Powys. "Systematic Discrimination in Peer Review: Some Reflections." Daily Nous, May 7, 2017. http://dailynous.com/2017/05/07/systematic-discrimination-peer-review-reflections/.

Wiegand, Wayne. *Part of Our Lives: A People's History of the American Public Library*. Oxford: Oxford University Press, 2015.

Williams, Mita. "Why I Think Faculty and Librarians Should Not Host Their Work on Academic.Edu or Researchgate.Com," November 20, 2015. http://librarian.newjackalmanac.ca/2015/11/why-i-think-faculty-and-librarians.html.

Willinsky, John. *The Access Principle: The Case for Open Access to Research and Scholarship*. Digital Libraries and Electronic Publishing. Cambridge, MA: The MIT Press, 2006.

Willinsky, John. *The Intellectual Properties of Learning: A Prehistory from Saint Jerome to John Locke*. Chicago: University of Chicago Press, 2017.

Wilsdon, James. "Independent Review of the Role of Metrics in Research Assessment," 2015. http://dx.doi.org/10.4135/9781473978782.

Windle, Joel. "Hidden Features in Global Knowledge Production: (Re)Positioning Theory and Practice in Academic Writing." *Revista Brasileira de Linguística Aplicada* 17, no. 2 (2017): 355–378. https://doi.org/10.1590/1984-6398201610966.

Winn, Joss. "Mass Intellectuality." *Josswinn.Org* (blog), June 4, 2014. https://josswinn.org/2014/06/04/mass-intellectuality/.

Winn, Joss, and Richard Hall, eds. *Mass Intellectuality and Democratic Leadership in Higher Education*. London: Bloomsbury, 2017.

Wolff, Christine, Alisa Rod, and Roger Schonfeld. "Ithaka S+R US Faculty Survey 2015." New York: Ithaka S+R, April 4, 2016. https://doi.org/10.18665/sr.277685.

Woodward, Colin. "Huge Number of Maine Public Records Have Likely Been Destroyed." *Press Herald* (blog), December 30, 2018. https://www.pressherald.com/2018/12/30/huge-number-of-maine-public-records-have-likely-been-destroyed/.

Woolhouse, R. S. *Locke: A Biography*. Cambridge: Cambridge University Press, 2007.

Working Group on Expanding Access to Published Research Findings ("Finch Group"). "Accessibility, Sustainability, Excellence: How to Expand Access to Research Publications," August 20, 2012. https://doi.org/10.2436/20.1501.01.187.

Worstall, Tim. "Facebook Is Free Therefore It Is You Getting Sold." Forbes, November 10, 2012. https://www.forbes.com/sites/timworstall/2012/11/10/facebook-is-free-therefore-it-is-you-getting-sold/.

Wouters, Paul Franciscus. "The Citation Culture." PhD diss., University of Amsterdam, 1999.

Wouters, Paul, Zohreh Zahedi, and Rodrigo Costas. "Social Media Metrics for New Research Evaluation." In *Springer Handbook of Science and Technology Indicators*, edited by Wolfgang Glanzel, Henk F. Moed, Ulrich Schmoch, and Michael Thelwall. Berlin: Springer International Publishing, 2019.

Wulf, Karin, and Alice Meadows. "Seven Things Every Researcher Should Know About Scholarly Publishing." The Scholarly Kitchen, March 21, 2016. https:

//scholarlykitchen.sspnet.org/2016/03/21/seven-things-every-researcher-should-know-about-scholarly-publishing/.

Yankah, Kwesi. "African Folk and the Challenges of a Global Lore." *Africa Today* 46, no. 2 (1999): 9–27. https://doi.org/10.1353/at.1999.0017.

Year Book of the Royal Society of London. London: Harrisons and Sons, 1908.

Young, Iris Marion. "Responsibility and Global Justice: A Social Connection Model." *Social Philosophy and Policy* 23, no. 1 (2006): 102. https://doi.org/10.1017/S0265052506060043.

Zajko, Mike. "The Copyright Surveillance Industry." *Media and Communication* 3, no. 2 (2015): 42. https://doi.org/10.17645/mac.v3i2.270.

Zanetti, Cristiano. *Janello Torriani and the Spanish Empire: A Vitruvian Artisan at the Dawn of the Scientific Revolution.* Nuncius Series: Studies and Sources in the Material and Visual History of Science, volume 2. Leiden: Brill, 2017.

Žarkov, Dubravka. "On Intellectual Labour and Neoliberalism in Academia—Or, in Praise of Reviewers." *European Journal of Women's Studies* 22, no. 3 (2015): 269–273. https://doi.org/10.1177/1350506815591920.

Zenodo. "Zenodo—Research. Shared." Accessed June 4, 2019. https://zenodo.org/.

Contributors

Eduardo Aguado-López is the general director of Redalyc and a member of the National System of Researchers SNI of Mexico. He holds a doctorate in higher education from the Center for Research and Teaching in Humanities, Mexico and earned a master's degree in sociology from UAEM. Eduardo is professor-researcher of the School of Political and Social Sciences at UAEM, a founder and director of the Network of Scientific Journals from Latin America and the Caribbean, Spain and Portugal, Redalyc. He is the cofounder of AmeliCA Open Knowledge S. C. He was awarded the distinction of "Doctor Caracciolo Parra and Olmedo, Rector Heroico" in 2011 by the Universidad de los Andes, Venezuela for the Dissemination of Latin American Science. He was awarded the National Book Award Venezuela, in the category of Scientific-Technical Book. He has published several research papers and books on bibliometrics, open access, alternative metrics and epistemology, among others; and he has participated in several keynote presentations at national and international conferences.

Denisse Albornoz is an international development specialist and sociologist from the University of Toronto. Her research addresses power dynamics and inequality in the production of technology, data, and knowledge and its impact on vulnerable or disenfranchised communities. She was a research associate for the IDRC and DFID-funded Open and Collaborative Science in Development Network (OCSDNet) (2014–2018), coeditor for the open-access book *Contextualizing Openness* (University of Ottawa Press), and one of the cofounders of the Knowledge G.A.P. project (2017–2018). Denisse is currently the research director of the digital rights NGO Hiperderecho (Lima, Peru) and is leading research and programs that champion access to justice for data and technology users in Peru, with a focus on women, the LGBTQ community, at-risk youth, and the urban poor.

Penny C. S. Andrews researches politics, fandom, internet cultures, gender, and social media. They have bylines as a freelance journalist in the Independent, Slate, New Statesman, Prospect, the Times, Popula, and more. On Twitter, they are @pennyb.

Dominique Babini is from Argentina, holding a doctorate in political science and a postgraduate qualification in scientific information. She is an open-access advisor at

CLACSO, where she has developed the digital repository and coordinates the International Open Access Campaign. Dominique is a member of the International Scientific Committee of REDALYC, of the REDALYC-CLACSO collection of 940 Latin American SSH journals, and the CLACSO representative in AMELI-Open Knowledge. She conducts research on open access scholarly communications at the University of Buenos Aires-IIGG and is a member of the Expert Committee of the National System of Digital Repositories-MINCYT of Argentina; the DORA-San Francisco Declaration on Research Assessment Advisory Committee, and Coalition Publi.ca (Canada) International Committee.

Arianna Becerril-García is full-time professor-researcher at the Autonomous University of the State of Mexico (UAEM). She is executive director and cofounder of the Network of Scientific Journals from Latin America and the Caribbean, Spain and Portugal, Redalyc, and a member of the National System of Researchers (SNI) of Mexico. She holds a PhD and an MSc in Computer Science from the Tecnológico de Monterrey, Mexico and is a computing engineer at UAEM. She is founder and chair of AmeliCA Conocimiento Abierto S.C. She is cofounder of the Mexican Network of Institutional Repositories (REMERI) and a member of the committee of InvestInOpenInfrastructure (IOI), and a representative member of Latin America in The Global Sustainability Coalition for Open Science Services (SCOSS). Her research output consists of numerous research papers, books, book chapters, and software applications on open access, technologies for scholarly publications, interoperability, artificial intelligence, information retrieval, the semantic web and Linked Open Data; as well as different keynote participations at national and international conferences.

Leslie Chan is an associate professor at the Centre for Critical Development Studies at the University of Toronto Scarborough. His teaching and professional practice centers on the role of "openness" in the design of inclusive knowledge infrastructure, and the implications for the production and flow of knowledge and their impact on local and international development. An original signatory of the Budapest Open Access Initiative, Leslie is active in the experimentation and implementation of scholarly communication initiatives of varying scales around the world. He serves as director of Bioline International, an international collaborative open-access platform since 2000. He was the PI of the Open and Collaborative Science in Development Network, and the PI of the Knowledge G.A.P project. He serves on the advisory board of the Directory of Open Access Journals and the San Francisco Declaration on Research Assessment. He is also a member of the steering group on Investing in Open Infrastructure. Leslie has published widely on topics related to open access, knowledge equity, and the South/North asymmetry in knowledge production and circulation.

Jill Claassen has worked at University of Cape Town (UCT) Libraries as the section manager of scholarly communication and research since November 2014. One of the sections she oversees is scholarly communication and publishing, which is responsible for implementing UCT's open-access policy by making UCT's scholarship discoverable through the institutional repository, OpenUCT, which already has over 25,000 scholarly works openly available. This section also has an open-access publishing service, which includes publishing open journals and open monographs and textbooks. The philosophy of this publishing service is to share African scholarship, by making it accessible to everyone on the continent and the world, thus ensuring that Africa's scholarly output is visible and contributes to the global knowledge economy. Currently there are five emerging journals, 10 monographs and two textbooks on the publishing platforms. Jill is the co-servicing officer of SPARC Africa's executive committee since 2017, which aims to advance scholarly communication on the continent. Prior to moving to UCT Libraries, she worked at the University of the Western Cape's library as the institutional repository manager from 2012 to 2014. During this period, the library played a significant role in advocating for open access at the university, including the signing of the Berlin Declaration and passing an open-access policy. Jill is a registered PhD candidate in Library and Information Science and her research is on developing an open-access publishing model for Africa.

Emily Drabinski is critical pedagogy librarian at the Graduate Center, City University of New York where she also serves as liaison to the School of Labor and Urban Studies. Drabinski sits on the editorial board of *Radical Teacher*, a journal of socialist, feminist, and antiracist pedagogy. She also edits *Gender and Sexuality in Information Studies*, a book series from Library Juice Press/Litwin Books.

Martin Paul Eve is professor of literature, technology and publishing at Birkbeck, University of London and visiting professor of Digital Humanities at Sheffield Hallam University. He holds a PhD from the University of Sussex, is the author of five books, including *Open Access and the Humanities: Contexts, Controversies and the Future*, and a cofounder and CEO of the Open Library of Humanities. In 2018, he was awarded the KU Leuven Medal of Honour in the Humanities and the Social Sciences for his work on open access and in 2019 was awarded the Philip Leverhulme Prize.

Kathleen Fitzpatrick is director of digital humanities and professor of English at Michigan State University and author of *Generous Thinking: A Radical Approach to Saving the University* (Johns Hopkins University Press, 2019), *Planned Obsolescence: Publishing, Technology, and the Future of the Academy* (NYU Press, 2011) and *The Anxiety of Obsolescence: The American Novel in the Age of Television* (Vanderbilt University Press, 2006). She is project director of Humanities Commons, an open-access, open-source network serving more than 20,000 scholars and practitioners around the world. She is a member of the board of directors of the Council on Library and Information Resources and of the Educopia Institute and is vice-president/president-elect of the Association for Computers and the Humanities.

Aileen Fyfe is a historian of science, technology, and publishing, and professor of modern history at the University of St Andrews, UK. She has written about the history of science communication and popularization in nineteenth-century Britain, including the prize-winning *Steam-Powered Knowledge: William Chambers and the*

Business of Publishing 1820–1860 (2012). Her current research investigates the history of academic publishing from the seventeenth century to the present day, including the financial models underpinning scientific journals, their editorial and reviewing processes, and the role of learned society publishers. She is the author of various articles about the history of Royal Society publishing, and lead-author of the 2017 briefing paper *Untangling Academic Publishing: A History of the Relationship Between Commercial Interests, Academic Prestige and the Circulation of Research*.

Jonathan Gray is lecturer in critical infrastructure studies at the Department of Digital Humanities, King's College London, where he is currently writing a book on data worlds. He is also cofounder of the Public Data Lab; and research associate at the Digital Methods Initiative (University of Amsterdam) and the médialab (Sciences Po, Paris). More about his work can be found at jonathangray.org and he tweets at @jwyg.

April M. Hathcock works at the intersection of libraries, scholarly communication, law, and social justice. She is currently the director of scholarly communications and information policy at New York University, where she educates the campus community on issues of ownership, access, and rights in the research lifecycle. Before entering librarianship, she practiced intellectual property and antitrust law for a global private firm. Her research interests include diversity and inclusion in librarianship, cultural creation and exchange, and the ways in which social and legal infrastructures benefit the works of certain groups over others. She is a 2018 *Library Journal* Mover and Shaker, as well as the author of the article "White Librarianship in Blackface: Diversity Initiatives in LIS" and the blog *At the Intersection*, which examines issues at the intersection of feminism, libraries, social justice, and the law.

John Holmwood is professor of sociology at the University of Nottingham. He was the cofounder of the Campaign for the Public University (https://publicuniversity.org.uk/), and the cofounder and joint managing editor of Discover Society (https://discoversociety.org/), a free online magazine of social research, commentary, and policy analysis. He writes on pragmatism and public sociology and is the author (with Therese O'Toole) of *Countering Extremism in British Schools? The Truth about the Birmingham Trojan Horse Affair* (Policy Press, 2017). He is academic adviser to LUNG Theatre company and their play, *Trojan Horse*, which won the Amnesty International Freedom of Expression Award at the Edinburgh Festival Fringe in August 2018.

Harrison W. Inefuku is the scholarly publishing services librarian at Iowa State University, where he directs the library's publishing program, the Iowa State University Digital Press. Prior to launching the press, he launched and managed Iowa State's institutional repository. He has published and presented on diversity, equity, inclusion, and social justice in scholarly communications and academic publishing, and in libraries and archives more broadly. He holds an MAS and MLIS from the University of British Columbia and a BFA in Graphic Design and BA in Visual Culture from the University of the Pacific.

Contributors

Eileen A. Joy is a research specialist in Old English literary studies and intellectual history, as well as a para-academic rogue publisher, with interests in poetry and poetics, ethics, affects and embodiments, queer studies, object/thing studies, the ecological, post/humanism, and scholarly communications. She is the founding ingenitor of the BABEL Working Group, coeditor of *postmedieval: a journal of medieval cultural studies*, and founding director of punctum books: spontaneous acts of scholarly combustion.

Bruno Latour is professor emeritus at Sciences Po medialab and curator of several exhibitions. He has been the principal investigator of the *AIME* project.

Stuart Lawson is a library worker at Edinburgh Napier University, and a researcher with a doctorate on the politics of open access. They have both research and practice expertise in open access, open data, and scholarly communication funding. Stuart is an editor of the *Journal of Radical Librarianship*.

Namhla Madini has been working for the University of Cape Town, Health Sciences library since 2007. She has an honors degree in library and information science from UCT in 2010. Her responsibilities include providing an array of information services to the library users. She is part of the team that publishes open-access monographs using Open Monograph Press.

Robin de Mourat is research designer at the médialab laboratory (Sciences Po, Paris). He has been embedded in *An Inquiry into Modes of Existence* as a participant observer since 2014, in the frame of a PhD research in arts & design examining the role of formats in academic publishing, at Université Rennes 2. He works at the intersection between academic equipment and inquiry practices, combining a background in product design, design history and theory, and human-computer interactions, with diverse material and discursive experiments in the humanities and social sciences. He has participated in the making of texts, things, and conversations about the epistemology of design activities, interdisciplinary methodologies in humanities and social sciences, and social and cultural studies of scholarly practices.

Thomas Hervé Mboa Nkoudou is a PhD candidate in public communication at the Université Laval in Quebec. His involvement as a coresearcher in the SOHA Project (Open Science in Haiti and French-speaking Africa) has allowed him to acquire a strong background in the field of scholarly communication. He is working on the African landscape of scholarly communication in order to improve, through commons of knowledge, the visibility of African researchers on the scientific web, to promote diversity and inclusion in open access, as well as to fight the neocolonial and neocapitalist hidden faces of open access. Due to this experience, he is part of many international and African organizations involved in open science and regularly invited to give lectures on the state of scholarly communication in Africa.

Bethany Nowviskie is dean of libraries and professor of English at James Madison University. She formerly directed the Digital Library Federation and served as research associate professor of digital humanities at the University of Virginia, where she was the founding director of the UVa Library Scholars' Lab and a special advisor to the Provost for digital humanities research. A long-time humanities computing practitioner, Nowviskie is a past president of the Association for Computers and the Humanities and a CLIR Distinguished Presidential Fellow.

Angela Okune is a doctoral candidate in the Department of Anthropology at the University of California, Irvine. She studies data practices and infrastructures of research groups working in and on Nairobi, Kenya in order to explore broader questions of equity, knowledge production, and socioeconomic development in Africa. Grounded in the context of Nairobi as a heavily saturated site of research where many participants question the benefits of research, Angela is interested in shifting notions of ethical scientific responsibility to "open up" knowledge held in tandem with considerations of data protection and privacy. Angela is a recipient of a Wenner-Gren fieldwork grant, a 2016 graduate research fellowship from the National Science Foundation, and 2018 UC Berkeley Center for Technology, Society and Policy fellowship. From 2010 to 2015, as cofounder of the research department at iHub, Nairobi's innovation hub for the tech community, Angela provided strategic guidance for the growth of tech research in Kenya. She was a network coordinator for the IDRC and DFID-funded Open and Collaborative Science in Development Network (OCSDNet) (2014–2018) and coeditor of the open-access book *Contextualizing Openness* (University of Ottawa Press). She currently serves as a student representative on the Society for Social Studies of Science (4S) Council and as a design team member of the Platform for Experimental Collaborative Ethnography (PECE).

Abel L. Packer is a Brazilian information scientist and expert in information technology and knowledge management. He is one of the cofounders of SciELO and current director of the FAPESP SciELO Program. He is also project coordinator at the Foundation of the Federal University of São Paulo (UNIFESP) and former director of the Latin American and Caribbean Center on Health Sciences of the Pan American Health Organization/World Health Organization (BIREME/PAHO/WHO). Abel has a bachelor's degree in business management and a master of library science from Syracuse University in the United States.

David Pontille is senior researcher at the French National Center for Scientific Research (CNRS) in the Centre de Sociologie de l'Innovation / i3 (UMR 9217) in Paris. His work is organized into two main topics: the evaluation technologies of scientific research (authorship and attribution of productions, journal rankings, bibliometrics, peer review), and the politics of maintenance dedicated to technologies and infrastructures. Founding member of Revue d'Anthropologie des Connaissances, he also co-leads a blog dedicated to ordinary writing practices: Scriptopolis (http://www.scriptopolis.fr/en).

Reggie Raju is the director of research and learning at the University of Cape Town Libraries. He has worked in academic libraries for more than 35 years. He holds a PhD in information studies and is the author of several publications in peer-reviewed national and international journals, chapters in books, and a book publication. His research focus is on research librarianship with an emphasis on open access and library publishing. He is currently a member of the Academic and Research Libraries Standing Committee of IFLA, as well as being the convener of its Special Interest Group: Library Publishing. Reggie is currently the chair of SPARC Africa and is driving the social justice agenda of open access for Africa. He serves on the editorial board of the *Journal of Librarianship and Scholarly Communication*.

István Rév is the director of the Vera and Donald Blinken Open Society Archives and professor in the Department of History at the Central European University.

Donato Ricci is a designer and researcher. He specializes in the use of design methods in human and social sciences. He followed the design aspects of Bruno Latour's *AIME* project, with whom he co-curated the ResetModernity! exhibition at ZKM Karlsruhe and at the Shanghai Himalayas Museum. From 2005 to 2012 he was involved in the development of the DensityDesign Lab's research programs. He is assistant professor of "Representação e Conhecimento" at the Universidade de Aveiro and part of the SPEAP Programme in Political Arts within SciencesPo School of Public Affairs. His work has been featured in several conferences and exhibitions (Medialab Prado—Visualizer; SIGGRAPH Conference; MIT Humanities + Digital Conference, The Art of Network), publications and showcases (Data Flow; Information Graphics; Visual Complexity; Visual Storytelling). He received a silver and a bronze at the Malofiej-Awards, and was selected, in 2018, for the ADI Design Index.

Charlotte Roh is the scholarly communications librarian at the University of San Francisco, where she manages the institutional repository, copyright advisory, open education program, library publishing program, and open access policy. Her work is at the intersection of social justice, libraries, and scholarly communication, and is informed by her personal experience and years of work in academic publishing.

Naomi Rosenkranz is the assistant director of the *Making and Knowing Project* at Columbia University. She serves as the main administrative liaison, supports the historical reconstruction research, oversees the Project's chemical laboratory, and maintains the digital collaboration systems. She studied physics at Barnard College, with research experience in material science, experimental condensed matter, and physical chemistry. She served as the inaugural Science Resident in Conservation with Columbia's Ancient Ink Lab, identifying and characterizing ancient carbon-based inks. She continued her investigation of inks at the Metropolitan Museum of Art, working with the departments of scientific research and paper conservation to examine medieval iron-tannate black inks through recipe reconstructions and spectral analysis of museum objects. She is coeditor of the *Making and Knowing Project*'s digital critical edition of BnF Ms. Fr. 640.

Claire Conklin Sabel received a BA in history from Columbia University and an MPhil in history and philosophy of science from the University of Cambridge. She is currently completing her PhD in history and sociology of science at the University of Pennsylvania, where her research focuses on the relationship between global commerce and the earth sciences in the early modern period. She is the author of "The Impact of European Trade with Southeast Asia on the Mineralogical Studies of Robert Boyle" in Michael Bycroft and Sven Dupré, eds., *Gems in the Early Modern World* (Palgrave Macmillan, 2019). Before her doctoral studies, she was a research associate with the *Making and Knowing Project* at Columbia, and subsequently project manager for Columbia's Center for Science and Society and History in Action initiative.

Dorothea Salo is a distinguished faculty associate in the University of Wisconsin at Madison's Information School. She has written and presented internationally on scholarly publishing, libraries in the digital humanities, copyright, privacy, institutional repositories, linked data, and data curation. Her "Recover Analog and Digital Data" project rescues audio, video, and digital data from obsolete or decaying carriers. As coinvestigator for the IMLS-funded Data Doubles project, she is helping investigate undergraduate students' perceptions of privacy relative to learning analytics practices. Salo holds an MA in library and information studies and another in Spanish from UW-Madison.

Maura A. Smale is chief librarian and professor at New York City College of Technology, and faculty in Interactive Technology & Pedagogy and Digital Humanities at the Graduate Center, both of the City University of New York. She holds graduate degrees in anthropology and library and information science, and her research interests include undergraduate academic culture, critical librarianship, open access and open educational technologies, and game-based learning. She has been codirector of the City Tech OpenLab, an open digital platform for teaching, learning, and collaboration. With Mariana Regalado, she published *Digital Technology as Affordance and Barrier in Higher Education*, exploring the ways students use technology in their academic work. Their edited volume *Academic Libraries for Commuter Students: Research-Based Strategies* examines US commuter undergraduate library use. She tweets intermittently @mauraweb, and blogs actively for the Association of College & Research Libraries' ACRLog.org.

Pamela H. Smith is Seth Low Professor of History at Columbia University, and founding director of the Center for Science and Society and of the *Making and Knowing Project* (www.makingandknowing.org). Her articles and books, especially *The Body of the Artisan* (2004), *Ways of Making and Knowing* (ed. P. H. Smith, A. R. W. Meyers, and H. Cook, 2017), and *From Lived Experience to the Written Word: Recovering Skill and Art* (forthcoming, Chicago), examine craft and practical knowledge. Her edited volumes include *The Matter of Art* (ed. C. Anderson, A. Dunlop, P. H. Smith, 2016), which treats materiality, making, and meaning, and *Entangled Itineraries: Materials, Practices, and Knowledges across Eurasia* (2019), which deals with the movement of materials and techniques across Eurasia before 1800. In the collaborative research and teaching initiative, the *Making and Knowing Project*, she and the Making and Knowing

Team investigate practical knowledge through text-, object-, and laboratory-based research.

Tamzyn Suliaman is a librarian at UCT Libraries, formerly a medical librarian who specialized in systematic reviews. It was through her efforts helping African scholars find African content that she discovered the importance of equitable open and accessible scholarship. In her current position in research and innovation, she is involved in open publishing, which allows for investigation of better measures to ensure that marginalized voices are heard through publishing African scholarship. Her particular focus is on ensuring that scholarship is inclusive and accessible to all.

Didier Torny is a senior researcher at the French National Center for Scientific Research (CNRS), in the Centre de Sociologie de l'Innovation / i3 (UMR 9217) in Paris. He currently works on a political economy of academic publications, with some aspects of this research being treated in his scientific blog (https://polecopub.hypotheses.org). He is also a project officer at the Information Sciences Direction of CNRS and copilot of the evaluation group of the French Open Science Committee.

Tianna Helena Uchacz is an assistant professor in the Department of Visualization at Texas A&M University and former postdoctoral scholar on the *Making and Knowing Project* at Columbia University. She has held fellowships at Utrecht University, the Zentralinstitut für Kunstgeschichte, and the Science History Institute, and her work has appeared in *Renaissance Quarterly* and *Nederlands Kunsthistorisch Jaarboek* as well as collected volumes (*Netherlandish Culture of the Sixteenth Century, Ornament and Monstrosity*). Her research uses experimental, performative, and digital humanities methods to interrogate the encoding of cultural values in early modern materials, artworks, and texts. Her current project asks how Netherlandish artists used the depicted body, and the sensual nude in particular, to articulate ethical questions and shifting social norms. She is coeditor of the *Making and Knowing Project*'s digital critical edition of BnF Ms. Fr. 640 and its Research and Teaching Companion.

John Willinsky is the Khosla Family Professor at Stanford. After working for some time on the educational implications of such knowledge systems as literary theory, historical dictionaries, and European imperialism, John has come to focus on both analyzing and altering scholarly publishing practices to understand whether this body of knowledge might yet become more of a public resource for learning and deliberation. John is most well known for founding the Public Knowledge Project, which produces the widely used software Open Journal Systems.

Jane Winters is professor of digital humanities and pro-dean for libraries and digital at the School of Advanced Study, University of London. She is coeditor of the open-access book series *New Historical Perspectives* and editor of a series on academic publishing, which is part of Cambridge University Press Elements: Publishing and Book Culture. She has led or codirected a range of digital projects, including *Big UK Domain Data for the Arts and Humanities, Traces Through Time: Prosopography in Practice* *across Big Data*, and *Digging into Linked Parliamentary Data*. Jane's research interests include digital history, born-digital archives (particularly the archived web), the use of social media by cultural heritage institutions, and open access publishing. She has published most recently on non-print legal deposit and web archives, born-digital archives and the problem of search, and the archiving and analysis of national web domains.

Index

aaaaarg.fail, 319
Academia.edu, 118, 258, 267, 269, 270, 351–352, 353
Academic freedom, 2, 317–318
Academic libraries, 174–176. *See also* Library publishing
  funding, 174–175
  institutional repositories in, 219, 352
  open access and, 55–56, 184, 272, 361
  preservation in, 219
Access to Research scheme, 166
Africa, 54, 62n3. *See also* Article processing charges (APCs), Global South and; Global South, research production in
  institutional repositories in, 31–32
  open access in, 27–37, 53–57, 60–61, 332
  research production in, 31–34, 37, 54, 70
  university system in, 32
African Journals Online (AJOL), 332
Afrofuturism, 195–197
Airbnb, 266–267
Alternative publication methods, 36–37, 105–106, 208, 255, 324. See also *An Inquiry into Modes of Existence (AIME)*; Format (of publication); *Making and Knowing Project*
Altmetrics, 256, 268, 347

Amazon, 266
AmeliCA, 288, 335
An Act for the Encouragement of Learning (1710). *See* Statute of Anne (1710)
An Inquiry into Modes of Existence (AIME), 106–111
Archives. *See also* Digital library design; Digital preservation
  digitization of, 240–241
  human rights issues and, 230–231, 237–238
  inclusivity in, 207–212
  integrity in, 238–240
  openness in, 229–231, 236, 244
  privacy and, 230–232, 234–238, 241–244
  provenance principle in, 236, 238
  retroactive redescription in, 231–234, 239–240
  silences in, 199, 205–207
Article processing charges (APCs)
  critique of, 4–5, 163, 324, 332, 337, 346, 354–355
  examples of, 157, 272, 320, 334
  Global South and, 29–30, 58, 59, 288, 331
  impact factors and, 29–30
  rationale for, 3, 29, 322
arXiv, 27, 118, 267, 269, 319, 357
SocArxiv, 268

Asia, open access in, 332
Augmented reality, 138
Author-pay schemes. *See* Article processing charges (APCs)

Beall, Jeffrey, 44–45
bepress, 267, 352, 353
Bibliometrics. *See* Citation metrics
BIREME. *See* Latin America and Caribbean Center on Health Sciences Information (BIREME)
Book processing charges. *See* Article processing charges (APCs)
Books, format of, 142–143. *See also* Format (of publication)
Boyle, Robert, 120
Browne Review, 185, 190n22
Budapest Open Access Initiative (BOAI), 2, 25, 27–28, 53, 56–57, 229, 251, 354

Career impacts of scholarly communications, 2, 47, 222, 223–224, 270, 277–279. *See also* Evaluation of research
Citation metrics, 115–118, 257, 310, 335, 347. *See also* Altmetrics; Evaluation of research; Impact factors
City University of New York (CUNY), 173
Clarivate Analytics, 272, 297, 334
CLACSO. *See* Latin American Council of Social Sciences (CLACSO)
Colonialism in scholarly communications, 42–43, 57–58, 163–165, 217
Coloniality of knowledge, 30–31, 35–36, 70, 209–210. *See also* Epistemic inequalities
Combahee River Collective Statement, 74
Confederation of Open Access Repositories, 246n21
ContentMine, 280–281

Copyright, 154, 270. *See also* Open access, copyright and; Piracy; Statute of Anne (1710)
legislation, 83, 95, 96, 155, 218, 281
CORE, 356, 359n14
Corpus analysis, 216. *See also* Distant reading; Machine learning
Craft. *See* "How-to books"
Creative Commons licenses, 7–8, 73, 84, 309

Declaration on Research Assessment (DORA), 30, 257, 278, 279, 335, 338
Defoe, Daniel, *Essay on the Regulation of the Press*, 91
Deposit libraries. *See* Legal book deposit
Depsy, 255
Digital humanities, 215–224, 347. *See also* Distant reading; *Making and Knowing Project*
NEH Office of Digital Humanities, 221
Digital library design, 196–201, 203n9
assessment measures, 199–200
privacy and, 200
Digital preservation, 137, 216–221, 362
Digital Science, 272
Directory of Open Access Journals, 258
Distant reading, 279–283
Diversity. *See* Colonialism in scholarly communications; Epistemic inequalities; Gender inequalities in scholarly communications; Global South; Labor in scholarly communications
Documenting the Now, 210
Dropbox, 218

Elsevier, 9, 42, 83–84, 267, 269, 271–272, 320, 351–352
Empiricism, rise of, 125, 127–129
Epistemic inequalities, 32–33, 36, 65–68, 70–73. *See also* Archives, inclusivity in and silences in; Coloniality of knowledge; Global South

Index

Evaluation of research, 9–10, 67, 223–224, 311, 344. *See also* Altmetrics; Citation metrics; Declaration on Research Assessment (DORA); Impact factors; Peer review; Research Excellence Framework (REF)
    Global South and, 30, 33, 37, 44–45, 299, 309, 338–339

F1000, 272
Facebook, 181, 258, 270
"Fake news," 182, 187, 205
FAPESP. *See* São Paulo Research Foundation (FAPESP)
Figshare project, 255
Finch Report (2012), 29
First World War in the archives, 232–233
Format (of publication), 103–105, 108–112, 138, 142–143, 362. *See also* Alternative publication methods; Print, hegemony of
Fourth Industrial Revolution (4IR), 271
Freedom of speech, 87, 234–235, 321. *See also* Academic freedom

Gender inequalities in scholarly communications, 45–46. *See also* Open access, social justice and
General Data Protection Regulation (GDPR), 218, 234–236
GitHub, 136, 144n3, 254, 267
Global South. *See also* Africa; Evaluation of research, Global South and; Latin America
    definition, xi, 74n1, 363n1
    research production in, 43–45, 57–59, 65, 70, 258, 285, 362
Google, 235, 270
    Drive, 136
    Scholar, 258, 309

Hacktivism, 175, 326n9
HathiTrust corpora, 206

"HowOpenIsIt?®," 290
"How-to books," 125–129
Humanities Commons, 268, 355, 356–357
Hypothesis project, 258

Impact factors, 9, 29–30, 185–187, 277–278, 288, 310, 323. *See also* Citation metrics; Evaluation of research
    alternatives, 278–279, 335
ImpactStory, 256, 278
Infrastructures of scholarly communication, 72–73, 251–253, 293, 324, 348, 355. *See also* Digital library design; Format (of publication); *Humanities Commons*; Labor in scholarly communications; Platformization; SciELO
    experiments in, 253–256, 257–259
Interdisciplinary research, 125–126, 133, 139, 140–141, 143
Internet Archive, the, 218, 246n21
ISIS database software, 300, 308

Joint Roadmap for Open Science Tools (JROST), 273
Journal Article Tag Suite (JATS), 287, 290, 294n2, 309, 313n11
Journal publishing, 9, 45, 47–48, 174–175, 217. *See also* Article processing charges (APCs); Impact factors; Latin America: journal publishing in; Peer review; SciELO
JSTOR Labs, 280

Labor in scholarly communications, 47–49, 165. *See also* Career impacts of scholarly communications
    diversity in, 211
Language issues in scholarly communications, 33, 34, 43–44, 67, 305, 310, 313n9
La Referencia, 297, 336

Latin America. *See also* Latindex; Redalyc; SciELO
  journal publishing in, 286–287, 290, 299
  open access in, 286–288, 292–293, 326n13, 331, 332–333, 335–338
  research production in, 69, 285–286
Latin America and Caribbean Center on Health Sciences Information (BIREME), 298, 299, 300, 308, 334, 336
Latin American Council of Social Sciences (CLACSO), 287, 288, 331, 335, 337
Latindex, 287, 333–334
Learned societies, 149, 343–345, 347–348, 353, 361, 362. *See also* Royal Society, the
Legal book deposit, 88, 89, 93–94
Leiden Manifesto, the, 257
LGBTQIA+ history, 207, 212n9
Libraries. *See* Academic libraries; Archives; Digital library design; Private libraries; Public libraries
Library of Alexandria, 238–239
Library publishing, 54, 55–58, 59–61
Licensing of the Press Act (1662), 85–87, 88–90, 93
Linked Open Data Cloud, 292, 295n18
Local Contexts project, 210
Locke, John, 84, 85–90, 95–96, 98n22, 99n34
LOCKSS Program, 246n21

Machine learning, 281–282. *See also* Semantic technologies
Making and Knowing Project, 126–127, 129–143
Mendeley, 258, 267, 351

Modern Language Association (MLA), 218. *See also* Humanities Commons
  Guidelines for Evaluating Work in Digital Humanities and Digital Media, 223
MLA Commons, 355–356
MS. Fr. 640, 126, 127–135, 140
Mukurtu project, 73, 210
Murray-Rust research group, 280–281, 284n8

Neoliberalism and higher education, 6–9, 183–188, 189nn7–8, 317, 324
New Historical Perspectives, 346–347, 349n11

OA2020 initiative, 29, 331
OCLC, 269
OntoOAI, 291–292
Open access. *See also* Academic libraries; Africa, open access in; Archives; Article processing charges (APCs); Journal publishing; Latin America, open access in; Open research practices; Public libraries; Royal Society, the, open access and; SciELO
  benefits of, 2–3, 41, 166, 176–178, 285
  business drivers for, 184–185
  copyright and, 83–84, 217
  data analytics and, 185
  definition of, 2–3, 55, 251, 354
  democracy and, 321–322, 323
  diamond, 54, 56, 60, 62n4
  dissertations and, 223
  economics of, 3–6, 7–10, 29–30, 268, 272–273, 324
  gold, 3, 29
  green, 3, 29, 37, 344
  human rights issues and, 332
  legislation on, 41, 319, 327n15, 333, 335–336, 349nn3–4

monographs and, 345–347, 349n9
origins of, 2, 26–27, 29, 128, 157
social justice and, 36–37, 41, 49, 53, 55
Open Access Button, 253–254
Open and Collaborative Science in Development Network (OCSDNet), 66, 68–71
Open Archives Initiative Protocol for Metadata Harvesting (OAI-PMH), 289, 291–292
Open Library of the Humanities (OLH), 268, 272, 319
Open research practices, 65–66, 69, 70–74, 208–209, 355. See also Open science
Open science, 36, 311, 338
Open Society Archives, 233–234, 237–238, 240, 246n17
ORCID project, 255
Outsourcing, 47, 48, 240
Oxford University Press, 42

Paywalls, 253–254
Pedagogy. See Teaching via research
Peer review, 46, 113–115, 116–120, 223, 328n25. See also Evaluation of research; Working papers
  anonymity in, 114
  open review, 116
  post-publication peer review, 117, 119
Pharmakon, 25–26
Philosophical Transactions. See Royal Society, the
Piracy, 90–91, 94, 100n44, 167, 172n48, 319–320. See also Copyright; Hacktivism; Sci-Hub
Plan S, 272–273, 331, 349n4, 349n9, 363
Platform for Experimental Collaborative Ethnography (PECE), 73
Platformization, 257–258, 266–273
Platforms, definition of, 257, 265–266, 267

PLOS ONE, 277
Principle of Respect for Context, 243
Print, hegemony of, 215, 221–224.
  See also Format (of publication)
Privacy Bill of Rights (2012), 243
Private libraries, 150
Public libraries, 161–167, 173–174
  class issues and, 163, 164
  colonialism and, 164–165
  funding, 162, 165, 166, 168n4, 174
  legislation on, 162, 164, 167n2, 168n6
  open access and, 166, 167, 177–178
  preservation in, 219
Publons, 255, 268
PubMed, 267
PubPeer, 119, 258
punctum books, 324, 328n30, 329n32, 346

Racial inequalities in scholarly communications, 46. See also Colonialism in scholarly communications; Epistemic inequalities; Global South
Radical OA Collective, 323–324
RDF (resource description framework), 290–291, 292
Reasons Humbly Offer'd for a Bill for the Encouragement of Learning, and the Improvement of Printing, 91–92
Redalyc, 285, 287, 288, 290, 297, 334–335, 337, 338
Red Archive, 237
Refugees and education, 171n41
Rehabilitation of Offenders Act (1974), 234
RELX, 269, 271
Research assessment. See Evaluation of research
Research Excellence Framework (REF), 6–7, 278–279, 319, 326n14, 344, 345
ResearchGate, 118, 258, 267, 269, 270, 272

Research Ideas and Outcomes (RIO) journal, 255
Right of erasure, 235
Right to be forgotten, 218, 234–235
Royal Historical Society. *See* New Historical Perspectives
Royal Society, the
  Fair Copying Declaration and, 155
  funding, 148–149, 156–157
  open access and, 157
  Philosophical Transactions, 147–156, 158n11, 158n15, 343
  Proceedings, 147, 152, 155, 156, 158n11
  reuse of research, attitude to, 154–155
Rwanda, Master Conform, 233–234

Samizdat Archive, 237
San, 68–69, 77n28
San Francisco DORA. *See* Declaration on Research Assessment (DORA)
São Paulo Research Foundation (FAPESP), 298, 299, 308, 334
ScholarLed, 323–324
ScholarlyHub, 258
SciELO, 44, 287, 290, 297–311, 313n9, 313n11, 334, 335
  Citation Index, 288
  international coverage, 297, 300–302, 305
  journal statistics, 302–305
  open access in, 298, 308–309, 326n13, 334, 338
  origins, 298–300
  thematic coverage, 304–307
Sci-Hub, 84, 167, 175, 319
Scopus, 285, 307, 335
Semantic technologies, 289–292
Social media, 181–183, 217, 242, 256, 258, 266
  metrics, 118, 120, 270
Social Science Research Network (SSRN), 267, 351, 353

SpringerNature, 9
Stationers' Company, 86–90, 91, 92–93, 94–95
Statute of Anne (1710), 83, 84–85, 92–96, 101n52, 101n57
Swartz, Aaron, 175

Teaching via research, 131–134, 136–137, 138–141
Technical Protection Measures, 281
Text mining. *See* Distant reading

Uber, 266–267
Ubuntu, 55, 61
United Nations Sustainable Development Goals, 332
Universities, 162, 183–185. *See also* Academic libraries; Archives; Neoliberalism and higher education; University presses
University of California and open access, 320
University of Cape Town, 56, 60–61
University presses, 6, 42, 99n35, 222, 287, 324

Virtual Health Library (VHL), 299, 336–337

Web of Science, 31, 285, 335
Working-class education, 162, 163, 164, 168n10
Working papers, 118–119

XML, 289–291, 294n2, 309, 313n11

Zenodo project, 254–255

www.ingramcontent.com/pod-product-compliance
Lightning Source LLC
Chambersburg PA
CBHW051240300426
44114CB00011B/826